COLLECTANEA SERICA •
3

Editor: ZBIGNIEW WESOŁOWSKI, S.V.D
Sankt Augustin

Lauren F. Pfister (ed.)

Polyglot from the Far Side of the Moon
The Life and Works of
Solomon Caesar Malan (1812–1894)

Portrait photo of Solomon Caesar Malan from A(rthur) N(oel) Malan, *Solomon Caesar Malan, D.D. Memorials of His Life and Writings* (London: J. Murray, 1897). Reprinted with permission of Staatsbibliothek zu Berlin, Preußischer Kulturbesitz, Signatur Aw 10866.

COLLECTANEA SERICA • NEW SERIES
——————— 3 ———————

Lauren F. Pfister (ed.)

Polyglot from the Far Side of the Moon

The Life and Works of Solomon Caesar Malan (1812–1894)

Monumenta Serica Institute • Sankt Augustin

Sumptibus Societatis Verbi Divini (S.V.D.)

Copy editors: BARBARA HOSTER, DIRK KUHLMANN, ZBIGNIEW WESOŁOWSKI
Cover and layout: JOZEF BIŠTUŤ

Arnold-Janssen-Str. 20
53757 Sankt Augustin, Germany
Fax: +49-2241-237486
E-mail: institut@monumenta-serica.de
www.monumenta-serica.de

First published 2022
by Routledge
2 Park Square, Milton Park, Abingdon, Oxon OX14 4RN

and by Routledge
605 Third Avenue, New York, NY 10158

Routledge is an imprint of the Taylor & Francis Group, an informa business

© 2022 Monumenta Serica Institute

The right of Lauren F. Pfister to be identified as editor of this work has been asserted by him in accordance with sections 77 and 78 of the Copyright, Designs and Patents Act 1988.

All rights reserved. No part of this book may be reprinted or reproduced or utilised in any form or by any electronic, mechanical, or other means, now known or hereafter invented, including photocopying and recording, or in any information storage or retrieval system, without permission in writing from the publishers.
Trademark notice: Product or corporate names may be trademarks or registered trademarks, and are used only for identification and explanation without intent to infringe.

British Library Cataloguing-in-Publication Data
A catalogue record for this book is available from the British Library.

Library of Congress Cataloging-in-Publication Data
A catalog record for this book has been requested.

ISBN: 978-1-032-13663-9 (hbk)
ISBN: 978-1-032-13686-8 (pbk)
ISBN: 978-1-003-23043-4 (eBook)

DOI: 10.4324/9781003230434

Typeset by Monumenta Serica Institute

Dedicated
to the Memory of

ROLF GERHARD ("GARY") TIEDEMANN
(1941–2019)

and

ROMAN MALEK, S.V.D.
(1951–2019)

productive colleagues whose works we admire
and whose friendship we have cherished

TABLE OF CONTENTS

Editor's Preface and Acknowledgements XI
Preface by the Rt Revd Dr. Graham Kings XV
Abbreviations XIX

CHAPTER 1
FRÉDÉRIC AMSLER
S. C. Malan's Familial and Ecclesiastical Context in Geneva 1

CHAPTER 2
† R. G. TIEDEMANN
S. C. Malan at Bishop's College, Calcutta, 1838–1840 17

CHAPTER 3
T. H. BARRETT
Malan as Dorset Worthy: Solomon Caesar and Valentine Ackland 35

CHAPTER 4
JOHN EDWARDS
Solomon Caesar Malan: Personality, Polyglossia and the Autistic Spectrum 47

CHAPTER 5
LAUREN F. PFISTER
Surprises within Solomon Caesar Malan's Christian Works and His Critical Advances
in Scholarly Christian Reflection 79

CHAPTER 6
THOMAS ZIMMER
Solomon Caesar Malan's Understanding of Chinese Sayings and Proverbial Wisdom:
A Preliminary Study of His Art and Technique of Translation 103

CHAPTER 7
WILLIAM YAU NANG NG
Discerning the Worldview in Confucian Proverbs: A Preliminary
Reflection on S. C. Malan's Selection of Confucian Proverbs from *The Four Books* 123

CHAPTER 8
LORETTA E. KIM
Malan's Manjurica 151

CHAPTER 9
RITA KUZDER
Initiating the Discovery of Tibetan Wisdom in the *Original Notes on the Book of Proverbs* 175

CHAPTER 10
JAMES M. HEGARTY
The Sanskrit of Solomon Caesar Malan: An Anglican Savant Reads the *Mahābhārata* 207

CHAPTER 11
GYULA PACZOLAY and LAUREN F. PFISTER
From Ladakh to Budapest via Broadwindsor: The Journey of an Unusual Gift
of Tibetan Books 229

CHAPTER 12
LAUREN F. PFISTER
Recovering the Now Invisible Malan Library 253

CHAPTER 13
LAUREN F. PFISTER

Breaking the Code of a Monstrous Codex: An Intellectual Journey into the
Hidden Secrets of *The Original Notes on the Book of Proverbs* 289

Notes on Contributors 337

General Index 341

List of Illustrations

Cover: Section of Figure 20, Bodleian Color Image (ONBP Ms), MS.Ind.Inst.Misc. 10, f. 573 verso. Reprinted with permission of the Bodleian Library, University of Oxford.

Frontispiece: Portrait photo of Solomon Caesar Malan from A(rthur) N(oel) Malan, *Solomon Caesar Malan, D.D. Memorials of His Life and Writings* (London: J. Murray, 1897). Reprinted with permission of Staatsbibliothek zu Berlin, Preußischer Kulturbesitz, Signatur Aw 10866.

Editor's Preface and Acknowledgements

p. XIII Fig. 1: Oxford Conference Participants, Display of S. C. Malan's Works (Photo by Mirasy M. Pfister, August 2012).

Chapter 1: S. C. Malan's Familial and Ecclesiastical Context in Geneva

p. 8   Fig. 2: Sketch of Lake Geneva by S. C. Malan. Reprinted with permission of The Getty Research Institute, Los Angeles. ID no.: gri_2013_m_25_b6_052.

p. 11   Fig. 3: Color Image by S. C. Malan / Sketch of Swiss Alps through a Wooden Window. Reprinted with permission of The Getty Research Institute, Los Angeles. ID no.: gri_2013_m_25_b6_051.

Chapter 3: Malan as Dorset Worthy: Solomon Caesar and Valentine Ackland

p. 37   Fig. 4: St. John the Baptist Church, Broadwindsor (Photo by Mirasy M. Pfister, August 2012).

p. 39   Fig. 5: The Vicarage, Broadwindsor (Photo by Mirasy M. Pfister, August 2012).

Chapter 4: Solomon Caesar Malan: Personality, Polyglossia and the Autistic Spectrum

p. 53   Fig. 6: Bodleian Color Image (ONBP Ms), MS. Ind. Inst. Misc. 10, f. 156 recto. Reprinted with permission of the Bodleian Library, University of Oxford.

Chapter 5: Surprises within Solomon Caesar Malan's Christian Works and His Critical Advances in Scholarly Christian Reflection

p. 89   Fig. 7: *ONBP*, vol. 1, pp. 352-353 (Prov. 7:22-23), "Long Note."

p. 90   Fig. 8: *ONBP*, vol. 2, pp. 46-47 (Prov. 11:21), "CKJV, Short Note."

p. 92   Fig. 9: *ONBP*, vol. 2, p. 376 (Prov. 16:4), "CKJV, Long Theological Reflection."

p. 93   Fig. 10: *ONBP*, vol. 2, p. 556 (Prov. 18:24), "Complicated Etymology, CKJV."

p. 94   Fig. 11: *ONBP*, vol. 3, p. 281 (Prov. 25:11), "CKJV, Cultural Etymology."

Chapter 6: Solomon Caesar Malan's Understanding of Chinese Sayings and Proverbial Wisdom: A Preliminary Study of His Art and Technique of Translation

p. 109 Fig. 12: *ONBP*, vol. 2, p. 367 (Prov. 16:1), "Ming h. dsi" (footnote 2).

Chapter 7: Discerning the Worldview in Confucian Proverbs: A Preliminary Reflection on S. C. Malan's Selection of Confucian Proverbs from *The Four Books*

p. 141 Fig. 13: *ONBP*, vol. 3, p. 159 (Prov. 23: 17-18), Chinese sources (footnotes 3-5, 7).

Chapter 8: Malan's Manjurica

p. 165 Fig. 14: Example of Manchu calligraphy. Source: Britta-Maria Gruber and Wolfgang Kirsch, "Writing Manchu on a Western Computer: (An Interim Report)," *Saksaha: A Journal of Manchu Studies* 3 (1998), p. 42. https://quod.lib.umich.edu/s/saksaha/13401746.0003.008/--writing-manchu-on-a-western-computer?rgn=main;view=fulltext (accessed March 16, 2021).

Chapter 9: Initiating the Discovery of Tibetan Wisdom in the *Original Notes on the Book of Proverbs*

p. 184 Fig. 15: *ONBP*, vol. 3, pp. 410-411 (Prov. 27: 12-14), Tibetan source (p. 410, footnote 2).

Chapter 10: The Sanskrit of Solomon Caesar Malan: An Anglican Savant Reads the *Mahābhārata*

p. 220 Fig. 16: *ONBP*, vol. 1, pp. 392-393 (Prov. 8:30-31), *Mahabharata* (p. 392, footnote 4).

Chapter 11: From Ladakh to Budapest via Broadwindsor: The Journey of an Unusual Gift of Tibetan Books

p. 250 Fig. 17: Image of Malan plaque, Broadwindsor (photograph by Mirasy M. Pfister, taken in August 2012).

Chapter 12: Recovering the Now Invisible Malan Library

p. 275 Fig. 18: Entrance door to Malan Library, Indian Institute, Oxford. BB66/00364. Reprinted with permission of the Historic England Archive.

p. 281 Fig. 19: Gallery and lecture hall, Malan Library, Indian Institute, Oxford. BB66/00376. Reprinted with permission of the Historic England Archive.

Chapter 13: Breaking the Code of a Monstrous Codex: An Intellectual Journey into the Hidden Secrets of *The Original Notes on the Book of Proverbs*

p. 334 Fig. 20: Bodleian Color Image (ONBP Ms), MS.Ind.Inst.Misc. 10, f. 573 verso. Reprinted with permission of the Bodleian Library, University of Oxford.

p. 335 Fig. 21: Bodleian Color Image (ONBP Ms), MS.Ind.Inst.Misc. 10, f. 580 verso. Reprinted with permission of the Bodleian Library, University of Oxford.

p. 336 Fig. 22: Bodleian Color Image (ONBP Ms), MS.Ind.Inst.Misc. 10, f. 831 recto. Reprinted with permission of the Bodleian Library, University of Oxford.

Back cover: Excerpt from a letter by S. C. Malan sent to Theodore Duka, dated 15 October 1883, LHAS Csoma 58 13/1. Courtesy of the Library and Information Centre of the Hungarian Academy of Sciences, Budapest.

EDITOR'S PREFACE AND ACKNOWLEDGEMENTS

This volume is a fulfilment of a long sought-after set of goals in my own life as a person engaged in comparative philosophical and comparative religious studies, bringing together like the confluence of many rivers a number of themes that have tested my patience, stretched my thoughts, and required me to rely heavily on the collegiality, scholarly acumen, and enduring trust of many persons.

Among the goals I have sought to embody through this work is a conviction that there is within a large range of practical wisdom much that is shared cross-culturally. This was a conviction that grew out of my initial studies of Solomon Caesar Malan's (1812–1894) final three-volume work, *Original Notes on the Book of Proverbs* (1889–1893), a conviction that had not been taught to me in my philosophical training, but had been demonstrated in profound and unexpected ways within that massive and complicated volume. Exactly how much of that practical wisdom could be shared cross-culturally was a matter that I could not by myself assess in any way comprehensively. I have needed companions along the way as I stretched toward reaching that goal, and those scholarly colleagues who have taken part in this volume served in those capacities admirably. As a consequence of taking up the editing work of this volume, I have learned so very much from the works of these colleagues, and so to them I offer my heart-felt gratitude.

Because little has been written about S. C. Malan since his death in 1894, and no single scholarly volume has ever been produced on his life and works, it was an unusual task to take up this unprecedented study. In many ways this involved immense challenges, all of which have been documented within various chapters of this book, but in particular in the last three chapters. The efforts of those who helped to bring this study into feasibility included the long-term efforts of my beloved wife, Mirasy Pfister, and several students who helped to prepare the electronic database based upon my wife's extensive notes. To those persons – Dr. Sophia Katz and Ms. Yip Wing-yan – I also offer my public expression of gratitude for their efforts in this regard. In addition, there have been extensive efforts made on the part of the late Prof. R. G. Tiedemann to arrange many aspects of the 2012 international conference on Malan's life and works held at Wadham College in Oxford, including a trip to Broadwindsor and connections with key persons in many places. Also, timely and multiform help has been gleaned over the years from the practical support offered by Dr. Gillian Evison, the Librarian of the Indian Institute Library and Chief of the Oriental Division of the Bodleian Libraries, the former being where S. C. Malan's works had been kept for many years.

Here a technical matter should be explained with regard to the terms of reference for the current institution of the Bodleian Libraries in Oxford. When S. C. Malan was alive, the singular was employed; Malan himself always referred to "the Bodleian Library." Nevertheless, under its continuing expansion in the 21st century, the plural form of reference was made its official title. So, within this volume, both forms of reference will be found, the former in contexts where the earlier institution is involved, and the latter for reference to the contemporary institution and our colleagues there who have greatly supported our research, collaboration, and the provision of a number of images that greatly enhance this volume.

Building upon the 2012 international conference, we have been able to bring together through the combined efforts of those who have committed themselves to this new area of research chapters within this volume exploring many historical insights into the life of S. C. Malan that come from scholarly assessments of his life spent at different periods in Switzerland, India, and the UK (especially in Chapters 1-3). In addition, we include within this volume a number of specialized studies related to his hyper-polyglossia, not only from the perspective of some of the major texts that he produced, but also from linguistic and psychological perspectives (see especially Chapter 4). Another leit-motif within our volume explores how S. C. Malan expressed his missiological interests and Christian worldview as he engaged in a vast cross-cultural exploration of proverbial wisdom (as found in Chapters 2, 5, 7, 10, and 12). On top of all these important contributions, we present within this volume some specialized studies in Malan's identification, translation, and interpretation of proverbial wisdom in Chinese classical and popular sources (Chapters 6 and 7), Egyptian hieroglyphic sources (one section of Chapter 4), Manchurian proverbs and his calligraphic art in that script (Chapter 8), his handling of the immense multivolume study in Sanskrit of the *Mahābhārata* (Chapter 10), and his use of Tibetan documents and their renderings into English (Chapters 9 and 11). Our study ends with two unusual accounts: the first in Chapter 12 dealing with the nature, extent, and institutional troubles of what was "The Malan Library" in the context of the Indian Institute at Oxford and later in the Bodleian Libraries, and the second seeking to provide extensive cues for dealing with the massive and complicated relationship between the manuscript version of the "Original Notes on the Book of Proverbs" (1833–1894, abbreviated in this volume as "ONBP Ms") and the published English version of that work with the same name (and abbreviated as *ONBP*). In no way does this offer a comprehensive account of Malan's extraordinary productivity, but it does provide the first scholarly and critical efforts to understand, evaluate, and critically appreciate what he did and did not accomplish. One hint of this lack of comprehensiveness is found in the index, where more than sixty languages are identified as those involving texts that S. C. Malan read, sought to understand, and linked ultimately to his comparative wisdom project based on the biblical book of Proverbs. If we add all the languages together that the scholars who have written chapters in this volume can read sensitively, I suspect that we would probably only reach less than half of that number of languages identified in the index.

Here again I must restate the fact that without the abiding trust and enduring collaboration of all of the colleagues who have contributed to this volume, along with many others (including those already mentioned), this volume would have been impossible to complete. Among the others I must also acknowledge at this time is Ms. Mary Siu, the Executive Office of the Centre for Sino-Christian Studies at the Hong Kong Baptist University, who has been a major administrative and communication aide in the midst of the many years that this project was pursued. Here those of us who have contributed to this volume also want to acknowledge the editorial insights and thorough reviews provided by a team of scholarly editors at Monumenta Serica: Jozef Bištuť, S.V.D., Dr. Barbara Hoster, Dr. Dirk Kuhlmann, and Prof. Dr. Zbigniew Wesołowski, S.V.D. In addition, a number of the photographs that are included in this volume have been taken by my beloved wife, Mirasy, to whom we all are indebted for the provision of these images that document our shared journey following in the steps of S. C. Malan.

Much to my own personal regret, this volume could not be published before one of our colleagues passed away from his own battle with cancer, R. G. Tiedemann. To him as a Protestant scholar with specialization in the history of Shandong Province in China, and to our Roman Catholic colleague at the Monumenta Serica Institute, Fr. Roman Malek, S.V.D., who passed away in the same year, we humbly and gratefully dedicate this volume.

Double Creek Rehsprung Meadows
Black Hawk, Colorado, USA
25 June 2020

Fig. 1: Oxford Conference Participants, Display of S. C. Malan's Works
(Photo by Mirasy M. Pfister, August 2012)

PREFACE

THE RT REVD DR. GRAHAM KINGS
Retired Mission Theologian in the Anglican Communion and
Honorary Fellow of Durham University

It is a delight for me, as a former Bishop of Sherborne, Dorset, to write a few words as a preface to this fascinating and illuminating book. I recall with great fondness my day together with the writers after they had travelled from their conference in Oxford to visit Solomon Caesar Malan's parish of Broadwindsor, on 24 August 2012.

With his colleagues, Prof. Lauren Pfister, the editor, is to be congratulated on raising into the light of contemporary scholarship the remarkable life of this hidden gem of a Dorset scholar-priest.

Solomon Caesar Malan was an orientalist of the highest order, embedded in a country parish in Dorset for forty years, 1845–1885. In him were found skills of over forty languages, watercolour painting, music, translation, book collecting and friendship.

In his magisterial second volume of *The Victorian Church,* Prof. Owen Chadwick set Malan in the context of a particular Anglican tradition:

> The country scholar-parson still had leisure. At Embleton Mandell Creighton wrote his great history of the papacy. At Crayke in Yorkshire Edward Churton made a serious contribution to the study of Spanish literature. At Warkworth in Northumberland R. W. Dixon wrote the standard Tractarian history of the English Reformation. At Navestock in Essex Stubbs acquired that master of medieval sources which helped to create the English school of history. At Broadwindsor, despite a mind which lacked critical sense, Caesar Malan became one of the English authorities on the study of oriental languages.[1]

In the enlightening Chapter Three of this book, Prof. Timothy H. Barrett quotes the biography of Malan by his son, showing the extraordinary contrast of high scholarship and humble mission. The shy and reserved scholar ministered amongst "stiff sons of toil, of a simple wit that seldom rose above the level of sheep, turnips, and sour cider."[2]

Barrett also mentions the well-known Moule family of Dorset. In my library, I have a precious book which I bought in a Sherborne antiquarian bookshop. It is the Greek and English concordance of the New Testament,[3] which belonged to the most famous member of the Moule family of Dorset, C. F. D. Moule (1908–2007). He became a good friend when I studied at Ridley Hall and Selwyn College, Cambridge. Moule was born in China of Church Missionary Society parents, went to school in Dorset and, as one of Britain's leading New Testament scholars, served

---

[1] Chadwick 1970, p. 166. Chadwick's comment about lacking "critical sense" seems to refer to his forceful attack on Westcott and Hort's Revised Version of the New Testament in 1881.

[2] *SCM DD*, p. 119.

[3] See Hudson – Abbot 1885.

as Lady Margaret Professor of Divinity at the University of Cambridge for twenty-five years. He spent the last few years of his life at the Old Rectory nursing home in the village of Leigh, not too far from Malan's Rectory in Broadwindsor.

So, what is Malan's legacy? During his lifetime he passed on two significant collections of his books to key academic institutions.

In 1884 he gifted to the Hungarian Academy of Sciences forty Tibetan books. These had been given to him, when he taught at Bishop's College Calcutta (1838–1840), by his friend, the Hungarian Tibetologist Alexander Csoma de Kőrös (1784–1842).

In 1885, to the delight of Sir Monier Monier-Williams, Boden Professor of Sanskrit at the University of Oxford, he entrusted to the newly founded Indian Institute at Oxford 4017 of his books.

Perhaps his legacy may also be found in a modern seminar in Dorset? When I served as Bishop of Sherborne (2009–2015), I wanted to encourage current "scholar-priests," in the tradition of Malan. I mentioned his iconic life to the ten clergy who joined me when I founded the "Harding Seminar." This met (and still meets) once a term for Evening Prayer at Sherborne Abbey, followed by dinner at the Eastbury Hotel, after which a theological paper would be presented and discussed.

St. Stephen Harding (ca. 1050–1134), after whom the seminar is named, was also a Dorset priest of surprising influence whose legacy needs appreciating more today.[4] He was a monk at Sherborne Abbey who later became the third Abbot of Citeaux, a mentor of St Bernard of Clairvaux, the writer of the Cistercian constitution, *Carta Caritatis*, and the founder of thirteen other Abbeys in France.

Solomon Caesar Malan delighted in and translated wisdom from Oriental Proverbs for the benefit and wider learning of many. On the website of the Mission Theology in the Anglican Communion project, which I now direct, we are collecting proverbs from around the world. One of my favourites is from China:

> An oil lamp becomes brighter after trimming, a truth becomes clearer after being discussed.[5]

May this book of deep research and eminent insight encourage many contemporary scholars to discuss truth with each other and, in the tradition of Malan, combine profound research with humble ministry.

Select Bibliography

Chadwick, Owen. 1970. *The Victorian Church Part* II. London: Adam and Charles Black.

Hudson, Charles F. Hudson – Ezra Abbot. 1885. *A Critical Greek and English Concordance of the New Testament*. London: Samuel Bagster and Sons.

---

[4] Kings 2015.

[5] Mission Theology in the Anglican Communion, http://www.missiontheologyanglican.org/resource/what-is-truth/ (accessed 21 December 2020).

Kings, Graham. 2015. "English Monk who Encouraged the Ministry of Women." *The Times* (UK) (31 January 2015), p. 85, available online at Fulcrum (renewing the evangelical centre), https://www.fulcrum-anglican.org.uk/articles/english-monk-who-encouraged-the-ministry-of-women/ (accessed 21 December 2020).

ABBREVIATIONS

ANM	Arthur Noel Malan (Solomon Caesar Malan's elder son)
CKJV	Corrections to the King James Version (by Solomon Caesar Malan)
CM	César [Jacques] Malan (Solomon Caesar Malan's younger brother)
CMGA	Gédéon Sabliet, *César Malan. Un gagneur d'âmes, 1787–1864, d'après l'ouvrage de C. Malan fils, les écrits de Malan et les documents de famille* (Dieulefit: Nouvelle société d'éditions de Toulouse, 1936).
GS	Gédéon Sabliet
JL	James Legge
KJV	King James Version
LRHES	Solomon Cæsar Malan, *A Letter to the Right Honourable the Earl of Shaftesbury, President of the British and Foreign Bible Society: On the Pantheistic and on the Buddhistic Tendency of the Chinese and of the Mongolian Versions of the Bible Published by that Society* (London: Bell and Daldy, 1856).
LWCK	Theodore Duka, *Life and Works of Alexander Csoma de Kőrös: A Biography Compiled Chiefly from hitherto Unpublished Data. With a Brief Notice of Each of His Published Works and Essays, as well as of His still Extant Manuscripts* (London: Trübner, 1885). Reprinted Abingdon: Routledge, 2000.
LYM	S. C. Malan, *Letters to a Young Missionary* (London: Joseph Masters, 1858).
ONBP	S. C. Malan (trans. and annot.), *Original Notes on the Book of Proverbs*, Vol. 1 subtitled *"according to the Authorised Version"*; Vols. 2 and 3 subtitled *"Mostly from Eastern Writing."* 3 vols. (London: Williams and Norgate, 1889–1893).
ONBP Ms	S. C. Malan, Manuscript version of *Original Notes on the Book of Proverbs*
SCM	Solomon Caesar Malan
SCM DD	*Solomon Cæsar Malan, D.D.: Memorials of His Life and Writings.* Published by his son, the Rev. Arthur Noel Malan (London: John Murray, 1897).
SCRR	S. C. Malan, *Seven Chapters [S. Matthew i-vi; S. Luke xi] of the Revision of 1881 Revised* (London: Hatchards, 1881).
STK	S. C. Malan (trans.), *The Three-fold San-tsze-king: or, The Triliteral Classic of China, as issued I. by Wang-Po-keou, II. by Protestant Missionaries in that Country; and III. by the Rebel-chief Tae-ping-wang*, put into English, with notes, by the Rev. S. C. Malan (London: D. Nutt, 1856).

VeTCM	*La vie et les travaux de César Malan, ministre du Saint évangile dans l'Église de Genève, pasteur de l'Église du Témoignage, Dr en théologie de l'Université de Glasgow.* Published by his son, César [Jacques] Malan (Geneva – Paris: Cherbuliez, 1869). Accessible online using the following URL: http://books.google.com/books?vid=BCUL1092579436 (accessed 21 December 2020).
WIGC	S. C. Malan, *Who is God in China, Shin or Shang-Te? Remarks on the Etymology of* אֱלֹהִים *and of ΘΕΟΣ, and on the Rendering of those Terms into Chinese* (London: Samuel Bagster and Sons, 1855).

1

S. C. MALAN'S FAMILIAL AND ECCLESIASTICAL CONTEXT IN GENEVA

Frédéric Amsler

1. Introduction

Two older biographies describe the familial context of César Jean Salomon Malan (in English, Solomon Cæsar Malan): one is the biography by Arthur Noel Malan (1846–1933), SCM being his father;[1] the other was by César Jacques Malan (1821–1889), SCM's younger brother, about Henri-Abraham-César Malan (1787–1864), their father.[2] Both biographies were written by sons to honor the memory of their fathers. This means, of course, that they were well informed about many details, but naturally lacked enough critical distance to reveal a comprehensive vision of either fathers' life and works. Undoubtedly, the strong character of the father of SCM dominated both of these accounts of the Malan family context in Geneva. During the 19th and 20th centuries, some more biographies were published about SCM's father, César Malan, and all continue to highlight this general impression. First came a short text by a leader of the Free Church Jean Augustin Bost,[3] then in 1936 one written in French by Gédéon Sabliet;[4] and in 1997 one in Dutch by W. van der Zwaag[5] and finally one from a revivalist point of view by Patrick Chenaux.[6]

Unfortunately, and somewhat ironically, all of the above volumes' documentation of Swiss Protestant life in Geneva is quite poor. Consequently, this contribution will be based primarily on materials from those older biographies, but I will add some interpretive elements which will place them into wider historical and cultural perspectives.[7]

---

[1] See *SCM DD*.

[2] See *VeTCM*.

[3] Bost 1865.

[4] See *CMGA*.

[5] See van der Zwaag 1997. Unfortunately, this volume remained inaccessible to me because, first of all, it is written in Dutch, and secondly, because the most accessible copy of this work is held in the Bibliothèque des Cèdres in Lausanne, which was closed when I initially pursued research for this chapter and, unfortunately, will remain closed for several more years. The lack of access to materials from this library is very regrettable, because it was the library of the Free Church in that part of Switzerland (l'Église libre vaudoise), a church close to the Réveil (Revivalism) which existed during the period of our study. Consequently, it contains a very rich collection of books and materials related to Swiss ecclesiastical history of the 19th century, and notably, possesses the Malan family archives. In the end, I was able to consult that family archive, but it did not provide any major information relevant for this study.

[6] Chenaux 2000.

[7] Amsler, forthcoming.

To begin, I will introduce the microcosmos of 18th and 19th century Geneva, starting with some remarks about the Malan family context there, and then move on to describe and discuss the larger political and ecclesiastical contexts which enveloped their lives.

2. The Malan Family and Its Historical Context

Both biographies about César and SCM highlight the Malan family's origins. ANM attributes some qualities of his father's character to features of his ancestors, who from late medieval times were located in the region of the Vallées Vaudoises in Piemont. He subsequently described his father in the following terms:

> [He maintained a] steadfast faith in the Bible, [with] stubborn resolution in its defence, enthusiasm regulated by faith, strong sympathy with the spirit of nature in mountain, torrent, and forest, [and] an instinctive tendency towards retirement.[8]

By this means the biographer refers back to the religious wars of the 1540s in the southern part of France, particularly in Mérindol, where a branch of the family Malan had been well established. Among their relatives were those who are counted as martyrs of the Protestant faith, especially after the Revocation of the Edict of Nantes (1685).[9] So, after his sister had been tortured, Pierre Malan, the great great grandfather of SCM, fled from persecution and re-established his family in the Protestant enclave of Geneva in 1722.[10]

In his biographical monograph César Jacques Malan indicates that "he [his father] always considered a real title of nobility to belong to this small group of confessors, and to have in his family the 'glorious blood of the martyrs'."[11]

Echoing these claims, ANM writes about his grandfather, César Malan, that he was

> known and revered in all the Christian world, endured persecution for his faith in the spirit of the Vaudois, not, indeed, of fire and sword, but of insult, scorn, and injury; coming out of the then Socinian Church of Geneva, and shining as a light in a dark place, boldly declaring the Divinity of our Lord, and suffering deprivation of all things rather than deny his faith.[12]

This is truly a hagiographic depiction stemming from a 19th century Victorian image of the "noble great man." Although I do not feel the need to deny that a family might be constituted as much by the blood relationship among its members as by its historically and genealogically constituted collective memory, it seems to me that this explanation is terribly insufficient for understanding the life of César Malan as well as that of his son, Solomon Caesar Malan.

---

[8] See *SCM DD*, p. 2.
[9] Consult *SCM DD*, p. 4 and *CMGA*, p. 26.
[10] See *SCM DD*, pp. 4-5 and *CMGA*, p. 26.
[11] *VeTCM*, p. 20. This author's translation.
[12] Quoting from *SCM DD*, pp. 5 and 11.

Furthering these doubts are the facts that certain strange gaps in the accounts of the father's life appear within these two older biographies. On the one hand, for example, in the work of Arthur Noel Malan, there is no mention at all of the religious conversion of César Malan, the author's grandfather, which is prominently displayed in the volume by the author's uncle. Also missing is any account of the larger political situation of Geneva in the early 19th century. On the other hand, in the work by César Malan about his father, who bore the same name, there is no mention that his father had at one point in his life joined a Freemasons Lodge in Geneva, a fact that begs for further explanation. In addition, it seems particularly unjustified for him to ignore the political, cultural and economical conditions which influenced and shaped the theological conflicts which clearly constitute much of the interpretive content of his biography.

So here I intend to propose another explanation of the familial and ecclesiastical context of the Malan family in Geneva. The focus of my attention will be on the life of the father, César Malan, and will include a discussion of the political and theological contexts in Geneva at the turn of 18th and 19th centuries.

3. The Political and Ecclesiastical Contexts of Geneva

At the beginning of the 19th century, the Church of Geneva, which had adopted the Reformation on May 21, 1536, had from that time onward been always governed by the Calvinist ecclesiastical prescriptions of 1541 (revised in 1576 and after). These laws established four types of ministries within the Church and the Genevan society: the ministries of pastors, deacons, elders and doctors.[13] Until its abandonment in 1725, all young Genevans continued to learn by heart Calvin's Catechism of 1542 during their Sunday School lessons. As a consequence, it was a strong and fundamental influence for building up Genevan Calvinist theology and ethos, and marked the personal identities of the city's residents.[14] Notably, the second article of the Constitution of the Republic of Geneva dated February 5, 1794, a very democratic Constitution mirroring this aspect of the French Constitution, granted Genevan citizenship only to those persons who belonged to the "Protestant or reformed religion."[15] Subsequently, in the revision of the Constitution published in October 6, 1796, it prescribed that "any public act of a religion different from the Protestant or reformed religion is not allowed in the Republic."[16] From these historical facts we can underscore just how much the city of Geneva was truly a reformed republic of the Calvinist sort. It required that those who lived there would accept the religious orientation of the rulers, and so in this sense it supported the post-Reformation political principle, *cuius regio, eius religio*. As a consequence, it also became a

---

[13] The doctors are the teachers and lecturers of the Academy. This ministry remained the least developed in this ecclesiastical project as conceived by Calvin himself, and remained underdeveloped afterwards as well.

[14] Consult Veuilleumier 1983, p. 77.

[15] *Constitution genevoise, acceptée par la Nation*, art. 2: 21.

[16] *Constitution genevoise, sanctionnée par le souverain*, Titel XV, art. 750: 158.

haven for those who sought freedom from persecution because they were Protestants, and so this added legal protection for these new immigrants exercising their *ius emigrandi*.[17]

3.1. The Regime of the Annexation (1798–1815)

The Napoleonic Annexation of the Geneva Republic took place on April 15, 1798, which essentially required its integration into the so-called "Département du Léman," through the *Traité de Réunion de la République de Genève à la République Française* of April 26, 1798.[18] Its purpose was to break apart the dominance of the Protestant reformed tradition, depriving that tradition of its political exclusivity and cultural privileges in the city. The Concordat of July 15, 1801 – conceived by Napoleon Bonaparte as the first consul and supported by the current pope Pius VII – included "organic laws" which established the free public exercise of Roman Catholic worship within all French territories. This was arranged, however, no longer as a "State religion," but only on the basis that it was the religion of the majority of the citizens.[19]

From a religious perspective, this Concordat produced a seismic change within Geneva. In essence, it allowed Roman Catholicism to regain a cultural foothold within the city, one that was officially and publicly supported for the first time since the abolition of the mass in 1535. As already mentioned, it supported the free exercise of Roman Catholic worship in areas under French sovereignty as guaranteed under the first article of the Concordat; consequently, the Prefect of the "Département du Léman" was responsible for its realization.[20] Subsequently, Roman Catholics became established once more in Geneva, including approximately 4,000 parishioners in 1800. By this means they were able to create a Roman Catholic parish within the city, having received the Saint-Germain church on loan for that purpose,

---

[17] It should be emphasized that it was hardly thinkable in the 16th century Holy Roman Empire that people would not have the same religion as the prince, or that there could be more than one religion under the same jurisdiction. For people who adhered to a religion differing from that of the prince, they had no other choices than to change their religious affiliation or emigrate as specified by the Augsburg Settlement of 1555. From this perspective, the Revocation of the Edict of Nantes was shocking, because it forbade Protestants from leaving the French Kingdom.

[18] As documented in Métral – Fleury 2011, pp. 133-134 (see p. 135 for bibliography and pp. 136-140 for the text of the treatise).

[19] "Le gouvernement de la république française reconnaît que la religion catholique, apostolique et romaine, est la religion de la grande majorité des Français. Sa Sainteté reconnaît également que cette même religion a retiré et attend encore, en ce moment, le plus grand bien et le plus grand éclat de l'établissement du culte catholique en France, et de la profession particulière qu'en font les consuls de la république. "En conséquence, d'après cette reconnaissance mutuelle, tant pour le bien de la religion que pour le maintien de la tranquillité intérieure, ils sont convenus de ce qui suit: Art. 1er. La religion catholique, apostolique et romaine, sera librement exercée en France; son culte sera public, en se conformant aux règlements de police que le gouvernement jugera nécessaires pour la tranquillité publique." See *Textes du Concordat*.

[20] Consult Ganter 1986, p. 353.

and being given grounds for a cemetery outside the city wall.[21] This small religious community was led for almost forty years (1804–1843) by the priest Jean-François Vuarin. His religious commitment in this revolutionary context was summed up in the following formula: "When you are the priest of Geneva, you go there, you stay there, and you die there!"[22]

Of course, from a legal and political point of view, the Annexation entailed the death of Geneva as a Protestant republic. Nevertheless, resistance to these political conditions was also organized. In fact, the Protestant Church in Geneva and its related school system were going to remain the two unique Genevan institutions which originated from what was referred to during the Napoleonic era as "the Ancien Régime." What this meant, then, is that the Protestant Church and the School were both institutions which would continue to carry and promote Protestant identity among Genevan citizens even during the Annexation, even in spite of the fact that the exclusive legal and political privileges they had previously included were no longer prevalent.

In the light of all these important political and cultural changes, we can now reflect on the status of the members of the Malan family. As a regent and pastor himself, and being the son of a previous regent and even a grandson of an even earlier regent, César Malan was a brilliant student and a promising leader nurtured within the Genevan school system. Being a descendant of Huguenot refugees added to his religious prestige, so that he had all the qualities required to carry on and extend the Protestant identity of Calvinist Geneva within its previous political context as a Protestant Republic. Consequently, the Napoleonic Annexation brought him and his family a major cultural and political challenge, which he and others like him needed to address.

3.2. The Constitution of 1815

While it was the case that some patriotic citizens in Geneva may have imagined that the Restoration of the Republic of Geneva on December 31st, 1813, would mean the end of the young Roman Catholic community and the return to the cultural and political conditions prevailing before the Annexation after the collapse of the Napoleonic empire and the surrender of its forces, in fact this was not a genuine possibility. The new Swiss canton of Geneva manifested on the religious and cultural level a certain amount of originality. It became a society mixed with different denominations of Christianity by the incorporation of the "Communes réunies," which meant that Sardinian and French territories were incorporated into the territory belonging to Geneva in order to create a less divided territory.[23] This territorial reorganization – required for the entry of Geneva to the Swiss Confederation at that

---

[21] See Ganter 1986, pp. 354-355.

[22] Cited from Ganter 1986, p. 357.

[23] At that time there were 22,300 inhabitants in the city, and in addition 9,139 lived within the 13 "communes genevoises," all of them being only Protestant. There were also 4,350 inhabitants within the six French communes, with another 12,700 residents also in the 16 communes under the sovereignty of the King of Sardinia, all of them being only Roman Catholic. In

time – marks from a legal point of view the definitive end of the cultural and political equation which had prevailed before the Napoleonic Annexation, i.e., that to be a Genevan was to be Protestant. So, from a cultural point of view, the Protestant Genevan "unanimimity" which was born in 1536 ended in 1815; from that time onward, more than 40% of the Genevan population was identified as Roman Catholic. The Roman Catholic populace would even become the majority for a short period of time in 1860, however, Genevan Protestant citizens generally remained the majority.[24]

In the light of these major changes in the cultural and political landscape of Geneva, a series of legal requirements were established to prevent a possible assimilation of Protestants by Roman Catholics,[25] and of Roman Catholics by Protestants.[26] These political measures are not easily understood by those of us in the 21st century because our political, religious and cultural values have been shaped by the Universal Declaration of Human Rights promulgated in 1948 by the United Nations. Nevertheless, these legal conditions raised no major problems for 19th century Genevans, and so would be ratified subsequently by other international treaties, as we will see. In fact, these legal measures highlighted the mutual mistrust prevailing between these two Christian communities; they had no intention whatsoever of allowing for any freedom of religion or freedom of conscience. What these political changes did require is that there could be no exclusive connection between the political and religious authorities, as had happened in the past within Geneva. The Genevan political authorities were responsible for civil order, but with regard

---

total, then, there were 31,439 Protestants and 17,050 Roman Catholics inhabiting Geneva at that time. Cf. Ganter 1986, p. 367.

[24] In 1860 there were 40,727 Protestants in Geneva (but among them were 4,825 foreigners) in contrast to 42,618 Catholics (among whom 24,506 were foreigners), as claimed in Ruchon 1953, p. 127. For a full assessment of the major changes of this period, consult Amsler – Scholl 2013.

[25] In the first article of the so-called "eventual laws" (in the case of possession by Geneva of new territories) joined to the Constitution of August 24, 1814, "the preservation, the free exercise and the maintenance of the [Roman] Catholic worship services for Genevans of the new territory" is guaranteed. See *Constitution pour la Ville et République de Genève*. On the civic level, the "eventual laws" limited the Roman Catholic representation in the Councils. Even if the Roman Catholic population outnumbered the Protestant populace in the old territory, its representation could not be more than one third of the 250 deputies in the representative Council.

[26] So, paragraph 1 of article 3 of the Protocol of Vienna of March 29, 1815 asserts that "the Catholic Religion will be maintained and protected in the same way as it is now in all the municipalities given up by S. Mr. King of Sardinia, and which will be gathered in the Canton of Geneva." See *Protocol de Vienne du 29 mars 1815*. One year later, article 12 of the Treaty of Turin of March 16, 1816 (made between the King of Sardinia, the Swiss Confederacy, and the canton of Geneva) asserts that "it was advisable that the laws and the current uses on 29 March 1815, with regard to the Catholic Religion in all the given up territory, will be maintained, except that it is differently adjusted by the authority of the Holy See." See *Traité de Turin entre Sa Majesté le roi de Sardaigne, la Confédération suisse et le canton de Genève du 16 mars 1816*.

to the religious affiliations of its citizens, the Roman Catholic citizens of the "Communes réunies" remained under the ultimate authority of the Holy See guaranteed by the King of Sardinia.[27]

The cultural coexistence of two forms of Christian worship within the same political jurisdiction obliged the Genevan State to specify the respective rights and duties of both parties. Nevertheless, on the basis of the new legal arrangements in the second decade of the 19th century, the Protestant community was far better integrated into the institutions of the Genevan State than those belonging to the Roman Catholic community.[28] Even though it seemed that the Protestant community had been extensively restricted by the new political treaties, the fact was that the Protestant Church in Geneva retained a considerable influence because the link between Protestant religion and Genevan citizenship was not directly challenged. What happened legally was the affirmation that nationals of the "Communes réunies" had the right to be Roman Catholic and Genevan, but they became Genevans with an implicit "second class" status.[29] Once again, this is shocking for those of us who live in the 21st century, but the Genevan oligarchic system was in reality perfectly in touch with its time and with the attitudes of European monarchs during the first half of the 19th century. During that period, political changes by means of constitutional restructuring were granted only with difficulty. For example, there was no interest in supporting universal suffrage.[30]

---

[27] These religious guarantees did not obviously facilitate the integration of the new populations, especially because the Roman Catholics depended on a Sardinian bishop, the bishop of Chambéry. Though determined in 1815, the difficult transfer of Genevan Roman Catholics of the diocese of Chambéry to that of Lausanne succeeded only in 1819. See Ganter 1986, pp. 376-385. Later on, the promulgation by the Genevan magistrate on January 1, 1822, of a new matrimonial law removing from parishes the marital registers provoked a strong reaction in Sardinia, which, through the federal Directory, later compelled the Genevan Legislative Council to exclude the application of this law in those municipalities that were formerly under Sardinian control.

[28] Article 2 of the title XI specifies that "at the head of the lay members [of the Consistory] will be two Advisors of State elected for three years by the aforementioned Council and the Company of the Pastors."

[29] In comparison, Roman Catholicism would remain the state religion in France until the end of the reign of Charles X (1824–1830). After the Uprising of 1830, Louis-Philippe I would not restore Roman Catholicism to its former status.

[30] As mentioned above, the Holy Roman Empire, which only officially disappeared at the Congress of Vienna, was from the 16th century governed by the principle of religious segregation, *cuius regio, eius religio*. The Genevan provisions are an adaptation of this old principle involving a dissociation of civil and religious powers in the new territories. At the beginning of the 19th century, it still was not self-evident that Roman Catholic territories were administered by Protestants, nor that the Geneva government had in fact integrated Roman Catholics into their political life. In other words, the fact was that that mixed territories were administered by a newly mixed government. In Geneva men's universal suffrage dates back to 1842.

Fig. 2: Sketch of Lake Geneva by S. C. Malan. Reprinted with permission of The Getty Research Institute, Los Angeles. ID no.: gri_2013_m_25_b6_052

4. The Theological Context of Geneva in the Early 1800s

I shall be much briefer in my discussion of the theological context of Geneva at the beginning of the 19th century, because the biographers we referred to above clearly favor the Protestant Revivalism (*Réveil*) of the period, and insist on underscoring its importance, especially because César Malan collaborated with that movement.

Summarily speaking, Genevan Protestantism was profoundly influenced by the ideas of the Enlightenment. There is a famous portrayal of this theological shift in the pages of the article entitled "Genève" within the seventh volume of the *Encyclopédie* edited by Diderot and Alembert:[31] "To describe it simply and straightforwardly, many of the pastors of Geneva have no other religion than what is a perfect Socinianism, rejecting all that they call mysteries."[32] We have also the claims made in *La seconde lettre de la montagne* (Amsterdam, 1764) written by Jean-Jacques Rousseau, where he elaborates the following scenario:

> It is asked of the ministers of the Church of Geneva if Jesus Christ be God? They dare not answer. It is asked, if he were a mere man? They are embarrassed, and will not say they think so. A philosopher, with a glance of the eye, penetrates their character. He sees them to be Arians, Socinians, Deists [...]. Oh, Genevans! Those gentlemen, your ministers, in truth are very singular people! They do not

---

[31] See *Encyclopédie ou Dictionnaire raisonné des sciences, des arts et des métiers*, p. 578, A.
[32] Consult both ANM, *SCM, DD*, p. 10 and *Encyclopédie ou Dictionnaire raisonné ...* .

know what they believe or what they do not believe. They do not even know what they would wish to appear to believe. Their only manner of establishing their faith is to attack the faith of others.[33]

The doctrinal charges contained in the article from the *Encyclopédie* stimulated a quick reaction from the "Compagnie des pasteurs" (the assembly of the Genevan Protestant ministers). They published a declaration on February 10, 1758, to defend themselves, but the ideological damage had been done, and their response was unable to counter the critical image produced by the *Encyclopédie*.

Historically speaking, this was the situation which the Genevan Revivalists sought to exploit in numerous ways.

5. Reconsiderations about César Malan's Influence on His Son

So now, in the light of all these political, religious and ecclesiastical explanations, what do we have to say about César Malan and his influence on his first son, Solomon Caesar Malan?

Henri-Abraham-César Malan was born in Geneva on July 7, 1787, the second of two sons, a gifted child who was already reading when he was only three and a half years old,[34] he received almost all of his schooling in Geneva, spending only one year in Marseille at the age of 17. It was at that time in his life that he appears to have decided to study theology. In 1809, he completed his studies very successfully subsequently becoming a regent or teacher for the fifth class of the College or middle school in Geneva, fulfilling what had become an intergenerational family tradition. As it had happened, his father, Jaques-Imbert Malan, had served as a regent of the fourth class in that same school, succeeding his father-in-law, Prestreau.[35] From this point of view, César Malan was a pure and brilliant product of Genevan education. As a regent, he introduced the educational method of "mutual education" promoted by Andrew Bell and Joseph Lancaster, teaching using this method in Yverdon in the school named for Henri Pestalozzi. César Malan was undoubtedly one of the best regents in the College of Geneva during this period of time. One historian adds the following note about this stellar teacher among the young Genevans:

> That same year [1809], he joined the Freemason Lodge which was called "L'union des coeurs" ("the union of hearts"). Its members, who all claimed to be Christians, made the Bible their favorite topic of study, practicing communal prayer as a daily discipline, and supported the rites of their order. [Malan himself] obtained in 1811 the status of "the rectified Scottish Regime" – a means to open up an impulse toward a spiritual life.[36]

---

[33] Cited from *SCM, DD*, p. 10.

[34] As claimed in *VeTCM*, p. 26.

[35] See *VeTCM*, p. 21.

[36] Cited from Mützenberg 1997, p. 90. For a complete study of freemasonry in Geneva in the 19th century, see Ruchon 1935, pp. 133-134. Ruchon indicates in particular that the pastor Charles-Etienne-François Moulinié had given to the oldest Genevan Lodge, the "Union of

On April 25, 1811, César Malan married Salomé Georgette Jeanne Schönenberger. They would have twelve children, among whom Salomon César Jean was the first. Everything seemed to be going very well for them. Still, I take it to be very important to underscore the fact that César Malan was a child of the Napoleonic Annexation. He completed all of his intellectual and professional training during the Annexation, which was a period when the Protestant reformed faith served as a very strong component for any traditional Genevan identity in the context of the new inter-denominational competition. Along with other theologically trained Protestant pastors of this period, he belonged to a generation of "patriotic pastors" who based the sustainability of the Genevan identity on the traditions of Protestant reformed religion.

If it is true that serious religious doubts in César Malan's life began in 1813, and that the activities associated with Revivalism in Geneva did not directly influence him, then it is justified historically to connect his future "conversion" of 1816 with some deep and troubled reflections about Genevan identity. During the two years period from 1813 to 1814, it seemed that the fate of Geneva was bound to Switzerland, and that Geneva would never again be the Protestant reformed Republic which she had previously been. How would someone like César Malan overcome this threatening political transition? The mainstream of the Genevan Protestants was to make the reunion with the Swiss political alliance a strategic and symbolic return to past religious and cultural conditions, as if nothing significant had changed, and so to maintain as strong a link as possible between the Protestant Church and the Genevan State. Consequently, one would intend to broadcast in this time the image of Geneva as the "Protestant Rome," the "Citadel of the Reformation" and the "city of Calvin." Even though this was more of a myth than a political, social or theological reality, it was a strategically attractive option. In fact, it became the main cultural solution for many Genevans, and so remains an influential interpretive emphasis even in the 21st century.

Hearts," a Christian orientation very close to revivalism. He also confirms that for pastoral reasons Malan had already resigned from the lodge in 1814.

Fig. 3: Color Image by S. C. Malan / Sketch of Swiss Alps through a Wooden Window. Reprinted with permission of The Getty Research Institute, Los Angeles. ID no.: gri_2013_m_25_b6_051

The option of the Revival and of Malan would be to "return sincerely to the original sources," to reinstate the strict doctrines of Calvin which had previously been associated with "the glory of the city." Due to his familial origins rooted in French Huguenot traditions, César Malan probably inherited an idealized and nostalgic image of Geneva as a city of refuge, something like a heavenly Jerusalem on the European continent. Having lost her Calvinist theological moorings during the 18th century, Geneva in the early years of the 19th century was also losing her political and cultural uniqueness, especially during the years between 1813 and 1815. Following the claims of his biographers, admittedly we can attribute the religious conversion of César Malan to the special work of the Holy Spirit. Nevertheless, we need to qualify the nature of this conversion much more precisely in both religious and cultural terms. César Malan was already a religious man and a respected pastor in Geneva. His transformed life involved a theological conversion which coincided exactly with the crisis of identity bound up with the advent of a new Geneva based upon the political conditions of the Congress of Vienna. Consequently, we should underscore that César Malan did not convert from atheism to a traditional Protestant form of faith, but from a form of rationalized Protestant theology to another Protestant theological orientation typified as being simultaneously strict Calvinist, mystical and romantic, meaning that it was more existential, rooted in biblical texts, and promoting the transformation of human life through the Spirit of Christ.

Immediately after his conversion, César Malan found a number of theological echoes and parallels with those involved in the Genevan Revivalism. His biographers count this as an advantage for Malan after his conversion, but here I want to focus on an alternative interpretation, considering what he was missing or losing during this process. Malan became involved with propagators of British Revivalism or Methodism in Europe (Robert Haldane, Richard Wilcox, Henry Drummond) and the young Genevan theological students who were their disciples (Emile Guers, Henri-Louis Empeytaz, Henry Pyt, and Ami Bost, among others), sharing the same theological concerns, but deviating from them on the ecclesiological level. The partisans of the Réveil were separatists; they wanted to establish a new Church; César Malan, on the contrary, opposed this move, prompted by his Genevan patriotism and his attachment to the Protestant Reformed Church of Geneva.[37] Although the case of his ministerial dismissal by the contemporary Genevan pastoral elders was only treated as a theological dispute, the real problem appears to me to be the threat of separatism. Since Genevan Protestants had remained unified for more than three centuries, we can understand why the ecclesiastical authorities undertook all means to avoid an internal division when Geneva became a denominationally mixed territory.

Consequently, in the context of his own independent congregation meeting at the Chapel of Witnessing, César Malan would exercise his talents as a clergyman, a teacher (by his catechisms), a hymn writer (producing more than a thousand new hymns), and a popular writer on theological, religious and moral topics within his many publications. All this he pretended to do in the context of the Protestant Reformed Church in Geneva which he sincerely appealed to. Nevertheless, the leaders

---

[37] "For Malan, whom [the authorities] had suggested to restrain, he hesitated for a long time. Though he was de facto forbidden from preaching, he felt freer towards his Church, without admitting however that he had lost any of his rights. He had no scruples in distributing the Last Supper to some brothers in Mr. Drummond's particular lounge on September 21, 1817, four months after the famous Règlement [dated from May 3, 1817]. This very independent act confused some observers, even as he later confused them even more by his strange act of submission. Indeed, in May 1818 he submitted to the requirements of the 'Respectable Company' [the Council of Genevan Protestant pastors], and signed the form. Having been openly orthodox, evangelical and a convinced convert for several years, he had in fact no separatist tendencies. [...] Subsequently in 1820 he [Malan] decided to build the Chapel of Witnessing [Chapelle du Témoignage] within his own property, for which he received generous subsidies from supporters. Still, he did not intend this as an act of ecclesiastical separatism. He preached there, gathering around him a certain number of persons to whom he fed the Word of life. Although he did accept the title of minister from them, in that chapel he neither baptized nor distributed the Last Supper. To preach the Gospel was his only concern; to assert the truth his only preoccupation." Quoting from Bost 1865, pp. 21-25, translation mine. "After this the Company dismissed him from the ecclesiastical ministry, and the Chapel of Witnessing was organized as an independent Church in 1824. The Church of Bourg-de-Four had already existed for six years, but Malan preferred for diverse motives not to connect his work directly with that of his brothers, even though all of them knew that they served in a common ministerial work." (As stated in Bost 1865, p. 25, translation mine). According to the will of César Malan himself, the Chapel of Witnessing was destroyed at his death in 1864. The only memory that remains in Geneva of these events is the name of the small "rue de la Chapelle" that ran alongside of it.

of that church refused to listen to him, did not want to have anything more to do with him, and he lost his wages overnight.

As we have seen, SCM, the first son of César Malan, was born on April 22, 1812, and had a very different personal history from that of his father. I generally agree with his son, A.N. Malan, when he writes about the youth of his father during the period of his grandfather's dismissal from the Genevan clergy, that it imbued him with a deep distrust of society, and probably of Geneva, but curiously not of religion![38]

Undoubtedly, from his father SCM received his piety. As one of the sons of César Malan wrote,

> It is this feeling that he printed in our children's hearts, that God is, not an *idea*, but an *alive reality*. [...] Our father was not content with saying this to us; he did much more than this, and did it in much better ways! He convinced us of it by means of the way he lived his life! He walked every day within our presence, and up to the end, as seeing the One who is invisible![39]

In this sense, then, the Malan family life was placed under the permanent eye of God, with a period for worship in the morning as well as one in the evening during every day, which no child could escape. Before every meal there was prayer, and when guests departed, they were offered a blessing and a wish for their return. Particularly as the first son of this Malan household with its very self-consciously affirmed history, SCM could only with difficulty choose a vocation that did not directly involve Protestant religious faith. But by becoming a missionary to India, and an international traveler, not to mention being later an Anglican vicar and Orientalist, SCM could persuade his immediate family members that he followed in the spiritual footsteps of his father, even though he undoubtedly had decisively moved away from his father's Protestant Genevan patriotism with its reformed and evangelical theological tradition.

---

[38] "Such were the external associations amid which the young Salomon received his earliest impressions. As his mind gradually dawned with powers of intelligence more keenly appreciative and observant than is usual in childhood, he must have formed strange views of society. Indeed, from the few allusions that he ever made to his experiences of those early years, it is clear that his first impression of the world was little else than abhorrence. Seeing his father the object of insult and persecution, which often rendered it advisable that his children should not go beyond the bounds of the garden at Pré l'Evêque (the name of the house was changed to 'Pré Béni' in 1827), his infant mind conceived vague notions of fear and dislike towards those who lived outside the garden-gate. His highly sensitive nature thus received a bias towards a spirit of antagonism; and this, being grafted on a determined will, developed with advancing years into strong resentment against oppression, and a resolute zeal to fight for the right." *SCM DD*, pp. 11-12.

[39] Quoting from *CMGA*, p. 150, translation and emphasis mine.

Select Bibliography

Amsler, Frédéric – Sarah Scholl (eds.). 2013. *L'apprentissage du pluralisme religieux. Le cas genevois au XIXe siècle*. Genève: Labor et Fides.

———. forthcoming. "César Malan, chantre à contretemps." In: Jean-Pierre Bastian, Christian Grosse and Sarah Scholl (eds.), *Les fractures protestantes en Suisse romande au XIXe siècle*. Genève: Labor et Fides, 2021, pp. 238-265.

Bost, Jean-Augustın. 1865. *César Malan: Impressions, notes et souvenirs*. Genève – Paris: Emile Béroud – Ch. Meyrueis.

Chenaux, Patrick. 2000. "César Malan à Genève: Le doux et l'amer de l'Évangile." *La Revue réformée* 51 (mars 2000) 2 (207), pp. 66-77.

Constitution genevoise, acceptée par la Nation le 5 février 1794, l'an 3 de l'Egalité, et précédée de la Déclaration des droits de l'homme. Genève: Pierre Francou, by J. J. Paschoud, 1794. Text available online: doc.rero.ch/record/7821 (accessed December 21, 2020).

Constitution genevoise, sanctionnée par le souverain le 5 février 1794, l'an 3 de l'Egalité: Modifiée et compléttée, Ensuite du vœu exprimé, le 31 août 1795, par un très-grand nombre de citoyens, le 6 Octobre 1796, l'an 5 de l'Égalité. Précédée de la Déclaration des droits et des devoirs de l'homme social, consacré par la nation genevoise le 9 juin 1793 l'an 2 de l'Égalité. Genève: L'imprimerie du Luc Sestié, 1796.

Constitution pour la Ville et République de Genève (adoptée le 24 août 1814) http://http://doc.rero.ch/record/7822?ln=de (accessed March 4, 2021).

Encyclopédie ou Dictionnaire raisonné des sciences, des arts et des métiers de Denis Diderot et Jean Le Rond d'Alembert, t. 7, (Paris: Briasson, David, Lebreton, Durand, 1758). https://fr.wikisource.org/wiki/L'Encyclopédie/1re_édition/Volume_7 (accessed March 4, 2021).

Ganter, Edmond. 1986. *L'Église catholique de Genève: Seize siècles d'histoire*. Geneva: Slatkine.

Métral, Véronique – Patrick Fleury (eds. and annot.) 2011. *Histoire de Genève par les textes des origines à nos jours*. Genève: Slatkine.

Mützenberg, Gabriel. 1997. *Grands pédagogues de Suisse romande*. Lausanne: L'Age d'homme.

Protocole de Vienne du 29 mars 1815. https://www.ge.ch/legislation/accords/doc/3001.pdf (accessed December 21, 2020).

Ruchon, François. 1935. *Histoire de la franc-maçonnerie à Genève de 1736 à 1900 d'après des documents inédits*. Reprint Genève: Slatkine, 2004.

———. 1953. *Histoire politique de la République de Genève: De la Restauration à la suppression du budget des cultes (31 décembre 1813 – 30 juin 1907)*. Vol. 2. Genève: Alexandre Jullien.

Textes du Concordat (15 juillet 1801/26 messidor an IX) et Articles organiques (8 avril 1802/18 germinal an X). Text available online: http://www.napoleon.org/histoire-des-2-empires/articles/le-concordat-de-1801 (accessed December 21, 2020).

Traité de Turin entre Sa Majesté le roi de Sardaigne, la Confédération suisse et le canton de Genève du 16 mars 1816. https://www.ge.ch/legislation/accords/main.html (accessed December 21, 2020).

Veuilleumier, Marc. 1983. "Politique et société à Genève en 1831." In: Olivier Fatio (ed.), *Genève protestante en 1831: Actes du colloque tenu en commémoration des 150 ans de la création de la Société évangélique de Genève et de la parution du journal "Le Protestant de Genève" [Genève, 12 et 13 juin 1981]*. Genève: Labor et fides.

Zwaag, W. van der. 1997. *César Malan (1787–1864): prediker van het frans-zwitsers Réveil*. Utrecht: Uitgeverij De Banier.

2

S. C. MALAN AT BISHOP'S COLLEGE, CALCUTTA, 1838–1840

† R. G. Tiedemann

> Let us then be charitable, and pitiful, and courteous towards our brethren just set free from the trammels of idolatry, who feel as yet imperfectly, and see men as trees, walking. Like our own Master, therefore, let us not rebuke them for seeing no better, but try and heal them a second time till they see clearly how they ought to walk. You cannot safely tear the prey from a lion's mouth. But if you change his nature he will let it go of his own accord.
>
> – Solomon Cæsar Malan (1858)[1] –

It may very well be that polyglots are not as rare as is sometimes assumed. The author of a recent book concluded his search for such creatures with the following remarks:

> Eventually I met a number of hyperpolyglots – perhaps more than anyone has ever met before – and researched others. From what I now knew about the beatific Mezzofanti, the crabby Krebs, the feisty Lomb, the obsessed Alexander, the excitable Helen, the shy Hale, and all the others, I built a picture of what qualities combined to make a polyglot. In accumulating languages, they followed their own interests and needs – refusing to bend either to an evolutionary logic or to social convention.[2]

Sadly, SCM was not among that number. But he has not been entirely forgotten. In 1975, under the heading "Ripley's – Believe It or Not," several local newspapers in the United States carried a syndicated cartoon-like image of SCM with the following message: "Solomon Caesar Malan (1812–1894) an English clergyman, wrote the same psalm in 80 languages – including Sanskrit, Chinese, Hebrew, Syrian, Arabic, Persian, Tibetan and Japanese."[3] Still, his otherwise rather low profile can be attributed to the relative paucity of material concerning his personal life. To a large extent, scholars have to rely on the biographical account prepared by his son, the school teacher Arthur Noel Malan (1846–1933).[4] This is particularly the

---

[1] SCM 1858, p. 68.

[2] Quoted from Erard 2012a, p. 212. Erard is referring to the Italian cardinal and linguist Giuseppe Gasparo Mezzofanti (1774–1849), and the "king of hyperpolyglots" named Emil Krebs (1867–1930), who worked for many years as interpreter in Germany's legation in Beijing and whose preserved brain was analysed in 2002. On Krebs, see also Erard 2012b. The other polyglots are more contemporary language wizards: Kató Lomb (1909–2003), Alexander Arguelles (b. 1964), Helen Abadzi (b. 1951) and Kenneth Locke Hale (1934–2001).

[3] One of these papers was the *Kingsport Times-News* (Kingsport, Tennessee) of 16 March 1975.

[4] Referring to *SCM DD*.

case with regard to the phenomenal linguist's rather brief career at Bishop's College in Calcutta, India.

1. The Origin and Objects of Bishop's College

The origin of the college can be traced to Thomas Fanshawe Middleton (1769–1822), first Anglican bishop of all the Indian territory under East India Company control.[5] In 1818, he launched his scheme for the education of Indian clergy from all parts of the subcontinent. He defined the objects of the college as follows:

1) To instruct native and other Christians in the doctrine and discipline of the Church, in order to their becoming preachers, catechists, and schoolmasters.
2) For teaching the elements of useful knowledge and the English language to "Musalmans" and Hindus, having no object in such attainment beyond secular knowledge.
3) For translating the Scriptures, the Liturgy, and moral and religious tracts.
4) For the reception of English Missionaries to be sent out by the Society for the Propagation of the Gospel in Foreign Parts on their first arrival in India.[6]

The establishment was to train Indian converts for ordination and produce Christian literature in the learned and vernacular languages of the country. To accomplish this task, at least two, and later three, permanent European professors or teachers would be needed. "When the scheme is in full working order, each Mission Station would have an English Missionary Clergyman, one or two Missionaries to be educated in the College and ordained as Missionaries, or Catechists or as Schoolmasters, all from the College."

From the start Bishop's College was, therefore, closely connected with the Anglican missionary enterprise in India. Consequently, initial funding for constructing and staffing the college at Sibpur near the East India Company's Botanical Garden in the Howrah district of Calcutta was received from the Society for the Propagation of the Gospel in Foreign Parts (SPG),[7] the Society for Promoting Christian Knowledge (SPCK), the Church Missionary Society for Africa and the East (CMS), as well as from the British and Foreign Bible Society (BFBS). In 1820, William Hodge Mill (1792–1853), a graduate of Trinity College, Cambridge University, and an ordained priest in the Church of England, was appointed by the SPG as the first principal of Bishop's College.[8] The professors selected by the SPG for the college were expected to be well qualified Anglican priests. "They should be, if not

---

[5] Passage of the East India Company's Charter Renewal Act of 1813 by the British Parliament had lifted the formal ban on the admission of missionaries into Company-ruled territories.

[6] The four chief aims are mentioned in Gibbs 1970, pp. 2-3.

[7] At that time frequently referred to as the Incorporated Society.

[8] Mills developed into a profound Oriental scholar and upon his return to England became Regius Professor of Hebrew at Cambridge University and – among his various clerical positions – canon of Ely. For further details, see Bendall 1894, p. 400.

distinguished for general scholarship, at least respectable divines, acquainted with the Scriptures in the Originals, of frugal and laborious habits and possessing a talent for languages. [...] They should be men of sedate habits and serious piety."[9] To promote learning at the college, its library contained about 5,000 volumes, besides a large and varied collection of manuscripts, in Syriac, Pahlavi, Arabic, Persian, Tibetan and Sanskrit.[10] In some ways it is easy to see why the learned polyglot Malan would find an appointment at Bishop's College attractive.

2. Solomon Cæsar Malan in Calcutta

However attractive the position at the college may have been, it is nevertheless surprising that young SCM was selected by the SPG, an organization reflecting the "high church" tradition in the Church of England. After all, César Jean Salomon Malan was a Swiss citizen from Geneva.[11] Moreover, his father Henri Abraham César Malan (1787–1864) was an Evangelical connected with the revival (*réveil*) movement within the Reformed Church and in conflict with the Swiss ecclesiastical authorities in Geneva.[12] Such a background would not normally have been favoured by the more conservative SPG. On the other hand, British Evangelicals, including Robert Haldane (1764–1842) and Henry Drummond (1786–1860), flocked to Geneva and interacted with César Malan in the years after 1815. Moreover, Malan père was warmly received in both England and Scotland during visits in the 1820s. Indeed, when César Malan was suspended from the Church of Geneva in 1823, he declared himself to be a member of the "English Church."[13] It may be significant that his contacts in British Evangelical circles included the "conservative Evangelical" Daniel Wilson (1778–1858), who mentions him in 1823.[14] In 1832, Wilson was consecrated Bishop of Calcutta and thus assumed a supervisory function as Visitor of Bishop's College. In any case, given the links with Geneva, it can be assumed that at least some Evangelicals in England would have been aware of SCM's promising potential.

Young SCM's contacts in Evangelical circles were extended through matriculation at St Edmund Hall,[15] Oxford, in 1833 and his marriage to Mary Marsh Mortlock (1813–1840), daughter of John Mortlock (1785–1837) and Mary Ann Louisa

---

[9] General Meeting of the SPG of 18 May 1819, Archives of the United Society for the Propagation of the Gospel, Special Collections (hereafter USPG Archives).

[10] *The Bengal and Agra Annual Guide and Gazetteer for 1841*, vol. 1, part III (Calcutta: 1841), p. 52.

[11] Having Anglicized his name to "Solomon Caesar Malan," he became a naturalized British citizen in 1845. See Certificate 262 issued 4 November 1845, HO 1/20/262, The National Archives, Kew.

[12] *Schweizerische Monaths-Chronik* 9 (1824), pp. 150-153. See also Chapter 1 in this volume.

[13] *Schweizerische Monaths-Chronik* 9 (1824), p. 153.

[14] See Stunt 2000, p. 47.

[15] Note that Bishop Daniel Wilson was also educated at St Edmund Hall and later, as vice-principal (1807–1812), continued to preserve the Hall as a fervent centre of Oxford Evangelicalism. Consult Bateman 1860.

Woodd[16] (1786-1828). The couple had met in the summer of 1830 when Mr. Mortlock and his daughter spent several weeks in Geneva. They were married in 1834 by the Rev. William Marsh (1775-1864), Vicar of Basildon (Berkshire) and godfather of the bride.[17] John Mortlock, "rose to wealth by industry, and spent his wealth in acts of Piety and Charity";[18] William Marsh and Basil Woodd were "honorary governors for life" of the Church Missionary Society, the Evangelical body within the Church of England.[19] It is worth noting that his marriage alliance must also have afforded SCM considerable financial security.[20]

After his encounter with the Mortlocks in Geneva, SCM went to Scotland in 1830 as tutor to the family of George Hay, 8th Marquess of Tweeddale. In 1833 he matriculated at St Edmund Hall, Oxford. Upon completion of his studies at Oxford University in 1837, which had been marked by the distinction of winning the Boden Sanskrit scholarship[21] (1834) and the Pusey-Ellerton Hebrew scholarship (1837), the versatile linguist SCM felt confident enough to apply for a teaching position at Bishop's College. The college was at this time facing an acute shortage of teaching staff. One of the junior professors, the Reverend Frederick Holmes (ca. 1791-1850) had returned to Britain in 1836. In that year, the principal, W. H. Mill, tendered his resignation and eventually sailed for England in October 1837, thus leaving the other junior professor, the Reverend George Undy Withers (1807-1873), in sole charge of the institution. According to the minutes of the SPG Standing Committee of 1 June 1837, it would seem that SCM initially offered himself as a candidate for the office of principal. The minutes of 7 July 1837 indicate, however, that he had subsequently applied for the junior professorship and was invited for an interview on July 10.[22] Having been appointed Classical Professor at Bishop's College, Calcutta, SCM was elected a Resident Member of the Royal Asiatic Society on 16 December 1837.[23]

---

[16] Her father, Basil Woodd (1760-1831), was a "conservative Evangelical" Anglican priest; he founded many schools and was an active member of several religious societies, including the Church Missionary Society and the British and Foreign Bible Society.

[17] For details on this episode, see ANM, *SCM DD*, Chapter III.

[18] "Inscriptions in the Churchyard of St. Mary's, Paddington Green, Middlesex," No. 112, in: Sherwood 1913, p. 39.

[19] See the *Proceedings of the Church Missionary Society for Africa and the East* (1824), p. v.

[20] See the Will of John Mortlock of Brighton, Sussex, 30 October 1837, PROB 11/1885/311; Will of Mary Marsh Malan, 07 August 1840, PROB 11/1932/322; both in The National Archives, Kew.

[21] The Sanskrit Chair had been founded by Lieutenant-Colonel Joseph Boden (d. 1811) who was of the opinion that knowledge of that language would assist his countrymen in "the conversion of the Natives of India to the Christian Religion." Joseph Boden's will of 15 August 1811 (Probate Date: 17 December 1811), Prerogative Court of Canterbury, Will Register, PROB 11/1528, The National Archives, Kew.

[22] See the minutes of the SPG Standing Committee, USPG Archives.

[23] *Proceedings of the Royal Asiatic Society* (January 1838), p. ii.

He left Portsmouth with his wife and two young sons in the ship *Malcolm* on 6 January 1838 and reached Calcutta on 10 May.[24] He reported to Archibald Montgomery Campbell (1790–1859), the SPG Secretary in London, a few days later: "We are delighted with the College and its situation."[25] His arrival had been eagerly anticipated by Bishop Daniel Wilson who, referring to the desire at Bishop's College to engage in translation work, wrote to the Society for Promoting Christian Knowledge in early 1838:

> The loss of Dr. Mill necessarily now cripples its exertions, but we hope for his powerful help from home; and we look forward to Mr. Malan's oriental fame, though so young, as opening, after a series of years, an endless vista of translated copies of the Scriptures, Prayer-Books, and religious books, for the gaping eager eyes of millions in India.[26]

On 18 May 1838 SCM took his seat as a member of the College Council in Calcutta. In addition to having been appointed librarian, the multitalented professor also offered his services as college organist.[27] On Trinity Sunday, 10 June 1838 he was ordained deacon by the Bishop of Calcutta, "having obtained letters dimissory from Bishop Sumner, of Winchester, to Bishop Wilson. He was thus enabled to take his full share in the duties entailed by his professorship."[28] Moreover, he was subsequently licensed by the bishop to officiate at the collegiate chapel of Bishop's College.[29] Writing to the SPG in London, the bishop certainly was pleased by SCM's arrival:

> The moment is now a critical one, I really think, for the full prosperity of the college. You have been most successful in your choice of Mr. Malan. He is a delightful person, more than answering our warmest expectations, so far as we can at present judge; quick, energetic, a genius for acquiring Oriental languages, sound-minded, pious, of a sweet open temper, enthusiastic in love to India and the college. The applications [of students] from various parts of India concur, with the reputation of professor Malan, to render it probable that the college may now take a new spring and rise to its proper influence and efficiency.[30]

---

[24] Letter from Mrs. Malan in ANM, *SCM DD*, p. 47.

[25] SCM to A. M. Campbell, Bishop's College, 15 June 1838, C. Ind. I 13 (1), USPG Archives

[26] Bishop Daniel Wilson to the SPCK, Shalimar Garden-House near Bishop's College, Epiphany (6 January) 1838, *The Ecclesiastical Gazette or Monthly Register of the Affairs of the Church of England, and of Its Religious Societies and Institutions* No. 1 (London, 10 July 1838), p. 3.

[27] Proceedings of the College Council, 18 May to 22 June 1838, C. Ind. I 11 (28A), USPG Archives.

[28] SCM to A. M. Campbell, Bishop's College, 15 June 1838, C. Ind. I 13 (1), USPG Archives.

[29] *Parbury's Oriental Herald* 2 (July–December 1838), p. 515.

[30] Extract from a letter of Daniel Wilson, Bishop of Calcutta, 30 November 1838, in: *The Church of England Magazine* Vol. 7, No. 181 (31 August 1839), p. 11. See also Bateman 1860, vol. II, pp. 144-145.

However, the Indian climate and illness soon undermined the effectiveness of the small European teaching staff (acting principal Withers and junior professor SCM). As Withers reported to the SPG in August 1838:

> [...] I would only beg of the Society to keep in mind not merely the diminution of energy for active labour which this climate occasions but the very precarious tenure of actual strength and health it allows of, and to consider, if a single individual should be left alone in this Institution amid its complicated labours and cares (as under present circumstances is continually liable to happen) whether any reasonable hope can be entertained by himself or others of his being able, I do not say to acquire or extend, but even to apply, Oriental knowledge, for which the demand is and must be on the increase.[31]

SCM, who presumably prepared the minutes of a special meeting of the College Council convened on 9 November 1838, also commented on the pressures created by the paucity of professors, concluding that "very serious injury must accrue to the designs of the Society and the general interests of the Church in India if this great Missionary Institution, the operations of which promise to become more wide and important every year, be not kept up in its fullest state of efficiency."[32] The minutes continue:

> For himself Professor Malan cannot avoid saying that he feels his strength quite inequal [*sic*] to the multifarious and harassing duties that will now press upon him and from his inexperience in the management of the College he cannot but fear that the interests of the Institution will suffer from its present destitute state. It is needless to observe that under such circumstances it is impossible for him to devote any attention to the increasing demands of the Translation Department.[33]

Indeed, in his report to A. M. Campbell, Bishop Wilson recognized "the partial indisposition of Professor Malan" who "has overworked himself so much, that an affection of his eyes has been so far aggravated as to render a total cessation from reading for four or five weeks needful." The bishop added that under the prevailing circumstances, another professor or principal should be provided by the SPG,

> always supposing that you can meet with a really proper individual, which I sincerely trust you may. Whether it be a Principal or a Professor is not perhaps so important, if only it be a devout, learned, meek, laborious, academical-minded, kind-hearted, frank person – one who will work in well with the present College Authorities, and raise the general reputation of this fine Missionary Institution.[34]

---

[31] Withers to A. M. Campbell, Bishop's College, 6 August 1838, C. Ind. I.12 (64), USPG Archives.

[32] Minutes of the Special Meeting of the College Council, 9 November 1838, C. Ind. I 11 (28B), USPG Archives.

[33] *Ibid.* SCM elaborates this point in his letter to A. M. Campbell of 22 August 1838, pointing out that he is liable "to be seized with sudden illness." C. Ind. I 13.2, USPG Archives.

[34] Wilson to A. M. Campbell, Calcutta, 30 November 1838, C. Ind (3) 12A, USPG Archives.

Because the SPG failed to send a suitable additional professor to Calcutta, SCM found it increasingly difficult to cope with the extra work, especially after Professor Withers was forced to go on an extended sea voyage to Bombay "for health reasons" in November 1838. As Mrs. Malan's letter, begun on 16 January 1839, points out:

> You will not be surprised to hear that my dear husband has suffered from his most harassing position as the only responsible person in this College, and from the crowd of duties that have devolved upon him. He has long since been complaining of extreme languor and inability for exertion, which is not natural to him, and for the last three months his eye has been decidedly affected, so that he could not use it without much pain and great indistinctness of vision.[35]

She added on 28 January:

> You will see by the above that we are again under the chastening hand of God, for it is no small trial to my dear husband to be suddenly stopped short in his studies and projects, and every pursuit in which he takes interest. [...] His object is to get as much change of scene and variety as possible. [...] Every day proves more strongly that nothing but his going away for a time will succeed. [...] at present he is thinking of the Straits of Malacca, and possibly China.[36]

Yet it was becoming clear that the climate of Calcutta did not suit the constitution of Mrs. Malan either, especially after the birth of a third son.[37] It was, therefore, decided that Mrs. Malan should return with her three sons to England. SCM would accompany them as far as the Cape of Good Hope, where he would stay some months to recover his health to be able to resume his duties at Bishop's College at the beginning of 1840.[38] The Malan family left Calcutta on the *Duke of Buccleugh* at the end of March 1839, and reached the Cape at the beginning of May 1839.[39] Although SCM did benefit from the voyage and the sojourn in southern Africa, "yet the evil effects of the Indian climate soon re-asserted their baneful influence."[40] Having spent just a short time in Calcutta after his return from the Cape on 20 November 1839, the doctors decided that he should leave India. SCM left India at the end of April 1840, never to return to that country. During the long voyage back to England, he learned later in September that year that his wife had died on 5 April 1840.

It was of little comfort to SCM that the teaching staff at Bishop's College had in the meantime been reinforced by the arrival in December 1839 of Professor Arthur

---

[35] Quoted in *SCM DD*, pp. 53-54. SCM himself refers to the painful symptoms as "amaurosis in my left eye." SCM to A. M. Campbell, Bishop's College, 9 February 1839, C. Ind. I. 13.4, USPG Archives.
[36] Quoted in *SCM DD*, p. 54.
[37] Basil Henry Malan (1839–1859) was born at Bishop's College on 30 January 1839.
[38] *SCM DD*, pp. 52-53.
[39] *The Bengal Directory and Annual Register for the Year 1839* (Calcutta 1840).
[40] *SCM DD*, p. 56.

Wallis Street (1809–1851),[41] the SPG having previously refused an application from the Anglican cleric Henry Edward Manning (1808–1892), the future cardinal in the Roman Catholic Church, because "he was an avowed Oxford Tract man."[42] Yet it is interesting to note Bishop Wilson's first impressions upon Street's arrival:

> Professor Street is about thirty years of age, ripe scholar, iron constitution, fine health, active, enterprising, zealous for missions, prodigal of his strength, rides twenty miles of a morning in the sun, manners good, no great talker, in short he would have been a capital professor if he had not been imbued for seven years – steeped – in Tractarianism.[43]

In fact, as a vociferous opponent of the Oxford Movement, which he regarded as Romanizing the Church, the militant Evangelical bishop at Calcutta resented Street's appointment, accusing him of Tractarian tendencies and generally made his life at Bishop's College a rather unhappy one. For one thing, this "diversion into wholly irrelevant Oxford Movement polarization" contributed to the college's difficulty in attaining the high reputation so confidently expected by Wilson at the end of 1838.[44] Unfortunately, in the absence of his personal writings, we do not know Malan's thoughts on this unfortunate affair. But his own more tolerant position within the Church of England was later expressed in his advice to a young missionary supposedly going to India:

> You know I dislike as much as you do party names, such as "High" or "Low" Church, all of which are wrong. For both "High" and "Low" make the Church say and do things never intended by any of her genuine children. Yet as we must adopt certain words in order to be understood, I would have you be rather of the "Broad" than of either the "High" or the "Low" Church. By "Broad" I mean strict as regards yourself and charitable towards others. [...] You will find that the "Broad" Church is the best, especially abroad, where parties and sects of all kinds hinder the kingdom of CHRIST far more than do either superstition or idolatry.[45]

3. SCM's Scholarly Endeavours in Calcutta

The rather brief period spent at Bishop's College notwithstanding, SCM nevertheless managed to pursue his lust for learning and pick up a few languages in the process. As his son put it,

> That prominent trait in his character – an unappeasable thirst for knowledge – had now full scope in prompting him to search out the hidden treasures of Oriental wisdom. With the sight of the left eye gone, and the warning of high

---

[41] Street arrived in December 1839 on the *Scotia* from London. *The Bengal Directory and Annual Register for the Year 1840* (Calcutta 1841), p. 527.

[42] Bateman 1860, vol. II, p. 185.

[43] *Ibid.*

[44] See O'Connor 2000, p. 78. In his obituary notice, Wilson had rather kind things to say about Street. See *The Gentleman's Magazine* 36 n.s. (August 1851), p. 214.

[45] *LYM*, pp. 16–17.

medical authority that excessive study would produce blindness of the right eye, his one determination was to employ his sight while it lasted. [...] The restless activity of his brain rendered idleness impossible; and now that the prescribed course of Oxford study was over, he at once threw himself heart and soul into the wider paths of linguistic culture. When not necessarily engaged in college duties he devoted his leisure hours to studying the native languages of India, and besides these, Tibetan and Chinese.[46]

SCM's introduction to Tibetan studies was stimulated by a chance meeting with the Hungarian scholar Kőrösi Csoma Sándor (or Alexander Csoma de Kőrös, 1784–1842) who afforded him access to a variety of Tibetan texts.[47] "Although I had to cross the river to come to him, I requested him at once to give me one lesson a week in Tibetan, and he agreed to do so most readily.... [Because] I happened to be the only person who was troubling himself about Tibetan, he and I became very good friends during the whole of my (alas! too short) stay in India."[48] Especially after Malan had been appointed Secretary to the Asiatic Society of Bengal in 1839, his intimacy with Csoma, the under-librarian to the same society, ripened into sincere friendship.[49]

SCM learned "the rudiments of Chinese" from He Jinshan 何進善 (1817–1871), also known as Ho Fuk-tong 何福堂, who had come to Bishop's College as companion of Edwin Evans (1820–1852) from the Anglo-Chinese College, an institution maintained in Malacca by the London Missionary Society.[50] In a letter dated 16 January 1839, Mrs. Malan wrote: "A Chinese student has just arrived, the first of his nation that has been admitted here, and indeed he is among the first that have embraced Christianity. He retains his national costume, which is very peculiar, and seems a very simple-minded Christian."[51] Professor Withers, who calls him "Chien Sing," left the following assessment:

> The Chinese Student Chien Sing beside receiving regular assistance in English from his friend Mr. Evans and another Student has read daily with the Revd. Krishna Mohan Banoorjea[52] and I have examined him weekly in the portions he had read. His progress is steady tho' not rapid and his acquaintance with English

---

[46] *SCM DD*, p. 51.

[47] For more details about the relationship between Csoma de Kőrös and SCM, see Chapter 11 in this volume.

[48] Quoted in *LWCK*, p. vii.

[49] *SCM DD*, p. 48.

[50] They had been admitted to the College at the beginning of 1839. See the letter from SCM to A. M. Campbell, 9 February 1839, mentioned in the Proceedings from 10 December 1839 to 17 January 1840, C Ind. I 11 (29), USPG Archives. Variations in the spelling of his name: Ho Tsun-sheen (as expressed in Cantonese) and Ho Tsin-shan (the personal name in Mandarin pronunciation).

[51] Quoted in *SCM DD*, p. 53.

[52] Krishna Mohan Bannerjee (1813–1885), who had converted to Christianity in 1832, studied theology at Bishop's College and became the first Indian to be ordained a priest in the Anglican Church in Bengal.

as yet very limited. He possesses however fair abilities while his general disposition and character seem remarkable for simplicity and goodness.[53]

The "Sinological Orientalist" James Legge (1815–1897) of the London Missionary Society, who later became He Jinshan's mentor in Malacca and Hongkong, has left the following account of the latter's interaction with SCM at Bishop's College:

> He [Ho Tsin-shan] told me that he had learned some English before he went to Calcutta, but that the Classical Professor at Bishop's College, a Mr. Malan, had taught him much more, and introduced him to the study of various other subjects, while Mr. Malan had employed him also to teach himself the rudiments of Chinese; that, in fact, nothing could exceed Mr. Malan's kindness to him, and the way in which he had sought to promote his improvement. The two young men – for Mr. Malan's age must have been considerably short of thirty years – had come together, each thirsting for the knowledge which the other possessed; and their mutual profiting was great and lasting. Ho continued his studies with myself for some years, and in time became a very able preacher and expositor of Christian truth.[54]

SCM's collaboration with He Jinshan was, however, of rather short duration, namely the first few months of 1839. When Malan returned from the Cape toward the end of that year, He Jinshan was preparing to return to Malacca. According to a letter from Archdeacon Thomas Dealtry (1795–1861) of Calcutta, Edwin Evans' father, John Evans (1801–1840) had requested the return of both his son and He Jinshan to assist with the pressing work at the Anglo-Chinese College at Malacca.[55] Whatever the extent of SCM's brief introduction to the Chinese language in Calcutta, he would later make use of this knowledge when venturing into the minefield of the so-called "term question" that was raging among Protestant missionaries in

---

[53] Withers to A. M. Campbell, Bishop's College, 15 August 1839, C. Ind. I. 12 (70), USPG Archives.

[54] Quoted in ANM, *SCM DD*, p. 52. By the time Legge wrote these lines, he had become Professor of Chinese at Oxford University. On He Jinshan's later career as Legge's student and colleague, see Pfister 2004 and *id*. 1999.

[55] Dealtry to Withers, Calcutta, 21 November 1839, USPG Archives. The background to this development is rather complicated. John Evans was still affiliated with the London Missionary Society but "desirous of conforming to the discipline of the Church of England and presented himself to the Bishop of Calcutta for Holy orders during His Lordship's visitation to the Straits at the close of 1838." Wishing to have his son instructed in the same discipline, he sent him to Bishop's College as a nominee of the Powerscourt Foundation, along with He Jinshan who was on the Begum Sumroo Fund. Withers to A. M. Campbell, Bishop's College, 14 February 1840, C. Ind. I 12 (77), USPG Archives. It is interesting to note that Edwin Evans completed his studies upon his return to England in the early 1840s and died as the Anglican consular chaplain at Amoy (Xiamen 廈門), China. He Jinshan, on the other hand, became a disciple of the Scottish Congregationalist, James Legge, first in Malacca and subsequently in Hong Kong. Charles Simeon (1759–1836), an Evangelical clergyman in the Church of England, created a fund of nearly £ 1,000 for the endowment of theological scholarship at Bishop's College as executor of the will of Richard Wingfield, 5th Viscount Powerscourt (1790–1823). The colourful Begum Sumroo (1751–1836) of Sardhana had made available a fund to the SPG for the maintenance of native students in India.

China in the middle of the nineteenth century.[56] Given his relatively short-lived exposure to the Chinese language, the translation into English of three versions of the *Sanzijing* 三字經 (Three-Character Classic) must have been a greater challenge for Malan. Not only did he translate the original version that was probably written by Wang Yinglin 王應麟 (courtesy name Wang Bohou 王伯厚, 1223–1296) as the first formal introduction to Confucianism for children, but also the Christian version produced by Protestant missionaries and the text created by Hong Xiuquan 洪秀全 (1814–1864), the leader of the Heavenly Kingdom of Great Peace (Taiping tianguo 太平天國, also called the Taiping Rebellion) which had certain Christian characteristics.[57]

Bishop's College had been conceived as a missionary college; several foreign and Indian men had been trained there and ordained as evangelists for the Indian missions.[58] SCM decided, therefore, to familiarize himself with the actual missionary enterprise and made a brief tour in the neighbourhood of Calcutta prior to his final departure from India. In his report, sent to the SPG from Alexandria on 26 April 1840, he proudly announced that at the mission station of Krishnaghur (or Kishnagur; now Krishnanagar) "I expounded the Scriptures to the inhabitants in Bengalee. I was certainly very much pleased with what I saw and heard, though my visit was far too short to enable me to form a correct judgment of things."[59] He similarly preached in the newly acquired language to the Christians at Barripore, Tallygunge and Mograhat "to a most attentive and orderly congregation."

> The very expression and countenance of those dear natives is changed by their sincere conversion to Christianity. The natural self-interestedness and wiliness in the men and false shame in the women make room for frankness and openheartedness in the one, and true modesty in the other. But this is only in those,

---

[56] See *WIGC*. This was in part a critical analysis of a work (神 *Shin v.* 上帝 *Shang-Te. Antagonistic Versions of the Chinese Scriptures. A review of the controversy respecting the proper rendering of ELOHIM and ΘΕΟΣ into Chinese, and statement of the evidence showing a large majority for SHIN. By a life-member of the Bible Society, of thirty years' standing.* London: Wertheim and Macintosh, 1854) that had been published anonymously by Jacob Tomlin (1793–1880), formerly a missionary of the London Missionary Society at Malacca and later a clergyman of the Anglican Church in England.

In SCM 1856a, he further elaborated his critique in a letter to the Earl of Shaftesbury. Malan adopted the position that *Shangdi* (上帝) is the true God, whereas *shen* (神) refers to "inferior spirits." See also SCM, *LYM*, p. 56.

[57] See SCM 1856b.

[58] For a "catalogue" of ex-students of Bishop's College working as missionaries in India in 1841, see "Bishop's College," *The Bengal and Agra Annual Guide and Gazetteer for 1841*, vol. 1, part III (Calcutta 1841), pp. 53-55.

[59] Extract from a letter of the Rev. SCM, dated Alexandria, 26 April 1840, published in *The Missionary Register* 28 (June 1840), p. 300. On the subsequent disappointments in the Krishnaghur district, see Stock 1899, vol. 1, pp. 314-316.

of course, who have really tasted that the Lord is good; the difference is great, even in appearance, between them and those who merely profess Christianity.[60]

While catechising some members of the congregation at Jangera and being "delighted with the correctness of their heartfelt answers," SCM was particularly impressed by the women whom he questioned. These females,

> who returned their answers with the modesty and decorum unknown to a heathen woman, struck me much by their knowledge of the Scripture and Articles of Faith, although most of them cannot read. This is an important point – the education of females. I have strongly urged our missionaries to devote much attention to that branch of their duties. It is by converting the mothers when young that we shall have influence over the rising generation. I shall endeavour in England to raise a fund specially devoted to that purpose.[61]

To be sure, SCM employs here the language expected of a missionary by readers back in England at that time. However, reflecting in later years on his fleeting experiences in the mission field in the vicinity of Calcutta, he offered more meaningful counsel in a series of thirteen letters addressed to a young missionary who was said to be going to India. Among other things, SCM told him that, when corresponding with those to whom he is responsible at home, he should be guided by the truth, and not the desire to see his "Report" in print.

> The incident you cherish most is having preached to a crowd of natives in the bazaar, where you distributed abundance of tracts that were eagerly received. [...] That would do admirably for the "Report," and gain one or two more subscriptions to the Society. But that is only one side of the picture. You ought to write the other; I mean the whole truth, which is, that when you went to that same bazaar two or three days after, you bought a pound of sugar of a grocer, who gave it to you wrapped in one of your own tracts, a pile of which you spied on a shelf in his shop, ready for other customers. Tell that too; and leave [to] the reporters the responsibility of printing it or not as they like.[62]

According to SCM, it was more important to send out appropriately prepared missionaries, and with proper authority – i.e., men ordained in the Church of England rather than Dissenters. Moreover, not every

> good man [...] is a fit individual for the arduous work, the lonesome toil, the firm self-denial, the unwearied devotedness, the unflinching purpose, the deep learning, the sound judgment, the enlightened zeal and steady perseverance – but also for the glorious reward – of a missionary. Truly, no man taketh such an office unto himself, but he who is called to it of GOD.[63]

Thus, for "this holy calling," the quality was more important than the quantity of men sent to India and China. "Both of them are wonderful lands, swathed in archaic

---

[60] SCM, letter dated Alexandria, 26 April 1840, *Missionary Register* 28 (June 1840), p. 300.

[61] SCM, letter dated Alexandria, 26 April 1840, pp. 300-301. The extract from the letter was reprinted in *SCM DD*, pp. 57-59.

[62] *LYM*, pp. 63-64. This passage, slightly altered, was also quoted in *SCM DD*, p. 60.

[63] *LYM*, p. 10.

traditions, and inhabited by nations of the highest interest for the sake of their origin, their literature, and their language."[64] Thus, he advises against a rush of missionaries to India in the wake of the Indian Insurrection of 1857, because such men would not be properly qualified. In any case,

> An unusual demonstration on the part of missionary societies at the present time, would also, I fear, be bad policy. It would look as if the Christian religion were forced upon the natives of India, when they can resist it the least; it would needlessly wound their prejudices or increase their fears; and the kingdom of CHRIST might ultimately be rather hindered than promoted by it.[65]

There are, therefore, indications in SCM's writings that he was an advocate of cultural accommodation to Indian cultures displaying a surprisingly progressive attitude with regard to the missionary enterprise – at a time when this kind of open-mindedness was quite rare among Europeans.

> First, then, seek to understand and to occupy your rightful position in your new country; you will work all the better for it. I do not wish needlessly to hurt your feelings, but you must nevertheless know and feel that in India or in China you are, and must be, what you yourself have often called others in your own country, – "a foreigner."[66]

Consequently, the newly arrived missionary must remember that educated Hindus are men of superior intellect and learning. In particular, the thought that "men of a different complexion are inferior [...] proceeds from gross ignorance."[67] Along these lines, SCM offers the following advice:

> Do not think or talk of "conquered nation," or of "conquerors," of "rulers," and of "subjects": that is practically of no service to you in your character of missionary, preaching the Gospel to heathen Hindoos. You come to dwell in their country, in which they have lived from time immemorial, and on which they think you an intruder. You come to them with many prejudices of your own, to encounter their prejudices. There must then be concession on both sides; but that is a work of time. You must learn to known them, and they you.[68]

The new missionary must expect to be treated like a Hindu is treated when arriving in England. The Brahmin, and the Kshatriya, the Vaishya, and even the Sudra think the new arrival inferior.

> The Brahmin who teaches you Sanscrit [*sic*] or Bengalee comes to you for the sake of gain, and pays you many compliments. But in truth he despises you in his heart; and no sooner is he gone home than he washes himself, from fear of defilement by contact with you.[69] [...] And in China you will fare no better. To

---

[64] *LYM*, p. 8.
[65] *LYM*, p. 7.
[66] *LYM*, p. 33.
[67] *LYM*, p. 37.
[68] *LYM*, p. 34.
[69] *LYM*, p. 35.

say nothing of "*Fan-kwei*" [番鬼], ("foreign devil") the name by which you will be commonly designated [...]."[70]

Alluding to his own experiences, SCM added:

> Unfortunately, I say this in consequence of what I both saw and heard when I was in India. Therefore, as you would wish that a Hindoo should behave to you, do you also behave to him; with courtesy and due respect. Overcome all those difficulties by Christian patience, forbearance, and humility. Win him by your Christian spirit, by gentleness, kindness of manner, and earnestness of speech; and thus show your real superiority over him.[71]

As part of the adaptation process to conditions in the mission country, the new missionaries should study the sacred texts of the local elite. The new missionary must "remember that the only way to bring them over to your side, is for you first to go over to theirs."[72] SCM continued: "Go and fetch them, meet them on their own ground, and show yourself acquainted with their writings and system of thought. Then win them over to yourself; inspire them with trust and confidence ...."[73] He added: "For remember, that one single quotation at the right place and time, in Sanscrit, if to a Hindoo, or in Pali, if to a Cingalese or Burmese Buddhist, or in Koo-wēn [*guwen* 古文], if teaching Chinese, will have more weight in your favour with them than hours of talk from your own head."[74] SCM goes on to say:

> But, from want of experience in the matter, it may not occur to you, perhaps, that the educated Hindoos or Chinese with whom you will come into contact are fully your equals, if not your betters, in intellect, in shrewdness, in quickness, in cleverness, and many of them vastly superior to you in learning – ay, learning you might well wish to possess, in order to turn it to the best account, but which you never will acquire. In addressing them, therefore, do it with deference, kindness, and courtesy; not as if they were your inferior, but as men at least your equals.[75]

In this connection, he insists that it is essential to distinguish between the real doctrine of the learned and the sensualities of popular religion that have sprung from it in India.

> If, like ignorant or prejudiced men, you only look at the gross idolatry of the people, and go no deeper into their native lore, you must of course conclude that there cannot possibly be any thing in common between you and them. And thus you lose the first and strongest hold you can have on them, which is the fact, that there is a great deal in common between you and them, and that they should be made to know and see it; so as to narrow, and not to widen, the gulf you fancy fixed between them and yourself. It is because so many well-intentioned,

---

[70] *LYM*, p. 36.

[71] *LYM*, p. 37.

[72] *LYM*, p. 38.

[73] *LYM*, p. 42.

[74] *LYM*, pp. 45-46.

[75] *LYM*, p. 38.

but either not very wise or not very well informed, missionaries, have only looked at the outward gross form of heathen superstitions, that they have addressed Hindoos or Chinese, as if they were little better than cannibals or South Sea Islanders of the last century.[76]

With this in mind, missionaries to China, when meeting Confucians, should acknowledge that the moral sayings "of that great and good man [Confucius] offer many points of agreement between you and themselves."[77]

SCM's letters to "a young missionary" also include some practical information, concerning, for example, the serious issue of climate. So, he states the reasons why the new missionaries should arrive in India during the cool season in November.[78] "I arrived there unfortunately in the month of May, when the heat was intense; and inevitable exposure to the sun, though under an umbrella, caused head-aches that never ceased for months, and it brought on ill-health, which obliged me to relinquish my post with the utmost regret."[79] Similarly, Europeans should emulate the natives who "are almost always dressed in white, or in some light colour nearly as cool; and it is a great pity that some distinctive dress for the English Clergy, consisting of a white robe and black scarf or belt, is not adopted, for convenience and health's sake."[80] Finally, missionaries should consult a physician who has lived long in India in order to gradually modify their diet.[81]

4. Conclusion

SCM is known, if he is known at all, for his command of an extraordinary large number of foreign languages. It is, therefore, not surprising that he stressed the importance of language training in connection with the Christian missionary enterprise in India. Besides Sanskrit, which he called "the finest, the richest, the most harmonious, and the most venerable idiom ever spoken or written on earth,"[82] Malan urged missionaries to the subcontinent to learn at least one other language, such as Bengali, Hindi, Oriya, Marathi, Telugu or Tamil. But there was much more to the Swiss-born polyglot. Among his several fields of interest, we may note, for example, the many of watercolours, pen and pencil drawings produced during his travels.[83] Collecting birds' eggs was another of SCM's special activities. Among several collections donated by him to the Royal Albert Memorial Museum and Art Gallery in Exeter, England, in 1878 was the important collection of 1,117 birds'

---

[76] *LYM*, p. 48.

[77] *LYM*, p. 55.

[78] *LYM*, p. 29.

[79] *LYM*, p. 30.

[80] *LYM*, p. 31.

[81] *LYM*, p. 32.

[82] *LYM*, p. 57.

[83] For a brief account of the collection at the Getty Research Institute, Los Angeles, see Bonfitto 2015, pp. 169-176.

eggs (283 different species) that he had collected himself. He was also skilled in bookbinding, carpentry and repairing musical instruments.[84]

Of special interest in this chapter is SCM's commitment to Bishop's College and the missionary enterprise connected with it. Upon his return from the brief visit to some of the mission stations in the vicinity of Calcutta, he was encouraged by progress that had been made since the arrival of the SPG two decades or so earlier. The work

> is prospering through the blessing of God. But when we reflect that these blessed fruits have been produced by Bishop's College, and that the Christians of Barripore, Tallygunye, and Bowescotty, in all about 2,000, owe their spiritual birth to the efforts of zealous men educated within the walls of the College, have we not cause to thank God from the bottom of our hearts, praying He may give increase to the seed we sow, and bid us take courage for the future?[85]

Although SCM's sojourn at Calcutta was cut short by illness, he continued to take an interest in both the college and the SPG mission after his return to England. He had, in fact, submitted a list of recommendations "with a view to the more complete development of the resources of Bishop's College and the Society"[86] prior to his departure from India. They were subsequently scrutinized by the former Principal Dr W. H. Mill and discussed by the College Council (consisting of Acting Principal Withers and Professor Street) for final consideration by Bishop Daniel Wilson. It was, however, found that some of these suggestions had already been implemented and others too ambitious, impracticable or premature in the context of the prevailing conditions in Bengal. Bishop Wilson, while appreciating SCMs "warmth of zeal and devotion to the highest interests of the College," had this to say:

> I confess I do not see any single proposal of Professor Malan's which requires or would warrant any change in the usual proceedings of the College Authorities. [...] Indeed it appears to me that it would be very unlikely that a Junior Professor like Mr. Malan who had resided only a few months should be able unless when on the spot and in conference with the other College Authorities, to draw up any scheme especially so sweeping an one as the present is intended to be that would at all meet the actual state of things or produce the least permanent good effect.[87]

As concerns his support of the missionary enterprise, it should be noted that SCM made a donation of 1,000 rupees (the equivalent of US$ 25,000 in the same period) toward the construction of the tower for the church built at Mograhat in the early 1840s.[88] At this time he published a tiny booklet, consisting of a brief history as well as an outline of the fundamental principles and constitution of the College which, "although too young to have reached as yet a state of full efficiency,"

---

[84] For these and other accomplishments, see Simpson 2004.

[85] SCM, letter dated Alexandria, 26 April 1840, *The Missionary Register* 28 (June 1840), p. 301.

[86] A. M. Campbell to Withers, London, 31 July 1840, USPG Archives.

[87] Wilson to Withers, 28 January 1841, USPG Archives.

[88] Consult Long 1848, p. 265.

nevertheless produced many Indian and other labourers to the Anglican missions.[89] The remainder of this publication is devoted to the work of the SPG mission in the Calcutta area, for which he was soliciting funds.

By this time it was clear that SCM, having been priested and accepted the curacy of Alverstoke in Hampshire in 1843, would not return to India. In the same year he married his second wife, Caroline Selina Mount (1821–1911), daughter of the Anglican clergyman, Charles Milman Mount. After a year (1844–1845) as perpetual curate of Crowcombe, Somerset, SCM accepted the living of Broadwindsor, Dorset, in September 1845. Its vicarage became his base of operations until his retirement to Bournemouth in 1885. His sojourn in India may have been lamentably brief, yet it introduced him to cultures and languages that were significantly different to those of Europe. The fruit of this exposure to the propagation of the Gospel in a Bengali cultural environment as well as his engagement with Tibetan and Chinese studies are reflected in some of his abundant publications. In other words, the brief Indian sojourn was an important episode in the long and productive scholarly career of the remarkable Swiss-born Anglican clergyman, Solomon Cæsar Malan.

Select Bibliography

Bateman, Josiah. 1860. *The Life of the Right Rev. Daniel Wilson, Late Lord Bishop of Calcutta and Metropolitan India*. 2 vols. London: John Murray.

Bendall, Cecil. 1894. "Mill, William Hodge (1792–1853)." *Dictionary of National Biography*, Vol. 37, p. 400; revised by Parvin Loloi in the *Oxford Dictionary of National Biography*, 2004.

Bonfitto, Peter Louis. 2015. "'Harmony in Contrast': The Drawings of Solomon Caesar Malan." *Getty Research Journal* No. 7 (January 2015), pp. 169-176; http://www.jstor.org/stable/10.1086/680744 (accessed 21 December 2020).

Erard, Michael. 2012a. *Babel No More: The Search for the World's Most Extraordinary Language Learners*. New York: Free Press.

———. 2012b. "King of the Hyperpolyglots." *The Morning News* 10 January 2012. http://www.themorningnews.org/article/king-of-the-hyperpolyglots (accessed 21 December 2020).

Gibbs, Mildred Eleanor. 1970. "The First Hundred and Fifty Years." In: *Bishop's College Calcutta 1820–1970*. Calcutta: The College. An online version was produced by "Project Canterbury" in 2006: http://anglicanhistory.org/india/bishops 1970/ (accessed 21 December 2020).

Long, James. 1848. *Hand-Book of Bengal Missions in Connexion with The Church of England: Together with an Account of General Educational Efforts in North India*. London: John Farquhar Shaw.

Malan, Solomon Cæsar. 1843. *An Outline of Bishop's College, and of Its Missions in the Neighbourhood of Calcutta*. London: Burns.

---

[89] SCM 1843, p. 13. A list of catechists and missionaries who studied at the college is found on pp. 14-16.

O'Connor, Daniel (ed.). 2000. *Three Centuries of Mission: The United Society for the Propagation of the Gospel 1701–2000*. New York: Continuum.

Pfister, Lauren F. 1999. "A Transmitter but not a Creator: The Creative Transmission of Protestant Biblical Traditions by Ho Tsun-sheen (1817–1871)." In: Irene Eber – Sze-Kar Wan – Knut Walf – Roman Malek (eds.), *Bible in Modern China: The Literary and Intellectual Impact*. Monumenta Serica Monograph Series, 43. Sankt Augustin – Nettetal: Steyler Verlag, pp. 165-197.

———. 2004. *Striving for "The Whole Duty of Man": James Legge and the Scottish Protestant Encounter with China. Assessing Confluences in Scottish Nonconformism, Chinese Missionary Scholarship, Victorian Sinology, and Chinese Protestantism*. Scottish Studies International, Publications of the Scottish Studies Centre of the Johannes Gutenberg Universität Mainz in Germersheim, 34. 2 vols. Frankfurt a.M.: Peter Lang.

Sherwood, George (ed.). 1913. "Inscriptions in the Churchyard of St. Mary's, Paddington Green, Middlesex." *The Pedigree Register* 3 (September 1913) 26, p. 39.

Simpson, R. S. 2004. "Malan, Solomon Caesar (1812–1894)." *Oxford Dictionary of National Biography*. Oxford: Oxford University Press. See also http://www.oxforddnb.com/view/article/17854 (accessed 21 December 2020).

Stock, Eugene. 1899. *The History of the Church Missionary Society: Its Environment, Its Men and Its Work*. 3 vols. London: Church Missionary Society.

Stunt, Timothy. 2000. *From Awakening to Secession: Radical Evangelicals in Switzerland and Britain 1815–35*. Edinburgh: T&T Clark.

[Tomlin, Jacob]. 1854. 神 *Shin* v. 上帝 *Shang-Te. Antagonistic Versions of the Chinese Scriptures. A Review of the Controversy Respecting the Proper Rendering of ELOHIM and ΘΕΟΣ into Chinese, and Statement of the Evidence Showing a Large Majority for SHIN*. By a Life-member of the Bible Society, of Thirty Years' Standing. London: Wertheim and Macintosh.

3

MALAN AS DORSET WORTHY
Solomon Caesar and Valentine Ackland

T. H. Barrett

Solomon Caesar Malan's learning embraced, we are told, some forty or so languages, and his travels extended far over Europe, Asia and Africa. As an orthodox Victorian clergyman, moreover, his thoughts would naturally have extended to worlds unseen and the life beyond. Yet for all that his life encompassed, he lived most of it in a remote part of Dorset. It is with this contrast that the following remarks are concerned, with both how he lived and how he was remembered within the narrow confines of his parochial world. Dorset in the nineteenth century probably conjures up at best two interrelated images – of the Tolpuddle Martyrs, agricultural labourers transported to Australia for having dared to try to form a Trades Union, and of the Wessex novels of Thomas Hardy, novels that evoke the glories of the countryside while remaining utterly realistic about the trials of country life, especially for those at the foot of the Victorian social ladder. Thus, works such as *Jude the Obscure* document the plight of those in the countryside who sought broader intellectual horizons, though Hardy's own career from country cottage to respectable comfort showed that these could be achieved, given innate genius, a little luck, and the right contacts.

For learning was not unknown in Dorset in Hardy's youth, even learning that embraced some degree of knowledge of Asia – not perhaps among the country gentry, who tended to follow other pursuits, but in the vicarages of the Dorset clergy. The Reverend William Barnes (1801–1886), for example, author of the famous dialect poem *Linden Lea,* claims in his *Philological Grammar* of 1858 to have drawn on material in over sixty languages, including Japanese, Chinese, Mongol and Manchu; he certainly cites the work of Jean-Pierre Abel-Rémusat (1788–1832) on the first language, though generally there is not much indication in the body of the work of a thorough grasp of the more unusual tongues listed in his preface.[1] His daughter's memoir of his life shows that while he was able to study Indian languages and also Persian and Arabic in Dorset with a retired army officer from India, his more easterly researches were the result of periods of residence at St. John's College, Cambridge, when he was able to make use of the University library.[2] We should recall from works such as Jane Austen's *Sense and Sensibility* that by the nineteenth century the English countryside could easily harbour figures like her Colonel Brandon who had spent time in South Asia, and some of these might conceivably assist their local clerical friends with their philological explorations. But this was not the case for East Asia. The Chinese grammar she names as having been consulted by

---

[1] Barnes 1854, pp. vii-viii.

[2] Baxter 1887, pp. 60, 110.

him at Cambridge in January 1850 was the German work by the Hungarian Stephan Ladislaus Endlicher (1804–1849), which draws on earlier studies such as those by Stanislas Julien (1797–1873); no instruction was then given in Cambridge in the languages of East Asia, nor had Sir Thomas Wade (1818–1895) yet donated his Chinese library to the University.[3]

Barnes' friend and clerical neighbor, the Reverend Henry Moule (1801–1880) of Fordington (now part of Dorchester), seems to have possessed a practical rather than philological disposition, but one suspects that his eloquent advocacy of the earth closet as an efficient alternative to the water closet owed something to reports of the value of night soil sent back from China by his missionary sons, George Evans Moule (1828–1912) and Arthur Evans Moule (1836–1918).[4] He certainly took a close interest in his sons' activities and even published materials on China provided by them.[5] It was in fact Moule's large family, including especially the black sheep of the family, Horatio ("Horace") Moule (1832–1873), who gave Thomas Hardy vital experience of the possibilities of a literary life (as all of his biographers have recognized). Biographers also have recognized echoes of the Moules in some of his novels.[6] Arthur Evans Moule, as it happens, was a pioneer in the study of Chinese proverbs, publishing on the topic as early as 1874, well ahead of Arthur Smith, whose better-known researches in this field did not start to appear till 1882.[7] But his essay on this point looks back not to any avowed knowledge of Malan's work, but rather to the immediate problems of engaging the attention of Chinese audiences.[8]

The evidence suggests, indeed, that though he may have been aware of these Dorchester-based clerics, SCM did not participate in this small but fascinating coterie. The life of SCM by his son certainly mentions George Moule, whose missionary efforts eventually saw him raised to a bishopric based in Hangzhou, but he is quoted as having written to a correspondent of the biographer, "I had long known by report the name of Dr. Malan, and had reverenced it both for his manifold accomplishments, artistic and musical, as well as linguistic, and for his reverent conservatism in questions of sacred criticism."[9] George Moule is also incidentally frank

---

[3] For Endlicher and Julien on grammar, see Führer 2001, pp. 50-52; on Wade, see Aylmer 1989.

[4] For a good account of his role as inventor, see Ted Ward, *Henry Moule of Fordington, 1801–1880, Radical Parson and Inventor (Friend of Thomas Hardy)*, published privately by the author, Poole, no date.

[5] H. Moule 1868.

[6] For instance, Gittings 1975, pp. 61-71.

[7] For the course of Smith's work, see his remarks on his contributions to the *Chinese Recorder* from 1882 to 1885, in the opening to his "Preface to the Original Edition," in Smith 1965, p. i. For a bibliography of publishing on Chinese proverbs I have drawn upon Rohsenow 2002, pp. 201-210.

[8] A. E. Moule 1874b, refers back to an earlier contribution to the same journal and volume, "What is the Best Form of Address to a Heathen Audience?" 5 (January–February 1874) 1, pp. 33-41.

[9] *SCM DD*, p. 389; cf. p. 400.

in confirming the justice of Malan's diffidence about his command of Chinese: he had studied with a Chinese informant while in Calcutta, but he knew that he had much more to learn, and in Dorset none with whom to study.[10] Archival research may yet unearth correspondence between SCM and Barnes or the Moules, but at the very least George Moule's form of expression implies that he was not well known in person to him, and so probably not to the other Moules either.

Fig. 4: St. John the Baptist Church, Broadwindsor
(Photo by Mirasy M. Pfister, August 2012)

The reasons are not far to seek in his son's remarks about their situation in Broadwindsor, where even "a visit to Bridport or Chard was a thing to be talked about."[11] Dorchester was another world, whilst Malan was trapped in a financially rewarding but remote living where his parishioners were, to quote his son again, "stiff sons of toil, of a simple wit that seldom rose above the level of sheep, turnips, and sour cider."[12] No wonder he referred to his sojourn there as his "forty years in the wilderness."[13] Maybe there were compensations, such as days spent fly-fishing on the Frome at Toller Porcorum.[14] There would also have been some meetings with other local clergy, including perhaps the Dorchester clergy, but in these SCM

---

[10] *SCM DD*, p. 52.

[11] *SCM DD*, p. 120.

[12] *SCM DD*, p. 119.

[13] *SCM DD*, p. 137; cf. p. 281.

[14] *SCM DD*, p. 138. One notes that in George Eliot's *Middlemarch*, to which we return for some further comparisons below, as well as a country clergyman mired in pedantic scholarship in his library there is also depicted a clergyman whose study is full of fishing tackle, who also runs a small workshop as a hobby, Mr. Cadwallader: Eliot 1965, p. 92.

seems to have made less of an immediate impression than might be expected. One of his curates, a Mr. F. Parham, is quoted as saying "At clerical meetings he had not the weight which he ought by his learning to have had. He was too shy and reserved to go to teach them."[15]

All this we learn from the pious efforts of his biographer, and it must be said that his depiction of his father's career, in its scenes of parish life in particular, so redolent as they are of Hardy's Dorset, is well executed and informative. He is, however, not the sole source for SCM's Dorset life, as a glance at local archives demonstrates. In the parish records of his day he makes a perhaps predictable appearance, for almost all mentions of his name duly confirm his son's remarks on his abiding concern for the children of Broadwindsor, since they are concerned about the establishment and staffing of a primary school in the part of the parish known as Blackdown.[16] One entry that is not connected with the school concerns a letter of appreciation from the Secretary of State to SCM in response to a letter from him expressing the loyalty of the parish as shown in a recent address, which condemns Chartist outbreaks. This is dated 4 May 1848.[17] We should note that however innovatory SCM's Asian studies were for his day, in politics he was, in the words recorded by his filial biographer "a Tory to the backbone."[18] In his fear of Chartism, moreover, he was far from alone, as any survey of the mood of Britain up to and in the volatile months of spring 1848 makes clear; even some quite liberal persons viewed any prospect of democracy with unmitigated horror.[19]

The online catalogue of county records held at the Dorset History Centre also reveal a further manuscript relating to SCM, not from Broadwindsor, but from Lytchett Matravers, far away in the east of the county between Bere Regis and Poole, the eventual home of a Rev. William Mortimer Heath (1822–1917), on the last loose leaf of whose reminiscences we find these words:

> In one of the Forties, being in search of a Curacy, I visited the Rev. S. C. Malan at Broadwindsor – the only time I ever saw him. I was not engaged by him. I remember being very struck by his wonderful talent as an artist, shown by his watercolour drawings on his walls. I was not then aware of his gift for languages,

---

[15] *SCM DD*, p. 291. Emphasis in original.

[16] These are catalogued online, http://www.dorsetforyou.com/dorsethistorycentre (accessed 22 December 2020), which has a "Search our catalogue" function, wherein entering "Malan" produces a fine batch of parish records connected with the school, viz. PE/BDW/SC 3/1, PE/BDW/SC 3/2. PE/BDW/SC 3/3, PE/BDW/SC 3/4, PE/BDW/SC 3/5 and PE/BDW/SC 3/6. I am grateful to the staff of the Centre for all their help. I am also grateful to Mrs. Aileen Bishop, former churchwarden of Broadwindsor, who hosted the International Conference on SCM there on 23 August 2012, for confirming that local school records also attest to the close attention paid by Malan and his wife to school affairs.

[17] Call mark PE/BDW/IN 4/3.

[18] *SCM DD*, p. 416.

[19] Houghton 1957, pp. 54-56, for example, provides a succinct account of this.

but I remember his personal appearance well. I think this must have been in 1847.[20]

Arthur Noel Malan states that SCM had fourteen curates in all, and as we have seen, draws on their view of his father.[21] This brief encounter, then, hardly adds to our picture of the man.

Fig. 5: The Vicarage, Broadwindsor
(Photo by Mirasy M. Pfister, August 2012)

But not all catalogues held by the Dorset History Centre are available online. A set of files entitled "Record Office Notes" contains biographical gleanings accumulated over the years, and there is one entry under SCM's name, citing a *Bridport News* headline dated 25 July 1984, "Magyars remember Malan." I have not checked the article concerned, but it plainly refers to the anniversary of his donation to the Hungarian Academy of Sciences in September 1884 of the books he had been given many years earlier in Calcutta by the pioneering Hungarian Tibetologist Alexander Csoma de Kőrös (1784–1842). This is mentioned in his son's book, as is the newspaper obituary in Hungarian that he was subsequently accorded in 1895.[22] The website of the Academy makes it clear that the Hungarian Lutheran medical doctor and scholar, Theodore Duka (1825–1908), played an important part in this, though I leave further research into Malan, Csoma and Duka to others (as it would take one no doubt out of Dorset to Budapest and elsewhere, even if Duka, who had an

---

[20] Call mark D.1/OM/32.

[21] *SCM DD*, p. 137, and cf. n. 12 above.

[22] *SCM DD*, pp. 343 and 370.

English wife, died in Bournemouth).²³ But that a library of works from Ladakh now in Budapest should have sojourned forty years in the wilderness in Broadwindsor is no doubt something to be remembered in both Hungary and Bridport.

This almost exhausts what may be learned immediately from the Dorset History Centre, though no doubt substantive longer-term archival research might add to these findings. But on its shelves in the Local Studies Library it also holds a publication dedicated to SCM produced by a body located at its sister organization down the hill, the Dorset County Museum, namely the *Dorset Natural History and Archaeological Society*.²⁴ It is a small pamphlet of four pages, and is still apparently obtainable from the Society, according to the website of the Museum, for fifty pence, whereas some other issues in the series in which it appears, "Dorset Worthies," such as the pamphlet on the Tolpuddle Martyrs, are marked as out of print.²⁵ The work in question, "Solomon Caesar Malan," by Valentine Ackland (1906–1969), produced as number eleven in the series in 1969, though slight, does show that SCM's life in Dorset during the century after his death was not only recalled by Hungarians.

This brief life opens with the following words:

> In 1951 I found a tiny book, about two and a half inches by one and a half inches, on my mother's shelves. She had bought it in the 80s for one penny. It is the *Manual of Daily Prayers Translated from Eastern Originals*, by the Rev. S. C. Malan, MA, Vicar of Broadwindsor. The copy is the fourth edition. It was issued by Masters, London, in 1885.

The first edition, according to the researches of Lauren Pfister, was issued by the publisher in 1866, but it is interesting to learn that this minute work, overlooked (as Ackland observes), in the bibliography prepared by his son, saw a certain popularity, as evidenced by these reprints. The prayers plainly made an impression on Valentine Ackland, too, for she quotes two of them, as well as briefly describing the contents of the whole book. For the rest, however, she draws solely on the son's biography to fill out her four pages, though her conclusion does bear quotation:

> It is curious that the name of Caesar Malan should have been forgotten. Even if the bearer of it had not been brilliantly distinguished, such a name, once heard, could scarcely be mislaid; but for some reason this strange near-genius has all but vanished from memory, and that in less than a hundred years.

Who was the author of these generous and sympathetic words? Today Valentine Ackland, originally Mary Kathleen Macrory Ackland, might herself count as a "Dorset Worthy," since she at least merits an entry – admittedly a somewhat unenthusiastic one – in the *Cambridge Guide to Women's Writing in English*.²⁶ But in her own time she was probably seen as a more marginal figure, overshadowed by

---

²³ I have made use of Anon. 2006.
²⁴ This copy is bound into a volume with the call mark 942.08.
²⁵ See Dorset County Museum 2015.
²⁶ Sage 1999, p. 2.

the fame of her partner, the novelist Sylvia Townsend Warner (1893–1978).[27] One searches in vain for any indications of an interest in Asian Studies or (to use the contemporary term) Orientalism in published accounts of Valentine Ackland and her writings. The best that I have been able to come up with is that in her earlier years she was "loved by Anna May Wong," and that presumably coincidentally rather than consequently one of her last compositions was a piece entitled "Poem in the Chinese Manner."[28] The Chinese American actress Anna May Wong (1905–1961) was certainly in Britain during Ackland's time in London before her move to be with Warner in Dorset, and I have heard of at least one academic career in Chinese Studies that was prompted by an infatuation with her image on the silver screen, but that is about all that can at present be said.[29]

The case of Sylvia Townsend Warner is slightly more complex. The well-known travel writer and educator, Chiang Yee 蔣彝 (1903–1977), in *The Silent Traveller in Oxford* presents two poems in English by his recently deceased friend the historian, activist, and founder of *Dushu zazhi* 讀書雜志 Shelley Wang, that is, Wang Lixi 王禮錫 (1901–1939): both poems are followed by the notation "Translated by Miss Sylvia Townsend Warner."[30] Warner had some linguistic ability and was at one time commissioned to revise the first English translation of Proust, but I doubt that she knew Chinese. Her published correspondence includes a wonderfully vivid description of how Wang was the guest of the two women when he came to address the Dorchester Labour Party.[31] Such a trip was part of much broader efforts on his part to promote the cause of China in Britain.[32] But while her letter will be of interest to anyone researching the life of this intriguing but ill-fated individual, there is nothing in it to show that its writer was in the least aware that the reason why he addressed the good Labour Party members of Dorchester on matters relating to early Chinese history was because (as Arif Dirlik has shown) he was a key figure in initiating debate as to how Marxist views of the past might relate to China.[33] The "translations" provided by Chiang Yee are most probably like those of Witter Bynner (1881–1968) in the pioneering Chinese poetry anthology *The Jade Mountain*, in which he was entirely dependent on the explanations of the Chinese given to him in English by his Chinese collaborator.[34]

---

[27] Sage 1999, pp. 652-653.

[28] Ackland 2008, pp. 17, 198, and cf. p. 185. This edited anthology of her poems contains a fair scattering of biographical material in the introduction and notes evidently based on extensive archival reading, including "limericks and diary entries" (*sic*) as evidence in this instance of her early London life, so I have relied on it here for my understanding of Ackland's life and personality.

[29] For Anna May Wong, see Leong 2005, pp. 83-88, which covers this period in Wong's life, but does not comment on her private life.

[30] Chiang Yee 1944, p. 13.

[31] Maxwell 1982, p. 50.

[32] Buchanan 2012, p. 68.

[33] Dirlik 1978, pp. 207-212.

[34] Bynner – Kiang 1929.

In all the published letters and diaries of Ackland and Warner there is no mention of the latter's little pamphlet on SCM, though this may simply be because much of the archive remains unpublished, and editors have generally found other topics such as the relationship between the two women themselves much more important than possible references to their thoughts on neglected clergymen of Victorian Dorset. These, should they be unearthed, may well date to some time considerably prior to the date of publication, which may have been delayed: 1969 was the year in which the author died of breast cancer. But barring the discovery of further evidence one can only assume that the initial interest in SCM that stimulated Valentine Ackland to learn more about him may have been religious. Her mother, Rose Mcrory, who died in 1961, seems to have been conventionally Victorian in her own religious sentiments, but Valentine was rather more exploratory: after converting twice to the Roman Catholic church without lasting effect, the daughter ended her days attending a Quaker meeting.

But having said this, I should admit that whether out of consideration for her prospective readership or not, her summary of ANM's biography does not dwell on the religious issues of his father's day brought forward there, but rather on the human element in the tale. As such it forms an excellent introduction to the man and his life. But it also does a little bit more, in that Ackland ends by pointing out that she has heard of, but not seen, another account of Malan by a contemporary, Rev. William Tuckwell (1829–1919), in his *Reminiscences of Oxford*. This work, a fund of anecdotes that is now widely available on the Internet and in a recent reprint, turns out to have a brief but very helpful sketch of SCM based on acquaintance sustained during three separate periods of his life. These span first his appearance "as a young man at [...] St. Edmund's Hall, where prevailed tea and coffee, pietistic Low Church talk, prayer and hymnody of prodigious length [...]" and go on to recount how:

> Twenty years later I recall him as a guest in Oxford Common Rooms, laying down the law on questions of Scriptural interpretation, his abysmal fund of learning and his dogmatic insistency floated by the rollicking fun of his illustrations and their delightful touches of travelled personal experience. Finally, in his old age I spent a long summer day with him in his Broadwindsor home, enjoying his library, aviary, workshop, drawings [...]"[35]

Tuckwell's overall verdict – and one should remember that as a Christian Socialist he came from a rather different corner of the overarching Anglican Church of the time – states: "He was a benevolently autocratic vicar, controlling his parish with patriarchally imperious rule, original, racy, trenchant in Sunday School and sermons."[36] Tuckwell's independent witness to SCM's career and Broadwindsor life, though mildly condescending, has been found valuable enough to at least one recent blogger – among the many now rediscovering his scholarship thanks to the

---

[35] Tuckwell 1900, p. 96. It will be noted from the date of Tuckwell's birth that the "reminiscences" of Malan as an undergraduate must derive from second hand information, though there is no need to doubt his later observations.

[36] Tuckwell 1900, p. 97.

circulation of non-copyright SCM translations on the Internet – for it to have been posted in full.[37] But in some ways the most intriguing aspect of his portrait of SCM is the context in which he introduces it. For Tuckwell certainly had the opportunity to meet some of the finest scholars of the day, and his recollections, while partial, afforded him a wide range of possible comparison, making his praise of SCM's ability particularly well informed, and indeed impressive. Specifically, he introduces him as an undergraduate, allegedly "speaking as yet broken English" immediately after noting his contemporary Mark Pattison (1813–1884), "in those years, not yet disappointed, melancholy, and vindictive."[38]

Pattison's is not a name from Victorian times that lives on today, but to those best equipped to weigh up the matter he appears as a true scholar's scholar, a man of extraordinary learning, concerned to raise standards at a time when in retrospect they were in some areas, such as command of Latin and Greek, already staggeringly high.[39] But what intrigues most of all is that this man was widely supposed to have furnished the model for the bloodless and irrelevant clerical pedant Casaubon in George Eliot's (i.e., Mary Anne Evans, 1819–1880) *Middlemarch*. The late A. D. Nuttall (1937–2007) argues that while no simplistic association can be made between the Edward Casaubon of the novel and Pattison, expert on the Hugenot Humanist scholar Isaac Casaubon (1559–1614), the fact that George Eliot knew the Oxford don does suggest – well, an element of connection. True, the novel came out before Pattison's study, but it is clear that when George Eliot asked Pattison what he was up to as she was writing, "Casaubon" would have been the answer.[40] One may suspect more: Pattison seems to have had charm, but despite Tuckwell at no point is it likely that he could ever have been mistaken for a little ray of sunshine. At the time he was – as we say – "working on" Isaac Casaubon he had been already forced to abandon a more ambitious work on J. J. Scaliger (1540–1609); Isaac Casaubon was in his mind no doubt a step down – and yet he most probably doubted whether he could finish even this lesser task. One might even suspect an element of teasing in George Eliot – finish at least *that* book, or else you will simply be remembered, my friend, as a dry, old, and ultimately unproductive scholar with a much younger wife.[41]

Of course, it may not have been so at all, and in any case the question has no immediate relevance to SCM's case. William Tuckwell does not mention Eliot and

---

[37] See Pearse 2011.

[38] Tuckwell 1900, p. 95 – note as pointed out above (n. 35) that this particular assertion must be taken *cum grano salis*.

[39] This point is very effectively made in Nuttall 2003, p. 86.

[40] Nuttall 2003, p. 83, following John Sparrow.

[41] Note Eliot 1965, p. 454: "That was the way with Mr. Casaubon's hard intellectual labours. Their most characteristic result was not the 'Key to all Mythologies', but a morbid consciousness that others did not give him the place which he had not demonstrably merited – a perpetual suspicious conjecture that the views entertained of him were not to his advantage – a melancholy absence of passion in his efforts at achievement, and a passionate resistance to the confession that he had achieved nothing."

may well not have read *Middlemarch,* despite its treatment of social issues that might have interested him. Still his juxtaposition conjures up a contrast between the gloomy Pattison transmuted into Edward Casaubon, a country clergyman with a large house and a "long library," and the scholar of Hugenot descent, SCM, who may have been in like circumstances a didactic old Tory, but at least had something undeniably convivial about him.[42] And yet if we seek comparisons, there is an even greater contrast than that. For were we to seek a figure from the twentieth century to compare with SCM, we might well choose Arthur Waley (1889–1966), if not for the range of his publications then at least for the singular fact that he shared with SCM the remarkable disability for a scholar of having eyesight in only one eye.[43] But for Waley there was the compensation of living in Bloomsbury, minutes from the British Museum. Broadwindsor was no Bloomsbury: it was not even a Middlemarch or a Casterbridge. Apart from his family and his curate, SCM had no one, even if the local Pinney family, which seems to have had connections extending even as far as Bristol, were no doubt supportive.[44]

His son puts the situation well in describing his arrival at his new home from an earlier curacy in Crowcombe, in the Quantocks:

> When Mr. and Mrs. Malan set out on a visit of inspection before deciding to accept the living, they were accompanied by the Rev. W. F. Chilcott, Vicar of Monksilver, and Rural Dean. The party drove to Ilminster, and thence, with a change of horses, to Broadwindsor. The first impression as they passed up the village street was one of dismay at the general aspect of the place, so different from Crowcombe; but the Rural Dean encouraged them with the remark, "You will have to spend your lives here, so you had better make the best of it."[45]

That is the unpromising background against which his achievement needs to be measured. But the evidence of his work is there: not only was he productive – he seems to have been happy.

Select Bibliography

Ackland, Valentine. 2008. *Journey from Winter: Selected Poems.* Ed. Frances Bingham. Manchester: Carcanet.

Anon. 2006. "Theodore Duka, the First Biographer of Csoma." http://csoma.mtak.hu/en/dukativadar.htm (published 2006, accessed 22 December 2020).

---

[42] Eliot 1965, pp. 58-59, describes Casaubon as living in an inherited mansion in ample grounds almost as grand as an Oxford college.

[43] De Gruchy 2003, p. 54.

[44] Again, I am grateful to Mrs. Bishop (cf. n. 16 above) for confirming that the Pinney family has continued to benefit the parish with its largesse even into recent years. From stray references I have seen, their support for Malan and his family would form an excellent topic for further local research.

[45] *SCM DD*, p. 122 and the note on p. 378, that on his mother the son was asked to maintain a devout silence.

Aylmer, Charles. 1989. "Sir Thomas Wade and the Centenary of Chinese Studies at Cambridge, 1888–1988." *Hanxue yanjiu* 漢學研究 7 (1989) 2, pp. 405-422.

Barnes, William. 1854. *A Philological Grammar*. London: John Russell Smith.

Baxter, Lucy. 1887. *The Life of William Barnes*. London: Macmillan.

Buchanan, Tom. 2012. *East Wind: China and the British Left, 1925–1976*. Oxford: Oxford University Press.

Bynner, Witter – Kiang Kang-hu. 1929. *The Jade Mountain: A Chinese Anthology*. New York: Alfred A. Knopf.

Chiang Yee. 1944. *The Silent Traveller in Oxford*. London: Methuen.

Dirlik, Arif. 1978. *Revolution and History: Origins of Marxist Historiography in China, 1919–1937*. Berkeley: University of California Press.

Dorset County Museum. 2015. "Proceedings of the Dorset Natural History and Archaeological Society, Cumulative Index: Occasional Publications of DNHAS," consulted at http://www.palmyra.me.uk/DNHAS/occasional-pubs.html (published 2015, accessed 22 December 2020).

Eliot, George. 1965. *Middlemarch*. Harmondsworth: Penguin.

Führer, Bernhard. 2001. *Vergessen und verloren: Die Geschichte der österreichischen Chinastudien* [Forgotten and Lost: The History of Chinese Studies in Austria]. Bochum: Projekt Verlag.

Gittings, Robert. 1975. *Young Thomas Hardy*. Harmondsworth: Penguin Books.

de Gruchy, John Walter. 2003. *Orienting Arthur Waley: Japonism, Orientalism, and the Creation of Japanese Literature in English*. Honolulu: University of Hawai'i Press.

Houghton, Walter E. 1957. *The Victorian Mind*. New Haven: Yale University Press.

Leong, Karen J. 2005. *The China Mystique: Pearl S. Buck, Anna May Wong, Mayling Soong and the Transformation of American Orientalism*. Berkeley: University of California Press,

Maxwell, William (ed.). 1982. *Letters of Sylvia Townsend Warner*. Edinburgh: Clark Constable.

Moule, A[rthur]. E[vans]. 1874a. "What is the Best Form of Address to a Heathen Audience?" *Chinese Recorder and Missionary Journal* 5 (January–February 1874) 1, pp. 33-41.

———. 1874b. "Chinese Proverbial Philosophy." *Chinese Recorder and Missionary Journal* 5 (March–April 1874) 2, pp. 72-77.

Moule, Henry. 1868. *A Narrative of the Conversion of a Chinese Physician*. 2nd ed. London: James Nisbett.

Nuttall, A[nthony]. D[avid]. 2003. *Dead from the Waist Down: Scholars and Scholarship in Literature and the Popular Imagination*. New Haven – London: Yale University Press.

Pearse, Roger. 2011. "From My Diary [19 July 2011]." Weblog "Thoughts on Antiquity, Patristics, Information Access, and More." www.roger-pearse.com/weblog/2011/07/19/from-my-diary-132/ (accessed 22 December 2020).

Rohsenow, John S. 2002. *ABC Dictionary of Chinese Proverbs*. Honolulu: University of Hawai'i Press.

Sage, Lorna (ed.). 1999. *Cambridge Guide to Women's Writing in English*. Cambridge: Cambridge University Press.

Smith, Arthur. 1965. *Proverbs and Common Sayings from the Chinese*. Facsimile reprint of the 1914 American Presbyterian Mission Press edition. New York: Dover.

Tuckwell, William. 1900. *Reminiscences of Oxford*. London: Cassell.

Ward, Ted. N.d. "Henry Moule of Fordington, 1880–1880, Radical Parson and Inventor (Friend of Thomas Hardy)." Poole: published privately by the author.

4

SOLOMON CAESAR MALAN
Personality, Polyglossia and the Autistic Spectrum

JOHN EDWARDS

Part 1
Malan: A Life in Languages

1.1 A Prefatory Note

This section does not aim to be anything like a fully biographical description of Solomon Caesar Malan. I have been quite selective, attending centrally to two aspects of his life: his linguistic abilities, and the apparently dominant features of his personality. I am leaving aside, then, the ordinary details of SCM as a vicar, husband and father, most of his extensive travels, many of his non-linguistic achievements, and almost all of his religious activities and productions. The information here comes largely, though not exclusively, from the biography written by his son, Arthur Noel Malan. The simple fact is that we have very little to go on apart from this biography. There is a pamphlet by Valentine Ackland (1906–1969), in which the author regrets the neglect of SCM – whom she characterizes as both "brilliantly distinguished" and a "strange near-genius" – but it is essentially a four-page précis of ANM's book.[1] Beyond these, one finds only very brief references to SCM in the literature.

Since a son's biography is likely to be a work framed in respect and admiration – and, indeed, ANM's book rests upon an acknowledged foundation of "filial veneration" – we should remember Samuel Johnson's famous caution "in lapidary inscriptions a man is not upon oath." Sons' biographies of their fathers are often lengthy lapidary statements – that being so, however, we may perhaps give particular weight to any hints of criticism that ANM has recorded.

1.2 Malan the Linguist

Born in Geneva as César Jean Salomon Malan, SCM had from an early age been spoken to in Latin by his father. Indeed, ANM suggests that his grandfather spoke only in that language to his father: "Therefore, Latin was the child's father-tongue."[2] By age eighteen, he had fluent French, German, Spanish and Italian, and

---

[1] Ackland 1969. Valentine Ackland was born as Mary Kathleen, changing her name to the less gender-specific Valentine in her early twenties. She had a forty-year relationship with Sylvia Townsend Warner (1893–1978).

[2] *SCM DD*, p. 22. One thinks immediately here of Montaigne (1533–1592), whose mother tongue was Latin. He was taught in that language by Horstanus, a German physician, and his parents and servants also spoke to him only in Latin. This was the linguistic aspect of a strict pedagogical regime created by Montaigne's father. In his essay "Of Presumption," Montaigne

some English. He was also "well advanced" in Hebrew, Sanskrit, Arabic and other oriental varieties. We also note here the development of an "unrivalled calligraphy" in languages such as Chinese, Amharic, Egyptian hieroglyphic, Hindustani and Coptic. Before going up to Oxford, SCM worked as a tutor in Scotland. His English was still "imperfect" and his mastery of it was "gradual and laborious"; nonetheless, by the time he was twenty-five, a friend remarks on his good English and "very good accent."[3] It is instructive to note that the undergraduate asked if he might write some of his papers in French, German, Spanish, Italian, Latin or Greek – rather than in English. (His request was denied.)

In his *Reminiscences of Oxford*, William Tuckwell (1829–1919), a politically active Victorian cleric, describes SCM as an undergraduate whose inadequate English prevented him from taking a first-class degree in *literae humaniores*. Tuckwell also provides a brief summary of the linguistic skills of a man later described by a Syriac teacher in this way: "God must have made his brain of a brick from the Tower of Babel."[4] This summary makes a good general introduction to SCM's linguistic capabilities:

> In 1833 Solomon Caesar Malan matriculated at St Edmund Hall [...] speaking as yet broken English, but fluent Latin, Romaic [sic], French, Spanish, Italian, German, and a [sic] proficient at twenty-two years old in Hebrew, Arabic, Sanskrit [...] became Professor in Calcutta, gathered up Chinese, Japanese, the various Indian, Malay, Persian tongues [...] came home to the valuable living of Broadwindsor [...] amassing a library in more than seventy languages, the majority of which he spoke with freedom, read familiarly, wrote with a clearness and beauty rivalling the best native caligraphy [*sic*]. In his frequent Eastern rambles he was able, say his fellow-travelers, to chat in market and bazaar with everyone whom he met. On a visit to the Bishop of Innereth he preached a Georgian sermon in the cathedral. He published twenty-six translations of English theological works, in Chinese and Japanese, Arabic and Syriac, Armenian, Russian, Ethiopic, Coptic. [...] He left behind him a collection of 16,000 Proverbs, taken from original Oriental texts, each written in its native character and translated [...] experts could not be found even to catalogue the four thousand books which he presented, *multa gemens*, with pathetic lamentations over their surrender, to the Indian Institute at Oxford.[5]

---

 refers to the delight he takes in languages, although, with characteristic modesty, he suggests that his own French is corrupt and that his Latin mother tongue was lost for lack of practice. Consult Montaigne 1580 [1949].

[3] Quoted from *SCM DD*, pp. 30 and 38.

[4] Quoted from *SCM DD*, p. 115.

[5] Quoted from Tuckwell 1900, pp. 96-97. After reading this passage from Tuckwell, I attempted to discover where "Innereth" was. I found that C'innereth (Chinnereth; Kinneret) was a community on the western shores of the Sea of Chinnereth, otherwise known as the Sea of Galilee. It seemed hardly likely, however, that there was a cathedral there, much less one in which SCM could preach in Georgian. Luckily, his son describes an 1872 visit to the Bishop of Imereth – which, as Imereti, is a province in western Georgia, towards the Black Sea. Such are the toils and rewards of scholarly detective work.

ANM notes that his father felt "disembowelled" as declining health forced him to give away this large library.[6] A requirement of the bequest was that the books were to remain as an intact collection, and that a catalogue was to be made. However, as Monier Monier-Williams (1819–1899), the Keeper and Curator of the Indian Institute, wrote, in a letter to the *Times* – "where can be found any one cataloguer competent to deal with so great a variety of languages?"[7] Several experts were clearly required here, but it seems as if the stipulated cataloguing was never done. Just before his library moved, however, SCM did send along an "abstract" of it. This list reveals, again, the scope of his linguistic interests and abilities. Among the donated material are grammars, dictionaries, manuscripts, collections of proverbs, and other literature in 34 European, 11 Semitic, 47 Asiatic, 10 African and 3 Pacific languages.

SCM prepared a collection of psalms and prayers "in more than eighty languages and scripts"; with its numerous specimens, this was "a perfect miracle of magnificent writing."[8] He also made translations of the Lord's Prayer in 71 languages: these range from the biblical varieties, to Asian, European and even two Pacific languages (Fijian and Maori). The former collection, unpublished, was eventually presented to the Bodleian; the latter formed an appendix to Malan's work on seven chapters of the Bible.[9] His controversial *Vindication of the Authorised Version of the English Bible*[10] was "fortified by the vast resources of his scholarship and acquaintance with the 'versions of every nation, and kindred, and tongue, and people'."[11] Further evidence, in print, of his linguistic fluencies is found in the list of eleven varieties that forms part of his work on St John's gospel.[12] A contemporary review of the work made particular mention of the fact that SCM made all the necessary translations himself. A year later, he published three more religious studies, these involving Coptic, Armenian and other eastern languages.

SCM was not only a linguist on the printed page. Travelling in 1872, he wrote to his wife: "This is life! Talking thirteen languages a day – Jews, Turks, Infidels – I like the Turks best."[13] His son, ANM, then provides a similar note:

---

[6] *SCM DD*, p. 359.

[7] Cited in *SCM DD*, p. 371.

[8] Quoting from *SCM DD*, pp. 162 and 357. "Dr. Malan's book is like the bow of Ulysses," one scholar wrote (*ibid.*, p. 357): "Who now could be found strong enough to bend it?" ANM notes that, just before his death, his father was asked to bend the bow himself, being requested to at least "write out a list of the languages included in the volume. But no reply was elicited." ANM suggests that "the gradual failing of his intellectual powers was known in all its bitterness only to his own heart," but one evidence of it was a lack of pleasure in what once had been a consuming passion (*ibid.*, p. 358).

[9] See *SCRR*.

[10] Consult SCM 1856a.

[11] Quoted from *SCM DD*, p. 215.

[12] As found in SCM 1862.

[13] Quoted from *SCM DD*, p. 273.

> At a certain railway-station in Hungary, having tried in vain to take his ticket in English, French, German, Turkish, Armenian, Russian, Hungarian, Modern Greek, Italian, and Spanish, he [S. C. Malan] at last said, "Da mihi symbolum," etc., and, finding it successful, he rated the ticket-clerk soundly for only knowing the *linguam* [sic] *sicariorum*, "the language of cut-throats."[14]

It is perhaps unsurprising, then, that the Sanskrit scholar, Arthur MacDonell (1854–1930), described SCM as "without doubt by far the most accomplished Oriental linguist in English," a description now inscribed in SCM's church in Broadwindsor.[15] MacDonell became the Keeper of the Indian Institute but, at the time of writing this encomium, he was the deputy to Monier-Williams – who, in that letter to the *Times*, also described the recently deceased SCM as "an Orientalist absolutely unequalled, and never likely to be equalled, in respect of the marvelous diversity of his linguistic attainments and the profundity of his scholarship."[16] Robert Sinker (1838–1913), the Chaplain of Trinity College, Cambridge, also wrote on the occasion of SCM's death; remarking on "works which, I suppose, no other man in England could have done," he goes on to add:

> Of course, it is not hard to find men who are profound experts in a group of languages – the marvel in Dr Malan's case was that he mastered a group as most men would master a single language: and this not as a mere Mezzofanti, but with the keenest appreciation of the literature into which he broke, as well as the purely linguistic side of the matter.[17]

There were some slightly more cautious views of SCM's talents. MacDonell was clearly an admirer, suggesting that only "an Adelung or a Mezzofanti" could have surpassed his linguistic abilities.[18] He nonetheless writes:

> that, with so wide a range, he could have attained a high standard of scholarship in any one of them [i.e., languages], is doubtful [...] the intellectual limitations of even the most gifted render it impossible for any man to learn half a dozen languages thoroughly [...] had Dr. Malan concentrated his powers he would doubtless have acquired the eminence as a scientific scholar which he actually attained as a linguist.[19]

Owen Chadwick (1916–2015), the eminent theologian and historian of Christianity, was blunter. He first notes that "the country scholar-parson still had leisure" in the

---

[14] Quoted from *SCM DD*, pp. 273-274.

[15] MacDonell 1895, p. 453. When visiting Saint John the Baptist Church – where Malan was vicar for forty years – I noted that his name on the list of incumbents was given as "Soloman." This spelling is also found on the church's website (via www.achurchnearyou.com [accessed 9 March 2021]).

[16] As in *SCM DD*, p. 370.

[17] Quoted from *SCM DD*, p. 400.

[18] Mithridates (134–63 BCE), a king of ancient Pontus, was said by Pliny the Elder to speak all the languages of the 22 "nations" under his control. Johann Christoph Adelung (1732–1806) wrote a multi-volume account of this polyglot ruler; only one volume appeared before his death; see Adelung 1806. Mezzofanti I shall return to.

[19] MacDonell 1895, p. 456; see also Simpson 2004, pp. 274-275, footnote 52.

closing years of the nineteenth century, although scholarly studies were increasingly open only to "those with a comfortable benefice or with private means." (While some of SCM's decisions suggest fairly limited private means – see also the following section – ANM also documents a great deal of foreign travel, various purchases of high quality, and so on.) Chadwick then provides several examples of such rural clerics, and notes that "at Broadwindsor, despite a mind which lacked critical sense, Caesar Malan became one of the English authorities on the study of Oriental languages."[20]

When SCM left Oxford, in 1837, he became Classical Professor in Bishop's College, Calcutta, a missionary institution where his study of oriental languages continued. He now became particularly interested in Tibetan. By 1839 he was the Secretary of the Asiatic Society of Bengal, where the Hungarian orientalist Csoma de Kőrös (1784–1842) worked as a librarian.[21] Csoma was a formidable Tibetologist and a great influence upon SCM, to whom he gave "the whole of his Tibetan books, some thirty volumes."[22] When SCM presented his library to the Indian Institute, he kept back these Tibetan volumes, and they were gratefully accepted by the Hungarian Academy of Sciences.[23]

The penultimate chapter of the son ANM's biography is devoted to his father's *magnum opus*, the three-volume set of *Original Notes on the Book of Proverbs*.[24]

---

[20] See Chadwick 1970, pp. 165-166. Chadwick notes that the scholarly studies of country parsons did not always help much in "the work of the parish," and adds an interesting footnote provided by Jessopp 1891, pp. 38-39. A village resident observes that "to hear that there Reverend of ours in the pulpit you might think we was all right. But bless you, he ain't same as other folk. He do keep a horoscope top o' his house to look at the stares and sich." This "Reverend" is not SCM, but the many and various interests of the latter might be seen as analogous to those of the astronomical parson, Samuel Johnson (*fl.* 1885), who built a small observatory in his vicarage. Johnson was the vicar of Melplash from 1881 to 1905, and it is very likely that SCM knew him. Melplash and Broadwindsor, where SCM remained until May 1885, are each about two miles from the larger center of Beaminster (the birthplace of ANM) – Broadwindsor to the west and Melplash to the south.

[21] This is the "Asiatick Society" founded in 1784 by Sir William Jones (1746–1794) – whose studies in Sanskrit, Greek and Latin led him to the conclusion that the first was the parent in a family including the other two (and their descendants). "No philologer," he wrote, "could examine them all three without believing them to have sprung from some common source" (Edwards 1995, p. 26). The grouping is, of course, the Indo-European family of languages.

[22] Quoted from *SCM DD*, p. 50. Csoma was a pioneer in the study of Tibetan language and culture, and has been memorialized and honored in several parts of the world. In the philological arena he is undoubtedly a much more central figure than SCM, and a serious rival in terms of personal linguistic expertise. ANM cites James Gerard, a physician in the Bengal Medical Service, who wrote of Csoma's remarkable range of language proficiencies: "Hebrew, Arabic, Sanscrit, Pushtu, Greek, Latin, Sclavonic [sic], German, English, Turkish, Persian, French, Russian, Tibetan [...] Hindostani, Mahratti and Bengalee" – these, in addition to his native Hungarian. See also the biography of Theodore Duka published in 1885 (*LWCK*), and other relevant details in von Schiefner 1882.

[23] More about this gift to the Hungarian Academy of Sciences is elaborated in Chapter 11 in this volume.

[24] That is, the *ONBP*.

These notes were bound, expanded and re-bound over more than fifty years. There are more than 16,000 of them, and SCM's guiding impulse here was "that there is not a verse in the Book of Proverbs which does not find abundant parallels in Eastern literature."[25] Consequently, "each verse is illustrated with gems of Oriental wisdom for the most part, though Occidental languages are freely taxed for contributions."[26] Every note was taken from the original, "which I also copied, whole or in part, in its native character."[27] The vast majority of the notes are from oriental and non-Christian sources, reflecting more than 50 different languages. SCM's original was written on "sheets of blue foolscap, every quotation being written with marvelous symmetry and power [...] bound into a massive volume."[28] This was presented to the Indian Institute, and it may be consulted today in the Bodleian archives.

Any inspection of the work reveals a massive labor of love, one that extended well beyond the demands of that "greater accuracy" that SCM said had animated him.[29] It is clear that he loved scripts, lettering, and the demonstration of his prowess for their own sake. MacDonell remarks on his talent: "[S. C. Malan] was a master of Oriental calligraphy. His writing of the Devanāgari character few have probably ever seen equalled; and his Chinese hand it would be hard to excel."[30] And a review of ANM's book refers to his father's manuscript as "a marvel of penmanship."[31] Accompanying the gift of the manuscript version to Oxford, SCM wrote a prefatory note (in October 1894):

> These notes number about 16,000: they were all taking [sic], translated and copied whole or in part from their several originals, by me, S. C. Malan. I present it [sic] to the Indian Institute as witness of the use I made of some of the books I gave to that library. This book was also bound by me.[32]

---

[25] As found in *SCM DD*, p. 398.

[26] Quoted from *SCM DD*, p. 403.

[27] Quoted from *SCM DD*, p. 396.

[28] Quoted from *SCM DD*, pp. 397-398.

[29] See *SCM DD*, p. 396.

[30] MacDonell 1895, p. 455.

[31] See the anonymous review of *SCM DD*, Anon. 1898, p. 93.

[32] I read SCM's brief prefatory note in the Bodleian (Radcliffe Science) Library, where I also saw many pages of the manuscript version of the *Notes* themselves. I can certainly attest to the author's calligraphic skills, although his crammed and crowded arrangements make an odd accompaniment to those remarkable abilities. Upon seeing a sample page that is also reproduced here in this volume, a clinical colleague remarked that the minute and congested detail immediately suggested some variety of obsessive-compulsive disorder (OCD). See below, for some further brief mention of this syndrome.

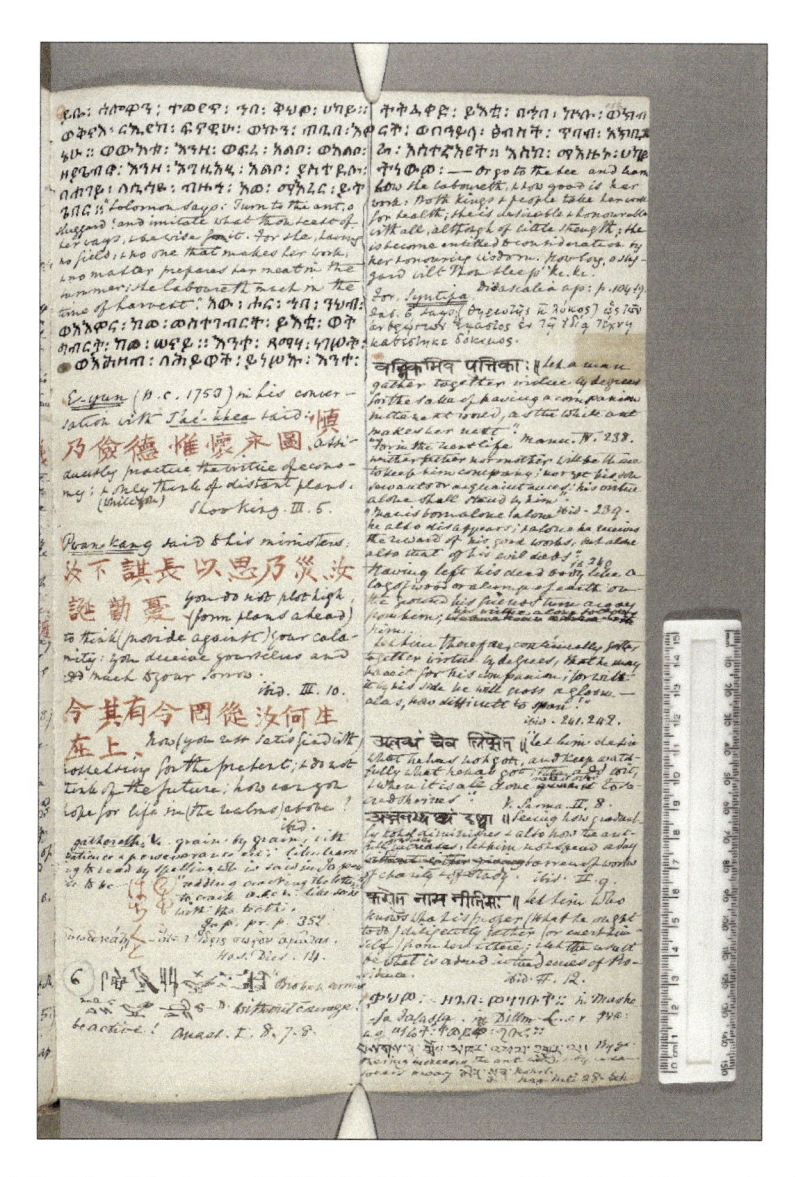

Fig. 6: Bodleian Color Image (ONBP Ms), MS. Ind. Inst. Misc. 10, f. 156 recto. Reprinted with permission of the Bodleian Library, University of Oxford

For all the time and effort that SCM devoted to his master work, the *ONBP* attracted "meagre notice."[33] In a reply to an admiring letter, he wrote that "reviewers have agreed among themselves that it shall be still-born; either because they are too stupid to see anything in it; or, rather, they ignore it from prejudice, which is more

---

[33] See the anonymous reviewer who writes that the *Book of Proverbs* is the work that will "live longest, and which, though it may never be popular, will be deeply prized by scholars" (Anon. 1898, p. 92).

likely."[34] In a rather question-begging statement, the son ANM suggests that his father's work is fittingly met with praise "by such of his friends as could best estimate its worth."[35] More than that, he acknowledges that only experts could interpret the *ONBP*, and that supplementary information about the provenance of the many proverbial quotations would have been helpful. He adds that "it had been his way to gather the choice fruits from the immensity of the store at his disposal, simply for his own delectation, without consideration for the deficiencies of lesser intellects."[36] This is the son defending the father, of course, but his choice of words might also be seen to imply some criticism. In any event, few scholars – and certainly not SCM – would find in their own enjoyment alone the fullest possible reward for their published labors.

It may be relevant to point out here that, before going to the comfortable living at Broadwindsor, SCM had two brief curacies: the first was in Alverstoke (on the Gosport side of Portsmouth Harbour), the second in Crowcombe (a few miles west of Taunton, the county town of Somerset). His Hampshire curacy was shared with two others, one of whom was Richard Chenevix Trench (1807–1886), and it is interesting to speculate that SCM's linguistic interests may have been furthered by his association with this fellow curate. Eventually becoming the Archbishop of Dublin, Trench was a philologist of some repute: works like *On the Study of Words* and *English Past and Present* were best-sellers in Victorian England. Even more relevant here, perhaps, is Trench's *On the Lessons in Proverbs*.[37]

Finally here, we can note that SCM had quite an enlightened view of translation. While Cicero's famous caution about translating *verbum pro verbo* has long been recognized, there have always been those who cautioned against the caution. For example, Nabokov argued that, in poetry at least, anything but the "clumsiest literalism" is fraudulent.[38] The tension between literal fidelity and literary felicity is constant, but SCM would have endorsed what Émile Rieu (1887–1972), the founder of the famous *Penguins Classics* series, called the "law of equivalent effect." This implies a rejection of Nabokov's literalism because, in his translations of proverbs, SCM was in a realm closer to poetry than to prose. ANM cites an analysis of his father's posture here:

> the object in translating is to convey as nearly as possible into the new language the exact ideas of the original. This requires, first that the force of the original

---

[34] Cited in *SCM DD*, p. 402.

[35] Quoting from *SCM DD*, p. 403.

[36] As found in *SCM DD*, p. 403.

[37] See the three volumes by Richard Chenevix Trench: *On the Study of Words* (1851), *On the Lessons in Proverbs* (1853), and *English Past and Present* (1855), all published in London by a publisher named Parker. Dermot Trench, a grandson of the reverend philologist, became a friend of James Joyce, and the model for Haines in *Ulysses*. The fictional Haines is a student of Irish, and in 1907 the real Trench published a pamphlet arguing for the revival of the language.

[38] As cited in Edwards 1995, p. 51.

word should be well ascertained, and then that the most appropriate term for it should be sought in the language which is to receive the translation.[39]

SCM's view of English is more dated, however. In commenting on the superiority of the English Bible, he not only hints at a literalism apparently rejected in his translations of proverbs – remarking on its "devout adherence to the original texts" – but he also suggests that its medium enhances its message. "It stands unrivalled among all other modern versions," he wrote, in part because of "the dignified and easy flow of a language that was in a great degree formed from it."[40] He also cites

> the nature of the English language, which is alike firm and flexible, elegant and manly; and so far, infinitely superior to the flippancy of the French, to the ponderousness of the Germans, and to the soft or effeminate character of the Italian, as a channel to convey the sense of the sacred texts.[41]

These sorts of linguistic stereotypes have long disappeared from the academic cloisters (although they linger, of course, in more popular quarters).[42]

1.3 Malan the Man

The Victorian clergyman who wrote about his early meetings with SCM also described seeing him again, in his middle years, "as a guest in Oxford Common Rooms, laying down the law on questions of Scriptural interpretation, his abysmal [*sic*, in the more literal sense it once had: simply "deep"] fund of learning and his dogmatic insistency floated by the rollicking fun of his illustrations and their delightful touches of travelled personal experience."[43] The words after "insistency" soften things a bit, but there is more. At their third meeting – in Broadwindsor, with SCM now elderly – Tuckwell remarks upon his library and aviary, his workshop and his drawings, being greeted with "hospitality stimulated by the discovery that in some of his favourite pursuits I was, *longo intervallo*, an enthusiast like himself." But he is also obliged to write that SCM was "a benevolently autocratic vicar, controlling his parish with patriarchally imperious rule, original, racy, trenchant in Sunday School and sermons."[44]

SCM was clearly of strong conservative tendencies, and these extended well beyond theological positions *per se*. He felt that "the transliteration of Oriental languages in Roman characters [was] … a kind of barbarism, and could hardly bear to

---

[39] Quoted from *SCM DD*, p. 166.

[40] Noted in *SCM DD*, p. 215.

[41] Quoted from *SCM DD*, p. 218.

[42] Elsewhere – and presumably with his tongue at least somewhat in cheek – SCM suggested that "Sanscrit [*sic*] … is the language of angels, which I hope we shall talk in heaven. Turkish is the language of gentlemen; English is the language of men; Greek is the language of philosophy." And what about Hebrew, someone asked? "Oh, too sacred to be mentioned." Cited in *SCM DD*, p. 274.

[43] Tuckwell 1900, p. 96.

[44] Tuckwell 1900, p. 97.

look at a book in which an Eastern language was thus degraded."⁴⁵ This seems rather elitist, to say the least, while his disapproval of "lady students" at Oxford merely part of a strong male tenor of the time. Needless to say, his politics were "Tory to the backbone."⁴⁶

ANM writes that "Dr. Malan's claim to distinction rests mainly upon his pre-eminence as an Oriental scholar. In him profound linguistic ability was combined with an insatiable eagerness for knowledge […] energy of resource […] indefatigable zeal for literary labour."⁴⁷ A strong intellect, then, fueled by marked curiosity and the drive to satisfy it. Like others, SCM had his preferred scholarly areas; unlike quite as many others, perhaps, "when conscious of limitation he ignored the subject."⁴⁸ More pointedly, not only did he have extremely poor mathematical ability (to cite what is apparently a particularly egregious example), we discover that, for history, "he professed contempt, declaring it to be based on 'lies'."⁴⁹ This is surely rather odd, given his regard and concern for ancient peoples and languages.

From an early age, SCM's literary and religious interests led to an essentially bookish nature and, ultimately, the assembly of his important library. Throughout the son's biography, we read of a man who was devoted to learning and to the written word in particular. As he grew older, so he spent more and more time in his study: "he lived in his books."⁵⁰ He greatly prized this part of life, taking his meals hurriedly, "grudging the waste of time" involved and liable to irritation if his work was interrupted.⁵¹ The strong disapprobation that SCM expressed for interests and concerns that were not his own extended to the printed word. "He never read a novel, nor cared for any book of common light literature. Magazines and reviews for the most part he eschewed, denominating them 'trash'," and it is surely significant that his regular reading of the *Saturday Review* came to an abrupt halt when he read an article to which he took offence. The son also tells us that his father "never went to a theatre in his life, nor to a ball."⁵²

This bookish and scholarly man was also interested in music (he played several instruments, and was able to repair them), in ornithology (he kept an aviary, and had a very fine collection of birds' eggs), in bookbinding, in "mechanical handicraft" and in carpentry. With "tools of the best manufacture, many of them mounted in rosewood handles," he produced fine small articles of cabinetry.⁵³ Nonetheless,

---

[45] MacDonell 1895, p. 457.

[46] Noted in *SCM DD*, p. 416.

[47] Quoted from *SCM DD*, p. 416.

[48] As cited in *SCM DD*, p. 116.

[49] Found in *SCM DD*, p. 117, the son goes on to describe a trifling problem that any beginner in algebra could solve – but which his father could not.

[50] Quoted from *SCM DD*, p. 255.

[51] Noted in *SCM DD*, p. 266.

[52] Quoted from *SCM DD*, p. 145.

[53] Cited in *SCM DD*, p. 145. Noting that SCM's collection of birds' eggs, presented to the Exeter Museum, was "judged one of the finest in the country," Simpson in his biographical account of SCM (2004, p. 275) lists some of his other interests and activities, partly attributing

it is notable that most of his non-literary interests were solitary ones. He never played team sports, although he appreciated the accuracy of archery and admired a perfectly made arrow. He also came to like croquet and riding, and he enjoyed fly-fishing, particularly by himself. When first introduced to the "elegance" of angling, he "forthwith wrote to London for a set of the best tackle" – ANM reminding us yet again here that his father "could scarcely put up with anything except of the best."[54] Solitary pursuits, solitary inclinations.

Perhaps it is not surprising, then, that in old age SCM said, "I have been alone all my life, and I shall be alone to the end."[55] This reflects sadness and regret, to be sure, but it is also a rather maudlin invitation to the son to reflect upon a life of insufficiently appreciated work, a direction to which the father has nevertheless remained true – to reflect upon, to value and to admire. It is the cry of the lone but steadfast scholar. It is true that SCM was not a Casaubon, for he published a great deal and received much acclaim as a linguist and an orientalist. At the same time, we read in several places of lack of recognition. Beyond the "meagre notice" taken of his large work on proverbs, mentioned above, we can also note that he produced "a long list of translations from devotional works of Eastern ritual, published at his own discretion and expense, with indifference to the fact that they did not meet with much appreciation from the public." Here again, it is surely noteworthy that his biographer son then immediately adds that "never did he seek or take advice upon the subject from a friend."[56]

For someone who reacted strongly to criticism, it seems strange that SCM failed to accept positions that would have certified his scholarly eminence. His son writes that "not a few" found it surprising that his father should have remained at Broadwindsor "without further preferment," especially since SCM himself described his time there as "forty years in the wilderness."[57] Edward Pusey (1800–1882), whose importance in the "Oxford Movement" for Anglo-Catholicism was such that "Puseyism" became a virtual synonym, wanted SCM to succeed him as the Oxford professor of Hebrew, suggesting that a readership in Arabic would be a useful first step. Still, the young SCM declined the offer. Samuel Wilberforce (1805–1873) suggested the Bishopric of Mauritius (in what seems a very odd offer, and one that ANM merely mentions in passing): this offer was also declined.[58] SCM felt, we are told, that he had to hang on to the more remunerative Broadwindsor living to cover his considerable family expenses (see previous section – but see also the "princely tastes" noted below), but his son adds, as well, that "he shrank from

---

his lack of "real eminence" to energies too widely dispersed. See also footnote 19, as well as Owen Chadwick's account (1970, p. 166).

[54] Noted in *SCM DD*, pp. 148-149.
[55] Quoted from *SCM DD*, p. 115.
[56] Cited in *SCM DD*, p. 255.
[57] As found in *SCM DD*, p. 281.
[58] "Soapy Sam" Wilberforce is best known as the opponent of Darwinian evolution who participated in the famous 1860 debate with "Darwin's bulldog," Thomas Huxley (1825–1895).

sacrificing independence of opinion."[59] Was his bluff manner hiding some scholarly insecurity? Did SCM fear that his "independence of opinion" – often, as his son and others pointed out, expressed in strong terms – might be inconveniently challenged by scholars who could not be ignored, and to whom one could not condescend? It is also of interest that, when discussing his father's famous work on proverbs, ANM describes a "life-long solace […] enjoyed in the solitude of his sanctuary – where none might intrude to criticize or hazard a suggestion."[60] Later on, SCM did accept an honorary degree from Edinburgh in 1880, but such recognition does not of course involve the continuing public commitment to research, teaching and writing that important university appointments reflect and require.

ANM describes his father as completely self-reliant, so "centralised" that he was:

> defiant of all opposition. He could not bear even the rebuff of a contrary opinion. He never would admit the possibility of two sides to a question. Those who ventured to disagree with him placed themselves beyond the pale of reason. Argument, as a rule, he disdained and eschewed. To him his conclusions were self-evident and unquestionable.[61]

A little later, the son returns to this arrogant intractability, this dismissal or denial of contrary opinion: "he had a peculiar way of putting his eye-glass to his eye, and looking intently for a few moments at an object, and then pronouncing a verdict comprehensive and final, from which he would never swerve."[62] SCM might have acknowledged some limitations, but he clearly felt that his abilities were wide-ranging; they were broader, indeed, than one might have predicted. Here is his son again:

> It afforded him much amusement to recount how he had to teach the village artisans their various trades. The blacksmith had to be shown how to shoe horses so as to avoid hurting the frog of the foot […] the carpenter had to be shown how to use the plane so as to save the tracing.[63]

SCM also seems to have had a sense of entitlement, no doubt based upon a feeling that strength of intellect and scholarship justified some perquisites. "His tastes were princely, and he gratified them with lavish hand," his son writes.[64] After noting the vicar's contempt for money – "money! – dross! – filth!" – a neighboring curate adds that "he could scarcely put up with anything except of the best […] no one was more alive to the elegancies of life, and these can wealth alone command."[65] This curate is described as an "intimate" friend of SCM.

---

[59] Noted in *SCM DD*, p. 281.

[60] Noted in *SCM DD*, p. 403.

[61] Quoted from *SCM DD*, p. 117.

[62] Cited from *SCM DD*, pp. 146-147.

[63] Quoted from *SCM DD*, p. 141. In fairness, one should also cite ANM's observation that some of his father's blacksmithing advice was adopted thereafter.

[64] Cited from *SCM DD*, p. 170.

[65] Noted in *SCM DD*, p. 149.

One of SCM's avocational pursuits was sketching, drawing and painting, and I think we must see in this something more than an idle and amateurish hobby. His son writes that he was never satisfied with his own work, and that he "insisted that he never drew for pleasure."[66] This is very odd: apart from jobbing professionals, it is difficult to imagine artists who find no intrinsic pleasure in their work. So why did SCM sketch? His drawings were essentially records of his extensive travels, so that his son notes both his "indefatigable zeal" here and the fact that he "*never drew at all*" during his forty years at Broadwindsor.[67] The zeal extended to the ordering and the protection of his large portfolio, which eventually ran to more than 1,600 drawings, collated and mounted in ten volumes.[68] The work was kept "under lock and key" and visitors were not allowed to examine the drawings unless SCM was present. "Ladies were requested to remove their gloves before handling a volume; tea-cups were tabooed on the table, and never a finger was allowed to be laid on any drawing."[69] He believed that "character" was revealed by both drawing and handwriting, and, while he sometimes worked in water-color, he disdained oil painting – it was like "spreading butter" and not, presumably, suggestive of artistic character.[70] His strong views here extended to disdain of fashions in art, and some of them will be found in his *Aphorisms on Drawing*; the final maxim in this little book is that "the end of drawing is to praise Him, in our work."[71]

We have evidence, throughout his son's biography, that SCM was quite an accomplished artist. He had exhibitions, at Burlington House (the home of the Royal Academy) and the Crystal Palace, for example, some of his work was sold, and his sketches were considered very good.[72] More specifically, there are indications that professional painters thought well of his work. Benjamin Leader (1831–1923), a landscape artist whose works hang in the Tate and the Victoria and Albert Museum, told ANM that his father's were "the most clever amateur sketches I have ever seen," adding that he could have become more "had he devoted his whole time to art."[73] Philip Traub discusses SCM's art in an issue of *The Connoisseur*, and one can easily find mention of his paintings and sketches on the web (including on

---

[66] Quoted from *SCM DD*, p. 211.

[67] Quoted from *SCM DD*, p. 211, the italics in the original.

[68] The provenance and the number of SCM's drawings provide a rough record of the extent of his travels, and of the relative levels of interest that different parts of the world had for him. Here are the geographical divisions covered in the ten volumes of his work, with the number of sketches found in each: India (175 drawings), Egypt (122), the Holy Land: volume I (135) and volume II (280), Turkey (102), Italy (192), Italy and Sicily (151), Armenia and Nineveh (274), Spain and Greece (90), and "Home" (93). It is of course the careful collation and description that I find most relevant here.

[69] Quoted from *SCM DD*, p. 205.

[70] Noted in *SCM DD*, p. 205.

[71] As found at the end of SCM 1856b; cited again in *SCM DD*, p. 193.

[72] See Simpson's biographical note on SCM (*id.* 2004). (This Crystal Palace was the redesigned version, built in Sydenham in 1854.)

[73] Recorded in *SCM DD*, p. 214.

eBay!).⁷⁴ The most important holding of SCM's work is that of the Getty Research Institute in California – it has six of the ten albums of drawings (as referred to in footnote 68), acquired from the rare-book trade in 2013 (for examples, see Figs. 2 and 3 in Chapter One).⁷⁵ Peter Bonfitto, who was involved in the acquisition, is a researcher at the Institute; in correspondence with me, he writes that, while SCM and his contemporaries may have seen him as a talented amateur,

> that can only be accepted in a nineteenth-century context. He had an incredible command of the medium of watercolor. The drawings are simply superb. I have had the opportunity to show the drawings to a number of curators and art historians. Everyone agrees about the high level of their quality.⁷⁶

1.4 Malan Summarized

I believe that a fairly clear picture of SCM emerges here, one in which descriptions in the biography are complemented by the other sparse resources. First, he was obviously a talented man – particularly, but not solely, where languages are concerned. Where linguistic skills are concerned, it is not unreasonable to place him with the Mezzofantis of the world (and others, to whom I shall shortly turn). At the same time, one feels that his talents were, as several scholars suggested, too widely dispersed, and that his impact as a scholar was consequently lessened. Chadwick is most pointed here, when he refers to a mind lacking in "critical sense."⁷⁷ Deficiencies in this vital capacity do indeed undercut scholarship and, when shortcomings here are accompanied by a lack of focus, a dilution of scholarly effectiveness is entirely predictable.⁷⁸ Energetic application and a powerful work ethic are insufficient remedies. Indeed, it is also predictable that the major effect of sustained effort,

---

⁷⁴ Consult Traub 1968, p. 580.

⁷⁵ The Getty's albums have been digitized: http://hdl.handle.net/10020/2013m25 (accessed 11 March 2021). The location of two of the other four is known: one is in the British Library (where it has recently been examined by Lauren Pfister); another was acquired by Stellenbosch University (South Africa) in 1967. The latter is the "India" volume, which also has drawings made in Sri Lanka and South Africa; see Schröder – Trümpelmann 1971. Incidentally, the Stellenbosch connection is not as random as one might suppose. A branch of the Malan family has lived in South Africa since the late seventeenth century, becoming prominent in religious and political circles. D. F. Malan, Prime Minister from 1948 to 1954, lived in Stellenbosch. SCM reportedly came across "many of his own name during his sojourn at the Cape" in 1839, but told an enquirer that "I had nothing to say to them" (*SCM DD*, p. 56). If their politics and opinions were as narrow and prejudiced as those of the twentieth-century Malans – including the Prime Minister, an ardent nationalist and supporter of apartheid – then SCM did well to avoid them.

⁷⁶ My correspondence with Bonfitto began in October 2014, when he advised me that he was preparing a short piece about SCM, that was published the following year. See Bonfitto 2015, pp. 169-176.

⁷⁷ As characterized by Chadwick 1970, p. 166.

⁷⁸ SCM may have spread himself too thinly, linguistically and otherwise, but his biblical argumentation and his "proverbial" work hardly suggest a lack of focused concentration.

when it is felt to be inadequately recognized and rewarded, will be to foster or heighten a sense of grievance and neglect.

The most interesting personality characteristics attributed to SCM are ones that reinforce this picture, and they can be easily gleaned from the information presented here. He was an intelligent and hard worker, capable of long periods of unremitting scholarly labor, and – although not explicitly touched upon by his son – obviously blessed with a fine memory.[79] At the same time, he was disdainful and sometimes arrogant about intellectual and other pursuits that were not his own.[80] It is not, of course, anti-intellectual to focus one's activities in a fairly restricted field: all endeavors are reductionist, in that sense, and no one can study everything. It is anti-intellectual, however, to be dismissive of work outside a topic area simply because it is not one's own. Given the scope and polymathic nature of SCM's undoubted abilities, it is perhaps a little surprising to find this posture.

SCM was also solidly and unswervingly opinionated, possessed of a self-righteous sense of certainty. We also find the obsessive collector's desire for completeness. These qualities can be seen in his vigorous (and sometimes excessively fine-grained) attacks on what he thought of as inappropriate or inaccurate renderings of scripture and religious interpretation generally, as well as in the scope and intensity of his linguistic productions. He seemed unwilling to place himself in positions where he might be observed and found wanting, even when one or two of these positions were of very high status, and much sought after by scholars. Here we may recall Chadwick once more, and suggest that SCM felt himself lacking in that critical sensibility which is (or should be) a *sine qua non* for posts of scholarly significance. In a word, it seems that SCM was, despite his many obvious talents and robust opinions, an insecure man once outside his self-generated and self-sustained borders. Insecurity, after all, can very easily coexist with disdain, intractability and external indications of personal and intellectual strength. Also fitting in with this developing picture is SCM's sense of entitlement and, consequently, his thin-skinned lashing out at criticism, in reactions that were sometimes of an *ad hominem* nature.

If we consider his productions, particularly those – like his *Gospel According to St. John* and the *Original Notes on the Book of Proverbs*[81] – that draw upon and highlight his very extensive linguistic capacities, we see specific examples of his learning, his application, his energy and his obsessive concern with completeness. He was a man who valued "system," order, routine and categorization, and, in the productions just mentioned, we see a marriage of these with his language fluencies

---

[79] SCM's fine memory is particularly evident, of course, in his linguistic breadth – and so I shall return below to the significance of memory.

[80] We can recall here, too, that SCM was said never to draw "for pleasure," that he never went to the theatre or read novels (not English ones, at any rate) – further evidence, perhaps, of a rigorously self-limiting nature and one, perhaps, overly concerned with maintaining the appearance of a rejection of "lowly pastimes."

[81] Referring to works produced by SCM in 1862 and in the three-volume work published during 1889–1893.

– all in the ultimate service of an almost archival concern with what are essentially elaborate lists. And, if I may be allowed to call on Chadwick yet again, we may be seeing in SCM's works the fruits of a type of intelligent activity that does not rely chiefly upon originality or innovation, upon that critical sense. I should add here that this does not detract from the potential usefulness of the work. It is one of the roles of archivists, after all, to assemble, collate and sometimes interpret material that will be grist for the mills of others.[82]

In this connection, I am reminded of Sir Cyril Burt (1883–1971), a celebrated English educational psychologist and statistician who became infamous for allegedly falsifying data. Like SCM, he was also something of a polymath, fluent in several languages and of very broad interests and knowledge. In a review of Hearnshaw's 1979 biography of Burt, Crawford makes the interesting point that "despite his almost incredible erudition ... [Burt] may not have been very creative."[83]

Part 2
Polyglossia, "Savantism" and the Autistic Spectrum

2.1 A Prefatory Note

One point should be borne in mind throughout this section. The amazing and sometimes seemingly incredible musical, linguistic and mathematical capabilities found in some individuals – whether clearly autistic or not – must surely suggest something beyond strangely intense and prodigious attention to detail, allied to heightened powers of memory. Or, at least, such attention and such powers must rest upon certain special or atypical neural processes. How, after all, does a retarded individual "decide" to become an amazing calculator, how do extraordinary proclivities arise, where does the motivation for highly specific application come from? Some comments made by Michael Howe and Julia Smith may be mentioned here, as they bear upon the broader discussion. They point out that one of the obvious difficulties faced by investigators is that most of their informants are not, after all, very informative: they may be reticent to talk or, much more likely, may be unable to discuss how they perform their rapid calculations. Howe and Smith nevertheless suggest that a great deal of time is spent on memorization, that visual imagery of some sort seems often to be involved, and that – while essentially self-taught – the "calculators" sometimes receive encouragement from those around them. Howe pays some attention to this fundamental matter; see also his remarks on child prodigies.[84] Darold Treffert highlights three pivotal features of the "savant syndrome": neurological anomalies, inherited and/or acquired aptitudes, and powerful and

---

[82] Archivists are not the only benefactors of later critical scholarship. Quite regardless of their own abilities, the great collectors have often created museums and libraries of inestimable value, thereby becoming philanthropists and patrons of the arts and sciences.

[83] Quoted from Crawford 1980, p. 100.

[84] Consult Howe – Smith 1988, as well as Howe's two monographs, *The Origins of Exceptional Abilities* (Oxford: Blackwell, 1990) and *Fragments of Genius: The Strange Feats of Idiots Savants* (London: Routledge, 1991).

reinforced motivation – and we could almost invariably add excellence in memory and systematization to the list.[85] As with other conjectures, even those based upon the most recent psychopathological studies, Treffert's are more descriptive than explanatory, and his three "pivotal features" are not equally present in all cases. Indeed, there is some agreement that the achievements of many, perhaps most, savants (non-autistic ones, at any rate) are in fact based upon "an essentially normal mental-processing capacity allied to unusually intense and long-lasting attention, concentration and involvement in particular interests."[86] This takes nothing away from those extraordinarily rare achievements, of course, but – coupled with the fact that they generally coexist with normal (or, in some instances, sub-normal) abilities in other spheres of life – it does suggest that we are not dealing with miracle-workers. Still, "the demonstration that an individual can be simultaneously gifted and retarded continues to be a source of bafflement."[87]

2.2 On Autism

In April 2014, BBC-2 aired a program called "Living with Autism," presented by Uta Frith.[88] It revealed that, while about 80% of autistic individuals are unable to live independently, many have quite special talents. While perhaps one in ten has extraordinary abilities – the calendrical or "lightning" calculators, for instance – as many as one in three seems to have some notable skills (in music, memory, etc.).[89] Beyond memory, other common autistic traits include task repetition and practice (often obsessive), generally in the service of creating systems and patterns, as well as social inadequacies in which communication is impaired. Monologic communication, especially when scripted, means that making formal presentations – including, most interestingly, discussing one's own autism – on familiar subjects, in familiar settings, is possible for some.

Frith defines autism as a "lack of a social navigation system." There is a deficient "theory of mind" (she calls it "mentalising") – an inability, that is, to fully grasp the feelings of others or, in some instances, to even attribute feelings to others. At a simple level, then, autistic individuals may lack those "normal" social sensibilities that make fluent interactions possible. Neurological research suggests that autistic people show less activity in brain regions associated with "mentalising." While clinical diagnosis is currently only possible at two or three years of age,

---

[85] Consult Treffert 1989.

[86] Quoted from Howe 1991, p. 162; see also Foer 2011.

[87] As found in Howe 1991, p. 65.

[88] See also Frith 2014. In that article Frith introduces a whole issue of *The Psychologist* (a monthly publication of the British Psychological Society) which is largely devoted to autism. It provides the then most recent succinct treatment of the topic.

[89] Within that same issue, Christian Jarrett suggests, drawing upon estimates provided by the (British) National Autistic Society, that "approximately .05 per cent of the autistic population has an extreme talent." He refers here to a very small number of people – those who have a "genius-level gift" – and not to the larger number who "have islands of relative or impressive strength." See Jarrett 2014, p. 746.

investigations are now looking at the brain-wave patterns of infants: while some variant activity has been detected, it is certainly not the case that all infants with "markers" suggestive of autism actually develop the disorder. Genetic influences also seem significant here; recent research in the "reading" of DNA has uncovered linkages between a number of genes and autism.[90] Finally here, it is noteworthy that the neurological underpinnings of autism may be connected with those that lead to epilepsy: Daniel Tammet (see also below) suffered epileptic seizures himself, and he writes that "about a third of children with an autistic spectrum disorder develop temporal-lobe epilepsy by adolescence."[91]

Autistic individuals often have frustrating and anxious social lives, in which they cannot understand the actions and words of others, and where they fail to understand jokes, banter and metaphor. Imitation can reduce stress here – a process not unlike the social "modelling" that is so useful for all people. Still, one autistic informant said that "I don't miss other people when they're not present," and describes her lack of emotional commitment to others; nonetheless she is actually able to say this, to live with a partner, and to realize that others do manage strong and context-free emotional commitments. She provides an excellent example of why "Autism Spectrum Disorder," a term that captures the very wide variability, in both abilities and disabilities, observable across individuals, is such an improvement on the simple label, "autism."

A spectrum implies that determining prevalence is difficult. Frith suggests that the rate half a century ago was about 5 in 10,000; now it is twenty times greater. This probably says much more about diagnosis and reporting than about actual rate changes. Furthermore, some of the features common on the spectrum are very widely distributed indeed. Frith describes herself as obsessive in her work, sometimes socially awkward, and so on. It is not difficult, then, to find "autistic-like" traits – including compulsiveness, perfectionism, systematicity, eccentricity, and energetic devotion to specific tasks – in a great many individuals, particularly among scholars and others of above-average intelligence whose work often rests upon these qualities. Michael Erard suggests that tendencies to systematize might "help explain why scientists score higher than nonscientists on a test that measures autistic traits."[92] Systematicity is also associated with difficulties in dealing with or understanding abstractions or departures from what is concrete or literal. In a useful journalistic overview, Steve Jones writes that, on measures of emotional sensitivity, "those with autism proper do worst, then Asperger's patients, followed by the high-functioning [autistic] group, and then – in order – by scientists, professors and men. Women come top."[93] Simon Baron-Cohen, interviewed in the BBC program,

---

[90] For those interested, consult Abraham 2014, A1.

[91] Quoted from Tammet 2007, p. 39.

[92] Cited in Erard 2012, p. 230.

[93] Quoted from Jones 2012. Asperger Syndrome, a disorder on the autistic spectrum, involves the familiar repetitive behavior patterns, restricted interests, and difficulties with social interaction, but those suffering from it often seem to have more or less unimpaired cognitive and

argues in fact that very few of us would be at zero on any plausible scale of autism. The criteria on which clinical diagnosis rests, of course, have to do with traits whose strength interferes with normal social functioning. In another context, therefore, Baron-Cohen describes extreme "systematizing [...] the search for grand patterns [...] even though it is accompanied by an excessive narrowing of focus that reduces its usefulness."[94]

A spectrum of possibilities also allows us to bring in those interesting cases in which extraordinary abilities seem to coexist with an absence of any marked autistic tendencies. Anthony Smith, for instance, highlights the ability of the New Zealand-born professor of mathematics, Alexander Aitken (1895–1967). Asked to "make 4 divided by 47 into a decimal," Aitken began to respond after four seconds, then gave another digit every three-quarters of a second; in a minute or two he had provided the decimal to forty-six places, noting that this long sequence then repeats.[95] As we see in other cases, Aitken's ability was virtually automatic; he writes that, seeing a car with 731 on its registration plate, he "cannot help observing that it is 17 times 43."[96] Within the world of "lightning calculators," Aitken is unique in providing details of his methods of procedure.[97] Further discussions of Aitken's memory, which was almost as remarkable as his mathematical manipulations, are provided by Ian Hunter, and by Evan Brown and Kenneth Deffenbacher.[98] Howe points out that, while displaying abilities also found in savants, Aitken was not autistic. This is of course a most important point, and Howe goes on to suggest that remarkable achievements can in some instances be

> the outcome of an essentially normal mental-processing capacity allied to unusually intense and long-lasting attention, concentration and involvement in particular interests.[99]

Smith makes the same point: some "lightning calculators" are autistic savants, others – like Aitken – are not.[100] Smith notes that "savants [are] people with an island of startling ability in a sea of disability: people like 'Rainman' made famous by

---

linguistic development. Language use, however, may reveal everything from abnormal verbosity to lack of comprehension of anything departing from the literal.

[94] As cited in Wilson 2012, p. 45. This narrowness of focus was highlighted by Robert Ebisch (1989), in his useful review of Treffert's *Extraordinary People* (1989).

[95] Documented in A. Smith 1984.

[96] Cited in Sweeney 2000, p. 9.

[97] For those interested, consult Aitken 1954; see also Hunter 1962, and subsequently his book, entitled *Memory* (Harmondsworth, Middlesex: Penguin, 1966). Alexander Luria's volume, *The Mind of a Mnemonist* (Harmondsworth, Middlesex: Penguin, 1975), offers a famous account of "the mind of a mnemonist" that remains the most widely-known account of exceptional feats of memory. See further details in what follows, and also check specific passages in Luria's volume mentioned in footnote 115 below.

[98] See Hunter 1977, and Brown – Deffenbacher 1975.

[99] Quoted from Howe 1991, p. 154.

[100] Consult S. Smith 1983.

Dustin Hoffman's portrayal of an autistic savant in the film of that name."[101] How are we best to understand such people, this coexistence of extraordinary, if narrow, talent with broad incapacities? Smith goes on to say they are not to be thought of as some high-class "peep show," their varying personalities and abilities simply lumped together in one cabinet of human curiosities. They are fascinating, of course, both intrinsically and for what they may reveal about more "ordinary" individuals.

Smith also provides a summary of the sorts of talents most often displayed by savants. There are, for instance, the calendrical and numerical calculators – people who can tell you what day of the week Christmas fell on in the year 1359, who can multiply seven-digit numbers in their head, who can mentally extract cube roots, and so on.[102] There are, too, those with extraordinary musical abilities: think of the many stories of severely retarded, often speechless, people being able to play complex pieces of music after hearing them just once or twice. Besides memory skills, Smith suggests that what he calls "structure dependence" is central in these feats – a dependence, that is, upon regularity and precision which, coupled with memory and a great deal of "time-on-task," produces apparently magical results.[103] The crucial factor is a system which can, however laboriously, be analyzed. In this regard, Smith writes about a savant who almost flawlessly reproduced a piece of tonal music, but who fared much worse when asked to play back some of Bartók's atonal music.

---

[101] Quoted from N. Smith 2005, p. 39. Kim Peek (the real "Rainman"), one of those who used to be called "idiot savants," died in December 2009, aged 58. He apparently memorized thousands of books (including the Bible), and reportedly could read left- and right-hand pages simultaneously (one with each eye), taking only a few seconds per "pair." He was also a "calendrical calculator" – see below. Nonetheless, he was unable to look after himself or manage his own affairs. He had motor-skill deficiencies, too. Peek was damaged at birth: of particular interest, the corpus callosum – the nerve-bundle connecting the two hemispheres – was missing. (Lack of this commisure, or abnormalities therein, has long been associated with autism varieties.) Daniel Tammet describes meeting Peek in *Born on a Blue Day* – one savant encountering another – and Peek, in turn, had met Dustin Hoffman, the "Rainman" of the movie. An academic consultant on the film was Darold Treffert, whose 1989 book was an early attempt to bring current knowledge about savants under one roof.

[102] Discussed in S. Smith 1983 and Howe 1991, but also in Heavey *et al.* 1999, pp. 145-160.

[103] See N. Smith 2005. There are individuals with remarkable memories who are not autistic savants – although they do show the obsessive-compulsive behavior that is common among the latter. Kayt Sukel therefore describes a condition known as "Highly Superior Autobiographical Memory" and, more formally, as "hyperthymesia" (consult Sukel 2012.) A thirty-four-year-old informant, for instance, is able to recall events, day by day, that have happened over the past two decades. Such a memory – not founded in any mnemonic exercises – is not, of course, an unalloyed benefit; the title of a recent book – *The Woman Who Can't Forget* (by Price and Davis, 2008) – suggests the point here; see also footnote 115. There are, equally, those whose memory functions are notable for other reasons. A classic study by William Scoville and Brenda Milner discussed a patient whose epilepsy-relieving surgery interfered with his ability to form new memories. While in touch with his early life, he had to be re-introduced to his doctors every morning. Consult Scoville – Milner 1957.

Research suggests that synaesthesia – a condition in which sensory experiences are "mixed" – could reasonably be added to the list of common autistic traits. Baron-Cohen and his colleagues have noted that the disorder might occur in as many as 20% of autistic individuals (compared with about 4% in the non-autistic population).[104] While there are historical references to synaesthesia dating (at least) to the early eighteenth century – and John Locke (1632–1704) makes what may be a reference to the condition in his *Essay Concerning Human(e) Understanding* (1690)[105] – the first scholarly account seems to be that of Georg Sachs (1786–1814), in a medical dissertation recording observations of himself and his sister – both albinos.[106] Written in Latin, the work was published in German by Julius Schlegel, and has been given close attention by Jörg Jewanski and his colleagues.[107] A good general overview is provided by Richard Cytowic; see also Cytowic and David Eagleman.[108] In a brief but useful treatment, Jack Dutton discusses a number of varieties – including "lexical-gustatory" synaesthesia, with which words have tastes.[109] He also touches upon the possibility that, while the condition has neurological underpinnings, recently revealed by magnetic-resonance imaging,[110] the condition may not be entirely hereditary, in which case it might be possible (he suggests) for people to learn and acquire it. Would this be a good thing, given the link between synaesthesia and autism? There is no suggestion, of course, that attempts to induce some level of synaesthesia will have autism as a consequence, only that some of the cross-modality experiences found in many autistic people might prove valuable to others. Dutton draws here upon work by Nicolas Rothen and Beat Meier, and by Jamie Ward and associates, scholars who have proposed that synaesthesia may be linked to artistic creativity, and to enhanced memory and cognitive functioning.[111]

Referring to observations by Francis Galton (1822–1911), Julia Simner and her colleagues discuss "temporal-spatial" synaesthesia, in which sequenced units – letters and numbers, for example, but also days, weeks, months and years – are "seen" and "mapped" in particular spatial arrangements: the days of the week might be "seen" as occupying segments of an ellipse, and not necessarily equally-sized ones.[112] The title of their piece suggests that such synaesthesia is at once beneficial,

---

[104] Baron-Cohen *et al.* 2013.

[105] As found in Locke 1690, p. 118.

[106] See Sachs 1812.

[107] Consult Schlegel 1824; Jewanski – Sidler 2006. There being no classical Latin word for "albino," Sachs used Pliny's famous term for the "white Ethiopians" of Libya: *leucaethiopes*.

[108] See Cytowic 2002 and Cytowic – Eagleman 2009.

[109] Consult Dutton 2015; see also Cytowic 1993.

[110] Also discussed by Simner – Mayo – Spiller 2009.

[111] Discussed in Rothen – Meier 2014, and Ward – Thompson-Lake – Ely – Kaminski 2008.

[112] Simner – Mayo – Spiller 2009 treats the article by Francis Galton "Visualised Numerals," *Nature* 21 (1880), pp. 252–256 and 494–495 and its fuller exposition published in the following year. In passing, the authors seem to imply that some "mild" form of visuo-spatial synaesthesia might be quite widely distributed – a point reinforced by my own experience in mentally

a pillar of "savantism," and part of the hyperthymestic syndrome.[113] It is related, therefore, to both powerful memory and obsession-compulsion.[114]

Alexander Luria's famous little book about Solomon Shereshevskii (1886–1958) remains one of the best-known studies of a synaesthete-mnemonist. Shereshevskii described someone's voice as being "crumbly" and "yellow." He also associated numbers with things: "Take the number 1. This is a proud, well-built man; 2 is a high-spirited woman; 3 a gloomy person [...] as for the number 87, what I see is a fat woman and a man twirling his moustache";[115] similar discussions are found in Howe, and Yaro and Ward.[116] In fact, *audition colorée* is a fairly common form of synaesthesia, with Vladimir Nabokov and other lesser lights describing their "coloured hearing."[117]

2.3 On Polyglossia

Erard provides a useful overview of polyglots and "hyperpolyglots." The latter term was applied earlier, by Richard Hudson, to describe individuals knowing more than six languages. Erard raises the ante to eleven, but the precise number need not detain us here: the point is simply that, among multilinguals, some few have quite extraordinary abilities. Erard builds his book around Mezzofanti, as did Charles Russell – a century and a half earlier, and when SCM was in his middle age. Russell takes the first hundred pages of his book to discuss polyglots, ancient and modern, from Europe and the Near East, before turning to Mezzofanti himself.[118]

Cardinal Giuseppe Mezzofanti (1774–1849), who became a librarian in the Vatican, spoke – as nearly as one can determine[119] – about fifty languages with some fluency. He took every opportunity to talk with native speakers; beyond this, it is clear that he devoted a great deal of time to learning languages, sometimes in ways that most would find extremely tedious. For example, when visiting the library in Bologna where Mezzofanti worked before going to Rome, Erard found stacks of

---

visualizing the months of the year as a linear series of unequally-sized compartments, reflective of the academic calendar.

[113] See also footnote 103 above.

[114] Simner – Mayo – Spiller is one of seven articles on synaesthesia in a thematic section of this number of *Cortex* (45 [2009] 10); an earlier issue (42 [2006] 2) was given over completely to the subject. For those interested, consult Ward – Mattingly 2006.

[115] Quoted from Luria 1975, pp. 25 and 30. Synaesthetic memory or, indeed, extraordinary memory in general, is not always a welcome quantity. Luria's mnemonist, for example, was in many ways a prisoner of his powerful and retentive mental imagery; see also footnotes 97 and 103 above.

[116] Consult Howe 1991 as well as Yaro – Ward 2007. We see that some of the imagery here is not unlike the visualizations that "ordinary" people would suggest (for the numbers 1, 7 and 8), suggesting that synaesthetes too can take obvious paths; see, however, Tammet's numerical visualizations as described below.

[117] As discovered in Nabokov 1996.

[118] For their accounts, see Erard 2012, Hudson 2003, and Russell 1858.

[119] See Watts 1859.

flash cards in many languages, most of them written in the Cardinal's own hand.[120] When Pope Gregory XVI (1765–1846) surprised Mezzofanti with dozens of international students, he was able to chat with them in their own languages. While clearly a very atypical linguist, Mezzofanti's actual capabilities are not particularly clear, and some of the more detailed information that we have of him reveals considerable variation in estimates of his linguistic scope and depth. The several articles by Thomas Watts (1811–1869) will repay close study here.[121] Erard pays too little attention to Watts, in particular, and makes no reference to Russell's review essay – a pity, because they throw an early and quite sustained light upon the important matter of just what it means to "know" a language.[122] Their citations of first-hand observations made by prominent people who visited Mezzofanti are especially apposite. Watts provides, for example, details of a dozen eminent visitors, including Lord Byron.[123]

Drawing upon research that extends well beyond a reading of Mezzofanti, Erard suggests four basic cornerstones of polyglossia: (a) a capacity for sustained study; (b) a "superior ability to switch among languages"; (c) an excellent memory; (d) some advantageous neurological underpinnings. While some of the fascination that "super-linguists" have for us is that they "seem to have leapfrogged the banality of method," they tend in fact to use very banal methods, but "they make the banality more productive. Their minds *enjoy* the banality." Erard reports criticisms, along the lines that Mezzofanti never came out with anything creative: "He has not five ideas," one fellow priest said. Mezzofanti reminded one German visitor of a parrot: "He does not seem to abound in ideas" and he often repeats himself.[124] A Transylvanian lady said that he "rather studies the words than the subject of what he reads" and referred to his "empty unreflecting word-knowledge": he is, she wrote, best understood as "one of the curiosities of the Vatican."[125] Watts himself, while styling Mezzofanti "the greatest linguist the world has ever seen," yet points out that "he was a linguist only and not a philologist," and that "in an age which was remarkable for the vastness of its discoveries in the field of philology, the great linguist did

---

[120] Consult also Pasti 2006.

[121] Besides Watts 1859, see also his other two articles: "On the Extraordinary Powers of Cardinal Mezzofanti as a Linguist," *Proceedings of the Philological Society* 5 (1852) 115, pp. 111-125, and "On M. Manavit's Life of Cardinal Mezzofanti," *Transactions of the Philological Society* 1 (1854) 7, pp. 133-150. Thomas Watts, a prominent member of the Philological Society, and Keeper of Printed Books at the British Museum, was something of a polyglot himself. Consult also Russell 1858; Manavit 1853, and Mitterrutzner 1891.

[122] This is of course a central issue for Erard: he writes, for instance, about Ziad Fazah, reputed to know about 60 languages, who failed miserably when confronted on *Viva el Lunes*, a Chilean television talk show, in 1997. Fazah flubbed questions in Finnish, Mandarin and Russian (in the last, he was simply asked to respond to "What day is it today?"). His performance can still be seen on the internet (see Fazah 1997).

[123] As documented in Watts 1852.

[124] Quotations from Erard 2012, pp. 5 and 268-269. Emphasis in original.

[125] Cited from Watts 1852, pp. 119-121 *in passim*.

absolutely nothing."[126] He remakes the point later, writing that Mezzofanti never really did anything with all his languages: he never wrote a book, "his correspondence appears to have been scanty in quantity, and in quality little better than commonplace," and his sole publication appeared in 1820.[127]

Without wishing to needlessly multiply examples, we might note one or two other notable linguistic stars. John Bowring (1769–1856), from Devon, was said to have been able to speak about one hundred languages: he was a translator, anthologist, literary executor of Jeremy Bentham, statesman – and governor of Hong Kong from 1854 to 1859.[128] Another example is John Leyden (1775–1811), a Scottish polymath, physician and friend of Alexander Murray (1775–1813), author of an important history of European languages.[129] A more contemporary figure is Hans Eberstark (1929–2001), an interpreter who worked for the International Labour Organization, and who knew about a dozen languages well enough to translate in and out of them.[130] Erard discusses Ken Hale (1934–2001), well-known in modern linguistics circles: while he was said to "know" 50 languages, Hale himself claimed only three, saying that he could converse in English, Spanish and Warlpiri; all the others he could merely "say things in" – another distinction to be borne in mind.[131]

2.4 Autism *and* Polyglossia

Erard cites Simon Baron-Cohen (see also above): some hyperpolyglots seem "near-autistic," some have an "extreme male brain" (possibly higher levels of testosterone, that is to say), and other neurological features and anomalies have been suggested as underlying factors. Erard also reminds us of Baron-Cohen's argument that "systematising" is a frequent element in autism. Maleness and making lists: one of Erard's informants said that "I don't know many women who collect stamps or coins," suggesting to the author that perhaps we might see "polyglottery as a kind of collecting behavior, perhaps an obsessive one." In any event, Erard observes that "famous language learners, language accumulators and language geeks tend to be men."[132] Another author notes, too, that "autism and Asperger's are more common in males than females, and have been linked with prenatal exposure to testosterone."[133] Collecting often involves a search for completeness, or perfection, and Obsessive-Compulsive Disorder (OCD) – referred to in passing in footnote 32 – is not uncommon among savants.

---

[126] Quoted in Watts 1852, pp. 124-125.

[127] As claimed in Watts 1859, p. 245. He may not have been entirely correct, however, since Celestino Cavedoni noted that Mezzofanti's *Discorso in lode del P. E. Aponte* ... was not his only scholarly production. See Cavedoni 1861, p. 179.

[128] See these claims in Youings 1993.

[129] Consult Kelly 2010; see also Murray 1823 and Edwards 2005.

[130] As described in Bernstein 1993.

[131] See Erard 2012.

[132] Quotations found in Erard 2012, pp. 101 and 128.

[133] Cited from Wilson 2012, p. 45; see also S. Smith 1983.

Erard also describes Emil Krebs (1867–1930), a German polyglot who may have suffered from a mild form of Asperger Syndrome; see footnote 93. Analyses of Krebs's brain, donated by his wife to a German research institute in Düsseldorf, revealed some overdevelopment of the areas most directly concerned with speech and language.[134] Krebs was often compared to Mezzofanti, but Erard cites a scholar who said that his "wonderful talent bites its thumb ... [at] the Mezzofantis, who know all languages, but none fundamentally" – a German scholar, not surprisingly, but the statement does hint at the great difficulty in ascertaining skill levels, to say nothing of individual comparisons.[135]

Autistic reliance upon rule-governed systems – and the memory capacities that they both rest upon and facilitate – commonly underpins outstanding linguistic abilities, and two contemporary individuals highlight the point. Smith and his colleagues discuss Christopher Taylor, a Yorkshireman born in 1962.[136] Taylor is quite fluent in French, Spanish, Greek, German and Dutch, and has some command of Finnish, Swedish, Turkish, Danish, Norwegian, Welsh and Hindi. These talents coexist with a very low measured IQ, and Taylor suffers from a number of specific disabilities. He is uncomfortable in social situations, and most at ease in contexts in which his behavior is restricted and repetitive. He suffers from apraxia – a neurological condition whose most general characteristic is an incapacity to do things that the individual wants to do, and is not physically prevented from doing. Taylor cannot remember the way to his local pub, for example.

Daniel Tammet (b. 1979) recited from memory some 22,000 decimal places of *pi*. (Eberstark, noted above, was also a *pi*-memorizer, reaching about 12,000 places; neither, incidentally, comes close to the record here). A "high-functioning" autistic savant, Tammet is a member of the very small group – perhaps 100 worldwide – of so-called "prodigious savants."[137] He has been the subject of television documentaries and is a published author. His articulate capacity for self-description

---

[134] In her review of Erard's *Babel no more*, Hoge writes that it is unclear "whether the alterations in the brain of [Krebs] enabled, or resulted from, his exceptional linguistic aptitude" – a point to bear in mind in almost all cases. Also to be remembered is that brain structures and processes are so intertwined that finding some area or anomaly unique to polyglossia is unlikely. For the quote and the review, consult Hoge 2012.

[135] Cited from Erard 2012, p. 153.

[136] See Smith – Tsimpli 1995, and more recently Smith – Tsimpli – Morgan – Woll 2011.

[137] In discussing the possibility that intense application and the use of mnemonic techniques may be sufficient to account for even the most (seemingly) amazing feats of memory, Foer, in his *Moonwalking with Einstein* (2011), registers some skepticism about the "savant" status of Daniel Tammet – and, by implication, of some others. It is interesting, however, that Foer's book is devoted entirely to memory, with no mention made of extraordinary musical abilities or linguistic capacities, and only passing attention given to mental calculation. One infers, however, that Foer would be inclined to put all such skills down to practices and techniques which are available – in some degree, at least – to almost anyone of normal intelligence. Steven Smith in *The Great Mental Calculators* (1983) writes in a similar vein, even though Aitken in his article, "The Art of Mental Calculation" (1954), as well as other "lightning calculators," have tried to explain their techniques and suggest how others might employ them.

makes him a particularly valuable subject for scientific study. Tammet knows ten languages and, in a famous demonstration, he learned Icelandic in a week, becoming sufficiently fluent to be interviewed on television in Reykjavik. Nonetheless, he cannot (for example) drive a car: he would be overwhelmed by all the detail. Tammet also has synaesthesia. He sees numbers – thousands and thousands of individual numbers – as having particular shapes, colors, textures and other attributes. While "333" is an attractive number, "289" is ugly and "25" is energetic – shades of Shereshevskii. As well, his synaesthesia assists his language learning: "the Finnish word *tuli* is orange to me."[138] Multi-channel categorization seems key to Tammet's phenomenal memory.

Part 3
Some Concluding Remarks

I have already provided some summary comments about SCM himself, and need only repeat one or two that now seem especially salient. I think it is quite reasonable to call him a hyperpolyglot and, as was suggested, the use that he made of his skills exceeds that of Mezzofanti and most other linguistic prodigies. It is clear that he had a great capacity for sustained application, and dogged persistence, whether in the exhaustive compilation of his *Notes* or in his relentless religious arguments. At the same time, he was more a collector and a systematizer than he was a creator or an innovator. Some have argued that he spread himself too thinly across too many areas, others that he lacked the critical and incisive mind that marks the true scholar (these are not mutually exclusive descriptions). Nonetheless, his talents in several areas, most notably in music and art, were well above the average. More pointedly, both his biblical exegeses and his work on proverbs reveal deep and longstanding commitment.

It might be more accurate to say that SCM's talents and skills were at once wide and narrow. They were certainly wide, encompassing language and translation, art (both calligraphic and representational), biblical scholarship and exegesis, literature and music, and ornithology – to say nothing of above-average gifts in cabinetry and other artisanal pursuits. At the same time, his disdain for interests other than his own was often vehement, and his dismissal of light entertainments, plays and novels suggests narrowness and intemperance.

At a personal level, we find SCM to be extremely conservative and unswervingly opinionated. He was dismissive of individuals who displeased or failed to appreciate him, and, as just noted, of activities that were not his own. Unsurprisingly, then, he rarely solicited advice and was unreceptive to criticism. His bluntness in these regards, coupled with his refusal to consider highly prestigious university posts, suggest that – beyond the strong personal and intellectual perimeters that marked his life – SCM was a rather insecure person. I noted earlier that he was not a Casaubon, because, unlike that fictional pedant, he published and engaged in spirited academic debate. Nonetheless, he *was* something of a Casaubon. Unwillingness

---

[138] Quoted from Tammet 2007, p. 14.

to move fully into the public realm of scholarship, energies unmatched by originality, and obsessive aspiration to detailed completeness – these highlight the uncertainty and self-doubt we observe in both Middlemarch and Broadwindsor.

If we now consider SCM in the light of current knowledge about autism, it seems quite easy to place him on the spectrum of that disorder. Many of his traits suggest a connection here – as do, of course, those found in other creative and intelligent people. There may even be hints of synaesthesia, although we have no specific evidence of this in SCM's case.[139] We must of course agree with Frith, Baron-Cohen and other contemporary scholars who argue that virtually everyone will occupy some point on the autistic continuum. What is the explanatory value of a range of possibilities that includes all of us? Why is SCM worth discussing in this connection? The answer to the first question is that trying to understand where and why individuals occupy the positions they do has always been a central concern: in this sense, the autistic spectrum is like all other important dimensions of personality. The answer to the second is that SCM's life and works reveal a combination of abilities and limitations that are characteristic of what we might see as "mid-range" locations along the spectrum. Indeed, he seems to be a particularly interesting example of a combination that – while varying in the type and degree of its constituents – falls at neither scalar extreme and is in fact quite common in driven and ambitious individuals.

The "case" of SCM, then, is one of illustrative interest to all those concerned with patterns of extraordinary talents, but who at the same time understand that such talents can (and often do) coexist with less exceptional personal qualities. Thomas Carlyle wrote about genius resting upon the ability to take great trouble, which has given rise to the more common aphorism that it is an "infinite capacity for taking pains." The achievements of many savants, wherever they may fall along the autistic spectrum, very often reveal assiduous and unremitting application to tasks, and SCM's life's work is a clear case in point. At the same time – considering matters of creativity and originality, and again thinking of him in connection with similar and like-minded others – we might be a little hesitant to bestow the title of

---

[139] Consider, first, the personal reference I made in footnote 112 – one that I believe applies to many people. A "mild" synaesthesia would be in line, after all, with the other "mild" autistic traits that are so widespread among the population. Consider, too, this interesting note from Lauren Pfister: "There are points in [S. C. Malan's] proverbial statements where something like [...] synaesthetic elements arise – perhaps more indirectly and with a literary flair that may camouflage [them], but nevertheless present. [...] Malan could sketch at great speed, and – having only one normal eye to employ – his ability to capture scenes imaginatively, and so to recreate whole images with a calculatively discerning freshness, including his skills with water-colors, hints at something potentially very rich here. [...] Even while having such a "weak" form of interest in mathematics, he was nevertheless able in the 1860s to build a complicated church sanctuary along lines that were both traditional and informed in modern architectural features. There is something here very interdisciplinary and synthetic, perhaps involving dimensions of synaesthesia that have not been previously considered" (Pfister, personal communication, January 2015).

"genius."[140] Indeed, if we go back to Carlyle's rather unpoetic formulation, we read that the "transcendent capacity of taking trouble" is a necessary but insufficient condition for works of genius: the words "first of all" immediately follow what I have just cited.[141]

Genius is not, then, something attainable through extraordinary application alone. On the contrary, as we have seen here, such application unaccompanied by a high degree of critical intelligence is not likely to produce works of creativity and original vision. It can produce quite remarkable demonstrations of one sort or another and – to bring things back to SCM himself – it can also produce comprehensively assembled knowledge, collected scholarship from disparate sources, cultures and linguistic traditions, exhaustive catalogues and lists, and so on. As already noted above,[142] rich collectors have often left incredible legacies for critical scholars to work with. The work of SCM and others like him shows that such legacies are not solely the gifts of moguls of industry and finance.

Select Bibliography

Abraham, Carolyn. 2014. "Researchers Develop a Search Engine – for DNA." *Globe and Mail* [Toronto] (19 December 2014), A1.

Ackland, Valentine. 1969. *Solomon Caesar Malan 1812–1894*. Dorchester: Dorset Natural History and Archæological Society.

Adelung, Johann Christoph. 1806. *Mithridates, oder allgemeine Sprachenkunde*. Berlin: Voss.

Aitken, Alexander. 1954. "The Art of Mental Calculation, with Demonstrations." *Transactions of the Royal Society of Engineers* 44 (1954), pp. 295-309.

Anon. 1898. Review of *Solomon Cæsar Malan* (Arthur Noel Malan). *Church Quarterly Review* 46 (April 1898), pp. 73-94.

Baron-Cohen, Simon – Danielle Johnson – Julian Asher – Sally Wheelwright – Simon Fisher – Peter Gregersen – Carrie Allison. 2013. "Is Synaesthesia More Common in Autism?" *Molecular Autism* 4 (2013) 40, pp. 1-6.

Bernstein, Jeremy. 1993. "In Many Tongues." *Atlantic Monthly* 272 (October 1993) 4, pp. 92-102.

Bonfitto, Peter. 2015. "'Harmony in Contrast': The Drawings of Solomon Caesar Malan." *Getty Research Journal* 7 (2015), pp. 169-176.

Bonifazi, Filippo. 1851. *Catalogo della libreria dell'eminentissimo Cardinale Giuseppe Mezzofanti*. Rome: Librajo Romano.

---

[140] We might note here that the original sense of "genius" had to do with the characteristic nature of individuals or groups – divinely-inspired and tutelary, but not necessarily of outstanding quality in itself. (Places, too, could possess a particular spiritual resonance: the *genius loci*.) The use of the term to indicate exceptional manifestations of that nature seems to date from the earliest days of the Roman Empire.

[141] Citing from Carlyle 1859, p. 407.

[142] See footnote 82 above.

Brown, Evan – Kenneth Deffenbacher. 1975. "Forgotten Mnemonists." *Journal of the History of the Behavioral Sciences* 11 (1975), pp. 342-349.

Carlyle, Thomas. 1859. *History of Friedrich II of Prussia, Called Frederick the Great*. London: Chapman and Hall.

Cavedoni, Celestino. 1861. "Rimembranz e della vita e degli studi del Card. Giuseppe Mezzofanti, di chiara ed immortale memoria." *Opuscoli Religiosi, Letterarj e Morali* 9 (1861) 26, pp. 161-194.

Chadwick, Owen. 1970. *The Victorian Church: Part II (1860–1901)*. London: A. and C. Black.

Crawford, Charles. 1980. "The Mind Was Strong But the Body Was Weak." *Canadian Journal of Psychology* 34 (1980) 1, pp. 97-101.

Cytowic, Richard. 1993. *The Man who Tasted Shapes*. New York: Putnam.

———. 2002. *Synaesthesia: A Union of the Senses*. Cambridge, Mass.: MIT Press. 2nd edition.

Cytowic, Richard – David Eagleman. 2009. *Wednesday is Indigo Blue: Discovering the Brain of Synesthesia*. Cambridge, Mass.: MIT Press.

Dutton, Jack. 2015. "The Surprising World of Synaesthesia." *The Psychologist* 28 (February 2015) 2, pp. 106-109.

Ebisch, Robert. 1989. "A Flash in the Dark – The Savant Phenomenon: When Intelligence is Incredibly Intense but Tragically Narrow." *Globe and Mail* [Toronto] (13 May 1989), D5.

Edwards, John. 1995. *Multilingualism*. London: Penguin.

———. 2005. "Language Families and Family Languages." *Journal of Multilingual and Multicultural Development* 26 (2005), pp. 173-186.

Erard, Michael. 2012. *Babel No More: The Search for the World's Most Extraordinary Language Learners*. New York: Free Press.

Fazah, Ziad. 1997. "'El políglota' en *Viva el Lunes*." https://www.youtube.com/watch?v=6fUSuXHX5Kc (accessed 4 January 2021)

Foer, Joshua. 2011. *Moonwalking with Einstein: The Art and Science of Remembering Everything*. London: Penguin.

Frith, Uta. 2014. "Autism – Are We Getting any Closer to Explaining the Enigma?" *The Psychologist* 27 (October 2014) 10, pp. 744-745.

Galton, Francis. 1880. "Visualised Numerals." *Nature* 21 (1880), pp. 252-256 and 494-495.

———. 1881. "Visualised Numerals." *Journal of the Royal Anthropological Institute of Great Britain and Ireland* 10 (1881), pp. 85-102. Includes appendices.

Hearnshaw, Leslie. 1979. *Cyril Burt, Psychologist*. London: Hodder and Stoughton.

Heavey, Lisa – Linda Pring – Beate Hermelin. 1999. "A Date to Remember: The Nature of Memory in Savant Calendrical Calculators." *Psychological Medicine* 29 (1999), pp. 145-160.

Hoge, Kerstin. 2012. "Hyperpolyglottery." *Times Literary Supplement* (1 June 2012), p. 30.

Howe, Michael. 1990. *The Origins of Exceptional Abilities*. Oxford: Blackwell.

———. 1991. *Fragments of Genius: The Strange Feats of Idiots Savants*. London: Routledge.

Howe, Michael – Julia Smith. 1988. "Calendar Calculating in 'Idiots Savants': How Do They Do It?" *British Journal of Psychology* 79 (1988), pp. 371-386.

Hudson, Richard. 2003. "A 'Gene' for Hyper-polyglottism?" *Linguist List* (26 October 2003). http://linguistlist.org/issues/14/14-2923.html (accessed 4 January 2021).

Hunter, Ian. 1962. "An Exceptional Talent for Calculative Thinking." *British Journal of Psychology* 53 (1962), pp. 243-258.

———. 1966. *Memory*. Harmondsworth, Middlesex: Penguin.

———. 1977. "An Exceptional Memory." *British Journal of Psychology* 68 (1977), pp. 155-164.

Jarrett, Christian. 2014. "Autism – Myth and Reality." *The Psychologist* 27 (October 2014) 10, pp. 746-749.

Jessopp, Augustus. 1891. *The Trials of a Country Parson*. London: T. Fisher Unwin.

Jewanski, Jörg – Natalia Sidler. 2006. *Farbe, Licht, Musik: Synästhesie und Farblichtmusik*. Bern: Lang.

Jewanski, Jörg – Sean Day – Jamie Ward. 2009. "A Colorful Albino: The First Documented Case of Synaesthesia, by Georg Tobias Ludwig Sachs in 1812." *Journal of the History of the Neurosciences* 18 (2009), pp. 293-303.

Jones, Steve. 2012. "Science and the Roots of Faith." *Daily Telegraph* (21 August 2012), p. 25.

Kelly, Stuart. 2010. *Scott-land: The Man who Invented a Nation*. Edinburgh: Polygon.

Locke, John. 1690. *Essay Concerning Human Understanding*. London: Basset.

Luria, Alexander. 1975. *The Mind of a Mnemonist*. Harmondsworth, Middlesex: Penguin.

MacDonell, Arthur. 1895. "Dr. S. C. Malan." *Journal of the Royal Asiatic Society* 27 (April 1895) 2, pp. 453-457.

Malan, Solomon Caesar. 1856a. *A Vindication of the Authorised Version of the English Bible, from Charges Brought against It by Recent Writers*. London: Bell and Daldy.

———. 1856b. *Aphorisms on Drawing*. London: Longman, Brown, Green, Longman and Roberts.

———. 1862. *The Gospel according to St. John, translated from the Eleven Oldest Versions, Except the Latin, viz., the Syriac, Ethiopic, Armenian, Sahidic, Memphitic, Gothic, Georgian, Sclavonic [sic], Anglo-Saxon, Arabic, and Persian, with Foot Notes to Every Translation, and a Criticism on All the 1,340 Alterations Proposed by "the Five Clergymen" in Their Revision of that Gospel*. London: Masters.

Manavit, Augustin. 1853. *Esquisse historique sur le cardinal Mezzofanti*. Paris: Sagnier et Bray.

Mezzofanti, Giuseppe. 1820. *Discorso in lode del P. E. Aponte della Compagnia di Gesù, detto in occasione del rinnovamento degli studi l'anno MDCCCXIX*. Bologna: Pontifica Università.

Mitterrutzner, Johannes. 1891. *Joseph Cardinal Mezzofanti der grosse Polyglott: Eine Lebensskizze*. Vienna: Pichlers Witwe und Sohn.

Montaigne, Michel de. 1580 [1949]. *Montaigne: Selected Essays*. Ed. Blanchard Bates, trans. Charles Cotton. New York: Random House.

Murray, Alexander. 1823. *History of the European Languages*. Edinburgh: Constable.

Nabokov, Vladimir. 1996. *Novels and Memoirs, 1941–1951*. New York: Library of America.

Pasti, Franco. 2006. *Un poliglotta in biblioteca: Giuseppe Mezzofanti (1774–1849) a Bologna nell'età della restaurazione*. Bologna: Pàtron.

Price, Jill – Bart Davis. 2008. *The Woman Who Can't Forget*. New York: Free Press.

Rothen, Nicolas – Beat Meier. 2014. "Acquiring Synaesthesia: Insights from Training Studies." *Frontiers in Human Neuroscience* 8 (2014), p. 109.

Russell, Charles. 1855. Article II [an untitled review of Manavit's *Esquisse historique*, of Watts's "On the Extraordinary Powers ..." and of Bonifazi's *Catalogo della Libreria* ...]. *Edinburgh Review* 101 (1855) 205, pp. 23-71.

———. 1858. *The Life of Cardinal Mezzofanti, with an Introductory Memoir of Eminent Linguists, Ancient and Modern*. London: Longman, Brown.

Sachs, Georg Tobias Ludwig. 1812. *Historiae naturalis duorum leucaetiopum: auctoris ipsius et sororis eius*. Ph.D. diss., Friedrich-Alexander Universität, Erlangen.

Schiefner, Franz Anton von. 1882. *Tibetan Tales Derived from Indian Sources*. London: Trübner.

Schlegel, Julius Heinrich Gottlieb. 1824. *Ein Beitrag zur nähern Kenntniß der Albinos*. Meiningen: Keyssner.

Schröder, Otto – Georg Trümpelmann. 1971. *Solomon Caesar Malan: Aquarelles / Akwarelle*. Kaapstad [Capetown]: Human and Rousseau.

Scoville, William – Brenda Milner. 1957. "Loss of Recent Memory after Bilateral Hippocampal Lesions." *Journal of Neurology, Neurosurgery and Psychiatry* 20 (1957) 1, pp. 11–21.

Simner, Julia – Neil Mayo – Mary-Jane Spiller. 2009. "A Foundation for Savantism? Visuo-spatial Synaesthetes Present with Cognitive Benefits." *Cortex* 45 (2009) 10, pp. 1246-1260.

Simpson, Robert. 2004. "Malan, Solomon Caesar." In: H. C. G. (Colin) Matthew – Brian Harrison (eds.), *Oxford Dictionary of National Biography*, vol. 36. Oxford: Oxford University Press, pp. 274-275.

Smith, Anthony. 1984. *The Mind*. London: Hodder and Stoughton.

Smith, Neil. 2005. *Language, Frogs and Savants*. Oxford: Blackwell.

Smith, Neil – Ianthi-Maria Tsimpli. 1995. *The Mind of a Savant*. Oxford: Blackwell.

Smith, Neil – Ianthi-Maria Tsimpli – Gary Morgan – Bencie Woll. 2011. *The Signs of a Savant: Language Against the Odds*. Cambridge: Cambridge University Press.

Smith, Steven. 1983. *The Great Mental Calculators*. New York: Columbia University Press.

Sukel, Kayt. 2012. "They Never Forget: The Strange Gift of Perfect Memory." *New Scientist* No. 2878 (18 August 2012), pp. 34-37.

Sweeney, Brian. 2000. "Alexander Aitken, The Human Computer." http://www.nzedge.com/legends/alexander-aitken (accessed 4 January 2021).

Tammet, Daniel. 2007. *Born on a Blue Day: A Memoir of Asperger's and a Extraordinary Mind*. London: Hodder.

Traub, Philip. 1968. "Solomon Caesar Malan: Artist, Scholar, Theologian." *The Connoisseur* 169 (October 1968), p. 580.

Treffert, Darold. 1989. *Extraordinary People: Understanding "Idiot Savants"*. New York: Harper and Row.

Trench, Dermot. 1907. *What is the Use of Reviving Irish?* Dublin: Maunsel.

Trench, Richard Chenevix. 1851. *On the Study of Words*. London: Parker.

———. 1853. *On the Lessons in Proverbs*. London: Parker.

———. 1855. *English Past and Present*. London: Parker.

Tuckwell, William. 1900. *Reminiscences of Oxford*. London: Cassell.

Ward, Jamie – Jason Mattingly. 2006. "Synaesthesia: An Overview of Contemporary Findings and Controversies." *Cortex* 42 (2006) 2, pp. 129-136.

Ward, Jamie – Daisy Thompson-Lake – Roxanne Ely – Flora Kaminski. 2008. "Synaesthesia, Creativity and Art: What is the Link?" *British Journal of Psychology* 99 (2008), pp. 127-141.

Watts, Thomas. 1852. "On the Extraordinary Powers of Cardinal Mezzofanti as a Linguist," *Proceedings of the Philological Society* 5 (1852) 115, pp. 111-125.

———. 1854. "On M. Manavit's Life of Cardinal Mezzofanti." *Transactions of the Philological Society* 1 (1854) 7, pp. 133-150.

———. 1859. "On Dr. Russell's Life of Cardinal Mezzofanti." *Transactions of the Philological Society* 6 (1859) 1, pp. 227-256.

Wilson, Glenn. 2012. "Delusions and Grandeur." *Times Higher Education* (1 November 2012), pp. 42-45.

Yaro, Caroline – Jamie Ward. 2007. "Searching for Shereshevskii: What is Superior about the Memory of Synaesthetes?" *Quarterly Journal of Experimental Psychology* 60 (2007), pp. 682-695.

Youings, Joyce (ed.) 1993. *Sir John Bowring, 1792–1872: Aspects of His Life and Career*. Exeter: Devonshire Association.

5

SURPRISES WITHIN SOLOMON CAESAR MALAN'S CHRISTIAN WORKS AND HIS CRITICAL ADVANCES IN SCHOLARLY CHRISTIAN REFLECTION

Lauren F. Pfister

In April 1880 Solomon Caesar Malan was presented with an honorary doctorate from University Edinburgh for his achievements as an "eminent linguist and Biblical scholar" who, according to Professor Charteris' *laudate*, had studied "many subjects, each one rarely mastered by any scholar of our country, and all of them, I believe, never before combined in the record of one student's life."[1] Significantly, this honor came before he published his *magnum opus*, the three volumes of his collected quotations and briefly stated critical reflections entitled *Original Notes on the Book of Proverbs* (1889–1893).[2] One might expect consequently that these honors were given in the light of some outstanding standard works in Christian theological studies by this former Anglican missionary to India (in Calcutta [Kolkata], 1837–1840), but there was more than this standard reason for honoring the man.

From the angle of SCM's biographers, which include a thoughtful biography by one of his sons in 1897, the Vicar of Broadwindsor held a long and principled preference for the King James Version (or "Authorized Version") of the English Bible.[3] So strong was this tendency in earlier works,[4] but especially during heated debates over the Revised English version of the New Testament in 1881 and 1882,[5] that later biographers considered SCM's part in the debates surrounding questions regarding the integrity of the Revised English Version of the New Testament as indicating how "out of touch" he was with current scholarly trends in that sphere.[6]

---

[1] *SCM DD*, pp. 309-310 *in passim*.

[2] Referring to *ONBP*.

[3] As seen at some length in the discussion related to the challenge made by Dean Burgon in his articles entitled "Revision Revised," where it is shown how that author was personally indebted to SCM and recorded that indebtedness numerous times. Subsequently, SCM as the vicar of the Broadwindsor Anglican church community added his own critical assessment in a focused study on certain chapters of the Gospels of Matthew and Luke, which are similarly quoted from at length. Consult *SCM DD,* pp. 313-327.

[4] There are three larger works published in the 1850s and 1860s that indicate SCM's intellectual concerns as an Anglican vicar related to this problem. See SCM 1856. The second was SCM 1862. Being a rather large tome, this book included over 400 pages of translations and critical exegetical notes. Finally, the third volume was SCM 1869c.

[5] Consult *SCRR* and SCM 1882a.

[6] See the brief but poignant statements of this sort in the obituary for SCM written by A. A. MacDonnell in the *Journal of the Royal Asiatic Society of Great Britain and Ireland* (MacDonnell 1895), and in R. S. Simpson's later account in the *Oxford Dictionary of National Biography* (Simpson 2004). Simpson ends his article by stating that SCM maintained a

Yet there is in fact more to discover about SCM's Christian scholarship in both historical periods before and after 1880. What one finds among SCM's publications appearing before 1880 are some notable critical advances on the frontiers of biblical research and intra-denominational Christian studies which reveal another facet to what previous biographers tended to portray as his staunchly conservative Anglican theological stance. When other perspectives related to those previously achieved critical advances are applied to assessing the complicated text of the *ONBP*, there are even more matters to consider that raise numerous new questions about the multiform nature of that work and its inherent theological, etymological, and cross-cultural value within Christian studies of the late Victorian era.

1. Surprises in Malan's Advances in Engaging "Eastern" Churches

As we have learned from Frédéric Amsler,[7] SCM grew up in the home of a conservative evangelical pastor who had been politically ousted from the ecclesiastical structures of authority in Geneva. In his late teens and early twenties, SCM chose to align himself to the Anglican church as a consequence of both theological convictions and motivations tied to his first marriage. Undoubtedly, this was a move largely unanticipated by his father, and so initially it was also opposed; apparently after some years of adjustment, both father and son were able to accept these new conditions, and so continued to work along parallel trajectories of Christian service in their different contexts over the subsequent years. SCM's hyperpolyglot skills came into extensive use not only in his collecting parallel and antithetical proverbial sayings within his own private devotional texts, the largest being the manuscript version of the *ONBP* which was initiated in 1833 while he was a student as Oxford,[8] but also in his cross-cultural explorations of other non-European Christian denominations. Notably, these were churches which were still held in many conservative Christian circles of his day to be heretical in their religious status. In addition to all these texts which were produced before 1880, there were two others which revealed Malan's extensive interests in these non-European religious sources related to biblically-based traditions. The first was an unusual work found among Ethiopic sources for which he published an English version in 1882,[9] and in the latter he

---

"strongly conservative temperament and distrust of many developments taken for granted by later generations," which prevented him from attaining "real eminence in any one field." He continues then by stating, "This is shown most clearly in his condemnation of the Revised Version, and of the new Greek text of the New Testament published by Westcott and Hort (both 1881)."

[7] See the first chapter of this volume.

[8] It is easy to neglect the fact that the published version of *ONBP* was based on a manuscript version initiated in 1833, when SCM was 21 years old and studying at Oxford University as a student. The manuscript version of the work was the very last item donated in October 1894 from his personal library to form the future Malan Library housed in the Indian Institute in Oxford, just a few months before he passed away. Its call number in the Bodleian Libraries is "MS.Ind.Insti.Misc.10."

[9] This is an unusual work that links up ancient Ethiopic traditions with those found in later Jewish interpretations of the first chapters of the *Tanakh* (the Hebrew Bible). Consult SCM

offered an English rendering of the liturgical traditions of the "Holy Apostolic Church of Armenia" in 1887.[10] Here below I will focus on works published before 1880.

SCM's contributions in these spheres were generally to offer English versions of liturgical, theological and historical texts related to these non-European Christian traditions. Some volumes were prepared for devotional use by English parishioners, while others carried more theological and historical details that would be of interest to other Christian pastors and intellectuals. They also tended to follow cultural emphases in SCM's own linguistic explorations, so that there are groups of books from the same or similar languages which can be identified as being published in a definite chronological order. For example, one volume from Greek Orthodox and Russian Orthodox sources appeared in 1859,[11] followed by one related to Georgian Christian history in 1864,[12] and a subsequent volume from Syrian Christian sources.[13] From that point in time SCM's interests clearly shifted, so that he put extensive effort into producing five writings on the Armenian church, four being published between 1868 and 1872.[14] This was followed almost immediately by four volumes on the Coptic churches in Egypt, all published between 1872 and 1874.[15]

In addition to these volumes, there were three other tomes which could be described as offering a mixture of texts and discussions with these churches from ancient middle eastern and eastern Christian sources,[16] including his massive work

---

1882b. SCM's thorough engagement with the classical Jewish commentarial traditions here was unusual when compared with his other works on Eastern Christian sources, anticipating his further engagement with these and other ancient "Eastern" sources he would review especially within his etymological studies produced in his final work, the *ONBP* (as will be described in detail below).

[10] Consult SCM 1887.

[11] This is the volume of SCM's renderings in *id.* 1859.

[12] Consult SCM 1864.

[13] See the very small sized booklet of 71 pages translated by SCM 1866.

[14] The first four writings appeared as a group, there being two relatively short articles between two monographs. This was followed much later by the last volume, which was published in 1887, while Malan was already at work on producing the first volume of the *ONBP*. The first four writings are the book entitled *The Life and Times of Saint Gregory the Illuminator* (SCM 1869a); followed by *Instruction in the Christian Faith: According to the Orthodox Armenian Church of Saint Gregory the Illuminator* (SCM 1869b), which was 39 pages in length, and *The Confession of Faith of the Orthodox Armenian Church: Together with the Rite of Holy Baptism as it is Administered in that Church* (SCM 1872b), with a final volume produced under the title, *The Divine Ἐσχολογιον* [Eschologion] *and the Divine Liturgy of Saint Gregory the Theologian* (SCM 1875). Twelve years later SCM completed his work in this realm with the volume already mentioned earlier, dealing with the *Liturgy of the Holy Apostolic Church of Armenia*.

[15] See SCM 1872a, 63 pages in length; SCM 1873a, 91 pages in length; SCM 1873b, consisting of 115 pages, and finally SCM 1874.

[16] These three more complicated volumes include, first of all, SCM 1858, 135 pages in length. The second tome is the extensive volume mentioned in footnote 4 above, SCM 1862. The

on the Gospel of John. If SCM's three works on defending the "Received Greek Text" and "The Authorized Version" had attracted some of the University of Edinburgh's intellectual elite to his scholarship, the other fifteen volumes apparently gained their unanimous support for presenting him with an honorary degree. In fact, it was the volume constituted by renderings and notes on eleven ancient versions of the Gospel of John as they shed light on the character of the Authorized Version that particularly stood out in the *laudate* offered by Prof. Charteris in 1880. Noting SCM's unusual scholarship in languages generally unknown by other English citizens, Charteris went to the trouble of listing those renderings "from the eleven oldest versions, except the Latin, viz.: the Syriac, Ethiopic, Armenian, Sahidic, Memphitic, Gothic, Georgian, Sclavonic [*sic*], Anglo-Saxon, Arabic and Persian."[17] When there is further opportunity to review details about the character of the *ONBP*, as will occur later in this chapter and also in the latter chapters of this volume, it will become completely clear that many of these languages were also being used not only for New Testament studies, but also in SCM's life-long study of the biblical book of Proverbs.

Here a brief reflective note is also worthwhile adding at this point: SCM's choice not to refer to the Latin Vulgate was more a matter of Protestant conviction than of any linguistic limitations in Latin studies. From research pursued in the *ONBP*, particularly in its etymological studies which were a creative addition to that text when compared with the manuscript version of the work, SCM was obviously a capable reader in Latin and a critical interpreter of the Latin Vulgate.[18] Instead, his main purpose was to uphold the primacy of the Authorized Greek version of the New Testament by reference to these other ancient renderings of the Gospel of John, because (in his own words),[19]

> [...] these eleven Versions from all parts of the earth, independent, unknown to one another, speaking tongues for the most part unintelligible to each other, of origin often uncertain – bear one and the same witness, so firm, so constant, and so clear as to show that the truth they tell is one, as the light they reflect is one also.

Here his theological orthodoxy and hints about his metaphysical beliefs about the "deeper truths" that are revealed through even "all-too-human" translations offer suggestions about why he would also seek to locate in his *ONBP* alternative expressions in the more than 50 languages where statements paralleling or contrasting with sapiential apothems in the biblical Proverbs were found.

Such a translation strategy – using biblical versions in ancient languages other than the original Koiné Greek manuscripts of New Testament books to verify the readings of the Greek texts themselves – may seem to some as too indirect, or even

---

 third work within this group of publications was a shorter interpretive article entitled, SCM 1871, being only 24 pages in length.

[17] As cited from *SCM DD,* p. 309.
[18] Evidence for this claim can be found below in the fourth section of this paper.
[19] Quoted from SCM 1862, Preface, pp. xii-xiii.

farfetched. Nevertheless, it should be noted that precisely this strategy is now employed within scholarly annotated versions of the Greek New Testament as part of the critical apparatus to verify which words, phrases, and passages are the earliest and most reliable. In the most current version of the standard Greek New Testament that I could obtain, published in 2016, the editors and scholars who created the text and its annotations employ not only Greek manuscripts in papyri, manuscripts, and selected portions, but also evidence drawn from early versions in Latin, Syriac, Coptic, Armenian, Georgian, Ethiopic and Old Church Slavonic.[20] Without question, then, SCM not only was insightful in his use of this translation strategy, but anticipated what is now a standard practice of textual critical work on the Greek New Testament by as much as half a century.

Returning once again to SCM's claims about the nature and use of these early versions in ancient languages of the Gospel of John, it should be noted that this broad-minded cross-cultural vision of transferable and interpretable wisdom did not deny the unique expressions found in various languages, but instead relished in their creative efforts to portray in alternative modes what could be recognized as the same "deeper truth." This same attitude motivated his effort in producing fifteen volumes of English renderings portraying the liturgical, theological and historical accounts of "Eastern" Churches; this being understood, it indicates for us in a new way how his conservative orthodox Christian commitments could also become a springboard for critical advances in Christian scholarship.

2. Surprises in SCM's Critical Engagement with Bibles in East Asian Languages

As I have already mentioned elsewhere, SCM became acquainted with Chinese language, its ideographs and characters, so that he began reading Chinese texts during his time in Calcutta in 1839. He had offered lessons in Greek to a young Chinese student named Ho Tsun-sheen (He Jinshan 何進善, 1817–1871) in exchange for lessons received from that student regarding Chinese language.[21] More than ten years later – after SCM had endured the death of his first wife in 1840, being remarried after several years as a widower, and ultimately taking up a position as an Anglican vicar in the parish church of the Nativity of St. John the Baptist[22] in the small village of Broadwindsor in 1845 – he published three major works dealing with Chinese Christian terminological questions. The first was published in 1855, and focused on contemporary debates about the proper Chinese terms to be used in rendering key theological terms in the Christian Bible. The second work, published

---

[20] Consult the lists of these early versions in Aland – Aland – Karavidopoulos – Martini – Metzger 2016, pp. 30-36 in the "Introduction." This version is the fifth revised edition in its third corrected printing, prepared by the Institute for New Testament Textual Research in Münster/Westfalia, under the direction of Holger Strutwolf, and produced also in junction with the American Bible Society as well as the United Bible Societies.

[21] See the account given in Pfister 2012, pp. 11-13.

[22] An account of the church and brief reference to SCM as a vicar, along with an unusual picture of the man in "studious attire" is found in Thornburgh 1991. The picture appears on page 33.

in the following year, indicates how SCM in the interim had learned and read enough Chinese and Mongolian to begin to explore serious questions related to theological translations in both of these languages. It consisted of a lengthy monographic letter to the head of the British Bible Society, the Earl of Shaftesbury, expressing SCM's personal concerns about some of the theological implications of technical terminology chosen to render key theological terms in those languages.[23] Being sizeable works in their own right, they were followed soon afterward by SCM's study of three different versions of the Chinese *Sanzijing* 三字經 (Three Character Classic). In this third substantial work, he compared the Chinese original of the *Sanzijing* with the creative alternatives produced by 19th century Protestant missionaries in China and by Hong Xiuquan 洪秀全 (1814–1864), the king of the Taiping Insurgency (Taiping tianguo 太平天國, 1851–1864).[24] Though this did not end his interest in the biblical translations produced in East Asian languages, these were the most substantial works devoted particularly to Chinese sources that he published in his lifetime before he began to work on the published version in English of the three volume set, *ONBP*. What this indicates is that by 1857 SCM had become a competent reader of Chinese texts, a skill which he continued to explore as he documented numerous parallels to biblical proverbs from Ruist ("Confucian") and Daoist literary sources.

Unfortunately, even though these essays did receive some attention in Britain at the time, they have not been integrated into the larger story of the so-called "interminable question" related to the debates over which Chinese terms could best render the theological concepts of "God," "spirit," and other related terms in the Greek New Testament and the Hebrew Scriptures. In fact, SCM was actively engaged in the current debates, and was offering some critical advances in Christian scholarly reflection for English readers in Great Britain of his day related to biblical translation work in Chinese and Mongolian languages. Notably, he generally supported positions adopted by James Legge, the famous missionary-scholar from Scotland who resided in Hong Kong for more than thirty years (1842–1873), and later took up the first professorship in Chinese at Oxford University (1876–1897).

3. Surprises in Malan's Cross-Cultural Openness in Christian Missiology

Even as SCM was completing his major works dealing with Chinese and Mongolian translations of biblical and other texts, he was articulating his own preferred missiological principles for younger missionaries who were interested in following his own footsteps in travelling eastward as Protestant Christian missionaries. In his bundle of brief and articulate letters published as a single book entitled *Letters to a Young Missionary*, SCM worked out a perspective for Christian missions which was notably different from mission leaders who promoted a more aggressive and

---

[23] Consult SCM, *Who is God in China, Shin or Shang Te? ...* and *A Letter to the Right Honourable the Earl of Shaftesbury ... On the Pantheistic and on the Buddhistic Tendency of the Chinese and of the Mongolian Versions of the Bible ...* .

[24] See *STK*.

confrontational approach to cross-cultural Christian missionary strategies.[25] What is significant here is that his missiology engaged in a cross-culturally open approach, what should be seen as a Christian humanist approach, something which might not be expected by some who had categorized SCM's theology as strongly conservative and putatively unyielding. Instead, in these letters SCM highlighted in a number of different ways his appreciation of practical wisdom in different cultures and languages, and sought to promote the discovery of "cultural bridges" for Christian missionaries in other cultures (as opposed to the more confrontational missiological principles of those such as James Hudson Taylor [1832–1905] of the China Inland Mission).[26]

Research into the Malan Library held originally at the Indian Institute Library (1885–1967) and now dispersed within the Bodleian Libraries is only just beginning. Due to the existence of a hand-written book list that documents over 1,000 titles that were originally part of that library, we can gain some understanding of only a relatively small portion of the many other titles which were documented in cards found in three larger boxes. Those cards were rediscovered during 2012 because of the temporary relocation of reading rooms and staff from the New Bodleian Library for the sake of preparing it for computerized access. The rediscovery was initially confirmed by Dr. Gillian Evison in correspondence with this author during the Spring of 2012. What we previously had been told through ANM, the son and biographer of SCM, was the following: The vast majority of SCM's personal library became the "Malan Library" as a result of his donation of over 4,000 titles to the Indian Institute in 1885. All of these volumes or works were distinctively identified by means of a paper plaque normally found on the back side of the front cover of the volume or manuscript. That little notice indicated that the particular text in hand belonged to "the Malan Library," confirming also the former owner's name and the date when the text was donated. It has been confirmed by Dr. Evison that a complete catalogue of the Malan Library was never completed, apparently due to the simple fact that there were texts within that library from more languages than any one bibliographer could handle. Ultimately, therefore, no such printed catalogue was able to be prepared. Other evidence that corroborates this claim is the fact that the book lists for the Malan Library (not the cards, but other independent book lists) present groups of books, articles and manuscripts in a series of numerical subcategories starting with the number 88 and ending with the number 92, all written with red ink so that they are highlighted in both the record and the card catalogue. Each of these numbered categories possess their own subordinate categories ranked from A to F except in the last case, where it abruptly ends with B. Yet when the card catalogue is carefully reviewed, one is surprised to discover that there are volumes numbered with the same red ink sequence numbers which go up to the number 103, as well as a good number of other volumes without any numbers at all found in the card catalogue. All of these bibliographic cards are hand-written, and

---

[25] Consult *LYM*.

[26] See one account of this confrontational missiological approach in contrast to another advocate of a more open cross-cultural engagement by Christian missionaries in Pfister 2003.

there are obviously very different calligraphic styles found among these cards, suggesting that there were indeed many bibliographers who worked at the list at different times. One suspects, therefore, that much more now can be done rather quickly to reconstruct a conceptual account of much of the Malan Library. Nevertheless, there are also still a good number of works that will have to be "rediscovered" by identifying them because they have the Malan Library identification plaque found on the back side of the front cover or elsewhere within the text. These library plaques are also found in all of the manuscripts which Malan donated to the Indian Institute and the Bodleian Library, so that there are probably a majority of texts originally belonging to the Malan Library which now can be identified. How many remain unrecorded within the card catalogue would have to be determined by further bibliographic research.[27]

What we have been able to find is that there are a number of bilingual and trilingual texts which SCM had in his personal library, so that one of the ways he stretched his polylingual interests was by testing his reading of parallel passages in various classical texts. For example, he had copies of trilingual versions of the Ruist ("Confucian") classical texts in Chinese, Manchurian and Mongolian, texts and languages important for the Sinification of the nobility within the Manchurian tribes, also embracing the language of the Mongolians who ruled mainland China between the 13th and 15th centuries.[28] Within his etymological studies in the published version of the *ONBP*, as will be described in some detail below, there was evidence that he was reading Hebrew texts with Aramaic, Syriac, and Chaldean commentaries, indicating his interest in and concern for the cross-cultural renderings which helped to reveal concepts and cultural sensitivities not knowable through European language media. Similarly, one discovers within that same work that SCM was intrigued with the transpositions and creative turns of folk tales and moral stories which travelled from the Sanskrit of the *Hitopadesa* through Pahlavi into Arabic.[29] Though he also held in his library a good number of bilingual texts including English as the basic language, particularly among grammars and dictionaries in specific

---

[27] Significantly, however, I was surprised to find one volume within the card catalogue which was published in 1916, nearly two decades after SCM's death. This is something I did not find elsewhere in the portions of the cards I reviewed, but it suggests that even the card catalogue itself may have been "corrupted" by the addition of a few other tomes not originally found in that library. Find more complete details about "The Malan Library" in Chapter 12 of this volume.

[28] These texts I had first seen in research related to the Chinese aspects of the *ONBP* in the first months of 2008. I was particularly surprised to see in explanations he added to his footnotes that he was reading at times a Manchurian translation of a Daoist text, the *Taishang ganyingpian* 太上感應篇, something I had not previously anticipated as existing in China during that period, due to the limited scope of my own studies.

[29] When following the quotations of the *Hitopadesa* in the *ONBP*, for example, one will discover that SCM will occasionally also make reference to the Arabic translation or another rendering of the same saying after the quotation or within the footnote.

languages, he also had texts using Latin-Sanskrit,[30] Latin-Avestan,[31] and Russian-Mongolian[32] bilingual formats. These serve as textual evidence of SCM's intellectual curiosity and his ability to extend beyond normal linguistic realms found in his Dorset setting to explore many other forms of classical and cultural learning. Certainly SCM maintained a principled openness to such challenges, but it is important to underscore that he went beyond learning texts in different languages into other realms of learning as well.

In response to Frédéric Amsler's contribution (Chapter 1) on cultural and political contexts of the Malan family in 19th century Geneva, I am also intrigued by the facts that indicate some parallels between the lives of the father and his first son in various aspects that sometimes have been overlooked by historians and biographers. For example, both men travelled widely, and did so regularly with Christian concerns driving them. Where they actually travelled, however, was very different: the father, César Malan, travelled mostly in northern European contexts, including Great Britain, serving as an international evangelist for what would now be referred to as a Protestant evangelical worldview; the son, SCM, travelled more widely in the Middle East and Eastern European settings, but also often with the intention to meet Christian figures and to discuss major theological concerns.[33] In this regard, both expressed an openness to different cultures, and took adventuresome risks to discover what those differences meant for living out an active Christian witness in an apostolic mode. There are other parallels in their lives which we will mention briefly only in our final reflections, because they do not necessarily reveal other facets of SCM's critical advances in Christian scholarship, though they do reveal something about a shared form of spirituality, a factor only briefly addressed in Amsler's account.

Within the *LYM* we find principles of hermeneutic openness and cross-cultural appreciation that also undergird SCM's own comparative study of wisdom literature as we find it in the *ONBP*. So, it is all the more appropriate now to explore some seldom discussed aspects of that latter work in the light of this awareness.

---

[30] This involved a copy of the *Padma Purana* (published by Wollheim da Fonseca in 1831 from Berlin [Bodliean call number (IND) 4.5.3.Padma 3]).

[31] This being a Russian rendering of the Zoroastrian religious texts of the Avesta produced by the publisher W. Bezobrazow in 1871 (Bodleian call number [IND] 48 C 22). I have not seen this text, and found only one other Latin-Russian version of the Avesta (on worldcat.org) produced by the Russian Imperial Academy of Science by Kaetan Andreeevitsch Kassowitsch in 1861. Either the recorded details are incorrect, or this might be a rare edition of this or some other published work.

[32] Entitled *Grammatika Tatarskago iazyka*, it is a grammar of Mongolian language in Russian produced by Iosif Giganov in 1801 (Bodleian call number: [IND] 57 E 17/1).

[33] From the biography written by his son, ANM, we can identify trips made into North Africa and the Holy Land (1840–1842), then into the larger areas of Palestine (now Syria and Iraq) as well as Armenia (1850–1851), and then again into Georgia and Russia during the 1870s.

4. Surprises in Malan's Critical Scholarship within the *ONBP*

Up to this point in time there has been no attempt at a scholarly assessment of the three-volume work SCM took the last eight years of his life to produce, that is, the English version of the *ONBP*.[34] As far as I am aware, the first effort at systematically attempting to understand the text from various angles of analysis was that of my own article published in English in 2012, based on discoveries made earlier in 2007 and 2008.[35] Subsequently, an extensive database documenting the details of SCM's nearly 16,000 footnotes within the *ONBP* created by Mirasy Pfister had been put into an electronic format by 2009, so that a breakthrough in studying the details of this massive text has been effectively reached. We now know that there are texts in at least 54 languages referred to in the whole of the *ONBP*,[36] and can identify the texts and languages which are most often cited with great precision and detail. Unquestionably, the most often cited texts are in Chinese, amounting to about 11% of the total work; the next most prominent language sources are Sanskrit, Tibetan, Greek, Tamil and Arabic.[37] Beyond these six most prominent language sources, there are a notable number of texts cited in Hebrew (or Aramaic), Telegu, and "Cingalese" (Sri Lankan) languages. Other prominent language sources which are cited less often than all those already mentioned include Egyptian, Osmanli (the language of the Ottoman Empire), Mongolian, Japanese, Bengalese, Italian and Georgian. What this indicates is that the majority of these language sources are "Eastern" in the sense that they are identified as North African, Middle Eastern, Central Asian, Southeast Asian, and East Asian languages. Only two, Greek and Italian, stem from European cultural contexts. Therefore, in this regard the subtitle of the work found in the second and third volumes, "Mostly from Eastern Sources," is in fact a suitable description of the whole work.

---

[34] The fifteenth chapter of ANM's biography of his father produced in 1897 is devoted to describing facets of this work, and so offers not only a general introduction to its character, but also some special insights into how his father's extensive study of proverbial literature left its mark in the patterns of their family's conversations and intimate joking. Nevertheless, since that time there has been no overall assessment of the whole work for the past 120 years and more, even though there have been a few brief articles mentioning some limited aspects of the work. See *SCM DD*, pp. 395-418.

[35] Consult my critical reflections on ANM's account of the Malan Library in Pfister 2012, pp. 22-24.

[36] Find many more details and justifications for these determinations in the final chapter of this volume.

[37] Here I am very self-conscious of not being able, even after more than ten years of study in various aspects of SCM's life and works, to identify the language groups of some titles, but most of these are not as prominent (they are cited less often) than texts produced in the above languages. There are texts in various Indian languages and Middle Eastern language texts, especially Persian, as well as some others, which I myself cannot identify, and so would greatly welcome comments and insights of others in these areas. The summaries above are based only on what I and my wife (sometimes also with the help of others) have been able to identify.

| 352 | ORIGINAL NOTES ON | [vii. 22, 23 |

reins he will drop through passion for me. If he were Brahmā or Djānarduna, yet will I wound him to-day with the arrows of love. But she was cursed by the Rishi, and turned into a bird on the Vindhya mountains."[1]

"For to be (clever) able to let virtue have the upper hand and overcome, makes a man wise and good; but being clever at overcoming virtue makes the bad man," say the Chinese.[2] "Thus when the Brahman offered his daughter to P'hara Thaken, this one said: I will tell thee one thing; hearken. 'The Mān-nat [demon of pride, &c.] fought with me all the way from my hermitage in the sacred forest to the foot of the Ajjapala bo-tree [sacred fig-tree], but as he was not able to prevail against me, he fled. Then his daughter tried to seduce me with her wiles and 'Nat-tish' form, but she could not shake my mind. Thy daughter shall not touch the soles of my feet.'"[3] "For although woman's person was created by Maha Brahma, like a golden creeper that overcomes everything—yet, setting aside such qualities as she has, her heart reveals (or contains) a big stone."[4] "Trust no go-between; but do thine own business thyself; for know this, that man's [and woman's] nature is made up of craft, imposture and fraud."[5] "Whence can morals come to a man who is entangled with a woman?"[6] "Through בְּרֹב לִקְחָהּ, the abundance of her captivating talk;" Arab. 'through the multitude of her arts.'

22 He goeth after her straightway, as an ox goeth to the slaughter, or as a fool to the correction of the stocks;

23 Till a dart strike through his liver; as a bird hasteth to the snare, and knoweth not that it *is* for his life.

וּכְעֶכֶס אֶל מוּסַר אֱוִיל, lit. 'and like stocks (fetters, &c.) to the punishment of a fool'—an inversion of words, probably for the sake

[1] Markand. Pur. i. 5. [2] Ming Sin P. K. c. 3. [3] Buddhagh. par. v.
[4] Lokopak. 49. [5] Ahmed V. Timuri, c. xx. [6] Lokaniti, 136.

| vii. 22] | THE BOOK OF PROVERBS. | 353 |

of rhythm. A difficult passage, for which various interpretations are offered; as by Gesenius, who takes וּכְעֶכֶס with אִישׁ, understood—"and as a man (who deserves the) stocks, to the chastisement of the fool" [for 'of folly']. But this is far-fetched and unsatisfactory. The literal rendering seems best. As "money 'goes' to pay a bill," and "cloth 'goes' to make a garment," &c., so also do "the stocks 'go' to the punishment of a fool." The inversion in A.V. is clear enough. Arab. 'or like the silly [foolish] man to the stocks (fetters, &c.) of retribution [punishment].'

Ver. 23. עַד יְפַלַּח חֵץ כְּבֵדוֹ, 'until an arrow [rend] split his liver.' This clause properly belongs to the preceding verse, with which it is connected, and is thus rendered by the LXX.: 'As a dog to the collar, and as a hart shot through the liver with an arrow.'

Ver. 22. "*As an ox . . . . as a fool to the stocks*," &c. "He follows her, ἑκὼν δέκοντί γε θυμῷ,[1] 'will he, nill he.'" "He who follows his own desire (or inclination) commits a sinful action," said Gautama to Gahapati.[2] "And so it is that every man among mortals, one and all, is led like an ox to the slaughter."[3] "The man who has heard [learned] little of Buddha's law, grows old like an ox. His flesh increases, but not his intellect (or knowledge)."[4] "Whither are you going, then, Mrs. Fate?" asks the man. "I'll follow you," answers Fate; "go on."[5] [Every man being for the most part the author of his own 'fate,' fortune or misfortune in life.] "Follow the owl," say they in Egypt, "and it will bring you to ruinous places."[6] "Take the raven for thy guide," say the Arabs, "and he will soon bring thee to carcases of dead dogs."[7] "Yielding to the advice of one of the pigeons, the whole flock flew down upon the grain into the net, and were caught."[8]

"The fool who in his folly thinks, 'This woman loves me;' from that moment becomes her plaything, like a tame bluejay. Such a man is always thought little of in the world, whatever he may say or do; for such a man is a slave of women who will have him on no other terms. For they care

[1] Il. δ̓. 43. [2] Singhala V. Sutta, p. nè. [3] Sulla Suttam, 7.
[4] Dhammap. Jarav. 152. [5] Telugu pr. [6] Egypt. pr. [7] Meid. Ar. pr.
[8] Hitop. i. 206.

2 A

Fig. 7: *ONBP*, vol. 1, pp. 352-353 (Prov. 7:22-23), "Long Note"

While I have described elsewhere the complicated relationship between the massive manuscript version, the ONBP Ms, and its published English version in three volumes,[38] there are good reasons here to readdress matters related to the etymological notes which SCM himself claimed "do not deserve the name of criticism," that is, of scholarly critical notes.[39] As has already been mentioned previously, these generally brief etymological remarks were a completely new addition to the text, and were developed independently of the details drawn from the ONBP Ms. On the basis of what we have already learned about SCM's earlier published works, this portion of the *ONBP* resembles in many ways some of the extensive textual analyses found in his compilation of twelve renderings (including the English rendering of the King James Version) of the Gospel of John, completed in 1862. Twenty-five years later SCM was taking up the same kind of reflective thoroughness, and the results appear to portray more critical details than he was willing to admit at the outset of his work.

---

[38] Consult the discussion in Pfister 2012, pp. 25-28, and in Chapter 13 of this volume.
[39] This quotation is found in Pfister 2012, p. 27, citing *ONBP*, vol. 1, p. xi, n. 1.

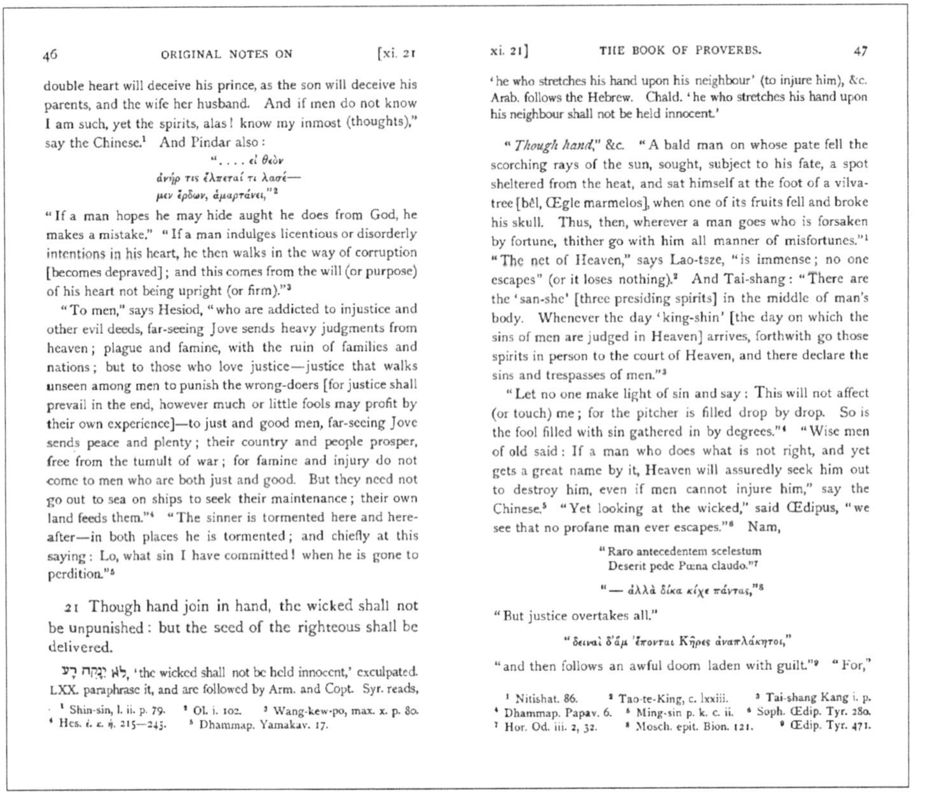

Fig. 8: *ONBP*, vol. 2, pp. 46-47 (Prov. 11:21), "CKJV, Short Note"

Within the 915 verses found in the modern renderings of the biblical book of Proverbs, which make up the basic structure of the thirty-one chapters in that text, there were just over 800 independent passages created (because some verses were grouped together with others when initially prepared in the manuscript and later printed in the English version). Among these more than 800 pericopes, 485 passages had etymological statements attached to the initial part of the pericope and printed in the smallest font found in the whole work, all of which sought to describe the meaning of the original Hebrew. Because the published form of the *ONBP* employed the King James Version of the English rendering of the book of Proverbs, these notes also served as critical reflections on the relationship of the standard Hebrew text and that 17th century English rendering found in the King James Version. In addition, those critical statements joined with other comments related to versions of the biblical book of Proverbs primarily studied by SCM in renderings in other Middle Eastern languages. What this means, then, is that within the *ONBP* as a whole, 347 verses had no such explanations following the initial presentations of the verse or passage in the KJV rendering of the scriptural text. Statistically speaking, SCM had worked to provide these extra critical elements within the published three-volume set to more than 55% of all the texts in the *ONBP*. If we go on to describe these critical etymological texts by their length, the vast majority of them were limited to just a few lines,⁴⁰ while just over 120 of those etymological comments ranged between being five to fourteen lines in length.⁴¹ The longest passages, those reaching 15 lines or more, were only ten in number throughout all three volumes. Intriguingly, most of these longer comments were not critical of the KJV rendering, but were elaborating cultural or linguistic questions related to the passages on hand.⁴²

Notably, among all these etymological notes and comments there are 147 passages which can be identifying as disagreeing with and/or qualifying the rendering of the English translation found in the KJV.⁴³ This is thoroughly unexpected by those who had assumed that SCM was a diehard theological conservative, but as has been pointed out in his comparative study of the Gospel of John in 1862, he already had indicated that human error could creep into various versions, and should be identified in order to reach the "deeper truth" which those versions sought to portray. This was one reason why he pursued assessments of many older renderings in various languages besides the original Greek (in the case of the Gospel of John) or Hebrew (in the case of Proverbs), because he believed where a consensus could be found within those other ancient renderings, an alternative way of reaching the "deeper truth" could be found. As a consequence, within these etymological comments in the *ONBP* SCM also criticized the distortive paraphrasing and arbitrary renderings he found in the Greek version of the Proverbs within the Septuagint (symbolized traditionally as LXX) and the Latin Vulgate, especially when they "misled" the translators of the KJV as well as translators in other ancient languages.⁴⁴

---

⁴⁰ Counting only on the basis of the lines in these etymological comments and not their content, there were 352 of the 485 passages which were this kind of brief note, amounting to just over 72% of all those additions. They appeared immediately following the scriptural verses and were produced in a smaller font, oftentimes including Hebrew terms along with some Greek and Latin phrases, when appropriate. More on the content of these notes will be offered in the following statements.

⁴¹ These are generally more substantial statements that include some very important critical comments, and amount to 123 of all the passages, or just over 25% of all these etymological comments.

⁴² These long etymological comments are found in the following passages, identified by their place in the book of Proverbs and then in the volume and page where they appear in the *ONBP*: 3:19 (vol. 1, p. 142); 7:22-23 (vol. 1, pp. 352-353); 8:22 – the longest with 51 lines (vol. 1, pp. 376-378); 8:30-31 (vol. 1, pp. 392-393); 9:10-11 (vol. 1, pp. 408-409); 11:25 (vol. 2, p. 65); 13:11 (vol. 2, p. 178); 16:4 (vol. 2, p. 376); 20:27 (vol. 2, pp. 708-709); and 26:10 (vol. 3, p. 327).

⁴³ Previously I had identified 123 passages with these criticisms of the English renderings of the King James Version, but this had included only those which stated so explicitly. In reviewing the original materials, it became clear that there were others where an alternative rendering was presented and confirmed without explicitly opposing the KJV, and so these have added to the total amount of passages. See my previous claim in Pfister 2012, pp. 28-29, with details in the footnotes.

⁴⁴ From SCM's point of view, the Septuagint had the more numerous errors, citing problems with its renderings 59 times throughout the *ONBP*, while with the Vulgate he only noted 16

> 376 ORIGINAL NOTES ON [xvi. 4
>
> being calm and at peace [from inward strength] is a proof that a man is perfect in wisdom."[1]
>
> **4** The Lord hath made all *things* for himself: yea, even the wicked for the day of evil.
>
> By referring the suff. הוּ in לְמַעֲנֵהוּ to 'the Lord,' A.V., the Vulgate, and the Armenian version, unwittingly make the Lord predestinate the wicked for the day of evil. But this cannot be. The construction here is similar to that of לְמִינֵהוּ and לְמִינוֹ at Gen. i. 12, and 21, לְמִינֵהֶם, where the suffix clearly refers to every grass, tree, and bird 'after its kind,' and to waters 'after their kind,' salt, fresh, still, running, &c. Here also לְמַעֲנֵהוּ cannot be taken for the prep. 'for,' 'propter;' but rather in its original meaning of 'after its purport, object, nature, what it answers or will come to.' And the sense of the passage will then be: 'The Lord hath made, כֹּל, all things; everything, לְמַעֲנֵהוּ, 'after its own account, purpose, or what it will come to.' Thus He made the man who is wicked, as He made the wolf that is cruel; but the wolf's cruelty, that makes him dreaded and hunted to death, does not come from God; since in a better state of things 'the wolf and the lamb shall dwell and feed together' [Is. xi. 6, lxv. 25]; so the wicked man's own wickedness works for him the 'day of evil.' This term, מַעֲנֵהוּ, occurs a little altered in every Arabic fable, for—'the purport, meaning, or moral of this is.' Chald. and Syr. render 'for himself,' by 'those who obey Him,' מִשְׁתַּמְעִין.
>
> "*The Lord hath made*," &c. "O Ahura Mazda, rule thou (or mayest thou rule) over thy creatures, according to [their] wishes and wealth (or health)."[2] "For all his works serve Him," said Enoch, "and do not vary. But according to what God has appointed, does everything come to pass."[3] "And no man," says Theognis, "is rich or poor, good or bad, νόσφιν δαίμονος, without the will, consent, or influence of the gods."[4] "O ye Pierides," says Hesiod, come and praise your father Zeus,
>
> Ὅν τε διὰ βροτοὶ ἄνδρες ὁμῶς ἄφατοί τε φατοί τε,
> ῥητοί τ' ἄρρητοί τε, Διὸς μεγάλοιο ἕκητι,
>
> [1] Saīn ūgh. fol. 9.   [2] Yaçna, viii. 10.   [3] Bk. Enoch, c. vi. 2.
> [4] Theogn. 167.

Fig. 9: *ONBP*, vol. 2, p. 376 (Prov. 16:4), "CKJV, Long Theological Reflection"

places where it had gone astray. In the former case, the LXX sometimes offered a paraphrase that was wide of the mark, as in 9:18 (vol. 1, p. 416), 11:26 (vol. 2, p. 70), 17:23 (vol. 2, p. 487) and 19:22 (vol. 2, p. 632), other times presenting something not at all found in the original Hebrew, as in 4:23 (vol. 1, p. 235), 11:30 (vol. 2, p. 82), 14:18 (vol. 2, p. 256), and 17:12 (vol. 2, p. 463). The most egregious problems in the LXX occured when the verses found in the Hebrew were simply overlooked, so that no rendering was found at all, as in 13:6 (vol. 2, p. 166), 16:2 (vol. 2, p. 368), 20:14 (vol. 2, p. 684), 20:15 (vol. 2, p. 685) and 27:9 (vol. 3, p. 397).

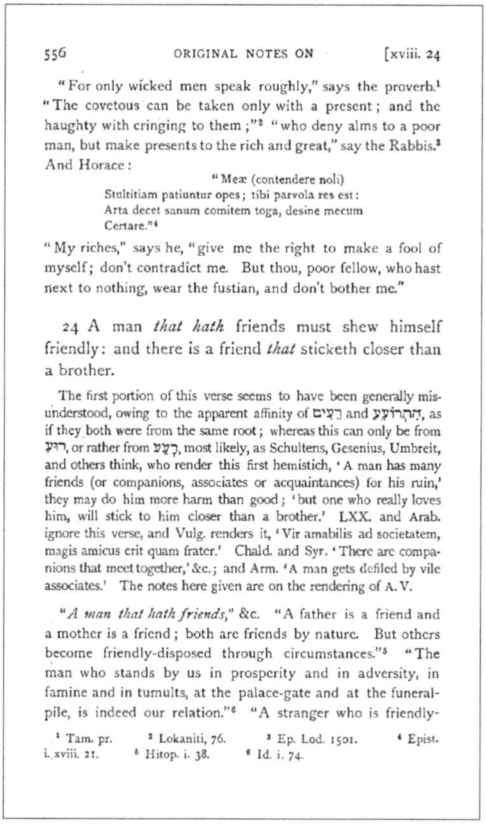
556 ORIGINAL NOTES ON [xviii. 24

"For only wicked men speak roughly," says the proverb.[1] "The covetous can be taken only with a present; and the haughty with cringing to them;"[2] "who deny alms to a poor man, but make presents to the rich and great," say the Rabbis.[3] And Horace:

"Meæ (contendere noli)
Stultitiam patiuntur opes; tibi parvola res est:
Arta decet sanum comitem toga, desine mecum
Certare."[4]

"My riches," says he, "give me the right to make a fool of myself; don't contradict me. But thou, poor fellow, who hast next to nothing, wear the fustian, and don't bother me."

24 A man *that hath* friends must shew himself friendly: and there is a friend *that* sticketh closer than a brother.

The first portion of this verse seems to have been generally misunderstood, owing to the apparent affinity of רֵעִים and הִתְרוֹעֵעַ, as if they both were from the same root; whereas this can only be from רוּעַ, or rather from רָעַע, most likely, as Schultens, Gesenius, Umbreit, and others think, who render this first hemistich, 'A man has many friends (or companions, associates or acquaintances) for his ruin,' they may do him more harm than good; 'but one who really loves him, will stick to him closer than a brother.' LXX. and Arab. ignore this verse, and Vulg. renders it, 'Vir amabilis ad societatem, magis amicus erit quam frater.' Chald. and Syr. 'There are companions that meet together,' &c.; and Arm. 'A man gets defiled by vile associates.' The notes here given are on the rendering of A. V.

"*A man that hath friends,*" &c. "A father is a friend and a mother is a friend; both are friends by nature. But others become friendly-disposed through circumstances."[5] "The man who stands by us in prosperity and in adversity, in famine and in tumults, at the palace-gate and at the funeral-pile, is indeed our relation."[6] "A stranger who is friendly-

1 Tam. pr. 2 Lokaniti, 76. 3 Ep. Lod. 1501. 4 Epist. i. xviii. 21. 5 Hitop. i. 38. 6 Id. i. 74.

Fig. 10: *ONBP*, vol. 2, p. 556 (Prov. 18:24), "Complicated Etymology, CKJV"

From the angle of the number of ancient languages sources employed in these etymological comments, there is a marked difference between the first and the last two volumes of the *ONBP*. In the first volume SCM would normally only mention three versions within these critical notes, making comments on the relevant Hebrew terms, and then referring to the Greek of the Septuagint, a Chaldean Targum, or perhaps an Arabic rendering. But from the beginning of the second volume, those initial etymological notes referred far more regularly to a wider group of readings, including besides those already mentioned above also other versions of the Proverbs in Syrian, Armenian, and Coptic, as well as explanations drawn from a number of classical Jewish commentators[45] and at least four notable modern Hebrew scholars.[46] In unusual circumstances one even discovers that he mentioned renderings in

45 The three which are mentioned by name are ranked here in the order of the frequency of SCM's references to their works: Rabbi Ibn Aben Ezra (17 times), Rabbi S. Yarchi (12 times), and Rabbi Levi B. Gershon (5 times).

46 These latter four are references to commentaries to the Proverbs produced by Chilon (14:8 [vol. 2, p. 226]), Schultens (found four times including 16:26 [vol. 2, p. 417] and 27:17 [vol. 3, p. 416]), Gesenius (cited five times, including 23:35 [vol. 3, p. 202] and 30:31 [vol. 3, p.

alternative Egyptian sources,[47] as well as versions in Osmanli,[48] Welsh,[49] and French.[50] Under these more advanced conditions it would be of great interest to have a biblical scholar review some of these comments to assess their scholarly worth. It would indeed seem hard to deny that some special linguistic and interpretive scholarly assessments do in fact appear within these comments, even though they ironically stand in contrast to SCM's own diffidence about them as mentioned in the preface to the first volume of the *ONBP*.

> xxv. 11] THE BOOK OF PROVERBS. 281
>
> and from children of tender years. Let a wise man, therefore, speak in their hearing with the utmost caution, after thinking it well over, and see if it is fit or unfit to be told."[1] Lastly, Theognis advises us:
>
> "Πρῆξιν μηδὲ φίλοισιν ὁμῶς ἀνακοίνεο πᾶσιν
> παῦροί τοι πολλῶν πιστὸν ἔχουσι νόον·"[2]
>
> "Do not communicate thy business to all thy friends indiscriminately, for few there are whose faithfulness can be trusted."
>
> "*Lest he that heareth thee*," &c. "Fall at the feet of your adversary (opponent), rather than at the feet of your witnesses," says the Tamil proverb.[3] "Better to blush once [for an offence committed]," say the Italians, "than to grow pale many times [from dread of disclosures and of punishment]."[4] "For a blot upon one's name (or reputation) can never be wiped off,"[5] say the Japanese.
>
> 11 A word fitly spoken *is like* apples of gold in pictures of silver.
>
> בְּמַשְׂכִּיּוֹת כָּסֶף may mean, according to the etymology, either 'apples of gold inlaid with silver ornamentation,' or 'apples of gold in a setting of silver filagree.' Chald. 'apples of gold inlaid with silver designs.' Syr. id. Vulg. 'mala aurea in lectis argenteis.' עַל־אָפְנָיו, 'at the proper time and fitly.'
>
> "*A word*," &c. "Though there be many forests, yet few are the places where sandal, the first (or best) of trees, grows. So also, though there be many wise men, yet it is difficult (or rare) to produce elegant sayings," says the Tibetan, who adds: "A horse is known by his step; gold and silver are known when melted; and a wise man is known by the composition of his elegant sayings."[6] "For the ornament of speech is worthy of honour,"[7] says Ebu Medin.
>
> "To get a good word from a good man," says Siün-tsze,
>
> [1] Pancha T. i. 113. [2] Theogn. 73. [3] Tam. pr. [4] Ital. pr.
> [5] Jap. pr. p. 507. [6] Legs par b. pa, 449, 450. [7] Ebu Med. 126.

Fig. 11: *ONBP*, vol. 3, p. 281 (Prov. 25:11), "CKJV, Cultural Etymology"

Beyond these unusual and important additions to the *ONBP*, which indicate one way in which SCM made critical advances in relationship to the 17th century English renderings of the KJV as well as more precise accounts of the Hebrew by various

---

558]), and Umbreit (mentioned once along with Schultens and Gesenius in 18:24 [vol. 2, p. 556]).

[47] As cited in his notes for the *ONBP* found in 20:1 (vol. 2, p. 646), 20:26 (vol. 2, p. 706) and 25:12 (vol. 3, p. 283).

[48] This occurred only once within the etymological comments in the *ONBP* at 12:22 (vol. 2, p. 142).

[49] Uniquely mentioned in the *ONBP* at 14:14 (vol. 2, p. 239).

[50] Found four times in the etymological comments of the *ONBP* at 5:12-14 (vol. 1, p. 264), 6:12-15 (vol. 1, p. 303), 12:4 (vol. 2, p. 98) and 15:19 (vol. 2, p. 341).

grammatical, etymological and comparative linguistic analyses, I have argued elsewhere that he was also probing into a new realm of comparative philosophical studies by suggesting the many parallels between the Hebrew text of the Proverbs and numerous passages in the Ruist (Confucian) canonical literature.[51] Those arguments I will not repeat here, but it would also be important to note that his use of Tibetan wisdom literature, drawn also from some of the nearly 40 Tibetan texts he received from Alexander Csoma de Kőrös, should also stand as a notable effort in comparing Tibetan Buddhist and Hebrew sapiential literature.[52] Instead of exploring further into either the Chinese or the Tibetan dimensions of this work, tasks which have been pursued in later chapters within this volume, I will focus instead on another critical advance suggested by SCM that has been completely overlooked by scholars for the past century, as far as I am aware.

That advance has to do with the identifiable parallels found in what in recent decades has been confirmed to be "thirty sayings" produced in the passage extending from Proverbs 22:17 to 24:22 and those found in a number of ancient Egyptian hieroglyphic texts. In English language renderings of the Proverbs, I have only seen the most recent revision of the New International Version (completed and published in December 2010) as distinctively identifying the thirty sayings in sequence within this particular section of the biblical book of Proverbs.[53] Though the details about parallel teachings I will identify from the *ONBP* in the following paragraphs should be weighed carefully and more precisely by a competent Egyptologist, I am able to at least offer an earlier assessment made by a 20th century Hebrew scholar as well as an extensive study produced more recently as part of a commentary to the biblical book of Proverbs that justifies my making some relatively precise claims regarding SCM's awareness in proverbial literature gleaned from Egyptian hieroglyphics. In order to clarify this matter, we need to consider the following points in order to understand the nature of this unusual contribution to the study of comparative wisdom literature which SCM made in relationship to the comparison of classical Hebrew and ancient Egyptian proverbial texts.

The Hebrew scholar, Robert Alden, had this to say in 1983 about the Egyptian textual parallels to this sequence of passages in the book of Proverbs:

> We do have some information about an Egyptian wisdom catalog which is divided into thirty sections and credited to [...] Amen-em-Ope. The Egyptian document is incomplete, however, including only seventeen of the thirty sections,

---

[51] This is the main concern of Pfister 2012, developed particularly in the last sections of that article, pp. 37ff.

[52] Though the history of the relationship of SCM to this great Hungarian Tibetologist has been explored by various Hungarian scholars, as well as his later connection with the Hungarian intellectual, Theodore Duka, which has been explored by Gyula Paczolay at length; only Rita Kuzder in Chapter 9 in this volume has sought to identify the Tibetan texts cited by SCM in the *ONBP* and weigh them for their accuracy in rendering or their significance in the context of the *ONBP*.

[53] See the text online at http://www.biblica.com/bible/niv/proverbs/22 (accessed 4 January 2021), where at 22:17 there is a section entitled "Thirty Sayings of the Wise" and each saying is subsequently numbered (such as "Saying 7" and "Saying 22").

each section being much longer than the individual verses or clusters of verses in Proverbs. Furthermore, many of the Egyptian proverbs sound more like verses outside this section of Proverbs than those in it. Generally the bulk of evidence disproves rather than proves the dependence of Proverbs on Amen-em-Ope.[54]

Alden made these comments on the basis of an incomplete Egyptian text, but his further suggestion that those Egyptian sayings "sound more like verses outside this section of Proverbs" has now also been shown to be insightful. For those like SCM who were concerned about the nature and status of the biblical Proverbs as well as questions related to those parallels and their interdependence, there has been a great deal of further work done in the last century that illuminates some aspects of those complicated problems.

On the basis of what I had learned through some secondary literature before coming to the expansive commentaries produced by Michael V. Fox,[55] a major debate was initiated in 1923 regarding apparent parallels between one Egyptian text of the above mentioned Amen-em-Ope (or simply Amenemope) and the specific verses mentioned above as found in Proverbs 22 to 24.[56] Fox cites a specific German study in 1924 as the pivotal point in these parallel studies, one that claimed more precisely that within this section of Proverbs there were portions that appear to be a "Hebrew translation" of selected sayings written down by the Egyptian sage, Amenemope.[57] Some other scholars have claimed, in contrast to Alden, that the Egyptian text was written down significantly earlier than the book of Proverbs,[58] suggesting that there was a complete reliance of the Hebrew writers on those of the earlier Egyptians. Nevertheless, these broader questions regarding intertextual reliance have proven to be more complicated and not easily resolved. In spite of all these contentious matters, all involved with these debates would agree with David Atkinson when he concludes his own discussion of this debate as follows:

> [E]ven if there is some borrowing, the "wise" have deliberately pressed their material into the framework of a faith in the covenant Lord who will take up the cause of the poor (22:23), and is the defender (go'el) of the fatherless (23:11, *cf.* Dt. 10:18).[59]

This assessment of Fox's own advanced research does not deny this claim in any way, but adds numerous details that are more precise and informed. Dividing the whole passage into two sections – the first constituted by Proverbs 22:17 to 23:11

---

[54] Cited from Alden 1983, p. 165.

[55] Referring to Fox 2009 and 2010.

[56] Consult Keimer 1926. According to Derek Kidner, the debate was initiated by Wallis Budge who published a version of the *Teaching of Amenemope* in 1923. Consult Kidner 1964, p. 23.

[57] Fox cites an article by Adolf Erman published in 1924 that made these more precise claims. Consult Fox 2010, p. 18.

[58] As argued by Kidner 1964, pp. 23-24.

[59] Quoted from Atkinson 1996, pp. 144-145. So even Kidner, who argued for the earlier date of the *Teachings of Amenemope*, concludes that "if Proverbs is the borrower here, the borrowing is not slavish but free and creative. Egyptian jewels, as at the Exodus, have been reset to their advantage by Israelite workmen and put to finer use" (Kidner 1964, p. 24).

– he notes that there are a good number of selected parallels with the Amenemope sayings, so that he refers to them as "The Amenemope Collection."[60] The remaining section – from Proverbs 23:12 to 24:22 – has parallels from other sources, but with a particularly notable parallel at the beginning of this section (23:13-14) with a well-known Aramaic text, the *Book of Ahiqar*, and another (23:29-35) from an ancient Egyptian text of sayings from "Anii."[61] Fox's own account of how these expressions of Egyptian wisdom literature became known by Hebrew scribes indicates the complexities involved in this theoretical attempt to identify those parallels.[62] Notably, he points to parallels with the sayings of Amenemope in thirteen other passages of the biblical book of Proverbs involving eighteen Hebrew verses,[63] and another fourteen passages (including the one mentioned above) of which there are parallels in other parts of the book of Proverbs to sayings of Ahiqar.[64]

There are several points that can be made to indicate to what level of self-consciousness SCM grasped that there were such parallels between Egyptian hieroglyphic texts of wisdom sayings and those in this special portion of the biblical book of Proverbs. First of all, SCM was very aware of the fact that the traditional way of identifying the structure of the Proverbs was to divide it into eight parts that did not recognize this portion as a distinct collection, a tradition of scholarship which he cited in detail in his commentarial note to *ONBP* 30:1.[65] Nevertheless, when he came to the passage in 22:17, he stated unequivocally, "This looks like another division of the Proverbs, although not so stated, as in ch[apters] x [and] xxv."[66] While SCM apparently did not know of the sayings of Amenemope, he cited those of three other collections noted by Fox very often. Using SCM's way of referring to them, these were the sayings attributed to "Ptah-hotep," those associated with "Ani," and those from "Kaqimna" (sometimes also referred to as "Kakimna").[67]

---

[60] For notes on "The Amenemope Collection," consult Fox 2009, pp. 707-733. A list of all the likenesses in selected portions and whole sayings is carefully documented in *ibid.*, pp. 757-760.

[61] Find notes for this section in Fox 2009, pp. 733-753. The introductory paragraph to this section points to the two parallels I have mentioned above.

[62] Discussed in Fox 2009, pp. 753-756.

[63] Put into a chart in Fox 2009, p. 762.

[64] Involving 16 Hebrew verses, as seen in the chart on Fox 2009, p. 767.

[65] The eight traditional "divisions" in the book of Proverbs were the (1) Introduction (1:1-7); (2) Preface (1:8-19); (3) the first major division or the dialogue of Solomon with his sons (1:20 to 9:18); (4) the second major division which is the first part with short proverbial statements which are thematically diverse (10:1 to 24:34); (5) the third major division with short proverbial apothegms (25:1 to 29:27); (6) the fourth but smaller division of similar materials but from non-Solomonic sources (30:1-33); (7) an even shorter fifth division from non-Solomonic sources (31:1-9); and (8) the final poem to the "noble wife" which is an acrostic based upon the order of the Hebrew alphabet (31:10-31). See SCM's own summary of these divisions in *ONBP*, 30:1 (vol. 3, p. 537).

[66] Quoted from SCM, *ONBP*, vol. 3, p. 105 at 22:17.

[67] These Egyptian hieroglyphic collections of wisdom are referred to by Fox as "Kagemeni," "Ptahhotep," and "Anii" (as cited and described in Fox 2010, pp. 19-22).

Within the following 150 pages of the *ONBP* devoted to this section, covering the full length of this previously unnoticed passage (Proverbs 22:17 to 24:22), SCM referred to parallels in Egyptian hieroglyphic texts within 59 separate footnotes, sometimes linking them in a series,[68] because of the thematic likenesses he recognized. In the third volume of the *ONBP*, this amounted to a remarkable 52% of all the citations from Egyptian hieroglyphic sayings in that one volume.[69]

Whether or not SCM was recognizing a set of parallels that was thirty years ahead of recognized biblical scholarship is a matter which should be taken up by competent Egyptologists and scholars of the book of Proverbs. Alden's comments in this regard are very enlightening, but he was unaware of what SCM had done in this realm of study. Nevertheless, more could be done by both Egyptologists and Hebrew specialists in this regard that go beyond my own linguistic and interpretive abilities, because in the ONBP Ms SCM wrote out the hieroglyphic texts before rendering them into English, making it possible to provide various levels of critical analysis including calligraphic correctness, an assessment of his hermeneutic understanding, translation accuracy from ancient Egyptian to modern English, and other critical interpretive insights related to these discoveries on his part. Whatever else might be suggested, we see again a critical advance in Christian scholarly reflection which SCM had made during the last years of his life, an advance that deserves further scholarly attention and interpretive appreciation.

5. Concluding Comments

Intensely interested in the liturgical dimension of Christian traditions, SCM nevertheless avoided and even argued against the sacramental theology undergirding the Anglo-Catholic Movement, which had been having an impact starting from Oxford in the mid-19th century. Instead he focused on a devotion to special revelation as revealed in the Bible, a spiritual focus also found as a major theme within his own father's published sermons. As a Protestant theologian and Anglican vicar, SCM was drawn more closely to the Oriental and Eastern Christian traditions, which offered positive parallels to Anglican traditions and did not include the theological debates involved in Roman Catholic understandings of the major sacraments. In this way he had added to his father's distinctive emphasis on the Bible this special emphasis on liturgical traditions.

---

[68] For example, the long list of quotations found in *ONBP* under 22:18 (vol. 2, pp. 105-106) involve eight different quotations linked together (see p. 106, footnotes 1, 3, 4, 6-10). Similarly, at 24:13-14 (vol. 2, pp. 235-236) there are six quotations linked together from two different Egyptian sources (as found on p. 236, footnotes 1-6).

[69] That is to say, there were fifty-nine citations of Egyptian hieroglyphic sayings made in the space of two chapters, while there were 114 citations within that whole volume, involving eleven chapters. When taken from the angle of the whole three-volume set of the *ONBP*, this amounted to a section of two out of 31 chapters (or about 6.5% of the whole text of the biblical book of Proverbs) and included in that small portion just over 22% of all the 265 citations of Egyptian hieroglyphics recorded in the whole work. The concentration of those kind of sayings in that small portion of the *ONBP* is very unusual statistically.

As we consider SCM's life from the broader angle of the inter-generational traditions which he resisted as well as affirmed, it is notable that even in the *laudate* address presented in Edinburgh, his life and work was briefly and admirably linked to the evangelical work of his father and the Christian devotional work of one of his own sons. Another realm which is not a "critical advance" in any sense, but did parallel his father's precedents, was in SCM's publication of prayer books and liturgical meditations from Eastern Christians for his fellow Anglican priests, as well as popular Christian literature published during his later years for children. Two volumes of the latter sort appeared in 1881 and 1882, one dealing with the parables in the Gospels, and the other with the miracles of Jesus Christ also recorded in those Gospels. This suggests not only that he pursued engagements with children within Sunday School contexts as a pastor, but also confirms his will and ability to address very different kinds of persons at different stages of their own spiritual journeys. In this regard, he was fulfilling a spiritual vision which escaped his father's problems in Geneva: while the father had been ousted from the pastoral elite in Geneva and continued to hope for their revival, the son worked within the evangelical framework of the Anglican communion and found ways to accomplish what could not be done so easily under the political and religious restrictions of the Swiss Genevan context after 1815.

Yet here we can also focus our attention once more on some of the distinctive scholarly contributions SCM made to the critical reading of the KJV within the *ONBP*. Notably, as he neared the end of his own life's journey, we discover what is basically unexpected by his biographers. Having characterized SCM's religious attitudes as being staunchly conservative in their Anglican orientation, especially in relation to the "Authorized Version" of the Bible, which he sincerely appreciated, there is no anticipation at all that the same man would ever critically analyze and reject any renderings found in the KJV. Nevertheless, when we take more seriously his understanding of the nature of Divine truth that could be transcribed into numerous languages with all their deficiencies, and how this did not lead him to skeptical agnosticism, but to a more vigorous search for "deeper truths" which he believed the Spirit of God would confirm even through human languages, there is adequate room for understanding why he would not feel that he was compromising his Christian principles by criticizing not only the KJV, but also the Greek Septuagint and the Latin Vulgate, when they misled the 17th century English translators in their renderings of the Proverbs.

When all of these advances in Christian scholarship are put together, we discover that SCM was a more complex Christian advocate than previous biographers have portrayed. His conservative adversarial stances related to the KJV did not prevent him from recognizing errors in that version of the Proverbs, and his cross-cultural openness toward appreciating different legitimate portrayals of basic spiritual principles made his missiology more culturally sensitive and engaging than might be expected from his conservative Anglican commitments. In addition, what he also promoted as a missiological openness to understanding the best and noblest ideas in other cultures was consistent with what he sought to achieve through the publication of his English version of the *ONBP*: that is, the appreciation of practical forms of wisdom within "Eastern" cultures, even in spite of their obviously different worldviews (or "theoretical wisdom").

What we have discovered within his *magnum opus*, the *ONBP*, is that there is more to this work than what one might suspect by a cursory review of its title and contents. In this chapter I have sought to demonstrate that there is an immense amount of critical etymological insight included in the *ONBP*, and in addition, there is a remarkable anticipation of scholarly discussions about the parallels found between ancient Egyptian and Hebrew proverbial wisdom, which deserves our attention as well as further critical study. The fact that SCM anticipated these discussions by at least thirty years through noting the parallels he could find during his personal studies of ancient Egyptian texts in the 19th century deserves serious consideration by biblical scholars and Egyptologists.

As a result, we can now arrive at a surprising assessment: though SCM could be seen as a conservative evangelical Anglican with a strong appreciation for liturgy and worship, he was also at the same time critical advancing Christian scholarship. He was an advocate of culturally sensitive Christian ministry and missions during an age when confrontational mission strategies were often preferred. Also, in spite of his preference for the KJV of the English Bible and the standard Greek text (the Textus Receptus) on which it was based, SCM was able in his later days to identify numerous infelicities and errors in the KJV renderings of the Hebrew Proverbs; as we have seen previously, he pointed out these critical assessments within over 140 of his etymological studies appended to the initial reflections on various passages in the book of Proverbs. In addition, he offered critical advances in studies of comparative sapiential literature. As asserted in this and other chapters in this volume, within his work in relationship to Chinese, Tibetan, Sanskrit and Egyptian sources, SCM was exploring and identifying themes which were following and anticipating certain scholarly concerns that extended far beyond his own era. In some cases he anticipated scholarly trends and questions that would be developed only later in the 20th century. Certainly, such a list of critical advances in Christian scholarship should justify our reconsideration of his place in both theological studies within Great Britain as well as internationally-oriented Oriental studies at the end of the 19th century.

Select Bibliography

Aland, Barbara – Kurt Aland – Johannes Karavidopoulos – Carlo M. Martini – Bruce Metzger (eds.). 2016. *The Greek New Testament*. Stuttgart: Deutsche Bibelgesellschaft.

Alden, Robert L. 1983. *Proverbs: A Commentary on an Ancient Book of Timeless Advice*. Grand Rapids: Baker Book House.

Atkinson, David. 1996. *The Message of Proverbs: Wisdom for Life*. Leicester – Downers Grove, Ill.: Inter-Varsity Press.

Fox, Michael V. 2009. *Proverbs 10-31: A New Translation with Introduction and Commentary*. New Haven – London: Yale University Press.

———. 2010. *Proverbs 1-9: A New Translation with Introduction and Commentary*. New Haven – London: Yale University Press.

Giganov, Iosif Гиганов, Иосиф. 1801. *Grammatica Tatarskago iazyka Грамматика татарскаго языка*. St Petersburg: Imperaotorskaja Akademija Nauki.

Keimer, Ludwig. 1926. "The Wisdom of Amen-em-ope and the Proverbs of Solomon." *The American Journal of Semitic Languages and Literatures* 43 (October 1926) 1, pp. 8-21.

Kidner, Derek. 1964. *Proverbs: An Introduction and Commentary*. Leicester – Downers Grove, Ill.: Inter-Varsity Press.

Macdonnell, A. A. 1895. "Obituary: S. C. Malan." *The Journal of the Royal Asiatic Society of Great Britain and Ireland* 27 (April 1895) 2, pp. 453-457.

Malan, Solomon Cæsar. 1856. *A Vindication of the Authorized Version of the English Bible from Changes Brought Against It by Recent Writers*. London: Bell and Daldy.

——— (trans. and comp.). 1858. *Prayers and Thanksgivings for the Holy Communion: Chiefly for the Use of the Clergy. Translated from Coptic, Armenian, and Other Eastern Rituals*. London: Joseph Masters.

——— (trans.). 1859. *Meditations for Every Wednesday and Friday in Lent on a Prayer of Saint Ephraem: Translated from the Russian, to Which are Added Short Homilies for Passion Week from Saint Chrysostom, Saint Severian, and Saint Ephraem*. London: Joseph Masters.

——— (trans. and comp.). 1862. *The Gospel According to S. John: Translated from the Eleven Oldest Versions Except the Latin, and Compared with the English Bible, with Notes on Every One of the Alterations Proposed by the Five Clergymen in Their Revised Version of This Gospel, Published in 1857*. London: Joseph Masters.

———. 1864. *A Short History of the Georgian Church*. London: Saunders and Orley.

——— (trans.). 1866. *Repentance: Chiefly from the Syriac of S. Ephraem, and other Eastern Sources*. London: Joseph Masters.

———. 1869a. *The Life and Times of Saint Gregory the Illuminator*. London: Rivingtons.

———. 1869b. *Instruction in the Christian Faith: According to the Orthodox Armenian Church of Saint Gregory the Illuminator*. London – Oxford – Cambridge: Rivingtons.

———. 1869c. *A Plea for the Received Greek Text and for the Authorized Version of the New Testament: In Answer to Some of the Dean of Canterbury's Criticism of Both*. London: Hatchards,

———. 1871. *On the Disagreement between the Greek and the Armenian Churches*. London: Rivingtons.

——— (trans. and comp.). 1872a. *The Divine Liturgy of Saint Mark the Evangelist: Translated from an Old Coptic Manuscript and Compared with the Printed Copy of that Same Liturgy as Arranged by Saint Cyril*. London: D. Nutt.

———. 1872b. *The Confession of Faith of the Orthodox Armenian Church: Together with the Rite of Holy Baptism as It Is Administered in That Church*. N.p.: n.pub.

———. 1873a. *The Calendar of the Coptic Church*. London: D. Nutt.

———. 1873b. *A Short History of the Copts and of Their Church*. London: D. Nutt.

———. 1874. *The Holy Gospel and Versicles: For Every Sunday and Other Feast Days in the Year. As Used in the Coptic Church*. London: D. Nutt.

———. 1875. *The Divine Ἐσχολογιον [Eschologion] and the Divine Liturgy of Saint Gregory the Theologian*. London: D. Nutt.

———. 1882a. *Selected Readings in the Greek Text of Saint Matthew Lately Published*. London: Hatchards.

——— (trans. and comp.). 1882b. *The Book of Adam and Eve, also called The Conflict of Adam and Eve with Satan, a Book of the Early Eastern Church: Translated from the Ethiopic, with Notes from the Kufale, Talmud, Midrashim and Other Eastern Works*. London – Edinburgh: William and Norton.

———. 1887. *Liturgy of the Holy Apostolic Church of Armenia*. London: Gilbert and Rivington.

Pfister, Lauren F. 2003. "Rethinking Mission in China: James Hudson Taylor and Timothy Richard." In: Andrew Porter (ed.), *The Imperialist Horizons of British Protestant Missions, 1880–1914*. Grand Rapids: William B. Eerdmanns, pp. 183-212.

——— [Fei Leren 费乐仁]. 2011. "Yi wei tongxiao duoguo yuyan de Ruishiren dui 'Zhongguo zhihui' de faxian" 一位通晓多国语言的瑞士人对'中国智慧'的发现 [A Swiss Polyglot's Discovery about 'Chinese Wisdom']. In: Pan Derong 潘德荣(ed.), *Guoxue Xijian: Guoxue dui Xifang de yingxiang guiji* 国学西渐——国学对西方的影响轨迹 [National Studies Heading Westward: Traces of the Influences of National Studies in the West]. Hefei: Anhui renmin chubanshe, pp. 81-112.

———. 2012. "A Swiss Polyglot's Discovery about the Chinese Search for Wisdom: Solomon Cæsar Malan's (1812–1894) Comparative Philosophical Contributions in his *Original Notes on the Book of Proverbs*." *minima sinica* 2012/1, pp. 11-52.

Simpson, R.S. 2004. "Malan, Solomon Caesar [formerly Cæsar Jean Salomon] 1812–1894." In: *Oxford Dictionary of National Biography*, vol. 36, Macquerie – Martin. Oxford – New York: Oxford University Press, pp. 274-275.

Thornbough, Richard. 1991. *A Guide to the Parish Church of the Nativity of St. John the Baptist, Broadwindsor, Dorset*. n.p.: n.pub.

Wollheim da Fonseca, –Anton Edmund. 1831. *De nonnullis Padma-Purani capitibus: Textum e cod. mst. bibl. reg. Berol. edidit versionem latinam et annotationibus illustravit annotationibus*. Berlin: Impensis Jonas.

Online Resource:

The Bible (New International Version). 1991. http://www.biblica.com/bible/niv/ (accessed 4 January 2021).

6

SOLOMON CAESAR MALAN'S UNDERSTANDING OF CHINESE SAYINGS AND PROVERBIAL WISDOM
A Preliminary Study of His Art and Technique of Translation

THOMAS ZIMMER

Looking at Solomon Caesar Malan's *Original Notes on the Book of Proverbs*, it becomes clear that he intended to create a polyglot collection of wise sayings from as many languages as he could learn to read in order to illustrate and to highlight the breadth of the wisdom found within the biblical book of Proverbs. As can be seen from SCM's three volumes united under the title of *ONBP*, the author has used a wide range of writings from Oriental and Asian sources in order to show the similarities between the book of Proverbs and proverbial sayings in other cultures. As far as Chinese texts were concerned SCM cited from prominent classical Confucian as well as from Daoist sources. But as we can see from his footnotes, SCM had access to a couple of less prominent sources of orthodox writing as well, namely, the *Taishang ganyingpian* 太上感應篇 (Folios on the Vibrant Responses of the Most High), the *Mingxin baojian* 明心寶鑒 (The Precious Mirror to Enlighten the Mind), and the *Mingxianji* 名賢集 (A Collection with Sayings from the Wise Men of the Past for Enlightenment).

In this chapter I will try to explore the question of how deep SCM's understanding of these classical Chinese sources really was, on what basis his translations were made, and how reliable the English versions of the Chinese texts are in order to get a fresh and new look at his achievements. To initiate this whole process, I will make some remarks on the Chinese sources and then come to the question of how good and adequate SCM's translations from Chinese to English really were.

1. Texts Sources in Chinese

Generally speaking, SCM's search for exemplary literary sources of wisdom from different Asian as well as Oriental cultures was pursued on the basis of a broad understanding of relevant textual materials. Regarding Chinese sources, as we can see from the footnotes in the three volumes of his *ONBP*, SCM quoted from canonical texts in both the Confucian and Daoist traditions. Apart from these, SCM also cited sayings from a couple of non-canonical texts related to Confucian, Daoist and even Buddhist traditions in literature, particularly focusing on pedagogical texts and various versions of some famous imperial edicts. The three texts that SCM employed in his *ONBP* and that I will study here within this chapter – the *Taishang ganyingpian*, the *Mingxin baojian*, and the *Mingxianji* – belong to the category of sapiential texts with a strong pedagogical orientation.¹ SCM's strong interest in this kind of literature that served as examples of the circulation of divine wisdom found in many societies – what theologically would be recognized as a part of "general revelation." This could be especially seen in his obvious interest in another important pedagogical text that I will not evaluate in any detail, namely the *Sanzijing* 三字經 (Classic of Three Characters).² In order to get a better impression of the nature of these three non-canonical texts and the textual and interpretive problems related to them, I will first briefly describe some of their most distinctive characteristics.

These three tracts served as a means of publishing shared wisdom in a popular form to common Chinese people. In fact, they are pointing back to an old tradition related to popular publications. With new developments in Chinese printing in the 11th century of the Song dynasty, involving the creation and use of "moveable metal type" (*jinshu huozi* 金屬活字, "metal moving characters") in the publication process,³ this form of literature became immensely influential, so that a great part of the literature read by the ordinary classes of society were in the form of these small booklets. Several of these books have come to be reckoned as classics. The *Sanzijing* that I have just mentioned, for example, has been the primary reader in traditional Chinese teaching, especially in the education of younger people, including both boys and girls in the late Qing and early 20th century.⁴ Traditionally – and

---

[1] In traditional China's elementary school teaching (the technical term for this being *mengxue* 蒙學) there existed a wide variety of texts with great differences in their foci. Some texts, like the *Sanzijing* or the *Qianziwen* 千字文 (Text in Thousand Characters), focused on the teaching of Chinese characters; others, like the *Qianjiashi* 千家詩 (Thousand Poems), stressed pronunciation and articulation. In addition, the *Lunyu* 論語 (Analects) and the *Mingxianji* were used for teaching literary style. Since "traditional teaching" after 1911 in particular was regarded as "backward" and old-fashioned, or in the PRC era "ideologically questionable," this literature has been neglected by many in mainland China for much of the 20th century. Only after some leaders started to become aware of the value of traditional Chinese culture (the term since the 1990s for this being *guoxue* 國學, "national learning"), these traditional teaching materials have become more popular. For example, see Zhang Shengjie 2012.

[2] As illustrated in *STK*.

[3] As described in detail by Pan Jixing 2001, pp. 14-37 and 53-62.

[4] These primers included quotations from the canonical texts and ancient histories, outlining by this means the basic Chinese system of moral values which allows us to call it "sapiential literature." Sometimes it is difficult to categorize this kind of literature, depending how the content and use of these texts are ascribed by the compilers. Texts like the *Sanzijing* seem to have been considered as an "official" reader in teaching young male students. (Nevertheless, to read these texts required a fair amount of knowledge of classical Chinese – unlikely to be found among small children. Consequently, it was actually more a book about childhood education than it was a volume of suitable readings for beginners.) Others texts, like the *Taishang ganyingpian*, seem to have been used more independently as a source of personal, relational, and even religious advice. This may be the reason why late 20th century scholars categorize the *Sanzijing* as part of "Neo-Confucian Education," while the *Taishang ganyingpian* is included under the category of "Morality Books" in a chapter devoted to "Self and Society in the Ming" (as found in de Bary – Bloom 1999, ch. 23, pp. 804-807 and ch. 24,

even nowadays – these tracts have been readily accepted by wide circles of Chinese society. These kind of leaflets and tracts have been probably more often and more carefully read than in similar settings in Europe and North America, where such productions are generally only lightly esteemed. The wide circulation and growth of tract literature – including especially moral maxims and essays, booklets issued in favour of special religious systems or particular deities – has to be seen in connection with persons who wished to accumulate merit for themselves. Consequently, they generously devoted money for the production and distribution of these works. Here I am assuming that this has also been the case with the three texts I will have a closer look at. It is especially this popularity and the wide range of circulation of these texts which poses a problem to scholarly research. Because they generally have not been categorized as belonging to the canonical tradition, we often do not know which version of these regularly republished tracts has been used in a work like SCM's *ONBP*. Let us take the *Taishang ganyingpian* as an example, since it is perhaps the most celebrated tract in the annals of Chinese literature, and may have been broadcast in copies numbering in the hundreds of millions. Normally, it was not sold in the ordinary way within street bookstalls or shops, but was obtainable in temples, both Buddhist and Daoist, the copies being placed there for gratuitous (and merit-earning) distribution. Larger editions of this kind of non-canonical literature, published together with commentaries, illustrative notes, and narratives, could be purchased from book sellers.[5]

Now let us have a look at the three texts I am dealing with in my essay one by one.

1.1 *Taishang ganyingpian*

The *Taishang ganyingpian* – better known by its abbreviation as *Ganyingpian*[6] – is a popular work of proverbial guidance in the form of a tract. The *Ganyingpian* is a

---

pp. 899-902 respectively). This kind of different categorizing can be useful, but we have to keep in mind that the "wisdom" in the texts was very similar. Morality books were used as a kind of "self-teaching": "In fact, so basic was their appeal to the denominator in ethical thought that they were read and used even by some scholars identified with the main schools of learning. The underlying idea of the morality books is that virtue is rewarded and vice punished. Besides [...] the morality books give homely tales drawn from the popular consciousness and imagination to illustrate them" (quoting from *ibid.*, p. 899).

[5] For these details see the introduction in Webster 1918, pp. 1ff. There seem to have existed countless different versions of the *Taishang ganyingpian*, because they differed in their use of commentaries, explanations and legends. The popularity of this text is further illustrated by the fact that some modern European visitors to China published Chinese editions of the *Taishang ganyingpian* (without translation, just the plain Chinese text together with the Chinese commentaries and only a very short introduction in some European language) through their own foreign presses. See, for example, Turrettini 1889.

[6] Several possible English translations for this title can be generated. For example a very literal translation would be "Folios on the Vibrant Responses of the Most High." Since the term "Taishang" (i.e., the Most High) is a respectful expression for the ancient Daoist philosopher who was subsequently divinized, Laozi, another possible translation would be "Lord Laozi's Book of Rewards and Punishments." SCM's own description of the text and translation of its

classical text from the Daoist tradition, representing editorial efforts that collected suitable texts into a single tract during the Song dynasty between the 10th to 13th centuries. In fact, however, many of the sayings in this small book – all of them being citations that are attributed to the ancient sage, Laozi – may be much older. In the original standard version that has also been used for most of the translations,[7] the *Ganyingpian* is a rather short collection existing of only twelve hundred Chinese characters. Numerous later editions have followed after the oldest extant edition published in the Song dynasty, variously packing the short tract with prefaces, instructions, and miraculous tales.[8]

The text itself belongs to the sort of instructional aids which had been devised in ancient China over the centuries in order to introduce broader circles of society to the tenets and practices of various Daoist traditions.[9] As can be discerned from the list of its editions across various centuries, the sapiential instructions of the *Ganyingpian* were supported by various publishing formats, but especially by "illustrations and remarks" (*tushuo* 圖説).[10] The pedagogic character of morality books like the *Ganyingpian*, and their links to values in contemporary society, can also be seen from a linguistic angle. For example, quite a number of phrases from the *Ganyingpian* have become proverbially well-known among Chinese sayings.[11] It should be safe to say that the *Ganyingpian* is not to be seen as a religious document, but that it "[...] offers the reader a moral code, a method of cultivating health and fulfilling spiritual needs while maintaining a conventional social and professional life."[12] This argument may be further strengthened by the distinct Chinese concept of "retribution" (*baoying* 報應), which is mentioned in the text many times; the idea that rewards and punishments were thought to be dispensed by a supreme being had its anchor in the ancient belief that Heaven presides over the moral order,

---

title can be found in the index to the first volume of his *ONBP*: "Tai-shang, 'the Sublime'; epithet of Lau-kiun, a celebrated Taouist philosopher, chiefly through his work Kang-ing-pien, on rewards and punishments" (cited from *ONBP*, vol. 1, p. 488).

[7] Find the whole English translation in Webster 1918, pp. 15-28. He also provides a list of "the principal translations into European languages," the first one published in French in 1816, and then followed by seven others, the last being published in 1904 (*ibid.*, pp. 11-12).

[8] For a list of various editions of this work, consult Bell 1992, p. 173, n. 1. The standard version of the early text with a commentary by Li Changling 李昌齡 (*fl.* 1233) is included in the *Daozang*, i.e., the Daoist Canon. But the stories found in various versions of the *Taishang ganyingpian* are not part of the classical work or the Daoist canon. Bell proposes the following translation for its title: "Treatise of the Most High on Action and Retribution."

[9] According to Li Ying-chang's historical introduction to the work, the *Taishang ganyingpian* belonged to the "Action and Karma School" that advocated charitable works and sacrifice of self to help others. One representative sect of this school dated back to the Southern Song dynasty in the 12th–13th centuries, and shows a strong influence from Mahayana Buddhism. See Li Ying-chang 1994, pp xx.

[10] See, for example, the fifteen illustrated stories of *Taishang ganyingpian* in Li Ying-chang 1994.

[11] See Appendix II in Webster 1918, p. 31.

[12] Quoted from Li Ying-chang 1994, p. xxvii.

rewarding the good and punishing the wicked. "But instead of relying on the belief that everything is dependent on the favour of a god, the morality books are based on the idea that one can control one's own destiny by achieving virtue and eschewing vice. One can judge the value of his own actions and be assured of an appropriate reward."[13]

Depending on the philosophical traditions of early commentators, very different sources could be included within such a collection of instructional aids. As a syncretic approach is a typical feature of many writings produced by Song dynasty authors, it is notable here as well that the promoters of Daoist teachings were drawing as well upon Confucianist and Buddhist tenets.[14] In connection with the *Taishang ganyingpian*, as is true for most of these kinds of texts, we do not know precisely who the original author was. Nevertheless, at least for a rather early stage of that tract's development, a certain Chinese resident of Sichuan province known as Li Changling 李昌齡 (*fl.* 1233) is mentioned who has produced important annotations for its claims and sayings.

The basic worldview underpinning the instructions found in the *Ganyingpian* is influenced by the Buddhist idea of "retribution" activated within the context of a cosmic nexus of "cause and effect" (*yinguo* 因果), which in Buddhist beliefs meant that any human's conduct in a previous life had already produced its effect in this life. While the Daoist worldview expressed in the *Ganyingpian* does not necessarily support reincarnation, it does offer advice based upon the impact of "cause and effect" in this life. The basic message within its pages is that anyone who does good things will be rewarded, and anyone who commits crimes will be punished (*shan you shan bao, e you e bao* 善有善報，惡有惡報). With regard to the Confucian traditions the idea of "self-cultivation" (*xiushen* 修身) – meaning to put into personal practice Confucian moral values, rituals and culture – appears as a clear message emphasized within the *Ganyingpian*. Other popular Confucian conceptions of society – including relationships between family members and within certain classes of society, extending to Confucian ideas of statecraft – are found throughout the text. Still, the Daoist notion of "cultivating the Dao" (*xiudao* 修道) – meaning to strive for profound virtue, and so to seek by culture and asceticism to become an immortal – serves as the basic ontological hope of the whole text.

Generally speaking, it should be safe to say that the *Ganyingpian* is a good example of syncretistic tendencies during the Northern Song dynasty, when thinkers were highly motivated to find appropriate means to manage the worldly affairs of society by relying on admonitions from Buddhist and Daoist religious traditions, even though they were framed within Confucian moral practices. Despite these many different religious influences that impinged on the general character of morality books, the *Ganyingpian* remained weak in its assertion of any particular religious worldview. These tracts were not like the socially radical religious literature produced at various times by printing presses of Europe, such as during the

---

[13] Cited in de Bary – Bloom 1999, p. 904.
[14] For more details see Boltz 1982 and 1985.

Reformation Period. This occurred in part because many aspects of traditional Chinese religious life were grounded in a this-worldly morality and shorn of almost all transcendent authority.[15]

1.2 *Mingxin baojian*

SCM's second source of popular Chinese wisdom was the *Mingxin baojian*, a popular text from early Ming dynasty (1368–1644) about religious doctrines collected from Confucian, Daoist and Buddhist sources.[16] The best translation for the title of this book – which was used to offer moral advice especially to young and uneducated people – would perhaps be "The Precious Mirror to Enlighten the Mind."[17]

What makes the *Mingxin baojian* interesting in the context of intercultural influences on the development of sapiential literature is that this little tract has not only developed some influence for centuries in many East Asian countries in China's neighborhood (like Japan, Korea or Vietnam), but that it also played an important role in the intercultural relationship between China and Europe. The *Mingxin baojian* is apparently the first Chinese book ever translated into a European language; the Spanish translation under the title, *Espejo rico del claro corázon*, was rendered by the Spanish Dominican, Juan Cobo (Gao Muxian 高母羨, ca. 1546–1592), and published in 1593.[18] It is very likely that SCM knew this translation or even possessed a copy of it.

---

[15] See Bell 1992, p. 185.

[16] The earliest version of *Mingxin baojian* (called the "master copy," *fanliben* 范立本) is from 1393. The rather short text comprises about 700 characters and has been divided into two *juan* with ten chapters each. The oral character of the sources can be seen from the rhythmic style of the entries.

[17] SCM's description and translation of the text is found in the index to the first volume of *ONBP*: "Ming-sin Paou Kien – 'Precious Mirror for Enlightening the Heart', a Collection of Wise Sayings" (*ONBP*, vol. 1, p. 483).

[18] A source for this information is Walravens 1987, p. 197. After becoming a priest of the Dominican order, Cobo travelled to Mexico in 1586 and to Manila in 1588. He was assigned by King Philip II to bring Christianity to China, and he translated several works of classical European philosophy into Chinese. Cobo also has the distinction of being the first to introduce European philosophy and science to China, at least in print. He was sent to Japan by the governor of Manila, and he died when his boat sank during his return from Japan. The original copy of the *Mingxin baojian* he used for his translation could have been a version which was brought to the Philippines by Chinese merchants. That this text was widely spread in East Asia can be seen from the fact that a copy printed in 1454 was found in Korea in 1974. The existence of the tract in Japan can be traced back to 1631, and there is evidence from 1574 that copies circulated among scholars in Annan (i.e., today's Vietnam). For these details consult Lou Chengzhao 1993, p. 37. Unfortunately, a Chinese version of the original text could not be found for this study. Even Chinese scholars only recently became interested in the *Mingxin baojian*, the first version with explanations in Modern Chinese seems to be from 2007. See Fan Chonggao 2008.

1.3 *Mingxianji*

SCM's last source of popularly expounded Chinese wisdom was the *Mingxianji*, a collection of mainly Confucian sayings which seems to have been written during late Song dynasty (i.e., corresponding to the Southern Song, 1127–1279). An appropriate translation could be "A Collection with Sayings from the Wise Men of the Past for Enlightenment."[19]

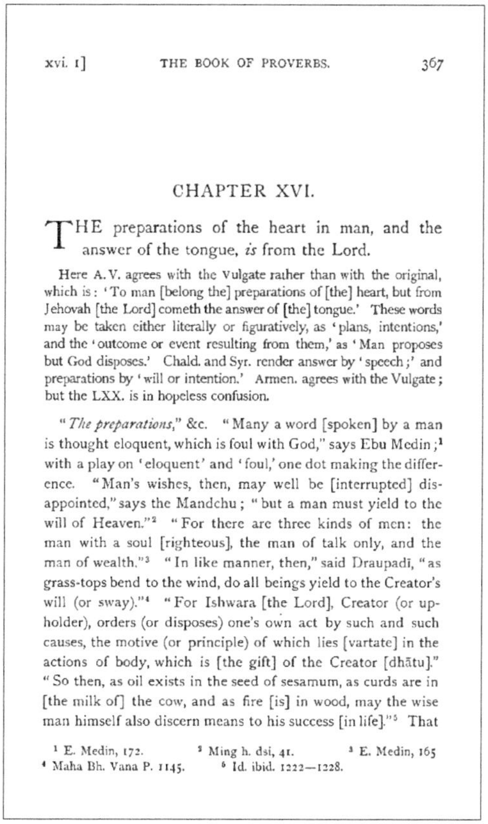

Fig. 12: *ONBP*, vol. 2, p. 367 (Prov. 16:1), "Ming h. dsi" (footnote 2)

---

[19] No bibliographic remarks can be found in SCM's *ONBP* on this text, which is referred to by the transcription "Ming hien dsi," either in the body of the text or his index to vol. 1. SCM's use of *dsi* for the third character in the title is unusual and problematic, and should normally correspond to the Pinyin *zi* or the older *tsu* in the Wade-Giles transcription. This would lead to a possible title like *Mingxianzi* 明賢(子?), but such a book can be found nowhere. Further investigation has led to the conclusion that the title should be *Mingxianji*, with the Chinese characters 明賢集, since a collection is found under this title in the internet (http://binchuan-chinese-traditional.blogspot.com/2015/04/blog-post_69.html, accessed May 12, 2021)). Notably, SCM's English translations from the *Mingxianji* found in the *ONBP* correspond to the Chinese internet version mentioned above.

This text is constituted by a number of proverbial sayings and quotations from popular poems written in lines of four to six Chinese characters. Its rhythmic style makes the entries easy to read and facile to remember. A complete proverbial saying in the *Mingxianji* consists of four phrases which have a certain inner logic. The rhythmic structure and the rhyme scheme add coherence to the whole volume as well. In traditional China the *Mingxianji* was supposed to be reading material for children and used for teaching at schools, but when viewed from its content the book offers advice about how to behave and how to deal with problems in the family, among other themes.[20] The many examples from the *Mingxianji* used by SCM in his *ONBP* suggest that he must have been fully aware of the great popularity of this text and its strong proverbial character. As we will see below, SCM's use of the rich variety of wisdom offered in the *Mingxianji* clearly manifests his attraction to the tome, although since he selected them only as they related to themes found in the biblical book of Proverbs, it may seem that he chose his examples randomly.

2. SCM's Renderings and "Art of Translation" within his *ONBP*

At least as far as the study of Chinese proverbial literature and morality books are concerned, dealing with SCM's translations of the texts he employed within his *ONBP* is quite challenging. The first difficulty is finding appropriate sources of the Chinese standard texts that have been popular reading materials at their time. The problem here is that, even though they were popular and read widely, they have not been included into larger literary collections such as *congshu*, making suitable copies difficult to locate. The second difficulty is to find the appropriate passages in the Chinese text after reading SCM's translation. Often in the *ONBP* SCM mentioned the title of the source and the page of the version he has access to, but if one does not have the same version, it can be very hard to trace back from his English translation to the actual Chinese apothegms referred to in any one of SCM's particular citations. Obviously, only by comparing the translation with the original passage will one be able to understand and reveal something about SCM's translation techniques and their "correctness." Precisely because of this shortcoming, since a Chinese text of the *Mingxin baojian* could not be located for this study, in the subsequent evaluations I had to rely on the comparative analyses of the other two texts with SCM's renderings to arrive at my various judgments.[21] In the following paragraphs, I will first give a short overview of the general features of SCM's translation in relationship to the two relevant sources described in the previous section. Following that, I will evaluate those passages that are of particular interest, and seek to come to various judgments about SCM's "art" or "style" of translation.

---

[20] Similar kinds of this early "literature of advice" in China have been *Sanzijing*, already mentioned above, as well as a number of other books, even though they involve slightly different emphases in the advice that is offered. See, for example, *Dizi gui* 弟子規 (Rules for Disciples, edited by Li Yuyan 李毓彥 from the Qing dynasty [1644–1911]) and the *Qianziwen*, which should even be older and is attributed to Zhou Xingsi 周興嗣 (propably died in 521 A.D.).

[21] I did so by consulting the sources I have mentioned above and a German version of the biblical text ("Die Sprüche Salomons," pp. 621-645).

Different from the other translators of these texts that have been mentioned above, SCM just picked various passages from the original in order to serve his purposes of finding parallels or contrasts to the biblical proverbs. This leaves the terms and contexts of the original text (which would normally have to be considered for a proper translation) unconsidered, and leads to the construction of a new context and understanding in the translation based on the dominating presence of the relevant passages from the book of Proverbs. A very obvious example for this technique can be found in SCM's quotations from the *Ganyingpian*: he always included as an introduction or identification of each quotation the phrase "[...], says Tai-shang, [....] ."[22] In fact, however, SCM's reference to the "speaker" Taishang is an invention, because in the original version that name appears only one time, just at the beginning of the whole text. Presumably, then, all the rest of the text consists of direct quotations.[23] As a consequence, and probably unintentionally, even if SCM did not directly translate "Taishang" as "God," his translation of phrases from the *Ganyingpian* take on a biblical tone by the frequent use of Tai-shang as the enunciator of wisdom.

Leaving out the context of certain expressions and not proceeding in a strictly philological manner, where the translation of a whole text is pursued, leads to another problem. Although the whole tract is rather short, the text of the *Ganyingpian* possesses an inner logic, a general system and context which is relevant for understanding each selected passage. Scholars and translators who offered the whole text in another language after SCM had published the *ONBP* have noticed this and elaborated on it in some cases. Webster, for example, describes this aspect of the text in the following way:

> At first sight the work seems almost beyond analysis of any kind; it appears to be a series of phrases strung together more or less loosely, the only connection being that of the subject of retribution, which clearly dominates the entire book. [...] But analysis is not altogether impossible: in spite of many instances of repetition and overlapping [...] there are certain leading lines of procedure and treatment which are clearly defined."[24]

These phrases and the inner argumentation of the *Ganyingpian* make it possible for Webster to add his own explicit structure to the text – starting with an introductory section, followed by various thematic sections, and finishing with "concluding remarks" and an exhortation. For Webster (and for me) it is crucial to notice these special dimensions within the whole text and to see/understand the context which is constructed accordingly in order to appreciate the "value" of certain expressions in the text. The crucial sections in question within the *Ganyingpian* are, according to Webster, "the good man exemplified" and "the bad man exemplified." The portrait

---

[22] For examples in *ONBP*, vol. 1, p. 100 (2:22), p. 185 (3:28), p. 188 (3:30), and p. 189 (3:32).

[23] See for example the translation by James Webster who stays very close to the original text. The first two line read: "The words of the Most High: Woe and weal have no doors, but come only at the call of men." Found in Webster 1918, p. 14. The term "Most High" does not appear a second time in the whole rest of the text.

[24] See Webster 1918, p. 12.

offered of the "good man" within the first portion of that section is that of the *junzi* 君子, i.e., the "princely man" – a gentleman, a wise man, and a man of complete virtue according to Confucianism. The important term, *dao* 道 (introduced in the proverb "if it is the right way, advance; if the wrong way, retire" [*shi dao ze jin, fei dao ze tui* 是道則進，非道則退]) here means simply "the path of rectitude," reflecting the idea of duty which has so large a place in the writings of Confucianism, and notably has none of the abstract import of philosophical Daoism here.[25] Nevertheless, the section related to this description of the "good man" is actually relatively short. Much longer and more detailed is the section about the "bad man" and his characteristics, being in itself a depiction of the "wrong way" (*feidao* 非道).[26] What is important about this change in the whole text of the *Ganyingpian* is that this part of the work "soon leaves the more strictly ethical character of Confucianism for the devious paths of Taoist accretion," according to Webster.[27] For example, in a later part of that section on "the bad man," the term *siming* 司命 turns up, it being a reference to a popular deity found mostly in Daoist contexts called the "Arbiter of Human Destiny."[28]

What I intend to highlight here by means of these examples is the ambivalent nature of a text like the *Ganyingpian* which poses a great challenge for every translator. At crucial moments a more philological approach to the translation, including more of the surrounding context or at least reference to it, seems the safest way in order not to distort the meaning of a certain passage (as well as the understanding of the text as a whole). Webster proceeds with that approach to the "art of translation" at least most of the time. To the contrary, SCM does something very different. It appears in his translation of sayings from the section about the "bad man" in the *Ganyingpian*, he is in fact constructing cross-cultural conceptual connections with the biblical concept of "sin": not to follow the way (*feidao*) or to neglect one's duty (*feiyi* 非義) is a sin according to SCM, giving his translation a very "biblical" tone once again. One could argue that this was in fact SCM's self-conscious intention, to find parallels or contrasts to biblical wisdom in proverbial form, but what I am seeking to underscore here is that he could have done so without suggesting reductionistic Christianized accounts of the meanings of non-biblical proverbs.

A typical translation from this Chinese tract in SCM's *ONBP* reads like this: "'And it is a sin,' says Tai-shang, 'to borrow a thing and not return it.'"[29] One

---

[25] See Webster 1918, p. 13.

[26] In the Chinese text of the *Ganyingpian* we learn that these "bad" characteristics are attributed to the man who acts "without duty" (*feiyi* 非義).

[27] Cited from Webster 1918, p. 14.

[28] In Webster's work we can find different renderings for this same term. In his translation of the main text of the *Ganyingpian* we can read: "For such crimes as these, the Minister of Life administers punishment according to the nature of the offence – curtailing life by twelve years or one hundred days." In the following footnote Webster explains the deity *siming* in the following way: "the Arbiter of Destiny, 上帝 [*shangdi*] God." See Webster 1918, p. 27.

[29] Quoting from *ONBP*, vol. 1, p. 185 (Proverbs 3:28). For more "sins" according to SCM see, e.g., p. 189 (3:32); p. 331 (6:29); p. 345 (7:12); and p. 350 (7:21). Again, every translation

possible answer to the question why SCM has identified "sin" with *feidao* might be found in influences from the German language and different terms used there. A passage from the book of Proverbs 10:11[30] according to the English version of the KJV used by SCM states: "The mouth of a righteous man is a well of life: but violence covereth the mouth of the wicked." The idea of *feidao* according to SCM's example here is connected with "the wicked." The German translation is different: "Des Gerechten Mund ist ein Brunnen des Lebens; aber den Mund der Gottlosen wird ihr Frevel überfallen."[31] Here the *feidao* is seen as an equivalent for the "Gottlosen," that is, "one without God." This German term "gottlos" seems much closer to the Chinese idea of *feidao*, and so could more easily be linked to "sin."

Now, even in spite of the interpretive reservations mentioned previously, I would like to take a closer look to see whether there is an interpretive equivalence between SCM's English translations from the *Ganyingpian* and his English renderings of the biblical book of Proverbs. I will start with some short general remarks, in order to point out at least one striking difference in the nature of these two texts. Perhaps the biggest difference between the Proverbs of the Bible and the text of the *Ganyingpian*, particularly after one has read them both in their entirety, is the tone of these two texts: The biblical Proverbs are addressed to everybody in person, i.e., the speaker addresses "you" which gives the text a very personal and intimate tone while the *Ganyingpian* is totally different in style, and does not personally address a reader as such. There is much more distance between the "speaker" and the reader in the Chinese tract, because "Taishang" only speaks about the "good man" and the "bad man." The *Ganyingpian* offers ideals which should be followed or bad examples which should be avoided, but the appeal to the reader to follow or to avoid is much more indirect and impersonal than those in the biblical Proverbs. Perhaps SCM had noticed this important difference, justifying why he invented the speaker "Taishang" in order to assert a stylistic equivalence between the two texts.

Therefore, let us ask very directly: how correct and representative are these English renderings of the relevant proverbs SCM found in the Chinese versions of the *Ganyingpian* and the *Mingxianji*?[32]

---

may have a different understanding of ambivalent terms in texts like the *Ganyingpian*. The term *guo* 過 when used as a noun in Chinese texts possesses meanings like "transgression," "error" or "fault." The term is found in the *Ganyingpian*'s passage, *jian ta shi bianbian shuo ta guo* 見他失便便說他過. It is Webster who translates *guo* here as "sin" ("The misfortunes of others he puts down to their sins [...]," as in Webster 1918, p. 23), whereas SCM translates *guo* as "fault" ("'Do not divulge the faults of others', says Tai-shang." From *ONBP*, vol.1, p. 439 [10:12]).

[30] Consult *ONBP*, vol. 1, p. 439.

[31] See "Die Sprüche Salomons," p. 627.

[32] As already explained in n. 19 above, I was unable to find a Chinese version of the *Mingxin baojian*, and so cannot analyze the relationship between SCM's rendering of passages from that work with a standard Chinese source.

2.1 SCM's English Translations of Proverbs in the *Taishang Ganyingpian*

In a broader sense (with regard to the syntactical structure and the "message of the text") most of the translations of passages from the *Ganyingpian* I have looked at and which I have compared with the Chinese originals seem more or less correct, manifesting in some of these cases SCM's impressive knowledge of cultural, philosophical, and religious topics in China. This makes it even more obvious that those shortcomings in his English translations rather involve questions about his intentions than those of his basic linguistic knowledge. Nevertheless, it becomes clear that Malan produces no "correct translation" in the strictly philological sense, but that he prefers renderings that reveal his own understanding of the basic message shared by both the Chinese and Hebrew texts.

Here I will illustrate what I mean by the following example. The *Ganyingpian* states (using SCM's English rendering): "'If a man commits a great fault,' says Taishang, 'the Spirit cuts off twelve years of his life; but for a small fault, only a hundred days.'" In this passage the term for assessing the penalty (*jisuan* 紀算) has a definite significance, namely, the duration of the sentence.[33] As far as the sentence as a whole is concerned, SCM's translation is generally correct, but it is still an incomplete translation. The fact is that he did not translate the whole title of the spirit involved in the Chinese passage. Instead, he referred only to "the Spirit," so that one might wonder by the use of the capitalization, is SCM intending to allude to the "Holy Spirit"?[34] This could obviously lead to a serious misunderstanding by uninformed readers.

Apart from the questions concerning the unusual character of SCM's translations in the *ONBP* already mentioned above, some logical twists become obvious when comparing examples cited from the biblical proverbs and those sayings chosen by SCM from the *Ganyingpian*. For example, the biblical text, "Say not unto thy neighbour, Go, and come again, and to-morrow I will give; when thou hast it by thee,"[35] is presented by SCM as conveying the same sense as "And it is a sin," says Tai-shang, "to borrow a thing and not return it." But according to my understanding of these passages, what is criticised in the biblical text is avarice, whereas the *Ganyingpian* expresses a warning not to become a thief. Similarly, the ruling principle behind the biblical saying, "Strive not with a man without cause, if he have done thee no harm,"[36] surely is love, whereas in the *Ganyingpian*'s "'Give way

---

[33] See an alternative rendering in Webster 1918, p. 16, n. 5. The quote can be found in *ONBP*, vol. 1, p. 100.

[34] The "Spirit" in question here should be the "Controller of Destiny" (i.e. *beidou shenjun* 北斗神君). That spirit resides in the Great Bear, and on the 3rd of the eighth month his feast of incarnation is celebrated. Accordingly, Webster's philologically complete and correct translation is "the Spirit ruler of the Dipper." Taken from Webster 1918, p. 16 (translation) and ns. 4 and 6 on the same page for the explanations.

[35] From Proverbs 3:28, presented in *ONBP*, vol. 1, p. 185. This same passage includes the quotation from the *Ganyingpian* that follows.

[36] From Proverbs 3:30, as found in *ONBP*, vol. 1, p. 188, with the susequent quotation also coming from the *Ganyingpian*.

over and over again,' says Tai-shang, '[lose much] and take little for yourself,'" it is generosity.[37]

Another kind of twist in logic comes up in connecting sayings drawn from chapter 7 of the biblical proverbs with those from the *Ganyingpian*. The former describes (according to the subtitle of the German version of the Bible) "the sad consequences of seduction to whoring."[38] SCM chose two sentences from an episode in that biblical context where a woman is described as approaching a man walking by and inviting him to come with her. The two passages from the Bible and their corresponding sentences from the *Ganyingpian* read as follows in their presentation in the *ONBP*:

> Now is she without, now in the streets, and lieth in wait at every corner. [...] "For it is a sin," says Tai-shang, "for a woman to have neither docility nor obedience." [...][39]
>
> With her much fair speech she caused him to yield, with the flattering of her lips she forced him. [...] "However, the wife is not alone to blame [for her adultery], [...] "Yet it is a sin in her not to show him [her husband] proper respect," says Taishang.[40]

The proverbs from the Bible are clearly describing the devious ways an adulterous woman employs to seduce a man. Again, SCM is "constructing" a sin in the saying of the *Ganyingpian* by leaving out the context and missing the Confucian connotation. The two passages chosen from the *Ganyingpian*, of course, are examples from the "bad man"-section in the text. The short Chinese passage portrays some extra features that make it quite different from the rather monotonous structure of the rest of that section. The two passages in Chinese when rendered in a different English translation read as follows: *nan bu zhong liang, nü bu rou shun, bu he qi shi, bu jing qi fu* 男不忠良，女不柔順，不和其室，不敬其夫 / "(For a man), all the loyal and upright feelings which distinguish a true man are lost; (for a woman), tenderness and obedience are unknown. (The man), he does not live in accord with his wife; (the woman), she does not respect her husband."[41] In the process of this argumentation the Chinese text changes from general observations about "everybody" to the distinctions between husbands and wives, and by this means characterizes the result of evil conduct as exemplified in the various intimate relations and duties which exist between a husband and his wife. This passage reveals a clear reliance

---

[37] The twist in logic becomes even more obvious when looking at the Chinese original of the *Ganyingpian*. SCM purposely (?) exaggerates when he translates the first two characters of the simple four character phrase, *tui duo qu shao* 推多取少, with "over and over again." Again, Webster's philologically correct translation reads "He gives much, and takes little" (found in Webster 1918, p. 18).

[38] See "Die Sprüche Salomons," p. 625. My English rendering.

[39] Quoting the KJV for Proverbs 7:12 and the *Ganyingpian*, both found in *ONBP*, vol. 1, p. 345.

[40] The initial text from the KJV of Proverbs 7:21, as seen in *ONBP*, vol. 1, p. 348; the text including the saying from the *Ganyingpian* appears later in *ibid.*, pp. 349-350.

[41] Quoted from Webster 1918, p. 25, with some slight revision.

on basic principles for married persons within Confucian ethics, but does not relate it to any religious dimension that would highlight these matters as "sinful actions."

2.2 SCM's English Translations of Proverbs in the *Mingxianji*

Regarding SCM's English translations of passages from the *Mingxianji* some things are different from what was found in his renderings of the *Ganyingpian*. One common feature of those renderings drawn from both Chinese tracts is the construction of a definite speaker for passages from the *Mingxianji* text. Quotations from this text are very often accompanied by phrases such as "say the Mandchus" or even "says Confucius," although no direct reference to either Manchus or Confucius can be found in the Chinese text. Another of SCM's constructions is the addition of the term "heaven," referring by this means to a divine power, even if the Chinese text does not mention it and remains vague about this. Typically, "Heaven" is added in the English translation of the *Mingxianji* if "the LORD" appears in the KJV rendering of the book of Proverbs. For example, in comparison to a well-known passage from Proverbs 3:5, "Trust in the Lord with all thine heart; and lean not unto thine own understanding,"[42] a subsequent contrastive saying is cited as coming from the *Mingxianji*: "For he who submits to Heaven is preserved; but he who opposes Heaven perishes" (*jishan you shanbao, ji'e you ebao* 積善有善報，積惡有惡報).[43] There is at least one instance where both "Confucius" and "the Mandchus" appear together in an unusual passage where SCM incorporates them into what are essentially his own observations from broader readings in Chinese and Manchurian sources. In relation to the biblical statement from Proverbs 4:2 ("Hear, ye children, the instruction of a father, and attend to know understanding. For I give you good doctrine, forsake ye not my law"),[44] SCM offers the following comments and quotation: "Confucius used to address his disciples as, 'My little children,' a term of affection yet, according to the Mandchu saying, 'among ten thousand disciples, there are but six dozen good ones'" (*sanqian tuzhong li, qishi'er xianren* 三千徒眾立，七十二賢人).[45] A literal English rendering from the *Mingxianji* would be, "While there are three thousand followers standing, [only] seventy-two are worthy and virtuous persons." So, here as well, we can see how SCM preferred a saying with some literary flair in his English rendering rather than a more literal (and perhaps less captivating) precision.

Nevertheless, I would also want to underscore the fact that there are quotations from the Proverbs which perfectly correspond with sayings from the *Mingxianji*,

---

[42] Found in *ONBP*, vol. 1, p. 114.

[43] This English translation can be found in *ONBP*, vol. 1, p. 115. Again, it is hard to say whether the original Chinese proverb really corresponds with the translation. I have looked through the Chinese text of the *Mingxianji* and remain unsure about some of the quotations, this being one of the unsure cases.

[44] Quoted in *ONBP*, vol. 1, p. 194. The subsequent quotations occur on the same page.

[45] Neither "Confucius" nor "the Mandchu" are mentioned in the Chinese text. In addition, the first five characters appear to be translated wrongly, at least according to this version of the *Mingxianji*, since the text only speaks about "three thousand disciples."

especially when the two texts are exemplifying the power of the Lord and of Heaven. One good example of this kind of parallel is found in the passages related to Proverbs 3:33, "The curse of the Lord is in the house of the wicked: but he blesseth the habitation of the just."[46] Observe how the principle of this biblical proverb is echoed in the English rendering from the *Mingxianji*: "If a wicked man wishes to make another man perish, Heaven will not let him. But if Heaven has resolved the ruin of a man [for his wickedness], how difficult it is to prevent it!" (*ren zhuo ren si tian bu ken, tian zhuo ren si you he nan* 人著人死天不肯，天著人死有何難).[47]

Another interesting formal feature of SCM's translations in the *ONBP* is that he sometimes splits the traditional Chinese saying and only uses part of a complex phrase in order to make the saying fit its supposed counterpart in the biblical Proverbs. An example of this is found in Proverbs 10:1 ("A wise son maketh a glad father: but a foolish son is the heaviness of his mother."), which is compared to the saying from the *Mingxianji*: "When the son is dutiful and obedient, the father's heart is at rest."[48] Nevertheless, this English rendering of the Chinese saying is only the second part of a clearly stated account of Confucian familial wisdom, which goes like this: "A virtuous wife reduces the burden of a husband; an obedient and respectful son leaves the father's heart at rest" (*qi xian fu huo shao, zi xiao fu xin kuan* 妻賢夫禍少，子孝父心寬). Obviously here, the biblical proverb only deals with sons in relationship to their parents, but the portion of the Chinese saying that refers to a "virtuous wife" is not relevant in this case, and so it is simply left unmentioned by SCM, without any explanation of the contextual difference.

The randomness of SCM's choices of proverbial wisdom sayings from the *Mingxianji* becomes obvious in other ways as well. There is a pertinent example found in a saying related to the "naughty person" and "wicked man," concluding in the judgment found in Proverbs 6:15:[49] "Therefore shall his calamity come suddenly; suddenly shall he be broken without remedy." In fact, in the subsequent three quotations, SCM forms one new saying out of two different passages in the *Mingxianji*, and so collates the two different contexts into a single saying.[50] That quotation is divided into two quoted sayings, but nothing about their varying contextual framework is described. The material in the *ONBP* appears as follows:

---

[46] Found in *ONBP*, vol. 1, p. 189.

[47] See *ONBP*, vol. 1, p. 190.

[48] The passage from the KJV appears in *ONBP*, vol. 1, p. 420, with the English rendering of the saying from the *Mingxianji* found on the following page.

[49] In this case, this is a set of sayings drawn from Proverbs 6:12-15, with the quotation being the last of the four sayings that is linked together in this spot. See *ONBP*, vol. 1, p. 303.

[50] SCM refers to the sources in his *ONBP*, vol. 1, p. 306 as "Ming h. dsi 167, 170." My problem has been that the version of the work that SCM employed remains unclear, and unfortunately, newer versions of the *Mingxianji* that I have found do not have any page numbers. Consequently, one has to make an educated guess about which saying may be the Chinese original SCM was rendering into English. In spite of these interpretive problems, the two passages shown above should be the right versions.

"'Assuredly,' say the Mandchus, 'he who goes about troubling and deceiving others, will inevitably become poor. From the beginning, Heaven has not granted pardon to such men.' 'The wicked man thinks of deception, because his heart is bad.'" Though one might ask further questions related to how these two sayings relate to the biblical proverb, and noting that SCM does document the fact that he took the two sayings from two very different sources in the one footnote connected to them, there is an arbitrariness of selections there that should be a concern for those interested in his style of translating these Chinese materials.

Coming to the question of the logical relationship between passages from the book of Proverbs and those quoted from the *Mingxianji*, it is obvious that SCM sometimes proceeded in ways that could be challenged. An important example of this can be found in the connections he made when reflecting on Proverbs 2:22: "But the wicked shall be cut off from the earth, and the transgressors shall be rooted out of it."[51] The basic sense of this saying must be framed in the worldview that is fundamental and assumed within the whole of the book of Proverbs, and is made explicit in Proverbs 2:6: "For the Lord giveth wisdom: out of his mouth cometh knowledge and understanding." Wisdom in this biblical context comes from the Lord, and humans are required to accept that wisdom, learn from it, and live on the basis of it. So, the meaning of the proverb cited above that comes at the very end of the second chapter of that biblical text, one that stands alone and is not directly linked to other proverbs in that same chapter of the *ONBP*, manifests one of the terrible consequences happening to those who do not care about and even resist that kind of wisdom. It is in this context, then, that SCM cites two parallel statements from the *Mingxianji* that are given close to each other in the Chinese text:[52]

> When fortune is favourable to a man whose heart is not good, he assuredly comes to a miserable and untimely end" (*ming hao xin bu hao, zhong tu yaozhe le* 命好心不好，中途夭折了).

> But when a man's fortune and his heart are both bad, then even to his old age he lives in poverty and wretchedness [trouble and sorrow] (*xin ming dou bu hao, qiong ku zhi dao lao* 心命都不好，窮苦直到老).

The "wisdom" expressed in these passages of the *Mingxianji* is of a totally different kind compared to that found in the biblical passage with which they are associated, and so here the logical connection is questionable. Where the proverb based on biblical wisdom asserts that there will be an assured punishment for the "wicked" and those living in opposition to "the Lord," the *Mingxianji*'s wisdom is grounded on the presence of a mighty power behind all things and events, something that is described as a vague "fate" or "fortune" (*ming* 命). Undoubtedly, SCM was aware of these differences in worldview commitments, but he should have explained how he understood the relationship of these two forms of wisdom, especially in their reliance on two very different accounts of the ultimate powers in human life.

---

[51] As quoted from the KJV in *ONBP*, vol. 1, p. 99.

[52] As found in *ONBP*, vol. 1, p. 100, cited as coming from pp. 105 and 106 in the version of the *Mingxianji* that SCM was employing (*ibid.*, ns. 2 and 3).

Without this kind of an explanation, the connection between these various sayings remains logically questionable.

Similarly, in the translations SCM offered from the *Ganyingpian* as well as in the *Mingxianji*, there are a lot of examples from the *ONBP* where SCM selected texts which seem to correspond to each other quite well at first sight, but do show striking differences in their fundamental meanings after a closer examination. Due to limitations of time and space, I will choose only one more example cited from the *Mingxianji*. In Proverbs 3:29 it is stated in the KJV version of that saying:[53] "Devise not evil against thy neighbour, seeing he dwelleth securely by thee." The parallel proverb selected by SCM from the *Mingxianji* is given the following English rendering: "By all means settle near a good neighbour; by all means make friendship with a good man" (*ju bi ze lin, jiao bi liangyou* 居必擇鄰，交必良友). According to my understanding of these sayings, the advice given in the Proverbs expresses a stronger moral demand, whereas the Chinese proverb is not so much an exhortation, as a wise recommendation about choices in human relationships that will allow one to stay safe and unmolested from any kind of trouble. Though there is an obvious conceptual connection related to one's neighbours, it is hard to explain why SCM would bring together such very different kinds of proverbs, because their intentions and exhortative ranges of expression involve totally different assumptions.

3. Conclusion

In this contribution I have introduced four Chinese works that SCM quoted from within his *ONBP* that are unusual because they are not part of the normal canonical literature of traditional China. Among these four texts, the *Sanzijing*, or what SCM called *The Triliteral Classic*, had a semi-canonical status among Confucian traditions as a pedagogical tool for teaching young men (and by the late 19th century, also young women) in traditional Chinese cultural settings. The other three works were popular pedagogical tracts that included many sayings expressed in proverbial-like form: the *Taishang ganyingpian*, the *Mingxin baojian*, and the *Mingxianji*. Due to the fact that I had access only to Chinese standard copies of the first and third of these works, my study of SCM's general approach to these translations, and some specific critical analyses of selective renderings of proverbial statements from those two works constituted the main concerns of my research and reflections here.

What I have discovered as a result of this research is of some vital interest in understanding SCM's "art" or "style" of translation as it is revealed within the first volume of the *ONBP*. Though the scope of my study is limited to that first volume, and so may not be generalized without further research done in the latter two volumes, some important interpretive discoveries could already be made regarding both the general framework of SCM's translation work in the *ONBP* as well as his

---

[53] Cited from *ONBP*, vol. 1, p. 187. The subsequent rendering of the Chinese proverb also occurs on the same page.

specific approaches to, and self-conscious stylistic tropes found within specific translations from Chinese into English that he adopted within that work.

As we have seen through the comparisons of SCM's English renderings of Chinese proverbs from the two popular works that I have analysed, SCM intentionally made changes or added terms to suit his needs for finding corresponding wisdom and related messages in those two popular Chinese tracts. The most fundamental problem I am trying to bring to light here has little to do with the accuracy or inaccuracy of SCM's English renderings of any particular Chinese passage, or with the fact that there are a limited number of choices with which a translator must work to get the best possible rendering. Rather, both SCM's careful choice of examples from far more complex original texts in Chinese and his self-conscious effort to change certain aspects of those wisdom sayings by both indirect and direct means have advanced a silent argument for a particular commitment that he wanted to underscore: that is, he intends for his readers to come to recognize that there are similar expressions of wisdom in the form of proverbial sayings in ancient literary documents found in the Bible as well as in those popular tracts that were composed in traditional China.

Seen from a broader perspective of cultural and political encounters and confrontations between traditional Chinese people and modern European and North American persons in the 19th century, SCM's technique of translation clearly developed out of a very different approach towards foreign cultures and people in comparison with the imperialistic approach which dominated many realms of those cross-cultural engagements. Though this has not been the main theme of discussion in this chapter, it has been addressed elsewhere in this volume;[54] I understand my own contribution in this chapter as a critical addition to those discussions from the angle of a Sinologist who is looking at how SCM presented those Chinese texts discussed here within his *ONBP*. In fact, translation was regarded as a necessary precondition of cross-cultural communication in those 19th century contexts, but it was not necessarily regarded as being done in an "objective" way. Especially those experts in the fields of politics or the natural sciences often chose to present non-English documents in literal translations in order to establish a kind of radical incommensurability between Chinese and European languages. Their "art" or "style" of translation may have had some similarities with SCM's, but surely their worldview and attitudes toward Chinese culture were very different from his.[55]

---

[54] See discussions of SCM's missiology as expressed in his *Letters to a Young Missionary* in Chapter 2 and of SCM's critical advances in Christian scholarship in Chapter 5 for those extended arguments.

[55] For different ideological questions in connection with translations in the 19th century, consult Liu 2004.

Select Bibliography

de Bary, Wm. Theodore – Irene Bloom (trans. and comp.). 1999. *Sources of Chinese Tradition, Volume One: From Earliest Times to 1600*. New York: Columbia University Press.

Bell, Catherine. 1992. "Printing and Religion in China: Some Evidence from the *Taishang Ganying Pian*." *Journal of Chinese Religions* 20 (1992), pp. 173-186.

Boltz, Judith M. 1982. "Opening of the Gates of Purgatory: A Twelfth-century Taoist Meditation Technique for the Salvation of Lost Souls." In: Michel Strickmann (ed.), *Tantric and Taoist Studies in Honour of R. A. Stein*. Mélanges chinois et bouddhiques, 21. Bruxelles: Institut Belge des Hautes études chinoises, pp. 488-510.

———. 1985. *A Survey of Taoist Literature, Tenth to Seventeenth Centuries*. Berkeley, Cal.: University of California.

Fan Chonggao 范崇高. 2008: "*Mingxin baojian* ciyu jieshi zhixia" 明心宝鉴词语解释指瑕 [Some Remarks on the Flaws Found in the Explained Terms within the *Mingxin baojian*]. *Kaoshi* 考试 41 (2008), pp. 210-211.

Li Ying-chang. 1994. *Lao-tzu's Treatise on the Response of the Tao*. Trans. Eva Wong. San Francisco: HarperCollins.

Liu, Lydia H. 2004. *The Clash of Empires*: *The Invention of China in Modern World Making*. Cambridge, Mass. – London: Harvard University Press.

Lou Chengzhao 娄承肇. 1993. "*Mingxin baojian*: Zuizao yicheng Xifang wenzi de Zhongguo shu" 明心宝鉴——最早译成西方文字的中国书 (*Mingxin baojian*: The First Chinese Book Translated into a Western Language]. *Liaowang xinwen zhoukan* 瞭望新闻周刊 11 (1993), p. 37.

Pan Jixing 潘吉星. 2001. *Zhongguo jinshu huozi yinshua jishushi* 中國金屬活字印刷技術史 (A History of Moveable Metal Type Printing Technology in China). Shenyang: Liaoning kexue jishu chubanshe.

"Die Sprüche Salomons." 1935. *Die Bibel oder die ganze heilige Schrift des Alten u. Neuen Testaments*. Nach der deutschen Übersetzung D. Martin Luthers, Stuttgart: Privileg – Württembergische Bibelanstalt, 1935, pp. 621-645.

Turrettini, François. 1889. *Livre des récompenses et des peines avec commentaire et légendes: Ouvrage Taoiste*. Genève: H. Georg.

Walravens, Hartmut. 1987. *China illustrata: Das europäische Chinaverständnis im Spiegel des 16. bis 18. Jahrhunderts*. Weinheim: Acta Humaniora, VCH.

Webster, James. 1918. *The Kan Ying Pien. Book of Rewards and Punishments*. Shanghai: Printed at the Presbyterian Mission Press.

Zhang Shengjie 张圣洁 (ed.). 2012. *Mengxue Shisanjing* 蒙学十三经 (Thirteen Classics of the Traditional Chinese Elementary School Teaching]. Beijing: Wenhua yishu chubanshe.

DISCERNING THE WORLDVIEW IN CONFUCIAN PROVERBS
A Preliminary Reflection on S. C. Malan's Selection of Confucian Proverbs from *The Four Books*

WILLIAM YAU NANG NG

1. Introduction: Proverbs in Comparative Perspective

Confucianism has very often been taken as a representative school of humanism, yet humanism is a complex concept with many layers of accumulated meaning.[1] While some do argue that humanism is essentially atheistic (or agnostic), particularly among some modern humanists, there are also those who recognize that there are other forms of humanism that have existed in different periods and cultures, and so they conceive of the fact and further possibilities of identifying and developing a religious form of humanism. Nevertheless, Confucian humanism, especially in its modern expressions, has very often been understood as a kind of secular thought deprived of any religious dimension. Consequently, some scholars persist in claiming that even classical Confucian works are books that essentially express a form of secular wisdom.

However, Confucianism – especially in its ancient pre-imperial expressions – was not always being understood as a secular philosophy. An examination of classical canonical Confucian works in particular suggests that Confucianism not only provides wisdom about secular life, but also conveys insights about religiosity.

Solomon Caesar Malan in his *Original Notes on the Book of Proverbs* collected many proverbs from literary works in many languages created and developed in numerous countries around the world.[2] Notably, Confucian works, and especially canonical texts in the ancient Confucian tradition, were not missing from his collection, but formed a substantial and significant part of the comparative proverbial literature in the *ONBP*.[3] This chapter's main aim is to identify and describe the worldview reflected in the classical Confucian proverbs selected and quoted in SCM's *ONBP*. As Confucian proverbs in general within his work were culled from

---

[1] For a discussion of the historical development of humanism in the West, see Bullock 1985.

[2] For further details about SCM's linguistic studies in the *ONBP*, consult Chapters 12 and 13 in this volume.

[3] According to Lauren Pfister, about 13% of all citations in the *ONBP* are from Chinese sources, and though these included some Daoist and a few Chinese Buddhist sayings, most were from either canonical Confucian scriptures or Confucian-related texts. Some non-canonical Chinese works were cited by SCM as well, as discussed in Chapter 6 in this volume. For details about the statistics of Chinese sources in the *ONBP*, consult Pfister 2012, p. 19, footnote 31.

a relatively wide range of Chinese sources, amounting to over twenty different major titles, it is not feasible to treat them all in detail here. Rather, I intend in this chapter to focus on the proverbs drawn by SCM from the classical set of Confucian scriptures called *Sishu* 四書 (Four Books): *Lunyu* 論語 (Analects), Mengzi 孟子 (Mencius), *Daxue* 大學 (Great Learning) and *Zhongyong* 中庸 (Doctrine of the Mean).[4] To be more precise, in this chapter I will seek to reconstruct and study the specific worldview mirrored in those proverbs selected and rendered into English by SCM from the Confucian *Sishu* for the sake of comparing their claims with those of biblical proverbial wisdom. By this means I also intend to demonstrate and argue that this ancient Confucian worldview manifested a clearly religious dimension and, therefore, it can be better understood as a kind of religious humanism. Although the term "religious humanism" itself is open to diverse interpretations,[5] we may define classical Confucian humanism as religious humanism in the sense that it is opposed to any kind of secular humanism which denies the possibility of transcendence.

In order to accomplish this task, I must first explore and explain several preliminary matters that will lead us ultimately into our discussion of that ancient Confucian worldview, one that can be identified and reconstructed from the quotations provided by SCM within his *ONBP*.

1.1 On the Nature of Proverbs

Etymologically speaking, the word "proverb" has a Latin origin, "proverbium," and is a combination of the prefix, "pro" ("before," or "in front of") and the word, "verbum" ("word"). In this sense, then, a proverb, should be regarded as an important saying "noted from the beginning," that is, a saying that should be taken as basic material for pursuing more detailed studies into the nature of human wisdom in any particular cultural context. Wolfgang Mieder, a contemporary authority of the study of proverbs, defines the term in a way that can be summarized as follows: A proverb is a short, generally known sentence produced and popularized by a group of people using the same language, a saying which contains wisdom, truth, morals, and traditional views expressed in metaphorical, literary, fixed and memorizable forms, so that they can be handed down from generation to generation.[6]

From this account we can see that Mieder's definition identifies a few prominent aspects belonging to the class of sayings we should identify as proverbs. He highlights that the essential character of any proverb lies not merely in its stylistic form,

---

[4] SCM used what we might now consider to be non-standard English titles to refer to these works, including *Lunyu* (Analects) and *Mengchi* (Mencius).

[5] The term "religious humanism" has also been used to refer to the kind of humanism which opposes traditional expressions of religion. Typical examples of this form of humanism have been published in the *Humanist Manifesto I* (1933) and *Humanist Manifesto II* (1973). These two manifestos first appeared in *The New Humanist* and *The Humanist* respectively, but can also be found in Lamont 1993, pp. 285-300. In this article, the term "religious humanism" denotes a humanistic philosophy which embraces the concept of transcendence.

[6] Following definitions provided by Mieder 1993, p. 24.

but also in its conveyance of wisdom, truth, morals and traditional values. Similarly, the *Collins Cobuild English Language Dictionary* defines a proverb as "a short sentence that people often quote and that gives advice or tells you something about human life and problems in general."[7] Another dictionary defines a proverb as "a brief epigrammatic saying that is a popular byword; an oft-repeated pithy and ingeniously maxim."[8] These various definitions point to the important fact that proverbs are not just ordinary sayings or famous quotations, but reveal details that touch on many aspects of wisdom for living. Indeed, proverbs are so significant in many cultures because they highlight principles or clever sayings that enhance and direct those who desire to live well and wisely. Precisely in this way, the biblical book of Proverbs is constituted to a large degree as a collection of sayings and teachings about human morality and living wisely; according to the main themes developed in one commentarial account of the messages found within that book of Proverbs, there are found within it many contrastive and creative Hebrew sayings dealing with the nature of wisdom and folly, God and humans, humility and pride, wealth and poverty, as well as the most basic categories of life and death, while also addressing various aspects of marriage and family life, friendship, justice/righteousness, sexual morality, ways of speaking properly and wisely, and insights into a host of emotional displays that portray hints about a person's character and integrity.[9] Therefore, it is not far off the mark to say that proverbs are short sayings that are concerned about wisdom for life that usually include advice and insights into moral, ethical and/or spiritual realms. As proverbs are usually short and easy to remember, they are also easy to disseminate in numerous ways (such as teaching, sharing advice, clever sayings in story-telling, plays, popular literature, and modern media), and so create inter-generational intellectual and spiritual influences that can have profound and even transformative social impacts. In cultures found across many parts of our world – located in the so-called East and West as well as North and South of our planet – people across the ages have used orally-transmitted, written, and printed collections of proverbs to communicate and help guide others in solving problems they face in everyday life as well as other more unusual circumstances.

Obviously, SCM was convinced of the cross-cultural value of proverbs, knew of their presence in many cultures, and was interested in the ways they portrayed wisdom for living well. As has been documented elsewhere in this volume, he had begun working on a personal project of comparing other traditions of proverbial

---

[7] Quoting from *Collins Cobuild Advanced Learner's English Dictionary* 2006, p. 1150.

[8] Cited from *Webster's Third New International Dictionary of the English Language* 1963, p. 1827.

[9] In one summary statement David Atkinson observes that various sections of the biblical book of Proverbs involve sayings not only related to "the foundational values of love, justice and the fear of the LORD," but also "the more practical values associated with family, marriage, health, security and the use of the tongue" (Atkinson 1996, p. 144). There are other aspects of the book of Proverbs that distinguish some of its sayings by their use of natural symbols and observations of animal, plant and insect life to portray wisdom for human life.

lore with those found in the biblical book of Proverbs since his college years at Oxford, and he kept up this interest and expanded his studies in this realm during the rest of his life for a period of nearly sixty years. In his Preface to his *ONBP*, SCM mentioned clearly that "the Hebrew title of the book of Proverbs means not only proverbs, properly so called, but in general also parables, fables with a moral; apologues, couplets on moral subjects; maxims, aphorisms, riddles, etc."[10] By this means SCM underscored that his own understanding of the Hebrew title of the biblical text involved a much more flexible conceptual account of proverbs that could involve different styles of expression and even other literary genres. Whatever these differences in style or genre involved, SCM knew very well that the most distinctive content of proverbs was concerned with wisdom that dealt with many moral and spiritual matters.

1.2 On the Diversified Nature of Confucian Proverbs

There are many kinds of Confucian proverbs. Because the Confucian tradition with its long history and rich content exercised extensive influence especially within East Asian communities,[11] its ideas, concepts and values especially penetrated different levels of those Asian communities. As has been seen in an earlier chapter in this volume, SCM was aware of and quoted classical proverbs from Confucian canonical sources, but also was aware of at least three popular collections of wisdom proverbs that included those drawing upon different Confucian values. This is consistent with the broader cultural impact of Confucian education, self-cultivation, and their attendant values in those Asian communities.

Recognizing that Confucianism was not limited in its influences to the educated elite, it is important to note that the main tradition as well as many sub-traditions were also expressed in popularized proverbs that formed one of the traditional Chinese literary genres. For example, one collection of popularized Confucian aphorisms that was apparently not known to SCM, but was published during the later Ming dynasty, was *Caigentan* 菜根譚 (The Vegetable Root Discourses), authored by Hong Yingming 洪應明 (1573–1620). In fact, the *Caigentan* embodied wisdom drawn from all the three major trends of traditional Chinese thought – Confucianism, Buddhism, and Daoism (a synthetic option referred to during this period as *sanjiao heyi* 三教合一, or the "unity/harmony/unification of the three teachings") – and so included sayings related to the Confucian virtue of self-cultivation, Daoist and Buddhist concepts of enlightenment, as well as their doctrines that promoted returning to simplicity and the "unadorned truth."[12] Consequently, wisdom in *Caigentan* is actually a mixture of the three ideological systems mentioned above, being one special expression of a philosophy of life that has influenced Asian communities greatly in its own distinctive ways, and still thrives in China today. So, we can see that Confucian ideas have been popularized through these proverbs as well and are

---

[10] Quoted from *ONBP*, vol. 1, p. iii.

[11] As claimed in Shun – Wong 2004, p. 1.

[12] As promoted in Hong Yingming 2003, p. 19.

still very much used in Chinese daily conversations. Therefore, a somewhat detailed study of any of these varieties of Confucian proverbs can reveal important elements in the influence and character of Confucianism at any particular period of traditional and post-traditional Confucian societies.

1.3 Explaining the Scope of this Study

Within this chapter the reader will find neither a special treatment of the life of SCM nor a general study of Confucian traditions. Instead, this chapter has the rather limited intention of reconstructing and elaborating a worldview manifested within the classical Confucian proverbs cited in SCM's *ONBP*. Apparently SCM himself had hoped to accomplish such a broad ranging comparative interpretation of the quotations he cited within the *ONBP* from over fifty different linguistic corridors, but he died within a year after finishing the last volume of that major work, and so never was able to offer something containing this sort of interpretive richness. In this regard, then, this chapter offers a small contribution to that kind of cultural discussion, and so could be extended by others into Hebrew-Confucian comparative cultural studies. In this light, then, my choice to pursue this specialized topic is not arbitrary. In fact, the most direct way of studying SCM's life and works would be to study his whole corpus instead of looking at the *ONBP* alone.

Still, it must be added that this study is complicated by the very nature of the *ONBP*, because it is mainly a collection of proverbs from different civilizations accompanied by very limited commentary and comparative interpretation. The text as a whole was not intended to be a specialized study focused on a few general issues; instead, it provides a collection of proverbs, apothegms, and short stories or depictions that parallel or sharply contrast with themes addressed in the biblical book of Proverbs. In some sense it is a kind of source book for cross-cultural studies of proverbial wisdom, constituted mostly by quotations from sources in more than fifty languages, all rendered into English for the sake of the Anglophone audience it was intended to address. As a result, it is quite naturally difficult to use the *ONBP* to figure out a clear picture of SCM's own thought.

It is equally difficult to study the nature of Confucianism from SCM's work, even though he had cited several hundred quotations from Confucian classical texts. Notably, the passages SCM cited from the Confucian *Sishu* (Four Books) were not intended to show a complete and accurate picture of ancient or classical Confucianism; rather, as already mentioned, they were selected to illustrate, highlight or contrast certain principles, aspects, and themes found in the biblical book of Proverbs. Consequently, it is not possible to argue for a comprehensive Confucian worldview or even a general account of Confucian traditions from the Chinese Confucian proverbs SCM selected.

Taking all these issues into consideration, my purpose here is to elaborate certain aspects of the worldview illustrated by SCM's selection of Confucian proverbs. Because those Confucian proverbs found in *ONBP* come from a relatively wide variety of Chinese texts, it is not possible to treat them all in one study. Instead, this chapter will confine its scope of investigation to those proverbs and sayings taken from the Confucian *Sishu*. Though the *Sishu* were actually four separate works in the ancient Chinese past, they were taken collectively as a whole, becoming an independent four-fold *opus* starting from the 12th century (or the latter years of the Southern Song Dynasty), and so were often taken by so-called Neo-Confucians of that period to be a coherent and singular set of Confucian Classics that contained within it a standard Confucian worldview. It was in fact largely this Neo-Confucian sub-tradition that SCM encountered when he studied Confucian texts and their commentaries. Not only did he consult quite often the commentarial works of Zhu Xi 朱熹 (1130–1200) on the *Sishu*, that Confucian scholar being the creator of the *Sishu* during his career, and so a seminal representative of Neo-Confucian traditions, he also actually possessed a whole set of (*Zhuzi quanji* 朱子全集 (The Complete Works of Master Zhu [Xi]), a set that is still in the Oriental Division of the Bodleian Libraries in Oxford. These suggest further reasons for focusing on those quotations he chose from the *Sishu* and published in the English version of the *ONBP*, all for the purpose of reconstructing a coherent worldview, as far as that is possible, from the selection of classical Confucian quotations SCM used.

1.4 Methodological Considerations and the Concept of Worldview

Paul Ricoeur (1913–2005) has advocated the idea of the autonomy of any text in his hermeneutic theory.[13] This autonomy is not a total independence: it does not banish the author, and by implication, the original context and original audience, to irrelevance. Rather, it refers to the importance of active interpretations by varying people in different generations, signifying the text's escape from the finite horizon lived in by its author. Working with such an assumption, I will not seek to conceive of a text without SCM and will explore the nature of the classical Confucian worldview that is not confined to SCM's own commitments, but one that is reflected in and refracted from the Confucian proverbs SCM selected.

The study of worldview is an important approach advocated especially by the late British scholar of religious studies, Ninian Smart (1927–2001). Nevertheless, I will not be following Smart's famous account of "worldview" that requires a suspension of judgment about the truth of various belief systems, accompanied by a methodological consideration that seeks "the neutral, dispassionate study of different religious and secular systems."[14] Rather, I use the word to refer to the framework of ideas and beliefs through which an individual, group or culture interprets the world and interacts with it. A worldview is often a network of presuppositions which is not verified by rigorous justifications but can be verified by means of human experience. The very nature of wisdom sayings, such as seen in the proverbs we are studying here, matches up well with the nature of a worldview, because they regularly reveal how ancient Chinese persons, as well as many others in later generations, have been guided to interpret their lifeworld and how they become engaged in lived relationships due to that interpretation of their culturally-loaded understanding of reality.

---

[13] See Ricoeur 2016, pp. 159-183.

[14] Cited from Smart 1999, p. 14.

Therefore, it is feasible to illustrate the worldview found within the Confucian proverbs cited in SCM's work. Still, before I offer an account of those Confucian proverbs, some brief account of SCM and his work on the biblical book of Proverbs is necessary.

2. Solomon Caesar Malan and His *Original Notes* *on the Book of Proverbs*

Since proverbs generally are simultaneously very useful and provocative rhetorically, people seek to understand and make use of them in different ways. Scholars like Aristotle tried to study them in their own right, so that his scholarly effort eventually started a discipline later known as "paremiology," that is, "the study of proverbs." Consequently, those scholars who have attempted to collect proverbs from various linguistic sources belong to a related discipline, one where collecting and grouping these sayings together is technically referred to as paremiography. SCM is unquestionably one of the most important scholars in the history of paremiography. His monumental work, *ONBP*, that was published in three volumes from 1889 to 1893, is huge and complicated; it relates a large selection of relevant proverbs from different languages and civilizations to those sayings found in the biblical book of Proverbs. So, before we proceed any further, it is relevant and wise to offer some brief account of SCM and his *ONBP*, though readers can also refer to other chapters in this volume to study other dimensions of his life and the creation, development, and publication of this major work in greater detail.[15]

2.1 The Man: Solomon Caesar Malan

Born in Geneva, SCM was by birth a Swiss citizen descended from an exiled French family, whose father, Dr. Henri Abraham Caesar Malan (1787–1864) enjoyed a great reputation as a Protestant divine.[16] SCM himself later became a British citizen and Anglican vicar, becoming a well-recognized orientalist scholar (especially as a translator of Middle Eastern, Eastern European and Asian texts) during his lifetime.

As described by his son, Arthur Noel Malan, in his biographical work about his father, "Dr. Malan's claim to distinction rests mainly upon his pre-eminence as an Oriental scholar. In him profound linguistic ability was combined with an insatiable eagerness for knowledge […]."[17] SCM manifested his talent for languages already during his youth. At the age of eighteen, he had already made notable progress in his studies of Sanskrit, Arabic and Hebrew.[18] At the age of 21, when he was

---

[15] For interested readers, please consult Chapter 13 in this volume, where detailed analyses of both the *ONBP* and the ONBP Ms are provided.

[16] A through account of SCM's father and the family in which he grew up is provided in the first chapter of this volume.

[17] Quoted from *SCM DD*, Preface, p. v.

[18] Consult "Malan, Solomon Caesar," *The 1911 Encyclopedia Britannica,* vol. 17, p. 461. Viewed at https://en.wikisource.org/wiki/1911_Encyclop%C3%A6dia_Britannica/Malan,_Solomon_Caesar (accessed May 20, 2021).

accepted as a university student at St. Edmund Hall, Oxford, he was still in the process of learning English in depth, and so he petitioned the matriculation examiners to allow him to use either French, German, Spanish, Italian, Latin or Greek to take the examination instead of English. By that age, then, he felt confidence in working in six other European languages besides English, indicating the degree to which he was a true polyglot.

After his university graduation in 1837, SCM travelled to India working there as a lecturer at Bishop's College.[19] Before his return to England in 1840, he had also laid the linguistic foundations for working with Chinese and Tibetan texts. Fifteen years later, in 1855, SCM published a work dealing with the theological terminology employed in contemporary Chinese Christian renderings of the Bible, entitling the work *Who is God in China: Shin or Shang-te? Remarks on the Etymology of Elohim and of Theos, and on the Rendering of Those Terms into Chinese*.[20] Having worked in India for nearly three years, his ability to learn different languages and understand various religions was all the more highlighted.[21] Therefore, SCM's knowledge about Chinese language and religions was not merely at an amateur level, but had developed to the point in the 1850s that he could participate in contemporary theological debates related to the Chinese translation of biblical texts.

2.2 The Book: *Original Notes on the Book of Proverbs*

Equipped with varying levels of his mastery of a remarkable multitude of languages, SCM pursued a life-long project of collecting proverbs from different traditions, initiated during his student years at Oxford as an act combining spiritual devotion, intellectual curiosity, and critical discernment. Such a life-long effort finally developed in the 1880s into what became the published English version of *ONBP*.[22]

By applying his knowledge of so many languages, the contents of SCM's *ONBP* followed this line of thought: he sought, among other things, to bring to his readership an understanding of the biblical book of Proverbs that was as close to the original meaning of the Hebrew text as far as he could discern it. For instance, in explaining "To know wisdom and instruction; to perceive the words of understanding,"[23] he started his explanation by providing the original meaning of the word in Hebrew for "wisdom":

---

[19] See Chapter 2 in this volume for many details about his time in Bishop's College.

[20] *WIGC*.

[21] Throughout his life, he continued his learning in languages, to the point of mastering some extremely difficult languages such as Georgian, Armenian, and Coptic. As noted already in Chapter 5 of this volume, SCM ultimately completed numerous translation works from foreign languages into English, all accomplished after he returned to England from India in the early 1840s.

[22] For further details about the nature and formation of the *ONBP*, please see Chapters 12 and 13 in this volume.

[23] See *ONBP*, vol. 1, p. 3, quoting the KJV of Proverbs 1:2.

Wisdom, [ḥakmah,²⁴ written in Hebrew] is originally "skill," and [ḥakam, another Hebrew term] "skilful" – *hoion Pheidian lithougon sophon* [written in Greek, and then rendered in English] as we call Phidias a clever [wise] sculptor; only signifying thereby that "*sophia – aretē technē esti* [written again in Greek, and then rendered in English] wisdom is the virtue [or merit, excellence] of art," says Aristotle.²⁵

Having made these initial claims, SCM went on to describe the meaning of the equivalent terms in Zoroastrian and Arabic texts, as well as Ciceronian Latin and Tibetan Buddhism. But even this did not complete his analysis of wisdom; he added to these claims further notes on philological parallels found in Anglo Saxon, German, Sanskrit, Latin and Greek languages.²⁶ Following Aristotle, SCM argued that wisdom implied order and judgment, and so possesses dimensions that are both intellectual and spiritual. Citing Cicero and a Tibetan text at that point, he compared their accounts of wisdom to biblical claims, for "real wisdom" is presented as "the right judgement in all things of a ready mind, wrought in us by the one principle of love and fear of God."²⁷ Notably, SCM adds, the wisest do all this "without deliberation."²⁸

With his expansive knowledge of so many different languages and cultures that were generally unknown by most of his Anglophone contemporaries, SCM sought out points of comparison of the biblical conception of wisdom with various other conceptions in Asian cultures, but also including among them the concept in ancient Chinese. So, in the same setting mentioned above, SCM located where Confucius spoke about wisdom. He noted that "'In teaching men,' says Confucius, 'always inculcate these five virtues: *jin*, humanity, *agapē* [written in Greek]; *i*, justice; *li*, propriety; *chi*, wisdom; and *sin*, faithfulness.'"²⁹ These five virtues are now identified in contemporary Chinese as *ren* 仁, *yi* 義, *li* 禮, *zhi* 智, and *xin* 信, indicating how very different the 19th century transcriptions employed by SCM are from our 21st century usage.³⁰ Frustratingly, after offering this citation, SCM did not offer any further explanation of the parallel between *ḥakmah* and its Chinese equivalent *chi* (*zhi*), but by means of this basicmethod of simply quoting relevant sources, SCM could at least confirm that wisdom – however it was conceived – was prized by Confucius as one of the five most noble virtues. Still, before we seek to

---

24 The "ḥ" symbol represents a guttural consonant in Hebrew that is differentiated from a soft "h" sound in English.

25 See *ONBP*, vol 1, pp. 3-4.

26 As found in *ONBP*, vol. 1, pp. 3-4.

27 Quoted from *ONBP*, vol. 1, p. 4.

28 *Ibid*.

29 *Ibid*.

30 For those who read the *ONBP* in detail, it will be found that SCM's transcriptions of key Chinese characters were not only different from our 21st century standard transcriptions, but also were inconsistent within the three volumes of the *ONBP* itself. So, there is a need to read the text carefully as well as in comparison with the Chinese standard texts he cites, requiring quite a bit of labor for the diligent student.

reconstruct the worldview manifested in SCM's selection of classical Confucian proverbs in the *ONBP*, it is also obligatory on my part to introduce briefly the nature of Confucian traditions and then provide some general account of the character of Confucian proverbs.

3. Confucianism and Confucian Proverbs

SCM collected proverbs from various traditions and quoted Confucian texts quite extensively. One of the reasons is the high reputation Confucianism enjoyed in Europe because of the promotion of some Enlightenment scholars such as Gottfried Wilhelm Leibniz (1646–1716) and Christian Wolff (1679–1754).[31] Clearly, SCM added to European and Anglophone readers' awareness of the extent to which Confucian proverbs addressed themes of shared wisdom with the biblical book of Proverbs even in spite of major cultural differences between Golden Age Jewish culture and classical Confucian culture. In order to underscore these points, I will now proceed to offer general depictions of the Confucian school and their classical Confucian proverbs.

3.1 The Confucian School

According to *The Cambridge Dictionary of Philosophy*, "Confucianism" is defined as "a Chinese school of thought and set of moral, ethical, and political teachings usually considered to be founded by Confucius."[32] Robert Audi, the author of that article, continued to elaborate on the nature of Confucianism by focusing on its ethical and political aspects, and its development in the line of different Chinese Confucian thinkers, including Mencius (Mengzi 孟子, ca. 372–289 BCE), Hsün Tzu (Xunzi 荀子, ca. 310 – ca. 255 BCE), Tung Chung-shu (Dong Zhongshu 董仲舒, 179–104 BCE), Han Yü (Han Yu 韓愈, 768–824), Chu Hsi (Zhu Xi), and Wang Yang-ming (Wang Yangming 王陽明, 1472–1527). Yet, the nature of Confucianism in fact deals with much more than a summary of basic themes and notable scholarly figures. Here below I will summarize some of the fundamental commitments that are shared by all expressions of Confucianism across its more than 2,500 years of cultural history in China, Korea, Japan, and Vietnam.

3.1.1 Self-Transformation

Confucianism does have its ethical and political aspects, however, both of them should not be considered to be the core elements of the major Confucian tradition. Yao Xinzhong has described the major tradition in the following manner:

> The Confucian tradition is both a tradition of literature and a way of life. [...] [Confucianism is] not only the philosophic discussion of human nature, but also devoted to self-transformation in relation to one's spiritual and cultural destiny.[33]

---

[31] As asserted in Ching – Oxtoby 1992.

[32] Quoting from Audi 1999, p. 173.

[33] Cited from Yao Xinzhong 2000, p. 11.

In this light, then, it should be underscored that "self-transformation" is a core dimension of Confucianism. If there is one concept that should be selected as the cornerstone of Confucianism, we have no doubt to say that it must be *ren* 仁 (variously rendered as "cultured humaneness," "benevolence," or simply "humaneness"). All other concepts in Confucianism are built upon this fundamental concept of *ren*.

Confucius (Kong *fuzi* 孔夫子) repeatedly taught that *ren* is a humaneness manifested in a sincere heart and a devoted spirit, so that it became an essential element within all rituals, political life, and every social relationship. With regard to rituals and music, he taught that "[I]f a person lacks humaneness (*ren*) within, then what is the value of performing rituals? [And] if a person lacks humaneness within, what is the use of performing music?"[34] In response to his best student, Yan Hui 顏回, Confucius explained *ren* in the following manner: "To subdue one's self and return to propriety, is perfect virtue. If a man can for one day subdue himself and return to propriety, all under heaven will ascribe perfect virtue to him."[35] To another disciple named Fan Chi 樊遲, Confucius explained the same concept in a different way, reflecting the need of that student: "It is to love *all* men."[36] In Confucius' view, the performance of good and proper behavior without *ren* is not possible, if it is to be truly "good and proper." So, he argued, if politicians or people in high positions have *ren* in their hearts, those people under their authority will follow their good conduct, and their society will be able to maintain a harmonious cultural environment. On the basis of these explanations and justifications, then, self-transformation to a humanely cultivated person (*ren ren* 仁人) is the true cornerstone of Confucianism.

3.1.2 Transforming Society

Though self-transformation is a core teaching within Confucian traditions, Confucius' teaching does not focus merely on individual growth and development. To re-establish humane social order was also one of his great concerns during his lifetime, when war and chaos was too often experienced. As suggested in the quotations above, transforming society cannot be accomplished without self-transformation. According to Cheng Chung-ying, "To Confucius and his followers a good society and a righteous government must start with and hence be founded on the moral perfection of the human person."[37] More precisely, it is the perfectibility of humans

---

[34] The author's rendering of *Lunyu* 3:3; see also Legge 1893a, p. 155 for an alternative translation.

[35] Quoting from Legge 1893a, p. 250, *Lunyu* 12: 1.

[36] Here citing *Lunyu* 12:22, as translated in Legge 1893a, p. 260. Italics in the original. The use of italics in Legge's translation here is not a matter of emphasis, but indicates that the word italicized is not found directly in the Chinese standard text. This should be assumed also in all subsequent quotations from Legge's English renderings.

[37] Quoted from Cheng Chung-ying 2004, p. 124.

– that is, the possibility that they may become morally exemplary – that is the foundation for a stable and humane society in Confucius' viewpoint.

In the *Lunyu* (Analects), we can see that the ideal society of Confucius relies on both the cultivation of people in high positions as well as those among the common people.

> Let your *evinced* desires be for what is good, and the people will be good. The relation between superiors and inferiors is like that between the wind and the grass. The grass must bend, when the wind blows across it.[38]

The stability of the society is built on the premise that the people in high positions behave properly and with sincere hearts, so that the common people will be influenced by their good conducts accordingly. The phrase, "people in high positions" (*zai shang wei* 在上位)[39] refers not merely to those holding political power; it literally means "those who take seats in the upper level." It can therefore refer to anyone who is respected by others and so is offered a seat of honor among them. Such a person may be an elderly member of a family, or a person of social status respected by others. The reason they are considered to be culturally important is because they offer good examples for the younger generation to learn and follow. The effectiveness of learning by following good moral examples is highly praised in the classical Confucian tradition. If a person is moved by these moral examples and is willing to follow them, he or she will eventually also become a moral person who may even be exemplary as well. Consequently, the effectiveness of moral lessons is contrasted positively in ancient Confucian teachings of the *Lunyu* and the *Mengzi* with the use of external coercion by punitive laws.

> The Master said, "If the people be led by laws, and uniformity sought to be given them by punishments, they will try to avoid *the punishment*, but have no sense of shame. If they be led by virtue, and uniformity sought to be given them by the rules of propriety, they will have the sense of shame, and moreover will become good."[40]

Leading society by virtuous conduct and rules of propriety would prompt common people to have a sense of shame, because they may identify themselves with such a humane figure and so become self-conscious of their failing to reach the moral quality exemplified by those involved with governance. In this way social chaos is devalued, because it can never harmonize the common person with those in governance when self-cultivation is their shared standard for the good life. Therefore, we can see that self-cultivation is the key to the transformation not only of oneself, but also of broader society.

---

[38] Quoting from the latter half of *Lunyu* 12:19, found in Legge 1893a, pp. 258-259. Italics in original.

[39] As seen in the *Zhongyong* (The Doctrine of the Mean *or* The State of Equilibrium and Harmony) 14, Legge 1893a, p. 395.

[40] Cited from *Lunyu* 2:3, Legge 1893a, p. 146, italics in original.

3.1.3 The Classical Works of Confucianism

According to the introductory section of one of the last chapters in the *Shiji* 史記 (Records of the Grand Historian), it is claimed that

> All the Six Arts (*liu yi* 六藝) help in governance. The *Book of Rites* (*Li* 禮) helps to regulate men, the *Book of Music* (*Yue* 樂) brings about harmony, the *Book of History* (*Shu* 書) records incidents, the *Book of Poetry* (*Shi* 詩) expresses emotions, the *Book of Changes* (*Yi* 易) reveals supernatural influence, and the *Spring and Autumn Annals* (*Chunqiu* 春秋) shows what is right.[41]

These in fact were the classical works Confucius used to teach his disciples. Subsequently, these books have been regarded as cultural standards for learning in Confucian traditions. The main reason that these books were considered to be "classics" is that some scholars believed Confucius had participated in the editing, annotating, and compiling of all of these scriptures. For example, Chen Lifu believed that

> Confucius edited the *Book of Songs*, and the *Book of History*, compiled the *Book of Rites*, and the *Book of Music*, annotated the *Book of Changes*, and wrote the *Spring and Autumn Annals*. These were called the Six Classics.[42]

Later on, other classical works were also added to this list of Confucian classics.[43] However, the *Lunyu*, the *Mengzi*, the *Daxue* and the *Zhongyong*, which together are known as the "Four Books," ultimately replaced the Five Classics (*wujing* 五經) as basic educational standards starting in the Southern Song dynasty (about the

---

[41] 六藝於治一也。禮以節人，樂以發和，書以道事，詩以達意，易以神化，春秋以義。 The translation is by this author. For the Chinese standard text, consult https://ctext.org/shiji/hua-ji-lie-zhuan/ens (accessed March 10, 2021). The text comes from the initial paragraph of the 126th *juan* of the 130 *juan* in the *Shiji*, a selection of which Burton Watson translated as "The Biographies of Wits and Humorists" ("Huaji liezhuan" 滑稽列傳). Though Watson did not translate this section, one can get a sense of the content of the whole *juan* by viewing his selection about the dwarf jester in the Qin court, Actor Zhan, from this portion of the *Shiji*. See Sima Qian 1993, pp. 215–216.

[42] Quoted from Chen Lifu 1972, p. 2.

[43] Besides these six classical texts, there were also some other works that over time have been viewed as classics within the long and extensive development of Confucian traditions. Ancient works such as the *Lunyu* and the *Xiaojing* 孝經 (Book of Filial Piety) were viewed as Confucian classics in the Later Han dynasty. Yao Xinzhong has described clearly the whole development of the "Classics of Confucianism" (Yao Xinzhong 2000, p. 57): "Taken as the textbooks in the Tang Dynasty (618–906 CE), the 'Nine Classics' were inscribed on stone tablets, namely, the *Book of Changes*, the *Book of History*, the *Book of Poetry*, the three commentaries on *the Spring and Autumn Annals*, the *Rites of the Zhou*, the *Rites of Etiquette and Ceremonial*, and the *Book of Rites*. The Nine Classics later became the Twelve Classics by taking in three more books, namely, the *Book of Filial Piety*, the *Analects of Confucius* and *Er Ya*. In the Song Dynasty (960–1279 CE), the *Book of Mengzi* was added to the Twelve Classics so that the 'Thirteen Classics' was finally established, which has been used as the standard collection of the Confucian classics ever since."

end of the 12th c. CE), and so became the most representative works of the mainline Confucian tradition.[44]

4. The Worldview Reflected in the Confucian Proverb Chosen by S. C. Malan

The Confucian quotations SCM selected in his *ONBP* form a picture that reflects some key features of Confucianism. The ideas of a "superior man" or "gentleman" (*junzi* 君子) and "holy man" or "sage" (*shengren* 聖人),[45] including how these people should act, form some of the most important foci of all the quotations selected by SCM from the Confucian *Sishu*. In fact, a relatively careful but brief review of all the Confucian proverbs cited in the *ONBP* reveals that at least 89 quotations (some of them repeated in different contexts) are directly related to these two concepts (sometimes including both concepts in a single quotation).[46] Taken statistically, those 89 quotations constitute nearly 17% of the full number of quotations from the *Sishu* found in the *ONBP*,[47] suggesting that the prominence of the presence of discussions and comments about the *junzi* and *shengren* in the *Sishu* impressed SCM enough that nearly every fifth quotation from the *Sishu* in the *ONBP* involved direct references to them.[48]

---

[44] As claimed in Sano Kōji 1988.

[45] Normally in 21st century renderings in European languages of the term *shengren*, the vast majority use the term "sage" or "wise man" or their equivalents. Nevertheless, Roman Catholic renderings in French and Latin, especially in earlier texts, rendered the term as the equivalent of "saint" (though the translations of the Four Books [*Les quatres livres*) in both languages by Séraphin Couvreur (1835–1919) systematically used the equivalents for "sage" (*le sage*) and "the most wise man" / *summe sapientissimus vir*). For examples, consult Couvreur, 1895, *Lunyu* 9:6 (p. 164) *Mengzi* 2A:2 (p. 366), 7B:25 (p. 641), *Zhongyong* 11 (p. 34), 27 (p. 57) and 31 (p. 62). While Protestants generally used the term "sage" and its equivalents, there was one exception: the Lutheran missionary, Richard Wilhelm (1873–1930 quite often rendered the term within both Confucian and Daoist classical texts in German also with the equivalent for "saint" or "saints" (*die Heiligen*). (See especially Wilhelm's very influential German rendering of the *Yijing: Das Buch der Wandlungen*.) SCM was aware of earlier Roman Catholic precedents in this regard, and so changed his renderings of key terms such as this one (as will be seen in what follows) according to the context, as far as he could understand it.

[46] Among these 89 quotations, 38 come from the *Zhongyong* (29 referring to *junzi*; 9 to *shengren*), 44 from the *Lunyu* (40 referring to *junzi*, 4 to *shengren*); 4 from the *Mengzi*, and 3 from the *Daxue*.

[47] Within the whole of the three volumes of the *ONBP*, there are 532 quotations from the *Sishu*: 274 from the *Lunyu* (or just over 51% of the total); 112 from the *Zhongyong*, 84 from the *Mengzi*, and 62 from the *Daxue*. The quotations directly referring to the *junzi* and *shengren* constitute 16.7% of all these quotations cited in the *ONBP*.

[48] The emphasis here is on "direct references," but it should be noted that there are also probably another 90 quotations referring to quotations in which Confucius is describing the virtues of his disciples, or of his own character and habits, as well as other quotations in which disciples describe qualities of their master. These certainly were relevant to any questions related to the qualities that distinguished *junzi*, and when in reference to Confucius, they were con-

Nevertheless, it would be generally true also to say that the concern for knowing situations accurately and truly, and becoming an educated person with wisdom and morality, seemed to be among the most important threads connecting most of the seemingly scattered and unrelated quotations of Confucian proverbs in the *ONBP*, precisely because they paralleled many similar emphases in the biblical book of Proverbs. How a human being relates to reality in these contexts is of paramount concern. Therefore, it would be helpful to explain briefly the Confucian notion of "transcendence" as exemplified in SCM's selections before we go deeper into the discussion on sages, saints, and gentlemen (that is, *junzi*).

4.1 Confucian Notions of Transcendence

There are more than thirty times that classical Confucian proverbs cited by SCM make direct references to the realm of transcendence, that is, proverbs from the *Sishu* that mention Heaven (*tian* 天),[49] Heaven and Earth (*tiandi* 天地),[50] as well as ghosts and deities (*guishen* 鬼神).[51] This realm is also sometimes referred to as the *Dao* (*Tao* 道) or "the Way," though that term can refer to many other ways besides those identified with transcendence.[52] In this regard, it is significant to note that the mention of transcendent beings in the biblical book of Proverbs that are referred to besides the dominant Hebrew deity named "Yahweh" (often translated in English versions as "the LORD") are minimal. While this name for the Hebrew deity occurs

---

sidered qualities of a sage or *shengren*. So, when including both direct and indirect references to these concepts from quotations taken from the *Sishu* and appearing in the *ONBP*, they come close to involving a third of all those quotations. Further study of the other 24 Chinese sources cited in the whole of the *ONBP* – including other Confucian scriptures, some Chinese collections of more popular wise sayings, and a few collections of literary idioms published in bilingual format by missionary-scholars – would certainly reveal even more citations involving these major concepts, but that range of study goes beyond my current focus of attention in this chapter.

[49] As a substantive called by SCM regularly as "Heaven," *tian* appears 15 times in *ONBP*. It also is used adjectively to describe something heavenly, such as the "heavenly mandate," "a heavenly knight" and "heavenly way," but these instances are not included here.

[50] This phrase referring to the whole of the natural order – as so generally seen as including something beyond the planet, but not necessarily including anything as extensive as what might be called "the universe" in the 21st century – occurs only three times in the *ONBP*. See *ONBP*, vol. 1, p. 23; vol. 2, p. 349; vol. 3, p. 268.

[51] This phrase appears 15 times in the *ONBP* and includes in its conception all levels of spiritual beings.

[52] SCM seemed to be aware of the different ways the term *Dao* could be portrayed, and so in varying contexts referred to it not only as "the Way," but also in other contexts as "the right way," "right principles," "good order," a particular person's "way," and even the "rule of conduct." Three out of the fifteen times it appears in the *ONBP*, SCM is dealing with *tiandao* 天道, which should definitely be seen as a reference to this realm of transcendence. SCM renders that phrase variously as the "Tao of Heaven," "Heaven's Way" and the "Way of Heaven" (found in SCM *ONBP*, vol 1, pp. 22, 364, and 474 respectively).

85 times in the book,⁵³ there are also whole chapters in the biblical book of Proverbs where it does not appear,⁵⁴ or where it appears only once.⁵⁵ Other conceptual terms of reference for the deity occur only seven times in the whole 31 chapters of that biblical book.⁵⁶ Intriguingly, though SCM had discussed the question of the appropriate terms in Chinese for the biblical God, he only once mentioned the term *shangdi* 上帝 ("Lord on High" or "Supreme Lord") within his quotations and notes in the *ONBP*.⁵⁷ Beyond this, the mention of "heaven and earth" only occurs once,⁵⁸ and only one time does the metonym "Heaven" represent the deity.⁵⁹ There is no mention of ghosts, but there is one saying where the "spirits of the dead" – a phrase which includes meanings overlapping with the Chinese conception of *gui* 鬼 – are referred to.⁶⁰ Consequently, it would be valuable to continue to ask about what prompted SCM to identify or link up these passages in Confucian texts with certain passages among the Hebrew proverbs, but this will not be done here.

In SCM's work, the most frequently quoted and retranslated section from the *Sishu* on the realm of transcendence comes from Chapter 16 of the *Zhongyong*.⁶¹ It is a uniquely emphatic description of the impact of spirits on human beings, nothing like its content being found elsewhere in the whole of the *Sishu*. Notably SCM not only found the passage but referred to it three different times within the *ONBP*,⁶²

---

53 According to a concordance for the New International Version of the English Bible, "The LORD" (YHWH or "Yahweh") occurs 18 times in the first nine chapters of the biblical book of Proverbs, 46 times in Chapters 10 through 20, and 21 times in Chapters 21 through 31. Consult Kohlenberger 2015, p. 702 for the details and p. 1406 for the Hebrew term (H3378).

54 Specifically, Chapters 4, 7, 13, 26 and 27.

55 Specifically, once again, Chapters 2, 5, 9, 23, 25 and 31.

56 The general term for deity (*ᵉlohim*) occurs five times within the whole of the biblical book of the Proverbs, while its philologically more basic term, *'ēl*, as well as a more poetic form of that basic term, *'ēloah*, both only occur once within the whole biblical text.

57 See *ONBP*, vol. 1, p. 123, in reference to the *Zhongyong* 19.

58 Found in Proverbs 25:3.

59 Seen in Proverbs 30:4. The same Hebrew term appears three other times in the text, but refers to the physical sky in all of those cases.

60 As cited in Proverbs 2:18.

61 子曰：「鬼神之為德，其盛矣乎。視之而弗見；聽之而弗聞；體物而不可遺。使天下之人，齊明盛服，以承祭祀。洋洋乎，如在其上，如在其左右。詩曰：『神之格思，不可度思，矧可射思？』夫微之顯。誠之不可揜，如此夫。」 *Zhongyong* 16. This passage reads in Legge's version reads as follows: "The Master said, 'How abundantly do spiritual beings display the powers that belong to them! We look for them, but do not see them; we listen to [*sic*], but do not hear them; yet they enter into all things, and there is nothing without them. They cause all the people in the kingdom to fast and purify themselves, and array themselves in their richest dresses, in order to attend at their sacrifices. Then, like overflowing water, they seem to be over the heads, and on the right and left *of their worshippers*. It is said in the Book of Poetry, 'The approaches of the spirits, you cannot surmise; – and can you treat them with indifference?' Such is the manifestness of what is minute! Such is the impossibility of repressing the outgoings of sincerity!" Cited from Legge 1893a, pp. 397-398. Italics in the original.

62 The passage appears in whole or in part in *ONBP*, vol. 1, p. 21; vol. 2, pp. 309 and 360.

rendering sections of it in various ways. The full citation in SCM's main English version goes as follows:

> Spirits, what virtue [power], and how great! You look, but you cannot see them; you listen, but you do not hear them; they are in the substance of things, and cannot be separated from it. They cause men appareled everywhere to offer them sacrifices. Those spirits are a countless host on the right hand and on the left.[63] One knows not when they draw near. Were it better if they were treated slightly? Their subtleness [invisibility] is evident; the truth [perfection] of it cannot be hid.[64]

Comparing SCM's various renderings of this passage to that of the Scottish Sinologist, James Legge (1815–1897), it is possible to notice differences that reveal some of the flexible qualities, as well as some of the shortcomings, of SCM's approach to the translation of this Chinese passage.[65] Nevertheless, there is no question that this passage presents an unusually direct account of the influences and capacities of ghosts and deities within the classical Confucian worldview. It clearly struck SCM's memory as an unusual passage that deserved the repeated references he made to it.

Because of the all-powerful nature of the Way, humans cannot live separately from it. The Way is always with us. But the problem is that human beings do not always follow the Way, to the point that some regularly neglect or oppose it. Since according to Confucian teachings humans possess the free will to decide either to follow the course of a *junzi* or become an unworthy person, it is up to each human to determine whether they will follow and promote the Way or not.

---

[63] This sentence is presented in different renderings in the two other places where the passage is mentioned. In *ONBP*, vol. 2, p. 309, it reads, "They [the spirits] are like the waves of the ocean around us, immense, infinite! They are as it were above, they are as it were on the right hand and on the left." Subsequently, he retranslates the last sentence seen above as "The spirits! On the right hand and on the left, worship them as if they were present" (*ONBP*, vol. 2, p. 360). The former rendering is a more detailed attempt to capture the imagery of the passage, though in the latter portion the rendering is more liberal in its interpretation; the latter is only a brief selection but adds the verb "worship" and focuses on the peoples' responses, where the text describes how they are present to those offering sacrifices to them.

[64] Cited from *ONBP*, vol. 1, p. 21. This English version is worth comparing to Legge's rendering found in n. 56 above.

[65] Most notably as a shortcoming, SCM did not apparently realize that within this passage there was a citation from an ancient classic, referred to in Legge's rendering as the *Book of Poetry*. Nevertheless, while Legge's translation is more verbose, one sees how SCM sought to craft his English into a terse style that reflected the style of the Chinese original. Also, in the one section that he rendered three times, SCM (like Legge) was willing to explore other ways of portraying the meaning of the sentence in English, manifesting a high degree of flexibility. Also, in the earlier section, the unstated subject is rendered by Legge as "we," but SCM prefers "you," making the rhetorical aspect of the passage more provocative for the reader. Had SCM referred to Legge's rendering when he added the verb "worship" to his final version of that one retranslated sentence? Perhaps.

4.2 Confucian Values Promoting Sincerity and Faith

When responding positively to the realm of the transcendent as presented in the Confucian classics, human beings should demonstrate "faith/faithfulness" (*xin* 信) and "sincerity" (*cheng* 誠). A well-known saying illustrating Confucius' attitude towards rituals and sacrificing that also reveals his teaching regarding these attitudes is presented in *Lunyu* 3:12. Recognizing this, SCM cited the passage four times in the *ONBP*,[66] sometimes with interpretations that aligned the claims within the passage more easily to an explicit Jewish monotheistic worldview.[67] This passage in Legge's rendering states that the Master

> "sacrificed *to the dead*, as if they were present. He sacrificed to the spirits, as if the spirits were present." The Master said, "I consider my not being present at the sacrifice, as if I did not sacrifice."[68]

The importance of "being present," or the highlighting of his attentiveness during these events, clearly opposes any superficial formality in performing rituals and sacrifices. Rather, Confucius emphasized an attitude of sincerity in one's spiritual cultivation. As it is stated in *Zhongyong*, there is nothing left if there is no sincerity (*bu cheng, wu wu* 不誠無物).[69] Sincerity, therefore, can be summarized as being the inner state of mind required for cultivation, growth, and self-transformation. To be sincere is to be wholly involved in ritual expressions,[70] while simultaneously being free from self-deception.

---

[66] Found in *ONBP*, vol. 1, p. 21 (where the passage is attached to a previous saying, but not given a footnote), and p. 279; also vol. 3, p. 44 (where it appears amid quotations from a series of passages that constitute most of *Lunyu* 3:11-13) and p. 159 (where it is wrongly ascribed to represent *Lunyu* 3:18).

[67] In his renderings of this passage (*Lunyu* 3:12), several times he rendered the term *shen* 神 in the singular and with the first letter capitalized, translating it as "the Spirit" (*ONBP*, vol. 1, 21 and vol. 3, p. 159), and one time as "Deity" (*ONBP*, vol. 3, 44). The term for sacrifice (*ji* 祭) is regularly translated as "worship," adding especially to the parallels with the Jewish sacrificial system. When these Confucian proverbs are found in the context of his discussion of "the fear of the LORD" (Proverbs 1:7, *ONBP*, vol. 1, p. 21) or "the LORD" (Proverbs 5:21b and 23:17 as in *ONBP*, vol. 1, p. 279 and vol. 3, p. 159), the plurality of "the spirits" in regular Confucian practice (which SCM does refer to elsewhere, and in other contexts) is essentially lost.

[68] Quoting from Legge 1893a, p. 159. Italics in original.

[69] Legge renders this sentence as "Without sincerity, there would be nothing." See Legge 1893a, p. 418, from the midst of *Zhongyong* 25.

[70] Intriguingly, SCM does capture this attitudinal emphasis of being "wholly involved" in *ONBP*, vol. 3, p. 44. He renders *Lunyu* 3:12 there in the first-person plural, which is not explicit in the Chinese version, as "In all events, we ought to worship as in the presence of Deity, and give ourselves wholly to the act of worship; otherwise it is no worship at all."

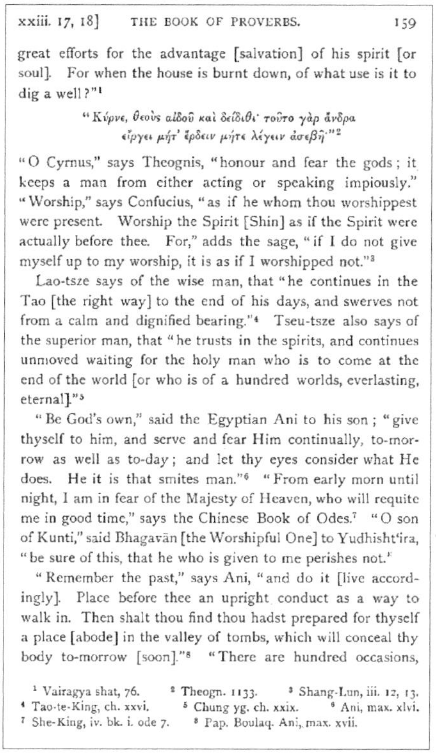

Fig. 13: *ONBP*, vol. 3, p. 159 (Prov. 23: 17-18), Chinese sources (footnotes 3-5, 7)

4.3 Differing Conceptions of the "Superior Man" and "Sages"

SCM also was aware of the differences between the "superior man"[71] or *junzi* (transcribed as *kiün-tsze*[72] and most often translated as "wise man,"[73] but also "the good man,"[74] "the wise and good man"[75] and "the honourable man"[76]) and sages or *shengren* (transcribed as *shin-jin*[77] and most often translated as "holy man,"[78] sometimes as "saint,"[79] and at least one time also as "holy man [or sage]"[80]). In one of the

---

[71] A rendering appearing 18 out of 75 times that *junzi* appears in the quotations from the *sishu* within the *ONBP*.

[72] As found eight times in the *ONBP*, often with one of his preferred English translations.

[73] Used 30 times out of the total 75 times that *junzi* appears within those quotations.

[74] Found six times.

[75] Used eight times.

[76] Translated in this manner six times.

[77] As found in *ONBP*, vol. 1, p. 69.

[78] Out of 14 times the term is found in the *ONBP*, 12 times SCM uses this rendering.

[79] Seen only twice in *ONBP*, vol. 1, pp. 69 and 461.

[80] Where only the single term, *sheng*, appears in the Chinese standard text, but is used twice in a passage, the first one being translated with this English rendering (in *ONBP*, vol. 1, p. 67).

passages from the *Zhongyong* that SCM cited more than once,[81] the Confucian sages possess great powers that appear to be mystical powers of extraordinary status.[82] The late Lee Chair Professor Julia Ching (1934–2001) had argued successfully that the classical Confucian concept of "sage" referred to Sage Kings who were shaman-kings supposed to possess certain kinds of mystical powers.[83] But eventually, this mystical dimension was very much overshadowed in later Confucian traditions by a more humanistic vision that emphasized one's moral and ethical achievements.[84]

Nevertheless, a Confucian sage is still often taken to be a person with a high level of moral and spiritual cultivation, usually manifested as being capable of attaining a great harmony (*taihe* 太和, or "ultimate harmony") or achieving centrality in an advanced stage of equilibrium (*zhonghe* 中和).[85] This is exactly where the difference between a sage and a superior man lies. Even though wise, good, and superior humans may possess great virtues, they may not be able to attain this stage of equilibrium. The stage of great harmony can only be achieved through complete moral and spiritual cultivation; the achievement of this centrality in an advanced stage of equilibrium leads to an optimal cosmic order that allows the myriad things to all achieve their proper positions and functions.[86]

4.4 The Classical Confucian Notion of "Cultivation"

In spite of their differences, both sages and wise/superior men according to the classical Confucian texts need to maintain a good connection with the transcendent. To attain and subsequently maintain this connection, "cultivation" is necessary.

One seeks the virtue of Heaven not outwardly, but in relationship to Heaven directly. A Confucian adept should seek inwardly from the depths of the human mind-and-heart to attain heavenly virtues. As is clearly stated in one classical Confucian proverb, all the four Confucian cardinal virtues are rooted in the human mind-and-heart (*ren yi li zhi gen yu xin* 仁義禮智根於心).[87]

In this regard SCM did not always comprehend these particular claims related to classical Confucian understandings of self-cultivation. One should point out that some "creative translations" occur within the *ONBP* in this sphere of the classical

---

[81] *Zhongyong* 27 (see Legge 1893a, pp. 422-423, cited in *ONBP*, vol. 1, pp. 69 and 461.

[82] In a passage not cited by SCM, the sage is described as knowing things before they occur or to "foreknow" (*qianzhi* 前知) things, and so being "like a spirit" (*ru shen* 如神). For these English translations, see Legge 1893a, pp. 417-418.

[83] Consult Ching 1997, "Son of Heaven: Shamanic Kingship," pp. 1-34.

[84] Claimed in Ching 1997, "The Moral Teacher as Sage: Philosophy Appropriates the Paradigm," pp. 67-98.

[85] As presented in *Zhongyong* 1. Consult Legge 1893a, pp. 384-385.

[86] As described in *Zhongyong*, at the end of Chapter 1, found in Legge 1893a, p. 385.

[87] See the final section of the *Mengzi* 7A:21. In Legge's rendering of the whole saying, "What belongs by his nature to the superior man are benevolence, righteousness, propriety and knowledge" (Legge 1893b, p. 460).

Confucian worldview. When reflecting on the difficulties of moral and spiritual cultivation, SCM rendered a passage from *Lunyu* 7:3[88] in the following manner:[89]

> Virtue alone is not able to keep men from evil. Those who hear of righteousness are unable to follow it, and the wicked are not able to alter their course. It is a grief to me.

Checking the standard Chinese text reveals that the first sentence in SCM's rendering above is not a literal translation from the Chinese, but appears to be more like a comment or reflection upon Confucius' saying in that context. In fact, it should not be presented as being part of the Chinese text and his translation. This lack of fidelity to the standard texts by SCM deserves further critical assessment.

From the original context, it is not clear what the occasion was when Confucius made this comment. However, commentators regularly interpret the passage from the perspective that Confucius is making this remark to teach his disciples four important ways of cultivation: namely, practice cultivation, discuss what has been learned, follow righteousness, and correct wrongdoings. Instead of merely expressing a lamentation about his own weakness in being unable to keep himself from evil, Confucius is teaching his disciples ways of attaining success in cultivation. Both SCM's comments and JL's rendering of this passage suggest an affirmation of the weakness of human moral ability, while the mainline Confucian interpretation of this same proverb suggest something quite different. After all, traditional Confucianism regularly places much faith in the good inclinations of human beings, to the point that in the context of Neo-Confucian metaphysics, they talk about the "original goodness" of human nature. SCM's comment contains a distrust of human nature that is quite alien to this mainline interpretation of Confucian tradition. This questioning of human nature is also reflected in another of SCM's renderings of a different Confucian saying: "I have not yet seen one man love virtue as he loves pleasure."[90] However, other classical Confucian proverbs suggest a more positive judgment of human beings. "'If a man,' says Confucius, 'will bend his will towards

---

[88] The Chinese text is: 德之不修, 學之不講, 聞義不能徙, 不善不能改, 是吾憂也. This passage is rendered by Legge as, "The Master said, 'The leaving virtue without proper cultivation; the not thoroughly discussing what is learned; not being able to move towards righteousness of which a knowledge is gained; and not being able to change what is not good: – these are the things which occasion me solicitude.'" See Legge 1893a, p. 195.

[89] Cited from *ONBP*, vol. 1, p. 6. Several things should be noted about this passage and its annotation in this location. First, SCM renders the passage as a description of others and not of Confucius himself, as found in Legge's rendering (that is consonant with Chinese commentaries) seen in the previous footnote. Secondly, the second Chinese phrase is dropped out by SCM, probably inadvertently. Finally, the footnote has only "c. vii" or "chapter 7," so that the precise location of the proverb (*Lunyu* 7:3) cannot be easily found by those who are not accustomed to this form of general reference.

[90] Cited from *ONBP*, vol. 2, p. 472. The standard Chinese text is 子曰: 吾未見好德如好色. This passage reads in JL's version as follows: "The Master said, 'I have not seen one who loves virtue as he loves beauty'" (see Legge 1893a, p. 222).

virtue, he will abstain from evil.'"[91] In this proverb, the capacity of humans' will power is more highly regarded. It may be inferred that, according to the worldview manifested in these proverbs, while the limitations of human beings are noted, the power of human beings to carry out self-transformation is still positively asserted.

But it would be wrong to think of such a transformation as confined within one's own self. Rather, part of the first paragraph of *Daxue* – which asserts an ever-expanding set of realms of personal cultivation involving familial, national, and global concerns[92] – is cited four times in the *ONBP*.[93] As the immediate realm of cultivation outside of one's self is the family, Confucians of all ages and dynasties have regularly emphasized the importance of familial relationships and their related virtues, writing extensive commentaries and books on those various relationships. Notably, then, there are more than a couple dozen classical Confucian proverbs dealing with familial relationships quoted and referred to within the *ONBP*. Among them, a good number of them are about filial duties, a topic that was considered so significant that a later Confucian text was devoted to its elaboration, and given the name, *Xiaojing* 孝經 (Book of Filial Piety).[94]

5. Concluding Remarks

Having worked through the three volumes of the *ONBP* to identify the proverbs quoted from the *Sishu*, I have faced a number of challenges in working with SCM's text. As other chapters in this book clarify in greater detail, in some ways the *ONBP* was not only SCM's *magnum opus*, but also somewhat of an unfinished and inconsistent work. That is to say, while the *ONBP* brought together parallels and anti-proverbs from a range of cultures and literatures unsurpassed in his own day, SCM's presentation and accounts of classical Confucian proverbs do also provoke a number of research challenges for the 21st century Sinological scholar. There are times SCM's English renderings are brilliant and insightful,[95] but other times there

---

[91] As cited from *ONBP*, vol. 1, p. 253. The Chinese standard text is 子曰：苟志於仁矣，無惡也. JL's rendering is even more strongly worded, "The Master said, 'If the will be set on virtue, there will be no practice of wickedness'" (see Legge 1893a, p. 166).

[92] See this chain of "eight steps" in Legge 1893a, pp. 357-359.

[93] The full "eight steps" were never referred to completely by SCM. Instead, he dealt with only selected parts of those steps, and sometimes also adding notes from special commentaries on that classical Confucian text. In *ONBP*, vol. 1, p. 77, he only referred to the will and the heart (steps 3 and 4), while in *ONBP*, vol. 1, p. 434, SCM referred to four of the steps in a sequence (the nation, the institution [family], the personal self, and the heart). One time he referred to the commentary of the Song Confucian scholar, Zhu Xi, on "rectifying the heart" (*ONBP*, vol. 1, p. 242), and another time he gave commentaries by Master Cheng (*Chengzi* 程子) on the four steps mentioned above (but reversing the order of the "heart" and "personal self," as found in *ONBP*, vol. 2, pp. 718-719).

[94] For an English rendering of the whole text of *The Classic of Filial Piety*, see Legge 1879, pp. 449-488. Legge's transcription of the title is "Hsiao King."

[95] Consider the following six cases for their brevity and style, in comparison to the renderings of JL: *Lunyu* 2:12 君子不器. "The accomplished scholar is not a utensil" Legge 1893a, p. 150); "An honourable man is no common thing" (*ONBP*, vol. 2, p. 66). *Lunyu* 9:4 子絕四,

are a number of peculiar problems in how he rendered those sayings. Sometimes, and not often, but at certain points, he simply missed the meaning of the ancient Chinese sayings. Other times, he presents them in ways that are difficult to locate in the standard Chinese versions of the *Sishu*. In addition, how he referred to those passages in the extensive footnotes found at the bottom of each page in the *ONBP* are at times complicated and inconsistent. For all of these reasons, then, some comments in this conclusion about the nature of the *ONBP* text as it portrays these classical Confucian proverbs are worth presenting to those who are yet uninitiated in reading SCM's monumental work.

For those aware of the problems of deciphering transcriptions of Chinese characters in texts written by European and North American missionary-scholars and Sinologists, the inconsistencies in the various systems create a number of quandaries. Since SCM was reading those materials in a number of languages, the inconsistencies between various transcribed names that he read, the terms he himself transcribed using his preferred system, and what is now in the 21st century considered to be the standard – the mainland *Pinyin* transcription system – are numerous and sometimes highly problematic.[96]

In working as I have done to identify the Chinese source texts related to specific English quotations found in the *ONBP*, there are some problems within the texts that require some discernment, but also at times some diligence in figuring out exactly what SCM had done. The fairly common manner in which SCM cited a

---

毋意，毋必，毋固，毋我. "[Confucius] had no forgone conclusions, no arbitrary predeterminations, no obstinacy, and no egoism" (Legge 1893a, p. 217) "Confucius [...] was free from four things: he had no 'will,' no 'must,' no 'shall,' and no 'I' (*ONBP*, vol. 1, p. 121). *Lunyu* 14:29 君子恥其言而過其行. "The superior man is modest in his speech, but exceeds in his actions" (Legge 1893a, p. 2860); "The superior man, however, is [ashamed] reserved in his words, but he surpasses them in his actions" (*ONBP*, vol. 2, p. 498). *Lunyu* 15:26 巧言亂德. "Specious words confound virtue" (Legge 1893a, p. 302); "Crafty words disturb virtue" (*ONBP*, vol. 3, p. 361). *Lunyu* 15:34 子曰：當仁，不讓於師. "The Master said, 'Let every man consider virtue as what devolves on himself. He may not yield his performance of it *even* to his teacher'" (Legge 1893a, p. 304); "Hold fast virtue," says Confucius, "do not yield in anything opposed to it – no, not even to your teacher" (*ONBP*, vol. 1, p. 140). *Zhongyong* 2 君子中庸，小人反中. "The superior man *embodies* the course of the Mean; the mean man acts contrary to the course of the Mean" (Legge 1893a, p. 386); "The good man keeps invariably to the middle path of virtue [righteousness]; the vulgar transgress it" (*ONBP*, vol. 3, p. 476).

[96] Most of the transcriptions SCM employed came close to following JL's early transcription system, and so they are generally able to be deciphered by someone who knows the standard Chinese and is experienced in working with texts in European languages about China from the 19th century in particular. For those who are not aware of these problems, the identification of certain names and/or concepts may be very difficult. Two examples, both of which involve errors in the English transcription of Chinese names and titles, are illustrative of what these problems are like. In one passage, the disciple of Confucius named Jilu 季路 is inappropriately transcribed as "Kee-Too"; in another, the title of a respected scholar and teacher in classical Confucian texts is *fuzi* 夫子, but it is transcribed as "Hoo-tsze," making it sound like a name of a particular "Master." Find these in *ONBP*, vol. 3, p. 4 and Vol. 1, p. 67 respectively.

passage was to take a small sentence from a much larger section within the *Sishu*, and then to cite it by the sectional numbering system that had been developed by notable sinologists such as JL in his *Chinese Classics*. So, for example, when referring to the "nine thoughts" that distinguish a wise man (*junzi*), SCM in one place refers only to the fifth item, and in another only to the eighth.[97] The reference is to the same passage in the *Lunyu*, but one must search carefully to identity the particular saying within that passage that is actually quoted in the *ONBP*. In another passage he quotes only one out of four pieces of advice to a disciple,[98] and in still another, only the second of "three joys" (*san le* 三樂) that typifies a cultivated scholar's (*junzi*) life.[99] A more difficult situation occurs for a diligent researcher when SCM cites a small passage in a much longer section of a Chinese classic, such as when he translates only a single sentence from the fifth paragraph in the tenth chapter of the *Zhongyong*, but refers to the passage only by the chapter number.[100] There are dozens of such passages from all language sources within the *ONBP*, and a sizeable number that use this technique for translating and annotating quotations SCM culled from the *Sishu*.

Sometimes what is found within the *ONBP* is more like a paraphrase than a literal translation,[101] where in other cases there is an arbitrary or unintentional deletion of part of the passage.[102] In one case it is found that a saying is said to be given by "Confucius," but in fact it comes from his disciple, Zengzi 曾子.[103]

More frustrating are the few times that the passage SCM cites is incorrect. The vast majority of these relatively minor mis-citations can be properly discovered by reading nearby verses in standard English renderings or by means of the Chinese text itself, but a few remain unidentifiable. Sometimes the form of notation, following

---

[97] This is in reference to *Lunyu* 16:10. See *ONBP*, vol. 1, p. 363 and vol. 2, pp. 595-596. For cross-references that make the problem even more clear, see Legge 1893a, p. 314.

[98] See *Lunyu* 2:18, and its related quotation in *ONBP*, vol. 1, p. 627.

[99] Cited from the *Mengzi* 7A:20 (as found in Legge 1893b, pp. 458-459) and quoted *ONBP*, vol. 3, p. 164.

[100] Found in *ONBP*, vol. 3, p. 247, with the full passage found in Legge 1893a, p. 390.

[101] See three examples in *ONBP*, vol. 1, p. 451; vol. 2, p. 497; and vol. 3, p. 44, dealing with *Lunyu* 2:10, 13:3, and 3:11-13 (though cited as 3:18) respectively. For comparison, check Legge 1893a, pp. 149, 263-264, and 158-159 respectively.

[102] In one case SCM skips over the middle of the three main stays in the first section of the *Daxue* (*ONBP*, vol. 1, p. 69, in contrast to Legge 1893a, p. 356); in another case he unexplainedly skips over one phrase in the middle of the passage in the *Zhongyong* (*ONBP*, vol. 1, p. 461, revealed by comparing it with Legge 1893a, pp. 422-423.

[103] As seen in *ONBP*, vol. 2, p. 177, *Lunyu* 8: 5 (compare Legge 1893a, p. 210).

precedents in Chinese literature, cites only the chapter of a section where there are many verses,[104] but more often the citation numbering is simply wrong.[105]

All these textual challenges make studying SCM's presentation of these classical Chinese proverbs more complex. Whether or not similar problems occur in the other texts coming from texts written in more than fifty other languages would have to be determined through a collaborative research project where all relevant languages can be read by various persons in that research group.

Some concluding statements can now be made about the classical Confucian proverbs identified and considered by SCM in his *ONBP* and reviewed in this chapter.

It is clear that SCM's selection of classical Confucian proverbs from the *Sishu*, though limited in number, has already been successful in demonstrating the humanistic nature of the classical and pre-imperial periods of Confucianism. While the emphasis on the capacity of human beings to make meaningful moral achievements is properly asserted, he also points out that the fallibility of human beings is also noted within them. It is not difficult to recognize, therefore, that SCM's choices of Chinese proverbs that hinted at human fallibility undoubtedly echoed the basic evaluation of the status of human nature in Christianity and, to some extent, also within classical Hebrew proverbial literature.

Significantly, then, SCM's selection of classical Confucian proverbs also reveals that classical Confucian traditions were not supporting merely a secular humanist worldview, but instead they emphasized the importance of a person's relationship with transcendence or transcendent beings. In this regard, several summary points can be highlighted.

---

[104] For example, within the first citations from the *Lunyu* (*ONBP*, vol. 1, p. 5), only chapter 20 of the *Lunyu* is cited, when the actual quotation comes from 20:3, but there are three relatively long passages that constitute the chapter. More challenging is the citation of the twelfth chapter of the *Lunyu* in an anomalous manner ("xii, p. 10," as if it comes from a particular page), but it is in fact from the first saying in that chapter (12:1), while the whole chapter consists of 24 sayings (see *ONBP*, vol. 2, p. 243).

[105] Some are merely one verse off, discovered by following a text like Legge's of the same work (such as in *ONBP*, vol. 1, p. 67, where he cites *Lunyu* 9:5 when it should be 9:6). Sometimes the numbering of such passages is a problem caused by references to different translations of the *Lunyu*, but most of these times are simple mistakes. Far more troublesome are the citations that are relatively far off from the actual location of the quotation, and so only those who have more than average familiarity with the Chinese texts and at least one of their standard renderings, or have access to concordances or other research tools related to these texts, will be able to locate their actual sources. For example, in relationship to the *Lunyu*, SCM makes a number of disorienting mis-citations: he cites *Lunyu* 1:2 when it should be 1:8 (*ONBP*, vol. 3, p. 382); *Lunyu* 3:18 when it is actually most of the connected passage from 3:11-13 (*ONBP*, vol. 3, p. 44); *Lunyu* 14: 16, when it actually is 4:16 (and so an additional "1" was inadvertently printed, (*ONBP*, vol. 1, p. 477); *Lunyu* 14:42 when it is actually 14:45 (*ONBP*, Vol. 2, p. 53); *Lunyu* 15:2 when it should be 15:26 (and so the last number was inadvertently missed, *ONBP*, vol. 3, p. 361). Other examples are related to citations from the *Zhongyong*. In one place SCM cites chapter 20 when it should be chapter 6 (*ONBP*, vol. 2, p. 326); in another, chapter 14 when it should be chapter 16 (*ONBP*, vol. 3, p. 246); and in still another, chapter 23 when it should be chapter 33 (*ONBP*, vol. 3, p. 207).

First of all, some of those classical Confucian proverbs reveal an emphasis on the necessarily close relationship with and communication between cultivated human beings and the transcendent realm. It signifies a classical worldview in which spirituality, much more than speculative philosophy, occupies a dominant place. Seen from this perspective, SCM's selection of classical Confucian proverbs reveals the ancient Confucian emphasis on cultivation, faith/faithfulness and sincerity that continued to have a cultural influence for more than two millennia within Confucian-influenced societies.

It is clear from SCM's collection of these sayings that ancient pre-imperial Confucian scholars valued self-cultivation not merely for the advancement of their own personal growth, but also for the betterment of their society and larger realms of human communities. In other words, SCM realized that classical Confucianism advocated a balanced emphasis on the importance of self-transformation, familial and social transformation, and even conceived of what might be called "world-transformation." SCM's selections from *Daxue* in particular demonstrated clearly this expanding realm of interests within the classical Confucian concern for cultivation.

What is even more important within this chapter's discussion is SCM's realization that classical Confucian cultivation is not limited to the betterment and growth within only the human realm. Rather, he demonstrated how it manifests a deep acknowledgement of the transformative capacities of the realm of transcendence. As has been indicated above, the great power of Heaven (*tian*) as well as ghosts and spirits (*guishen*) is underscored several times from an important passage SCM found in the 16th chapter of the *Zhongyong*. Within this passage SCM revealed a particular transcendent dimension within the pursuit of sagehood. It refers not merely to moral advancements, but also to a special kind of transformation that is not simply confined to human persons and their relationships in their contemporary societies. Rather, this passage points to a communal transformation that aims at not only the transformation of self and society, but ultimately includes the transformation of the universe. Therefore, it is clear that the nature of the classical Confucian worldview reflected in SCM's selection of proverbs from the *Sishu* manifests a religious humanism that affirms and engages the realm of transcendence. Notably, this is a perspective that has sometimes been denied, or simply overlooked, in late 20th century and early 21st century studies of classical Confucian texts.[106] Consequently, it is a valuable contribution to the continued studies of these ancient works and their attendant worldview.

---

[106] For documentation of this secular and sometimes explicitly anti-religious interpretive bias, consult Ames – Hall 2001. For alternative translations and interpretations, consult Plaks, 2003 and Johnston – Wang 2012. For another resource for the critique of this modern secularists' approach to classical Confucian texts, including specific reference to interpretations in contemporary Chinese settings, consult Pfister 2009, pp. 53-65, and *id*. 2010, pp. 29-59.

Select Bibliography

Ames, Roger T. – David L. Hall. 2001. *Focusing the Familiar: A Translation and Philosophical Interpretation of the Zhongyong*. Honolulu: University of Hawai'i Press.

Atkinson, David. 1996. *The Message of Proverbs: Wisdom for Life*. Leicester, England and Downers Grove, Ill.: Inter-Varsity Press.

Audi, Robert. 1999. *The Cambridge Dictionary of Philosophy*. 2nd ed. New York: Cambridge University Press.

Bullock, Alan. 1985. *The Humanist Tradition in the West*. New York – London: W.W. Norton.

Chen Lifu. 1972. *The Confucian Way: A New and Systematic Study of the 'Four Books'*. Trans. Liu Shih Shun. Taipei: The Commercial Press.

Cheng Chung-ying. 2004. "A Theory of Confucian Selfhood: Self-Cultivation and Free Will in Confucian Philosophy." In: Shun – Wong 2004, pp. 124-147.

Ching, Julia. 1997. *Mysticism and Kingship in Ancient China: The Heart of Chinese Wisdom*. Cambridge – New York: Cambridge University Press.

Ching, Julia – Willard G. Oxtoby. 1992. *Discovering China: European Interpretations in the Enlightenment*. Rochester, N.Y.: University of Rochester Press.

Collins Cobuild Advanced Learner's English Dictionary. 2006. Ed. John Sinclair. Glasgow: HarperCollins.

Couvreur, Séraphin (trans. and comm.). 1895 [1992]. *Les quatres livres avec un commentaire abrégé en Chinois: une double traduction en français et en Latin, et un vocabulaire des lettres et des noms propres*. 5th ed. Taipei: Kuang-ch'i Press.

The Encyclopedia Britannica. 11th ed. Cambridge – New York: Cambridge University Press.

Hong Yingming. 2003. *Tending the Roots of Wisdom*. Trans. Paul White. Beijing: New World Press.

Johnston, Ian – Wang Ping (trans. and comm.). 2012. Daxue *and* Zhongyong*: Bilingual Edition* Hong Kong: The Chinese University Press.

Kohlenberger, John R. III (ed.). 2015. *NIV Exhaustive Bible Concordance*. Grand Rapids: Zondervan.

Lamont, Corliss Lamont. 1993. *The Philosophy of Humanism*. 7th ed. New York: Continuum.

Legge, James. 1879. *The Sacred Books of the East: The Texts of Confucianism, Part I*. Oxford: Clarendon Press.

———. 1893a [1960]. *The Chinese Classics, Vol. 1: Confucian Analects, The Great Learning, and the Doctrine of the Mean*. 2nd ed. Hong Kong: Hong Kong University Press.

———. 1893b [1960]. *The Chinese Classics, Vol. 2: The* Works *of Mencius*. 2nd ed. Hong Kong: Hong Kong University Press.

Mieder, Wolfgang. 1993. *International Proverb Scholarship: An Annotated Bibliography, with Supplements*. New York: Garland.

Pfister, Lauren F. 2009. "Testing the Modern Chinese Secularists' Mirage: Hermeneutic Blind Spots in Justifying Master Kong's Irreligiosity." *minima sinica* 2009/2, pp. 53-65.

———. 2010. "Trumping the Myth of Ruist Secularity: The Missiological Significance of Independent Evidence about Theistic Yearnings among Chinese Literati in the Ming and Qing Dynasties." *minima sinica* 2010/1, pp. 29-59.

———. 2012. "A Swiss Polyglot's Discovery about the Chinese Search for Wisdom: Solomon Cæsar Malan's (1812–1894) Comparative Philosophical Contributions in His *Original Notes on the Book of Proverbs*." *minima sinica* 2012/1, pp. 1-52.

Plaks, Andrew H. 2003. Ta Hsüeh *and* Chung Yung: *The Highest Order of Cultivation, and On the Practice of the Mean*. London: Penguin.

Ricoeur, Paul. 2016. "The Model of the Text: Meaningful Action Considered as a Text." In: John B. Thompson (trans. and ed.), *Hermeneutics and the Human Sciences: Essays on Language, Action and Interpretation*. Cambridge – New York: Cambridge University Press, pp. 159-183.

Sano Kōji 佐野公治. 1988. *Shishogakushi no kenkyū* 四書学史の研究 (A Study of the History of the Learning of the Four Books]. Tōkyō: Sōbunsha.

Shun Kwong-Loi – David B. Wong (eds.) 2004. *Confucian Ethics: A Comparative Study of Self, Autonomy, and Community*. Cambridge – New York: Cambridge University Press.

Sima Qian. 1993. *Records of the Grand Historian: Qin Dynasty*. Trans. Burton Watson. Hong Kong – New York: Columbia University Press.

Smart, Ninian. 1999. *Worldviews: Crosscultural Explorations of Human Beliefs*. 3rd ed. Upper Saddle River, New Jersey: Pearson.

Webster's Third New International Dictionary of the English Language. 1963. Ed. Philip Babcock Gove. Springfield, MA: Merriam-Webster.

Wilhelm, Richard. 1924. *I Ging: Das Buch der Wandlungen*. Jena: Eugen Diederichs.

Yao Xinzhong. 2000. *An Introduction to Confucianism*. Cambridge – New York: Cambridge University Press.

8

MALAN'S MANJURICA

Loretta E. Kim

1. Introduction

At the present time "Manjuristics" is a relatively small field, but one that is also highly diversified. Scholars in East Asia, North America, and Europe pursue studies of various topics, including Manchu linguistics, literature, history, and culture. Often known as "Sinologists," or "China specialists," or perhaps only by their disciplinary identities, scholars of Manjuristics come together for international conferences that reflect their national, cultural, and academic heterogeneity. Bibliographies of their collective scholarship also embody the profound breadth of work carried out by a proportionately small number of individuals.[1]

Manjuristics' long-standing reputation as an obscure but vibrantly expanding discipline partially stems from the fact that contemporary academics show less interest in and possess less knowledge of the Manchu language, especially when compared to other East Asian languages such as Chinese and Japanese. Even Mongolian, its cousin in the Tungusic language family, carries more weight in international academia. As in the cases of the European classical languages today, Latin and Greek, Manchu has become a language that is studied, but its use as a medium of producing original scholarship is rarely found. Also, since many Manchu-language texts are bilingual or multilingual, it has not been considered a primary language required to pursue many research topics related to Manchuria. While a certain number of scholars have cultivated strong traditions of teaching Manchu in greater China, Japan, Europe and North America during the twentieth and twenty-first centuries, factors such as institutional support, access to Manchu-language archival documents, and student interest based on career prospects have generally limited their ability to heighten Manjuristics' profile and influence.

Therefore, it is striking that the nineteenth-century divine Solomon Caesar Malan included Manchu among the languages in the published version of his *Original Notes on the Book of Proverbs*. Although it is imaginable that as a polyglot who achieved varying degrees of literacy in over fifty languages, SCM purposefully designed the parameters of this work to encompass a wide selection of common and rare languages, with Manchu fitting into the latter category, it is still remarkable that among all possible choices, Manchu would attract his attention. His son, Arthur Noel Malan, also took notice of his father's knowledge of Manchu, as well as

---

[1] Exemplary works are found in Giovanni Stary's four volume work produced over a number of years, entitled *Manchu Studies: An International Bibliography* (Wiesbaden: Harrassowitz, 1990–2003), and Yan Chongnian's 阎崇年 bibliography, *Ershi shiji shijie Manxue zhuzuo tiyao* 20 世纪世界满学著作提要 [Abstracts of 20th century International Scholarship on Manjuristics] (Beijing: Minzu chubanshe, 2003).

Mongolian, and cited both among the languages of original source texts that SCM used in the *ONBP* within the biography that he wrote of his father. There ANM added the praise that an anonymous writer for the *Oriental Review* had expressed: "Few readers will be able to gather from the simple and unpretending references at the bottom of each page the marvellous extent of Oriental reading which has furnished the author with parallel passages from the vast literature of the East."[2]

SCM's knowledge of Manchu and Mongolian, as displayed in his handwriting of phrases in these two languages, was impressive. Although several Europeans preceding him could assert their mastery of reading these Tungusic scripts, no clear evidence remains that they could write them. Even in China, from the Qing dynasty (1644–1912) onward, most individuals able to read and write Manchu and Mongolian claimed them as their native languages. Therefore, that someone who was not exposed to these linguistic communities directly could replicate the scripts deserves attention. This chapter will therefore concentrate particularly on analysing the varying degrees of SCM's comprehension of Manchu and in doing so, break ground on understanding his interest in including this language in the *ONBP* as well as in other works, especially his *Sacra Privata*, in which he wrote out private meditations on psalms and prayers composed between 1851 and 1853.[3]

Even more noteworthy is that SCM chose to incorporate Manchu sayings in his *ONBP* at a time when the Manchu language was seen by others as being in decline. The as-yet prevalent scholarly assessment of the Manchu spoken language and writing system from the end of the Qianlong reign (1735–1796) to the legal termination of the Qing dynasty in 1912 is that both became endangered and then effectively moribund.[4] Since the end of the Qing dynasty, progressively fewer individuals were able to utilize them as their primary means of communication, and more significantly for historians and linguists, few have chosen to learn them, thereby perpetuating trends toward its decline.[5] The last monarch of the regime, the Xuantong 宣統 emperor, claimed in his autobiography that he could only utter the command, "Ili! (stand up)," which he learned as a set phrase in the context of dealing with court ministers.[6] Manchus of humbler rank had already been reproached by preceding rulers, notably the Qianlong emperor, for composing poor and unsophisticated

---

[2] Cited from *SCM DD*, p. 397.

[3] Consult SCM, *Sacra Privata*, a beautiful manuscript completed in 1853, and then later in 1859 bequeathed to the Bodleian Library. It is now found in the Bodleian Libraries under the call number "MS.Or.Polygl.f.1."

[4] As elaborated in Ch'en Chieh-hsien 1976, pp. 137-54.

[5] Even scholars who have argued that Manchu culture was more robust and durable than proponents of the view that the Manchus became Sinicized from the early Qing dynasty onward, such as Ding Yizhuang, acknowledge that the decline of Manchu was based on pragmatic calculations of the language's utility and pressure from the cultural environment in which Manchus of the late eighteenth and nineteenth centuries lived. See Ding Yizhuang 2003, p. 268.

[6] As documented in Aisin-Gioro Puyi 1985, p. 64.

documents, and not speaking the standard form of their ostensible mother tongue.[7] Therefore, the conventional assumption that Manchu had become merely a *pro forma* language for drafting government documents by the nineteenth century arose from substantial evidence that a progressively diminishing usage had occurred by that time for more than two generations.

At the same time, a robust body of scholarship has mitigated this view and proven that Manchu was a living language in the nineteenth century and even continues to be utilized in spoken and written forms today, if not only for its original and prime purposes as a governmental language (the Qing dynasty's "national language," or *guoyu* 國語, Manchu: *gurun i gisun*), but also as a marker of Manchu ethnic identity.[8] Throughout the Qing dynasty, Manchu became the lingua franca of soldiers (known as bannermen) in many of the frontier garrisons, such as those in the northeast quadrant of the empire;[9] many of these populations, including several non-Manchu ethnic groups, continued to use Manchu as a written language into the mid-twentieth century.[10] Among Manchus, the spoken language was still maintained in dialects throughout the eighteenth century.[11] Although fewer than one hundred living Manchu persons may be considered to be fluent native speakers, the Sibe population of Xinjiang has preserved a coherent derivative of Manchu that individuals as young as thirty years old still employ in daily life.[12] The transmission of Manchu as a spoken and written language has also carried on in Taiwan after the end of the Qing dynasty, particularly from the mid-twentieth century to the present-day, through the work of several scholars including Kuang Lu 廣祿 (1900–1973),[13] Ch'en Chieh-hsien 陳捷先,[14] Chuang Chi-fa 莊吉發,[15] and their students.

Whether one concludes that during SCM's lifetime Manchu was an important ethnic minority language employed primarily for official rather than colloquial functions, or a language on the verge of extinction during the Qing dynasty, SCM's interest in and knowledge of the language merits examination. The most unique trait of his case is that he wrote Manchu script, as well as the other languages, in his

---

[7] For a general discussion of how emperors of the early and mid-Qing periods utilized their multi-lingual abilities strategically and acted as arbiters of Manchu language, see Kim 2007, pp. 83-88.

[8] The abbreviation "Man." will indicate that terms in subsequent references are transliterated from Manchu.

[9] As documented in R. G. H. Lee 1970, pp. 22, 81-82.

[10] Manchu also had symbolic value in the borderlands, as evident in the discovery of a Manchu-language passport dated to 1927. Described in Hauer 1929, pp. 153-56.

[11] Confirmed in Ki-moon Lee 1973, pp. 99-132.

[12] Manchu is widely recognized as a language that is no longer transmitted to new speakers and has been static for several decades, whereas Sibe continues to be a living language that evolves to fit contemporary circumstances. For further details consult Enhebatu 1995 and An – Guo 2007.

[13] Consult Kuang – Li 1965, pp. 1-165.

[14] Documented in Ch'en Chieh-hsien 1976 as well as in his later work, *id*. 1988.

[15] Found in the prolific work of Chuang Chi-fa 1997–2016.

own hand. SCM's decision to write Manchu is of academic value because Manchu handwriting samples that are decisively attributable to a particular individual are uncommon.[16] Therefore, the following sections of this chapter will reconstruct the environment in which SCM may have gained exposure to the language, evaluate his proficiency in writing and translating Manchu, and consider how his work is a worthy contribution to Manjuristics. Although he did not conduct any original or analytical scholarship on Manchu language, literature, or philosophy, his compilation of Manchu wisdom sayings and his assertion of their connection to synonymous adages in other languages has produced significant information and claims that enhance all three areas of inquiry I will pursue in this chapter.

2. S. C. Malan's Garden of Manchu Knowledge

Since no verifiable records have come to light about how SCM learned Manchu or whether he maintained relations with Manjuristics scholars in Great Britain and Europe, much of this section is purposefully speculative. Further investigation of his social and professional network may yield some more clues about his intentions and means of studying Manchu. Yet, even with the known facts about resources available during his lifetime, as will be presented below, it is possible to understand how SCM may have developed his aptitude in the language.

In fact, SCM was in good company for his study of Manchu as a scholar in Europe, which was and is still a vibrant base of Manjuristics. During the late nineteenth and early twentieth centuries, the leading figures in European Manjuristics were Vasilii Vasil'evich Radlov (Friedrich Wilhelm Radloff, 1837–1918), Erich Haenisch (1879–1966) – author of a still-respected German grammar of Manchu, Haenisch's contemporary, Erich Hauer (1878–1936) – who compiled a Manchu-German dictionary[17] – and the French explorer, Paul Eugène Pelliot (1878–1945).[18] The next generation, born and working right before or within two decades after SCM's death, included Németh Gyula (1890–1976), Ligeti Lajos (1902–1987), Walther Heissig (1913–2005), Herbert Franke (1914–2011), and Gerhard Doerfer (1920–2003). At present, many of their students and colleagues are active in Germany and the Russian Federation, while a fewer number of no less significant persons are carrying on Manjuristics research in France and Italy.[19] Several of these

---

[16] Imperial rescripts on Qing government documents and the works of literati such as the poet and prose translator, Bujilgen Jakdan (birth and death dates unconfirmed), active in the late eighteenth and early nineteenth centuries, are the few kinds of texts with definitively identifiable Manchu orthography. For the work of Jakdan, see Bosson – Toh 2006, pp. 13-26.

[17] See Haenisch 1961 and Hauer 2007.

[18] Enough knowledge of Manchu existed in Europe during the mid and late nineteenth century so that scholars undertook comparative linguistic studies. See, for example, Hermann 1881.

[19] Russian specialists include Tatiana A[leksandrovna] Pang at the Institute of Oriental Manuscripts of the Russian Academy of Sciences and Konstantin S. Yakhontov [Konstantin S. Iakhontov]. German scholars include Michael Weiers, professor emeritus of the University of Bonn. Leading French experts include Françoise Aubin (1932–2017), former Research Director at the French National Centre for Scientific Research (CNRS).

individuals have published definitive works of scholarship on Tungusic language and literature, one notable example being Liliya M. Gorelova's edited work, *Manchu Grammar*.[20]

SCM could have learned Manchu through interaction with one or more of his contemporaries who were known experts of the language, although there is no affirmation that this occurred. Otherwise, he could have gained access to the language through self-instruction, utilizing any number of texts that were available in Europe during his lifetime. Possible educational materials existed that were produced in modern languages in which SCM was fluent.[21] The earliest work was in French and produced in 1828 by Julius von Klaproth (1783–1835), *Chrestomathie Mandchou*, a German scholar studious in Asiatic languages, working during his adulthood with both Russian and French academies, and who had travelled to the Qing empire with a Russian embassy in 1805 and 1806.[22] This would be followed by another French volume prepared by another German, Hans Conon von der Gabelentz (1807–1874), and published in 1832, dealing with the "elements" of Manchu grammar.[23] Though many other relevant works published in French would appear many decades later, the next linguistic tool related to Manchu language was produced in English by Alexander Wylie (1815–1887), a London Missionary Society printer working in Shanghai. Wylie's contribution was an English translation of a Manchu grammar originally written in Chinese, which he published in Shanghai in 1855.[24] Subsequently, there were four other works dealing with Manchu language produced during the last three decades of the 19th century, two in French,[25] and one each in Russian[26] and English.[27] Unfortunately, as I have already indicated, there is no evidence among the notes within any of his works that confirms that SCM had access to any of these volumes.

---

[20] See Gorelova 2002.

[21] All of the works that will be mentioned in this paragraph are described in Sinor 1963, pp. 163 and 167.

[22] Consult Klaproth 1828.

[23] See von der Gabelentz 1832.

[24] For those interested, see Wylie 1855. Here it is appropriate to also mention that the *Man Hanzi Qingwen qimeng* 滿漢字清文啟蒙 was compiled by Wuge Shouping 舞格壽平 and published in 1730 after revision by Cheng Mingyuan 程明遠.

[25] These are Adam 1873, and a volume by the Belgian Roman Catholic priest and Orientalist, Charles de Harlez, or more formally, Charles-Joseph de Harlez de Deulin (1832–1899), consult Harlez 1884.

[26] That is the volume produced by Ivan Il'ich Zakharov (1816–1885), a Russian diplomat who lived in Beijing from 1839 to 1850. His work was entitled *Grammatika man'chzhurskogo iazyka* [Grammar of the Manchu Language] (Saint Petersburg: Imperial Academy of Science, 1879).

[27] See the volume produced by the Prussian scholar trained in Germany and later having a colorful diplomatic career in the Qing and Korean empires, Paul Georg von Möllendorf (1847–1901), *A Manchu Grammar, with Analysed Texts* (Shanghai: American Presbyterian Mission Press, 1892).

The only certain information about how SCM developed his knowledge of the Manchu language is that he collected various learning aids and texts related to his study of wisdom and Christianity. In his personal library, subsequently bequeathed in 1885 to the Bodleian Library at Oxford University, were bilingual Chinese-Manchu instructional materials such as an incomplete volume of the *Man Hanzi Qingwen qimeng* 滿漢字清文啟蒙 / *Manju Nikan hergen-i Cing wen ki meng bithe* (Manchu script / Chinese Character Primer of the Qing Language), and bilingual Manchu-Chinese versions of Chinese classics such as the *Daxue* 大學 (Great Learning), *Yijing* 易經 (Book of Changes), and *Shijing* 詩經 (Book of Poetry).[28] SCM also possessed Manchu texts such as *Toumen tschaki ounengi segiyen / Wanwu zhen yuan* 萬物真原,[29] edited by Giulio Aleni S.J. (1582–1649). Embarking upon rational speculation from this point forward, it is plausible that SCM started his study of Manchu as a student at the University of Oxford or during subsequent visits to the campus. Although the acquisition dates of the university's Manchu-language holdings have yet to be matched with SCM's lifetime, the majority were likely available for his consultation.[30] He could have read several multilingual lexicons, including the *Yuzhi siti Qingwen jian* 御製四體清文鑑 / *Han-i araha duin hacin-i hergen kamciha Manju gisun-i buleku bithe* (Imperially Commissioned Four-language Manchu Mirror), and literary reference works like the *Man Han chengyu duidai* 滿漢成語對待 / *Manju Nikan fe gisun be joforo acabuha bithe* (Manchu–Chinese Concordance of Idioms).[31]

Many other resources were available further afield in Great Britain, as attested in the catalogue of Chinese and Manchu books in the University of Cambridge Library, published in 1898,[32] and the 182-page bibliography published in 1977 by the British Museum and entitled *Manchu Books in London*, compiled by (Julian) Walter Simon (1893–1981) and Howard G.H. Nelson.[33] Many of the Manchu language materials in these collections, however, were not directly related to SCM's

---

[28] Special thanks to Gillian Evison, David Helliwell, and Joshua Seufert at the Bodleian Libraries, University of Oxford, for granting access to a list of their Manchu-language holdings. For Qing-period texts with two synonymous titles in Chinese and Manchu languages, the titles are cited in "Chinese title / Manchu title" order.

[29] Rendered into standardized Manchu, the title should be *Tumen jaka-i unenggi sekiyen (-i bithe)*; in Latin it was known as *Rerum omnium vera origo*.

[30] SCM probably did not see at least eight out of twenty-eight texts because he was already elderly when they were published. Four were produced in 1878, one in 1888, one in 1889, and one in 1891.

[31] The publication date of the *Man Han chengyu duidai* is unknown.

[32] Consult Herbert A. Giles, ed., *A Catalogue of the Wade Collection of Chinese and Manchu Books in the Library of the University of Cambridge* (Cambridge: Cambridge University Press, 1898).

[33] The Simon and Nelson bibliography includes holdings in the British Library, India Office Library and Records, Public Record Office, British and Foreign Bible Society, Royal Asiatic Society, and Royal Geographical Society, and the School of Oriental and African Studies (University of London). Unfortunately, the bibliography only mentions acquisition dates for some of the cited materials, so it is difficult to identify all the texts SCM could have seen.

principal interests in philosophy and theology. Nevertheless, some of them – such as the Manchu-Chinese translation of the Gospel of St. Matthew and a Manchu translation of the 1677 [*Yuzhi*] *Rijiang sishu jieyi* [御製]日講四書解義 / *Han-i araha inenggidari giyangnaha sy su-i jurgan be suhe bithe* (Explanations of the Four Books of Confucianism for Daily Tutoring) – may have attracted his attention.

SCM could have also obtained additional resources through contacts in France, the German states, and Eastern Europe. Substantial collections of Manchu texts were stored in Berlin, as described by Julius von Klaproth in his catalogue published in Paris in 1822,[34] those details being confirmed in the catalogue produced by the Russian Orientalist, Tatiana A. Pang.[35] Notably, SCM's romanization of Manchu in the *ONBP* and in his handwritten catalogue of his own library collection indicates that he was at least aware, if not purposefully influenced by, the conventions of French Sinologists, such as using "ts" to represent "j" and "ou" for "u."[36] He may have also learned his transliterations from publications such as the article produced by the German linguist and customs officer for the Qing and Joseon governments, Paul Georg von Möllendorf, "Essay on Manchu Literature."[37] In Eastern Europe, SCM may have consulted items from repositories such as those found in the Hungarian Academy of Sciences, where a prodigious collection of Mongolian and Manchu manuscripts had been amassed. As catalogued by György Kara and current as of 2000, this collection included 42 works of Mongolian language, 49 pieces of Mongolian folk and classical literature, as well as 24 Buddhist texts in Mongolian language,[38] as well as twelve Chinese classics translated into Manchu, 19 Manchu dictionaries, three Manchu grammars, and seven works of Manchu literature.[39]

Among these possible sources, it is likely that SCM read works of Christian theology translated into Manchu, Chinese classics translated into Manchu, and Manchu language original works on wisdom in order to choose appropriate entries for his *ONBP*. Within the first category were many texts that representatives from different denominations of Christianity had rendered. It is well known that Roman Catholics from among the Jesuits had exchanged Western knowledge of science for information about Chinese religion and philosophy during the Qing dynasty.[40] Several of these individuals became trusted advisors to the imperial throne, their

---

[34] That is, *Verzeichniss der Chinesischen und Mandschuischen Bücher und Handschriften der Königlichen Bibliothek zu Berlin* [Chinese and Manchu Books and Manuscripts in the Royal Library in Berlin] (Paris 1822).

[35] Consult Pang 1998.

[36] Special thanks to Timothy Barrett for pointing out this tendency in Malan's library catalogue. The Romanization follows the convention that was standardized by Séraphin Couvreur of the École Française d'Extrême-Orient in 1902.

[37] See von Möllendorf 1889–1890.

[38] For the Mongolian title list by thematic category, see Kara 2000, pp. 495-500.

[39] For the Manchu title list by thematic category, see *ibid.*, pp. 531-533. Notably, these do not include materials cross-referenced in Mongolian, so that they are counted only once, rather than twice.

[40] For further details, consult Mungello 1988, pp. 252-273.

credibility undoubtedly enhanced by their ability to communicate in Manchu.[41] Although they did not succeed in their ultimate mission of gaining numerous converts among both the political elite and common people, this intention motivated the translation of theological expositions composed during the sixteenth through eighteenth centuries. A representative list of such works is found in the table below.

Table 8.1 Select Manchu Language Christian Texts[42]

Manchu name	Chinese name	Latin name	Compiler	Compiler Life Dates
Abkai ejen-i enduringge tacihiyan-i oyonggo gisun	天主聖教約言	*Sanctae legis compendium*	João Soeiro	1566–1607
Abkai ejen-i tacihiyan-i hešen-i bithe	天主教要	Unconfirmed	François Furtado	1587–1653
Abkai ejen-i tob tacihiyan-i temgetu-i šošohon	天主正教約徵	Unconfirmed	Luigi Buglio	1606–1682
Abkai ejen-i toktobuha geren yargiyan temgetu	主制群徵	Unconfirmed	Johann Adam Schall von Bell	1591–1666
Abkai-i ejen unenggi jurgan [-i bithe]	天主實義	*Vera de Deo doctrina [~ ratio]*	Matteo Ricci	1552–1610
Abkai enduri hūi-i kicen-i yarugan	天神會課	Unconfirmed	Francesco Brancati	1607–1671
Enduringge beye be kenehunjehengge de jabuha bithe	聖體答疑	*De Sancto Corpore (seu de Eucharistia) responsa ad dubia libellus*	Ferdinand Verbiest	1623–1688
Enduringge beye-i oyonggo gisun	聖體要理	*Tractatus de Sancta Eucharistia*	Giulio Aleni	1582–1649

---

[41] The utility that both Qing emperors and Jesuit consultants derived from the use of Manchu as a medium of communication is apparent in specific acts of cooperation, such as in the Kangxi emperor's employment of Jesuit negotiators to resolve the first major Qing–Russian conflict leading to the 1689 Treaty of Nerchinsk. For details, consult Sebes 1962. Jesuits viewed the mastery of Manchu as a means to an end, such as reading Manchu translations of Chinese classics which they considered simpler than the original, literary Chinese versions, but by knowing Manchu, they could also convey their opinions to the emperors in a more direct manner.

[42] The data for this table is from Stary 2000, pp. 305-310. Another detailed bibliography of Christian literature, some of the entries overlapping with the ones on this list, is found in Walravens 2000, pp. 453-468. Other studies dealing with Manchu-language Catholic catechisms include Mish 1958, pp. 361-371, and Walravens 1974–1975.

Manchu name	Chinese name	Latin name	Compiler	Compiler Life Dates
Šeng niyan guwang i	聖年廣益	Annus sacer, seu vitae Sanctorum totius anni [abbreviated version]	Joseph Marie Anne Moyria de Mailla	1669–1748
Šeng ši cu nao	盛世芻蕘	Saeculo aureo humilis tractatus seu Sententiæ hominis rudis ad litteros	Joseph Marie Anne Moyria de Mailla	1669–1748
Sing lii jen ciyan bithei hešen	性理真詮	Philosophiae naturalis vera explication	Alexandre de La Charme	1695–1767
Weile be geterembure jingkini kooli	滌罪正規略	Lavandorum peccatorum recta norma	Giulio Aleni	1582–1649

Translations of portions of the Bible into Manchu were also being produced piecemeal in Great Britain during SCM's lifetime, so he may have referred to a draft or final version of some of these works.[43] Robert Pinkerton of the British and Foreign Bible Society received the original commission to start the translation in 1821, but he delegated the task to a member of the Eighth Russian Orthodox Mission in Beijing, a person named Stepan Vasil'evich Lipovtsov (1770–1841).[44] Lipovtsov concentrated on the New Testament, completing the whole translation in 1825.[45] Putting together the Old Testament in Manchu required the labours of George Borrow (1803–1881) and William Swan (1791–1866), who visited St. Petersburg to find earlier translations, and Edward Stallybrass (1794–1884), who finished a second draft of Borrow and Swan's work by 1850.[46] Borrow then completed and published a translation of the whole New Testament (Man. *Musei ejen Isus Heristos i tutabuha ice hese*, literally "The Surviving New Edicts of Our Lord Jesus Christ") in 1836. Reprints of the Manchu translations of the Gospels of Matthew and Mark were subsequently produced in Shanghai in 1859.[47]

These Manchu translations of theological texts and the whole Bible embodied noteworthy blends of pragmatic transcriptions, interpretations based on the literal meaning of the Greek and Hebrew standard texts and manifest a cultural concordance with Manchu indigenous ideas. Several Latin terms were rendered into forms that Manchu native speakers could pronounce fluently, such as *subota* (Lat.

---

[43] For characteristics of the completed text, see Matsumura Jun 1976.
[44] Described in Stary 2000. See also Walravens 1977–1978.
[45] Noted in Walravens 2000, p. 447.
[46] As documented in *ibid*.
[47] Once again, found in *ibid*.

sabbata, sabbath) and *eglesiya* or *egere siya* (Lat. *ecclesia,* church).[48] Most Biblical personal names also belong to this category, like *Bonksio Bilado* (Pontius Pilatus). Others were translated literally utilizing relevant Manchu vocabulary, like *enduringge beye be alimbi* ("to receive the holy body," Holy Communion) and *enduringge baita-i songko* ("evidence of a holy event," sacrament).[49] Yet other Christian concepts retained their original meanings, but were modified to resemble Manchu native ideas, such as *misa wecen* ("Mass offering," Mass,)[50] and *abkai ejen* ("Lord of the Sky," meaning "God" like the Chinese term *tianzhu* 天主).[51] SCM's selections of proverbs from the Manchu language published in the *ONBP* suggest that he favored the second and third forms of translation, since there are minimal traces of overtly foreign vocabulary in them.

The second category of Manchu texts preserved within major European archives and libraries that is pertinent to SCM's project are translations of Chinese texts. Multiple translations exist for many of the Chinese classical canon, such as the *Yuzhi fanyi sishu* 御製翻譯四書 / *Han-i araha ubaliyambuha duin bithe* (*Sy su bithe*) (Imperially Commissioned Translation of the Four Books).[52] Manchu-Chinese versions of the *Xiaojing* 孝經 (Book of Filial Piety) and the *Sanzi jing* 三字經 (Three-character Classic) were similarly accessible.[53] Other Chinese texts related to wisdom that were translated into Manchu are the *Si ben jianyao* 四本簡要 / *Duin felehe oyonggo šošohon* (Four Volumes of Pithy Sayings) first published in 1652, *Fanyi liushi zhenyan* 繙譯六事箴言 / *Ubaliyambuha ninggun baita targabun gisun* (Admonitions Regarding Six Subjects), and the Daoist tract *Guansheng di jun jueshi baoxun jing* 關聖帝君覺世寶訓經 / *Enduringge di giyūn kuwan mafa-i jalan de ulhibure boobai tacihiyan-i nomun bithe* (Precious Teachings for the Edification of the World).[54]

Texts originally composed in Manchu, particularly containing Manchu indigenous wisdom, comprise the smallest category of research materials that SCM may have examined. The most representative work of Manchu folk knowledge is the *Emu tanggū juwan sakda gisun sarkiyan* (*Bai er laoren yulu* 百二老人語錄; Words of One Hundred and Twenty Old Men) by Songyun 松筠 (1752–1835). Official works to demonstrate rulers' erudition, such as the Kangxi emperor's 1724 *Shengyu guangxun* 聖諭廣訓 / *Enduringge tacihiyan neileme badarambuha bithe* (The Sacred Edicts] and the Manchu monolingual *Šengdzu gūsin hūwangdi-i boo-i tacihiyan-i ten-i gisun* (*Shengzu jiaxun gaolun* 聖祖家訓高論 [The Kangxi Emperor's Noble Family Precepts], published in 1730), would have also been suitable

---

[48] Pointed out in Stary 2000, p. 312.

[49] Noted in *ibid*.

[50] *Ibid*.

[51] As noted in Walravens 2000, p. 450.

[52] For a description of the text, see Pang 1998, p. 37. SCM may have also read related scholarship, such as von der Gabelentz 1864.

[53] See von Möllendorf 1889–1890, pp. 16, 17, 19.

[54] As cited in *ibid*., pp. 22-23, 27.

references, since multiple versions were available at various European sites.[55] Moreover, as the table below shows, certain sources were derivatives of Chinese compositions or multi-lingual concordances that provided culturally significant and linguistically helpful translations.[56]

Table 8.2 Select Texts of Manchu Language Wisdom Literature

Manchu name	Chinese name	English translation and year of publication
Fan yi lei biyan bithe	繙譯類編	Collection of Translated Miscellanies, 1740 (compiled by Nimača Guanjing 尼瑪察觀景, published by Wenyuantang 文淵堂)
Han-i araha sain be hūwekiyebure oyonggo gisun	御製勸善要言	Imperially Commissioned Sayings to Promote Goodness, 1655
Ilan hacin gisun kamcibuha gebungge saisa isabuha bithe	三合名賢集	Manchu, Mongolian, and Chinese Trilingual Collection of [Sayings of] Notable Worthies, 1879–1880
Inenggidari sahangge be acamjaha gisuren bithe	[滿文]日知薈說	[Manchu-language] Collection of Daily Knowledge (Qianlong reign, publication year unconfirmed)
Inenggidari sahangge be isamjame gisurehe bithe	日知薈說	Collected Daily Knowledge, 1881 (two versions)
Nadan tacihiyan be urunakū hūlabure bithe	七訓須讀	Compulsory Readings of Seven Teachings [of Confucian Ethics], 1764

3. Manchu in the Miscellany

More definite and comprehensive evidence must be uncovered about the extent of SCM's overall exposure to Manchu texts that were already present in Europe, as well as those acquired from other parts of the world before firm assessments about his competence in the language may be made. Still, available anecdotal evidence as well as some basic evaluations of how he wrote and paired selected Manchu sayings in the *ONBP* with synonymous passages in other languages can suffice to posit that he attained at least an intermediate level of comprehension of both Manchu and Mongolian. According to his son, SCM could argue coherently about equating Christian concepts with Mongolian indigenous terms. For example, SCM disagreed with the British and Foreign Bible Society about the translation of the term for "God" in the Mongolian-language translation of the New Testament. He believed

---

[55] See again von Möllendorf 1889–1890, pp. 21–22.

[56] The data for this table is primarily derived from Pang 1998.

that *Tegri* (or the term more commonly pronounced as *Tngri*) was more suitable, being a word of confirmed indigenous invention over *Burčan* (also known as *Bodzha*), a term used to refer to the Buddha.[57] Consequently, SCM objected to the Bible Society's preference for the use of the latter.[58] He was also active in exchanging knowledge of Manchu language with specific individuals, such as the Chinese missionary-scholar, the Rev. Walter Henry Medhurst (1796–1857), with whom he corresponded about the meanings of the Chinese terms used in Chinese Bible translation, the main terms being *shin* (or *shen* in today's Pinyin transcription) 神 (god, spirit or deity) and *shang-te* (or *shangdi*) 上帝 (God, Lord on High or Supreme Lord).[59]

Turning to the manuscript version of the *Original Notes to the Book of Proverbs* (subsequently "ONBP Ms," to distinguish it from the published version in English that is *ONBP*) to analyse his handwriting and translation ability, there are numerous samples to evaluate since SCM recorded Manchu sayings throughout most of the manuscript. To contextualize the frequency of their appearance in the text, the tables below compare the quantity of Manchu and Mongolian entries found in ONBP Ms. Although SCM sometimes paired phrases with the same meaning in both languages, in most of the text he rarely placed Manchu and Mongolian passages together on the same pages. Since his main purpose was to find parallel or antagonistic sayings in alternative languages and texts related to proverbial themes found in the biblical book of the Proverbs, one must assume that SCM distributed his references to Tungusic proverbial sayings throughout the manuscript primarily based of their thematic relevance to those biblical proverbs.

Table 8.3 Aggregate Distribution of Manchu and Mongolian Sayings in ONBP Ms[60]

Language	Number of Citations/Pages
Manchu	106 citations
Mongolian	151 citations
Manchu and Mongolian (appearing on the same page but not the same content)	15 pages in the whole of the ONBP Ms

---

[57] An issue SCM briefly discussed in *ONBP*, vol. 2, p. 38, where he added after a quotation from a Buddhist text entitled "Tonilkhu Yin" the following parenthetical comment: "This and like passages show that 'Burkhan,' as it is used in the Mongolian Bible, is a bad equivalent for 'God'."

[58] See *SCM DD*, p. 179. SCM expressed such views in *A Letter to the Right Honourable the Earl of Shaftesbury, President of the British and Foreign Bible Society: On the Pantheistic and on the Buddhistic Tendency of the Chinese and of the Mongolian Versions of the Bible Published by that Society* (London: Bell and Daldy, 1856).

[59] Medhurst, writing from Shanghai on 6 March 1855, expressed his intention to send a part of a "Mandchu manual" to SCM. See *SCM DD*, p. 170.

[60] Data for this table and the following three are all from the original, unpublished manuscript (ONBP Ms), now stored in the Bodleian Libraries and given the call number "MS.Ind.Inst.Misc.10."

Merely identifying all these instances of SCM's Manchu and Mongolian calligraphy are significant because it is rare to confirm so many samples of Manchu handwriting that are definitively attributable to a particular individual. Of course, it is also important because SCM determined that so many Manchu sayings should not only be recorded in his own hand within the ONBP Ms, but also were rendered into English and documented in the published version (that is, the *ONBP*). The first issue related to the handwritten passages of Manchu proverbial sayings is extraordinary because it remains inconclusive whether students of Manchu language living outside of Qing territory learned how to write the script. From the conventional practices of Manchu language pedagogy transmitted to learners in the twentieth and twenty-first centuries, one can surmise that writing was not a core component of such instruction.[61] Orthographic errors in certain excerpts suggest that SCM may have learned to write on his own and gradually improved with increased practice and familiarity with the script's mechanics. The second issue mentioned above – that Manchu proverbial sayings were utilized in relative abundance within both the manuscript as well as in SCM's English renderings of them in the published version – must also be explored by determining their sources of origin.

Starting my own more in-depth analysis with this second issue, it is notable that SCM only listed four of his sources in the manuscript's preface as written in Manchu: *Ming hican ji 157 tze*, *Kong dai kicūn-i bithe*, *Juwan jakūn acangga sere tacihiyan*, and *Ioi gung jun (run)-i bithe*.[62] The title of the first text is the easiest to decipher. Since *Ming* is not a native word, and *hican* ("frugal" or "simple") and *ji* (the imperative form of the verb, "to go") do not make grammatical sense in that order, the title is obviously foreign, and with some strategic deduction, identified as the *Mingxianji* 名賢集 (A Collection of Well-known Worthies' Sayings), a compilation of aphorisms based on Confucian precepts. The 157 *tze* likely refers to the 157 fascicles (Chin. *ce* 冊) of that work. In the second title, *Kong dai kicūn-i bithe*, only the genitive particle "*i*" and the word for book, "*bithe*," are indisputably Manchu. The term *kicūn* seems to be a Manchu word, but since it cannot be found in any lexicon, it might be a misspelling of *kicen*, meaning "diligent" or "lesson." Therefore, *kicen-i bithe* can be understood as "lesson book" or "book of lessons." The first two elements of the title resemble Chinese words, so the first step is to reverse-transliterate them into their Chinese morpheme equivalents, which is *gong* (or *kong*) *dai*. Guessing what *gong dai* or *kong dai* means is more uncertain and

---

[61] Even today, the majority of current Manchu language courses are centred on translation and pronunciation, but not penmanship and original composition in Manchu.

[62] Here I need to explain a problem with regard to identifying certain pages in the ONBP Ms. I did some independent work on the manuscript while in Oxford some years ago, but the records I have are sometimes incomplete. Unfortunately, due to the pandemic alerts that have affected so much of normal life, institutional access, and international travel as this chapter was being finalized, I could not get access to the manuscript for a final confirmation. The editor did have images made from nearly 300 pages of the ONBP Ms, but in some cases, the pages I refer to are not among them. Where this occurs in the following footnotes, I will explain that the pagination "may be" in a particular range of pages. In this case, the text of the bibliographic notes is in ONBP Ms, probably between 6 recto and 7 verso.

ultimately inconclusive. In the third title, *Juwan jakūn acangga sere tacihiyan*, linking the individual elements of *Juwan jakūn* ("ten" + "eight" = "eighteen"), *acangga* ("harmonious" or "fitting"), *sere* ("being"), and *tacihiyan* ("teaching"), the phrase refers to a collection of eighteen lessons. The fourth and final title, *Ioi gung jun (run) i bithe* could be the story of Yu Gong 愚公 from the *Liezi* 列子 ([Writings of] *Master Lie*) written in the fifth century BCE by Lie Yukou 列禦寇.[63] SCM did mention other sources in citations attached to certain entries, as will be discussed below, but did not indicate specific references to texts and pagination for many of the Manchu sayings.

A prime factor in solving the mysteries involved in deciphering the two latter source titles involves working through the particularities of SCM's Manchu penmanship. A significant number of words in the Manchu sayings are formed incorrectly, easily misleading all but persons who have extensive knowledge of Manchu orthography. Like many learners of Manchu, SCM encountered two major problems in developing mastery of the script. The first issue involves writing along a vertical axis with accurate curvature and angles as appropriate for each letter. In different samples, SCM inscribed letters that are too round and conversely, too thin, to be identified decisively. As can be seen in the sample text below, letters have different shapes and details such as serifs. Each word must be symmetrical and uniform in style with the ones preceding and following it. Although this example was produced by means of computer software, it reflects the homogenous precision that Manchus valued in standard handwriting.

---

[63] The years of the birth and death of this author are unknown. It is possible that SCM meant to refer to another text, but that discovery would depend on deciphering accurately the Chinese characters that the Manchu syllables have transliterated.

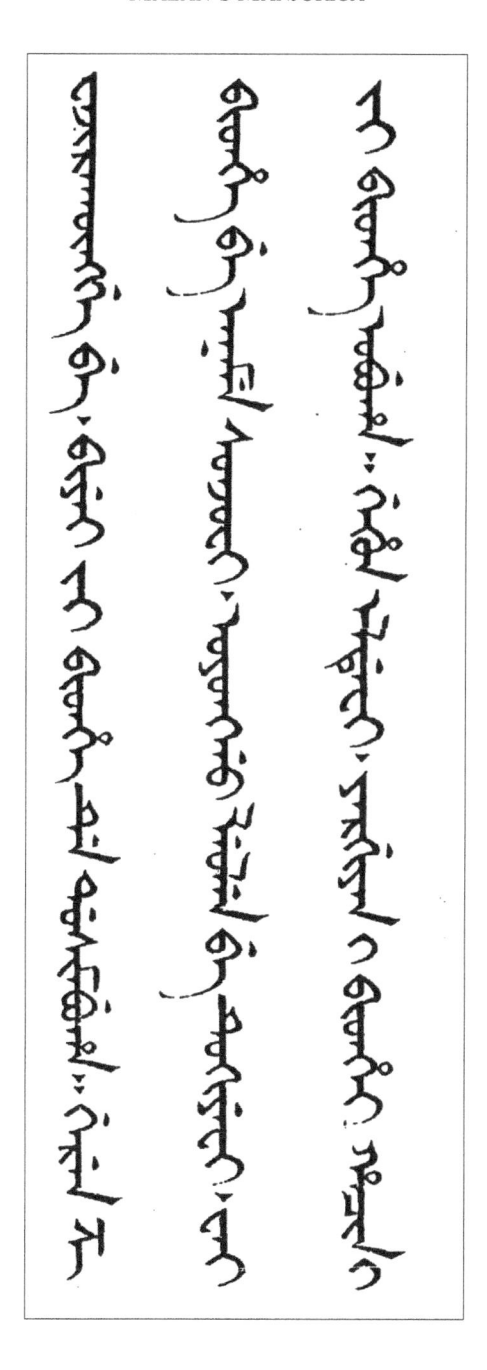

Fig. 14: Example of Manchu calligraphy. Source: Britta-Maria Gruber and Wolfgang Kirsch, "Writing Manchu on a Western Computer: (An Interim Report)," *Saksaha: A Journal of Manchu Studies* 3 (1998), p. 42. https://quod.lib.umich.edu/cgi/p/pod/dod-idx/writing-manchu-on-a-western-computer.pdf?c=saksaha;idno=13401746.0003.008;format=pdf (accessed June 24, 2021)

Over time SCM's handwriting went through a discernible evolution, changing in style and varying in accuracy as seen in the comparison of excerpts.[64] Some excerpts are composed so that even linear and angular letters are rounded out and difficult to distinguish from the normally elliptical letters. In other excerpts, the elliptical letters are flattened as if stretched out on the invisible vertical axis running through the words so that they become asymmetrical.[65] SCM also struggled with the common error of either omitting or misplacing the diacritical marks associated with some letters, known as "dots and circles" (Man. *tongki fuka*). He was also uncertain about the placement of punctuation, thereby breaking up or creating grammatically awkward phrases. While reading many of the passages, one must perform mental corrections in order to understand certain morphemes. Here below I will seek to illustrate this problem by means of the following sample, inserting my own critical comments in the bracketed statements.[66]

> *Nenehe saisa-i kubaliyambuha* [this is a non-existent word; the closest matching word is *kūbuliyambuha*] *fe jisen be benjifi acabume folofi gūnin adali gurse* [*gurse* is not a known word; by context one guesses that it should be *urse*] *de uhelehe buyerengge ere bithe be tuwarangga. ere beye be dasime bahara de mangga. jabšan de taifin neyin* [*neyin* is not a known word; the closest match is *nergin*] *urgun sebjen-i forgon de banjinjiha be safi. bithe-i dorgi geren baita be hergen toma* [*toma* is missing a dot; it should be *tome*]. *gisun tome. mojilen* [*mojilen* is missing a dot; it should be *mujilen*] *de dursuleme. baita de yarkiyalame* [*yarkiyalame* is missing a dot; it should be *yargiyalame*] *geli erinteri* [*t* in *erinteri* should be a *d* and changing the second *e* to *a* is necessary so the word should be *erindari* which is an actual word, unlike *erinteri*] *gimcime* [this word has an extraneous dot; it should be *kimcime*] *baicame. urunakū fulehe be baimbi.*

The misspelling of lengthy or unusual words may be justified as resulting from one's unfamiliarity with Manchu or the technical difficulty of linking all the individual letters in a word correctly. Notably in this regard, SCM also miswrote many common terms, such as *gūnin* (heart, mind),[67] *niyalma* (person),[68] and *kemuni*

---

[64] Even separate passages on the same page were rendered in varying styles of handwriting, such as with the three sayings on ONBP Ms, p. 276 recto, so it is likely that they were written at different times.

[65] Two examples of this tendency are "*abka-i* [which is written in a way that looks like *abin*] *irgen be feihugeleme* [*feihugeleme* should be *weihukeleme*] *oihorilara*" (ONBP MS, p. 282 verso) and "*makdame* [should be *maktame*] *saišaici hūturi banjinambi. firume gisureci jobolon banjinambi*" (ONBP Ms, p. 533 recto).

[66] ONBP Ms, p. 12 verso.

[67] See "*erdemu be isabure guin* [should be *gūnin*] *be iktambure.*" ONBP Ms, probably somewhere between 30 verso and 33 recto.

[68] Two examples are "*ambasa saisa jurgangga babe ulhimbi. buye iyalma* [*iyalma* is missing a "n" dot at the top of the word; it should be *niyalma*] *aisingga babe ulhimbi*" (ONBP Ms, p. 282 verso) and "*hūsun getugun* [*getugun* should be *getuken*] *oci iyalma* [as in the previous example, *iyalma* is missing a "n" dot at the top of the word and should be *niyalma*] *be gidašambi ambasa saisa toose jafaha de hūturi be isebu*" (ONBP Ms, probably between 557 verso and 562 recto).

(often, still, yet).[69] Omissions or distortions of letters in certain passages also lead to the conclusion that SCM was either copying from inaccurate sources, or did not know Manchu well enough to correct what he might discern to be a problematic spelling.[70] The latter interpretation is more probable, since in certain cases of similar or identical phrases repeated on different pages, he would not spell the same word correctly in every instance. For instance, in three citations of the maxim about not becoming angry because people age rapidly ("Do not quarrel [kindle] three inches of anger; the young head soon grows hoary), the word for "youths," *asihata*, is spelled correctly only two out of three times.[71]

The source texts for passages may have also been where SCM's errors originated. Many of these texts were not written or printed legibly and accurately, and so it would be a reasonable explanation that SCM may have replicated the errors contained in them, especially since most of those textual sources were translations of Chinese philosophical works. Most of the Manchu language sayings are attributed to the *Mingxianji* (both in the ONBP Ms as well as in *ONBP*);[72] that text was variably identified as "*Ming hien dsi*," "Ming h. dsi," or even "*M.H. dzi*." In part 1, 74 out of 138 discrete items in Malan's *ONBP* manuscript are citations from the *Mingxianji*. This figure excludes at least six illegible ones and three that are indirectly associated with ones from the *Mingxianji*, written either directly next to them or on the same page, but without separate references. The proportion of *Mingxianji* quotations (30 out of 35 items) is greater in part 2 of the ONBP Ms. Among the assortment of sources that provide the minority of sayings are the Manchu preface to the *Zigong shizhuan* 子貢詩傳 (Zigong's Book of Songs)[73] and a translation and

---

[69] See "*niyalma de gemuni* [*gemuni* has an extraneous dot; spelled correctly, it should be *kemuni*) *sain baita be yabuci* ..." (ONBP Ms, p. 300 recto).

[70] The possibility that he was writing by imitation but not fully aware of spelling is evident in his stylistically flawless rendition of the phrase "*niyalma-i mujilen selei gese bicibe hafan-i fafun hija-i adali* [orthographic errors corrected]" (ONBP Ms, p. 607 recto). His calligraphy meets the high standards that would be upheld by Qing official scribes, but there are several misspelled words, such as *mūcilen* instead of *mujilen*, *tafan* instead of *hafan*, and *hita* instead of *hija*.

[71] Compare the same phrase, quoted from the *Mingxianji*, fascicle 45, on ONBP Ms, pp. 392 recto, 411 verso, and 580 verso. The incorrect spelling of *asihata* is on p. 392 recto. Interestingly, other words besides *asihata* are variably misspelled in the three versions of the phrase.

[72] Though the printed version of the English renderings of these passages are not the focus of this study, it is worth noting that in *ONBP*, vol. 1, there are thirty references to this work, and only ten of them refer to the Manchu translation or commentary. This is only revealed if one reads the quotations and comments in the body of the work, because SCM did not mention whether he was referring to the Chinese or the Manchu in the footnotes. A simple example occurs where on the same page there is one reference that is apparently based on the Chinese, and the other is clearly from "the Mandchu" (consult *ONBP*, vol. 1, p. 31, n. 9 and 11 respectively).

[73] See, for example, the references on ONBP Ms, pp. 310 recto and 470 verso. The author of this single-fascicle work is Duanmu Ci 端木賜, known to be a disciple of Confucius. A reference to this work is also found in *ONBP*, vol. 1, p. 49, footnote 3.

elaboration of the popular Daoist treatise, the *Taishang ganyingpian (tushuo)* 太上感應篇(圖說) / *Tai sang-ni acabume karulara bithe* (Illustrated Books of Rewards and Punishments).[74] Other Confucian and Daoist texts are also represented,[75] but many of the passages are marked illegibly.[76]

Another point that should be made here is that some errors in SCM's writing and comprehension were due to mistranslations in the Manchu–Chinese texts he consulted. Although many texts were translated meticulously or at least sufficiently to represent the main ideas, several were full of minor errors, and yet by dint of their quantity and context, they are significant errors. One of these texts is the *Qingwen zhiyao* 清文指要 / *Manju gisun-i oyonggo jorin-i bithe* (Main Points of the Manchu Language), first published in 1789, containing many such mistakes. For example, the sentence "*ini ama-i gese urehe banjhabi*" is translated as 生的活像他阿媽一樣 (He lives like his mother). The problematic element is *ama*, which is the Manchu word for "father," but may be confused by someone only familiar with Chinese to be the equivalent of the colloquial Chinese word for "mother" (*a ma* 阿媽).[77] Translated correctly from Manchu to Chinese, the sentence is actually, "He lives like his father."[78] Also, throughout the text, *umesi sain* (very good) is written incorrectly as *hen hao* 狠好 (literally translatable as "ruthless-good," rather than *hen hao* 很好 that means "very good").[79] The character *hen* 狠 ("ruthless") is also misused in phrases such as *labdu acarakū*, translated as *hen bu duidang* 狠不對當 (literally "ruthless inappropriate/unfitting" rather than 很不對當 "very inappropriate").[80]

---

[74] See, for example, the references on ONBP Ms, pp. 867 verso, 914 verso and a page somewhere between 622 verso and 625 recto. Two versions of the *Ganying pian* are stored in the British Library. References to the Manchu version of this work appear in *ONBP*, vol. 1, pp. 223, 241, and 265, as well as in vol. 2, pp. 17, 66, and 88.

[75] Abbreviations for more obscure texts are difficult to decipher because these Romanized titles are not cited together with their original language names. Within the printed version of the ONBP, there are a few references to the Manchu commentaries to the *Zhongyong* 中庸 or *The Doctrine of the Mean* in James Legge's initial rendering of the title (cf. *ONBP*, vol. 1, p. 221, n. 9), the *Daxue* 大學 or *The Great Learning* in Legge's rendering of that title (cf. *ONBP*, vol. 2, p. 388, n. 4) and some popular collections of proverbial sayings that include Confucian, Daoist and sometimes Buddhist sayings.

[76] Unmarked or poorly marked passages are numerous, such as two discrete entries on ONBP Ms, p. 768 verso.

[77] *Qingwen zhiyao*, volume (*ce* 冊) 4, *xia* 下, p. 12a. The more well-known "first edition" of this text was published in 1809 by the Sanhuaitang 三槐堂.

[78] The transliteration of the Manchu *ama* as 阿媽 occurred in late Qing texts like *Qingwen zhiyao*, so SCM probably translated the Chinese characters as is, without understanding that the term is Manchu in origin, as Chinese people in areas like Beijing would recognize. See Zhang - Qi 2017, p. 145.

[79] See *Qingwen zhiyao*, vol. 4, *xia*, p. 1a.

[80] *Ibid.*, p. 6b.

Although SCM may have inadvertently committed many orthographic errors because he copied the Manchu sayings from translations or bilingual versions of Chinese texts, rather than writings originally composed in Manchu, he took great care to translate them accurately into English and to pair them appropriately with synonymous phrases in other languages. One example, which SCM uniquely marked out as a "Tartar adage," but which comes from the *Mingxianji*, is the saying, "*Baita bici damu ambasa saisa-i jakade hebdeme uru waka ocibe buya niyalma-i gisun be ume donjire*" (with orthographic errors corrected).[81] His translation into English conveys the general idea accurately, "If thou hast a business on hand, consult about it with wise men [...] never listen to the words of wicked men." Slight modifications, if one articulates all the literal meanings, are that one should only (*damu*) consult with officials and sophisticated gentlemen (*ambasa saisa*), and that by doing so one can discern what is right and wrong (*uru waka ocibe*). Rather than assuming there is a connotation of "wickedness," which would be commonly translated as *ehe*, the modifier for the kind of person from whom one should not solicit advice is written here as being "small" or "insignificant" (*buya*). Therefore, although the moral principal is essentially the same in both versions of the saying, the nuances involved i seeking out powerful persons rather than weak or marginalized individuals – the former being likely to be knowledgeable, and the latter being petty and ignoble – are nearly lost in translation. Nevertheless, this example reflects SCM's ability to understand Manchu sayings well enough to translate them coherently. He could also comprehend Manchu sufficiently to render similar phrases in Manchu with some precision and distinctiveness. For example, the phrase *ehe be mudere de obure*, which SCM translated as "to do evil with all our might" and a related phrase, *oshon kokirakū be jempi yabure*, was translated both as "to act with cruelty, brutality, evil intentions" and "to place one's powers in evil."[82]

4. Conclusion

SCM's Manchu language selections – even though most of them are not originally Manchu proverbs but drawn from Manchu renderings of Chinese proverbs – do raise many questions that should provoke deeper inquiries. Firstly, since I am unable to read SCM's mind or uncover the full extent of his exposure to Manchu language materials, I can only speculate why he drew most of his Manchu selections from relatively few sources. Certainly, Manchu translations of Chinese wisdom sayings were more relevant for achieving his overarching goal of drawing parallels between multiple linguistic and cultural traditions in relationship to those found in the biblical book of Proverbs. However, it is imperative to determine more precisely whether SCM read any works of indigenous Manchu philosophy and folklore.[83] Entries

---

[81] ONBP Ms, p. 425 verso.

[82] ONBP Ms, p. 30 recto.

[83] Even from the perspective of the printed version of the *ONBP*, most of the Manchu sayings are taken from commentaries to various classical Confucian and Daoist works. Up to this point in time, the only text found within that work that SCM cites and may be an indigenous

without explicit citations added into the large volume of the ONBP Ms may have the greatest potential to be native Manchu idioms or close derivatives, but such a hypothesis can only be confirmed after an exhaustive combing of texts that will lead to making appropriate matches and discoveries.

That SCM included Manchu as one of the featured languages in both the ONBP Ms and his published English rendering of relevant Manchu proverbs in the *ONBP* in and of itself should also inspire more research into Manchu proverbial sayings. Most scholarship on indigenous Manchu knowledge has concentrated on the translation and linguistic parsing of the texts, rather than their cultural origins and literary value.[84] Future research should emulate the work already undertaken in the area of Mongolian literature, whether by translating and pairing Chinese idioms with literal Mongolian translations and synonymous native terms, or by producing philologically informed translations of Mongolian aphorisms.[85]

Just as significant as the above analysis of some of the content of Manchu proverbs found in the ONBP Ms is the opportunity to assess SCM's handwritten recordings of Manchu sayings. The calligraphic errors that he made initially, and the progress he manifested in developing an elegant hand, provide insights into the challenges of writing Manchu, and prompt further questions about whether these problems were similar or different for linguistic natives and non-natives.[86] Although there are many errors in SCM's Manchu calligraphy as seen in the ONBP Ms, comparing different entries within that manuscript as well as within other works where Manchu script has been written by SCM suggests that his Manchu handwriting improved markedly over time. In the *Sacra Privata* he completed by 1853, SCM wrote in a steady and flourishing hand with few errors. His Manchu script resembles the Qing imperial court scribe standard in form and style, and on one particularly magnificent page in which he surrounded the Chinese character for "end" (*zhong* 終) with a rectangular "frame" of Manchu, SCM's only orthographic error was the

---

Manchurian work is entitled "*Yui-gang jin enduri*" (identified by SCM as "Mandchu" and cited in *ONBP*, vol. 2 p. 166, n. 6).

[84] The arguably most prolific scholar of Manchu literature and linguistics to date, Giovanni Stary, has produced a prodigious corpus of English, German, and Italian translations and commentaries on original Manchu language works, but both the breadth and depth of his achievements are extremely unique in the field of Manjuristics.

[85] Regarding native terms, see Baoligao 1973. For more details about Mongolian aphorisms, see Yoshitake 1928, pp. 689-702.

[86] SCM's progress in learning various languages offers rich avenues for comparison with his study of Manchu. E. Wyn James notes that while SCM generally reproduces Welsh words accurately in standard Welsh orthography in the printed version of the *ONBP*, there are a few examples where he seems to have miscopied or misunderstood a word in the written source from which he was copying, and there are one or two examples where he seems to spell a Welsh word as he would have heard it orally, rather than copying it from a written source in standard orthography. Similarly, James Hegarty has stated that SCM's Sanskrit in the *ONBP* was legible, but not sophisticated. These perspectives were expressed at the "International Conference on Solomon Caesar Malan (1812–1894)," held at Wadham College, University of Oxford on 24 August 2012.

placement of a diacritical dot on the left rather than the right-hand side of the word *oyorongge* (important).[87]

SCM's investment of time and repeated efforts to write Manchu correctly and elegantly in the ONBP Ms is a significant contribution to Manjuristics. The field has previously centered on the reading and interpretation of Manchu texts, with relatively negligible attention paid to how scholars may have cultivated their understanding of the linguistic and cultural attributes of the language through copying and other acts of reproduction. Just as the actions of finding and arranging aphorisms facilitated SCM's meditation on universal wisdom, his handwriting of these sayings can be seen as a means of reflecting on the inherent beauty and value of the languages in which they were expressed.

Select Bibliography

Adam, Lucien. 1873. *Grammaire de la langue Mandchou* (Grammar of the Manchu Language). Paris: Maisonneuve.

Aisin-Gioro (Aixin Jueluo) Puyi 爱新觉罗・溥仪. 1985. *Wo de qian bansheng* 我的前半生 (From Emperor to Citizen; literal translation: The First Half of My Life). Beijing: Qunzhong chubanshe.

An Chengshan 安成山 – Guo Yuan'er 郭元尔. 2007. *Xiboyu Manyu kouyu jichu* 锡伯语满语口语基础 (Foundations of Spoken Sibe-Manchu). Urumqi: Xinjiang renmin chubanshe.

Anonymous (ed.) 1789. *Qingwen Zhiyao* 清文指要 *Manju Gisun-i Oyonggo Jorin-i bithe* (Major Points of the Manchu Language). Beijing: Shuangfengge. 4 *ce* 册.

Baoligao 宝力高 (ed.) 1973. *Han Meng chengyu xiao cidian* 汉蒙成语小辞典 (Concise Dictionary of Chinese-Mongol Idioms). Huhhot: Nei Menggu renmin chubanshe.

Bosson, James – Hoong Teik Toh. 2006. "Jakdan and His Manchu Poetry." In: Stephen Wadley – Carsten Naeher (eds.), *Proceedings of the First North American Conference on Manchu Studies (Portland, Oregon, May 9–10, 2003), Vol. 1: Studies in Manchu Literature and History*, Tunguso-Sibirica, 15. Wiesbaden: Harrassowitz, pp. 13-26.

Ch'en Chieh-hsien 陳捷先. 1976. "The Decline of the Manchu Language in China during the Ch'ing Period." In: Walther Heissig (ed.), *Altaica Collecta (Berichte und Vorträge der XVII PIAC)*. Wiesbaden: Harrassowitz, pp. 137-154.

———. 1988. *Manchu Archival Materials*. Taipei: Linking Publishing.

Chuang Chi-fa 莊吉發. 1997–2016. *Qing shi lunji* 清史論集 (Collected Essays on Qing History), vols. 1–26. Taipei: Wen shi zhe chubanshe.

Ding Yizhuang 定宜庄. 2003. *Qingdai Baqi zhufang yanjiu* 清代八旗驻防研究 (Research on the Qing Eight Banners Garrisons). Shenyang: Liaoning minzu chubanshe.

---

[87] As found in SCM, *Sacra Privata*, probably p. 582 recto. The exact page where this image occurs, I have not been able to verify, since no access to the manuscript is currently available under the restrictions of the Covid-19 pandemic.

Enhebatu 恩和巴图. 1995. *Manyu kouyu yanjiu* 满语口语研究 (Research on Spoken Manchu). Huhhot: Nei Menggu daxue chubanshe.

von der Gabelentz, Hans Conon. 1832. *Élements de la grammaire Mandchoue* (Elements of Manchu Grammar]. Altenbourg: Comptoir de la littérature.

———. 1864. *Sse-schu, Schu-king, Schi-king in mandschurischer Übersetzung* (The Four Books, The Classic of History, and The Classic of Poetry in Manchu Translation). Abhandlungen der Deutschen Morgenländischen Gesellschaft, 3. Leipzig: F.A. Brockhaus.

Giles, Herbert A. 1898. *A Catalogue of the Wade Collection of Chinese and Manchu Books in the Library of the University of Cambridge*. Cambridge: Cambridge University Press.

Gorelova, Liliya M. (ed.). 2002. *Manchu Grammar*. Leiden – Boston: Brill.

Haenisch, Erich. 1961. *Mandschu-Grammatik: mit Lesestücken und 23 Texttafeln* [Manchu Grammar: With Reading Selections and 23 Texts]. Leipzig: Verlag Enzyklopädie.

Harlez, Charles de. 1884. *Manuel de la langue Mandchou, grammaire, anthologie et lexique* [Handbook of the Manchu Language and Grammar, with an Anthology and Glossary]. Paris: [n.p.].

Hauer, Erich. 1929. "Ein Reisepaß in Mandschusprache aus dem Jahre 1927" [A Passport in Manchu from 1927]. *Mitteilungen des Seminars für orientalische Sprachen, Ostasiatische Studien* 32 (1929), pp. 153-156.

———. 2007. *Handwörterbuch der Mandschusprache* [Concise Dictionary of Manchu Language]. Ed. Oliver Corff. 2nd ed. Wiesbaden: Harrassowitz.

Hermann, K[arl] A[ugust]. 1881. *Die Mandschusprache, verglichen mit dem Finnisch-Estnischen* [The Manchu Language, Compared with Finnish-Estonian]. Dorpat (Tartu): n.p.

Kara, György. 2000. *The Mongol and Manchu Manuscripts and Blockprints in the Library of the Hungarian Academy of Sciences*. Budapest: Akadémiai Kiadó.

Kim, Loretta E. 2007. "Illumination and Reverence: Language, Identity, and Power in the Prefaces of the Manchu Mirrors." In: Stephen Wadley – Carsten Naeher (eds.), *Proceedings of the First North American Conference on Manchu Studies (Portland, Oregon, May 9–10, 2003), Vol. 2: Studies in Manchu Linguistics*, Tunguso-Sibirica, 16. Wiesbaden: Harrassowitz, pp. 67-112.

von Klaproth, Julius. 1828. *Chrestomathie Mandchou, ou recueil de textes Mandchou […]*. (Manchu Chrestomathy, or a Collection of Manchu Texts […]). Paris: L'imprimerie royale.

Kuang Lu 廣祿 – Li Xuezhi 李學智. 1965. "Lao Manwen yuandang yu Manwen lao dang zhi bijiao yanjiu" 老滿文原檔與滿文老檔之比較研究 (Comparative Studies of Old Manchu Literary Source Archives and the Old Manchu Archives), *Zhongguo Dongya xueshu yanjiu jihua weiyuanhui nianbao* 中國東亞學術研究計劃委員會年報 / *Annual Bulletin of The China Council for East Asian Studies* 4 (1965), pp. 1-165.

Lee Ki-moon 李基文. 1973. "Sibpal segi eui Manju-eo bangeon jaryo" 十八世紀의滿洲語方言資料 [A Manuscript in the Manchu Dialect of the Eighteenth Century], *Jindan Hagbo* 震檀學報 36 (1973), pp. 99-132.

Lee, Robert H.G. 1970. *The Manchurian Frontier in Ch'ing History*. Cambridge, Mass.: Harvard University Press.

Malan, Solomon Cæsar. 1853. *Sacra Privata*. Manuscript, Bodleian Libraries: call number MS.Or.Polygl.f.1.

———. 1856. *A Letter to the Right Honourable the Earl of Shaftesbury, President of the British and Foreign Bible Society: On the Pantheistic and on the Buddhistic Tendency of the Chinese and of the Mongolian Versions of the Bible Published by that Society*. London: Bell and Daldy.

Matsumura Jun 松村潤. 1976. "Manshūgo yaku no seisho ni tsuite" 満州語訳の聖書について [On the Manchu Version of the Bible], *Tōyō bunko shohō* 東洋文庫書報 7 (1976), pp. 37-53.

Mish, John. 1958. "A Catholic Catechism in Manchu." *Monumenta Serica* 17, pp. 361-71.

Möllendorf, P[aul]. G[eorg] von. 1890. "Essay on Manchu Literature." *Journal of the North China Branch of the Royal Asiatic Society* 24 (1889–1890), pp. 1-45.

———. 1892. *A Manchu Grammar, with Analysed Texts*. Shanghai: American Presbyterian Mission Press.

Mungello, D[avid] E[mil]. 1988. "The Seventeenth-Century Jesuit Translation Project of the Confucian Four Books." In: Charles E. Ronan, S.J. – Bonnie B.C. Oh (eds.), *East Meets West: The Jesuits in China (1582–1773)*. Chicago: Loyola University Press, pp. 252-273.

Pang, Tatiana A[leksandrovna]. 1998. *A Catalogue of Manchu Materials in Paris*. Wiesbaden: Harrassowitz.

Sebes, Joseph. 1962. *The Jesuits and the Sino-Russian Treaty of Nerchinsk (1689): The Diary of Thomas Pereira*. Bibliotheca Instituti Historici, 18. Rome: Institutum Historicum S.I.

Sinor, Denis. 1963. *Introduction à l'étude de l'Eurasie centrale* [Introduction to the Study of Central Asia]. Wiesbaden: Harrassowitz.

Stary, Giovanni. 1990–2003. *Manchu Studies: an International Bibliography*. Wiesbaden: Otto Harrassowitz. 4 vols.

———. 2000. "Christian Literature in Manchu." *Central Asiatic Journal* 44 (2000) 2, pp. 305-316.

Walravens, Hartmut. 2000. "Christian Literature in Manchu: Some Bibliographic Notes." *Monumenta Serica* 48 (2000), pp. 445-469.

———. 1977–1978. "A Little Known Russian Manchurist." *Manchu Studies Newsletter* 1-2 (1977–1978), pp. 65-74.

———. 1974–1975. "Zu zwei katholischen Katechismen in mandjurischer Sprache" (On Two Catholic Catechisms in Manchu). *Monumenta Serica* 31 (1974–1975), pp. 521-549.

Wylie, Alexander. 1855. *Translation of the Ts'ing Wan K'e Mung* [清文啟蒙]: *A Chinese Grammar of the Manchu Tartar Language*. Shanghae [*sic*]: London Mission Press.

Yan Chongnian 阎崇年 (ed.) 2003. *Ershi shiji shijie Manxue zhuzuo tiyao* 20 世纪世界满学著作提要 (Abstracts of 20th century International Scholarship on Manjuristics). Beijing: Minzu chubanshe.

Yoshitake, S. 1928. "Some Mongolian Maxims." *Bulletin of the School of Oriental and African Studies* 4 (February 1928) 4, pp. 689-702.

Zakharov, Ivan Ilich. 1879. *Grammatika man'chzhurskogo iazyka* (Grammar of the Manchu Language). Saint Petersburg: The Imperial Academy of Science.

Zhang Meilan – Qi Jin. 2017. "The Decline of Manchu in Its Contact with Late Qing Chinese: A Case Study of Several Editions of *Qingwen Zhiyao*." In: Xu Dan – Li Hui (eds.), *Languages and Genes in Northwestern China and Adjacent Regions*. Singapore: Springer Nature, pp. 141-152.

9

INITIATING THE DISCOVERY OF TIBETAN WISDOM IN THE *ORIGINAL NOTES ON THE BOOK OF PROVERBS*

RITA KUZDER

1. Dealing with the Obvious and the Unexpected: Initiating the Discovery

Already in Budapest in the late 19th century it was known that the Hungarian scholar, Csoma de Kőrös (ca. 1784–1842), had given an extraordinary gift of numerous Tibetan documents to the young Solomon Caesar Malan sometime in the late 1830s.[1] At that time, SCM was teaching at Bishop's College in Calcutta.[2] From what has now been confirmed through careful research, the number of Tibetan documents SCM donated to the Hungarian Academy of Sciences in 1884 came to 39 documents consisting of 65 different texts.[3] That is to say, SCM had access to those Tibetan documents for more than forty years before he arranged to have them sent to Budapest. Consequently, when he began to prepare the English version of his *Original Notes on the Book of Proverbs* in the mid-1880s, SCM was working from the calligraphed passages and notes made in the huge manuscript in which he had written parallels to proverbial sayings found in the biblical book of Proverbs.[4]

Because of all these historical connections related to SCM's access to Tibetan writings and his relatively long period of studying, reading, and writing in Tibetan, it was assumed that he would have referred to many proverbial sayings in the three-volume set of the published *ONBP* (1889–1893) from the documents he had received from Csoma de Kőrös. Nevertheless, there were complications related to such an assumption that have puzzled me and others who have tried to document this line of transmission. On the one hand, it is well known that SCM sent at least 36 Tibetan documents to Budapest in 1884, and on the other hand, as this volume documents in some detail, the Malan Library was created in Oxford from the relatively large donation of manuscripts, books, and written materials that had previously constituted SCM's unusual personal library.[5] So, naturally, several questions arose from these circumstances. First of all, how many of the Tibetan documents SCM received from Csoma de Kőrös did he quote in the ONBP Ms and ultimately translate into English as part of the citations from Tibetan sources in his published version? Secondly, another matter that has remained unclear is whether SCM donated all the

---

[1] Details about this story have been recorded and elaborated in Chapter 11 of this volume.

[2] See Chapter 2 in this volume for an account of SCM's activities in Bishop's College.

[3] Confirmed and explained in Chapter 11.

[4] This is the manuscript known as "MS.Ind.Inst.Misc.10" in the Oriental Division of the Bodleian Libraries. I will refer to it subsequently as the "ONBP Ms."

[5] Details about history and content of the Malan Library are presented in Chapter 12 in this volume.

Tibetan documents he had received in Calcutta to the Hungarian Academy of Sciences. Assuming that he did not obtain any other Tibetan documents after those he had received from Csoma de Kőrös in the late 1830s, is there any evidence that SCM did not send certain Tibetan documents to Budapest in 1884, but kept them in his personal library for his own use until they were sent to Oxford in 1885? These have become the basic questions that initiated my own research into SCM's understanding of Tibetan language and assessing evidence found within the Tibetan proverbs cited in the *ONBP*.

By comparing items listed as "Tibetan" or "Buddhist" texts in the Index found at the end of the first volume of *ONBP* with the bibliographic list of the documents that constitute the "Csoma Bequest,"[6] I have identified two Tibetan documents from that special collection held now in the library of the Hungarian Academy of Sciences that were apparently used by SCM in creating his published version of the ONBP Ms.[7] Those two documents are identified by SCM in that Index, though his description of them do not mention anything about their being part of the Csoma Bequest. He referred to them there in his 19th century transliteration as "Byam-chub-lam-gyi-sgron-ma"[8] and "Snan-ngag me-long, etc."[9] Using Tibetan as well as a standard 21st century Tibetan transliteration of those titles, those two documents can be identified as follows:

- བྱང་ཆུབ་ལམ་གྱི་སྒྲོན་མ། – transliteration: *byang chub lam gyi sgron ma*.[10] This is a document written by Atisha, and is known in its Sanskrit version as *Bodhipathapradipa*, that is, "Lamp for the Path to Enlightenment" or "Lamp for the Path to Full Awakening." In the library of the Hungarian Academy of Sciences, it is identified as "Csoma-bequest No. 18."

- སྙན་ངག་མེ་ལོང་། – transliteration: *snyan ngag me long*. An English translation of the title of this work is "The Mirror of Sweet Words." In the library of the Hungarian Academy of Sciences, it is found under the call number "Csoma-bequest No. 37." This text is only cited once within the *ONBP*,[11] as far as I have

---

[6] This bibliographic list is provided in Orosz 2008, vol. 1, pp. 1-25.

[7] The section of the Index related to "References" is found in *ONBP*, vol. 1, pp. 481-485. It is not a comprehensive list of all works found even in that initial volume of the *ONBP*, much less the whole three-volume set, but it fortunately did have some references to certain Tibetan works.

[8] Found in the bottom of the right-hand column of the Index at *ONBP*, vol. 1, p. 481. It is further described there by SCM, following the title of the work, as "Lantern on the road to the Buddha; a Buddhist work."

[9] This work is recorded at the bottom of the right-hand column of the Index at *ONBP*, vol. 1, p. 484. SCM describes it further as "Commentary on 'The Mirror of Sweet Words.'"

[10] Here from the outset, it should be explained that the spelling of Tibetan words are not the same as their pronunciation; as in the case of English, there are letters within a word that are not pronounced. So at times I will refer to a pronunciation of a word first, and then follow it with its Tibetan transliteration. Scholarly articles in Tibetology are based on Turrel Wylie's system, see https://en.wikipedia.org/wiki/Wylie_transliteration (accessed March 16, 2021).

[11] Seen at *ONBP*, vol. 1, p. 16, n. 10.

been able to identify it. Nevertheless, it is an important treatise on the theory and principles of Sanskrit poetics, written by the Indian *pandita*, Dandin (Skt., Daṇḍin) (ca. 6–7th c.). It was introduced to Tibetan scholars in the 1220s by Sakya Pandita, so that from that time it served as the standard guide for the literary composition of poetry, philosophy, biography and letter writing. What we have in this text within the Csoma Bequest is a commentary to that original text composed in 1667 by the Fifth Dalai Lama, Ngawang Lobsang Gyatsho (*nga dbang blo bzang rgya mtsho*, 1617–1682).[12]

Of some interest is the fact that SCM also referred to Csoma's Tibetan grammar in the *ONBP*, because what Csoma included within the grammar were some of his own translations of Tibetan proverbs.[13] Nevertheless, these are probably not as important as the other surprising and unexpected result of this initial research into SCM's use of Tibetan proverbs. Since SCM had access to nearly 40 Tibetan documents from the Csoma Bequest, why did he only cite two of them? Were the others written in styles that did not include what he counted as "proverbial"? Or were there other reasons for such a numerically small number of Tibetan sources related to the Csoma Bequest to be quoted in the *ONBP*?

Secondly, from what can be seen by comparing how SCM described the works and the titles mentioned above, the first title is rendered somewhat awkwardly, while the second document he explicitly (and precisely) describes as a "commentary" to the work with that title. There are here hints of some further questions that could be raised about the level of understanding SCM had of those Tibetan sources, but here I will not address those matters, reserving these responses for a later point in this chapter.

When I had opportunity to pursue some research at the Oriental Division of the Bodleian Libraries, where the volumes associated with the former Malan Library are now held in a dispersed and unsystematized form, I made a further discovery. The three most cited Tibetan texts in the *ONBP* are found there, and are not located in the Academy's library in Budapest. Immediately I considered the possibility that these three works were formerly documents in the Tibetan gifts given to SCM in Calcutta in the late 1830s, and suspected that SCM kept them so that he could verify his footnotes to their content for the *ONBP* during the time between the departure of the Csoma Bequest to Hungary in early 1884, and the delivery of his personal library to Oxford in 1885. From all that is currently known about SCM's access to Tibetan works, this reason for his keeping three major Tibetan manuscripts from the Csoma Bequest in his personal library is probably the most justified of all the

---

[12] As documented in Terjek 1976, pp. 128-129.

[13] Cited and identified as coming from Csoma's Grammar or Csoma's translation in *ONBP*, vol. 2, p. 103, n. 4, and vol. 3, p. 260, n. 9, and p. 598, n. 11. This document was created along with a Tibetan-English Dictionary that was supported by the funding of William Moorcroft in India. Both works were published in 1834. Csoma's Tibetan grammar dealt with articles that were considered essential for obtaining a fundamental knowledge of the language. He presented within that volume the various parts of speech within Tibetan and produced lists of terms based on what he had learned at that time.

explanations that would be considered possible under the circumstances and limitations with which SCM lived. Those three major Tibetan documents are identified as follows, the first two being well-known texts in Tibetan Buddhist literature:

- ལེགས་པར་བཤད་པ། – transliteration: *legs par bshad pa*. This is a document written by Sakya Paṇḍita. Another title for the work is *Sakya Legshe* (Elegant Sayings). SCM did cite this work in the Index to his first volume of *ONBP* and gave the title as "Treasury of Good Words."[14] This text is cited 263 times in the whole of the *ONBP*, referring to 270 different passages.

- རྒྱ་ཆེར་རོལ་པ། – transliteration: *rgya cher rol pa*. This is a Tibetan translation of the Sanskrit text named the *Lalitavistara* (Extensive Play Sutra). Once more, SCM did cite this work in his *ONBP* Index for the first volume, referring to the Sanskrit original, and describing the text as "a Buddhist account of the birth and doings of Shakyamuni, the last Buddha."[15] Second to the former text in number of citations, it appears in the footnotes throughout the whole of the *ONBP* 167 times, and includes 170 passages.

- མཛངས་བླུན། – transliteration: *mdzangs blun*, a document also known as མཛངས་བླུན་ཞེས་བྱ་བའི་མདོ། – transliteration: *mdzang blun zhes bya ba'i mdo*. This document is known in Sanskrit as the *Damamūka-nidāna-sūtra* (The Sutra of the Wise and the Foolish). Once again, this text is mentioned in SCM's *ONBP* Index for "References," the title being given as "The Wise and The Fool. A Collection of Stories."[16] This document is cited 103 times in the whole of the *ONBP* and includes references to 107 passages.

What I mean by stating that these are the most often cited Tibetan documents in the published version of the *ONBP* can be demonstrated by reference to the statistics worked out by Lauren and Mirasy Pfister more than ten years ago.[17] According to their statistical analysis at that time, there are thirteen Tibetan documents mentioned in the three-volume set of the *ONBP*, with 659 total citations. The three Tibetan texts mentioned above as the most often cited are presented in the order of their citations: the first was cited 265 times throughout the three volumes; the second, 143 times; the third, 102 times. Together they were cited 510 times, which amounts to a little more than 77% of all the Tibetan citations. Ten other Tibetan documents share in the remaining 149 citations, and the one closest to these three has only 49

---

[14] See *ONBP*, vol. 1, p. 483, middle of left-hand column. He refers to the author as "Saskya pandita."

[15] Found in *ONBP*, vol. 1, p. 484, middle of the left-hand column. His transliteration of the title there is "Rgya-tcher-rol-pa."

[16] As cited from *ONBP*, vol. 1, p. 482, near the bottom of the left-column.

[17] The work done by Mirasy Pfister and others to prepare the database by which these statistics have been generated is described briefly in Chapter 13 of this volume. The statistics based on this database have been extremely helpful for initiating further research into the published version of the *ONBP*, but it should be seen as only an initial statistical foundation for pursuing this research work. More recent assessments of the content of the footnotes of the *ONBP* in relationship to Tibetan sources reveals several other problems that I will describe in detail later in this chapter.

citations. In research pursued for this chapter, I have determined more precise accounts of the number of Tibetan documents mentioned by SCM in the *ONBP*, as well as other statistics drawn from research into the content of the *ONBP*'s footnotes, and so will update those numbers and statistics in later portions of this chapter.

2. Further Questions about S. C. Malan and His Understanding of Tibetan Language and Tibetan Sources

From all these initial explanations there arises a number of questions that are prompted by what has been seen so far. How technically accurate was SCM's understanding of the Tibetan language and the Tibetan documents that he had possessed for much of his adult life? Sometimes his rendering of the titles of those works in his bibliography have provoked questions about the precision of his renderings. Beyond this, however, there is a more extensive problem related to how he referred to the titles of the Tibetan texts and documents that he read and cited. In the initial section I have only referred indirectly to a few of those problems, such as his inconsistency in referring to titles of works he referred to most often, but there are also other more significant problems that I will describe in some detail later in this chapter. Larger and culturally more significant problems also remain. What terms in Tibetan are equivalent for the concept and content of "proverbs" that SCM was searching for? Did he discuss this problem at all? Furthermore, how, and in what ways did the *ONBP* in its own day contribute to scholarship in Tibetan research? Are there any significant contributions that remain important for 21st century Tibetan research? Culturally speaking, how well did SCM grasp the different worldview portrayed in the Tibetan sayings he included in the *ONBP*? Did he "Christianize" or "Judaize" the content of Tibetan proverbs so that they would match up better with sayings and passages in the biblical book of Proverbs?

In the remainder of this chapter, I will seek to answer all of these questions, as far as that is possible for me to do so. To start out with, therefore, I will approach the question of what it was that SCM was seeking when he was pursuing proverbial literature and sayings in the Tibetan texts that he was reading.

3. Solomon Caesar Malan's Account of the Concept of a Proverb and Possible Tibetan Equivalents

In his preface to the initial volume of the *ONBP*, SCM offered an extensive account of not only the nature of the Hebrew term for "proverb" (*māšāl*) and "proverbs" (*mᵉšālîm*),[18] but also indicated the vast amount of proverbial resources found among

---

[18] SCM refers to these two terms directly in n. 2 of *ONBP*, vol. 1, p. iii, adding both the Hebrew terms in their Hebrew spelling as well as their transliterations. There one will find the transliteration he employed for the plural form of the word is "*meshālim*," but here above I use a more updated transliteration. The Hebrew term for the single word "proverb" appears six times in its Hebrew expression between three pages in that preface (*ONBP*, vol. 1, pp. ix-xi).

numerous "Eastern authors."[19] Generally speaking, SCM takes a broader view of the concept of "proverb" than some might take, but also opposes the equivalence made by some ancient authors between "proverbs" and "parables."[20] For him, proverbs may include "fables with a moral,"[21] "wise sayings,"[22] "apologues, couplets on moral subjects; maxims, aphorisms, riddles,"[23] even more distinctively "friendly or proper advice,"[24] and more technically, "distichs."[25] Precisely in this sense, then, proverbs are not "vulgar sayings," but are "ornament[s] to a discourse" that become both "lights (or lanterns) to conversations," but also "a seal to a wise man's word."[26]

Notably, within this wide-ranging discussion of many ancient sources,[27] SCM does refer to the fables found in the Tibetan classic work, *Dsang-Lun* (or in modern transliteration, *mdzangs blun*, The Sutra of the Wise and the Foolish), as an example of what the "proverbs" can and should include.[28]

Within Tibetan language there are two words in common use for this genre associated with "proverbs." First, there is the term *tampe* གཏམ་དཔེ་ (*gtam dpe*)[29] which refers to a proverb, common saying, and maxim; secondly, there is the term *khape* ཁ་དཔེ་ (*kha dpe*), which is regularly found in dictionaries and refers to a proverb. What distinguishes the meaning of these two terms is very slight: the original sense of the prevailing term, *tampe*, is that it is a "speech example"; the term *khape* is described as a "mouth example." While this etymological analysis does not offer much insight, it is more helpful to understand how they function within Tibetan language and culture. What these two terms refer to are stories or allegories related

---

[19] Cited from *ONBP*, vol. 1, p. xi.

[20] For his argument against the equivalence of these two terms, see *ONBP*, vol.1, pp. ix-xi.

[21] Quoted from *ONBP*, vol. 1, p. iii.

[22] Stated in particular reference to ancient Egyptian proverbial sources, citing from *ONBP*, vol. 1, p. v.

[23] Here again from *ONBP*, vol. 1, p. iii.

[24] A phrase that translates the meaning of the classic Indian text called the "Hitapodesa," a title SCM notes that is used in Sanskrit also for the Christian translation of the biblical book of Proverbs. See *ONBP*, vol. 1, p. vi.

[25] This term SCM defines as "consist[ing] of two hemistichs in apposition the one to the other," involving "a saying both short and frequently used," with equivalents in Arabic, Sanskrit, and Persian. See his discussion and these quotations from *ONBP*, vol. 1, pp. x-xi.

[26] Quotations taken from *ONBP*, vol. 1, pp. viii, where SCM quotes from Arabic and Persian sources for these descriptions.

[27] Within the twelve pages of the preface to the *ONBP* SCM refers to works in Arabic, Armenian, Chinese, Egyptian, Georgian, Greek, Hebrew, Latin, Persian, Sanskrit, Tibetan, Turkish and Welsh.

[28] Seen in *ONBP*, vol. 1, p. v.

[29] The initial word *tampe* reveals how the word should be pronounced, while the transliteration provided in parentheses presents the technical way to refer to the Tibetan term. This way of referring to phrases and titles will be employed here and in the rest of this chapter.

to mundane examples that are often handed down by older generations and employed to illustrate religious truth (*chos*) or common sense. Notably, this genre of literature is found in and elaborated within both Buddhist sutras as well as in Tibetan Buddhist narrative literature.

My own research work has focused on the classification of Tibetan proverbs,[30] and so allowed me the opportunity not only to read many documents in Tibetan language, but also to explore other terms that are used in Tibetan to refer to what SCM described as "proverbs." During that research work I discovered two more Tibetan terms that are applied to "proverbs": *pechoe* དཔེ་ཆོས་ (*dpe chos*) and *doedra* ཟློས་སྒྲ་ (*zlos sgra*). According to Christopher Cüppers and Per K. Sørensen, the term *pechoe* (*dpe chos*), which is used to refer to a "parable" or "allegorical simile," is defined in a variety of ways, but can be basically described as a short lesson in the form of a religious topos (*chos*) that is exemplified, illustrated or allegorized (*dpe*) and often takes the form of a brief story or tale (*gtam rgyud*).[31] Notably, in the preface of a dictionary of *pechoe*s the following account of this genre of Tibetan literature is described in detail.

> [*Pechoe*s] are not *tampe*s, but they stand very close to them. [They are composed of] brief and tight expressions, containing mostly just nouns. No verbs can be found in them. They are generally four to ten syllables long. The most important feature regarding them is that there is a story behind them, and the *pechoe* is the essence of that story. In order to understand the meaning of any *pechoe*, one should learn about the whole story that it refers to. The main difference between *tampe* and *pechoe* is that *tampe*s are disseminated orally, while *pechoe*s are disseminated mostly in written form.[32]

While these four Tibetan terms are all relevant to the study of Tibetan proverbs, there is another word that refers to sayings that are "cited," because it is known who stated them or who created them. In European terminology this kind of saying is called an "adage." Even though this Tibetan term is not very often used, the *ngag gyun* ངག་རྒྱུན་ (*ngag rgyun*) is a term that includes all the other more precise terms, and yet refers to the fact that all of them have a known source. Since all of the Tibetan proverbs cited in SCM's *ONBP* are cited from well-known books and authors, this seems to be the best term to use in describing the Tibetan proverbs found there.

In fact, what SCM has done to collect Tibetan proverbs within his *ONBP* was far in anticipation of later studies produced in European languages about Tibetan proverbs and folklore. Although the scholarly realm of paremiology, or the study of proverbs, is international in scope, and there is reference to some Tibetan proverbial sayings, but still no major general survey of them all has been published.

---

[30] Consult Kuzder 2012. This is a Ph.D. dissertation completed in 2012 and written in Hungarian at the Eötvös Loránd University, located in Budapest.

[31] Summarized from Cüppers – Sørensen 2000, pp. xiii, n. 5.

[32] The translation is by this author. For the original text, consult *dpa' ris sangs rgyas* [Pari Szangye] 1999, pp. 5-6.

For example, there is a short survey of Tibetan folklore literature in one volume of the *Enzyklopädie des Märchens* written by Ulrike Roesler.[33] Although Roesler mentions some different genres and texts within her article – Buddhist stories including the Gesar epoch, and various other folktales, legends, and hagiographies – she does not write anything about the proverbs. Nevertheless, she does mention the witicisms found in the *Sakya Paṇḍita* and its religious parables, all of which are well-known among Tibetan people. In another article written sixty years ago about Tibetan "folk-literature,"[34] Frederick Thomas described a different set of literary genre that included prognostication methods and texts, proverbs, songs (including love songs, wedding songs, beer songs, working songs), tales (including animal tales, corpse tales, and fairy tales), the epic of *Gesar*, Tibetan opera texts, and texts for the *'cham* dances. Within that volume Thomas had produced a translation of a text that is the earliest extant text of Tibetan "folk-literature," "Sumpa Mother's Sayings," a text that possesses features that could be counted as "proverbial" under SCM's broad categorization of proverbs.[35] It is dated back to the period of the 7th or 8th centuries CE and was discovered in a Dunhuang cave by the European explorer, Aurel Stein (1862–1943). Its 76 sayings bear a remarkable similarity to an ancient Sumerian wisdom text called the *Instructions of Suruppak*,[36] yet this ancient Tibetan text is composed with old Tibetan grammar and contains advice and admonitions that are not always equivalent to proverbial sayings. As far as I have been able to discover, SCM never referred to this earliest Tibetan text in the *ONBP*, but he did refer to many others of a later era.

From this perspective, then, SCM was collecting sayings from Tibetan documents that very few scholars of Tibetan literature had focused on, especially in the 19th century. What I will now seek to document are the titles and characteristics of those Tibetan texts cited in the *ONBP*, and then offer some initial assessments of his translations, his understanding of those Tibetan sayings and their Buddhist claims, and the range of genre he included within "Tibetan proverbs."

4. Revealing More about the Tibetan Texts Cited Relatively Often in the *Original Notes on the Book of Proverbs*

While the *ONBP* is a remarkable document because of the manifest hyperpolyglossia that equipped SCM to be able to identify and record proverbial sayings from texts involving more than fifty languages, it is also a difficult work to read, because very few persons know enough about so many languages and their related cultures to appreciate the deeper cultural aspects that appear within the proverbs representing

---

[33] See Roesler 2007, vol. 13, pp. 523-530.

[34] Consult Thomas 1957.

[35] See Thomas 1957, pp. 103-112.

[36] This is a significant example of Sumerian wisdom literature. The *Instructions* date to the early third millennium BCE, being among the oldest surviving literature. The context consists of admonitory sayings of Suruppak addressed to his son.

any particular culture. Very seldom does SCM discuss, or even point out any historical details, about the authors he mentions in the body of the work or the texts that he so extensively cited within the nearly 16,000 footnotes that reveal the sources of his readings and recordings. Yet, because of his remarkably fortunate relationship forged with Csoma de Kőrös in Calcutta in the late 1830s,[37] and what SCM continued to learn through reading Tibetan documents, grammars, dictionaries, and other related materials for what amounted to nearly another fifty years after he departed from India in 1840, there can be a lot of interest generated in seeking to comprehend to what level of understanding and insight in Tibetan language and culture SCM had attained through reading, interpreting, and translating those Tibetan proverbs and fables into English.

To initiate such a worthwhile venture, I would like to record in this section some of the historical, religious, cultural and proverbial details related to a number of the texts that SCM cited and which I can identify. There are also some terms of reference for Tibetan book titles as well as some Tibetan or Indian authors that SCM employed that I cannot easily decipher, but because they do occur also within the index and among the footnotes of the *ONBP*, it is at least worth noting what they might be and why I cannot easily identify them. On this basis, then, there will be a large range of cultural and textual information that can be used to start another level of study and discernment, that is, using that information to weigh how accurately and perceptively SCM rendered those Tibetan Buddhist texts into English within the *ONBP*.

By reviewing both the incomplete Index found at the end of the first volume of the *ONBP* and the footnotes to that three-volume work, I have been able to identify eight documents that SCM employed in his *ONBP*, including the Tibetan grammar produced by Csoma de Kőrös.[38] Though that grammar has its own special historic value, especially for SCM, I will focus here on the other seven Tibetan documents that he cites within the *ONBP*, to reveal more about the character of their writings, their authorship (whenever possible), their proverbial content, and how often they were referred to by SCM in the *ONBP*. On this basis, it will be possible in subsequent discussions within this chapter to ask further questions about how well SCM understood and portrayed Tibetan Buddhist claims and other cultural features found in those works within his English translations of selected passages from those works within the *ONBP*.

Here below I will take each Tibetan document and provide a general account of its content and other matters that would be of interest for our further reflections on SCM's English renderings of selected sayings and passages taken from them and put into the *ONBP*. They will be presented in an order reflecting their relative use

---

[37] For more information on the relationship between Csoma and SCM, see Chapter 11 of this volume.

[38] As already seen above in n. 13, SCM cited Csoma's grammar three times within the *ONBP*, because it included some translations of Tibetan proverbial sayings that he included (and so properly cited their origin).

within the *ONBP*, from the one most often referenced within the footnotes, to the one least often found there.

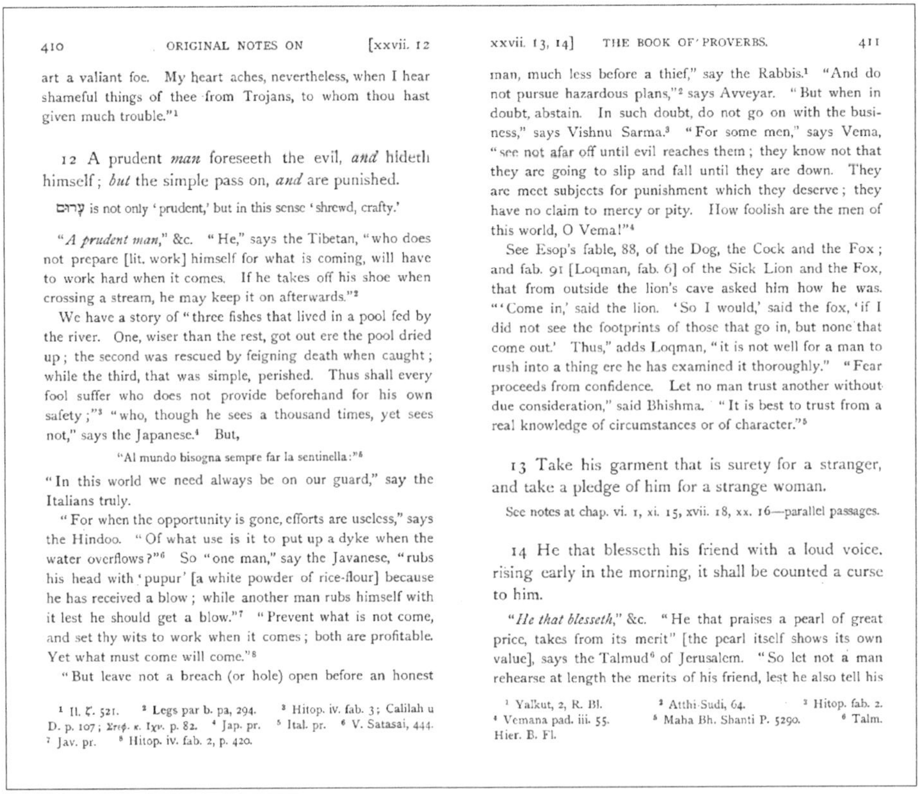

Fig. 15: *ONBP*, vol. 3, pp. 410-411 (Prov. 27: 12-14), Tibetan source (p. 410, footnote 2)

As has already been indicated above, the most often cited Tibetan work within the *ONBP* is the following document: ལེགས་པར་བཤད་པ། (*legs par bshad pa*), written by Sakya Paṇḍita, known also as *Sakya Legshe* (Elegant Sayings). This collection of moral precepts is written in verse, and was considered to be such an excellent work that it was imitated by others, and also translated into Mongolian.[39] The person Sakya Paṇḍita, also known as Kunga Gyeltsen Pal Sangpo (ཀུན་དགའ་རྒྱལ་མཚན་དཔལ་བཟང་པོ། transliteration: *kun dga' rgyal mtshan dpal bzang po*, 1182–1251), was a Tibetan spiritual leader and Buddhist scholar. He is considered to be the fourth of the Five Venerable Supreme Sakya Masters of Tibet, and so is generally known simply as Sangye Paṇḍita. This title was given to him in recognition of his scholarly achievements and knowledge of Sanskrit. Within Tibetan traditions he is believed to have been an emanation of the Bodhisattva Manjushree, the embodiment of the wisdom of all the Buddhas. He became known as a great scholar in Tibet, Mongolia, Coastal China

---

[39] The title of that work in Mongolian is Эрдэнийн сан Субашид (transliterated as *Érdéniïn san subashid*), meaning something like "Treasured Sayings."

and India, and was proficient in the five great sciences of Buddhist philosophy, medicine, grammar, dialectics, and sacred Sanskrit literature, while also having learned much about the so-called "minor sciences" of rhetoric, synonymies, poetry, dancing, and astrology. Sakya Paṇḍita's wisdom and writings have been so much admired that they have greatly influenced other authors, inspiring them to write new works. As a consequence, many of his sayings are well-known even by common persons who would not know that they originated from his writings.

The *Sakya Legshe* are part of a major Tibetan literary genre offering ethical advice, called *legshe*, a form of literature that is a very popular genre. These sayings are formally linked to Indian *subhāṣita* literature, which have been unusually influential also in Tibetan literature. The poetic form of these ethical sayings appears usually in four-line stanzas, where there are seven syllables in each line. From the perspective of Tibetan religious education, students are required to learn and memorize these sayings in monastery schools. As a consequence, they are not only repeated among monks, but are also known to uneducated Tibetans as well. Their literary content often involves figures representing the wise *khepa* (*mkhas pa*), the noble, *yarab* (*ya rabs*) and the stupid, *lünpo* (*blun po*). These sayings present many proverbial claims related to people's character and behavior, while also offering other advice related to common social problems. This advice is often expressed in a metaphor or principle that relates to similar situations in everyday life. In most of the four-line stanzas, it is the first line, or perhaps the first two lines, that have become proverbial.

SCM was obviously attracted to many of the Tibetan proverbs found in the *Sakya Legshe*, partly because the Hebrew sayings found in the biblical book of Proverbs are also composed of many distiches, or sayings in two lines. Similarly, their content overlapped in many ways, and so he found much to compare between them. It is significant, then, that it is in the latter two volumes of the *ONBP* that the majority of Hebrew proverbs are preserved as distiches (from chapters 11 to 31 in the book of Proverbs), and that there were more citations from the *Sakya Legshe* (119 times in the second volume, and 102 times in the third). In the first volume of the *ONBP*, where there are longer sections dealing with other themes, SCM cited this work the least among the three volumes (only 42 times).[40]

The second most cited Tibetan work in the *ONBP* is of a rather different character. It is the རྒྱ་ཆེར་རོལ་པ། (*rgya cher rol pa*), the full title of this text in Tibetan being འཕགས་པ་རྒྱ་ཆེར་རོལ་པ་ཞེས་བྱ་བ་ཐེག་པ་ཆེན་པོའི་མདོ། (*'phags pa rgya cher rol pa zhes bya ba theg pa chen po'i mdo*). It was originally a Sanskrit text known as the *Lalitavistara Sūtra*, and its 27 chapters were translated into Tibetan in the 8th century by Jinamitra. The meaning of the main term in the title, *Lalitavistara*, has been rendered as "Play in Full" or "Extensive Play," referring to the Mahāyāna view that the Buddha's last incarnation was a "display" or "performance" given for the benefit of all sentient

---

[40] This amounts to 263 citations of this classic Tibetan work throughout the whole of the *ONBP*, including 270 passages (because in some citations there were more than one passage rendered into English). The Pfisters' statistics were very close, claiming there were 265 citations of this work in the *ONBP*.

beings in this world. Throughout the whole of the document the story of the Buddha from the time of his descent from the Tushita heaven until his first sermon in the Deer Park near Benares is described and elaborated. Within this text, therefore, there are fewer proverbial sayings related to ethical advice, but a host of traditional accounts of the various reincarnations of the Buddha and his attainment of an enlightenment that released him from the cycles of those reincarnations. Here, then, a Mahāyāna version of a Buddhist worldview is expansively described, and so it would be a cultural and conceptual challenge for SCM to articulate its claims. He appeared to take that task seriously, since he quoted this Tibetan text rather evenly across the whole of the *ONBP*: 53 times in the first volume, 70 times in the second, and 40 times in the third.[41]

The third most often cited Tibetan text deals with a theme that forms one of the major leit-motifs of the biblical book of Proverbs. In Tibetan it is known as མཛངས་བླུན། (*mdzangs blun*) or as མཛངས་བླུན་ཞེས་བྱ་བའི་མདོ། (*mdzang blun zhes bya ba'i mdo*), following a Sanskrit original, entitled *Damamūka-nidāna-sūtra*, and is also known in Pali as *Bala-Paṇḍita Sutta*, both of which in English is rendered as "The Sutra of the Wise and the Foolish." So prominent is this theme in the Hebrew book of Proverbs, that one commentator identifies eleven words in Hebrew that cover some aspect of "wisdom," and six words for "folly."[42] The whole work is popularly described by another title, "An Ocean of Narratives," because it consists of *Jātaka* stories in fifty-one chapters, that is, stories of the previous reincarnations of the Buddha in human and animal form. From this important religious perspective, this classic Buddhist work traces the causes of present tragedies in human and animal lives to events which took place in former lifetimes. The theme of each narrative is the same: first it portrays something of the tragedy of the conditions of life for sentient beings, explaining the reason(s) for these tragedies, and then finally points to the possibilities of transcending them all. For centuries, the Tibetan version of "The Sutra of the Wise and the Foolish" has been a source of inspiration, instruction, and pleasure for all who have read it. So, from this angle, SCM chose a truly popular and classical text that portrays Buddhist wisdom based upon its concerns regarding the suffering involved in reincarnation and the goal of liberation through enlightenment.

Notably, the history of this unusual scripture is still uncertain. Legend has it that the tales were heard in Khotan by Chinese monks, who translated them into Chinese. Part of the documentation that supports these claims is that in Dunhuang, located in what is now northwestern China in Gansu Province, there are many wall paintings within the famous caves there illustrating stories from "The Sutra of the Wise and the Foolish." In addition, many painted scrolls discovered there portray the same themes.

Passages from this famous text are found spread throughout the three volumes of the *ONBP* in a relatively balanced way (35 citations in the first, 40 in the second,

---

[41] This involved 167 citations including 170 passages across the three-volume set. The Pfisters in this regard had only counted 143 citations, and so their numbers were significantly less than what is reported above.

[42] As discussed in Fox 2010, pp. 28-43.

and 28 in the third), with the largest amount occurring in the largest volume of SCM's opus.[43] Along with the other two Tibetan documents that are most often quoted in the *ONBP*, the sum of the citations drawn from these first three Tibetan texts constitute more than 70 percent of all the Tibetan citations found in the three volumes of the *ONBP*.[44]

The next Tibetan text made significant by being referred to nearly fifty times in the whole of the *ONBP* is another famous Buddhist text: ཐར་རྒྱན། or དམ་ཆོས་ཡིད་བཞིན་གྱི་ནོར་བུ་ ཐར་པ་རིན་པོ་ཆེའི་རྒྱན། that is, the *thar rgyan* (or in a more lengthy and precise title, *dam chos yid bzhin gyi nor bu thar pa rin po che'i rgyan*, meaning in English "The Jewelled Ornament of Liberation." It was composed by a famous Tibetan Buddhist monk, Gampopa Sonam Rinchen (*sgam po pa bsod nams rin chen*, 1079–1153). This Tibetan text is a famous survey of the ground, path, and fruition of the Buddhadharma, the author being the foremost disciple of the famous yogi and poet, Milarepa (ca. 1030–1120). Gampopa Sonam Rinchen was equally well known in Tibet as Dagpo Lhaje (*dvags po lha rje*), "the Physician from Dagpo," and Nyamed Dakpo Rinpoche, that is, the "Incomparably Precious One from Dagpo." Through his efforts the Dagpo Kagyu School was founded in 1125. More precisely, "The Jewelled Ornament of Liberation" is said to capture the essence of both the Kadampa and Kagyupa lineage of Mahāyāna teachings. The content of this famous text is summarized (for the sake of memorization) in six topics: "the cause, the support, the circumstance, the method, the result, and the activity." Put into more elaborate statements, those six points can be described in the following manner. First, the cause is buddha-nature, and its support comes from the most precious human body. Circumstance is one's spiritual friend. The method consists in these instructions. The result consists of the *kayas* (literally, "that which is accumulated," or the "bodies") of perfect Buddhahood.[45] Finally, activity is the spontaneous accomplishment of any sentient beings' benefits.

This is certainly one of the most technical Tibetan Buddhist texts that SCM consulted, one that would challenge him to make appropriate renderings of the content, methods, and goals along the way toward Buddhist liberation. From this perspective, then, it is perhaps understandable that he did not delve so deeply into these

---

[43] Here the Pfisters' statistics were remarkably close: they documented 102 citations of this work in the whole of the *ONBP*, and I have found 103 citations, with 107 passages involved.

[44] Based on the most recent statistics determined from a thorough rereading of the many footnotes in the three volumes of the *ONBP*, there are 724 Tibetan citations involving 744 passages from as many as 30 Tibetan documents, one third of them only being cited once. Consequently, the 533 citations associated with these three most often referred to Tibetan texts constitute 73.6% of the total number of citations found in SCM's English renderings in the whole of the *ONBP*.

[45] There are normally three "bodies" of the Buddha that are explored under this rubric: the *Dharmakaya* or "body of truth," the *Sambhogakaya* or "body of enjoyment (of the fruit of Buddhist practices)," and the *Nirmanakaya*, the "body of emanations."

complicated Buddhist accounts, but only cited proverbial sayings from this text less than fifty times within the three volumes of his *ONBP*.[46]

Similarly popular in broader realms of Mahāyāna Buddhism, but also less often cited in the *ONBP*, is *The White Lotus Sutra* (*Holy Sutra of the Greater Way*), or *Heart of the Perfection of Wisdom*, known in Tibetan as དམ་པའི་ཆོས་པད་མ། (*dam pa'i chos pad ma*), or more extensively as either དམ་པའི་ཆོས་པད་མ་དཀར་པོ་མདོ། (*dam pa'i chos pad ma dkar po mdo*) or བཅོམ་ལྡན་འདས་མ་ཤེས་རབ་ཀྱི་ཕ་རོལ་ཏུ་ཕྱིན་པའི་སྙིང་པོ། (*bcom ldan 'das ma shes rab kyi pha rol tu phyin pa'i snying po*). The earliest known Sanskrit title for the sutra is the *Saddharma Puṇḍarīka Sūtra*, which translates to "The Good Dharma Lotus Flower Sutra." In English, the shortened form of *Lotus Sutra* is used very often instead of the longer title. Unquestionably, the *Saddharma Puṇḍarīka Sūtra* or *Lotus Sutra* is one of the most popular and influential Mahāyāna sūtras in East Asian contexts; it is the basis on which the Tiantai 天臺 Buddhist school in China and the Nichiren 日蓮 schools of Buddhism in Japan were established.

Ancient traditions in Mahāyāna Buddhist literature state that the sutra was written down at the time of the Buddha and stored for five hundred years in a realm of snake gods (*nāgas*). After this, they were reintroduced into the human realm. The *Lotus Sūtra* presents itself as a discourse delivered by the Buddha toward the end of His life. The oldest parts of the text (Chapters 1–9 and 17) were probably written down between 100 BCE and 100 CE; most of the text had appeared by 200 CE.

From the angle of the Buddhist traditions that SCM read and studied, it seems that he was more inclined to document Buddhist texts from the Theravadan and Tibetan traditions rather than those from the Mahāyānan traditions; that is, he preferred those from Burma, Sri Lanka, Mongolia, and Tibet, rather than those later traditions as they developed in China, Japan, and Korea. Consequently, he only cited this particular text seven times in the whole of the *ONBP*.[47]

A final Tibetan document that is well-known, but was not cited very often by SCM in his *ONBP*, is བྱང་ཆུབ་ལམ་གྱི་སྒྲོན་མ། (*byang chub lam gyi sgron ma*), known in Sanskrit as the *Bodhipathapradīpa*, and in English as "Lamp for the Path to Enlightenment" or "Lamp for the Path to Full Awakening." This is one of the Tibetan documents from the Csoma Bequest that is now found in the Library of the Oriental Collection of the Hungarian Academy of Sciences.[48] Its shorter name is *Lamrim*, which means "stages of the path." Within this Tibetan Buddhist scripture all the stages of the complete path to enlightenment as taught by Buddha are presented, and so it has features that are similar to those found in the "Jewelled Ornament of Liberation." As will be seen, it was connected to the author of that later Buddhist treatise. Culturally and historically speaking, there have been many different versions of *Lamrim* produced in Tibetan Buddhist history, versions presented by dif-

---

[46] Nineteen times in the first volume, seventeen times in the second, and only ten times in the third tome.

[47] That is, once in the first volume, and three times in both the second and third volumes.

[48] It is known there as "Csoma-Bequest No. 18."

ferent teachers of the Nyingma, Kagyu and Gelug schools. However, all those versions of the *Lamrim* are elaborations of the 11th century original, the *Bodhipathapradīpa*.

When Atisha (982–1054), the originator of the *Lamrim* moved from India to Tibet, he was asked by king Jang Chub Jeshe Ö (byang chub ye shes 'od) to give a complete and easily accessible summary of the doctrine in order to clarify wrong views, especially those resulting from apparent contradictions between the sutras and their commentaries. Based upon this request Atisha taught what became known as the *Lamrim* by Tibetans, as already mentioned above. He was subsequently honored for this by the pandits of his *alma mater* in India, the monastic university of Vikramaśīla. Atisha's presentation of the doctrine later became known as the Kadampa tradition in Tibet. Gampopa, the Kadampa lineage monk mentioned above as the author of the "Jewelled Ornament of Liberation" and student of the famous yogi, Milarepa, introduced the *Lamrim* to his disciples as a way of developing the mind systematically. Notably, Gampopa's exposition of *Lamrim* is known to be still studied in the various Kagyu schools of Tibetan Buddhism. Tsongkhapa, the founder of the Gelug school which stems historically from Atisha's Kadampa school, wrote one of his masterpieces on the *Lamrim*; it is entitled *lam rim chen mo* (The Great Treatise on the Stages of the Path of Enlightenment), a literary document of about 1,000 pages in length. There is a medium-length *Lamrim* text composed also by Tsongkhapa that is about 200 pages long, while a very short version, called *lam rim bsdus don* (The Condensed Meaning of the Graded Path), only ten pages in length. This latter work is recited daily by many Gelugpas.

How much was SCM aware of all these cultural and historical facts? Generally speaking, I cannot confirm anything clearly about this matter. We have no indication that he studied the history of Tibetan Buddhism in any detail, even though he undoubtedly read all these texts in search of the proverbial wisdom that he wanted to compare with that found in the biblical book of Proverbs. In this light, then, it may be particularly significant that this famous Tibetan Buddhist scripture was only cited five times in the whole of the *ONBP*.[49]

5. Problems in Identifying some Tibetan Texts Cited in the *Original Notes on the Book of Proverbs*

There are several problems in identifying some of the texts described above within the footnotes of the *ONBP*, but there are also a number of citations that I find difficult to decipher. What is important to note is that these problematic citations only involve about ten to twelve percent of all the citations of Tibetan materials within the *ONBP*, so that most of the references are traceable. Nevertheless, it is worth noting some of the details of these problems and complications for the sake of future scholars who would study this vast and monumental work produced by SCM.

---

[49] Though it was cited three times in the first volume, and two times in the second, it was not even referred to once in the third volume.

First of all, it is sometimes disorienting, and at other times outright frustrating, that SCM chose to refer to texts from foreign languages generally not known by Europeans or Anglophone readers in their transliterated titles or by means of abbreviations of those titles. For example, the *Extensive Play Sutra* (*rgya cher rol pa*) is referred to by SCM by its full title as "Rgya-tcher rol-pa,"[50] but also as "Rgya tcher r.p."[51] and "Rgya tcher r. pa,"[52] or simply as "Rgya-tcher."[53] These ways of abbreviating the reference to this work are not terribly difficult to decipher in this case, but others are not so easily discerned. Consider SCM's ways of referring to *The White Lotus Sutra* (*dam pai'i chos pad ma dkar po mdo*): He sometimes referred to it simply as "Dkar padma,"[54] or "Padma dkar byeng wa,"[55] but also as "Dam pai chos – dkar padma,"[56] or "Dham pai padma dkar pa,"[57] or even "Dam pai ch'hos padma, etc."[58] A far more egregious problem exists, even for those with training in Tibetan studies, in identifying appropriate references for the *Jewelled Ornament of Liberation*. Part of the problem is that this Tibetan document has both a shorter and popular name in Tibetan – *thar rgyan* – and a longer and more complicated name – *dam chos yid bzhin gyi nor bu thar pa rin po che'i rgyan*. Throughout the whole of the *ONBP*, SCM used reference terms and abbreviations related to both Tibetan forms of reference, so that an uninformed person may be confused by believing these are two different Tibetan documents. For example, he referred to the popular name of the document as "T'hargyyan," "Thargyan," and "Th'argyan";[59] while on the other hand he could refer to the same document as simply "Dam chhos," or "Dam ch'hos," or "Damch'hos,"[60] but also by longer titles such as "Dam chhos yid b."[61] or "Dam chhos yit bj."[62] or even "Dam chhoes rin po."[63] When all these variants are placed within a context where texts from more than fifty

---

[50] Seen in *ONBP*, vol. 1, p. 3, n. 4.

[51] Occurring very often, but first seen in *ONBP*, vol. 1, p. 22, n. 11.

[52] As in *ONBP*, vol. 1, p. 42, n. 1.

[53] Found in *ONBP*, vol. 1, p. 141, n. 4.

[54] Occurring twice in *ONBP*, vol. 2, p. 434, n. 8, and p. 463, n. 2. One wonders if SCM simply forgot how he had referred to the same text when it had been published three years earlier (volume one was published in 1889, and volume two in 1892).

[55] Seen only once in *ONBP*, vol. 2, p. 292, n. 1.

[56] Seen only once in *ONBP*, vol. 3, p. 312, n. 5.

[57] Found only once in *ONBP*, vol. 3, p. 233, n. 1.

[58] See *ONBP*, vol. 1, p. 358, n. 2.

[59] These three renderings account for 35 citations involving 38 passages across the whole of the *ONBP*, which is a relatively large amount of citations, ranking as the fifth most frequently referred to in the list of Tibetan documents cited in the *ONBP*.

[60] See other problems with these three very brief phrases in the Appendix to this chapter.

[61] Found in the very first reference to this work, *ONBP*, vol. 1, p. 70, n. 1.

[62] Noted as the second reference to this work, *ONBP*, vol. 1, p. 116, n. 4.

[63] Seen in *ONBP*, vol. 2, p. 54, n. 4.

other languages are also being cited, it is not always easy to remember to which of these Tibetan documents those abbreviations actually refer.

I have made a list of other conundrums I found in the footnotes that I will add to the appendix of this chapter, for those who are interested in following up some of those items I found either difficult to identify with any particular Tibetan text or having titles or reference terms that are so general that they are also hard to specify.

6. S. C. Malan's English Renderings of Tibetan Proverbial Wisdom

How well did SCM manage such a vast array of proverbial lore, when he essentially "reduced" them into an English version by means of his translations? Did he simply erase the unparalleled concepts or terms, and so make them more palatable for an Anglophone audience? Or did he find other ways to present them that left a sense of their "foreignness," their "authenticity," and an obvious underscoring of his own self-conscious effort to confront those stranger elements within the *ONBP*?

In general, SCM made explicit and brief mentions within the main text of the *ONBP* that a particular saying came from a Tibetan source, one of the most basic ways to highlight the foreign source of any saying. Those references within the main text would include simple statements accompanying specific proverbs, appearing only about forty times among the 684 citations I have reviewed. They are added at the end of a proverb, or within a natural break within the saying, and put in the form of "says/asks the Tibetan"[64] or "say the Tibetans."[65] These statements parallel many other similar statements referring to those from other languages or cultures. Once there is a statement attributed to "the dge-long [Tibetan priest],"[66] and another time attributed to persons who are identified in the footnotes with known Tibetan texts.[67] Less clear are those that refer to specific sayings attributed to "the Buddha,"[68] "the Buddhisatwa," [*sic*] "the Buddhist,"[69] "wise men" and even "the brahman."[70] In all, one out of every ten citations from Tibetan sources has one of these

---

[64] The phrase "says the Tibetan" appears 26 times among the passages I have reviewed, while the phrase "asks the Tibetan" occurs only once.

[65] This phrase occurs eleven times among the passages I have reviewed. There does not appear to be any consistent or obvious reason why the plural occurs in these cases instead of the singular.

[66] As found in *ONBP*, vol. 3, p. 354; cited from the *Dsang-Lun* (The Sutra of the Wise and The Fool, also known as *Mdzangs blun*), chapter 15, accompanying Proverbs 26:25. Here and in the subsequent footnotes, I will refer to the Tibetan texts using the transliteration SCM himself provided.

[67] So reference is made to a person named "Chānakya" in the midst of proverbial sayings collected under Proverbs 21:25, and quoted from *Legs-par-bshad pa* (Treasury of Good Works), p. 223, appearing in *ONBP*, vol. 3, p. 33.

[68] Occurring five times among the passages I have reviewed.

[69] Occurring 19 times in various formulae added to the proverbial sayings.

[70] This last reference occurs five times among the passages I have reviewed, while all the others not footnoted only occur once in the form that is mentioned above.

descriptive statements added to the presentation of SCM's English version of their proverbial expressions.

Without question, SCM's motivation across sixty years of his life – from 1833 till the publication of the last volume of the *ONBP* in 1893 – was to bring all his linguistic prowess to bear in order to identify what would serve as a comparative platform in which proverbial literature could be brought together. Of course, this involved a basic assumption that material of this sort existed, and it could be used to compare within similar sayings found in other languages across the portions of the globe that he could come to know through their written or published texts.[71] All this effort was pursued on the basis of what was already a fairly long tradition among educated and literary elites in a number of cultures, and so SCM was undeniably self-conscious that he was taking up a very similar polyglot interest in shared wisdom literature and moral tales, following those cross-cultural trends as much as he could find them in relevant materials that he was able to obtain. Now in the 21st century, such studies continue to be unusual, but with the formal creation of the "study of proverbs" under the neologisms of "paremiology" and "paremiography,"[72] we all should be able to confirm that SCM set precedents that are worth considering even further, because he not only "located" those sayings in texts from over fifty languages, but also learned to write them in the scripts of those languages, most of the time also adding his own English renderings for those proverbial sayings in languages that were little known in Great Britain or Europe in his own day.[73] Ultimately, especially when considered from other angles informed by (1) cross-cultural judgments related to shared aspects of knowing, (2) diversities and commonalities in understanding, and (3) various rhetorical points of creativity that capture insights into human behavior in its variety, excellence, ironies and paradoxes, the portrayal of all these proverbs leaves an impression of an immense amount of shared recognition among human beings about many aspects of what we might refer to as "practical wisdom." Yet, simultaneously, an admirable linguistic and literary creativity is evident in these collected sayings, along with some unique elements in

---

[71] This would be one aspect of "domestication" that Venuti describes as a "strategy" within translation. Consult Venuti 2005.

[72] This is in reference to the bibliographic tome produced under the visionary guidance of Wolfgang Mieder, and with the collaboration of numerous other persons, entitled *International Bibliography of Paremiology: Collections of Proverbs, Proverbial Expressions and Comparisons, Quotations, Graffiti, Slang, and Wellerisms* (Burlington: The University of Vermont, 2011). A further example of a more focused collection of proverbs that follows more or less self-consciously in the footsteps of SCM, but with a radically different set of principles in ordering the paremiographic materials, is found in Gyula Paczolay, *European Proverbs in 55 Languages with Equivalents in Arabic, Persian, Sanskrit, Chinese and Japanese* (Veszprém: Veszprém Nyomda Rt., 1997).

[73] The handwritten exemplars of proverbial lore, almost always without any reliance on European transcription systems, appeared only in the manuscript version, the ONBP Ms, as described in the last chapter of this volume. In the published English version, only English language renderings of those passages appeared, with more or less accurate footnotes referencing the vast majority of the sayings.

their expressions, some verging on the level of cultural and linguistic untranslatability.[74]

In what follows, I will bring together some exemplary passages of SCM's English renderings of Tibetan proverbial sayings and stories, so that some more precise answers to the issues raised above might be addressed in our concluding statements.

In the context of the contrasts between the "wise" and the "foolish" – a theme I have already noted above is a major leit-motif within the biblical book of Proverbs – I have already documented the fact that SCM had discovered a whole text that was a Tibetan translation of a Sanskrit original referred to in English as the *Sutra of the Wise and the Fool*.[75]

"A fool is at his best when he says nothing."[76]

"There are some men," says the Tibetan, "who think that lust is happiness, although the practice of it is misery and ruin. But he who places his happiness in drinking wine, must think that a madman alone is happy."[77]

"Great people need not be proud (or haughty); and what does pride profit the low and mean? A gem needs no praise; but who would buy a counterfeit one, even if it were praised ever so much?"[78]

"Foolish talk," says the Buddhist, "is manifold: when it is false; when it is mere worldly nonsense; when it is true, yet only foolish talk. The mutterings of brahmans, worthless talk, and thoughtless, senseless talk, not worthy of respect. The fruit of it when "fully ripe" is – to be born a devil; or if one be born a man, he will have a speech base and contemptible, to which no one will pay attention. But of all foolish talk, the most sinful is to unsettle, or cause those who love the law [of Buddha] to waver."[79]

"For to wish for the smartest clothes when poor, to be proud while living on alms, and to dispute without knowledge, only make people laugh."[80]

"Who, then, is said to be his own enemy? He who makes no efforts towards purity and common sense," says the Tibetan.[81]

Notably, it is only in the fourth saying that the concept of reincarnation is linked to certain attitudes and actions among humans. The rest appear to share in a more

---

[74] As discussed in Guo Jianzhong 1995. See also Pym – Turk 2005. Within this volume some specific ways have been addressed to show points of tension or even misapprehension that SCM struggled with in Chinese, Manchurian, and Sanskrit sources (see Chapters 6-8 and 10).

[75] Find the basic English title in the index of *ONBP*, vol. 1, p. 482, left column. In Tibetan SCM referred to it most often as *Dsang-Lun*; in Sanskrit, this text is known as *Damamūka-nidāna-sūtra*.

[76] See *ONBP*, vol. 2, p. 502, related to Proverbs 17:28, from *Legs-par-bshad pa*, p. 219.

[77] See *ONBP*, vol. 2, pp. 646-647, quoted in parallel to the biblical saying found in Proverbs 20:1, from *Legs-par-bshad pa*, p. 268.

[78] See *ONBP*, vol. 2, p. 172, related to Proverbs 13:7, from *Legs-par-bshad pa*, p. 202.

[79] See *ONBP*, vol. 2, pp. 268-269, related to Proverbs 14:23, from *T'hargyan*, vol. 5, folio 43.

[80] See *ONBP*, vol. 2, p. 172, related to Proverbs 13:7, from *Legs-par-bshad pa*, p. 257.

[81] See *ONBP*, vol. 3, p. 522, related to Proverbs 29:16-17, from *Phreng Wa*, p. 15.

commonly extended understanding of wisdom and foolishness. Whether this appearance is actually portrayed by these various Tibetan texts is something that could be studied in greater depth.

Another prominent set of images built upon the basic metaphor of identifying actions and attitudes that would serve as a "door to religion," was drawn from the Tibetan version of the Sanskrit text, *Lalita Vistara* (or the *rGya Tcher Rol Pa*, the second most often cited Tibetan text in the *ONBP* as noted above). Here the question of whether "religion" is the most appropriate term to render the Tibetan term in that phrase is worth asking, but I will not address that problem here. Though at one point SCM parenthetically indicated that there were 108 "doors into religion" described within the fourth chapter of that particular Tibetan religious text,[82] I have found that he referred to only twenty-seven of them in the passages reviewed for this study.[83] This was due, undoubtedly and primarily, because they paralleled passages within the biblical book of Proverbs. All of these statements came in the regular form of "A^1/A^2 is a door to religion [...], [so that] it leads to R^1/R^2"; where A^1 would be "a particular kind of action or achievement" and A^2 would be "a particular adopted attitude," and R^1 referring to anticipated "impact or results" of those actions and achievements, and R^2 being the resulting "positive attainment" achieved due to adopting and sustaining that attitude in one's life. Adding specificity to these sayings, SCM sometimes also even indicated the number in the sequence of "the 108 doors" that a particular action/achievement or attitude represents.[84]

> "The restraint of the body is the fifth door of entrance to religion; it purifies altogether the three kinds of bodily vices."[85]

> "In the afterthought [continually thinking] of Buddha, lies the eighth door of entrance to religion. For a clear perception of him creates perfect purity."[86]

---

[82] As seen in *ONBP*, vol. 2, p. 13, related to Proverbs 21:8, from *rGya Tcher Rol Pa*, ch. 4. The metaphor varies at times, so that it is referred to as "a door to religious enlightenment" four times, or a "door to religious brightness" twice. Once it is "a door of entrance to the doctrine of morals," and another time as a "door of entrance to religion." In all cases, however, the basis metaphor of the "door" is found.

[83] Out of the 684 cited passages from Tibetan sources I have identified in the *ONBP*, I have studied more than three hundred of them in order to prepare this summary of SCM's Tibetan scholarship. In that light, then, it is possible that there are other relevant passages within this category of sayings that I have missed, and so those interested in this particular text and its English renderings should review all the other cited passages in order to have a comprehensive account of this particular kind of saying.

[84] This assumes, of course, that there is only one sequence of 108 passages of this sort of sayings in that particular chapter of the relevant Tibetan work. Whether or not this is the case, I have not been able to confirm by reference to a standard version of that Tibetan work.

[85] As presented in *ONBP*, vol. 1, p. 83, related to Proverbs 2:11, from *rGya Tcher Rol Pa*, ch. 4.

[86] Quoting from in *ONBP*, vol. 3, p. 161, related to Proverbs 23:18, from *rGya Tcher Rol Pa*, ch. 4.

"To examine well what is or is not cause for sorrow," says the Buddhist, "is one door [19th] to religion. It divides [severs] entirely our prayers [from worldly motives]."[87]

"In truth lies a door [24th] to religious enlightenment; it leads us to deceive neither God nor man."[88]

The last of these sayings cited above appears to have used a biblical phrase, "neither God nor man," rather than a more suitable phrase drawn literally from the Tibetan passage. This serves as a kind of "domestification" of certain foreign elements, such as a reference to "gods" rather than to "God." Most of the "achievements" found in the 27 sayings of this sort that I have identified have to do with the attaining of "knowledge" or a "great knowledge,"[89] while the "actions" vary from practical matters such as "curbing the tongue"[90] and "acknowledging what we have done amiss"[91] to ritualized efforts such as having "constant memory of the law."[92] In this last reference, there is a Hebrew parallel to "the Law" as the Torah, and so once again a more subtle form of domestification may be at work here. Positive attitudes that are highlighted include "respect,"[93] having a "compassionate heart,"[94] "joy"[95] and "benevolence,"[96] while attitudes created by the rejection or overcoming of unacceptable states of mind include "absence of a wicked mind"[97] and "a mind free from feelings of anger,"[98] and so also holding "no resentment." In all of these instances, one can discern how carefully and thoughtfully SCM read through that single chapter in the Tibetan scripture before him, revealing simultaneously in some cases aspects of a Tibetan Buddhist worldview that were distinct from the unelabo-

---

[87] Cited with all the parenthetical details in *ONBP*, vol. 2, p. 374, related to Proverbs 16:3, from *rGya Tcher Rol Pa*, ch. 4.

[88] Found in *ONBP*, vol. 2, p. 379, related to Proverbs 16:6, from *rGya Tcher Rol Pa*, ch. 4.

[89] Including "knowledge of our own action," "knowledge of the time (or times) and a right application of present circumstances," "knowledge of men," and "real knowledge of the 'self'." Find these respectively in *ONBP*, vol. 2, pp. 25, 229, 262, and 659 related to Proverbs 11:12; 14:8; 14:21 and 20:8. All of these passages are claimed by SCM to come from some portion of *rGya Tcher Rol Pa*, ch. 4.

[90] See *ONBP*, vol. 2, p. 162, related to Proverbs 13:3, from *rGya Tcher Rol Pa*, ch. 4.

[91] See *ONBP*, vol. 3, p. 461, related to Proverbs 28:13, from *rGya Tcher Rol Pa*, ch. 4.

[92] Referred to twice in *ONBP*, vol. 1, p. 175, and vol. 2, p. 187, related to Proverbs 3:21 and 13:13 respectively, both coming from *rGya Tcher Rol Pa*, ch. 4.

[93] See *ONBP*, vol. 2, p. 25, related to Proverbs 11:12, from *rGya Tcher Rol Pa*, ch. 4.

[94] See *ONBP*, vol. 2, p. 113, related to Proverbs 12:10, from *rGya Tcher Rol Pa*, ch. 4.

[95] Cited three times, but the first time appearing in SCM, *ONBP*, Vol. 2, p. 141, related to Proverbs 12:20, from *rGya Tcher Rol Pa*, ch. 4. In another place there is a reference to "great joy"; consult *ONBP*, vol. 2, p. 322, related to Proverbs 15:13, from *rGya Tcher Rol Pa*, ch. 4.

[96] See *ONBP*, vol. 2, p. 244, related to Proverbs 14:14, from *rGya Tcher Rol Pa*, ch. 4.

[97] See *ONBP*, vol. 3, p. 45, related to Proverbs 21:27, from *rGya Tcher Rol Pa*, ch. 4.

[98] See *ONBP*, vol. 2, p. 595, related to Proverbs 19:11, from *rGya Tcher Rol Pa*, ch. 4.

rated but manifest monotheism undergirding their biblical parallels. Even while recognizing a good number of those differences, however, SCM continued to link up these Tibetan proverbs to all the relevant passages that came from the book of Proverbs, biblical texts that he had carefully memorized and assiduously meditated on for nearly sixty years.

Where Tibetan sayings were found that contrasted the character of the wise from the traits of the foolish, and so portrayed insights that seemed to be more easily generalizable across cultures and linguistic corridors of proverbial literature, one can locate many more distinct cultural elements when various kinds of metaphors were applied. Here follows a set of Tibetan proverbs applying metaphors from inanimate things.

> "It is always by good men that good qualities are most praised. The sweet smell of the sandal-wood of Malaya is diffused [by the wind] to the ten quarters of the earth." And "good qualities, though they be hidden, yet are spread everywhere in the world. The flower of the nutmeg, though dry, yet scatters a sweet scent all round." [99]

> "But everything at its proper place. A head ornament is not tied to the feet; neither will anklets do to be worn on the head." [100]

> "O Radjor, if there were as many Ganges as there are grains of sand on the bank, and as many heaps of jewels and other precious things as there are grains of sand on the banks of all those Ganges, their joint value would not equal the value of one four-line verse of this lore." [101]

> "A good man in reduced circumstances shines all the more through his patience. If a torch be held downwards, the flame nevertheless always rises upwards." [102]

> "He that continues in pride, whether he be god or man," says the Buddhist, "is but a grain of mustard-seed, or a drop of water in the footprint of a cow, only a glow-worm – in these three thousand worlds." [103]

> "A good man walking along with an evil one is being slain by that one's wickedness. The water of the Ganges, though sweet to the taste, nevertheless becomes brackish by mingling with the water of the sea." [104]

> "What is life then? (1) It is an arrow shot upwards into the air, that soon returns to whence it came. (2) It is water running down a precipitous mountain. (3) It is like prisoners stepping together to be put to death. Many chances befall this life

---

[99] These two proverbs are presented in this sequence in *ONBP*, vol. 1, p. 434, related to Proverbs 10: 7, from *Legs-par-bshad pa*, pp. 25 and 36 respectively.

[100] See *ONBP*, vol. 2, p. 53, related to Proverbs 11:22, from *Legs-par-bshad pa*, p. 392.

[101] See *ONBP*, vol. 1, pp. 366-3677, related to Proverbs 8: 10, from *Ther-wa chhen po*, p. 148.

[102] See *ONBP*, vol. 3, p. 446, related to Proverbs 28:5-6, from *Legs-par-bshad pa*, p. 30.

[103] See *ONBP*, vol. 2, p. 404, related to Proverbs 16:19, from *rGya Tcher Rol Pa*, ch. 8.

[104] See *ONBP*, vol. 2, pp. 202-203, related to Proverbs 13:20, from *Legs-par-bshad pa*, p. 137.

from the air, from the flitting of a bubble, or from some trifle amiss in breathing."[105]

"The three worlds," says the Buddhist, "are not lasting; they are like an autumn cloud. The birth and death of living beings is like looking at a dance."[106]

Within this set of Tibetan sayings, SCM is not only sensitive in making verbal references to items found in Indian and Tibetan social and natural contexts, but also was more careful in referring to spiritual matters that bear out a Tibetan Buddhist worldview.

Here below are other passages in the *ONBP* that employ metaphors related to sentient beings in the animate world:

"A mean man, though he be great and very rich, is yet outdone by a smaller man of good family. When the old tiger begins to roar, the monkeys fall [from fright] from the top of the tree." "Fools, however many, yet being deprived of wisdom, fall into the power of the enemy. A herd of powerful elephants was destroyed by a hare gifted with intellect."[107]

"Many animals (or people) joined together and of one mind, though they have small power, bring about great results. It is said that a lion's whelp was killed by a quantity of ants."[108]

"Evil men, as a rule, impart their evil qualities to others. When a crow has eaten some unclean things, it wipes its beak on the clean earth."[109]

"Even if a man is learned, but by nature evil, eschew him; what wise man would take into his bosom a poisonous snake, though with a gem ornament on its head?"[110]

"Wealth gotten by force or craft," say the Tibetans, "is not wealth; just as the dog and the cat, while living, are but the incarnation [emancipation in transmigration] of impudence and shame."[111]

"You may judge of the relative merits of dge-longs [Buddhist priests in Thibet] by comparing them to the amra-fruit [mangoe]. Someone may have an agreeable demeanour, possess great qualities, inwardly following the moral precepts of moral virtue, be given to profound meditation, and be endued with deep knowledge; such a one is like the amra-fruit, both outwardly and inwardly ripe. Another dge-long, who subsists on charity, is also like that other one, endued

---

[105] Unusually, SCM cites two sources for this same quotation. See *ONBP*, vol. 3, p. 364, related to Proverbs 26:1, from *Dam chhos yid bjin gyi nor-wu*, vol. 3, folio 24 and *rGya Tcher Rol Pa*, ch. 13.

[106] See *ONBP*, vol. 3, p. 363, related to Proverbs 27:1, from *rGya Tcher Rol Pa*, ch. 13, p. 155.

[107] The two texts cited here appear in this order within the passage, but there is only one footnote given at the end of both. Consult in *ONBP*, vol. 3, p. 457, related to Proverbs 28:11, from *Legs-par-bshad pa*, 97 and 82 [respectively].

[108] See *ONBP*, vol. 1, p. 297, related to Proverbs 4:6-8, from *Legs-par-bshad pa*, 201.

[109] See *ONBP*, vol. 2, p. 202, related to Proverbs 13:20, from *Legs-par-bshad pa*, 58.

[110] See *ONBP*, vol. 2, p. 516, related to Proverbs 18:9, from *Legs-par-bshad pa*, 161.

[111] See *ONBP*, vol. 3, p. 10, related to Proverbs 21:6, from *Legs-par-bshad pa*, 49.

with great qualities, whom everybody honours and respects on account of his perfect and accomplished virtues."[112]

Here is a saying about the value of the monastic life:

"Speaking of the advantages of living in a monastery, for those who have neither governor nor patron," Hodsrung says: "In like manner as an arrow that meets with no obstacle hits the mark, by killing the robber who was carrying away household goods; so also does solitude kill desire, love of riches, etc."[113]

Some even more culturally colorful and dramatic passages are found in the Tibetan moral stories that were included within the *ONBP*.

"When Bchom-ldan-hdas [Gautama] came to Indrawami, he made eight great streams (or canals) to flow around the tank that was formed by the water with which he rinsed his mouth. Those streams flowed round and back into it. And those streams, while running, [caused to be heard] murmured voices (or sounds) of all manner of law and of wisdom."[114]

"In the Buddhist stories of Dsang-Lun, we read that 'a dge-long [priest] was born with both his fists closed, each holding a piece of gold, which was renewed as often as it was spent. This happened to him because in a former birth he had offered all he had, a small coin, to Buddha.'"[115]

"When the novice [dge-tshul] was sent by his superior [dge-long] to his house for food, and his daughter, who was very beautiful, was there alone, the monk warned the novice to keep watch over himself. The maid used all her artifices to ensnare him; but he bravely went into an inner chamber, and there, having rehearsed to himself all that good monks had done under such circumstances, he put an end to himself, rather than fall a victim to the wiles of that woman."[116]

"[A] poor old woman having begged the whole day, and having only got a small coin, went to an oil merchant for some oil, but he said it was not enough money. Someone then gave her some oil, with which she went to Buddha's temple and lit a lamp, praying that henceforth she might receive the light of wisdom. When Mangalya went into the temple the next morning, he found all the other lamps gone out except this one, which he tried to put out. But he found that, for all he tried, he could not put it out. Then Buddha said to him: 'If thou pour upon it the water of the four seas, thou canst not extinguish it; for it is for the chiefest use of man.'"[117]

"The king asked the wise tamer of elephants, how he had managed to tame so fine a one. 'I was one day hunting with him,' answered the man, 'and although he ran about wildly through passion, yet with my hidden charms I brought him into subjection to my power. And when he tries to break his fetters, a kind word

---

[112] See *ONBP*, vol. 2, p. 189, related to Proverbs 13:15, from *Legs-par-bshad pa*, 201.
[113] See *ONBP*, vol. 2, p. 506, related to Proverbs 18:1, from *rGya Tcher Rol Pa*, ch. 24, p. 327.
[114] See *ONBP*, vol. 2, p. 512, related to Proverbs 18:4, from *Dsang-Lun*, ch. 13, folio 50.
[115] See *ONBP*, vol. 2, p. 617, related to Proverbs 19:17, from *Dsang-Lun*, ch. 8, folio 34.
[116] See *ONBP*, vol. 1, p. 324, related to Proverbs 6:25, from *Dsang-Lun*, ch. 16, folio 96.
[117] See *ONBP*, vol. 2, p. 176, related to Proverbs 13:10, from *Dsang-Lun*, ch. 37, folio 207.

quiets him.' Thus one can tame a stiff-necked elephant, but not stiff-necked passion, which is either raised by one evil example, or set at rest by another good one."[118]

"We have read in the Dsang-Lun, that the great rishi Drang-srong [Vyāsa], having retired from Varanasi to the jungle in order to practice austerity, was visited there by the king, who asked him what he was doing in such a place. The rishi answered: 'I am practicing patience (or endurance).' Then the king cut off his hands and his feet, and said, 'What about this now?' The rishi replied, 'My mind does not falter; I am 'Zod-pa-chan, the enduring one' [such a man is then called 'De-dgra bshom-pa,' one who has overcome his enemies']."[119]

Within the *ONBP* I have also found one story that reads more like one of the moral tales from Aesop's fables; from SCM's perspective, this was not at all a mere coincidence. So, in relating the Sanskrit version of a moral story found in the *Hitopadesa* (as seen below), SCM was intellectually provoked to reveal how what was essentially the same story appeared with different details in various other linguistic corridors. In this particular case, then, SCM added comments on what he recognized as being very similar stories from Arabic, Syriac, Persian, Hindustani, Turkish, Greek, Latin, Tibetan, Mongolian, Cingalese and Chinese (in that precise order). Rather than deal with all those details, I will simply add his brief comments on the Tibetan and Mongolian versions of the story; they appear here below after the ellipsis.[120]

"[There is a] story of the Two Geese and the Tortoise, friends that lived together in the same pond. But fishers preparing to catch them [*sic*], the two geese agreed to take the tortoise to another pond. They each seized one end of a stick in its beak and told the tortoise to bite and hold tight the middle of the stick, warning the tortoise not to let go. They flew away, the tortoise hanging by its beak to the stick. But some cow-herds shouted, at so strange a sight, that when the tortoise fell they would kill and eat it. The tortoise, enraged at this, opened its beak, let go the stick, fell, and was killed." [...] "[T]he Tibetan makes two crows do the work, and the Mongolian turns the tortoise into a frog."

Here then SCM was intent on underscoring the principle of the tale, while also indicating how some of the details were shifted to what would be considered culturally more suitable elements. Another set of Tibetan stories imbued with distinctive Buddhist visions are portrayed by SCM in the following English renderings:

"When the god of the sea appeared to Dges-nen with his handful of water, the god asked him which was most, his handful of water or the whole ocean. 'This handful,' said Dges-nen. 'Why?' asked the god. 'Because,' said the other, 'at

---

[118] See *ONBP*, vol. 1, p. 267, related to Proverbs 4:12-14, from *Dulva*, vol. 2, p. 492.

[119] The parenthetical statement is an addition derived from a handwritten copy of the texts as cited below. The story comes from the first source, and the additional comments from the second. See *ONBP*, vol. 2, p. 435, related to Proverbs 16:32, from *Dsang-Lun*, ch. 11, p. 51, "ed. Schm." and ch. 2, folio 16, "native copy."

[120] See *ONBP*, vol. 2, pp. 124-125 *in passim*, related to Proverbs 12:15, the Tibetan text referred to coming from *Legs-par-bshad pa*, p. 87.

the end of a "kalpa" [a day and night of Brahma, or 4,320,000,000 years of mortals], seven suns shall dry up the ocean, but this much of water offered to Buddha shall endure forever.'"[121]

"When the nuns came to Yud-pa-laimdong, the abbess of the convent, they said to her: 'Although we are nuns, yet are we like other women, full of wickedness; teach us the law.' She answered, 'I will teach you everything, past, present and to come.' To this the nuns replied, 'Let alone for a while both the past and the time to come, and teach us about the present; and help [repair] us by explaining our doubt.'"[122]

"The wish to learn is not alone sufficient," said the brahman to king Ts'hang-pha-la; "but to learn, when one is taught, is very difficult, and only through tasting many troubles." "The poor king found it so to his cost; for his apprenticeship in Buddhistic law was by making parchment of his skin, reeds of his bones, and ink of his blood, with which he wrote the law on his own skin."[123]

Though there are many other examples of these Tibetan proverbs rendered into English by SCM, particularly in relationship to various virtues that religious and righteous persons embody, I take it that the examples already offered provide a representative sampling of these passages. From all these materials it seems justified to conclude that SCM appears to have gained a fairly broad sense of the distinctive characteristics of Tibetan Buddhism, many aspects of that tradition's worldview, terminology, and literary diversity being found articulated in his translations of those unusual texts. At certain points, however, he appears to have domesticated his Tibetan original into a more Jewish-like or Christian-like set of terms, but this way of translating does not appear very often. In this sense, then, one may be able to learn quite a bit about the cultural and religious distinctiveness of Tibetan wisdom from these selections included in SCM's *ONBP*.

7. Concluding Statements

Throughout this study I have tried to indicate various characteristics of SCM's awareness of Tibetan language and Tibetan proverbial lore as seen in his depictions of them within various passages of the *ONBP*. Relying on the texts found in the Oriental Collection of the Hungarian Academy of Sciences in Budapest, I have examined a number of Tibetan texts and compared them with those put into English within the *ONBP*, and so can state that on the basis of that small sampling of comparative analysis, SCM knew Tibetan language quite well. His translations are often stylish, and generally are grammatically correct. Many times, he portrays some distinctive Buddhist elements within his renderings, so that he appears to have a relatively clear sense of the Buddhist worldview that he encountered and could provide them in English by means of some technical Buddhist terminology that was not merely a "Christian paraphrase" of those passages. Nevertheless, as I have sought

---

[121] See *ONBP*, vol. 2, p. 335, related to Proverbs 15:16, from *Dsang-Lun*, ch. 5, folio 25.

[122] See *ONBP*, vol. 2, p. 489, related to Proverbs 17:24, from *Dsang-Lun*, ch. 24, folio 131.

[123] See *ONBP*, vol. 2, p. 470, related to Proverbs 17:16, from *Dsang-Lun*, folios 9 and 11.

to indicate in several places within this chapter, at certain points he had some tendencies to "domesticate" the Tibetan sayings into something more biblical and monotheistic, but this did not appear as a regular feature of most of his English renderings.

There is much more comparative study that could be done by carefully identifying the many other Tibetan documents and passages that SCM quoted in the *ONBP*, and then comparing how he rendered those passages from Tibetan into their English versions. Persons who could also add insight into SCM's account of the Hebrew text itself, and how this also alerted him to parallels in Tibetan and other sources, would contribute even more to this comparative study than I am able to do. My sincere hope is that this initial study will encourage more rigorous and systematic study of SCM's identification, use and interpretation of Tibetan proverbial lore.

Appendix

Other Notes and/or Unrecognizable Titles of Tibetan Documents in the *ONBP*

Below I will first add the transliteration term or phrase that SCM employed in his *ONBP* – sometimes in his index to the first volume, and many times in the footnotes to the *ONBP* – and then follow this by writing beneath those terms and phrases what I take to be the Tibetan equivalent of them (using both Tibetan language and its transliterations, when possible). Subsequently, I will offer a critical note about what I believe the term or phrase refers to, when it is possible to do so, and otherwise will try to explain why I cannot currently decipher it or relate it to a particular Tibetan Buddhist document or text. All of these terms, phrases, and titles are found in the footnote sections of the *ONBP*, sometimes with multiple renderings (which are also provided, when relevant), and for those that have appeared more than two times, I will indicate how many times they have been used in citations in the *ONBP*.

1. "Bslas-cha gches-pa, etc." / "Bslav cha gtsam pa" / "Bslav cha chen pa" / "Bslav cha"

    This text/these texts were cited 13 times in the ONBP, but I am unable to identify them with a particular Tibetan work.

2. "Bslavs pa" / "Bslav cha-btso"

    These may be referring to the same text(s) seen in the first item above, but I am unable to identify them with a particular Tibetan work.

3. Bstan-hgyur

    This text is cited only twice in the whole of the *ONBP*,[124] but is mentioned as a larger work that includes "Tibetan classics."[125] The contemporary transliteration would be *btsan 'gyur Tengyur* (བསྟན་འགྱུར་ btsan 'gyur), which in English

---

[124] As found in *ONBP*, vol. 2, p. 41, n. 4, and vol. 3, p. 260, n. 9.

[125] Described in this fashion in the Index to *ONBP*, vol. 1, p. 482, under the putative title of one part of that work called *Dri-med-dkon-segs*.

can be referred to briefly as "The Translated Treatises." This work actually consists of a collection of several hundred volumes of scriptures explaining the *Kangyur*, the translated words of the Buddha (the number of volumes of the *Tengyur* is 225 – by some other sources 228 – and that of the *Kangyur* is 108). As a consequence, unless the reference is very precise, it would be hard to locate a quotation from such a huge collection of works.

4. "Chanakya-Niti (in Tibetan translation)"
Probably from a bilingual Sanskrit-Tibetan text, including the Tibetan translation of the Chanakya Niti in the Tengyur, entitled ཙན་ཀའི་རྒྱལ་པོའི་ལུགས་ཀྱི་བསྟན་བཅོས་ (*tsa na ka'i rgyal po'i lugs kyi btsan bcos*).

5. "Dam chhos "/ "Damchhos "/ "Dam ch'hos"
དམ་ཆོས། (*dam chos*), which is a very general term that means "noble doctrine" or "holy teaching." It is such a general term of reference that it could refer to a number of specific works, and so is difficult to identify precisely.

6. "Dmar-khrid"
དམར་ཁྲིད། (*dmar khrid*), which in English means "pure method," or "telling the meaning directly," and so is describing a direct instruction on experiential meditation, and could be even a final instruction in religion or medicine. SCM refers to it as "Practical Instruction";[126] it appears only once within the body of the *ONBP*.

7. "Dri-med-dkon-segs"
དྲི་མེད་དཀོན་ཤེགས། (*dri med dkon shegs*). This title is not known at all, and is not cited in the body of the *ONBP*, but only in the Index. It is claimed there to be a part of a larger work called the *Bstan-hgyur*.[127] It could be about a number of topics. From the linguistic point of view *dri med* means in Tibetan "spotless," "immaculate," and therefore "faultless," "free from impurity," and so on. There is another document entitled དྲི་མེད་བཤགས་རྒྱུད། (*dri med bshags rgyud*), which in English would be rendered as the "Immaculate Confession Tantra" or "Stainless Confession Tantra." Nevertheless, it is unclear if this is the proper reference that SCM intended to indicate.

8. "Drislan phreng wa" / "Drislan p'hreng wa" / "Dris lan phr. wa" / "Drislan p'hr. wa"
དྲིས་ལན་འཕྲེང་བ། (*dris lan 'phreng ba*) can be rendered in English as "A Garland of Questions and Answers." SCM referred to it as a "Chaplet of morals, etc., in questions and answers."[128] It is cited five times in the whole of the *ONBP*, but I cannot otherwise identify it.

9. "Dszu-tung gyan"

---

[126] In the Index to *ONBP*, vol. 1, p. 482, left column; appearing in vol. 1, p. 320, n. 1.

[127] As found in *ONBP*, vol. 1, p. 482, left column.

[128] In the Index within *ONBP*, vol. 1, p. 482, left column.

This particular phrase or title I cannot identity. It occurs only once in the whole of the *ONBP*, in the third volume. SCM translated the title as "Sweet Rewards."[129]

10. "Dulva" / "Kah-gyur Dulva" / "Dulwa" / "Hdul-wa"
Because this source is cited 13 times in the *ONBP*, it stands as one of the minor texts that SCM did refer to occasionally. This is the *dulva* (*'dul ba*), which in Sanskrit is the title for one of the three major categories of Buddhist sutras: the Vinaya, or compilations of various monastic discipline and rules. It is an important source of the Buddha's teachings that includes many practical principles, comprising some presentation and discussion of what we would now count as ethics, and depending on the text, may be directed toward laypersons or ordained monks.

11. "Hjam-dpal"/ "Hjam-dp." /"Hjam-dpal mst-han brjod"
འཇམ་དཔལ། (*'jam dpal*/) In my opinion this is a proper name and not a book title.

12. "P'ha-rol-tu, etc."
ཕ་རོལ་ཏུ། (*pha rol tu*). This phrase is only used once by SCM in the body of the *ONBP*,[130] and is mentioned in the Index as a text "on transmigration."[131] Nevertheless, it is too short for being a title. I cannot properly identify the title of such a document from this abbreviated reference. Perhaps it could be the བཅོམ་ ལྡན་འདས་མ་ཤེས་རབ་ཀྱི་ཕ་རོལ་ཏུ་ཕྱིན་པའི་སྙིང་པོ། (*bcom ldan 'das ma shes rab kyi pha rol tu phyin pa'i snying po*), which would be the famous Mahāyāna sutra, *Prajñāpāramitā Hṛdaya* (the Heart Sutra)

13. "Phreng wa" / "Phreng-wa" / P'hreng-wa"
འཕྲེང་བ། (*'phreng ba*). It is cited 18 times in the whole of the *ONBP*, and so is a relatively important minor text referred to by SCM. Nevertheless, this title is simply too short to indicate what document it refers to. In his own rendering of the title, SCM calls it "A Garland of Wise Sayings."[132] The phrase does refer to a "garland."

14. "Rdo dje ch. Pa" / "Rdo-rje-gchod pa" / "Rdo-rdje-kchod pa"
Cited only four times in the whole of the *ONBP*. Its contemporary transliteration is *rdo rje gcod pa*, and its full title is འཕགས་པ་ཤེས་རབ་ཀྱི་ཕ་རོལ་ཏུ་ཕྱིན་པ་རྡོ་རྗེ་གཅོད་པ་ཞེས་བྱ་བ་ ཐེག་པ་ཆེན་པོའི་མདོ། (*'phags pa shes rab kyi pha rol tu phyin pa rdo rje gcod pa zhes bya ba theg pa chen po'i mdo*). In Sanskrit it is known as the *Vajracchedikā-Prajñāpāramitā-Sūtra* (The Exalted Sutra on the Perfection of Wisdom entitled The Diamond Cutter).

---

[129] See *ONBP*, vol. 3, p. 161, n. 3.
[130] See *ONBP*, vol. 1, p. 96, n. 11.
[131] See *ONBP*, vol. 1, p. 484, left column.
[132] See *ONBP*, vol. 1, p. 484, left column.

The fact that SCM did not cite it very often suggests that he may have found its doctrinal and worldview differences, as well as the style of the sutra, too technical for the proverbial literature he was exploring.

This sutra presents the teachings of the Buddha to a senior monk, Subhūti. In the sutra, the Buddha has finished his daily walk to Sravasti with the monks to gather offerings of food, and he sits down to rest. Elder Subhūti comes forth and asks the Buddha: "How, Lord, should one who has set out on the bodhisattva path take his stand? How should he proceed? How should he control the mind?" What follows is a dialogue regarding the nature of the 'perfection of insight' (*prajñāpāramitā*) and the nature of ultimate reality (which is illusory and empty). The Buddha begins by answering Subhūti by stating that he will bring all living beings to final nirvana – but that after this "no living being whatsoever has been brought to extinction." This is because a bodhisattva does not see beings through reified concepts such as "person," "soul" or "self," but sees them through the lens of perfect understanding, as empty of an inherent, unchanging self. As a consequence, the major themes of this sutra are *anatman* (not-self), the emptiness of all phenomena (though the term *śūnyatā* itself does not appear in the text), the liberation of all beings without attachment, and the importance of spreading and teaching the *Diamond Sutra* itself.

15. "Sdom pa sum pai, kon segs" / "Sdom pa sum pai mdo, kong segs" / "Kon-segs" / "Sdom pa, kon segs" / "Dkon seks" / "Dkon segs"

    This text is cited nine times in the whole of the *ONBP*. In contemporary Tibetan transliteration, it is known as *sdom pa gsum pa'i dkon brtsegs*, and in Sanskrit it is entitled the *Trisamvaranirdesaparivarta-sutra* (The Three Vows of the Jewel Mound Sutra).

16. "Smon-lam bchu-tham" / "Smon-lam, bchu-tham, etc."

    སྨོན་ལམ་བཅུ་ཐམ། (*smon lam bcu tham*). This document is only referred to once in the body of the *ONBP*,[133] and is rendered as "Buddhist prayers" by SCM.[134] Its title is once again too short to be identified with a particular sutra. In English it literally means "Ten Prayers."

17. "Taranatha"

    ཏ་ར་ན་ཐ། (*ta ra na tha*). Here we have something rather unusual. Tāranātha (1575–1634) was a Lama of the Jonang school of Tibetan Buddhism. His original name in Tibetan was Kunga Nyingpo (*kun dga' snying po*), and he was born in Tibet. What is odd is that this is not the title of a text, but the name of a specific person. What SCM describes in his Index is another text written by Taranatha, but he does not provide the Tibetan title for it. There he describes

---

[133] See *ONBP*, vol. 1, p. 465, n. 6.
[134] See *ONBP*, vol. 1, p. 484, right column.

the text as *On the Introduction of Buddhism into Tibet*.[135] Notably, however, it is only cited once in the whole of the *ONBP*.[136]

18. "Thar wa" / "Ther-wa chhen po" / "Ther-wa" / "Thar-wa, Mahajana" ཐར་བ། (*thar ba*). This is a text cited four times in the whole of the *ONBP*, and is admitted by SCM to be a title for "several treatises on the subject" regarding "emancipation."[137] In fact, once again, it is too short of a title to identify it with a particular sutra. In English, the term means "to escape" or "to become free."

19. "Ts'he-hpho-va etc."
This text is cited only twice in the whole of the *ONBP*. It may be referring to a sutra in the Kangyur tradition, which is ཚེ་འཕོ་བ་བསྟན་པའི་མདོ) *tshe 'pho ba btsan pa'i mdo*).

Select Bibliography
(not including any Tibetan texts found in this chapter)

Cüppers, Christopher – Per K. Sørensen (eds.) 2000. *A Collection of Tibetan Proverbs and Sayings: Gems of Tibetan Wisdom and Wit*. Stuttgart: Franz Steiner.

dpe chos tshig mdzod. [Dictionary of Proverbs] 1999. Ed. dpa' ris sangs rgyas [Pari Szangye]. Xining: Mtsho sngon mi rigs dpe skrun khang.

Fox, Michael V. (trans. and comm.). 2010. *Proverbs 1-9: A New Translation with Introduction and Commentary*. New Haven – London: Yale University Press.

Guo Jianzhong. 1995. "Translatability in CE/EC [Chinese-English/English-Chinese] Translation." In: *An Encyclopaedia of Translation: Chinese-English – English-Chinese*, ed. Chan Sin-wai and David E. Pollard. Hong Kong: The Chinese University Press, pp. 1057-1067.

Kuzder, Rita. 2012. "A tibeti proverbiumok klasszifikációja" [Classification of Tibetan Proverbs]. Ph.D. diss. Budapest: Eötvös Loránd University.

Orosz, Gergely. 2008. *A Catalogue of the Tibetan Manuscripts and Block Prints in the Library of the Hungarian Academy of Sciences*. 2 vols. Budapest: Library of the Hungarian Academy of Sciences.

Paczolay, Gyula. 2000. "Some Notes on the Proverbs." In.: Ilona Nagy – Kincső Verebélyi (eds.), *Folklore in 2000: Voces amicorum Guilhelmo Voigt Sexagenario*. Budapest: Universitas Scientiarum de Rolando Eötvös nominata, pp. 315-328.

Pym, Anthony – Horst Turk. 2005. "Translatability," in *Routledge Encyclopedia of Translation Studies,* ed. Mona Baker. London – New York: Routledge, pp. 273-277

Roesler, Ulrike. 2007. "Tibetische Erzähungen." In: Rolf Wilhelm Brednich, Heidrun Alzheimer *et al*. (eds.), *Enzyklopädie des Märchens*. Band 13. Berlin – New York: de Gruyter, pp. 523-530.

---

[135] See *ONBP*, vol. 1, p. 485, left column.
[136] See *ONBP*, vol. 1, p. 71, n. 2.
[137] See the Index at *ONBP*, vol. 1, p. 485, left column.

Terjek, József. 1976 *Körösi Csoma dokumentumok az Akadémiai Könyvtár gyűjteményeiben*. [Körösi Csoma Documents in the Collections of the Academic Library]. Budapest: MTA.

Thomas, Frederick William. 1957a. *Ancient Folk-Literature from North-Eastern Tibet (Introductions, Texts, Translations and Notes)*. Berlin: Akademie-Verlag

———. 1957b. "Sumpa Mother's Sayings." In: Thomas 1957a, pp. 103-112.

Venuti, L. 2005. "Strategies of Translation." *Routledge Encyclopedia of Translation Studies*. Ed. Mona Baker. London – New York: Routledge, pp. 240-244.

10

THE SANSKRIT OF SOLOMON CAESAR MALAN
An Anglican Savant Reads the *Mahābhārata*

JAMES M. HEGARTY

Solomon Caesar Malan, missionary, minister and scholar, spent more than fifty years of his life on his great work, *Original Notes on the Book of Proverbs mostly from Eastern Writings*. Having put his short-lived missionary career in India behind him in 1840, SCM, from the light-filled and leafy vicarage of Broadwindsor in Dorset, embarked on an "armchair" exploration of the religious literature of the world. His quest: to find analogues for every one of the *meshālim*, the pithy aphorisms, contained in the biblical book of Proverbs. SCM was no Francis Younghusband (1863–1942), or Sven Anders Hedin (1865–1952), who some years after SCM's death would physically cross the vast deserts of Central Asia, but his quest – amendable though it was to breaks for tea and vespers – was quite as epic. SCM read materials in more than eighty languages in the original. He did so at a time when lexica and grammars were not always easily available or entirely accurate. The undertaking was connected to a missionary agenda, but it was not exhausted by it.[1] The quest to find the traces of "divine wisdom" in all the religious literatures of the world, while of course Christocentric, was marked by its openness to alien patterns of thought. It was also suffused with a deep appreciation, a "feeling of reverence for those eminent writings,"[2] indeed something of a luxuriation, in religious expression *tout court*.

In this chapter, I will take up the rich and extended engagement between SCM and the Sanskrit epic poem *Mahābhārata* (The Great Bhārata, henceforth *Mbh*), as it is reflected in his great work. I will consider, first of all, the range and extent of SCM's knowledge of Sanskrit literature. I will then focus on the editions and translations of the *Mbh* that would have been available to him during the course of the nineteenth century. I will also consider the form and extent of Sanskrit Studies in Europe in that period and the range and extent of grammatical and lexicographical works that would have aided SCM in his studies. The main body of this chapter will consider, in detail, a representative selection of SCM's translations from the *Mbh*. I will show that SCM's competence in Sanskrit should not be in doubt, but that his goals as a translator, and his overarching hermeneutical orientation to the *Mbh* lead, inevitably, to the distortion of his source material. I will show that there is a conflict between SCM's search for trans-cultural *meshālim* and the complexity of the *Mbh*'s ideological agenda and narrative structure.

---

[1] Articulated in *ONBP*, vol. 1, Preface, pp. xi–xiv.
[2] Quoting from *ONBP*, vol. 1, p. xiv.

1. Introducing the *Mahābhārata*

As SCM is the subject of the present volume in its entirety, he requires no further introduction.[3] However, the *Mbh* does: The *Mbh* is a vast epic poem that tells of the enmity of two groups of cousins, the Kauravas and the Pāṇḍavas. They are locked in a conflict over succession that culminates in a horrific war, resulting in the slaughter of almost the entire kṣatriya (the "warrior" caste). The war is divinely justified as a rescue mission for an earth overrun with demonic beings (the Asuras), who are incarnate as warriors. Viṣṇu and the other gods (the Devas) themselves incarnate to rid the world of these troublesome beings. Viṣṇu's incarnation is as the god-hero, Kṛṣṇa. The text is also a repository of diverse tales and asides, involving political, philosophical, and theological speculations.

The text of the *Mbh* is prodigious in its length. The oft-quoted statistic is that it is eight times the combined length of the *Illiad* and *Oddyssey* and five times the length of the Bible.[4] Its author, in traditional lore, is said to be one Kṛṣṇa Dvaipāyana Vyāsa, a Brahmin sage who is also credited with the arrangement of the four Vedas, amongst other things.

The *Mbh* has been consistently drawn upon by generations of South Asians in Sanskrit and the many Indian vernaculars. Its point of origin is obscure, but we can say – on linguistic and contextual grounds – that it emerged in something like its present Sanskrit form around the beginning of the Common Era (notwithstanding the likelihood of a textual and oral pre-history) and that it has continued to develop (though how much and in what ways is open to question) throughout its history. From an initial period of composition and redaction, the cultural emphasis within South Asia shifted to the preservation of the text (albeit in multiple redactions). That this is the case is reflected in our first epitome of the *Mbh* (the *Bhāratamañjarī* of the Kaśmīri pandit, Kṣemendra, which dates to the eleventh century CE), which seems to be based on a text not dissimilar to the critical edition of the Sanskrit text. It is also reflected in the early manuscript evidence (the earliest of which is Newar, that is to say from the Kathmandu Valley in modern-day Nepal, and dates to the eleventh century), which again has much in common with the critically established text (on which I will explain more below). It is also clear from the manuscript evidence that there is a distinct Southern recension of the text, which is the *textus ornatior*.

The earliest known evidence for the content of the *Mbh* is a list of its constituent books, which was found in central Asia (on the back of a Buddhist philosophical text) and dates to the early part of the third century (ca. 230 CE). The list does not agree with the catalogue of the books as it is preserved in later manuscript tradition (the *parva-saṃgraha*), though what this tells us about the history of the text is a matter of scholarly dispute.[5]

---

[3] Informed historical accounts of his life in Geneva, India, and Dorsetshire are found in Chapters 1–3 in this volume.

[4] Though this is a very instructive set of comparisons, I cannot vouch for these statistics.

[5] As discussed in Hegarty 2012, p. 28.

The Sanskrit text of the *Mbh* achieved a maximally inclusive form in the so-called "vulgate" edition of Nīlakaṇṭha in the second half of the seventeenth century, which sought to record all variant readings, but which was not a "critical" edition in the modern sense of that term.

The *Mbh* was critically edited, however, only in the twentieth century. The goal was to establish an approximation of the archetype of the Sanskrit text. In this regard, the critical editors, led by the great V.S. Sukthankar, were not entirely successful (the stemma being too multi-branched to admit of unequivocal statements). However, the critical edition, containing, as it does, a faithful record of all the manuscript variants found in the editorial process – both short and long – is an extraordinary scholarly resource. It may not have established an archetype for the *Mbh* on the basis of the manuscripts thus far surveyed (which number in the hundreds), but it suggests that such an archetype might have existed.

On this basis, what can we say about the overarching ideological agenda of the *Mbh*? Little that is brief. However, there is no doubt that the Brahminical establishment, which was the custodian of the Veda and of the sacrificial system based upon it – was assailed by challenges from both within and beyond itself from at least the third century BCE. The "gnostic" teachings of the late-Vedic Upaniṣads, with their questioning of the significance of ritual activity, combined with the new, anti-Vedic, religious teachings of the Jains and the Buddhist, were proving popular. Indeed, it is clear from inscriptional and material cultural evidence that the Buddhists were enjoying considerable royal patronage from at least the time of the Mauryan monarch, Aśoka (272–232 BCE); it is worth noting that his father had been a patron of the Jains. In this context, the *Mbh* stands as an encyclopaedic riposte to a religious "modernity" that was untasteful to at least some sections of the religious and intellectual elite of the day. The *Mbh* is – and please forgive the oxymoron – an epic of revolutionary conservatism: in it one finds, for the first time, a cohesive vision of the peoples and places of South Asia combined with a Brahmin-centred religious ideology which co-opts new ideas and presents them as having a hoary Vedic antiquity. Even as it does this, the *Mbh* foregrounds the vagaries and the moral and practical *aporia* of human existence. Combined with the more doctrinaire Laws of Manu, the *Mbh* laid the foundations for what we now refer to as "Hinduism."

This might seem like an odd bedfellow for a compilation of pithy aphorisms such as the biblical book of Proverbs. The connection was clear for SCM, however, for whom the *Mbh* was almost as much of a constant companion as the former text. Before turning to SCM's engagement with the *Mbh*, I will say a few words about his wider engagement with Sanskrit literature and his historical context.

2. S. C. Malan's Knowledge of Sanskrit and Indic Literature

SCM made use of a wide variety of Sanskrit materials. Chief amongst these were the following: first of all, epics – including, of course, the aforementioned *Mbh* (his favourite, as will be shown below), and the *Rāmāyaṇa*;[6] secondly, didactic literature ("mirrors for princes" etc.), such as the *Kathāsaritsāgara* and the *Hitopadeśa*;[7] thirdly, there were the various examples of the Artha and Nīti Śāstric literature, which are manuals of politics and policy; fourthly, the *Vedas* – the *Ṛg* and *Sāma* in particular – which are ancient compilations of hymns for ritual use; fifthly, the *subhāṣitā* literature, which are the Sanskritic equivalent of a modern dictionary of quotations. SCM also made use of a wide variety of Pāli sources: amongst them were the *Dhammapada*, which is a famous digest of Buddhist teachings, and the *Jātaka*, which are the stories of the former lives of the Buddha. He also made use of materials in a variety of Indian vernaculars.[8] Given that he commenced his work during the early period of Sanskritic and Indological studies (to be discussed in detail below), the range of these materials cited is quite extraordinary.

When these affirmations are framed within the broader awareness we now have of the fact that his personal library amounted to just over 4,000 texts in various formats that included works in just over 100 different languages,[9] and that within the manuscript version of the *ONBP* SCM wrote out in the original scripts passages from texts in over fifty languages (representing at least something like seventy different cultures),[10] one can be overwhelmed by the seemingly Herculean task that the manuscript and published versions of the *ONBP* represent. Nevertheless, precisely because of these astounding claims, there are also good reasons for us to ask some more penetrating questions. How well did he actually know each of those languages and texts in which he studied them? Here I will focus on only some representative passages in one part of his Sanskrit knowledge, that is, SCM's handling of the selected passages taken from the extensive texts of the eighteen books within the *Mbh*.

3. Sanskrit in Nineteenth Century European Scholarship

The manuscript version of the *ONBP*, which was also entitled "Original Notes to the Book of Proverbs," was completed over a period of sixty years from 1833 and 1893. During this period, Sanskrit scholarship in the European context developed from its infancy to its "coming of age."[11] It had its beginnings in the early colonial

---

[6] So, for example, SCM cited the *Mbh* in the third volume of *ONBP* nearly 170 times, while in the same volume he cited the *Rāmāyaṇa* only nine times.

[7] Because the biblical book of Proverbs contains a good amount of proverbial sayings about kings and rulers, among other relevant themes, SCM cited the *Hitopadeśa* nearly 110 times in the third volume of the *ONBP*, indicating the level of interest he retained in that particular work.

[8] A list of works cited by Malan may be found at the end of *ONBP* vol. 1, pp. 481-489 and vol. 3, pp. 601-603.

[9] For further details, please consult the discussion of the Malan Library found in Chapter 12.

[10] The manuscript version of the *ONBP* is discussed in detail within Chapter 13.

[11] This is not to overlook the contributions of earlier – largely Jesuit – scholarship that predate the efflorescence of Sanskrit studies at the beginning of the nineteenth century. Such scholarship produced the first translations into any European language of Sanskrit sources, as well

period. For example, Charles Wilkins published his pioneering English translation of the *Bhagavad Gītā* in 1785, and William "Oriental" Jones blazed a trail with his oft-quoted statement of the historical relationship between Greek, Latin and Sanskrit, which was published in 1786.[12] This was followed by the pioneering works of German scholars such as August Wilhelm von Schlegel (1772-1829) and Franz Bopp (1791-1867), who placed the discipline of Indology and Comparative Indo-European Philology on a scientific footing. By the middle of the nineteenth century the field had established chairs in several major European seats of learning (the first chair being established in the rather new University of Bonn in 1818, followed by Oxford in 1832, amongst others). F. Max Müller (1823-1900) contributed greatly to the profile of Sanskrit as a field of study as the nineteenth century progressed with his edition of the *Ṛg Veda* and his broader deliberations on South Asian religion and culture. By the close of the nineteenth century, Sanskrit was an established area of scholarly endeavour, if still something of a specialized minority pursuit.

Even in this context of burgeoning activity, SCM was a well-respected figure. A. A. Macdonell, a celebrated Sanskritist of the day, in his eulogy for the former Broadwindsor vicar published in the *Journal of the Royal Asiatic Society*[13] stated that SCM was an oriental linguist of "incomparable achievements." In an age paradoxically full of such incomparables, this is high praise indeed.

4. Orientalists, Missionaries and Imperialists

Beyond the rather narrow field of Sanskrit Studies, SCM in his early years developed as a linguist in the context of a bitter ideological dispute with regard to the future direction of British colonial policy in India. The "Orientalist" lobby, established by Warren Hastings, proposed to govern India in the light of its local laws and customs, however distorted it may appear to us in retrospect. Its high watermark was the foundation in 1800 and ensuing activities of the College of Fort William in Calcutta, "the Oxford of the East," with its program of Persian, Sanskrit and vernacular studies. However, "Orientalists" were firmly challenged in these kinds of claims by both parliament and public opinion, partly because the contemporary spectre of the Nabob – the half-native company man – loomed large in the public imagination.[14] The publication of Mill's *History of British India* in 1817, with its

---

as Europe's first grammars of Sanskrit (notably produced in Latin). For details see Van Hal – Vielle 2013.

[12] In fact, that hypothesis was not original to Jones. He had borrowed it from Nathaniel Brassey Halhed, who was resident in Bengal as an employee of the East India Company between 1771 and 1785. Halhed translated *A Code of Gentoo Laws* from Persian into English, which was a digest of Sanskrit legal sources that had been compiled by eleven pundits at the request of the then Governor General of India, Warren Hastings. In the preface to his English translation of the *Code* Halhead made the observation that Jones was subsequently to make so famous.

[13] Consult Macdonnell 1895, pp. 453-457.

[14] This was a subject of dramatical invention even by the late eighteenth century. Consult Samuel Foote, *The Nabob: A Comedy in Three Acts,* which was first performed in 1772. Reprinted in Gregg 2005, pp. 111-146.

aggressive disparagement of Indian civilization, led to a growing lobby supporting cultural chauvinism in British dealings with its subject peoples. Such an orientation was not without its critics, however. Horace Hayman Wilson (1786–1860), fulsomely demonstrating his "Orientalist" credentials, remarked in his editor's preface to a later edition of Mill's *History*:

> With very imperfect knowledge, with materials exceedingly defective, with an implicit faith in all testimony hostile to Hindu pretensions, [Mill ...] has elaborated a portrait of the Hindus which has no resemblance whatever to the original, and which almost outrages humanity.[15]

Despite all this, Hastings' preference for the cultivation of a class of Englishmen who knew and loved India and her languages had been by 1835 almost wholly inverted. Lord Macaulay in his now infamous notes on English education called for an end to the study of Sanskrit and Arabic, and instead placing a new attention to the "intellectual health" (and not the "intellectual taste") of the "natives."[16] Hastings wanted to cultivate a class of Indians that loved Britain and her languages (which ironically included, of course, Greek and Latin).

As well as political tensions, there was also a debate concerning the role of missionary activity in India. The East India Company had blocked the entry of missionaries into India until the renewal of its Charter Act in 1813. It seems, however, that by the 1830s, the scholarly and the missionary agendas had become – at least for some – integrated. This is reflected in the founding requirements of the Boden chair of Sanskrit at Oxford. Joseph Boden explicitly mentioned the necessity for the "conversion of the natives of India" in his founding bequest to the University.[17] How one combined "mission" and "scholarship," was, however, very much in the hands of individual scholars.

How should we situate SCM in this somewhat agonistic context of "Orientalism," "Occidentalism," and Christian missionary activities? It is undoubtedly significant that Wilson was SCM's referee for the latter's only posting in India, a teaching position at the Anglican Bishop's College in Calcutta.[18] Notably, SCM was also secretary to the Asiatic Society of Bengal for a brief period during his time in India,[19] which suggests that he maintained "Orientalist" sympathies. It is also worth noting that the departing principal at Bishop's College at the time of SCM's appointment there, Dr. W. H. Mill, was considered for the Boden chair, but was

---

[15] Mill 1840–1848, preface of the editor, pp. vii-viii.

[16] Found in item 18. For the full text, consult "Minute by the Hon'ble T. B. Macaulay," February 2, 1835, http://www.columbia.edu/itc/mealac/pritchett/00generallinks/macaulay/txt_minute_education_1835.html (accessed March 17, 2021).

[17] It is not without interest to note here that SCM was a recipient of a Boden scholarship while studying in Oxford.

[18] SCM wrote to thank Wilson and to advise him of his imminent departure to India. These letters, from SCM to Wilson, are kept amongst the H. H. Wilson letters in the British Library. See his private papers, call number EUR E 301, vol. 3, pp. 35-36 and 81-82. For further details about SCM's experiences and work in Calcutta, see Chapter 2 in this volume.

[19] See Neill 2002, p. 458, appendix 27.

passed over in favour of Wilson (losing by only seven votes, 207 to 200 – as the Times reported at the time).[20] Mill's achievements as a Sanskritist were not of the order of Wilson's (he had co-authored only a single Sanskrit poem, an original work entitled the *christa-saṃgīta* or *History of Our Lord Jesus Christ in Sanskrit Verse*), but his missionary credentials were well established. SCM seems to reflect something of the agendas of both these men.

It seems, then, that the links between missionary activity, scholarship and politics (and the capacity for one to masquerade as the other) were as well developed in the nineteenth century as they are today.[21] SCM's *ONBP* must be understood in this context, yet we must also approach his *magnum opus* – in so far as it is possible – on its own terms. Before this is done, however, I will provide a brief overview of Sanskrit and, in particular, *Mbh* scholarship during the period of composition of the manuscript version of the *ONBP*.

5. Nineteenth-century Editions and Translations of the *Mahābhārata*

Given that this period spans six decades, from the 1830s to the 1890s, I will focus only on the editions of the Sanskrit text of the *Mbh* that would have been available to SCM, and not elaborate the scholarly debates that surrounded the text (which SCM makes no mention of, in any case). The version of the *Mbh* that SCM was most likely to have consulted is known to scholarship as "The Calcutta Edition," which was produced in Calcutta by the Asiatic Society in Nāgarī characters in four volumes between 1834 and 1839. It would therefore have been completed while SCM was residing in Calcutta. This version is based on that of Nīlakaṇṭha, the most inclusive of the versions of the *Mbh* (see the discussion above for details).

The only other edition that was produced in SCM's lifetime was again based on the Nīlakaṇṭha version and contained his commentary. This was the Bombay Edition of 1863. This is in *pothi* form (with horizontally extended pages that mimic the form of a palm leaf manuscript) with the text printed in bold Sanskrit letters in the middle portion and Nīlakaṇṭha's commentary at the top and bottom in small letters.

Numerous translations from the *Mbh* had been produced from the late eighteenth century onwards (in French, English and German) by luminaries such as Wilkins, Jones, Bopp, Müller, Monier-Williams and many others. It is worth noting in this regard that the perennially popular *Bhagavad Gītā* is itself drawn from the *Mbh*. The first translation of the Nīlakaṇṭha text (without his commentary) was not com-

---

[20] Please refer to "University Intelligence," *Times* [London, England], issue 14802, Saturday, March 17, 1832, p. 4, *The Times Digital Archive*, http://find.galegroup.com.lib-ezproxy.hkbu.edu.hk/ttda/infomark.do?&source=gale&prod Id=TTDA&userGroup-Name=hkbu&tabID=T003&docPage=article&searchType=AdvancedSearchForm&docId=CS67657329&type=multipage&contentSet=LTO&version=1.0 (accessed May 20, 2021).

[21] Especially if one is willing to use the term "missionary" in a slightly extended sense to encompass non-Christian and non-religious ideologies.

pleted, however, until 1894, the year SCM passed away.[22] If SCM had access to this text (which began to appear within the late 1880s), it was only in the very final stages of the preparation of the *ONBP* for print.

5.1 Sanskrit in 19th Century Scholarship – Lexicons and Other Scholarly Apparati

Like the field itself, the range of support materials that a scholar could call upon in the nineteenth century developed greatly. Of critical importance was the production of grammars and lexica. The pioneering work of Dutch scholars in the seventeenth century led to their being several largely reliable grammars of Sanskrit available in Europe (mostly in Latin, but translated also into German and Dutch).[23] Nevertheless, the monumental work of this sort during the nineteenth century was, without doubt, the St. Petersburg *Wörterbuch* compiled by Otto von Böhtlingk and published between 1855–1875 in seven volumes.[24] However, while SCM may have made use of this lexicon it is more likely that his primary reference tool was the Sanskrit to English dictionary produced by Wilson, which was published in 1819. Indeed, SCM was self-conscious of this work, and so had asked Wilson in 1843 if he was preparing a new edition of his dictionary.[25]

5.2 Sanskrit in India: The Figure of the Pandit

Given that SCM was Professor of Classical Languages at Bishop's College in Calcutta during the years between 1838 and 1840, one might also speculate as to his exposure to traditional Sanskrit scholarship as it was practiced in South Asia (though one should note that his health was poor at this time).[26] A suitably educated pandit might serve the function of Grammar, Dictionary and Thesaurus[27] regardless of the state of the European scholarly apparati (grammatical and lexicographical) of the period. However, SCM's sojourn in India was quite brief, and the *ONBP* notably does not document or reflect on any engagement with the contemporary and past Sanskrit commentarial tradition.

---

[22] Consult Rāya – Ganguli 1889–1894, consisting of ten volumes including all eighteen tomes within the work.

[23] For details see Winternitz 1977 [1927], pp. 8-25.

[24] Consult von Böhtlingk 1855–1875, in 7 volumes.

[25] In a letter dated July 9th, 1843. In fact, Wilson's dictionary was reissued in 1932, long after both men had passed away. For the letter, see again the correspondence of H. H. Wilson in the British Library: Private Papers EUR E 301, vol. 7, pp. 163-164. The revision of Wilson's dictionary was an ill-fated project: it was taken up by Theodor Goldstücker, but stalled after the publication of the first revised volume in 1856. For details about this story, consult the *Grammatica Grandonica*.

[26] See Ms. M. E. Gibbs, "Project Canterbury: Bishop's College Calcutta 1820–1970: 'The First Hundred and Fifty Years'," http://anglicanhistory.org/india/bishops1970/ (accessed March 17, 2021).

[27] For a description of the mode of education of the pandit, see Filliozat 2000 [1992], p. 75.

Having introduced the ideological context and the state of the art of Sanskrit and *Mbh* Studies in the period from the 1830s to the 1890s, I will now turn to a careful consideration of SCM's translations from the *Mbh* and their place in the *ONBP*.

6. S. C. Malan's Translations from the *Mahābhārata*

SCM's engagement with the *Mbh* is rich and sustained. He cites material from almost all of its eighteen books that constitute the *Mbh*. For the purpose of exposition, I have selected verses from three of the major books of the *Mbh*, the ones apparently most often cited in the *ONBP*, for consideration in this chapter.[28] The three books are:

The Vanaparvan – "The Book of the Forest" (book three of the *Mbh*)
The Udyogaparvan – "The Book of the Effort" (book five of the *Mbh*)
The Śāntiparvan – "The Book of Peace" (book twelve of the *Mbh*)

Each of these books contains a vast amount of didactic material. In each case, the *Mbh*'s central protagonists are presented in crisis and the teachings offered – at least ostensibly – address the particulars of their situation. In the *Vanaparvan* (also known as the *Āraṇyakaparvan*), the hero of our tale, King Yudhiṣṭhira, is in exile with his wife and brothers and laments his situation. This provides a rich range of opportunities for homilies from a variety of the great sages of the day (and of the distant past, for sages in ancient Indian literature tended to be very long-lived). In the *Udyogaparvan* – which was the book of the *Mbh* from which SCM quoted most[29] – we find the same king, returning now from exile only to find that his conniving cousin, Duryodhana, will not return his ancestral lands to him. The book is largely taken up with the mission of Kṛṣṇa to the court of King Duryodhana to sue for peace. It provides a foil for a vast variety of teachings on the nature of the good life and the path of the warrior as well as an opportunity for Kṛṣṇa to reveal his divine form, as he will do again so famously in the *Bhagavad Gītā*. The *Śāntiparvan* finds King Yudhiṣṭhira triumphant, but at a terrible cost. He has slaughtered his kinfolk and is overcome with grief. In this book, Yudhiṣṭhira's honorary grandfather, the sagacious Bhīṣma, empowered by the divine insight of Kṛṣṇa, offers the king a variety of teachings on the nature of kingship, of the universe and of liberation from rebirth that are designed to console the king and to oblige him to take up his role as ruler of the known world. Each of these books, as well as having a rich range of didactic content, captures one of the three critical moments in the plot development of the *Mbh*: exile; war (at least the eve of it); and victory (and its aftermath).

---

[28] From a thorough study of the footnotes in the third volume of the *ONBP* (dealing with Proverbs 20-31), eleven of the eighteen books in the *Mbh* are cited. The total number of citations of those books of the *Mbh* within this volume come to over 160, including 46 citations of the *Udyogaparvan*, 34 citations of the *Vanaparvan*, and 28 citations of the *Śāntiparvan* (that is, 108 of the more than 160 citations from the whole work). In fact, they are the three most cited books from the *Mbh* in that volume.

[29] So, it is found that in *ONBP*, vol. 3, the *Udyogaparvan* (referred to in the footnotes by the abbreviation "Maha Bh. Udyog. P.") is referred to 46 times in reference to 47 passages, the most citations and translations of any of the eighteen books of the *Mbh*.

6.1 From the *Vanaparvan*

I turn now to the nitty gritty of SCM's engagement with the *Mbh*. SCM cites, in relation to Proverbs 18:14 ("The spirit of a man will sustain his infirmity; but a wounded spirit who can bear?")[30] the following verse:

> *priye nātibhṛśaṃ hṛṣyed, apriye na ca saṃjvaret |*
> *na muhyed arthakṛcchreṣu, na ca dharmaṃ parityajet || 3.198.41 ||*[31]

This is partially translated by SCM (who does not translate the second line of the *śloka*) as:

> Let him not feel overjoyed with pleasant things (or in agreeable circumstances), nor yet be cast down when the reverse happens.[32]

How accurate is this as a translation? I would render the verse – rather literally – as follows:

> Do not rejoice (*na hṛṣyed*) excessively (*ati-bhṛśam*) in happiness (*priye*). In unhappiness (*apriye*), do not be melancholic (*na ca saṃjvaret*, lit. "to be fevered," but commonly used to express depression or sorrow in Sanskrit).

The verse is a simple one, marked by the use of the optative to formulate a prohibition – a feature typical of Sanskrit legal texts as well. SCM appreciates this and his translation is free, but faithful. The verse continues:

> You should not be perplexed (*na muhyed* – lit. "to become stupefied, or bewildered") as a consequence of calamity (*artha-kṛcchra*);[33] do not abandon (*na parityajet*) virtue (*dharma*)![34]

It is somewhat odd to translate only half a *śloka*; the *śloka* – developed from the Vedic *anuṣṭubh* metre – is the basic verse form of the *Mbh*. It is composed of thirty-two syllables in two lines of sixteen with four feet of eight syllables. It is marked by a series of permissible combinations of syllables of different "weight" or length.[35] It is also the basic unit of expression; that is to say, a *śloka*, more often

---

[30] His quotations of the biblical book of Proverbs always relies upon the King James Version, though this did not prevent him from criticizing that 17th century English rendering, as is documented in Chapter 5 of this volume.

[31] *Mbh*.3.198.41a (Calcutta Edition 13743) – the verse is repeated at 12.94.11. All references, unless otherwise indicated, are to the Critical Edition of the *Mbh*. As seen above, the portions of each *śloka* are divided by a single line (|), and completion of the full *śloka* is indicated by a double line (||), followed by the numbering of that passage in the Critical Edition of the *Mbh*.

[32] Cited from *ONBP*, vol. 2, p. 529 (in reference to Proverbs 18:14).

[33] *Artha-kṛcchra* – a compound noun, combining the word for "reason" or "cause" – *artha* – with that for calamity or trouble – *kṛcchra* – with the whole given in the locative case. "On account of calamity" is perhaps the equivalent English construction.

[34] *Dharma* as a term has an enormous semantic range, but broadly refers to lawful, virtuous or meritorious activity. It can also simply mean a religious teaching.

[35] It should be added here that one also finds *ślokas* with an extra line, bringing the total to 48 syllables. With regard to these "truncated translations" presented from the *Mbh* by SCM, this pattern of translation tends to dominate his use of quotations from this classical Indian epic.

than not, is complete unto itself and is grammatically independent of the verse that follows. This extends, more loosely, to the semantics of the *śloka*, which tends also to encapsulate a complete "thought." It is therefore exegetically dangerous to translate a half-verse. Here in this particular case, however, SCM is on relatively safe ground, as the second half of the verse largely repeats the sentiment of the first, and the two are grammatically independent of one another (with the whole verse being a sequence of short and sharp exhortations).

Allow me to move to assessing SCM's grasp of the narrative context of the verse. SCM identifies the interlocutors at this point in the *Mbh* to be the Brahmin Kaushiki and the king of Mithilā, Janaka, but in fact it is a hunter (Skt. *vyādha*) from Mithilā that is teaching Kauśika (the modern transliteration of the name who, in turn, is having his tale told by the sage Mārkaṇḍeya to the hero of the main story of the *Mbh*, Yudhiṣṭhira).[36] SCM's mis-identification of the interlocutors is a more serious lapse than his partial translation of the verse. While it would be of interest to have a dialogue in which a king offers religious instruction to a Brahmin (the traditional religious elite), it is not as arresting as having a hunter in a teaching role. In fact, SCM places the Brahmin in the teaching role, as is manifest from his further translations below. The occupation of the hunter, with its intimate connection to the taking of life, was a wholly impure undertaking in early Indian thought. The hunter in the present tale explains that he had been a Brahmin in a previous life, but that he had shot a hermit, which led to his current rebirth into this impure status. However, far from rejecting his occupation as a hunter, he emphasises the necessity for one to do one's hereditary duty. Subsequently, he discourses on the true nature of virtue to the proud Brahmin, who recognises the wisdom and power of the hunter's words. The content of the hunters's teaching is something of a compendium of early South Asian ethical and philosophical thought. It blends Buddhistic and other elements with a heavy emphasis on the authority of Vedic scriptures. It is one of many colloquies (Skt. *saṃvāda*) that appear in the *Mbh*, in which new religious ideologies are blended with Vedic orthodoxy.[37]

That is to say, taking only a selected portion of a full "saying" is a normal pattern found in SCM's translation of passages from the *Mbh* as they are presented in the *ONBP*. He apparently did so on the basis that the passage quoted is specifically relevant to the biblical proverb being compared. Still, when only a half of a *śloka* from the *Mbh* is presented by means of translation, but without any explanation of this way of presenting the passage, the exegetical danger addressed here is a serious hermeneutic problem.

[36] One should also not forget that the *Mbh* is always a story within a story within a story. That is to say, any particular passage is "framed" by two narrative contexts. The first is that of Ugraśravas – a professional bard – and the Brahmins of the Naimiṣa forest, who request a recitation of the *Mbh* during the intervals of their great Vedic sacrifice that occurs once every twelve years. Ugraśravas immediately introduces a further narrative context, in which the author of the poem (Kṛṣṇa Dvaipāyana Vyāsa) deputises one of his students, Vaiśampāyana, to recite the *Mbh* to a descendent of its central protagonists – one King Janamejaya! These "tellings" frame the entire text.

[37] See Hegarty 2012, pp. 112-118, for more details of this type of colloquy in the *Mbh*.

While still discussing an earlier passage from the book of Proverbs (18:4), SCM goes on to cite further verses from this portion of the *Vanaparvan:*

> "Yet let him [the wise man] not lose heart when his means diminish, neither let him abandon virtue. Let him not feel overjoyed with pleasant things (or in agreeable circumstances), nor yet be cast down when the reverse happens," said Kaushiki to the king of Mithilā. "Nothing comes to him that complains (or grieves); he only makes himself miserable," said Vyasa. "There is no end to being dissatisfied; whereas contentment is very great happiness." "But the mind ought not to be thrown down [dejected]. Such a state is real poison. It kills the man who gives way to it, like an angry snake kills a child. He who loses courage at starting, no good can come to him thus bereft of his energy," said Vyāsa.

This is a partial translation of *Mbh.*3.206.19-23:

parityajanti ye duḥkham, sukham vāpy ubhayam narāḥ |
ta eva sukham edhante, jñānatṛptā manīṣiṇaḥ || 3.206.19 ||

asaṃtoṣaparā mūḍhāḥ, saṃtoṣam yānti paṇḍitāḥ |
asaṃtoṣasya nāsty antas, tuṣṭis tu paramaṃ sukham |
na śocanti gatādhvānaḥ, paśyantaḥ paramāṃ gatim || 3.206.20 ||

na viṣāde manaḥ kāryam, viṣādo viṣam uttamam |
mārayaty akṛtaprajñam, bālam kruddha ivoragaḥ || 3.206.21 ||

yaṃ viṣādo 'bhibhavati, viṣame samupasthite |
tejasā tasya hīnasya, puruṣārtho na vidyate || 3.206.22 ||

avaśyaṃ kriyamāṇasya, karmaṇo dṛśyate phalam |
na hi nirvedam āgamya, kiṃ cit prāpnoti śobhanam || 3.206.23 ||

Which I would translate (again rather literally) as follows:

Men (*narāḥ*) who abandon (*ye parityajanti*) both (*ubhayam*) pleasure (*sukham*) and pain (*duḥkham*), they – satisfied by their knowledge (*jñāna-tṛptā*) and wise (*manīṣiṇaḥ*) – increase (*ta eva edhante*) [their] joy (*sukham*).

Fools (*mūḍhāḥ*) [are] wholly discontented (*asaṃtoṣa-parā*), while the learned (*paṇḍitāḥ*) achieve (*yanti*) contentment (*saṃtoṣam*). Of discontentment (*asaṃtoṣasya*) there is no end, but satisfaction (*tuṣṭis*) [is] the highest happiness (*paramaṃ sukham*). Those who have walked the path (*gatādhvānaḥ*), beholding (*paśyantaḥ*) the ultimate goal, (*paramāṃ gatim*) do not grieve (*na śocanti*).

The mind (*manaḥ*) should not be left (*na kāryam*) in despair (*viṣāde*); despair [is] the ultimate poison (*viṣam uttamam*); it kills (*mārayati*) one who is ignorant (*akṛta-prajñam*) just as the angry snake (*kruddha uragaḥ*) [kills] a child (*bālam*).

When trouble comes (*viṣame sampaṣṭhite* – lit. "in the arising of trouble"), despair (*viṣādo*) overcomes (*abhibhavati*) him; his vital force (*tejasā*) [is] depleted (*hīnasya*); he no longer understands (*na vidyate*) the purpose of life (*puruṣārtho*).

The fruit (*phalam*) of action (*karmaṇo*) – once done (*kriyamāṇasya*) – undoubtedly (*avaśyam*), is seen (*dṛśyate*); one obtains (*prāpnoti*) nothing (*na kim cit*) good (*śobhanam*) having given in to (*agamya*, lit. "having gone to") despondency (*nirvedam*).

Again, there is no doubting SCM's basic grasp of the Sanskrit of the verses in question. SCM's emphasis in his exegesis of Proverbs 18:4 is on patience, humility and strength in the face of the vicissitudes of human existence and on the preservation of spiritual integrity. The verses he selects from the *Vanaparvan* here are certainly relevant to this broad theme, but the virtue which one must never abandon – in Sanskrit, the *dharma* that one must never give up – is an uneasy blend of the relatively new theory of *karma* (the consequences of actions across successive lifetimes) with a socially conservative model of Vedic orthodoxy (which is itself largely post-Vedic and is derived from Sanskrit legal texts, the *Dharmaśāstras*). This is exactly the form of "revolutionary conservatism" that I suggested was characteristic of the *Mbh* as a whole. That new elements are being introduced in this teaching is obliquely indicated by the inversion of the normal pedagogical hierarchy, i.e., a Brahmin, rather than teaching, is taught (albeit by a former Brahmin). Indeed, Kauśika offers us the following radically counter-hierarchical sentiment:

yas tu śūdro dame satye, dharme ca satatotthitaḥ |
taṃ brāhmaṇam ahaṃ manye, vṛttena hi bhaved dvijaḥ || 3.206.12 ||

[...] but that *śudra*, always preeminent (*satata-utthitaḥ*) in truth (*satye*), self-restraint (*dame*) and virtue (*dharme*), I judge (*aham manye*) him a Brahmin; [It is] by conduct (*vṛttena*) that one becomes (*bhaved*) a Brahmin (*dvijaḥ*)!

Which we might compare with the content of a Buddhist text, the Pāli *Dhammapada*:

yassa kayena vacaya, manasa natthi dukkataj |
sajvutaj tihi thanehi, tam ahaj brumi brahmanaj || 391 ||

The one who does no wrong
Through body, speech or mind,
Restrained in three ways,
Him I call a Brahmin.[38]

SCM apparently cannot be detained by such inter-religious details, but one is left wondering whether the "wisdom" he so assiduously identifies works in entirely the same way in Hindu and Buddhist contexts (despite the similarities in the above) or across one or many lives. Nor does he seem to grasp fully the essential role of equanimity, as opposed to patience, in the face of everyday life in some branches of Indian philosophical tradition (or what this means in terms of the interpretation of physical reality as largely illusory, which is a hallmark of some of these traditions).

The other feature of SCM's exegesis is that it suppresses doctrinal differences. Indeed, in the very material from the *Vanaparvan* that he takes up, there is evidence of a doctrinal debate and synthesis that is subordinated by SCM to his vision of the overarching thematics of the book of Proverbs. He is utterly explicit in this regard, but this does not alter the way in which this acts on the text of the *Mbh*, which is reduced to an echo of a proverbial call for forbearance and spiritual fortitude. Having said this, one should not disregard the extent to which SCM has nonetheless selected relevant and apposite material. For what could be more conducive to forbearance than an impact on not only one, but numberless, lives?

---

[38] *Dhammapada* 16.391 as translated in Roebuck 2010, p. 76.

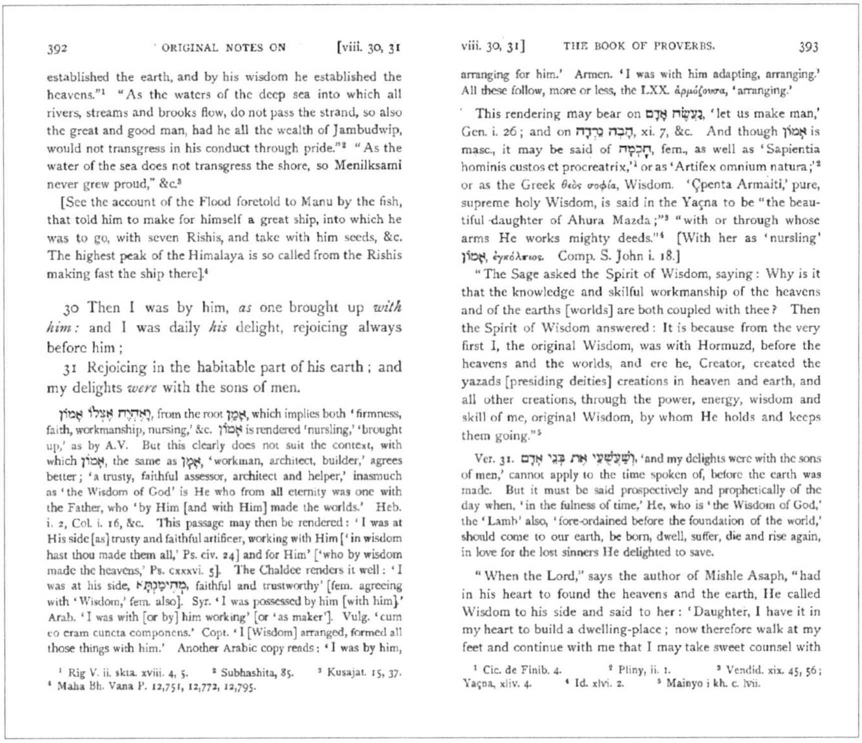
392 ORIGINAL NOTES ON [viii. 30, 31

established the earth, and by his wisdom he established the heavens."[1] "As the waters of the deep sea into which all rivers, streams and brooks flow, do not pass the strand, so also the great and good man, had he all the wealth of Jambudwip, would not transgress in his conduct through pride."[2] "As the water of the sea does not transgress the shore, so Menilksami never grew proud," &c.[3]

[See the account of the Flood foretold to Manu by the fish, that told him to make for himself a great ship, into which he was to go, with seven Rishis, and take with him seeds, &c. The highest peak of the Himalaya is so called from the Rishis making fast the ship there].[4]

30 Then I was by him, *as* one brought up *with him:* and I was daily *his* delight, rejoicing always before him;

31 Rejoicing in the habitable part of his earth; and my delights *were* with the sons of men.

וָאֶהְיֶה אֶצְלוֹ אָמוֹן, from the root אָמַן, which implies both 'firmness, faith, workmanship, nursing,' &c. אָמוֹן is rendered 'nursling,' 'brought up,' as by A.V. But this clearly does not suit the context, with which אָמוֹן, the same as אָמָן, 'workman, architect, builder,' agrees better; 'a trusty, faithful assessor, architect and helper,' inasmuch as 'the Wisdom of God' is He who from all eternity was one with the Father, who 'by Him [and with Him] made the worlds.' Heb. i. 2, Col. i. 16, &c. This passage may then be rendered: 'I was at His side [as] trusty and faithful artificer, working with Him [' in wisdom hast thou made them all,' Ps. civ. 24] and for Him' ['who by wisdom made the heavens,' Ps. cxxxvi. 5]. The Chaldee renders it well: 'I was at his side, מְהֵימַנְתָּא, faithful and trustworthy' [fem. agreeing with 'Wisdom,' fem. also]. Syr. 'I was possessed by him [with him].' Arab. 'I was with [or by] him working' [or 'as maker']. Vulg. 'cum eo eram cuncta componens.' Copt. 'I [Wisdom] arranged, formed all those things with him.' Another Arabic copy reads: 'I was by him,

[1] Rig V. ii. skta. xviii. 4, 5. [2] Subhashita, 85. [3] Kusajat. 15, 37. [4] Maha Bh. Vana P. 12,751, 12,772, 12,795.

viii. 30, 31] THE BOOK OF PROVERBS. 393

arranging for him.' Armen. 'I was with him adapting, arranging.' All these follow, more or less, the LXX. ἁρμόζουσα, 'arranging.'

This rendering may bear on נַעֲשֶׂה אָדָם, 'let us make man,' Gen. i. 26; and on הָבָה נֵרְדָה, xi. 7, &c. And though אָמוֹן is masc., it may be said of חָכְמָה, fem., as well as 'Sapientia hominis custos et procreatrix,'[1] or as 'Artifex omnium natura;'[2] or as the Greek θεὸς σοφία, Wisdom. 'Çpenta Armaiti,' pure, supreme holy Wisdom, is said in the Yaçna to be "the beautiful daughter of Ahura Mazda;"[3] "with or through whose arms He works mighty deeds."[4] [With her as 'nursling' אָמוֹן, ἐγκόλπιος. Comp. S. John i. 18.]

"The Sage asked the Spirit of Wisdom, saying: Why is it that the knowledge and skilful workmanship of the heavens and of the earths [worlds] are both coupled with thee? Then the Spirit of Wisdom answered: It is because from the very first I, the original Wisdom, was with Hormuzd, before the heavens and the worlds, and ere he, Creator, created the yazads [presiding deities] creations in heaven and earth, and all other creations, through the power, energy, wisdom and skill of me, original Wisdom, by whom He holds and keeps them going."[5]

Ver. 31. וְשַׁעֲשֻׁעַי אֶת בְּנֵי אָדָם, 'and my delights were with the sons of men,' cannot apply to the time spoken of, before the earth was made. But it must be said prospectively and prophetically of the day when, 'in the fulness of time,' He, who is 'the Wisdom of God,' the 'Lamb' also, 'fore-ordained before the foundation of the world,' should come to our earth, be born, dwell, suffer, die and rise again, in love for the lost sinners He delighted to save.

"When the Lord," says the author of Mishle Asaph, "had in his heart to found the heavens and the earth, He called Wisdom to his side and said to her: 'Daughter, I have it in my heart to build a dwelling-place; now therefore walk at my feet and continue with me that I may take sweet counsel with

[1] Cic. de Finib. 4. [2] Pliny, ii. 1. [3] Vendid. xix. 45, 56; Yaçna, xliv. 4. [4] Id. xlvi. 2. [5] Mainyo i kh. c. lvii.

Fig. 16: *ONBP*, vol. 1, pp. 392-393 (Prov. 8:30-31), *Mahabharata* (p. 392, footnote 4)

6.2 From the *Udyogaparvan*

Moving to the *Udyogaparvan,* in the context of his commentary on Proverbs 2:11 ("Discretion shall preserve thee, understanding shall keep thee"), SCM cites the following verses:

> "Shame (or bashfulness)," said Vaiśampayana, "when killed [overcome], kills virtue; and virtue, when killed, ruins one's good fortune. He who is without shame or is crazed, whether man or woman, excellence in virtue is not his; he is like a Sudra. But the bashful (or modest) worships the gods, honours his ancestors and [*namati*] bows to himself [respects himself]."[39]

The Sanskrit is as follows (combining verses *Mbh* 5.70.19 and 38-39), with the interlocutors being Yudhiṣṭhira and Kṛṣṇa. SCM's attribution of the passage to Vaiśampayana misrepresents the fact that he only "says" the verse, in the sense that he is the primary narrator of the main plot of the *Mbh*.[40]

hrīr hatā bādhate dharmaṃ, dharmo hanti hataḥ śriyam |
śrīr hatā puruṣaṃ hanti, puruṣasyāsvatā vadhaḥ || 5.70.19 ||

[39] Quoted from *ONBP*, vol. 1, p. 78. Sudra (*śudra*) is the lowest of the four castes comprising peasants, artisans and other menial workers.

[40] For an explanation of this problem of framing any *Mbh* quotation properly, see n. 36 above.

ahrīko vā vimūḍho vā, naiva strī na punaḥ pumān |
nāsyādhikāro dharme 'sti, yathā śūdras tathaiva saḥ || 5.70.38 ||
hrīmān avati devāṃś ca, pitṝn ātmānam eva ca |
tenāmṛtatvaṃ vrajati, sā kāṣṭhā puṇyakarmaṇām || 5.70.39 ||

The loss (*hatā*) of shame (*hrīr*), prevents (*bādhate*) the rule of law (*dharmam*), the loss of virtue (*hataḥ dharmo*) mars (*hanti*) [one's] royal dignity (*śriyam*). The loss (*hatā*) of one's royal dignity (*śrīr*) kills (*hanti*) a man (*puruṣam*), the absence of property (*asvatā*) [is] the death (*vadhaḥ*) of a man (*puruṣasya*).

Either shameless or mentally imbalanced (*ahrīko vā vimūḍho vā* – these are both adjectives, while the repetition of a postposition is common in Sanskrit, and is here *metri causa*), neither a woman (*na eva strī*) nor again (*na punaḥ*) a man (*pumān*), his prerogative (*adhikāro*) is not [established] in law (*dharme*), he [is] exactly like a *śūdra*.

[He who is] possessed of modesty (*hrīmān*) sustains (*avati*) the gods (*devāṃś*) as well as the ancestors (*pitṝn*) and the individual (*ātmānam*). By it (*tena*), one attains (*vrajati*) immortality (*amṛtatvam*); the goal (*sā kāṣṭhā*) of the pious (*puṇyakarmaṇām*).

Again, SCM's selection is adroit and his translation largely faithful. His discussion of the semantic range of the terminology of the book of Proverbs does seem to raise interesting questions about the Sanskrit terms *hrī* (shame), *hrīmat* (to be possessed of shame and thus modest or bashful) and *ahrī* (shamelessness). However, once again, SCM truncates the verses from which he translates and fails to take due note of their narrative context. At this point in the *Mbh*, Yudhiṣṭhira is bitterly complaining about his loss of his ancestral lands to Kṛṣṇa. SCM is actually translating from within a debate over royal prerogative. It is for this reason that I translate *dharma* as the "rule of law" here. Much of Yudhiṣṭhira's characterisation of shamelessness is directed at his cousin, Duryodhana, who has robbed him of his kingdom. In choosing not to translate the final line of verse 5.39, SCM also robs Yudhiṣṭhira's speech of its culminatory promise of immortality (which, owing to the royal context of the speech, is more likely to refer to a heavenly abode rather than a transcendental state). It is worth noting, however, that SCM might – at least implicitly – be exploring the shared "royal" context of the book of Proverbs and the *Mbh*. This might, in turn, provide some explanation of his fascination with the *Udyogaparvan* – the book from which he quotes most in the *Mbh* – with its explicit discussion of the rights and prerogatives of kings and its attempt to reconcile these with the demands of the religious life.

6.3 From the *Śāntiparvan*

Moving to the *Śāntiparvan* and SCM's commentary on Proverbs 10:22[41] ("The blessing of the Lord it maketh rich, and he addeth no sorrow with it"), we find

---

[41] As Fox notes, the section of the biblical book of Proverbs from 10:1 to 22:16 is given the title, "Proverbs of Solomon," and so this verse appears in the first chapter of that major section of the book. See Fox 2009, p. 509.

SCM exploring the following verse from the twelfth book of the *Mbh*, which he translates:

> "The fruit of virtue," said Manibhadra to Kundadāra, "always is superiority [influence] and happiness of various kings. Let the Brahman eat these fruits free from bodily suffering."[42]

In the Sanskrit this is:

> *maṇibhadra uvāca*
> *yadā dharmaphalaṃ rājyaṃ, sukhāni vividhāni ca* |
> *phalāny evāyam aśnātu, kāyakleśavivarjitaḥ* || 12.263.26 ||

I translate this as follows:

> The result of virtue (*dharma-phalam*) [is] always (*yadā*) dominion (*rājyaṃ*), and diverse forms of happiness (*sukhāni vividhāni*). Let him enjoy (*ayam aśnātu*) [these] very outcomes (*phalāny eva*) free of physical suffering (*kāya-kleśa-vivarjitaḥ*).

SCM seems to stumble in his Sanskrit here: he appears unsure of how to interpret *rājyam* and takes it to mean "kings" (though it is not a plural), which he construes with *sukhāni vividhāni* (which is grammatically improbable).

Turning to the narrative context, I have already introduced the *Śāntiparva* in general terms. The verse in question is part of an enquiry by Yudhiṣṭhira into the three "ends of life" (*dharma*, *artha* and *kāma* – "virtue, wealth and pleasure") and their relative status. In order to answer his question, the prostrate and dying Bhīṣma – full of the divine insight of Kṛṣṇa – relates an ancient narrative (known as an *itihāsaṃ purātanam* in Sanskrit) of the rain-cloud and the Brahmin. The story takes up the relationship between Kuṇḍadhāra (the cloud) and a penniless Brahmin who seeks his favour as an intermediary to the gods (as a means of generating wealth, Skt. *dhana*). The cloud, pleased at the devotions of the Brahmin, petitions on his behalf to the king of the Yakśas (a subordinate class of semi-divine being – a nature-spirit, if you will), Maṇibhadra. The semi-divine lord of wealth hears the entreaties of the cloud and offers to make the Brahmin wealthy. The cloud, however, is inclined to virtue (Skt. *dharma*) as a superior religious path. He rejects wealth. He asks that the Brahmin be made inclined to virtue. Maṇibhadra states (and this is the material cited by SCM) that prosperity is the consequence of virtue. The Brahmin receives his boon, but fails to recognise it as such (because he had anticipated the outcome of great wealth). However, the cloud is feted by the gods. The Brahmin, unaware of the nature of his boon, surrounded now by worldly goods, rejects them (thus calling into question the words of the Yakśa king). He retires to the forest to lead a life of ascetic activity. He progressively divests himself of the need for either food or water. He is granted a vision of the kings of the earth sunk into hell as a consequence of their cupidity. He then recognises the grace of the cloud – and of the gods – in inclining him to virtue and prostrates himself before the cloud. He states that there is little happiness in wealth, but that there is great happiness (indeed ultimate joy or *paramaṃ sukham*) in virtue.

---

[42] See *ONBP*, vol. 1, p. 464.

In addition to SCM's mild mistranslation (he also introduces the Brahmin – not explicitly mentioned in the verse in question – into his translation) of the present verse, his grasp of its context is somewhat flawed. SCM is in fact citing a statement by the king of the Yakṣas – that virtue generates property (a more general translation of the term *rājya*, which specifically refers to the territories of a king or chieftain) and happiness – that the story itself belies. The goal of the cloud is to teach the Brahmin of the redundancy of physical possessions, and so he shows the kings of the earth sunken into hell as a consequence of their concern with temporal power. This tale is itself part of a series of teachings in which Bhīṣma imparts knowledge to Yudhiṣṭhira, who is attracted to the mendicant life, even as he seeks to persuade him to take up the royal sceptre in the aftermath of the latter's bloody victory over his cousin, Duryodhana. There is also a very real possibility that this narrative is directed to a Brahmin constituency that were seeking to obtain and hold property, and that it therefore might also have a political purpose behind it. Here, SCM is quoting "out of context," so that his translation actually distorts the argument of the materials from which he is drawing.

Having considered, very briefly and from just a few representative examples, SCM's translations from the *Mbh*, I will turn to a few more general statements about his relationship with this classical Indian epic and the ideological agenda of his *ONBP*.

7. S. C. Malan, *Meshālim* and the *Mahābhārata*

SCM is a competent Sanskritist, but his approach to the *Mahābhārata* within the context of the *ONBP* denudes it of its thematics, subordinating his selected texts to the content of the biblical book of Proverbs. It would be tempting to interpret this *à la mode* as a form of cultural imperialism, but this would, I think, be mistaken. SCM is engaging – above all – in an act of translation. In this regard, it is worth considering his approach to the translation of the lexeme as much as to the larger text.

In a letter dated May 28th, 1855, SCM wrote to Wilson, thanking him for his favourable review of a recent work of his. He quickly moves on to a broader discussion of translation and etymology. He offers first of all something that might stand as the missionary Orientalist's *credo:*

> Now how can one <u>translate</u> one language into another, who knows only one of the two? [43]

He follows this comment with a discussion of Bopp's etymology of *theos*, contending that the idea that the Sanskrit term, *deva*, is cognate is untenable, and advancing instead that the Sanskrit term *div/dyu* (nominative *dyaus*) is the more likely candidate. This correction conceals a more far reaching critique of the philological derivation of meaning, however. SCM suggests that learned (e.g., etymologically informed) discussion of the most appropriate equivalent for "God" in a given

---

[43] This is SCM's underscore. Unpub. correspondence: British Library: Private Papers EUR E 301, vol. 13, p. 125.

language would have more weight "if there were no previous notions of him among the people for which the translation is made."[44] This suggests a sociolinguistic emphasis rather than an etymological one. It also explains, in part, his concern to reach out to extant "eastern writings" and to demonstrate that they are in sympathy with Christian revelation. His missiology is, it seems, pragmatic and contextually sensitive. Indeed, SCM makes this goal explicit in his introduction to the *ONBP*:

> The manifold meaning of the Book of Proverbs led me to think that the kindred passages from the writings of some of the "children of the east country" – brought together, as it were, a tribute to the king "whose wisdom excelled them all" – might form a more useful and appropriate commentary on the wisdom of his words, than adding one more to the many practical helps or critical works already published.[45]

In this context the example of St. Paul as linguist and exegete is important to SCM, and so he argues that Paul "met them on their own ground."[46] This seems a more honest assessment of his own endeavour than his contention that the *ONBP* provided "a rough pen and ink outline of what was intended to be a true picture of Eastern thought and wisdom."[47] The centrality of the book of Proverbs mitigates against the achievement of even an outline of the type he suggests. This is largely because the book of Proverbs for SCM existed both as a conglomeration of verses and as a series of – largely unexpressed – surmises about its key themes. "Eastern Writings" are – if the *Mahābhārata* is a reliable guide in this – subordinated to these themes, albeit necessarily given SCM's explicit agenda.

The *Mbh* consequently becomes an exegetical extension of the biblical book of Proverbs for SCM. What this ends up doing to the *Mbh* is significant interpretively. The form of the dialogue or *saṃvāda* in the *Mbh* (with its tendency to hierarchical inversion), the complex interlocutory structure of the *Mbh* (with the capacity for the value of wisdom teachings to be internally questioned – impossible in the format of the biblical book of Proverbs), and the debate over the nature of the true Brahmin[48] are all absent from the *ONBP*. This is, of course, because SCM's agenda is not historically or culturally reconstructive, but it does lead to a distortion of the content of the *Mbh*, regardless of the fidelity of his translations or the real parallelisms he sometimes identifies.

---

[44] British Library: Private Papers EUR E 301, vol. 13, p. 126.

[45] Cited from *ONBP*, vol. 1, p. xi.

[46] Quoted from *ONBP*, vol. 1, p. xiii. This is taken up in Pfister 2012, pp. 31ff.

[47] Cited from *ONBP*, vol. 1, p. xiii.

[48] In this setting, the "true Brahmin" becomes precisely associated with a commodity that one might very well translate as "wisdom," rather than "ritual," which had been the stable domain of the sacerdotal class in India since before the time of the Buddhists, Jains and the writing of the Upaniṣads (that is to say, up until around the fifth century BCE).

7.1 Polyglot Inspiration?

The inspiration for SCM's undertaking might have come from a notable polyglot Bible. One need only consider, for example, a page from the *Biblia Sacra Polyglotta*, edited by Brian Walton and published between 1653 and 1657[49] and compare it with a page of the autograph manuscript of the *ONBP* to see that the form and manner of presentation is somewhat similar. The Polyglot Bible was both a Catholic and a Protestant undertaking, largely concerned with the correction of the Latin Vulgate, but also with the presentation of "Oriental" translations of biblical materials. It is also possible that Erasmus' *Collectanea Adagiorum*, constituting his compilation of ancient Greek and Latin proverbs, might have been an influence.[50] That is to say, in the *ONBP* SCM provides a quintessentially Protestant transformation of the polyglot endeavour. Stated summarily, the principle of *sola scriptura* is expanded to include all sacred literature and with a special Orientalist touch is made universally inclusive, insofar as it stands as a witness to the perspicuity and veracity of biblical wisdom.

8. Conclusions

I can now draw a number of fairly concrete judgments from this study, as well as a few more inferential and generalised conclusions as a result of this enquiry into SCM's readings of the Sanskrit *Mahābhārata*.

First of all, SCM's Sanskrit was good and his translations, if not literal, were by and large faithful (at least on the basis of the materials considered here).

Secondly, SCM had a detailed knowledge of the entirety of the *Mahābhārata*. This is borne out by the sheer range of citations selected from that classical Sanskrit epic that pepper the pages of the published *ONBP*. As pointed out in part within several of the earlier footnotes, there were over 181 passages from eleven books of the *Mbh* that SCM referred to in the third volume of the *ONBP*, all presented and referred to within 168 citations that are identified from the footnotes to that volume. In comparison to quotations from works in the many other languages that appear in the *ONBP*, this is one of the largest amount of citations from any particular work. His mode of selection was also highly strategic; he focused on precisely those parts of the *Mbh* that were richest in the sort of pithy aphoristic statements that he sought so diligently while leaving shorter, more plot-driven, books unquoted (such as the final books of the *Mbh*).

Thirdly, SCM identified real proverbial parallels between the content of the biblical book of Proverbs and the *Mbh*.

Fourthly, SCM failed to take full notice of the complex interlocutory structure and ideological agenda of the *Mbh*. One consequence of this lack of recognition is that he frequently misattributed the statements he adduced from it. As has been argued in some detail from the examples I have provided, this shortcoming led to the distortion of some of its content of these texts in their English translations as

---

[49] Consult Walton *et al.* 1657.
[50] See Erasmus *et al.* 1500.

they appeared in the *ONBP*. There is a danger, however, of interpretive anachronism here. One aspect of *Mbh* studies that I have not taken up here was its scholarly interpretation in the nineteenth century. This would have to be the subject of quite another study. Put summarily, at the time SCM was reading, translating and interpreting the *Mbh*, the scholarly consensus (which only took shape in the 1880s) was for a *Mbh* that had evolved gradually and orally over a long period of time. In addition, that scholarly assessment confirmed that the *Mbh* had been subject to some quite radical redactions during its long history of transmission. Only Josef Dahlman in 1895 had argued for an approach to the *Mbh* that took it as a literary whole.[51] Significantly, this faultline in *Mbh* studies has never fully closed.

Fifthly, SCM's missiology was marked by a pragmatic orientation to his materials, so that he manifested impatience with highly abstracted forms of linguistic enquiry, especially those involving semantic complexities.

SCM's endeavour in the *ONBP* – to provide an encyclopaedic demonstration of the universality of the wisdom contained in Christian revelation, and specifically in the biblical book of Proverbs, by means of translation from Oriental languages – is perhaps one of the clearest demonstrations of the combination of "British Orientalism" (in the sense it acquired as a political lobby in the early nineteenth century) with a missionary hermeneutic. SCM interpreted Oriental literature referred to in the *ONBP* as variations on a set of themes that were perfected in Christian literature, but he does not reject the value of those materials on that basis. This is because, notwithstanding SCM's great love of Oriental literatures, his was an essentially pragmatic missionary endeavour. SCM wished to communicate as fulsomely and widely as possible the wisdom of the biblical book of the Proverbs and of Christianity more broadly, though admittedly for the most part from the sleepy confines of his Dorset parish. The *ONBP* should therefore be seen as a polyglot assemblage of "analogous" texts that are based on a theologically and linguistically driven assumption of mutual intelligibility.

Consequently, SCM is an important, and much neglected, figure in the history of the reception of Sanskrit knowledge in Europe, and most particularly in Britain. His combination of a missionary agenda with an Orientalist's sensibilities and competencies created a work that stands as an implicit rebuttal of the cultural chauvinism that emerged in Britain in the 1830s. Yet it is still a work that aggressively decontextualises and, as I have demonstrated at least in part, distorts that which he selected for inclusion in the *ONBP*. SCM's polyglot compendium of religious wisdom stands as a monument to a particular form of missionary inclusivism, which takes its place in an interesting and varied spectrum of engagements with Sanskrit sources in the nineteenth century. All of these reflections, then, should remind us that we generalise as to the nature, form and function of "Orientalism" and "Mission" in nineteenth-century Europe at our own risk.

---

[51] For those interested, please see Dahlman 1895.

Select Bibliography

Böhtlingk, Otto von (ed.). 1855–1875. *Sanskrit-Wörterbuch*. 7 vols. St. Petersburg: Buchdruckerei der Kaiserlichen Academie der Wissenschaften.

Dahlman, Josef. 1895. *Mahābhārata als Epos und Rechtsbuch*. Berlin: Felix L. Dames Verlag.

Erasmus, Desiderius *et al*. (ed.). 1500. *Veterum maximque insignium paroemiraum, id est adagiorum collectanea*. Parijs: Johann Philippi de Cruzenach.

Filliozat, Pierre-Sylvain. 2000 [1992]. *The Sanskrit Language: An Overview*. Trans. T. K. Gopalan. Varanasi: Indica.

Fox, Michael V. (trans. and comm.). 2009. *Proverbs 10-31: A New Translation with Introduction and Commentary*. New Haven – London: Yale University Press.

Gregg, Stephen H. (ed.). 2005. *Empire and Identity: An Eighteenth Century Sourcebook*. Basingstoke: Palgrave Macmillan.

Hegarty, James M. 2012. *Religion, Narrative and Public Imagination: Past and Place in the Sanskrit Mahābhārata*. London – New York: Routledge.

Macdonnell, A. A. 1895. "Obituary: S. C. Malan." *The Journal of the Royal Asiatic Society of Great Britain and Ireland* 27 (April 1895) 2, pp. 453-457.

Mill, James. 1840–1848. *The History of British India*. 9 vols. Ed. Horace Hayman Wilson. London: James Madden.

Neill, Stephen. 2002. *A History of Christianity in India 1707–1858, Vol. 2*. Cambridge: Cambridge University Press.

Pfister, Lauren F. 2012. "A Swiss Polyglot's Discovery about the Chinese Search for Wisdom: Solomon Caesar Malan's (1812–1894) Comparative Philosophical Contributions in his *Original Notes on the Book of Proverbs*." *minima sinica* 2012/1, pp. 1-52.

Rāya, Prathāpacandra – Kisai Mohan Ganguli (trans.). 1889–1894. *The Mahabharata of Krishna-Dwaipayana Vyasa: Translation into English Prose*. 10 vols. Calcutta: Bhārata Press.

Roebuck, Valerie. 2010. *The Dhammapada*. London: Penguin.

Sukthankar V. S. *et al*. (eds.). 1933–1972. *The Mahābhārata*. 27 vols. Pune: Bhandarkar Oriental Research Institute.

Van Hal, Toon – Christophe Vielle (eds.). 2013. *Grammatica Grandonica: The Sanskrit Grammar of Johann Ernst Hanxleden S.J.* (1681–1732). Potsdam: Universitätsverlag Potsdam.

Walton, Brian – Wenceslaus Hollar – Pierre Lombart (eds.). 1657. *Biblia Sacra Polyglotta: Complectentia textus originales, Hebraicum, cum Pentateucho Samaritano, Chaldaicum, Graecum: versionumque antiquarum, Samaritanae, Graecae, LXXII interp. Chaldaicae, Syriacae, Arabicae, AEthiopicae, Persicae, Vulg. Lat. quicquid compari poterat*. 6 vols. Londini: Imprimebat Thomas Roycroft.

Winternitz, Moriz. 1977 [1927]. *History of Indian Literature*. 2 vols. Delhi: Motilal Barnarsidass.

11

FROM LADAKH TO BUDAPEST VIA BROADWINDSOR
The Journey of an Unusual Gift of Tibetan Books

GYULA PACZOLAY AND LAUREN F. PFISTER

Proverbially it has been stated that "great things proceed and increase from small and obscure beginnings."[1] So, too, few people at the time in mid-May 1838 would have recognized that a "great thing" was taking place in Calcutta (now Kolkata) when a weathered Hungarian researcher in his fifties, who had studied Tibetan language and culture with lamas in the far northern Indian region of Ladahk, met a young Swiss immigrant to Great Britain in his late twenties, a relatively new graduate from Oxford University, in the garden of the colonial Anglican institution of Bishop's College.[2] Few there in Calcutta or in India at the time would have expected that something monumental would have grown out of that initial friendly encounter within the confines of such a colonial Christian bastion.[3] In fact, the person known in English as Alexander Csoma de Kőrös[4] (or in Hungarian as Kőrösi Csoma Sándor [1784-1842], or in Tibetan as "Sekunder Beg"[5] [and in contemporary Tibetan transcription the same name is presented as Sken-dher-bheg[6]]) has been recognized not only in Hungary, but also internationally, as one of the earliest scholars of

---

[1] A modern rendering of the saying of the 16th century Englishman, Richard Eden, in *The Decades of the Newe Worlde*, as quoted in Stevenson 1948, p. 1036. A similar saying is attributed to Publilius Syrus in his *Sententiae*, "The greatest things must have the smallest beginnings."

[2] As far as we know, the unique source for details about this encounter is Arthur Noel Malan's biography written after his father's death, *SCM DD*, pp. 48-51.

[3] Approaches to our topic could take a "post-colonial" or "postcolonial" interpretive spin, but since this has been done particularly by Donald S. Lopez and others in works we will cite in what follows, we will approach the matter primarily, but not exclusively, from relational and historical perspectives that go beyond those interpretive angles. For the difference between "post-colonial" and "postcolonial" interpretive positions, consult the introduction to Ashcroft – Griffiths – Tiffin 2006.

[4] In the Bodleian Library's "Descriptive Catalogue of the Tibetan Manuscripts held at the Bodleian Library, Oxford," his name is presented as "Alexander Kőrösi-Csoma."

[5] As found in a letter written in 1823 by one of his patrons, William Moorcroft, referring to the Hungarian scholar by both his Anglified Hungarian name and his Tibetan name, cited in Duka 1885, p. 34. The most important Tibetan lama (the last of three lamas he studied with) with whom Csoma de Kőrös worked to finalize the details of his Tibetan grammar and dictionary and other smaller works during the period from 1827 to 1830 in the Kanum Monastery, is presented by the following name in this same biography as "Bandé Sangs-GFyas PHun-Tsogs." See Duka 1885, p. 126.

[6] This rendering of his Tibetan name in contemporary transcription is found in Orosz 2008, p. 2, in the content description of item #3.

Tibetan Buddhism in modern Europe.[7] Though he was not the first European to learn the Tibetan language and read Tibetan Buddhist texts,[8] Csoma de Kőrös was the first to produce a Tibetan grammar in English as well as a bilingual English-Tibetan dictionary, and so on this basis has been given the title of the "Father of [European] Tibetology."[9]

What intrigues anyone who seeks to follow these various traces of cross-cultural history is that most scholars of contemporary Tibetan studies may not know much, or anything at all, about Csoma de Kőrös and his experiences in Kashmir and Ladahk during the 1820s. As a consequence, none of those contemporary scholars manifest any awareness of knowing the name of his young friend and Tibetan student, the Anglican priest from Switzerland, Solomon Caesar Malan.[10] Part of the reasons used by some to justify these blind spots in intercultural history is that Csoma de Kőrös was too intimately connected to colonial institutions, and so was deemed as being compromised intellectually due to the Orientalist ideology in which he was assumed to have taken part. In fact, Csoma de Kőrös did serve as a researcher and compiler of Tibetan lore under arrangements agreed upon by officials within the British colonial government in the 1820s,[11] and during the 1830s moved

---

[7] There is some debate about whether Csoma de Kőrös was the very first European to learn the Tibetan language and transmit what he had learned in a European linguistic medium, but it is also the case that SCM himself as well as many biographers of the Hungarian scholar have referred to him as the "father of European Tibetan studies." Reference to Malan's claim will be documented later in this chapter. The most substantial biography of Csoma de Kőrös in the 19th century was produced by another Hungarian polyglot and medical expert, an immigrant to Great Britain, Theodore Duka (1825–1908), already mentioned in n. 5 above. This is an unusual resource that will be cited numerous times within this chapter because of its thoroughness in research and insights drawn from interviews and correspondence with numerous persons in Hungary, England and India. More recent and more concise accounts of Csoma de Kőrös and his contribution to Tibetan studies are Le Calloc'h 1987, Lopez 1995, esp. pp. 256-258, and Buswell – Lopez 2014, p. 200.

[8] Lopez documents the fact that a Jesuit named Ippolito Desideri (1684–1733) was the first to meet Tibetan monks, learn Tibetan and subsequently came to understand much about their Buddhist worldview. Unlike Csoma de Kőrös and Lopez himself, Desideri lived and studied in the capital of Tibet, *Lha sa* (Lhasa), for a period of five years, from 1716 to 1721. He had been given that opportunity by his patron, the Mongolian ruler of Tibet at that time, Lha bzang Khan (d. 1717), the last ruler of the Khoshut khanate of the Oirat Mongolian people in Tibet. Consult Lopez 1995, pp. 253-256.

[9] As claimed also in the dictionary article on Csoma de Kőrös in Buswell – Lopez 2014, p. 200.

[10] Those among Tibetologists and biographers who do mention, and sometimes elaborate, more about the relationship between Csoma de Kőrös and SCM include, as mentioned elsewhere in this chapter as well, Malan's son and posthumous biographer, A. N. Malan; the Hungarian biographer of Csoma de Kőrös, Theodore Duka; and the Hungarian biographer, József Terjék in his Hungarian monograph (Terjék 1976).

[11] So that Csoma de Kőrös received a monthly sum of fifty rupees (perhaps equivalent at the time to about US$ 1,250, and so quite a reasonable stipend) from that government for a number of years while he was pursuing research within monasteries in the Ladahk (1824–1825) and "Upper Besarh" regions (1827–1830). See Duka 1885, pp. 78-79.

on to serve as the "under-librarian" responsible for cataloging Tibetan documents in the library of the Royal Asiatic Society of Bengal located in Calcutta, also under the patronage of the Indian colonial government.[12] Though the initial contract he made in 1823 related to the production of a dictionary and grammar of Tibetan language in English was with a British veterinarian and explorer working for the Indian government, William Moorcroft (1765–1825),[13] the complete cost for the publication of 500 copies of those two major works in 1834 was also covered by the coffers of the British colonial government in India.[14] Unquestionably, then, as a consequence of all these factors, Csoma de Kőrös had been attached to institutions that could be denigrated by post-colonial critics. In their view, his claims to "know Tibetan language and culture" are undercut by his association with colonial institutions and their "ways of knowing." All that they would expect to see within his published works, then, are fabrics of this epistemological distortion that would be unable to produce any revealing and sympathetic form of scholarship. Similarly, SCM as an Anglican priest, having graduated from a college in what would later become part of Oxford University and subsequently serving as the Classical Language professor at Bishop's College in Calcutta, was even more thoroughly associated with a major colonial religious institution. Besides, he was assigned there as a cross-cultural missionary, so that his willingness to learn Tibetan was obviously also associated with his own missionary interests, embedded intimately within the Anglican form of colonial education there in Calcutta.[15] So, even in spite of the fact that both men produced substantial scholarly documents that putatively not only manifest an impressive amount of learning, even if they constituted "break-

---

[12] Though he rejected receiving funds from the Royal Asiatic Society itself, he was supported at the level of 100 rupees per month by the colonial government for most of the decade of the 1830s. Details about these matters are provided in Duka 1885, pp. 103-104 and 112-113.

[13] This contract was initially made with support coming directly from William Moorcroft, as described in Le Calloc'h 1987, pp. 368-369. More than this, it can be said that Moorcroft's suggestions related to the study of Tibetan language and its value were pivotal for the Hungarian scholar, who had never known about this possibility before it was made explicit by Moorcroft. Indirectly he confirmed this fact by stating that "Providence" had led him to Tibet, because it was "not part of his original plan." See evidence supporting this understanding in Duka 1885, pp. 28-29, 37, and 125.

[14] The Dictionary was produced with a length of 345 quarto pages; the Grammar, 244 pages. The total cost born by the colonial government for their production was just over 6,410 rupies. Find these details in Duka 1885, pp. 120 and 124.

[15] The fact that it was a very rare matter to have any person interested in learning Tibetan at that time, no matter where they were located, is completely overlooked. Many years later Malan would also complain that he could find no one with whom to continue reading together the Tibetan texts he had in his personal library. Malan wrote that "I happened to be the only person who was troubling himself about Tibetan; he [Csoma de Kőrös] and I became very good friends during the whole, alas! too short, stay in India." On his part, Csoma de Kőrös wrote in the preface to his Tibetan language grammar, "The students of Tibetan have been most rare, if they existed at all." Both quotations are found in Duka 1885, pp. 128 and 142.

throughs" in realms of Anglophone Tibetology[16] and comparative proverbial literature respectively,[17] their association with mercantile and Christian colonial institutions have tainted their names. Perhaps it is due to these various kinds of cultural critiques, including colonialist ideological questioning and Orientalist skepticism, that the vast majority of scholars in Tibetan studies have not even read what these two men have produced, and in most cases would not even know about their existence.[18]

On the other hand, most persons involved in Anglophone biblical studies and Christian theology would also be almost completely unaware of the connections between Csoma de Kőrös and SCM. "Good reasons" for this can be raised because the former was a Hungarian scholar known almost exclusively for his Tibetan studies, and so we could imagine from that angle, they would assume that he had nothing to do with Christian studies. Beyond this, there is a practical matter involving linguistic corridors of scholarship: many of the substantial articles and books written about Csoma de Kőrös in the 20th century are either in Hungarian or another European language, rather than in English.[19] In order to illustrate this case very succinctly, we can refer to an article written in 1985 focusing on the numbers of biographies written in Hungarian about Csoma de Kőrös, who is described within the article as "a national hero" to Hungarian scholars. The author of that article identifies twenty-nine biographical monographs written in Hungarian on Csoma de

---

[16] Near the end of Le Calloc'h's article, he adds an appendix with details of 20 articles and monographs published between 1832 and 1840; some of them are very extensive (the longest article being 159 pages in length), written in English or English–Tibetan bilingual scripts by Csoma de Kőrös. The Tibetan-English Dictionary and the Tibetan Grammar appear as items 6 and 7 in that list. In addition, he notes three other posthumously published documents, the last of them being trilingual vocabulary lists in Sanskrit, Tibetan and English, drawn from the *Mahāvyutpatti*, that was published in three sections in 1910, 1916, and 1944. See Le Calloc'h 1987, pp. 385-386.

[17] Here we are referring to the last work produced by SCM, *Original Notes on the Book of Proverbs*.

[18] So, for example, the name of Csoma de Kőrös does not even appear in the index of Jeffery Paine's notable volume (*id*. 2004), where one might expect some sense of the historical precedent that Csoma de Kőrös had embodied in the early 19th century for that inter-cultural transplantation of Tibetan religious traditions. In another earlier work dealing with the "British discovery of Buddhism", Csoma de Kőrös is listed as one who gave "seminal" contributions to Buddhist studies, but only in one sentence, occurring without any footnote. Admittedly, he appears there in a list that included the notable French academician, Abel Rémusat, along with the names of Klaproth, Schmidt, Landresse and Hodgson; nevertheless, even though he is the only person noted as being involved with studies in Tibetan Buddhism, no further bibliographic details are provided. See Almond 1988, p. 25.

[19] Once again, in the final bibliographic section of Le Calloc'h's article, he cites 19 works in French (five published in the 19th century, the earliest being in 1833, and including eight of his own works published within the two-year period from 1984 to 1985) and 16 works in Hungarian, the only one in the 19th century being the biography written by Theodore Duka. Notably, there are books on Csoma de Kőrös published in Hungarian as early as 1907, and four others before 1945, so that the majority of them appeared from 1960 to 1987. Consult Le Calloc'h 1987, pp. 387-388.

Kőrös during the century from 1885 to 1985.[20] Notably, however, the only biographical monograph focusing on this Hungarian "Father of European Tibetan studies" in English was completed by Theodore Duka (1825–1908) in 1885, who also produced a Hungarian version during the same year.

In sum, then, even though the major 19th century biographer of Csoma de Kőrös, Theodore Duka, did write ground-breaking biographical studies regarding the pioneering Hungarian Tibetan scholar in both Hungarian and English, the vast majority of Christian scholars and European Tibetologists would not have become aware of those writings. In fact, Duka had served as a Civilian Surgeon within the Royal Bengali Army after having studied medicine at the University of London.[21] While serving in that capacity in various locations within the Bengal Presidency of colonial India,[22] he also published studies in both medical and Indian linguistic realms.[23] But how did this Hungarian doctor become associated with the British colonial system? In fact, Duka had received a degree in jurisprudence from Pest University, and then joined a military uprising seeking Hungarian independence from the Austrio-Hungarian Empire. Serving as an officer in the Hungarian forces under General Görgey, he fled the country after their defeat to the Austrian-Russian allied forces in 1849.[24] It was only at that period of time, then, having been accepted for medical training at the University of London, that he could adjust to a new identity as a political refugee to Great Britain.[25] Only after he graduated from medical school in 1853 did Duka become a naturalized British citizen.[26] Being both a Hungarian refugee immigrant to Great Britain and a Protestant intellectual, he was also somewhat awkwardly located on the margins of the standard Anglophone cross-cultural interactions within Anglophone Indian histories. Even though he was later made a full member of the Hungarian Academy of Sciences in Budapest, Duka's own associations with Malan also have been largely overlooked even by other notable academicians.[27] The triangulation required for re-imagining the cross-cultural

---

[20] Here referring to Le Calloc'h 1985.

[21] Here and in what follows we are offering summaries from the Hungarian biography written by Gyula Paczolay (*id.* 1998).

[22] Paczolay indicates that Duka served in the Bengali Army for twenty years, being joined there after one year by his English wife. They lived first in Comilla, where he established a hospital, and then later at Monghyr, Simla, Patna and Darjeeling. Consult Paczolay 1998, pp. 40-63.

[23] Find a full bibliography of Duka's publications in Paczolay 1998, pp. 118-126.

[24] Summarized from Paczolay 1998, pp. 20-30.

[25] Some indication of this is also found in the first pages of Aurel Stein's essay dealing with Duka (see details n. 27). That essay was privately published in 1914 after its presentation to the Hungarian Academy of Sciences, honoring Duka posthumously.

[26] This we learn from Paczolay 1998, pp. 35-37.

[27] So it is notable that the major address given by Aurel Stein, another Hungarian emigrant to Great Britain, honoring Theodore Duka at the Hungarian Academy of Sciences six years after his death, did not even mention how Duka had obtained from Malan the three dozen Tibetan documents that originally belonged to Csoma de Kőrös. Consult the 49 paged document by Aurel Stein (*id.* 1914). Notably, within Duka's biography of his notable Hungarian predecessor, Csoma de Kőrös, he refers to Malan six times, sometimes citing personal correspondence

linkages between Ladahk to Calcutta, and subsequently Calcutta to Oxford, Oxford to Broadwindsor, and ultimately Broadwindsor to Budapest, is simply beyond the scope of most "standard" expectations of Anglo-centric cross-cultural studies. Here in this chapter that unusual route of inter-cultural connections will be followed and explored through the lives and works that brought Csoma de Kőrös, Solomon Caesar Malan, and Theodore Duka together into a traceable line of historical connections, willing collaborations, and scholarly contributions.

1. From Ladakh to Calcutta, and Soon Afterwards to Great Britain

As a person gifted and intrigued with any new language that he could learn while in India, the 26-year-old Oxford graduate, SCM, was immediately intrigued with the unusual opportunity to learn how to read Tibetan from Csoma de Kőrös. Arrangements were made on May 10, 1838, the second day after the arrival of the Malan family in Calcutta, to meet on a "daily" basis.[28] We assume this means that they probably met around the same time from Monday to Friday, and possibly including some Saturdays, but not including Sundays, and did so often, if not always, in the small house where Csoma de Kőrös lived within the compound where the Library of the Royal Asiatic Society of Bengal was located.[29] It was because of these regular interactions that the two men developed a strong and warm friendship.[30] After engaging the young Anglican teacher of classical languages at Bishop's College for more than a year, Csoma de Kőrös was immensely impressed with the unusual gifts that Malan had in language acquisition. In fact, both men were polyglots of an unusual sort, what John Edwards here in this volume earlier has described more technically as "hyper-polyglots": Csoma de Kőrös knew and lived with as many as 17 languages,[31] and SCM learned many more over the period of

---

he had with the vicar of Broadwindsor. Consult Duka 1885, pp. 20, 66, 139, 142, 158, and 166-167.

[28] In an undated letter cited in his son's biography, SCM states "I went to learn Tibetan of him [sic] every day." Quoting from *SCM DD*, p. 48.

[29] This location is mentioned in a letter written by SCM and cited in Duka 1885, p. 142.

[30] Citing undated letters once again, SCM is quoted as saying that he and Csoma de Kőrös "became very good friends. [...] I used to delight in his company; he was so kind and so obliging, and always willing to impart all he knew. He was altogether one of the most interesting men I have ever met." Cited in *SCM DD*, pp. 50-51 *in passim*. Confirmed also in Duka 1885, pp. 142 and 167. In the latter location Duka claims, "Dr. Malan is presumably the only witness still living who knew Csoma face to face so well."

[31] According to an anonymous source cited by ANM, and possibly from a letter we have not seen but written by his father, the following claims are made, using names for several languages that are no longer current in 21st century Anglophone parlance: "The power of acquiring languages was the extraordinary talent of Csoma de Kőrös. He had studied the following ancient and modern tongues, and was proficient in many of them: Hebrew, Arabic, Sanscrit, Pushtu, Greek, Latin, Slavonic [sic], German, English, Turkish, Persian, French, Russian, Tibetan, with the addition of Hindostani, Mahratti, and Bengalee." Quoting from *SCM DD*, p. 50. We learn from Duka's study that Csoma de Kőrös purposefully had spent some months also learning how to speak two other "Sclavoinian" languages: "Getic" and "Sarmatic." See

five decades from the time he first arrived in Calcutta.[32] But there was more than the fascination with language that bound them together.

Indeed, there was something more adding to the quality and dimensions of the friendship that this pair of hyper-polyglots from different generations and distinct cultural backgrounds were able to forge. In fact, very little (if anything) is stated by any scholar of Tibetan studies who writes about Csoma de Kőrös regarding his religious background and educational training in Hungary and elsewhere in Europe, except for the astounding fact that just over ninety years after his death this pioneering Hungarian Tibetologist was declared to be a bodhisattva by Japanese Buddhists at Taishō University (Taishō Daigaku 大正大學) in Tokyo in 1933.[33] Yet there are also other matters here of great interest that can bring more light to understanding how the friendship between the weathered Hungarian sage and the eager Anglican student of proverbial lore could develop so freely and openly.

Csoma de Kőrös was born and grew up in a Protestant sub-culture in the Hungarian Transylvanian mountains, a form of Protestant spirituality deeply influenced by Calvinist traditions. He not only attended a Christian college named Nagy Enyed College for his middle school and early university training, but ended up serving there as a young lecturer in poetics for some years.[34] Subsequently, while in his

---

Duka 1885, p. 55. Also, after this unusual Hungarian hyper-polyglot died while en route to Lhasa, his "travelling library" included volumes (including many dictionaries and grammars) in twelve languages (all having been mentioned above). Consult Duka 1885, pp. 161-162.

[32] As indicated in Chapter 12 of this volume, when SCM had reached his 40th year of age in 1852, he wrote for himself a devotional of Christian prayers, scriptural passages, and liturgical writings in 82 languages, writing all the texts in those languages by his own hand and with the purpose of making it as beautiful aesthetically and calligraphically as he possibly could achieve. On the other hand, based on the thorough textual analysis made possible through the extensive documentation worked out by Mirasy Pfister and interpreted by Lauren Pfister, we now know that at the very least SCM referred to proverbial literature in 54 languages within his *ONBP*, probably including as many as 70 different cultures and intellectual or spiritual traditions. So, as John Edwards has clarified in his study of hyper-polyglots included in this volume (Chapter 4), we are dealing here with two extraordinarily gifted polyglots.

[33] This is one of the main themes discussed at length in Le Calloc'h 1987, pp. 358-363 and 373-384. What exactly his canonization within the Japanese Buddhist ranks of bodhisattvas has meant to contemporary Europeans is not completely understandable, especially since he himself was not a self-declared Buddhist. Still Le Calloc'h offers some hints for Francophone readers about how Csoma de Kőrös's Hungarian countrymen responded to this accolade. Next to his tomb in Darjeeling, India, Hungarian scholars of the Hungarian Academy of Sciences left a plaque that states (see Le Calloc'h 1987, p. 384, in our translation from the French): "Here lies the Hungarian sage, Alexandre Csoma de Kőrös, 1784–1842. Throughout the entire world he is one of the eminent within the academic discipline of Orientalism. For us, his compatriots, he is also an eternal example of patriotism and of abnegation. He sought to discover the cradle of our nation, and here his tomb is found. Nevertheless, here also there is found immortality."

[34] The parents of Csoma de Kőrös initially sent their son to Nagy Enyed College with the hope that he would become a minister in that tradition. Confirmed in Le Calloc'h 1987, p. 364. In fact, we learn from Duka's study that one of his cousins, Joseph Csoma, did become a Protestant pastor in the region. For further details, consult Duka 1885, pp. 3-8.

early thirties, the young Hungarian lecturer was given a scholarship to travel to Hanover so that he could study at the University of Göttingen during the years from 1816 to 1818, presumably to major in the field of theology.[35] It had been while he was there in a German speaking research environment that the highly motivated student from Transylvania was deeply influenced by two professors whose expertise were in anthropological methods, historical studies and Semitic languages and cultures.[36] As a consequence, he became all the more interested in linguistic and philological studies related to Semitic and Asian traditions, and to some degree at least, how they could reveal something about the historical and cultural influences that made Hungary and some of its people very unusual parts of the European continent.[37] It was these new interests that ultimately fueled his motivations to travel into Asian contexts to learn more about those languages and cultures.

In the case of SCM, as we have learned from Frédéric Amsler's essay (Chapter 1), French Calvinist teachings of a modern evangelical sort were the traditions that were deeply imbued in the Malan family life in Geneva as well. This unusual form of evangelical Calvinism was shaped also by developments in Geneva due to the impact of the Napoleonic wars that raged in Europe for some years before, as it was being transformed after 1815 from being a Protestant city-state independent of all other nations (a status it had maintained for nearly three centuries) into a canton of the Swiss Federation. Later, SCM had studied in Oxford, starting in the early 1830s, and gained the theological training adequate to prepare him for a life of Christian ministry in the Anglican tradition.

Though the Hungarian scholar was SCM's elder by nearly thirty years, their friendship was able to overcome that significant difference in age because of a number of factors we can now confirm: their unusual, and essentially informal, teacher-student relationship in Tibetan studies; their shared backgrounds in having received Protestant theological training,[38] including access to biblical languages; and an undeniable common interest in learning insights from a host of languages that became

---

[35] Details about how the young Hungarian lecturer earned that privilege, a scholarship that stemmed from English donors to the Nagy Enyet College, and how he pursued his studies while in Hanover (including taking his first lessons in English) are presented in Duka 1885, pp. 9-12. See also Le Calloc'h 1987, pp. 365-366.

[36] One of these two professors is identified by Duka as Johann Gottfried Eichhorn (1752–1827), a historian and Orientalist, who was the key goad in prompting the Hungarian scholar to envision a life-long search through Mediterranean and Central Asian lands and cultures. Another that is mentioned in that work is Prof. Florillo, the teacher of English language and literature there. Consult Duka 1885, pp. 6, 11-12.

[37] This search for the "source of Hungarian culture" is a theme found in many works, but it is notable that Duka in his biography written in 1885 emphasizes that this never was the only or most important realm of study that Csoma de Kőrös pursued. The fact that this theme continued to arise even a century after Duka sought to dismantle those claims, at the very least, indicates something about the importance of that quest for many of his Hungarian compatriots.

[38] In statements summarizing his background, Csoma de Kőrös indicated that he "finished [his] philological and theological studies in the Bethlen College at N. Enyed" during the years from 1815 to 1818. Cited from Duka 1885, p. 24.

accessible to them. While these all are solidly confirmed facts in Malan's case, it appears that few Tibetologists and other scholars would know that Csoma de Kőrös not only identified himself as a Protestant Christian, but was also involved in his later years in providing Tibetan translations of the Psalms and of the Anglican liturgy, including *The Book of Common Prayer*.[39] Added to all of these matters, both men shared the experience of being "expatriates" in British colonial India, residing within the vast and complicated city of Calcutta. The elder Hungarian had arrived there after many years of circuitous travelling and intense study and dialogue over Tibetan texts with at least three lamas in the Ladakh and Upper Basarh regions; the younger Swiss immigrant to Great Britain, having gained a new identity through studies in Oxford, had travelled there with his young wife and several sons.[40]

In all of these realms, we can now easily imagine, Csoma de Kőrös and SCM shared many dimensions of cross-cultural and inter-lingual studies, exploring also many fields of knowledge that embraced philosophical, religious, ethical and practical studies, particularly as they related to their interests in the development of languages and long lists of multilingual vocabularies. Understandably, then, all these factors enhanced the level of their friendship, and yet it is quite strange that after more than a hundred and seventy years following the death of that notable Hungarian Tibetologist, these factors have rarely, if ever, been mentioned in any study known to us discussing their relationship.

The simple fact that Csoma de Kőrös chose to entrust his extremely valuable collection of Tibetan materials into the hands of the young SCM – a massive gift that Theodore Duka admits was seen as "priceless" by Hungarian scholars[41] – is in itself a remarkable situation, one that should not be passed over too quickly, or left without further reflection. Was the Hungarian scholar incoherent in his choice of the recipient of such an unusual gift?

At least one contemporary Tibetan scholar, Pierre J. Marczell, has suggested by his written accounts and the tone of his comments that SCM was hardly worthy of what he himself counted to be "treasures" of Tibetan lore.[42] In fact, from a historical and economic point of view, all of the Tibetan manuscripts and block prints that Csoma de Kőrös had obtained during his years of study and interactions within specific Tibetan monasteries were purchased due to payments he received from colonial government officers or through that government's sponsorship. Being a man

---

[39] These matters related to translation are underscored briefly in Duka 1885, p. 140. Self-declarations of his own Christian heritage occur not only in letters where he recognized points of danger within Muslim dominated cultures in Central Asia, but also in letters where he discussed briefly various comparisons of Buddhist and Christian doctrines and practical morality. See the self-declarations, in Duka 1885, pp. 28 and 36, and for his comparisons of Tibetan Buddhism and Christianity, also consult *ibid.*, pp. 43–44, 55–56, 59–60, and 94.

[40] For details about this stage of SCM's life, the biography of his son is still informative and helpful. See *SCM DD*, pp. 26–60.

[41] Cited from Duka 1884, p. 492.

[42] This is particularly manifest in his article of 2002, mentioned above, published eight years after he himself had been in Oxford and celebrated the centennial of the death of SCM in Broadwindsor with a host of notable guests.

of high principle, to the point that he was sometimes seen as "eccentric" and even involving a kind of "meanness" that could offend his patrons,[43] one could imagine that the Hungarian Tibetologist might have felt obliged to hand over those Tibetan documents to suitable government officials. In fact, however, none of those officials knew Tibetan or could appreciate the value and content of those unusual documents. It was government officials who had suggested that Csoma de Kőrös contact those in the Royal Asiatic Society of Bengal to find a temporary home where he could serve their interests as a Tibetan consultant, and also place the many unusual Tibetan documents he had collected in a suitable library. Yet this is why Malan's presence in Calcutta was so timely and appropriate: by 1839 Malan had become the new secretary of the Royal Asiatic Society in Calcutta, and he was the one unique person who sincerely sought to learn Tibetan language and literature from the somewhat reclusive Hungarian scholar. Still, it is one thing to hand over a large set of rare documents to an official of a government-sponsored academic institution, and another to make them a personal gift to a specific student. Unexpectedly, Csoma de Kőrös took the latter course. Why?

What we should probably consider, then, or at least try to figure out by some way or another, is how much SCM benefited from and employed those Tibetan documents in his major three volume work *ONBP*. With this precise objective in mind, in 2014 Pfister requested a younger Hungarian Tibetan scholar, Rita Kuzder, to check if and when Malan had ever referred to any of those documents received from Csoma de Kőrös within his compilation of comparative proverbs, and she could not even find one unquestionable citation.[44]

Nevertheless, further study into the details of the *ONBP* unveiled several mentions of texts within the documents provided by Csoma de Kőrös to SCM. This occurred once within the main body of the text, and several times within the comments to the footnotes that garnish the bottom section of each printed page of the

---

[43] Once again, here, Duka's citations of private letters from other sources are extremely revealing. At the point when Csoma de Kőrös took up residence in Calcutta and was eager to have his dictionary and grammar published, there was a period of transition that was extremely awkward for all involved. One of his key supervisors, a person named Captain Kennedy, wrote in September 1829 to the then secretary of the Royal Asiatic Society of Bengal regarding "Mr. Csoma" as "a most eccentric character," one who seems to seek to "retain the incognito he lives in at the Monastery of Kanum" in Calcutta, and at times "received my advances, to be obliging, with a meanness not to be accounted for." At the same time, Csoma de Kőrös is portrayed as considering himself as "acting under a solemn pledge to Government to furnish the grammar and lexicon," so that he could "proceed to Calcutta to superintend their publication." To his credit Captain Kennedy adds that "[h]is needs are few, and I am informed his expenses on diet, &c., are of the most moderate description, in fact, not more than of one of the inhabitants of the village in which he resides." For this complex description and the quotations presented above see Duka 1885, pp. 104-105.

[44] Rita Kuzder did this on the basis of detailed information provided from the Pfisters' database related to the footnotes of the *ONBP*, revealing this startling fact. Her subsequent findings are documented in Chapter 9 of this volume.

ONBP.[45] The following passage appeared in the main body of the first volume of that three-volume work; because it is the one passage so far discovered of this sort, it is undoubtedly a very unexpected and significant section of the whole work. Within this paragraph SCM, who by that time in 1889 had already received an honorary doctorate from the University of Edinburgh, reflects on what he had learned from various Buddhist traditions, and how they compared to the claims of the Anglican Christian tradition which he advocated throughout his adult life.[46] It is written within the context of a single verse, Proverbs 10:28, that states (in the English of the King James version), "The hope of the righteous shall be gladness; but the expectation of the wicked shall perish."

> Referring to this, we read in the Dsang-Lun, that whereas Buddha spoke of "being wholly delivered from sorrow," in Dr. Schmidt's printed copy, in my native copy, given me by Csoma Korösi [sic], the same passage reads, "to be delivered from sorrow, together with the lord, or god." [Citing "Dsang-Lun, ch. i"] One letter makes the difference.[47]

Here we are particularly interested in this long parenthetical reference to two different versions of the text referred to as the "Dsang-Lun":[48] SCM explicitly

---

[45] The less direct references from Tibetan sources come also from another section of the *Dsang-Lun* and a single text from what SCM called the "Tibetan rendering of the Sanscrit Lalita Vistara": *Rygya-tcher-rol-pa*. In the former there is a brief note associated with the wise sayings linked to Proverbs 16:32, where he contrasts in footnote 6 the German rendering by Schmidt with the text found in the "native copy" noted in footnote 7. This appears in Volume 2 of the *ONBP*, p. 435. The latter appears in connection with the collected sayings following Proverbs 12:4 in Volume 2 of the *ONBP*, p. 103, n. 4. There SCM states that the long passage can be found in both that original Tibetan source and in English translation in "Csoma.Tibt.Gr.p.161," that is, on that particular page in the Tibetan grammar Csoma de Kőrös had published in 1834.

[46] Here we quote the first part of the passage, where the latter part is quoted in the following discussion. It comes from *ONBP*, vol. 1, p. 473, being located near the very end of that particular volume: "For whatever difference there may be between southern and northern, old and modern Buddhism, Nirvān, Nibbān, Nibbānam, Nirvānam, Engl. Nirvāna, means 'extinction,' and nothing else. So that the expressions, 'paramam nibbānam,' 'paramā gati,' &c, good, excellent Nirvāna, 'good passage,' or 'going hence, thither,' refer, probably, to the fewer transmigrations to be undergone, owing to a moral life on earth; for in any case, 'extinction' must be the same. The hope of the Buddhist, then, is extinction; the hope of the Christian is 'everlasting life' through Jesus Christ our Lord."

[47] *ONBP*, vol. 1, pp. 473-474. Because it is such a candid statement and involves references that are particularly important for our thesis here, we have quoted part of the passage here and the rest of it in our concluding section at the end of this chapter.

[48] This is a text now referred to by a contemporary Tibetan transcription as *Mdzangs blun*. It had been previously identified as *Dsang-Lun* by a German Tibetologist, Isaak Jakob Schmidt, and published in a German version in 1843, a German rendering that SCM also had obtained in his own personal library. It is apparently a Tibetan rendition of an original Sanskrit text knowns as the *Damomurkha-nama-sutra* (The Sutra of the Wise and the Fool). From a Wikipedia source we learn that this Tibetan text was in fact rendered from a Chinese original by a 9th century Tibetan Buddhist monk working in Dunhuang 敦煌 and named Chos grub (Facheng 法成). The version produced by the lama helping Csoma de Kőrös was, then, a

confirms that he had a "native copy" of it given to him by Csoma de Kőrös. This we understand to mean that it was a manuscript, and not a block print, as most of the works within the gift of Tibetan texts were in fact block prints. Nevertheless, when we have checked very thoroughly the descriptions of all the Tibetan manuscripts that are part of the "Csoma Bequest" and now held in the Library of the Hungarian Academy of Sciences, we cannot locate this particular text or its title. Nor do we find it mentioned among the titles of those Tibetan works also held at the Bodleian Library in Oxford, and referred to as part of the Malan Library, sent to that institution in 1885 (though we expect that it will probably be found there). Until we have a skilled Tibetologist who can decipher these matters in a more insightful manner, we are still left with an unusual quandary: a citation of a work claimed to be from among the manuscripts given to SCM by the Hungarian "father of Tibetology," and yet it cannot be identified among any of the bibliographies of the Tibetan texts in either the Hungarian Academy of the Sciences or the Bodleian Libraries.

Therefore, even though we have this singular text within the body of the first volume of the *ONBP* referring to one of the manuscripts given to SCM by Csoma de Kőrös, as well as two other direct references in footnotes, one might argue that precisely because there are only three identifiable references of these two kinds, all this should be quite enough to confirm Marczell's doubts that there was any significant connection between the two men.[49] Yet is this all there is to say about these matters? Certainly, there are also other questions to ask to follow up these previously unidentified discoveries. Did SCM cite any other Tibetan literature within that three-tome work? In fact, due to the work of Rita Kuzder, we know now that he did do so. At this point in our discussion, however, other questions about this problem should also be considered.

Were there any good reasons why SCM did not cite most of the documents given to him by Csoma de Kőrös in light of the orientation of his research for that massive compilation? Perhaps there were, since nearly all of the forty documents did not deal with apothemic or proverbial literature written in Tibetan. Notably, the particular text of the *Dsang-Lun* mentioned above cannot be found among them, as mentioned already. So, taking up a quite different perspective we can also ask, were there any indications that SCM himself had become dissatisfied with what he had learned and received from Csoma de Kőrös? Here we can give a strong denial, for we find no statement involving any note of dissatisfaction, but discover instead a continued admiration for that seminal Hungarian scholar of Tibetan language and cultures reaffirmed even forty years after his death. These statements come from

---

19th century manuscript reproduction in Tibetan of this text. The basic information mentioned here about this classical Tibetan text and its Sanskrit precedent is offered, without any further elaboration, at http://rywiki.tsadra.org/index.php/mdzangs_blun_zhes_bya_ba%27i_mdo (accessed March 17, 2021).

[49] Since we have composed these lines on the basis of what we could know, Rita Kuzder has found other details to confirm that SCM did use those Tibetan works in other ways. See Chapter 9 in this volume.

letters written in the 1880s to the biographer of Csoma de Kőrös, Theodore Duka, letters published in both the Hungarian and English versions of that biography. More about those letters and their content will be offered later in this chapter.

Finally, we should ask, could it be possible that SCM was willing to part with most of those Tibetan documents precisely because they had not been as useful for him in compiling that unusual three-volume collection of proverbial sayings known as the *ONBP*? This is certainly a possibility, but then if this was the main reason for doing so, it is not easy to explain why he did not give all of them to the Hungarian Academy of Sciences. From a later essay produced by Marczell with the help of others, we know that three Tibetan documents now remain in the Bodleian collection, and there are no doubts that at least two of the three documents were from SCM's personal library. Consequently, there is every good reason to expect that the third one was also officially donated by SCM in 1885 to the Indian Institute to become part of the Malan Library, and later in the 1960s became part of the Bodleian collections.[50]

So, having explored all these perspectives regarding the choice of Csoma de Kőrös to offer this gift to the talented young professor of classical languages at Bishop's College in Calcutta, who was at the same time the Secretary of the Royal Asiatic Society of Bengal, we can only surmise that the Hungarian scholar was convinced that those nearly forty documents would be employed reliably by SCM, his one gifted and eager Tibetan language student he had found while living in Calcutta. Whatever else was involved, Csoma de Kőrös was moved to commit that unique collection to SCM, and therefore, they all ended up by 1845 in the vicarage as part of SCM's personal library in Broadwindsor, a small country village in Dorsetshire. Notably, they remained there for four decades.

2. From Broadwindsor to Budapest: An Unexpected Arrangement

Having arrived in Calcutta on May 9, 1838,[51] SCM and his family soon afterwards showed signs of suffering from the hot climate and diseases picked up there, so that by the end of the year the family headed to South Africa for recuperation, arriving there in May 1839.[52] Believing himself to have regained his strength, SCM sent his wife, Mary, and their three young children to travel back to Great Britain in July of that year, while he himself returned in the fall to Calcutta to see if he could endure and thrive there in his teaching position at Bishop's College. It was probably

---

[50] I use the phrase "officially donated" because, on the one hand, SCM confirmed and sent just over 4,000 documents to Oxford in January 1885, but the Malan Library was not actually occupying its place in the Indian Institute until 1896, two years after the donor's death. For further details about these complications related to the Malan Library, see Chapter 12 in this volume.

[51] The sequence of events and their travel to Calcutta is documented in *SCM DD*, pp. 46-47. On this basis Duka's claim that SCM became the new Secretary of the Royal Asiatic Society of Bengal in 1837 is incorrect; it should have been 1838. See Duka 1885, p. 139.

[52] According to *SCM DD*, p. 55, Mary Malan began to suffer physically after the birth of their third child during their short residence as a family in Calcutta in 1838.

during this period that he arranged to meet with Csoma de Kőrös on the daily basis that they had mutually determined. Under the circumstances in which both of them were living in Calcutta without any family members, it is not hard to imagine why they would have become all the more close as colleagues and friends, particularly as they poured over various hand written and printed Tibetan texts. But once again, SCM's health began to fail, so that by April 1840 he had been given medical warnings about needing to leave and not return. Taking a relatively quick tour to various other places in India before he departed, SCM accepted the reality of his physical need, and left India for the last time.[53] During this period, and due to the slowness of international mail at the time, SCM was only aware that his wife, Mary, still suffered from a seriously compromised health, but in fact the disease proved to be fatal. She passed away on April 5, 1840, while SCM himself was taking his last tour of India and heading toward South Africa once again.[54] Unfortunately, he did not learn about her passing away until early September 1840, and then left immediately for Great Britain to take up his responsibilities with the children, and to discern what the future would now hold for him.

During the next three years SCM underwent a major transition in the basic orientation of his life, taking up positions of pastoral responsibility within Anglican churches in Great Britain as a means to sustain his family. Ultimately, and with the help of various other concerned friends, he married once again in October 1843. His new wife was also an English woman, Caroline Saline Mount, a daughter in another notable Anglican family, and one willing to take up the mothering of the three children coming from his previous marriage. So, from this period on, SCM's life began to regain some stability after nearly three years of living as a single parent with his three children.[55] During this same period, as we learn from other historical accounts, Csoma de Kőrös passed away in Darjeeling in April 1842, while trying to reach Lhasa.[56] What had begun as a remarkable relationship built upon interest in teaching and learning Tibetan had now been transformed into the quiet soliloquies that SCM would continue to have with the Tibetan texts that remained a part of his active research. Over the years from the early 1840s until 1884, when he felt pressed to consider what to do with his unusual personal library, SCM continued to read and identify Tibetan proverbs that paralleled sayings found in the biblical book of Proverbs, writing them down in a huge octavo volume using his own Tibetan calligraphy, and then adding translations in English for the sake of his own record and meditative consideration. This was done as part of his personal devotional study pursued daily over the years, which he started while he was a student in Oxford in 1833 and continued well into the 1880s. The result of all those many hours of thoughtful reading and writing was the creation of the manuscript version of the massive work he entitled *Original Notes on the Book of Proverbs*.

---

[53] Many other details of his efforts and travels within India are documented in *SCM DD*, pp. 56-60.

[54] Once again, this is documented in detail within *ibid.*, pp. 64-67.

[55] Details provided in *ibid.*, pp. 94-96.

[56] Documented with many details in Duka 1885, pp. 143-147 and 154.

As it happened,⁵⁷ Theodore Duka had already retired from active service in the Royal Bengali Army in 1874 as a Lieutenant-Colonel, returning to England where he and his family settled in London. Sometime later he was encouraged by the Hungarian Academy of Sciences to produce a biography on Csoma de Kőrös, since Duka knew quite a bit about a number of places where his Hungarian predecessor had been active, and also knew many British colonial officials who could help him locate relevant unpublished materials. For this reason, Duka returned to India in 1883 to pursue the research related to the life and works of Csoma de Kőrös. Notably, it was during that trip that Duka learned about the gift of the Tibetan documents given to SCM. In addition, he found the one authentic image of his Hungarian predecessor that remains a historical anchor in the midst of what was at the time a very uncertain portrayal about the man and his work.⁵⁸

By that time period much that was remarkable had also happened to SCM, events that increased his social status and the contemporary recognition of British academics of his being a scholar of unusual productivity and linguistic skill. In April 1880, SCM had been presented with an honorary Doctorate in Divinity by the *Senatus Academicus* of the University of Edinburgh.⁵⁹ It is not hard to imagine that at the age of 68 this accolade to his scholarly and popular writings must have brought SCM not a little satisfaction. Some three years later, after Duka had returned from India, the two men met each other for the first time in London and realized that they shared an admiration for the generally still unknown Csoma de Kőrös. Consequently, this initiated their correspondence, and ignited within SCM a fresh set of memories shared with Duka regarding what SCM himself had come to know of Csoma de Kőrös, including aspects of his character, details about his habits and personal dress, as well as his substantial contribution to Tibetan studies. Even memories that SCM had of his previous visit to the twin cities of Buda and Pest, experienced when he passed through the region in 1872, must have become once more alive in his thoughts.⁶⁰ Certainly, many other possibilities began to emerge through conversations and correspondence SCM had with this new Hungarian friend. Among those possibilities, we are told by Paczolay, was the suggestion first made by Duka that SCM consider sending the Tibetan documents he had received from the "Father of European Tibetology" to the Hungarian Academy of Sciences.⁶¹ Subsequently, citations from some of the letters of their correspondence appeared in Duka's work, and much later, citations from their correspondence also appeared in SCM's posthumously published biography written by his son, the Rev. A. N. Malan.⁶² Later

---

⁵⁷ Here and in the following sentences we are relying on the recent account of Duka's life in Paczolay 1998, pp. 64ff.

⁵⁸ As confirmed in Paczolay 1998, p. 92.

⁵⁹ Elaborated in *SCM DD*, pp. 308-310.

⁶⁰ As noted with some additional elaborations that include other cameos regarding SCM's sometimes eccentric character, in *ibid.*, p. 273.

⁶¹ Confirmed in correspondence with Paczolay by Pfister on July 12, 2016.

⁶² Duka quotes from at least four of the letters in *id*. 1885, pp. 20, 66, 142, and 158. Citations from two of these letters occur also in *SCM DD*, p. 342.

studies of their correspondence produced in the 1970s have cited twelve letters,[63] but Paczolay has also identified another twelve letters that passed between the two men and are now kept in the archives of the Hungarian Academy of Sciences.[64] The 24 letters we now have from their correspondence span a period from October 1883 to sometime in 1887.[65] From these generally brief letters we learn a number of details about the context of the lives of both SCM and Theodore Duka that reveal how and why the vast majority of the Tibetan documents received by SCM from Csoma de Kőrös were ultimately sent to Budapest.

Apparently sometime in the late Spring of 1883, SCM experienced a very serious bronchial infection, a disease that was quite unusual for his normally healthy condition. It put him into convalescence for at least three months, so that even by July 1883 he was struggling toward a full recovery.[66] At this time, then, SCM kept in mind two major projects: the first was to consider how to provide for an Anglophone audience an English version of his multi-lingual manuscript (the ONBP Ms) that he had used for his own personal devotions. This was a matter that had apparently been requested by some well-meaning friends, one which he took even more seriously once he realized that his health may prevent him from performing such a major task in the foreseeable future. The second matter on his mind was to locate a suitable institutional home for his very unusual personal library, within which were found also the gifts of the Tibetan documents received in 1839 from Csoma de Kőrös. Though he had not made this explicit in the first correspondence he had with Duka in October 1883,[67] these matters were raised by Duka in his interactions with SCM, as has been already mentioned, particularly in suggesting the possibility of offering the Tibetan manuscripts to the Hungarian Academy of Sciences.

From the content of their correspondence, we cannot find much direct discussion of the matter, something that must at first have only been suggested in private conversation. Nevertheless, the topic does come up directly in their correspondence, in a manner that almost appears as a sudden and nearly compulsive gesture; it appears in a brief letter written by SCM to Duka on April 5, 1884. It began abruptly, after the normal respectful greeting: "I am about disposing of my library. And I feel sorry to scatter about Csoma's Tibetan books and Mss which he gave me in 1839, which I have used and kept ever since for his sake." Having addressed his concern,

---

[63] Documented in both their original English and Hungarian renderings in Terjék 1976, pp. 38-61.

[64] Prepared in a typescript and sent to Pfister by Paczolay in 2012. The typescript is entitled "Twelve Letters Written by S. C. Malan to T. Duka," and in the first paragraph Paczolay clarifies, "These letters were not published earlier by Prof. József Terjék."

[65] In the typescript prepared by Paczolay, the last three letters appear to be sent during 1887, at the beginning and end of the year, but there is no accompanying year written down on the letters to verify this without any question. See also the back cover of this volume.

[66] This we learn primarily from *SCM DD*, pp. 335-341, but it sets the existential context for the subsequent events revealed in the correspondence between these two men.

[67] The full text of that English letter along with its Hungarian translation appears in Terjék 1976, pp. 38-39. Also found in *SCM DD*, p. 342.

Malan does not hesitate to confirm what had apparently been made known to him in conversation with Duka.

> [I]t strikes me that the University of Buda Pesth [*sic*] would be the proper home for those treasures. [...] There are some 30 vol[ume]s, and if you think they would prove acceptable to the University, and you would undertake to forward them[,] I will send them to you at once with pleasure.

Though the statements in this letter are put politely enough, one might sense at points that its straightforwardness extends beyond what propriety would require. Yet from the posthumously published biography about SCM we learn that this way of acting was consistent with his character. "The impulse of the moment was sometimes the motive which prompted action. He persuaded himself of the necessity and approached it by the shortest cut."[68]

No other plan could have been more demanding or personal for Duka, because he had spent a good number of years in India tracing down unpublished letters and documents written by and about Csoma de Kőrös. Though we have no copy of a letter from Duka to Malan, we find already within a week that another letter was sent by the Vicar of Broadwindsor to the retired Hungarian medical doctor, telling him in response to a letter from Duka that it would not be necessary for the medical doctor to go to Broadwindsor to retrieve the Tibetan documents.[69] At that time, as SCM indicates, he was already "arranging and ticketing Csoma's Tibetan books," and his intention was explicit. "When ready[,] they shall be sent to you at once." And so, the plan in SCM's mind had been set. Duka wrote another letter confirming his willingness to transport the Tibetan "treasures" to Budapest, and so in response, SCM wrote back on April 17, 1884. Indicating in that new letter that he had already packed them more than once, SCM hoped to give them as secure a passage as possible and would be sending them to London on the following day.[70]

Several aspects of this whole situation are notable, and worthy of further elaboration. First of all, the emotional attachment SCM had to these Tibetan documents was intensely linked to his reinvigorated memories of his Hungarian teacher. A flood of images that had been stored in his creative memory for more than four decades were once more relived within his very visual imagination. These erupted into descriptions of their interrelationship in Calcutta, elaborations of the mannerisms of Csoma de Kőrös, and even included details about his normal clothing. Indeed, as SCM once put it during the last decade of his life, "I lived in my books."[71] Also, a deep sense of the significance of the Hungarian scholar's achievements were reconfirmed through Malan's personal letters.

---

[68] Quoting from *SCM DD*, p. 117.

[69] A letter dated April 12, 1884 and appearing only in its original English and Hungarian translation in Terjék 1976, pp. 44-45. The quotations found in the next few sentences also come from this letter.

[70] See the full letter dated April 17, 1884 in Terjék 1976, pp. 46-47, and once again the whole English version of the letter in *SCM DD*, pp. 342-343.

[71] Cited in *SCM DD*, p. 281.

> I am looking [the Tibetan documents] over. They so remind me of him. There was something so kind, simple and winning about his manner. But my impression was, at the time, that he was not duly appreciated. [...][72]
>
> I remember dear Csoma's dress quite well. I never saw him in his best (if he had one) but I always met him in the library of the As[iatic] Society, of which I was Secretary during my stay in Calcutta. [...] He was much weather beaten, and his complexion evidently the worse for his exposure, and the hardship he had to endure. But I did enjoy my visits; he was so kind and genial; he certainly was pleased to find one interested in Tibetan. I gave him my Turkish Dictionary. But he never taught me the Magyar tongue – a most beautiful tongue – the little I know I learnt alone.[73]
>
> [Csoma de Kőrös] was devoted to his one object, was master of several languages, and over and above all, he has, and shall have to the end, the honour and credit of being the founder of Tibetan studies in Europe. [...] [H]e laid the foundation and others only build upon it.[74] [...] It has cost me a little to say goodbye to [his Tibetan gifts]. But I feel that they ought to rest in your University[,] where I trust they will be taken care of, and valued for poor dear Csoma's sake.[75]

There is a level of pathos here that descended on SCM also when he had prepared to send his personal library to the Indian Institute in Oxford in January 1885. Yet it should be noted here that this arrangement was made nearly eight months before that other event. We take this to be evidence of a self-conscious choice, a matter of honor and veneration for the Hungarian teacher that SCM himself had never again seen after he left Calcutta in 1840. This is reaffirmed twice already in the letters we have cited here, whenever SCM refers to sending the Tibetan documents to Budapest with Duka "for Csoma's sake," indicating a deep sense of personal indebtedness and interpersonal respect.

Notably, and here is another aspect of this whole remarkable process, Duka himself refers to this arrangement as "a spontaneous gift" presented to the Hungarian Academy of Sciences. What we now understand of this claim is that this was a "spontaneous" response to Duka's initial suggestion, suggesting that sometime in April 1884 Duka had explicitly raised the possibility of having the Tibetan documents taken to the Hungarian Academy of Sciences, and had promised to accompany them to their new location, if SCM chose to offer them to that institution's library. In the end, this did happen, and representatives of the Hungarian Academy of Sciences duly responded to the "great generosity" of SCM in both Hungarian and English, marking a new stage of usefulness for those unusual Tibetan documents.[76] We cannot help but add to this statement made in 1885 that the Tibetan documents and other unpublished materials, including Duka's correspondence with

---

[72] Quoted from Terjék 1976, p. 44.
[73] Citation from *ibid.*, p. 40.
[74] Found in *ibid.*, p. 46.
[75] Once again, quoted from *ibid*.
[76] Both of the above quotations appear in the main text of Duka 1885, p. 167.

SCM, now have their honored place within the Oriental Collection of the Library of the Hungarian Academy of Sciences.[77]

Yet another set of questions should be raised with regard to why SCM in 1884 chose not to send the vast majority of those Tibetan documents received from Csoma de Kőrös to the Indian Institute in January 1885 as part of what became the "Malan Library" there. There may have been a number of reasons, but among them was a persistent worry that SCM expressed more than once, that after his personal library would be taken to Oxford, its very diversified materials – including standard sets of materials in Christian classics as well as published or handwritten documents of classical works and missionary translations in numerous other language media, amounting to representative pieces from just over 100 languages – would be split up into many different libraries. Certainly, that fear was not unfounded, and eighty years after he had committed his over 4,000 tome personal library to the Indian Institute, his fears were realized in the 1960s.[78] Yet it would seem that far more positive reasons also were significant. Theodore Duka was an ethnic Hungarian emigrant to Great Britain who still maintained vital contacts with Hungarian scholars and was able to move those crates of Tibetan documents to the Hungarian Academy of Sciences under his personal observation. If anyone of that era knew the importance of the achievements of Csoma de Kőrös and could highlight these matters in Hungarian to contemporary scholars there, it was Duka. So, rather than send those Tibetan "treasures" to an uncertain future in Oxford, SCM wisely chose to entrust them to Duka's management. From a public and academic point of view, Duka proved to be exceptionally helpful as well. Before taking this "Malan bequest" to Hungary, Duka arranged for a public exhibition of the Tibetan documents under the aegis of the Royal Asiatic Society, and on that same night, 16 June 1884, presented a lecture explaining their content and significance to any who came to hear about this unusual international gift.[79]

The result was that, in terms of Hungarian scholarship related to Csoma de Kőrös, new research flourished beyond all expectations, and as has been mentioned previously, was the positive result of that sacrificial and perceptive set of decisions.

3. Quantifying the Gift of Csoma de Kőrös to S. C. Malan: Points for Clarification

How many "documents" were passed on by Csoma de Kőrös to SCM in Calcutta in 1839? There remains some small controversy about this matter due to the kinds of units used to count those documents, as well as evidence that the Csoma Bequest

---

[77] Both authors of this chapter have benefited greatly regarding the details of this chapter from the generosity and helpfulness of the current Head of the Oriental Collection of the Hungarian Academy of Sciences, Dr. Agnes Kelecsényi, and her staff.

[78] See the Chapter 12 in this volume for more details.

[79] This is documented not only in the *Journal of the Royal Asiatic Society*, but also in Paczolay 1998, p. 79.

sent to Budapest by means of Theodore Duka did not include all of those documents, though they were certainly the vast majority of them.

While there is no question that SCM was "an Orientalist absolutely unequalled, and never likely to be equalled" in his studies of so many non-European languages,[80] he was not always very consistent in portraying the number of those Tibetan documents he had received from the Hungarian "father of European Tibetan studies." This is certainly an awkward fact that requires some resolution, if that is at all possible. For example, at one point SCM indicated that there were "about three dozen" of those Tibetan texts of some sort;[81] yet in one of his letters cited above, he stated otherwise, claiming "there are some 30 vol[ume]s."[82] On the other hand, Theodore Duka in 1884 listed very carefully 40 documents. Yet some among those documents were in fact very limited in length, and so one might question whether they would be identified as particular "texts" or "monographs." Notably, Duka himself did not mention three other documents that SCM did not send through him to Budapest, and so this adds to the confusion. So, here below, a distinction between "documents" and "texts" will be made, and then further evidence given to show that there are some further documents originating from the gift of Csoma de Kőrös to SCM which were not sent to Budapest.

When reference was made above to "documents," this term is primarily intended to indicate the units of individuated manuscripts or blockprints kept by SCM in his personal library. Sometimes these were kept in individual boxes made for the particular document, and in other cases they were bound together by leather strings or other materials, with material on the top and bottom of the stack of documents to maintain them as a singular unit. Nevertheless, in each manuscript or blockprint there could be a series of different texts, so that the number of the documents would be expected to be less than the number of actual texts. So, for example, according to the catalogue of Tibetan documents identified as being part of the "Csoma-bequest" and currently held in the Library of the Hungarian Academy of Sciences, there are thirty-six documents in their possession, but these documents include within them forty-seven distinct texts.[83]

Another source of information regarding other Tibetan manuscripts held in the Bodleian Library in Oxford, confirming that they must have been part of the original gift of Csoma de Kőrös to SCM, was published by a Swiss Tibetologist, Pierre Marczell, in 2002.[84] One of the three documents Marczell describes is not merely

---

[80] This remarkable statement was made in a letter to *The London Times* written about SCM after his death by M. Monier-Williams, "Boden Professor of Sanscrit and Keeper and Curator of the Indian Institute," in December 1894. It is cited with this quotation in full in *SCM DD*, pp. 371-372.

[81] Quoting from a statement by SCM cited in *SCM DD*, p. 48.

[82] Citing the phrase found in SCM's letter to Duka dated April 5, 1884, and found in Terjék 1976, p. 42.

[83] Consult Orosz 2008, vol. 1, summarizing the content presented in the catalogue section, pp. 1-25.

[84] See Marczell – Rala – Gullu 2002, pp. 55-72.

a large singular text of 279 leaves in length, but includes seven different identifiable texts within it.[85] The second document is just over 400 pages in length, and is given the title of an "Outline of a Tibetan Dicty," the last word being the abbreviation for the word "dictionary." It is clearly indicated on its title page that this also belonged to Csoma de Kőrös.[86] A final box that counts as the third document is actually a set of ten texts that "are all rites from the cycle of Mahākārunika (Avalokiteśvara)."[87]

This being the case, the total gift of Csoma de Kőrös to SCM came to 39 documents, including 65 texts.

From 1839 till 1884 the host of Tibetan manuscripts and block prints – oblong rectangular texts, boxed in packaging about 6 inches wide, four to six inches deep, and nearly a yard long – were situated in the library-study rooms on the back side of the vicarage in Broadwindsor. Then, after receiving an honorary doctorate from the University of Edinburgh, SCM met that former Hungarian soldier and retired medical officer retired from the British army, Theodore Duka. As we have seen above, it was Duka who became the mediating agent, sending SCM's gift from Csoma de Kőrös to Budapest.

4. Concluding Notes

Our task here has been relatively simple: to retell, refine, and reassess a story that has been generally unknown within Anglophone worlds. Few have known that SCM had met and maintained such a significant friendship with the "Father of European Tibetology," Alexander Csoma de Kőrös. In addition, how the unusual gift of those Tibetan documents was kept in Broadwindsor, and then ultimately sent to Budapest, has been recounted in Hungarian and French, but very seldom in English. As we have pointed out, there have been also some questions about whether SCM really appreciated his teacher, whether he employed those Tibetan texts in his other work, and also confusions about how many documents and texts there were, as well as how many were ultimately sent to Budapest. All of these questions we have tried to answer here, but have left the more scholarly assessment of SCM's Tibetan knowledge to Rita Kuzder, who in Chapter 9 within this volume has provided a helpful account of what SCM had learned, which Tibetan texts he employed, and also some of the problems related to his references to texts that are difficult to identify as well as to certain claims drawn from those Tibetan documents.

What we can confirm from 19th century correspondence and secondary literature that is available is that SCM was self-consciously grateful for the learning and trust he maintained with his Tibetan teacher, and with the help of Theodore Duka, was able to honor his teacher by passing on the majority of the Tibetan texts given to

---

[85] Details regarding those seven texts within the one Tibetan document are presented in the latter of two appendices in Marczell – Rala – Gullu 2002, pp. 69-71. In the catalogue prepared for the Bodleian Library by John E. Stapelton Driver in 1970, and edited by David Barrett in 1993, this is known as "MS.Ind.Inst.Tib.1."

[86] In the Bodleian Library's call number system it's known as "MS.Ind.Inst.Tib.2."

[87] Quoting from Marczell – Rala – Gullu 2002, p. 55.

him as a gift by Csoma de Kőrös probably sometime in 1839. What we have not done is assess the level of competency in Tibetan language that SCM attained, but we have hinted at his awareness that the Buddhist worldviews that he encountered were radically different from the Christian worldview that he himself advocated. Whether or not his Tibetan teacher agreed with him would be worth considering. Fortunately, more details about how well SCM translated various Tibetan, Chinese, Manchurian and Sanskrit texts into English, and how openly he revealed those differences in worldviews, has been addressed to some degree in the chapters written by Rita Kuzder, Thomas Zimmer, William Ng, Loretta Kim and James Hegarty within this volume.

This account of the historical relationship between SCM and Csoma de Kőrös has underscored the unusual settings that drew those two men together, and their different fates that pulled them apart. While the historical story carries its own fascination, the larger impact of SCM's gift to academicians in the Hungarian scholarly world has not been forgotten. Just over twenty-five years ago, a group of Hungarian scholars travelled to the little town of Broadwindsor in Dorsetshire to offer a sign of thanks to SCM on the centennial of his death in 1994. In the entrance of the sprawling home that was once his vicarage, and is now a home for the elderly, they left a white marble plaque with a message carved into the stone. It states in glowing terms an encomium for the Anglican vicar, and is signed as follows (see Fig. 17):

Fig. 17: Image of Malan plaque, Broadwindsor
(Photograph by Mirasy M. Pfister, taken in August 2012)

Select Bibliography

Almond, Philip C. 1988. *The British Discovery of Buddhism*. Cambridge: Cambridge University Press.

Ashcroft, Bill – Gareth Griffiths – Helen Tiffin (eds.). 2006. *The Post-Colonial Studies Reader*. London: Routledge.

Buswell, Robert E. – Robert E. Jr. – Donald S. Lopez, Jr, (comps.). 2014. *The Princeton Dictionary of Buddhism*. Princeton: Princeton University Press.

Le Calloc'h, Bernard. 1985. "Les biographes d'Alexandre Csoma de Kőrös." *Journal asiatique* 273 (1985) 3-4, pp. 403-433.

———. 1987. "Alexandre Csoma de Kőrös, le bodhisattva hongrois." *Revue de l'histoire des religions* 204 (1987) 4 no. 4, pp. 353-388.

Duka, Theodore. 1884. "Some Remarks on the Life and Labours of Alexander Csoma de Kőrös, delivered on the occasion when his Tibetan Books and MSS. were exhibited before the Royal Asiatic Society on the 16th June 1884," *Journal of the Royal Asiatic Society of Great Britain and Ireland* 16 (1884) 4, pp. 486-494.

———. 1885. *Life and Works of Alexander Csoma de Kőrös: A Biography Compiled Chiefly from hitherto Unpublished Data*. London: Trübner.

Guo Jianzhong. 1995. "Translatability in CE/EC [Chinese-English/English-Chinese] Translation." In: Chan Sin-wai and David E. Pollard (eds.), *An Encyclopaedia of Translation: Chinese-English – English-Chinese*. Hong Kong: The Chinese University Press, pp. 1057-1067.

Lopez, Jr., Donald S. 1995. "Foreigner at the Lama's Feet." In: *id*. (ed.), *Curators of the Buddha: The Study of Buddhism under Colonialism*. Chicago: The University of Chicago Press, pp. 251-296.

Marczell, Pierre J. – Kusho Rala – Nicole Gullu. 2002. "The Tibetan Mss of the Malan Bequest in the Bodleian and Their Relation to the Life and Works of Csoma Kőrös." *Studia Asiatica* 3 (2002) 1-2, pp. 55-72.

Mieder, Wolfgang *et al.* (comp.) 2011. *International Bibliography of Paremiology: Collections of Proverbs, Proverbial Expressions and Comparisons, Quotations, Graffiti, Slang, and Wellerisms*. Burlington: The University of Vermont.

Orosz, Gergely. 2008. *A Catalogue of the Tibetan Manuscripts and Block Prints in the Library of the Hungarian Academy of Sciences*. 2 vols. Budapest: Library of the Hungarian Academy of Sciences.

Paczolay, Gyula. 1997. *European Proverbs in 55 Languages with Equivalents in Arabic, Persian, Sanskrit, Chinese and Japanese*. Veszprém: Veszprém Nyomda Rt.

———. 1998. *Duka Tivadar*. Budapest: Akadémiai Kiadó.

Paine, Jeffery. 2004. *Re-enchantment: Tibetan Buddhism Comes to the West*. New York: W. W. Norton.

Pym, Anthony – Horst Turk. 2001. "Translatability." In: Mona Baker and Kirsten Malmkjær (eds.), *Routledge Encyclopedia of Translation Studies*. London – New York: Routledge, pp. 273-277.

Stein, Aurel. 1914. *In Memoriam Theodore Duka, 1825–1908*. Budapest: Privately published.

Stevenson, Burton (comp.). 1948. *The Home Book of Proverbs, Maxims and Familiar Phrases*. New York: Macmillan.

Terjék, József. 1976. *Kőrösi Csoma dokumentumok az akadémia könyvtár gyüjteményeiben*. Budapest: Magyar tudományos akadémia.

Venuti, Lawrence. 2001. "Strategies of Translation." In: Mona Baker and Kirsten Malmkjær (eds.), *Routledge Encyclopedia of Translation Studies*. London – New York: Routledge, pp. 240-244.

Wilkinson, Endymion. 2013. *Chinese History: A New Manual*. Cambridge, Mass. – London: Harvard University Press.

12

RECOVERING THE NOW INVISIBLE MALAN LIBRARY

LAUREN F. PFISTER

Though my main purpose in this chapter is to offer both a general characterization and several specific details related to what was referred to as "The Malan Library," a special library associated with the Indian Institute in Oxford starting in the early months of 1885, I must also deal with a number of other factors that make this discussion all the more valuable. First of all, I want to indicate the extraordinary breadth of the languages and different kinds of documents that constituted that library. As the Rev. S. C. Malan himself described it (see Appendix I), it included codices, manuscripts and other forms of texts in many languages that had nothing to do with the subcontinent of India. This has much to do with his own self-conscious interest in Bible translation into foreign languages,[1] and his previous experience of living as a missionary-educator in Calcutta for most of the period from 1838 to 1840.[2] Precisely because of this, then, there should be some reflection about the relationship of SCM's library to a wide range of Christian missions in the 19th century, his Anglican commitments as both a former missionary and later vicar in Dorsetshire, and the significant problems related to how these interests were complicated and qualified by British imperial interests.[3] While I will approach the missiological interests only tangentially here, I will explore some documentable information about how SCM managed to obtain such an unusual collection of published and unpublished works from a wide range of sources, something that does inherently involve his religious, cultural and political affiliations. In addition, I will document the fact that the Malan Library had ultimately started to be dispersed in 1965 within the Bodleian Library, where it had never been previously located.[4] This relocation and dispersion of the library, in spite of previous agreements and the

---

[1] Not only did SCM write a number of books related to problems of biblical translations in various languages, but he also remained in contact with key persons in the British and Foreign Bible Society and at times participated in reviewing biblical materials in various languages before they were produced by them. See *WIGC*; SCM 1856; *id*. 1874; *id*. 1890. Consult also *SCM DD*, pp. 344-347, where SCM is shown to have corresponded with the Secretary of the British and Foreign Bible Society regarding matters related to biblical versions in Armenian, Calmuc, Georgian, Japanese, Korean and Tibetan languages.

[2] As described in Chapter 2 in this volume.

[3] An important study revealing how Oxford University was intimately tied to British imperial interests is Symonds 1986.

[4] To say that it had "started to be dispersed" in 1965 is a matter of conjecture on my part, because there were pictures taken of the Malan Library in the Indian Institute building in 1967, that seem to indicate that there were still many books present in that location at that later date. Nevertheless, it is clear that the whole library had been dispersed into varying parts of the Bodleian Library before the end of the 1960s.

undeniable value of a good number of its rare items, must be described briefly in order to comprehend the monumental effort involved in locating and then coming to understand many remarkable aspects of the Malan Library. What is presented within this chapter of our book, then, is a critical summary of the claims and content of major portions of the Malan Library, also including some new hopes that much of what can be identified by various means can bring an immense amount of light to various aspects of the life and works of the man, Solomon Caesar Malan.

Beyond all these important concerns that motivate the writing of this piece, I want to add a personal note related to key persons who made what appeared to be an impossible task – offering an updated and more critically precise account of the Malan Library – a reality. This involves expressions of gratitude that could only appear in a preface, but I want to underscore here that without the timely and diligent efforts of these various people,[5] the gargantuan and immensely complicated task of seeking to make proper sense of the many facets of SCM's life and works would have been literally beyond my ability to discern and assess. Of greatest importance to the whole research project was the special efforts of my beloved wife, Mirasy, who developed a thorough method of recording the nearly 16,000 footnotes in the published version of SCM's *Original Notes on the Book of Proverbs* (1889–1893), completing this task during the academic year of 2007–2008.[6] Without this very precise way of analyzing SCM's work, I would not have been able to begin to guess which texts within the massive collections of the Bodleian Libraries might have been originally part of the more than 4,000 texts offered to the Indian Institute in 1885. Secondly, I am profoundly indebted to Dr. Gillian Evison, the Chief of the Bodleian Libraries' Oriental Section as well as the current Librarian of the Indian Institute Library. Because of my persistent requests, starting in 2008, Dr. Evison continued to dig up important materials and artifacts related to the Malan Library. Before an international conference on SCM's life and works took place at Wadham College in Oxford in August 2012, she also relocated immensely important bibliographic materials that will be described later in this chapter. In addition, she made it possible for all our conference participants to have the opportunity to look through and analyze SCM's key texts as well as those bibliographic materials during a special session held within a private reading room in one part of the Bodleian, an event that immensely stimulated our comradery and underscored our shared comprehension of the importance of the Malan Library and some of his most unusual texts and works.[7] During the period approaching the international conference, the

---

[5] This is not to say that there were not others in the process of research over the years that have offered important guidance and cooperation in various realms and with specific tasks, but these figures have been critically significant for my own determination to pursue work related to SCM and his legacy.

[6] Mirasy has been my partner in research related to Malan over these years in other ways as well, but this was the most critical contribution that has continued to reap a harvest of new insights by myself and other scholars due to the details she has made available to us all.

[7] Dr. Evison's own reflections on these matters were framed within her essay presented at that international conference. See Gillian Evison, "The Bibliophile and the Bodleian," which can

personal involvement of Prof. Gyula Paczolay in Hungary in helping to unravel various aspects of the story of the Tibetan texts SCM ultimately donated to the Hungarian Academy of Sciences was undeniably critical.[8] Without his discernment regarding suitable scholars to contact, and his personal effort to locate texts, key persons, and relevant materials related to SCM as well as his unusual bequest to that Academy, it would have been impossible to resolve with any historical or archival certainty what has probably been one of the most important international discoveries related to the Hungarian contribution to Tibetan studies: the fact that the person who has been considered to be the Nestor of Tibetan studies in Hungary and Europe, Alexander Csoma de Kőrös (1788–1842), had given to the young SCM before he left Calcutta in 1840 a large set of Tibetan texts as a personal gift, a set of texts that had taken the Hungarian scholar a lifetime to collect. Finally, the diligent research support provided by a former student from the Department of Religion and Philosophy, Hong Kong Baptist University, Ms. Yip Wing-yan 葉詠恩, made it possible to digitize what my wife, Mirasy, had originally prepared as a large set of handwritten research notes, so that I could generate data searches related to specific languages, texts, and authors. This greatly increased the possibility of initiating new levels of interpretive work related to specific groups of proverbs coming from particular linguistic corridors. After the international conference on SCM took place in 2012, Wing-yan also created an extensive word document related to some materials made available to us by Dr. Evison, and so during the academic year 2013–2014 this task was also completed. Once again, many of the precise details and various insights I am now able to offer related to various portions of the former Malan Library have been made possible through this systematic work.

Having expressed my immense gratitude to these four important persons, I want to take up an existential perspective in revealing how the problem of the nature and extent of the Malan Library became a matter of scholarly interest within my own life and thoughts during the past decade.

1. Catching a Strong Scent of a Trail …

After more than a decade of flirting with the possibility of digging through a mesmerising mixture of thousands of more or less understandable footnotes in the English version of the three-volume set of the *ONBP*,[9] an unusual opportunity arose for me to teach during the academic year of 2007–2008 in the Religious Studies Institute of the University of Bern, Switzerland, that ignited my research motivations to study

---

be accessed by means of https://ora.ox.ac.uk/objects/uuid:ef937cf0-9254-4f44-8245-645115374a57 (accessed 28 January 2021).

[8] See Chapter 11 for an account of that unusual story of the Csoma Bequest. that was initially given to SCM in the late 1830s, and then in 1894 was transferred to the Budapest institution.

[9] It should be noted in passing here that the subtitle of the first volume ("According to the Authorized Version") varies from the subtitle found in the last two volumes, i.e., "Mostly from Eastern Writings." In fact, the subtitle in the first version makes the work sound far less adventurous and critical than the three-volume set actually is.

SCM and his works. As is told already above and elsewhere in this volume,[10] the difficult work that was pursued by my wife, Mirasy, in documenting and unravelling some of the mysteries bound up in the footnotes to SCM's three-volume *magnum opus* set the stage for other advances. Here I cannot avoid revealing some of the more colorful dimensions of that long journey of discovery, all of which were made realizable due to that one fecund year in association with colleagues in the beautiful city of Bern.

My appointment to the University of Bern as a visiting faculty member was completely due to the generosity and collegiality of Prof. Karénina Kollmar-Paulenz, who was serving as Dean of a number of academic units at that university during that period. Mirasy and I gladly chose to go there from Hong Kong, because my paternal relatives lived merely three kilometres outside of the city, which is surrounded by the gorgeous River Aare, and so that year became simultaneously an international adventure as well as a special homecoming for us. Regarding my own position at the university there, we were given much leeway to pursue research, and so while I had the privilege of teaching in Switzerland for the first semester, during the second semester I was given freedom to do research and writing elsewhere. Consequently, having discovered other materials related to the Malan family in archives in Lausanne, I was also able to pursue initial work in January 2008 focused on SCM's huge gift of the vast majority of his personal library to the Indian Institute in Oxford. The research focus I adopted at that time, linked intimately to my own area of specialization, was determinedly centered on locating the Chinese sources employed by SCM in creating his *ONBP*. Afterwards, I sought to assess whether and how well he had handled those Chinese texts quoted in the *ONBP* when he rendered them into English and set them within the larger and far more complicated context of the multi-cultural study of proverbial wisdom that was at the heart of this unusual work. Subsequently, I completed a lecture tour involving eight lectures in various universities in the United Kingdom during the early months of 2008, speaking about themes related to Chinese philosophy and Ruist-Christian dialogue. Still, the more fruitful period related to SCM research came in the following months, when my wife and I were able to spend two months of research, teaching and writing at the Philosophy Department of East China Normal University in Shanghai during March and April of 2008. This was made possible through special arrangements by the Gadamerian scholar, Pan Derong 潘德榮, and so I took advantage of that opportunity to introduce graduate students and colleagues there to some works by missionary-scholars, including James Legge (Li Yage 理雅各, 1815–1897), and wrote out my first major article related to SCM's interest in Chinese wisdom.[11] Once the English version of that article was published in 2012,[12] I

---

[10] Please see Chapter 13 in this volume for further details about this unusual manuscript.

[11] For readers who know Chinese, please consult Pfister 2011. In this article I coined the Chinese name for SCM as Ma Zhiku 馬智庫, his family name being the relatively common surname among Muslims, "Mr. Horse," and his personal name meaning "a treasury of wisdom."

[12] See Pfister 2012, pp. 1-52.

felt assured that there had been ample progress to attract enough persons to hold an international conference in Oxford later that summer. The success of that conference led to the desire to collaborate in the production of this volume that is now before our readers.

As we have already learned from Frédéric Amsler's article in this volume (Chapter 1), the father of SCM, the Rev. Henri Abraham César Malan, was a person rejected by the Calvinist establishment of post-Enlightenment Geneva, taking up a conservative theological position in opposition to his teachers and elders in the early 19th century Genevan Protestant church community.[13] Yet beyond this critical reality that shaped his eldest son's life profoundly,[14] it should also be pointed out that it was the father who taught and nurtured his son privately[15] in multiple languages[16] as well as in the fine arts, and was similarly a prolifically published author in numerous and very different realms of Christian theology.[17] SCM's father arranged for his brilliant firstborn son, the first of eleven surviving children,[18] to have his own book bindery in order to create his own personally bound tomes.[19] In the first case,

---

[13] Described in detail within the second to the fourth chapters of C. Malan 1869.

[14] Some might expect that there were some significant theological differences between the dissenting father (who later in the 1830s became a pastor joined with a Scottish-inspired foreign Calvinist church within Geneva, rather than the Genevan Calvinist church itself), and his first son, SCM (who chose to join "the establishment" of the Anglican Church after initiating his studies in Oxford University). There were tensions between them, as adequately clarified in the first chapters of ANM's biography, but there was also a continued interaction between father and sons that developed through two visits of the eldest son to the 19th century Swiss canton later during his vicarage and before his father passed away in 1864. More about this cannot be explained here, but it would be a major topic worthy of critical reflection in a subsequent essay.

[15] One might mention many other aspects of this father-son influence, a longer list having been already written out in *SCM DD*, p. 16.

[16] According to his son, ANM, SCM by age eighteen was "fluent" in the modern European languages of "French, German, Spanish, and Italian, and less perfectly English," and was already "well advanced in the knowledge of Hebrew, Sanscrit, and Arabic." Quoted from *SCM DD*, p. 21.

[17] The father was a well-known Christian author of moral tales in modern French, some which were translated into foreign languages, and one also even into Chinese. Beyond the many writings in the Genevan Calvinist theological controversies in which he took part, César Malan also became well known for his new French hymns, many of which were sung in other places where he travelled as a European evangelist. Evidence of the prolific nature of his publications, many being published and bound at his own private press in Geneva, is manifest in the extensive bibliography provided at the end of C. Malan 1869a (one that does not appear in the English version, unfortunately).

[18] Twelve children were born to the Rev. César Malan, his father, and his Swiss-born wife, eleven of them surviving into adulthood and alive after his death in 1864. C. Malan 1869b, p. 28.

[19] For his eldest son, the Rev. César Malan set up "a bookbinder's workshop, completely furnished." Obviously, the binding of some volumes that we know were produced by SCM later in his life in England demonstrate that he learned this skill well, displaying exquisite taste and remarkable aesthetic and technical talent in this realm. Quoted from *SCM DD*, p. 14.

SCM spoke Latin as his "father-tongue,"[20] and his artistic talents particularly in sketching and water-colors proved to be notable far beyond the little Dorsetshire village of Broadwindsor, where he served as the Anglican vicar for forty years.[21]

Having now recorded both my own personal sense of gratitude to those who supported our work as well as this brief account touching on the influences between the Genevan father, the Rev. César Malan, and his Anglican son, I now will turn directly to discuss in detail the route toward rediscovering the Malan Library, the topic that will remain the focus of this chapter. It was in 2008 that my wife and I had finally gotten a strong sense of the research trail leading to the monumental effort of seeking to understand, sympathetically appreciate, and critically evaluate what SCM had accomplished by the end of his life.

2. Hints of the Library That Once Was There ...

Time spent in the Bodleian Library in early 2008 was crucial for my own commitments regarding what further could be learned from pursuing basic research related to SCM in that context. Through the details provided by his son, ANM, in his helpful biographical work published several years after his father's death, I knew that a "Malan Library" existed, and that there was a large manuscript related to the *ONBP* that had been donated to the Bodleian Library.[22] I did not realize at the time that this exceptionally unusual manuscript had been sent to the Bodleian just two months before SCM's death, a potent sign of his ultimate submission to his final sickness.[23] Due to the timely and informed guidance of Dr. Gillian Evison, I was pointed toward a special card catalogue including the lists of all donated manuscripts and there quickly found a number of manuscripts associated with the name of SCM.[24] This was the first concrete evidence that I had discovered of the remnants of a "Malan Library," but I was about to be startled into a number of unexpected traces of that library as I began to take out the manuscripts, one by one, and look over them.

---

[20] Quoted from *SCM DD*, p. 22.

[21] Find a very recently published affirmation of this fact in Bonfitto 2015, pp. 169-176.

[22] The lengthy thirteenth chapter of his son's biography, *SCM DD*, pp. 339-372, is devoted to describing "The Malan Library," documenting its presence especially up to the time of the founding of the Indian Institute in 1896. As will be seen in what follows, this is only the initial stage of a much more complicated story.

[23] Described in appropriate detail in *SCM DD*, p. 369. The huge manuscript was sent along with a letter from Bournemouth, where SCM and his wife had retired, dated 8 October 1894.

[24] Having been so intent on finding the manuscript version on which the *ONBP* was reliant, I had not realized at that time how many more manuscripts had been donated by SCM to the Bodleian as well as the Indian Institute over the years. More details about these matters will be forthcoming in what follows.

3. Walking in Reverse with a Mirror to See Behind ...

Once Mirasy and I began to pursue details of SCM's major work on the biblical proverbs and the family archives in Switzerland in 2007, my initial research intention was to seek to understand how his recordings of Ruist ("Confucian") and Daoist proverbial wisdom fit into the wider comparative wisdom project that the *ONBP* constituted. As a consequence, rather than follow the many lines of other possible research that his three-volume collection of proverbial sayings regularly suggested, when I visited the Oriental Division of the Bodleian Libraries in early 2008, the focus of my attention was primarily twofold: first, I hoped to discover the manuscript version of the *ONBP* (ONBP Ms) in order to understand its character and begin to grasp its relationship to the published three-volume work of English renderings of all proverbial sayings that constituted the *ONBP*; secondly, I wanted to find the Chinese texts in the Bodleian that SCM had employed to identify suitable Chinese proverbs and sayings, so that he could subsequently write them down in Chinese into the ONBP Ms. There were many other questions that related to these simple tasks, and some of them had haunted me for some time previously. For example, had SCM actually read his own Chinese texts, or was he relying primarily on secondary sources written by missionary-scholars and others in other languages? Did SCM leave any traces about which manuscripts he had employed? When SCM wrote out the Chinese text – something that also could be doubted – how well did he write the characters? Could he demonstrate that he had truly learned adequate Chinese to do basic research in a wide range of canonical and non-canonical Chinese texts?

All these questions I brought with me to the Oriental Reading Room in Oxford's Bodleian, and it was my good fortune, with the special suggestions made by Dr. Gillian Evison, to resolve many of those questions within the first few days of my research.

First, after learning about my interests in seeking to locate those key texts originally associated with the Malan Library, Dr. Evison pointed out that there was a catalogue within that reading room that contained a large set of cards indicating details about all manuscripts donated to the library.[25] Within that catalogue I was able to identify a significant number of manuscripts donated by SCM, and though they were only given certain call numbers and the dates they were donated, I could make some educated guesses about which ones were possibly related to my two major concerns. I was delighted to discover on the second day that one of the choices I had made was in fact the large ONBP Ms.

As I worked very carefully through that volume without any reference initially to the printed version, I could verify that what was found within that manuscript were writings of quotations in numerous languages, some of the most obvious (to me) being Chinese, Arabic, Tibetan, Sanskrit, and Egyptian hieroglyphics. Most of

---

[25] It is important to note that this information had not been input into the computerized catalogue at the time, and so it was "invisible" to me without her specific reference to that medium-sized wooden card catalogue cabinet.

the time, the Chinese texts were also written in red ink,[26] and it was clear that he was using a brush, and not a pen or pencil. So, what remained to be learned was whether the original texts he cited underneath those handwritten statements in the manuscript could be located in Chinese texts that had belonged originally in his personal library, and subsequently had become part of the Malan Library. All of this made me feel like I was pursuing a task like Perseus: attempting to cut off the heads of a monster by moving backward into a dark cave, viewing things only as reflections on his own hazy shield. In my case, the mirror was the initial historical cues obtained from the published *ONBP*, but now I was trying to guess on the basis of the titles of Chinese texts (recorded in non-standard transcriptions) and their dates of publications whether they were the actual tomes that held the exact passages that had captured SCM's interest perhaps as much as 150 years earlier. The guesswork involved was daunting, but due to other special cues, including the all-important book plates attached to all the volumes in the original Malan Library, it was possible to make some initial progress in all these realms during that first visit.

After some days of sending as many requests as I could related to possible Chinese texts, the key librarian involved with Chinese and Japanese documents, David Helliwell, sought me out in the Oriental Reading Room and found out more about what exactly it was that I was seeking to discover. Ultimately, and much to my own personal delight, he led me down into the stacks themselves, to point out the exact place where he recalled he had placed many Chinese tracts and other items that had originally belonged to the Malan Library. He gave me the privilege to review all those texts and find those that were relevant to my research, so that I could then request them without further delays caused by all that guesswork. As a result, I could review the Chinese texts more systematically and effectively. What I discovered at that time was this: there were many items among the Chinese texts in the Malan Library that were in fact Christian writings in Chinese, and not just the indigenous Chinese texts that I was searching for. Of course, all of this was another important but unexpected hint related to the content of the Malan Library.

Even though my focus was on finding and reviewing the Chinese texts referred to primarily in the footnotes (and sometimes in the main body) of the published *ONBP*, I simultaneously continued to make requests related to seeing more of the donated manuscripts associated with Malan's gifts to the Indian Institute and the Bodleian Library of his day. As I did so and considered all that I had also seen visually in the massive collection of proverbial literature he had written out in the ONBP Ms, I could not help but be dazzled by the multi-lingual talents of this Swiss hyperpolyglot. There was so much more to do! Stubbornly, I kept my focus on the Chinese source texts and was able ultimately to publish records of what I had

---

[26] Most entries in the foreign language versions of texts that SCM wrote into that massive volume were presented in black ink. Sometimes even the Chinese texts were also written in black ink, as can be seen in the four colored images of pages from that octavo-sized manuscript presented in Chapter 4 and found at the end of Chapter 13 of this volume.

discovered and how I evaluated them in two articles, one in a Chinese version and the other in the original English.[27]

Having learned that the Bodleian Libraries had undergone a major computerization process starting in 2011, I began seeking traces within the data input by computer technicians. Some items were designated in the online database as having been donated by SCM or having belonged to the Malan Library. When I arranged to see copies of these documents, I began to realize that somewhere within the manuscripts or documents that had originally been part of that unusual but ill-fated library there was a book plate attached to each of them, serving as a visual verification of this fact. What this suggested is that if someone could visit the stacks and check each relevant item, or scan through a set of possible items, one might be able to relocate more of those kinds of tomes. Nevertheless, not being a member of the Bodleian Libraries' staff, this very practical method would not be possible under any normal circumstances. In addition, it still was and is the case that many of those items that did belong originally to the Malan Library were not indicated as having that connection within the online databases now regularly employed in the Bodleian Libraries.

During and after the international conference held at Wadham College in Oxford in August 2012, another set of discoveries related to the content of the Malan Library were made. During our conference we were introduced to four boxes related to what was called "the catalogue" of the Malan Library. Due to Dr. Gillian Evison's endurance in sifting through materials that had been moved during the process of the computerization, she rediscovered these materials and allowed us to look at them in depth. In one of four boxes were two soft covered volumes given the title, "The Malan Library Book List";[28] in the other three boxes were handwritten cards constituting another catalogue.[29] A careful analysis of the handwritten book lists within the two volumes revealed that they identified just over 1,000 titles involving more than 1,300 texts.[30] Within the boxes we could estimate that there were about 1,800 titles mentioned, a good number of them bearing numbers in red pencil that aligned with numbers in the book list. By this means, then, the total sum of the volumes "relocated" through these incomplete library records came at most to about one half of the total number of volumes associated with the original Malan

---

[27] See Pfister 2011 and 2012.

[28] This box has been given the call number "MS.Ind.Inst.Misc.85."

[29] These boxes were given three separate call numbers, all with the same initial title, but differing in the sequence of the numbers. The first was "MS.Ind.Inst.Misc.82" and the last "MS.Ind.Inst.Misc.84," with the middle containing the number "83" at the end.

[30] On the basis of information Mirasy and I retrieved from the two volumes of "The Malan Library Book List" in August 2012, all of which Ms. Yip Wing-yan put into a word file for our more convenient use by the middle of 2014, we could identify 1,042 titles (some which were multiple copies and so may have been counted more than once) that included 1,370 tomes (a number made slightly higher due to some unwarranted repetitions in the counting process).

Library.³¹ Fortunately, my own previous research had already identified a good number of other texts, particularly among Chinese works containing primarily Ruist and Daoist scriptures and teachings.³² This all was enough to motivate a further pursuit of "the invisible library."

All this being extremely exciting in the thought that there would be so much more to discover, a careful review of the summary of the content of the Malan Library that SCM had prepared in August 1884 (see Appendix I) requires us to offer several critical comments regarding the value of those discoveries. Ultimately, this also moves us forward to offer further considerations related to the actual content of the Malan Library as it was when it went to Oxford in 1885. Most obviously, in writing up this "abstract" of his personal library, the elderly Broadwindsor vicar had emphasized collections he possessed of Greek and Latin classics, the church fathers, ecclesiastical histories, and "old" and "modern divinity," all of which were notably missing from the Malan Library Book List that Dr. Evison had rediscovered in 2012. In and of themselves, the number of tomes related to these various collections may well sum up to as much as a thousand volumes.³³

Nevertheless, SCM also mentioned first of all in his summary statement having "Bibles in several languages." In fact, there are a sizable number of Bibles and portions of Bibles in some "Semitic" and in many "Asiatic" languages that are found in what used to be his personal library. Within the Malan Library Book List itself,³⁴ there are five whole Bibles: two in "Singalese" or "Cinhalese," and one each in Orissa, Burmese, and Arabic languages. In addition, there are complete renderings of the "Old Testament" in "Bengalee," Persian, and the standard Hebrew, with special emphasis given to collecting different versions of the Psalms or

---

[31] According to SCM himself, the total number of texts he donated to the Indian Institute in January 1885 were just over 4,000 items, but there had been other manuscripts donated to the Bodleian Library previously as well, so that the total number of those texts associated with his private library in Broadwindsor was probably somewhere close to 4100 texts. In *SCM DD*, p. 353, the bibliophile himself claimed there were 4,017 volumes (in a letter to Monier Williams dated 11 December 1884 from Broadwindsor).

[32] Consult Pfister 2012.

[33] Because my own research has focused on the Chinese and Asian languages that SCM sought to explore for their proverbial wisdom, I have not begun to explore the many volumes of this portion of the Malan Library that should be identifiable from different portions within the current Bodleian Libraries.

[34] All of the following calculations have been carefully documented on the basis of the word document created by Ms. Yip Wing-yan after digital images of The Malan Library Book List were taken by Mirasy Pfister, with the consent of Dr. Gillian Evison.

Psalter,[35] and the biblical book of Proverbs.[36] While this emphasis indicates something about SCM's life-long interest in Bible translations and the study of the biblical book of Proverbs, what is found within this list related to versions of the New Testament is even more expansive. There are whole New Testaments in 23 languages, there being four version in Sinhalese (also "Singalese"), and three in Burmese, Persian, and Tamil. Pairs of New Testament volumes appear in "Gujarate," Punjabi, and Telugu, with one being a "polyglot," but without the details about the specific languages in which the text is rendered. Each one of these tomes is named under a separate title in the book list.[37]

The statistics developed from this short list reveal something very unusual about the portion of the Malan Library that is recorded within the Malan Library Book List. There are 25 titles related to Old Testament texts mentioned above, and 35 titles in 23 languages related to full New Testament renderings. Another 80 titles consist of portions of the Bible rendered into other languages. In addition to all this, there are six translations – most, if not all, by foreign missionaries – of John Bunyan's *Pilgrim's Progress*, and nine version of both the Anglican *Book of Common Prayer* and some form of Christian catechism, each prepared in six different languages. When one adds together all the other Christian tracts, published sermons, devotionals, and other Christian materials in translation to what has already been described, the list amounts to just over 200 titles. That is to say that, based on the content of the Malan Library Book List, one fifth of all the works found within it were renderings of Christian materials in a host of languages, most of them being associated with the Indian subcontinent. At the very least, this indicates the extent

---

[35] There are ten versions of the Psalms within this list, two of them with multiple editions. These include five versions of the Psalms in Tamil, one of the important southern Indian languages with a rich literary tradition, and three in Arabic (also with a similarly impressive literary tradition that SCM explored in great depth). In addition, there are eight other versions presented here in the alphabetical order of their languages as spelled by those who prepared the list: Bengali, Burmese, Malayalim, Maltese, Oriya (or Orissa), a Russian/Hebrew diaglot version, and two others in Sanskrit and Telugu. As is manifest here, then, five of the eight versions listed come from Indian subcontinent languages, and then in addition we have the other five versions from Tamil, a language found in both southern India and in Sri Lanka. So, the focus of the cataloguers was made obvious by recording these details.

[36] Of course, this was of particular value for SCM as he considered shared wisdom from various linguistic corridors and explored how the biblical Proverbs were consequently put into the media of these "Eastern" languages. Besides a recently retranslated English version of the Proverbs he had found in 1871, there were versions in six other languages: two in Tamil and Burmese, and one each in Arabic, Persian, Sanskrit and Telugu.

[37] In addition, there are full New Testaments in fifteen other languages, the most exotic being a Pali version written in Burmese script, and a version produced by early Baptist missionaries to the Karen tribe, hill people living in Burmese mountains, with the specific clarification that it was prepared in the Sgan dialect of the Karen language. The remaining versions are only found once within the book list. They included renderings in Arabic, Bengali, Canarese, Hindustani (or what would now be referred to as Urdu), Kashmiri, Maltese, Marathi, Movlan, Nepali, Peguan, Pushtu (or Afghan), Sanskrit, and Vikanra. Once again, it is notable that the vast majority of these remaining versions found in the Malan Library Book List were related to people groups or language groups located in the Indian subcontinent.

of the foreign missionary translation literature out of which the Malan Library was created, and by which, at least in part, SCM began to learn about many languages. It also indicates the obvious limitations of this list, at least as a means of reflecting the nature of the whole of the Malan Library. That is because, as I have already indicated in an earlier chapter,[38] the largest amounts of quotations found in *ONBP* were not from sources in a language from the Indian subcontinent, but from Chinese sources. In addition, though there were indigenous sources in Bengali, Sanskrit, Tamil, and Telugu that SCM quoted from in that massive work, among the most prominent linguistic corridors represented in that three-volume set were those from Arabic, Egyptian, Georgian, Greek, Italian, Japanese, Mongolian, Osmanli (the standard Arabic language of the Ottoman empire), and the unusual contributions from Tibetan sources.[39] All this is to say that the Malan Library Book List reveals details about only some of the books that SCM had collected within his personal library, but very notably they do not reveal the names or details of the tomes he used most often within his last and most laboriously produced work, *ONBP*.[40]

All this is quite disappointing and frustrating, when we consider this from the angle of an effort to offer some sort of reconstruction of the content of the Malan Library as it was in the year of its transfer to Oxford in 1885. The mirror I had been using as I "walked backward" into this historical cave was even less clear than I had previously assumed.

Still, there is more to consider. Allow me here to also note that the vicar of Broadwindsor, a person who normally required high standards of work for himself and others, obviously prepared this list in a relatively random manner. For example, there is no alphabetical ordering of any of the lists of Semitic, Asiatic, and African languages, something that makes these lists rather unwieldy, even though they are basically representative and not at all overstated in their details. On the contrary, and much more significantly for the sake of understanding the actual content of the Malan Library, there is an unusual number of details found in the Malan Library Book List that are missing in the Anglican vicar's overview. Here the specifics reveal much regarding the whole matter.

---

[38] See the details in Chapter 5, part 4, starting at p. 89.

[39] The sources cited in Tibetan are highlighted here because of SCM's early relationship made with the famous Hungarian Tibetologist, Alexander Csoma de Kőrös, which is elaborated in more detail within Chapter 11.

[40] A caveat should be immediately added to this judgment. This is not to say that "The Malan Library Book List" has no inherent value. Quite to the contrary, it has provided the most thorough documentation related to one major part of the original Malan Library domiciled in the previous Indian Institute at Oxford University as it was from 1896 till 1965. Nothing like this kind of detail had been previously known, for there had been no printed catalogue, and neither the book lists or the handwritten card catalogue relocated by Dr. Gillian Evison has been known before 2012. What I am offering here, then, are critical assessments about the content of the list in relationship to recent scholarship related to other aspects of the Malan Library that are not represented in either the book list or those texts catalogued in the three card file boxes previously related to the Malan Library.

For example, in his list of grammars, dictionaries and literature in "European" languages, SCM did not mention either Latin or Greek, though he had previously highlighted the fact that he had a large collection of classical works in both languages. In fact, within the book list there are 81 titles that reveal that the main working language used in those volumes is Latin, including a good number of grammars and dictionaries related to other languages.

In addition, while SCM did indicate his interest in "dialects" of three major European languages (English, French and Italian), he did in fact also have works within his library that were studies of dialectical differences in various other linguistic settings, including North African, Dravidian, and northern Burmese (among the Karen) linguistic contexts. In terms of the collection of proverbs from different languages, there is also mentioned in the book list those from the "Braj Bha'sha," Malabar, and Cittagong Hill people that are not mentioned in his 1884 summary.[41]

In still another category, among the grammars created for various languages – mostly written in the European languages of English, French, German or Latin, but some occasionally written in their indigenous languages, and amounting to nearly 120 titles – there are about a dozen languages not mentioned in Malan's 1884 summary.[42] These include languages that I was able to identify by various means – Assyrian, Kurdish, Maltese, Pahlevi or Pehlevi, Phonecian, Pushtu[n], and Zend – and those that I have never heard about previously, and so I cannot easily recognize them without pursuing quite a bit of further research – including Old Bactrian, Brāhūī, Braj Bhâkhâ, Huzuāresh, Sindhi and Tulu.

Therefore, it was a further surprise – and actually quite shocking for me – to discover that there were more than twenty Asiatic languages represented in the works found in the book list that are not mentioned in summary of 1884. It underscores for me the statement made by his son, the biographer ANM, that SCM had started to suffer from certain diseases in the Fall of 1883, and that the emotional turmoil he felt in sending away his personal library was complicated and profound.[43] Somehow, it would seem, that rather disorderly summary of his personal library symbolizes his sense of "dis-ease," and so has required me to approach the process of attempting any reconstruction of the Malan Library with a new respect for the unanticipated discoveries that are to be made.

---

[41] The first of these languages I take to be what is elsewhere in the list more commonly referred to as the "Braj Bhâkhâ" language; the last literary group is found in what is now located in contemporary Bangladesh.

[42] I am somewhat cautious here, because sometimes the same language medium is referred to by different names and spelling in SCM's works as well as in the works of others who produced them, and so there are a few ambiguities that suggest to me that I should not be as precise in numbering them as I would prefer to be. For example, I have recognized through exploring things a bit more that "Thai" can also be referred to as "Siamese"; much less clear to me is the relationship between "Sikh" language and what is called "Sindhi."

[43] Documentation of those emotional responses are indicated in *SCM DD*, pp. 339-341.

4. Digging up Treasures Long Forgotten

Discovering in January 2008 the list of donations in the Oriental Room of the Bodleian Libraries, all being recorded on four cards within a designated cabinet including the records of all donations, was a major leap forward in identifying specific items related to the Malan Library. As can be seen even with a quick glance over the content of those cards (see Appendix II), most of those items were specifically designated as having been donated by SCM in either "January 1885" or simply "1885."

Almost assuredly, these items were part of the huge collection transferred from the Broadwindsor vicarage to Oxford in that year. Nevertheless, the four items obviously donated at other times than 1885 – items 1, 3, 10, and 27 according to my own listing of those "documents" in Appendix II – were not to be discounted because of their dates. In fact, the tenth item donated on "2 October 1894" was the ONBP Ms, and so was one of the main goals for advancing my research into the Chinese sources SCM had employed.[44] At least one of the other three documents reveals much about SCM's linguistic efforts, and so I will refer to it in more detail in what follows, even though it did not officially belong to what became "the Malan Library" associated with the Indian Institute in 1885.

Regarding the brief descriptions of these various donated manuscripts offered to "the Bodleian" by SCM, I noted several other matters related to the recordings found on those four cards. First, most of the items are identified according to specific languages, but there is a category abbreviated as "Misc" indicating those items are "miscellaneous," and so most often included materials either in many languages or in languages not known by the cataloguers. As I now know, this was particularly the case for the ONBP Ms (known by its call number as "MS.Ind.Inst.Misc.10"), which included proverbial texts written down by SCM in at least 54 different languages.[45] Following this, it should be noticed that even though I now may speak about these documents being "donated to the Bodleian," most of these items have "Ind.Inst." in their call numbers, indicating that they first belonged to the Indian Institute, and not to the Bodleian. Beyond this, a closer review of the content of the four cards reveals that many of the "documents" that have been given a single number actually involve several items, each given specific call numbers. What this means, in fact, is that there were many more manuscripts donated to the Indian Institute as parts of the Malan Library than there are "documents" listed in those four cards. Here I must add further details and must direct readers once again to the content of Appendix II.

From the angle of the languages and numbers of manuscripts that were donated by SCM during the period from 1885 till his death in 1894, I can make the following summary from a closer reading of the content of the donation lists.

---

[44] This document is described in detail in Chapter 13 of this volume, and so it will not be addressed here except for the sake of clarifying issues in a very brief manner.

[45] For more details about these matters, see Pfister 2012 and Chapter 13 in this volume.

Language of Manuscripts	Number of Manuscripts Donated
Chinese	3
Arabic	2
Burmese	2
Coptic	9
Miscellaneous	9
Pali	1
Panjabi	3
Persian	10
Sanskrit	15
Sinhalese	6
Telugu	2
Turkish	2

If we do not count the "Miscellaneous" category as a single language because it always involves polyglot documents, then I can at least summarize that this list of donated manuscripts includes texts employing at least eleven different languages, most of them being languages originating from South Asian and East Asian cultures. Numerically, they amount to a total of 64 individual manuscripts, not including the two items found at the very beginning and the very end of the lists on these four cards.

Among these donated manuscripts two that are designated as Chinese language texts actually involve other languages as well,[46] and four of those categorized as "miscellaneous" are in fact written either exclusively or primarily in either Ethiopian,[47] Japanese,[48] Mongolian[49] or modern Syriac.[50] In addition, almost all of those

---

[46] These are "MS.Chin.d.6" and "MS.Chin.3.25," the former being a practice book where SCM was beginning to learn how to write both Chinese characters and Korean Hangul phonetic symbols, and the latter constituted by a series of bilingual treatises in both Chinese and Manchurian.

[47] A manuscript received by SCM from "the Rev. Js. Krapp" on August 13, 1875, a document of over 120 pages in length and written in some form of Ethiopian language ("MS.Ind.Inst.Misc.3").

[48] This is "MS.Ind.Inst.Misc.5," a text written in Japanese *kanji* with the phonetic *furigana* for indicating pronunciation of those characters, as well as *hiragana* script associated with indigenous Japanese words and grammar. It is a handwritten manuscript of selected poems.

[49] Obtained from Dr. R. Yuille in 1859, who was apparently living in Glasgow at the time, this large 470 paged work was given the Mongolian title "M ... San Belek." In correspondence between the two men the context of the request and the fact of the manuscript being sent to SCM is confirmed (see in the Bodleian Libraries "MS.Engl.lett c.730, fol. 100-105"). The manuscript itself is mostly written in Mongolian, but there are some rather extensive passages also written in Tibetan, accompanied at various points within the lengthy manuscript by a Chinese numbering that apparently relates to the pages of the texts being employed. The call number for this trilingual manuscript is "MS.Ind.Inst.Misc.13."

[50] A sizable text of nearly 600 pages, it is described as a "Modern Syriac" volume "on repentance, faith, etc." Within the tome there is a signature accompanied with notes explaining that

documents cited under the category of "Coptic" were bilingual texts produced in both Coptic and Arabic. From the angle of codicology, some of the most unusual manuscripts were the Burmese sutras SCM obtained,[51] because they are written on rectangular sections of palm leaves and were originally collated together by strings tying all the texts together in a sequence so that they could be flipped over, one on the top of the other, as one read through the sutras.

It is not only among the donated manuscripts that some remarkable texts belonging to the Malan Library are discovered. Both within the so-called "Malan Library Book List" and the online catalogue one finds a lexicon involving at least seven languages produced by a seventeenth century Cambridge professor of Arabic named Edmund Castell (1606–1685), with a publication date of 1669. It was a massive work written in Latin, and including materials published in Arabic, Aramaic, Ethiopian, Hebrew, Persian, Samaritan Aramaic, and Syriac.[52] Among the 34 titles identified as polyglot works within the Malan Library Book List (including the work just mentioned above), there are 14 works using three languages ("triglot" codices),[53] seven others using four languages,[54] and another seven that employed more than this number of languages and dialects, but oftentimes without indicating them precisely enough to be recorded. As I continued to discover, explore, and record the various codices and works collected by SCM, I could not help but feel rather overwhelmed by the diversity of linguistic media in which he was not only able to float, but also to swim with more or less facility.

Another aspect of the collection that I can at least indicate briefly here is the fact that there were at least 17 titles within "The Malan Library Book List" that involved works published before the year 1700.[55] Notably, most of these works were also

---

SCM obtained this manuscript in "Mosul" in "June 1850." The call number for this work is "MS.Ind.Inst.Misc.2."

[51] Those identified as "MS.Ind.Inst.Burm 6(R), 7(R)."

[52] This *Lexicon Heptaglotton* is found as the second item on the 145th page of "The Malan Library Book List," but the date of publication there is "1679," where the online source cites the date in Latin as "1669." The call number for this work from the online catalogue is cited as being "F c 4 (14)." This work bears a book plate confirming that it belonged to the Malan Library sent to Oxford in 1885 from Broadwindsor.

[53] The trilingual combinations of these works are fascinating, with eight of them using English as one of the three languages, three using French, and one each in German, Hebrew, Italian and Latin. Three of these triglot works contained no European languages at all, but compared materials in languages including Arabic, Burmese, Gujurati, Hindustani (or Urdu), Malayan, Persian, Thai, and Turkish. The number of languages involved in these works that did not include languages originating from the Indian Subcontinent or Western Europe were not insignificant: they included works involving Arabic, Burmese, Malayan, Pehlevi, Persian, Sinhalese, Thai, Tibetan, Turkish and Zend.

[54] Here the representative languages from the Indian Subcontinent included Hindi, Levgnata, Marathi, Prakrit, Sanskrit, and Sindhi. European languages within these works included English, French, German and Latin. Other languages found within these works are Arabic, Ancient Bactrian, Pâzend, Persian, Thai, Turkish, and Zend.

[55] The earliest text was published in 1591 in Rome and was a copy of the New Testament Gospels in both Latin and Arabic (found as the fifth item on page 194 of the list).

quite large, being at least 200 pages in length. Certainly, also among these works there were some unusual tomes. Beyond this more restricted realm of earlier texts, there were more than 160 titles that referred to works that were 300 or more pages in length. In this regard, even though SCM had collected a number of smaller works, including papyri and smaller manuscripts, there were quite a number of works of substantial size also within his personal library.[56] Among the topics of volumes found in his collection, SCM had a large group of histories about various kingdoms, empires, and rulers; in addition, he had obtained a sizeable collection of indigenous poetry,[57] an extensive collection of literary anthologies in more than a dozen languages,[58] as well as more technical studies in archeology, astronomy, geography, linguistics, medicine, philosophy, and religious studies. All of this makes good sense for someone who would want to translate proverbial sayings from foreign languages, because they provide the historical and cultural backgrounds that would help to reveal the meaning of particular words, especially those that were special or technical terms in a foreign language.

What made this even more astounding to me, after already encountering the cornucopia of languages represented in the huge ONBP Ms, was a text completely unexpected by anything I had read about this Genevan-born naturalized British hyperpolyglot. It was the last item mentioned in the list of donations, and since it was recorded there as having been donated very early, on September 19th, 1859, I was inclined to overlook it. Fortunately, my curiosity and desire for seeking to understand as much as I could within the limited time set aside for research in the Bodleian in 2008 overcame my initial hesitations, and they were more than amply rewarded by the aesthetic harvest obtained from viewing the text entitled by SCM as his *Sacra Privata*.[59] Initially referred to within a letter of 1884 by the author of the volume as "the MS. in limbo at the Bodleian," it was only briefly and sometimes incorrectly described in his son's biography.[60] Because it was a creative work published privately by his father, ANM did not include it in the list of the publications,[61] and so

---

[56] Within the list I found 165 titles that fit this description.

[57] Including examples in Afghan, Arabic, Bengali, Hindustani, Persian, Sanskrit, Tamil, and Telugu.

[58] Including Arabic, Assyrian, Bengali, Burmese, Canarese, Dukhnee, Hindi, Hindustani (Urdu), Malayalam, Parsee, Persian, Pali, Pushto, Singalese, Telugu, and Turkish.

[59] *Sacra Privata* was completed in 1853. Its Bodleian call number is "MS.Or.Polygl.f.1," and it appears as the last item in the card catalogue list of donations from SCM (the 27th item listed in Appendix II).

[60] See *SCM DD*, pp. 357-358. The letter by SCM was written to "Mr. Williams" of the Indian Institute, and was dated December 20th, 1884, according to the son on the first page mentioned above. After the brief description, the biographer cites a number of unnamed reviewers of the volume, who speak in glowing phrases about the beauty of the volume and any of the content that they could recognize: "a perfect miracle of magnificent writing," "like the bow of Ulysses, ... I scarcely know who else can be found strong enough [to bend it]."

[61] It should have been listed as being "privately published" in 1853, but this unusual tome was not even mentioned within the list of the 57 publications found in Appendix D. of *SCM DD*, pp. 436-438.

only a person who happened to read the relevant section of the biography would know that it even existed. Created to be a collection of devotional readings in as many languages as he could handle during his 40th year of life, the vicar of Broadwindsor worked hard to create calligraphic images as elegant and as accurately as he could produce them.[62]

So attractive is the relatively small but thick volume,[63] especially when it is first seen with its impressive binding and pair of book clasps, it is hard not to be captivated by the great variety of its beautiful black-and-red ink calligraphic texts. Though they include Christian prayers, biblical psalms, and other passages from selected scriptures in these various languages, each page of almost 590 folio pages is also simultaneously a piece of art. Consequently, I will take a little more effort to portray something of the remarkable character of this artistic achievement, before reflecting once more on what it has to tell us regarding SCM's linguistic endeavors.

The front and back covers are masterpieces of leather workmanship, following a complicated pattern of sacred Islamic geometry SCM had previously seen and copied while visiting the Alhambra in the southern Spanish city of Granada.[64] At the center of this pattern is an eight-pointed (and so sixteen-sided) star, highlighted by a black circular icon at its geometrical heart, with the whole star invisibly crisscrossed[65] by two sets of larger equilateral crosses set at 45 degree angles to each other, but also placed so that their geometrical center is the same as that of the star.[66] This unusually complicated but still symmetrical design is accompanied by

---

[62] An interesting aside related to the creation of this work was made by his son, the biographer, who watched his father practicing these calligraphic images page by page, while teaching Latin to two of his sons. In the process, the younger boy who later became his biographer picked up some of those practice pages that were considered unworthy of being included in the tome, just in order to admire their aesthetic qualities. See *SCM DD*, p. 162.

[63] Based on a very selective group of visual images obtained of this work, each page is about four inches wide and six inches long, so that an opening is only about eight inches in total length. There are 589 folio pages in the whole volume, though the numbering later given to the volume by some librarian missed numbering two pages (between 212-213 and 564-565).

[64] When SCM visited that place before 1853 is not completely clear, but it may have been while he was en route to join an archeological expedition in Syria during 1851. The reference to the "pattern copied [...] from the Alhambra" is found in *SCM DD*, p. 357.

[65] By "invisibly crisscrossed" I intend to describe the fact that the complete lines of the arms of the two crosses "disappear" when they reach the outline of the sixteen-sided star, but reappear on the opposite side, so that one's imagination can connect the geometric lines even though they do not appear in the design.

[66] A pattern very close to this geometrical image, without the additional artistic flairs that are described in the following sentences, is found in Critchlow 2004, p. 171, figure F. The ends of each of the four extensions of the cross are not squared off, but include a slightly levered upward angle, with the point in the middle of each rectangular side of those cruciform figures. What makes SCM's image even more artistically intriguing is that instead of having the crisscrossing equilateral crosses situated so that one has an arm of the cross stretching from the center of the top to the center of the bottom, SCM shifted these overlapping crosses another 22.5 degrees to one side, so that none of the arms of either cross is exactly vertical or horizontal.

two circles of golden points of light, the inner circle of eight placed in the center of the eight triangles created by the crisscrossing arms of the two crosses very nearby the edges of the central star, and the second set of larger golden dots appearing at the edge of unclosed triangular spaces in between the ends of the crosses. These two sets of eight golden lights are aligned with each other so that the top and bottom dots are set upon a vertical line, and the middle dots extended to the right or left are set upon a horizontal line of the cover's design.[67]

All the pages included in this elegant volume possess gilded edges, the longest side being further decorated so that each gilded edge fits into a pattern of parallel columns slanted at 45 degrees; in addition, a symmetrical wave pattern is found stamped within each column, garnished with small circles on opposite sides of the wave and regularly appearing along the whole slanted decoration. Since the width of the volume was something just over three inches, there were at least nine parallel columns running diagonally across the open side of the volume, producing a moving golden wave effect that dazzles the observer.

On the relatively thick spine made of the same morocco leather found on the front and back covers, there are six big parallel rows in which a series of black diamond quadrangles were connected from side to side, surrounded by a thin black boundary, so that it creates automatically half diamonds in between each of the connected diamonds, one above and one below. Shiny golden points of light, exactly the same size as those smaller dots found in the inner circle around the eight-pointed star, sit in both the center of the full diamonds and near the top and bottom of the half diamonds in each row. Only the second row is left without this design, so that the title appears in large capital letters and gold print,[68] and surrounded once again by a thin and clear black rectangular figure that fits precisely into the dimensions of that row. Below the sixth row is printed in smaller golden capital letters the name of the author and the date in Latin numerals.[69] The pair of metal book clasps that hook into metal hooks attached to the back side of the volume contain statements in Japanese *katakana*.[70]

The content of this collection of "private readings" of "sacred texts" is initiated with a flourish of forty introductory pages of calligraphic art, and then begins in earnest with the first of thirty-one days of devotional readings. Most of the daily readings extend to about fifteen to twenty folio pages in length,[71] and the vast

---

[67] Though more details would need to be added to indicate other aspects of the design, this description may at least indicate to some degree the geometrical elegance of the cover of this tome.

[68] That is, "SACRA PRIVATA." followed also by a period, as seen here.

[69] That is, "Rev. S. C. Malan. MDCCCIII."

[70] ANM claims the clasps are made of silver and that they bore "Tatar inscriptions"; the clasps may be of some form of tempered silver, but the characters found on the clasps are definitely Japanese *katakana*, that is, characters normally employed to portray the sounds of foreign words. The right clasp contains thirteen phonetic characters, and the left, ten. So far I have not been able to decipher their meaning. Consult *SCM DD*, p. 357.

[71] A few of the readings, numbered according to their day in an ideal 31-day month, are no more than ten folio pages in length, such as found in the texts prepared for the first three days

majority involve texts written in several different language media and employing different calligraphic styles.[72] At various points in these texts he will vary the use of red and black ink, sometimes with the simple purpose of highlighting names of God within the biblical addresses or references to specific passages (by putting them in red ink in the midst of prose passages calligraphed in black ink). Other times he varies the color of the ink according to the number of lines written horizontally across the page. When writing in Chinese, as occurs most obviously in the readings for day 29, there are texts primarily read from the top to the bottom, in a classical style, but even here he adds some variety that is very innovative and would be confusing for those who do not know the texts well.[73] In several places, prayers are written so that a cruciform figure appears on the page in red ink, flanked by the rest of the text written in black ink. Truly this is a cornucopia of calligraphic art!

The final devotional reading for the 31st day is the most extensive of all the readings, ordered according to the letters of the Hebrew alphabet, and so including 22 sections with what are probably 22 different languages.[74] After further inspection

---

of devotionals as well as the readings for the sixth and seventh day. All the rest extend well beyond this length, sometimes stretching well beyond twenty folio pages in length. For the shortest readings see *Sacra Privata*, 43 recto – 71 verso (for the first three days together) and 111 recto – 129 verso (for the sixth and seven days' readings).

[72] Though it is not always possible to identify the nature of the languages being written, the shift in calligraphy can be followed rather easily, and many times the notation and number of a particular psalm or a passage of scripture from a specific book in the Bible can be identified. Those daily devotionals that involve more than ten changes of this sort include the readings for day 5, day 12, day 24, day 28, and the last two days, 30 and 31, with the special case of the last day to be described in what follows. Among the ten languages appearing on day 5 are texts in Mongolian, Egyptian hieroglyphics, Uncial Greeks, a Germanic language, and an ancient form of Spanish; they include biblical texts from Matthew 16: 24, Luke 1: 46, and 1 Thessalonians 5: 15. Find these and the other more lengthy devotional readings with these numerous linguistic and calligraphic changes in *Sacra Privata*, 87 recto – 110 verso (day 5), 190 recto – 208 verso (day 12), 415 recto – 433 verso (day 24), 483 recto – 508 verso (day 28), and 530 recto to 580 recto (days 30 and 31).

[73] Because I could read the Chinese and follow the *katakana* (phonetic Japanese) texts in the readings for day 29, I found SCM presented the Apostles' Creed in a very unusual fashion. Each page involved five lines of nine characters each, but written in an order that is repeated for many pages in both Chinese and *katakana* in this section. All the characters on the top, bottom, right and left sides are printed in red ink, while the rest within this red rectangular figure are written with black ink. One starts by reading the first line on the left from top to bottom, and then returns to the top, but continues reading the letters from left to right on the top row, followed by reading the letters from top to bottom in the fifth row on the far right. Finally, one reads the last four characters in the bottom row from right to left, but not including the last character in the first line, which had already been read. Subsequently, one goes to the second character in the second line on the left side of the page, reading it to the eighth character in that line, and then moving to the second character in the third line from the left. In this way one reads to the eighth character in the fourth line, and then proceeds to the next page, starting the whole procedure over once again. The whole text presenting the Apostles' Creed here is found in *Sacra Privata*, 511 recto – 519 verso.

[74] Those I can either recognize or make an educated guess about their nature (but not in the order of their appearance) include Arabic, Armenian, Burmese, Chinese, Coptic, Classical

of the text was made, I realized that the content of this 31st day of devotional literature was the translation of each of the 22 strophes of Psalm 119 in those 22 different languages.[75] In a colophon placed at the end of this unusual volume, SCM himself wrote that he had spent "252 hours" in preparing this manuscript.[76] A very close estimate of the number of languages involved has been provided by his son, A. N. Malan: he estimated that it involves "more than eighty languages, dialects, and scripts."[77] At the very least, then, with all the aesthetic qualities set aside, this volume that does not technically belong to "The Malan Library" confirms that already by the time he was forty years of age, SCM was able to write and read in something like eighty different languages.[78]

A similarly rich and complex story about one of the major treasures of the former Malan Library, the ONBP Ms, is developed in the following chapter in this volume, and so I will not provide any further details about that massive work here.[79]

One other discovery that is worth clarifying, at least in a relatively brief manner, is the fact that among the many treasures included in the former Malan Library, there is found very little evidence to account for the more than thirty Tibetan works that were given to the young SCM by a Hungarian scholar named Csoma de Kőrös while he was teaching in Bishop's College in Calcutta. It is a historic gift of remarkable value, and so it is worthwhile to ask why it was that, in the end, the Csoma Tibetan Collection was not part of the Malan Library.[80]

Part of the answer to this question relates to the fact that it was most likely the case that many of these texts did not contain the kind of proverbial expressions that the Anglican vicar of Broadwindsor was searching for. Historically speaking, it is

---

Ethiopian, Georgian, Japanese *katakana*, Manchurian, Mongolian, Pali, Sanskrit, Tamil, and Tibetan.

[75] This realization came about because, as I reread the Chinese section, I finally comprehended that SCM had included written numbers for each verse, and so realized that this involved the length and form of the Hebrew acrostic poem that is Psalm 119.

[76] The colophon is found on *Sacra Privata*, 583 recto. It states there (without the breaks of the lines in which it was written) that SCM "began this M[anuscript] on the 2nd of August 1851 and finished it on the 22nd of March 1853. The time spent in writing it was altogether 252 hours." It is dated "July 12, MDCCCLIII" (July 12, 1853), and signed "S. C. Malan, Vicar of Broadwindsor, Dorset."

[77] Quoted from *SCM DD*, p. 357. One can add that in a later work where SCM challenged the dropping of the famous last sentence of "the Lord's Prayer" in the Revised English version, he illustrated the fact that Christians from all over the globe had included that last sentence within their recitations of that prayer and documented it by publishing the prayer in 71 languages. Consult *SCRR*. The context of his argument and the list of all of those languages is provided in *SCM DD*, pp. 321-322.

[78] What remains an interesting mystery and involves a quite different story, is the inquiry into why, after only using this devotional work for just over five years, SCM chose to donate it to the "limbo" of the Bodleian Library. Though I have my own suspicions about the motivations that had moved him at that critical moment, I will not address the issue here.

[79] For those interested, please read Chapter 13.

[80] An extensive account of the "Csoma Bequest" is presented in Chapter 11 in this volume.

clear that SCM was quite aware of what he was doing when he sent away those Tibetan works. Indeed, nine months before sending off the vast majority of his personal library to the Indian Institute in Oxford to form "the Malan Library," SCM wrote to a Hungarian friend, a former military surgeon in the British army and Protestant believer, Theodore Duka (1825–1908),[81] asking about whether "some thirty volumes" of Tibetan works "would prove acceptable to the University" in Budapest. Duka quickly agreed to take the large set of Tibetan Buddhist texts to the Hungarian Academy of Sciences, where it has remained to this day.[82]

In sum, then, what I have sought to do in this section is to indicate something of the unusual character and value of the former Malan Library. Currently, that unusual library is now dispersed within the Bodleian Libraries, and so is effectively "invisible." Nevertheless, what has been done here is meant to initiate a process that may lead to it becoming visible once more, because of its immense historical value both in-and-of-itself, and in relationship to the man known as the "greatest Orientalist in 19th century Britain."

In the following section I will present more historical and bibliographic details about how SCM managed to collect such an unusual set of codices, manuscripts, and other forms of texts, and what brought about the situation in Oxford University's administrative history that led to the dispersion of this remarkable collection within the Bodleian Libraries' various collections.

5. The Construction and De-construction of the Malan Library, 1885–1965

From the details included in the previous section it is not hard to imagine why one of SCM's teachers who taught him Syriac claimed, after observing how quickly the young Swiss student was able to learn that particular language, "God must have made his brain of a brick from the Tower of Babel!"[83] Yet what has been seen above already indicates that his thirst for learning languages was continually fuelled by his efforts to collect new and even exotic manuscripts, writings, publications and studies. So it is claimed that he even said of himself, "I lived in my books."[84] Citing

---

[81] Though Stein mentions the fact that Duka provided a "depository of most of the still extant letters, books and other relics connected with Csoma," he did not apparently know about the connection between Csoma and SCM. See Stein 1914, p. 30.

[82] Orosz claims that the Hungarian Academy of Sciences received the "Csoma Bequest" in 1887, but there is clear historical documentation that it arrived there in the Fall of 1884. In a letter to "Dr. Duka" from "S. C. Malan" dated October 27th, 1884, the latter thanked Duka not only for the "pamphlet" related to Csoma, but also that the "gift" of those Tibetan works "has given pleasure to you and your friends." See *SCM DD*, p. 344, and the contrasting claims in Orosz 2008, p. ix. In the same place Orosz suggests that Csoma may have given those works to SCM in 1842, but SCM himself claims they were given to him by Csoma in 1839. See *SCM DD*, p. 342.

[83] The exclamation mark has been added for the proper effect here and does not appear in the original. Quoted otherwise from *SCM DD*, p. 115.

[84] Both this quotation and the subsequent Latin sentence appears in *SCM DD*, p. 281. The Latin quotation is cited as the precedent from which the motto for a long-lasting grammar school in

statement from Seneca, his biographer added that SCM would agree with the sentiment expressed by that Roman Stoic, "Vita sine literis mors est" ("Life without letters [or less literally and more conceptually, 'learning'] is death").

Fig. 18: Entrance door to Malan Library, Indian Institute, Oxford. BB66/00364. Reprinted with permission of the Historic England Archive

So here I would like to explore how SCM managed to amass such an unusual library[85] before he determined to commit it into the care of the Indian Institute of Oxford University in 1885. Subsequently, it survived as a distinct library collection in its new home for eighty years, and then, due to other interests that emerged during the post-WWII environment of Oxford University, the original plan that had involved the Malan Library's independent existence was abandoned for the sake of

---

the United Kingdom was created. It claims to come from the 82nd letter of Seneca the Younger, in the collection of *Epistolae morales ad Lucilium*. This claim was found in https://en.wikipedia.org/wiki/Derby_School#School_motto (accessed 1 February 2021).

[85] A brief description of the character of the library as it appeared in the vicarage in Broadwindsor is colorfully presented in *SCM DD*, pp. 250-251.

purposes that will be briefly revealed here in what follows, referring to that process as its "de-construction."

Being an avid bibliophile and as a vicar receiving an annual support that was more than twice what some notable professors received as their annual salary,[86] SCM was able to bring together a huge range of works from many places, some being locations where he had never personally travelled. Of course, and this should be added in order to be fair to the man, this salary was only offered to him after he obtained the vicarage in 1845, when he was 33 years old, and had lost one wife due to illness after they had served in Calcutta at Bishop's College for the period between May 1838 and January 1840, when he was only in his late twenties.[87] Subsequently, SCM travelled further for both reasons of health and spiritual renewal, and then returned to work in Anglican churches in England, starting in the Fall of 1842. Only three years later was he offered the economic security and social status of a British vicar in the national church, a position he maintained for forty years until his retirement from Broadwindsor in 1885. Though I can demonstrate that some of his manuscripts and codices were purchased before 1845, possibly due to the fact that he had also received two scholarships at Oxford for his achievements in Sanskrit and Hebrew,[88] the vast majority of them came into his possession after he had settled into his life as the vicar of Broadwindsor.[89] Whether from the angle of his achievements in Oxford as an undergraduate student, his work as an Anglican missionary in Calcutta, or his subsequent positions as a curate and ultimately a vicar in the Anglican church, SCM was enabled to fulfil his bibliophilic desires because of his connections with the British national church during the period when the British empire was extended across much of the northern hemisphere, and his own position allowed him special privileges with national and international institutions

---

[86] It is reported that the Professor of Chinese language and literature in Corpus Christi College, James Legge, received an annual salary of between 200 to 300 pounds sterling. See Girardot 2002, p. 158. Based on records found in *Crockford's Clerical Directory* of 1874, p. 467, the "living" received by the Broadwindsor vicar was a "tithe commuted at" 750 pounds sterling, apparently something like a "gross income." The net income was placed at 400 pounds sterling, along with the vicarage and the land attached to it. Obviously, this gave him reasons to not take up offers even at Oxford to serve as a professor in Hebrew or in a position as a researcher or reader in Arabic. Consult *SCM DD*, p. 281.

[87] For details, see Chapter 2 in this volume. Solomon and Mary Malan arrived in Calcutta in May 1838, but had to leave due to sickness in May 1839. Very unfortunately, Mary succumbed to diseases after her return to England on April 5, 1840. Find details of these matters in *SCM DD*, pp. 52-55 and 64-67.

[88] Announcement of the news that he had won the Boden Sanscrit Scholarship came near the end of February 1834, while the Boden and Pusey and Ellerton Hebrew Scholarship was added to his achievements in 1837, the last year of his studies in Oxford. Consult *SCM DD*, pp. 34 and 37.

[89] This could be done by simply citing the year of publication of many of the titles found in "The Malan Library Book List." My general impression is that more than half of all the titles in that list were published, if they came in a published form, sometime after 1840. Of course, he could have purchased volumes published earlier than this year at a later time as well, but the general impression is adequate to underscore the point I am making here.

of Christian religious work, tertiary level education, and political connections within that empire. Also knowing that, according to his son and biographer, his father had "lavish interests" and his "tastes were princely,"[90] it is not hard to imagine that SCM willingly spent what was needed to add to his personal library, whether done during his personal travels or by means of the extensive network he developed through correspondence.

As I have already pointed out above, the 1884 summary of the content of SCM's library written by the bibliophile himself includes "a collection of Greek and Latin Classics," the series of the "fathers of the church," volumes on "ecclesiastical history," "old divinity (in Latin)" and "modern divinity (in English)," including studies about all these works.[91] Notably, all of these tomes would normally be accessible from publishers within Great Britain and Western Europe for the scholarly reader. Because they were technical works regularly involving at least bilingual texts, they were generally quite expensive, but would be accessible and relatively easy to purchase by normal correspondence and logistical provisions made by means of the national post office (and later also by some international mailing institutions). When one reviews the locations of the publishers documented in the details related to the titles of the works cited in "The Malan Library Book List," it should be underscored that 231 of those titles, or just over one fifth of the total number of works on that list, were publications produced in either London or Paris.[92] Another 169 titles were published in cities found within either Great Britain or continental Western European countries.[93] When these are added to the number of tomes related to the other fields of study mentioned above (almost none from those realms appearing in that book list), the number of published works that might have been relatively easy to obtain from British or nearby European publishers may have amounted to as many as one third of all the works found in SCM's personal library.[94] This suggests that the vast majority of works he purchased or obtained came from publishers and institutions that would not have been necessarily easy for him to access, but in this regard, we should consider other relevant matters as well.

---

[90] Quoted from *SCM DD*, p. 171.

[91] Here again I repeat that this may well have constituted as much as a thousand titles in SCM's personal library.

[92] According to my records after careful review of the book list, there were 158 titles published in London, and 73 published in Paris. Here I can also underscore the point: those titles published in London were the largest number published from a single location within that book list.

[93] Here I am only including those that included publications of more than ten titles from one location. According to my records and ranked from the relatively more to the relatively less number of volumes (the number after the name indicating the volumes obtained from that location), these involved publishers from nine other cities or locations: Leipzig (42), Malta (23), Berlin (18), Vienna (17), Hertford (16), Leyden (15), Bonn (13), Oxford (13), and Göttingen (12).

[94] That is, something like 1,400 titles.

For example, SCM spent a significant amount of time travelling widely throughout Western and Eastern Europe,[95] a good number of places in India and Arabic cultural settings,[96] while also spending significant amounts of time in South Africa[97] as well as Mediterranean locations.[98] Later during his vicarate he obtained permission also to take longer trips to visit sites within the Middle East and Central Asian contexts, including visits to Armenia, Georgia, and Russian lands.[99] It is not hard to imagine that during these travels he also brought along funds, or made arrangements, to have publications, manuscripts, and other artifacts purchased and shipped back to the Broadwindsor vicarage.

As a consequence, then, we should not be much surprised that there are volumes and collections purchased not only from places in Great Britain,[100] but also from

---

[95] He visited his parents in Geneva at least twice, once in 1837 before heading to India, and once again in 1864 as his father was dying. It is easy to imagine that he would have passed through various major cities along the way, especially during the latter period, and be on the lookout for important books. At one point during the Autumn of 1847, he also took off ten weeks to visit sites in Spain, including the Alhambra. These details are based on records found in *SCM DD*, pp. 43, 152-153 and 231-232.

[96] Not only did he teach in what was then called Calcutta from 1838 to 1839, but he travelled around the immediate area for the sake of his health, and before he left never to return to India in early 1840, he made a missionary tour of other places within central and south-eastern India. On the way back to the Mediterranean Sea he also visited sites in Ceylon (now Sri Lanka), the Arabian Peninsula including Mecca, and Egypt along the Nile to see the pyramids and other ancient sites. Consult *SCM DD*, pp. 54-64.

[97] In Cape Town with members of the Malan clan there in 1839, while recovering his health, he spent six months. Documented in *SCM DD*, pp. 55-56.

[98] Among his favorite spots were Malta and "the Holy Land," both of which he visited more than once. The first time he visited Israel and the surrounding areas was in the Spring of 1842, but he returned to visit other parts of that area during a longer trip that included visits to the Summer Palace of the Assyrian king, Sennacharib. His sketches and water-color images of those places were among his most prized creations, a good number of the sketches being later employed to accompany a republication of the Christian Scriptures in the late 1860s. His sketches of the Assyrian palace have remained exemplary images that are still put on display by the British Museum when they focus on that realm of the Middle East. For details of the earlier trip, consult *SCM DD*, pp. 72-93, and for the later trip lasting from July 1849 to July 1850, see *ibid.*, pp. 154-161.

[99] The former trip is mentioned in the previous footnote. The latter took place over a period of four months, lasting from April to July 1872, and took him by way of Budapest through the Caucasus (including Crimea, Sebastopol, and across the Black Sea to see Mt. Ararat), and ultimately through the Russian empire along the Volga River, in order to reach Moscow and St. Petersburg. See the account of this trip in *SCM DD*, pp. 273-278.

[100] Including volumes published in Cambridge, Edinburgh, Hertford, Leeds, London, Oxford, and Plymouth.

Denmark,[101] France,[102] Germany,[103] and Holland,[104] as well as those from Italy,[105] Malta,[106] Poland,[107] Spain[108] and Sweden,[109] though we might raise our eyebrows at those obtained from Eastern Europe,[110] Russia,[111] and the Ottoman empire.[112] Truly more unusual are the many places in India from which codices and manuscripts were obtained,[113] as well as those in Burma[114] (now Myanmar), Ceylon[115] (now Sri Lanka), China, Japan, and Siam[116] (now Thailand). Only a few come from places beyond these many lands, including Algiers, Beirut, and Jerusalem. And yet even this list of locations does not exhaust the places from which SCM gathered his remarkable personal library.

There are only a few records and hints about how the most unusual manuscripts and published texts were obtained by the Anglican vicar from Broadwindsor, but they are helpful in suggesting how he managed to obtain them. From within the biography written by his son, it is stated that SCM maintained a fairly interactive correspondence by letter writing with Protestant missionaries in Hong Kong and

---

[101] Specifically, Copenhagen.

[102] Including only those published from Lisieux and Paris.

[103] Here involving a much larger range of publishers from places including Augsburg, Bielefeld, Berlin, Bonn, Detmold, Erlangen, Frankfurt on the Oder, Gießen, Göttingen, Greifswald, Halle, Hanover, Leipzig, Munich (München), Münster, Potsdam, Stuttgart, Tübingen, and Weimar.

[104] Some notable works were published in the following places in the Netherlands or Holland: Amsterdam, Franeker, Leyden, Rotterdam and Utrecht.

[105] Involving tomes published in Livarno, Padua, Palermo, and Rome.

[106] Some simply described as published in Malta, others from the capital city of Valetta.

[107] Only from Warsaw, as far as I could assess.

[108] Involving only volumes produced in Madrid.

[109] Only from Stockholm.

[110] Including works published in Königsberg in Prussia, Pest (now part of Budapest) in Hungary, Riga from the Baltic States, and Vienna, the capital of the Austrian-Hungarian empire.

[111] Only involving works published in St. Petersberg.

[112] Tomes from Constantinople.

[113] There are seventeen cities in the Indian subcontinent that are identified as places where documents were published. These include, in the alphabetical order of the place names as employed in the 19th century book list, the following cities: Allahabad, Bangelore, Benaris, Bombay (now Mombay), Calcutta (now Kolkata), Kandy, Lucknow, Ludhiana, Mangelore, Madras (now Chinnai), Mirzapur, Nellore, Pondicherry, Sadiya, Saipur, Serampur, and Surat (or Sunyapur).

[114] Once again, in the 19th century spelling of these place names: Maulmain (now Mawlamyire), Mandalay, Rangoon (or Yangoon), and Toungro (or Taungoo).

[115] Specifically, the northern port town of Jaffra, the main town of Colombo, and two names ("Cotta" and "Cottayan") that may be early alternative names for the current capital that is known simply as "Kotte" (meaning "fortress") or formally as "Sri Jayawardenepura Kotte."

[116] Specifically, from Bangkok.

Shanghai, including letters from James Legge,[117] the Scottish Congregationalist who served in Hong Kong as the head of the London Missionary Society station there, and the senior LMS missionary from Shanghai, the Rev. Walter H. Medhurst (1796-1857).[118] What can be learned from this correspondence is that the Anglican vicar was not only in touch with fellow Anglican missionaries, but also missionaries from other Protestant denominations, pursuing questions of shared interest and seeking to obtain copies of handwritten or published documents that would support his own research.

With regard to some manuscripts that were part of the Malan Library, the bibliophile sometimes simply wrote his signature on one of the first pages of the document, citing also the date and place where the manuscript had been obtained.[119] Other times, he wrote the name of the person from whom he had received it.[120] Another example drawn from the manuscripts that originally came as part of the Malan Library is a multilingual text primarily in Mongolian, but including some Tibetan texts as well as some Chinese numerals for identifying sections of the texts.[121] Apparently, the person who obtained the document, Dr. R. Yuille, sent the document to Broadwindsor from Glasgow after a lively conversation had developed, with a series of letters testifying to their correspondence during this period.[122] Still another came from the British representative in Japan, and included a document written in *kanji* (with the accompanying *Furigana*, that indicated how these Chinese characters would be read in contemporary Japanese) and *hiragana* (the indigenous Japanese phonetic system for normal Japanese words.[123] From these examples it can be seen how the Anglican vicar would develop his network of scholarly and even political ties in order to obtain suitable manuscripts for his personal library. In these particular cases, then, the manuscripts obtained were possibly one of a kind, and so of unusual value with regard to their calligraphy and content.

---

[117] A series of letters dated during the two years of 1855 and 1856 were sent by JL to SCM, portions of them appearing in *SCM DD*, pp. 169-170, and 173-174.

[118] These are letters also dated during the two years of 1855 and 1856 and indicate that along with letters other documents and volumes were sent between them. See *SCM DD*, pp. 170-172, and 174-177.

[119] Two manuscripts have such identification statements on them. One with the Bodleian call number "MS.Ind.Inst.Misc.2" is described as a "Modern Syriac" manuscript "on repentance, faith, etc.," and then in the same hand we find "S. C. Malan Mosul June 1850" below that descriptive statement and put into three separate lines one above the other. In a bilingual Coptic-Arabic manuscript of the Psalms, carrying the Bodleian call number "MS.Ind.Inst.Cop.3," there are simply the following marks: "S. C. Malan Jerusalem 1841" in two lines, the signature above the place name and date.

[120] In a multilingual text probably from Ethiopian settings and given the Bodleian call number "MS.Ind.Inst.Misc.3," SCM writes on the title page that this was "from the Rev. Js. Krapp" and was received on "August 13, 1875."

[121] This is the manuscript with the Bodleian call number "MS.Ind.Inst.Misc.13."

[122] The six letters are kept under the call number "MS.Eng.lett c.730, fol. 100-105."

[123] This is the manuscript with the Bodleian call number "MS.Ind.Inst.Misc.5." The address of the letter indicates that it is from "H[er] M[ajesty's] Legion. Yedo Japan July 8, 1881."

Fig. 19: Gallery and lecture hall, Malan Library, Indian Institute, Oxford. BB66/00376. Reprinted with permission of the Historic England Archive

From all these pieces of information, then, something of the unusual character and bibliographic value of the Malan Library can be revealed. And yet an unavoidable irony remains to be faced. The vast majority of the very unusual set of Tibetan manuscripts and block prints given to him as a gift by Alexander Csoma de Kőrös had been sent to the Hungarian Academy of Sciences in Budapest in 1884 – that nearly priceless set of Tibetan works have remained a distinct part of the Oriental Library in Budapest.[124] Nevertheless, his own multilingual personal library of exemplars written or published in over one hundred different languages only lasted until 1965, and then was dispersed within the Bodleian Library's various collections. What exactly happened to bring this about?[125]

Even though the whole of SCM's personal library was promised to the Indian Institute's fledgling group of curators by 1885, it was not put into its proper place until sometime before the opening ceremony of the Indian Institute that took place on the first of July 1896. SCM himself had described the whole library as something that would offer "a good show, as there are many folios and 4tos – and all have

---

[124] For details about this unusual gift, read Chapter 11 in this volume.

[125] The following account is completely dependent on Evison 2012.

cost me much money, trouble, and pleasure."[126] Having died on November 25, 1894, SCM apparently never had the pleasure or the chance to visit the fully established Indian Institute in Oxford where his eponymous library was on display. Also, the promise made to complete a catalogue for the whole library was never fulfilled, even though there were obvious attempts at cataloguing parts of it relevant to Indian studies, as found in the incomplete but still helpful notebooks with the proud title, "The Malan Library Book List." As I also indicated previously, a card catalogue was also initiated, and probably included as much as half of the titles within the whole library. Nevertheless, a cursory review of the three box loads of cards revealed that they sometimes also included later additions to the "Malan Library," that is, volumes added after the personal library was bequeathed to the Indian Institute in January 1885.[127] As a consequence, a more careful review of the cards themselves would have to be completed before greater precision about the nature and extent of its contents could be provided.

A meagre annual sum of 250 pounds sterling was set aside for management of the Indian Institute's libraries, an amount that the curators already in November 1884 recognized was woefully insufficient.[128] Subsequently, it seems, and in spite of some efforts to get a catalogue prepared, nothing much was done related to the Malan Library for the subsequent three decades. Something like a wake-up call came, however, when thirty books from that special library went missing in 1925 and ended up being sold to a local book dealer, who dutifully returned them to the Indian Institute.[129] As a consequence, arrangements were made in 1927 to pay the Bodleian Library an annual sum of 275 pounds sterling to manage the Indian Institute's libraries, including the Malan Library. This arrangement was confirmed by the Head of the Bodleian Library, Dr. Cowley, who was already complaining in 1928 that the funds were inadequate and had also "involved a considerable expenditure from Bodleian funds."[130] One can begin to see the writing on the wall by this time, but the actual administrative challenges that led to the dispersion of the Malan Library came about through a much larger and more trenchant political battle.

The political lines were drawn when a new Oriental Institute was established by the Hebdomadal Council in 1955, a decision that required that the new Institute

---

[126] Quoted from a letter to Monier Williams dated April 14, 1884, and cited in *SCM DD*, p. 348.

[127] In contrast, I have found only one volume in "The Malan Library Book List" that was obviously published after 1894, that is, after SCM had passed away.

[128] As Evison wryly points out, "the problem of under-funding appears with monotonous regularity in the minutes from then on." Quoted from and relying on the text in Evison 2012, p. 2.

[129] As Evison indicates, even the Keeper of the Indian Institute, citing a situation in the minutes of the Institute's meeting for November 13, 1924, could rarely find either the chief librarian or his assistant in the library itself, so that the loss of those volumes was due to their negligence. A person named Mr. A. S. Domiak from Wadham had been able to take out the thirty volumes without even signing for them, it was later discovered. Cited from the narrative found in Evison 2012, p. 5.

[130] Quoting from Evison 2012, p. 5.

would make "full provision for Indian studies."[131] By the following year, a legal decision in favor of Oxford University was granted, allowing it to employ the buildings of the Indian Institute as "general property of the University"; in lieu of this privilege, a fund of 20,000 pounds sterling was set up to provide for a "permanent endowment for the promotion of Indian studies." Already by this time, then, a wedge between "Indian studies" and "The Malan Library" was being leveraged by the upper administrators of Oxford University. In fact, by 1960 this plan had been augmented, with an eye ultimately to having the Indian Institute broken down, and a new set of buildings on the site to serve as the new University Offices. That was the most radical of plans, and it could not be maintained. Nevertheless, by 1961, the Indian Institute Library was taken to be a "separate entity" that should not be "absorbed into the general collection of the Bodleian," but no such provision was made for the Malan Library.

In 1964 it was determined that the Indian Institute Library would be moved to "a roof extension" that was to be "built on the north range of the New Bodleian," a move that actually took place in 1965. It has remained there until this day. Because opposition was growing against amalgamating "Indian studies" within "Oriental studies," a political debate began to brew that brought about "one of the University's most notorious episodes of bloodletting in recent history."[132] Though the Indian Institute Library was moved to its new home, the political decision did not favor the continuance of the Indian Institute or the Malan Library. Once news got out about the decision, the reaction caused by Indian newspapers – enhanced by patriotism in the new modern country of India free from British colonial rule – was understandably negative. Consequently, on the last day of 1965, the Bodleian Librarian, Mr. Myres, resigned. In the midst of all this uproar, the Malan Library, representing the ideals and interests of "Britain's Greatest Orientalist in the 19th century," quietly began to be redistributed by unnamed staff members among the many collections of the Bodleian Libraries.

6. Rediscovering the Importance of S. C. Malan and His Eponymous Library

Since the period from 1965 to 1967, the Malan Library had essentially disappeared. Nevertheless, due to the new computerization of all the library materials in the Bodleian Libraries, there has been a little sign of hope in discovering some items that are marked down as original parts of "The Malan Library." More significantly, extensive studies on various parts of SCM's life and works have developed in the early 21st century, including efforts to analyze his massive work that ultimately led to the publication of his three-volume work in English, the *ONBP*. The connection of that work with the former Malan Library is intimate and multifarious. So, with the expert support of the Bodleian Libraries' Oriental Division's leadership and the collegial efforts in research collaboration made by the authors of this volume, as

---

[131] Here and below, all quotations come from Evison 2012, p. 7.

[132] Here and in what follows, quoting from Evison 2020, pp. 7-8.

well as a good number of others who have paved the way toward gaining new insights into the life and works of this unusual Anglican vicar, the hyperpolyglot SCM, we together have now gained a new appreciation for the exceptional quality, unusual character, and relatively clear vision of the scope of the former Malan Library. Without question, it was an institution representing the interests of Anglican Christian life and of the 19th century British empire, as has been indicated in this chapter, but it was also a tribute to the scholarly endurance, research intensity, and linguistic interests of a man we could rightly honor as the most significant "Orientalist" within Great Britain in that century.

Though the Malan Library no longer occupies its place in what used to be the Indian Institute, it seems now quite possible that a collaborating team of experts who would arrange to go to Oxford might be able to reconstruct the details of most of that now invisible collection. My suspicion is that there are still a number of surprises yet to be discovered by that means, and so it spurs one on with a yearning for such meaningful research developments in the near future.

Appendix I

Description of a Summary of the Content of the Malan Library prepared by Solomon Caesar Malan himself and dated 13 August 1884.[133]

The Library of the Rev. Dr. Malan, Vicar of Broadwindsor, consists of [some 4,000 volumes] on the following subjects:—

BIBLES in several languages, with Commentaries, Apparatus Criticus, etc.

A Collection of GREEK AND LATIN CLASSICS, with works related to them, on Antiquities, Mythology, Grammar, etc.

FATHERS of the Church.

ECCLESIASTICAL HISTORY, Councils, etc.

OLD DIVINITY (in Latin): MODERN DIVINITY (in English).

HISTORY OF THE EASTERN CHURCH, in different languages.

GRAMMARS, DICTIONARIES, and LITERATURE in the following languages:—

EUROPEAN.
Russian	Norse
Sclavonic	Danish
Bohemian	Feroese
Servian	Gaelic
Italian and dialects	Manx
Spanish	Irish
Portuguese	Welsh

---

[133] Quoting from the text found in *SCM DD*, pp. 354-356. The spellings of particular language groups and capitalization of major terms are all presented as they are found within *SCM DD*.

Basque
Bulgarian
Icelandic
Swedish
Modern Greek
Finnish
Hungarian
Romansch
Etrurian
German

Cornish
English and dialects
French and dialects
Albanese
Dutch, etc.
Wotjak
Syrgenian
Lappic
Tehuwash, etc.
Greenlandish

A Collection of PROVERBS in various languages, and DIALOGUES in very many, and sundry GRAMMARS.

SEMITIC.
Hebrew Bibles, and
Commentaries, and
Literature
Rabbinical Literature
Syriac
Modern Syriac
Samaritan

Ethiopic
Amharic
Tigre
Arabic
Chaldean
Phœnecian
Assyrian

ASIATIC.
Sanscrit
Pali
Bengali
Hindi
Hindui
Urdu
Orissa
Telugu
Tamil
Sinhalese
Malayalim
Mahratta
Gujarati
Persian
Parsi
Pehlevi
Zend
Javanese
Kawi
Bali
Macassar

Tatar
Turkish
Mongolian
Mandchu
Chinese
Jakutish
Japanese
Aino
Corean
Burmese
Karen
Malay
Siamese
Annamite
Assamese
Uighur
Kalmuck, etc.
Assetish
Armenian
Modern Armenian
Kurdish

Sikh
Canarese
Tibetan
Georgian

Altai
Grammars of several
other languages

AFRICAN.
Etyptian Hierogly-
phics; Facsimilies
of Papyri, etc.
Coptic
Berber
Wolofe
Yoruba
Kaffir

Zulu
Sechuana
Galla
———
Malagasy
Maori
Fijian
Tonga, etc.

MANUSCRIPTS.
Sanscrit, Purānas, etc.
Pali, Diga, Nikāya, Parajikam, etc.
Orissa, Ramāyana
Arabic, various
Persian, "
Sinhalese, "
Telugu, "
Coptic Liturgies, etc.
Panjabee, Adhi Grunth, and commentary, prayers, etc.
Modern Syriac
Mongolian
Writing copies in most of the above languages.

Appendix II

Manuscripts donated to Oxford under the name "Malan, Rev. S. C." itemized in four catalogue cards

Card #	Bodleian Call Number	Date Received	[Document #]
1	MS.Caps.Or.C.27	1837	1
	MS.Chin.b.12	January 1885	2
	MS.Chin.d.6	October 1894	3
	MS.Chin.e.25	1885?	4
	MS.Ind.Inst.Arab.26, 27	January 1885	5
	MS.Ind.Inst.Burmese 6(R), 7(R)	January 1885	6
	MS.Ind.Inst.Copt.3-11	January 1885	7
2	MS.Ind.Inst.Misc.1	January 1885	8
	MS.Ind.Inst.Misc.2-6	1885	9
	MS.Ind.Inst.Misc.10	2 October 1894	10

	MS.Ind.Inst.Misc.11-13	1885	11
	MS.Ind.Inst.Pali 1(R)	January 1885	12
	MS.Ind.Inst.Panj. 1, 2, 3	January 1885	13
	MS.Ind.Inst.Pers.22	1885	14
	MS.Ind.Inst.Pers.49	date not given	15
3	MS.Ind.Inst.Pers.55-58	1885	16
	MS.Ind.Inst.Pers.72	date not given	17
	MS.Ind.Inst.Pers.95-97	date not given	18
	MS.Ind.Inst.Sansk.8	January 1885	19
	MS.Ind.Inst.Sansk.75(R)-80(R),82(R)	January 1885	20
	MS.Ind.Inst.Sansk.94(R)	January 1885	21
	MS.Ind.Inst.Sansk.100(R), 102(R), 104(R), 123(R)	January 1885	22F
4	MS.Ind.Inst.Sansk.140(R), 141(R), 221(R)	January 1885	23
	MS.Ind.Inst.Sinh.1(R), 2(R), 4(R)-6(R), 8(R)	January 1885	24
	MS.Ind.Inst.Tel.4(i ii)	January 1885	25
	MS.Ind.Inst.Turk.23, 30	January 1885	26
	MS.Or.Polygl.f.1	19 September 1859	27

Select Bibliography

Bonfitto, Peter Louis. 2015. "'Harmony in Contrast': The Drawings of Solomon Caesar Malan." *Getty Research Journal* No. 7 (January 2015), pp. 169-176.

Critchlow, Keith. 2004. *Islamic Patterns: An Analytic and Cosmological Approach.* London: Thames and Hudson.

Duka, Theodore. 1885. *Life and Works of Alexander Csoma de Kőrös: A Biography Compiled Chiefly from hitherto Unpublished Data: With a Brief Notice of Each of His Published Works and Essays, as well as of His still Extant Manuscripts.* London: Trübner; reprinted Abingdon: Routledge, 2000.

Evison, Gillian. 2012. "The Bibliophile and the Bodleian: Solomon Caesar Malan and His Oriental Library." Retrieved by https://ora.ox.ac.uk/objects/uuid:ef937cf0-9254-4f44-8245-645115374a57 (accessed 1 February, 2021).

Girardot, Norman J. 2002. *The Victorian Translation of China: James Legge's Oriental Pilgrimage.* Berkeley: University of California Press.

Malan, César. 1869a. *La vie et les travaux de César Malan, ministre du Saint évangile dans l'Église de Genève, pasteur de l'Église du Témoignage, Dr en théologie de l'Université de Glasgow.* Genève – Paris: Cherbuliez.

———. 1869b. *The Life, Labours, and Writings of Cæsar Malan.* London: James Nisbet.

Malan, Solomon Caesar. 1856. *A Letter to the Right Honourable the Earl of Shaftesbury, President of the British and Foreign Bible Society: On the Pantheistic and on the Buddhistic Tendency of the Chinese and of the Mongolian Versions of the Bible Published by that Society*. London: Bell and Daldy.

———. 1874. *Buddha and the Mongolian Version of the British and Foreign Bible Society: An Independent Testimony: Reprinted from the Quarterly Record of the Trinitarian Bible Society (No. 57), for April, 1874*. London: W. MacIntosh.

———. 1890. *On the Corean Version of the Gospels*. London: C. Green.

Orosz, Gergely. 2008. *A Catalogue of the Tibetan Manuscripts and Block Prints in the Library of the Hungarian Academy of Sciences*. 2 vols. Budapest: Library of the Hungarian Academy of Sciences.

Pfister, Lauren F. [Fei Leren 費樂仁]. 2011. "Yiwei tongxiao duoguo yuyan de Ruishiren dui "Zhongguo zhihui" de faxian" 一位通晓多国语言的瑞士人对"中国智慧"的发现 [A Swiss Polyglot's Discovery of "Chinese Wisdom"]. In Pan Derong 潘德荣 (ed.), *Guoxue Xijian: Guoxue dui Xifang de yingxiang guiji* 国学西渐——国学对西方的影响轨迹 (Chinese [National] Studies Flowing Westward: The Tracks of Influences of Chinese [National] Studies in the West]. Hefei: Anhui renmin chubanshe, pp. 81-112.

———. 2012. "A Swiss Polyglot's Discovery about the Chinese Search for Wisdom: Solomon Cæsar Malan's (1812–1894) Comparative Philosophical Contributions in his *Original Notes on the Book of Proverbs*." *minima sinica* 2012/1, pp. 1-52.

Symonds, Richard. 1986. *Oxford and Empire: The Last Lost Cause?* Basingstoke: Macmillan.

13

BREAKING THE CODE OF A MONSTROUS CODEX
An Intellectual Journey into the Hidden Secrets of
The Original Notes on the Book of Proverbs

LAUREN F. PFISTER

1. Promptings to Studying S. C. Malan's
Original Notes on the Book of Proverbs

In 1993 my own initial interest in Solomon Caesar Malan came about as a consequence of discovering in the Scottish National Library his three large octavo published volumes constituting the *Original Notes on the Book of Proverbs*. Like the version that I later found in the British Library, none of these volumes had even had their pages properly opened; that is to say, they were published so that the books were bound while the pages still remained connected in groups of about four to eight pages. They could only be read at that time if I had a letter opener and could carefully cut along the edge of each set of pages, making each double-sided page visible to the eye for the first time. What I saw at that time was a complex text that was beyond my ability to understand comprehensively, but I could at least identify from the footnotes that there were many Chinese sources cited in English versions within the text, along with many other ancient foreign documents also in English versions, most of which I could not identify. By that time, I already knew that the Swiss polyglot, SCM, had served as a missionary teacher to the young Chinese student, Ho Tsun-sheen 何進善 (1817–1871) during the academic year of 1838 to 1839;[1] SCM had done this as a newly established professor of classical languages at Bishop's College in Calcutta, and had helped that young Chinese person become a self-conscious Christian in the process of his instruction.[2]

Ironically for me, my subsequent attempts during the 1990s to obtain copies of this massive three volume set were fruitless, even when searching through antiquarian stores. Only in 2004 a Xeroxed version of the three-volume work was successfully obtained from the British Library, so that I could begin to carefully peruse the

---

[1] Noted originally in *SCM DD*, pp. 50-51, but also mentioned in JL's memorial statement for his colleague after his death, entitled "Sketch of the Life of Ho Tsun-sheen," found in the Christian World Mission archives in the SOAS Library (CWM/South China/Personal/Legge/Box 7), pp. 1 and 3. JL wrote this piece in "Hongkong," completing it on March 13, 1872. See other citations in Pfister 2004, vol. 1, pp. 134 and 255 (n. 368). This was not a theme addressed in Chapter 2 in this volume, but more about SCM's work in Bishop's College can be discovered there.

[2] Later that Chinese student would become the missionary colleague of the Scottish missionary-scholar in Hong Kong, James Legge (1815–1897), and the first published Chinese Protestant theologian. For more details about his life and works, consult Pfister 1999, pp. 165-197, and the relevant passages from my two-volume work already mentioned above, Pfister 2004.

whole published work. After my first general review of the work, I recognized that it was structured along the lines of the biblical book of Proverbs, as something like a commentary to each of the verses. Nevertheless, the more I reviewed various passages within the three-volume published work, the more I realized that it was not at all a normal commentary. Instead, what I found was a collection of sayings from numerous language sources related one way or another to the basic themes addressed in one or more verses of the biblical book of Proverbs. I located these in the *ONBP* under the particular verses to which they were relevant. Though almost all of those quotations had been put into an English rendering apparently produced by SCM himself, I could not discern by any easy means whether or not these were translations done by himself or copied from sources that already rendered these passages into English. There were so many questions that confronted me at the time, I simply had to put the materials aside until a suitable opportunity came to figure out a means to pursue appropriate research in order to find out if the time involved in studying this massive and complex text would be worthy of a systematic study.

The opportunity I was awaiting came only in 2007, when I was invited by a Swiss colleague to join her and others in the faculty of *Religionswissenschaft* (Religious studies) for an academic year (2007–2008) at the University of Bern in Switzerland. Knowing that SCM was Swiss in heritage, and that this could be something that both my wife, Mirasy, and I could pursue together as a joint project due to her willingness to work through many of the details of the extensive footnotes, I began to study SCM's life, and coordinated with her to work out ways to decipher the relationship between the main text and the nearly 16,000 footnotes that populated the bottom margin of each page of the three volumes that constitute the *ONBP*.

At that time in 2007, not much at all was known about SCM; there were very few scholars who had taken the time to study any of his works, and even fewer who had published anything about them.[3] As can be imagined by anyone who understands the creative choices involved in initiating ground-breaking research, I found it a daunting task to "start from scratch" on research related to SCM, especially in the light of the mysteries already encountered in the published version of the *ONBP*. Why was it the case that such a huge work created and published during the last decade of the 19th century was simply put aside by SCM's contemporaries, and so essentially left unaddressed and unevaluated? Were there some cues that could be obtained from any study of his life or from other works he had produced during his prolific life?

As I started to pursue these kinds of research questions in 2007, and despite finding a few short and pithy reviews of SCM's life and works that appeared in standard bibliographic works and within a few published articles, the outlook was frankly bleak. Almost nothing new had been done on SCM's life for more than a

---

[3] There has been no scholarly monograph or article in English published on SCM based on new studies of his corpus since 1897. As Chapter 12 in this volume indicates, much more has been done in Hungarian and French that touches on SCM's role in relationship to European Tibetology, but once more these were all studies on other figures, and only tangentially mentioned SCM.

century, and literally no one had written anything significantly about the *ONBP* after his filial son, the Rev. A. N. Malan, completed the posthumous account of his father's life and works in 1897.[4]

What had been written about the *ONBP* by ANM was helpful in certain ways, but he was not the linguist that his father had been, and so he could only present some personal impressions based on a sympathetic but still largely uncritical reading of that three-volume work. Nevertheless, what he wrote was, at the very least, an important beginning for anyone who might be interested in the *ONBP*, if for no other reason than the historical fact that no one else had written anything about his father's monumental work related to cross-cultural collections of proverbial literature. Though the account presented by the younger ANM in the context of his biography for his father could only be an inchoate step toward comprehending that huge and complicated work, it did manage to portray something basic about the character of the work. Recognizing the importance of the work in his father's story, the younger ANM devoted the whole of the fifteenth chapter of his biography to describe and illustrate the main text and some of the most obvious features of the content of the *ONBP*.[5] So, in the light of all these factors, I want to point out some of the advantages of this first detailed description of the *ONBP*. They stem from the fact that there are numerous illustrations from all three volumes of the work that ANM collected into thematic lists and quoted at some length – manifesting that he had indeed actually read through the huge work. In addition, ANM as a son understood from personal experience the dynamic role many of those sayings drawn from the biblical and other proverbs took on as they were woven into the daily experiences and some unusual traditions of the Malan family. In these ways, then, ANM could reveal some intimate cameos from his father's life, perspectives that are so personal at times that they would be otherwise irretrievable. As a filial son, he did slip into a Victorian style of hagiography in various other sections of that biography, but because this chapter was dealing more with a printed text than his father's life, this descriptive account could at least provide hints about some of the unusual content of the work. What he could not offer were any insights into the scholarly value of the citations on the basis of his own academic training; neither could he provide any account of the nature of their original sources, or reveal any special secrets in decoding the vast array of footnotes that appeared in the bottom margins of every page. Consequently, and due to the fact of its unique contribution as being the first rather lengthy and published account of the three-volume work of his father, I will summarize the main points of this account of the general image of the *ONBP*. Subsequently, I will offer a few more critical comments to reveal both the positive value and interpretive limits of ANM's account.

First of all, SCM produced in the *ONBP* some critical notes related to the King James English version (produced in 1611)[6] and Latin Vulgate versions of the

---

[4] This is the volume cited earlier, *SCM DD*.

[5] See *ibid.*, pp. 395-418.

[6] See a number of details about these "critical notes" identified and evaluated in Chapter 5 in this volume.

biblical book of Proverbs.[7] As will be seen later in this article, much more than this had actually been done by SCM, but this was at least what ANM could recognize from his own reading of the text. What is important about this initial description of the *ONBP* is that those who knew SCM and his biblical studies would not have necessarily anticipated that he would produce "critical notes" on the King James English Bible. Most of his contemporary readers in Great Britain during the latter part of the 19th century knew of SCM because he was a serious and stubborn public advocate for the value and importance of the King James Version (or "Authorized Version") of the English Bible, particularly in contrast to the new and modern "scientific" attempts to produce the Revised version in the 1880s.

Beyond this relatively insightful point, ANM collected various lists of thematically arranged "cosmopolitan" proverbs from a variety of linguistic sources, done primarily to illustrate their wit and rhetorical power.[8] Nevertheless, as has already been indicated previously, he was apparently unable to add any critical notes about his father's English renderings of these proverbial sayings, about the original sources from which they came, or even how his father had managed to obtain so many unusual works about proverbial and wisdom literature originally written in so many different foreign languages. Subsequently, and to conclude the chapter devoted to the *ONBP*, the biographer-son added some personal notes about how his father, SCM, employed several poignant proverbial sayings as summary judgments of his 19th century contemporaries.[9] By this means ANM provided fodder for several other important analytical and interpretive questions related to this work. He had summarized some of its special features in a clever and sympathetic manner, but in the process he added very little critical light into the way in which it had been produced, and was not able to provide any linguistic or hermeneutic insights into the varying qualities of his father's English translations as they related to the classical and other texts produced originally in so many foreign languages.

Notably, none of the more recent brief statements about SCM's life or works, outside of one article published in Chinese and English by this author in 2011 and 2012,[10] have reached the level of descriptive detail or advanced beyond the interpretive limitations of this summary of ANM written in 1897. Beyond what I myself have published in those two articles, both of which focused primarily on the Chinese wisdom that SCM identified and documented in English renderings of those Chinese sayings within his text, there has never before been any other critically justified and systematic evaluation of the *ONBP*. Still more poignantly, no person since the death of SCM in 1894, including his biographer and son, ANM, has explained the relationship between the original manuscript version of the *ONBP* and the three-volume published work rendered into English under the same title.

---

[7] Illustrated in *SCM DD*, pp. 402-406.
[8] Found in *ibid.*, pp. 406-415.
[9] Documented in *ibid.*, pp. 415-417.
[10] See Pfister 2012 and in Chinese, Pfister 2011.

To come to some of my own convictions about these matters took a number of years of persistent study, reflection, and a growing number of scholarly exchanges about the significance of SCM's *ONBP*. More discoveries of great importance that further prompted my own study of the *ONBP* came about due to research accomplished during a seminal sabbatical year in association with the University of Bern.[11] While in Switzerland in the Fall of 2007, my wife, Mirasy, and I discovered the Malan family archive in Lausanne, an archive no previous researcher had accessed. This added a wealth of new bibliographic information, and so it also naturally stimulated new interests in obtaining a more precise comprehension of his family background and, in particular, some critical awareness about the significance of SCM's early life in Geneva.[12] In early 2008 I pursued further research related to SCM in Oxford's Bodleian Libraries, and discovered the previously mentioned ONBP Ms.[13] The importance of this discovery, and my careful effort to document the unusual character of that monstrous volume, cannot be underestimated as it relates to the creative effort taken by SCM to produce the published English version of the *ONBP* during the last years of his life. At that time, as a result, I became even more self-conscious that the differences between the ONBP Ms and the printed versions of the *ONBP* were vast and even more complicated than I had originally conceived.

With the immense help of the Director of the Indian Institute and the Chief of the Oriental Division of the Bodleian Libraries, Gillian Evison, I was able to see historical documents and pictures of what had been the Malan Library, but at that time in the early months of 2008 I could not uncover any records of the full content of that library.[14] Since that time, Dr. Evison in 2012 did find a partial catalogue of the Malan Library in several formats, something that provided an immense and new provocation for further studies in SCM's life and works. In addition, it set some new foundational information that could be used to explore various aspects of the resources employed by the Swiss polyglot when he studied and wrote down into the ONBP Ms thousands of proverbs in the languages in which he had read them.[15]

Up to the year 2008, as has been clarified earlier, no one had ever systematically attempted to analyze the scope of the multi-lingual presentations found in the *ONBP*, or to compare them with the ONBP Ms. Because more critical comparative work

---

[11] See a related account of the significance of that sabbatical year spent in Switzerland in Chapter 12 within this volume. There many details are provided that are not repeated here.

[12] Please see Chapter 1 in this volume to obtain more details about this period of SCM's life and the familial context in which he grew up.

[13] Known as "MS. Ind.Inst.Misc.10," this was a huge octavo-sized manuscript of more than 950 folio pages, and had been donated to the Indian Institute by SCM in 2 October 1894, about seven weeks before he died. For further details, please see the second section of this chapter.

[14] For a thorough account of the nature of the Malan Library, see Chapter 12 in this volume.

[15] During the international conference on SCM's life and works held at Wadham College in August 2012, Dr. Evison made arrangements for all those attending the conference to take several hours to review the ONBP Ms and the bibliographic lists of portions of the Malan Library. One of the outcomes of that collective experience of exploration is Chapter 4 in this volume by John Edwards, exploring the significance of SCM's hyper-polyglot experiences.

needed to be done after the ONBP Ms was discovered, it took several visits before a thorough comparative location chart could be devised to aid us in the research comparing the manuscript and published versions of this major work. Only at this point in time did I myself begin to appreciate in much greater depth and with far more precision the nature of the creative enterprise that was achieved by SCM when he set out to produce the published version of the *ONBP* in English. (Please see Appendix I at the end of this chapter for the comparative locations of biblical proverbs in the *ONBP* and the ONBP Ms.) What I have done in this chart is to provide locations for the foreign language proverbs in the ONBP Ms as they are related to any specific proverb or set of proverbs in the *ONBP* itself. The reasons why these were necessary are explained in much greater detail later in this chapter, but here I will provide a brief summary of those justifications. While the presentation in English of all the foreign language proverbs related to any particular biblical text are found in the *ONBP* immediately following the presentation in English of the King James Version of that text, they appear in their original scripts and with an initial English rendering produced by SCM both before and after the biblical texts are found in the ONBP Ms. Without knowing this simple fact, any attempt to locate the original quotations which SCM copied into the ONBP Ms would be extremely disorienting to the uninitiated researcher.

During the period from 2007 to 2009, Mirasy conceived of and created her own handwritten and systematic notes related to the nearly 16,000 footnotes found in the bottom margins of the *ONBP*. Subsequently, we had the help of devoted research assistants[16] in creating an electronic database that allowed myself and other interested scholars to access these materials in a thorough manner from a wide variety of perspectives (more than fifteen fields); this made possible the basis for an immense analytical and systematic breakthrough. As a consequence of these monumental efforts on the part of Mirasy Pfister and Yip Wing-yan, we were able to produce the database that has allowed for a far more precise account of the original sources SCM relied on than anyone has previously ever known. A large part of the numerical and statistical data that has been learned by analyzing the details produced through this database is included in the following descriptive statements and critical analyses of both the ONBP Ms and its published English version.

2. A Description of the Manuscript Version of SCM's *ONBP*

In order to understand more completely the nature of the published English version of the *ONBP*, it is right to first review the nature and content of the manuscript version of this same work from which SCM created the published volume. What surprised me most about this huge unpublished manuscript is the stark differences in its linguistic content, the order of the collected texts, and the inherent and yet unstated purposes involved in the creation of these two related works.

---

[16] Initial help and suggestions were offered by Sophia Katz, during the period of her Ph.D. studies in Hong Kong, but the vast majority of the data-input process was accomplished by a former undergraduate student of mine, Ms. Yip Wing-yan.

As has been noted previously, the ONBP Ms was donated to the newly established (but not yet built) Indian Institute in Oxford in October 1894, some six weeks before SCM died. Because of its multi-lingual content involving sources in more than fifty different languages, it was categorized in the Bodleian Libraries' catalogue for donations under the "catch-all" category of "miscellaneous."[17] Here in what follows is a detailed description of this gigantic manuscript.

According to SCM's own statement found on the inside of the back cover of the book, he bound this volume himself, and rebound it two more times after his initial conception of the work. In a note at the front of the large book, he wrote down three years: 1833 – 1852 – 1894 (for details see below).

On this basis then, we can know that the project that motivated the creation of this manuscript was begun in the first year, when SCM was a young man of twenty or twenty-one years of age, at a time when he was just about ready to start studying at Oxford.[18] What the second date refers to is not very clear from his biographical history, but it was his 40th year, when he also prepared his elegant work in more than 80 languages called the *Sacra Privata*.[19] Nevertheless, the third date happens to be the year that he donated the volume to the Indian Institute in Oxford. That year, 1894, was just one year after SCM had completed the third and last volume of the *ONBP*, the published English version of the work.

On the inside flyleaf of the front cover of the ONBP Ms, there is the following note in the calligraphy of Solomon Caesar Malan (representing in font size and the order of wording the way it appears there):

Original
Notes on the Book of Proverbs

———

S. C. Malan.

———

1833—1852—1894
These notes number about 16000; they

---

[17] In that catalogue, the Bodleian manuscript number does not refer to the actual title SCM gave to the manuscript, but instead used "MS.Ind.Inst.Misc.10," with "Misc." referring to the miscellaneous category.

[18] Besides the introductory note found above, I found a 2 x 4 card located between pages 452 and 453, written in black ink with the following statement that was apparently written by someone other than SCM himself, perhaps by a librarian: "Original Notes on the Book of Proverbs / S. C. Malan / 1833 – 1852 – 1894. / These notes number about 16000; they / were all taken, translated and copied / whole or in part from their several / originals by S. C. Malan. D. D." (The slashes indicate the separate lines of this text.) Another similar card is found between pages 498 and 499, and carries the title, "Temporary Label." The title and the final statements differ slightly from the text above. The title is "Manuscript Notes on the Book of Proverbs / by the Rev. S. C. Malan D.D." The last sentence, added to the other statements found above, reads as follows: "This book was also bound by him."

[19] This is the manuscript known in the Bodleian Libraries as "MS.Or.Polygl.f.1."

> were all taken,[20] translated and copied whole
> or in part from their several originals, by
> me[,] S. C. Malan. I present it to the Indian
> Institute as witness of the use I made of
> some of the Books I gave to that library.
> This book was also bound by me.
>
> Octr. 2, 1894   Witness my hand
>   S. C. Malan. D.D.

Within another introductory note, SCM revealed that he had "bound [this book] for myself for the third and last time, March 27, 1879." So, from all these autobiographic sources we have a clear sense that this gigantic volume was a project that took up over sixty years of SCM's disciplined research and writing.

But why do I continue to refer to it by adjectives such as "huge," "gigantic," and (more dramatically) "monstrous"? Here a characterization of the physical dimensions of this self-made volume reveals the answer.

This immense leather-bound volume is approximately six inches thick, generally including pages within it that are about twelve inches in length and eighteen inches in height. Protected by thick front and back covers that are created out of a light leather, it already possessed in 2008 a worn light brown color on the front cover, but on the back cover it bears a color more like carmillion red. This is particularly evident in the small places under the two wide leather strips that constitute the base of the two clasps (to be mentioned below); under these protected places, the color of the leather is burgundy and the leather's texture is smooth.

Prepared so that it might last for many years, the volume possesses two leather clasps stretching from the back cover on the right side, which also bear a metal hook at their ends. These hooks fit into a metal tongue which is at the end of a simple but ornate metal clasp bar of about an inch and a half in length; two of these adorn the front cover about three inches from the top and bottom of the cover, held down by two bronze screws. In order to "open" the book, one needs to press down on the front cover in order to release the metal clasp from the tongue at the top on both of the book clasps, and then the clasp naturally swings away from the book and the body of the manuscript, so that it can be opened at leisure. Closing involves the same kind of procedure in reverse: pressing down from the top and inserting each of the clasps over the metal tongue.

On both the front and back covers there are larger brass end-covers, ornately embossed, two covering the outside corners and fixed by brass screws; those screws on the inside of the end-covers are not directly on the corner, but placed about one quarter of an inch away from that inside corner. In each case, then, the end-covers are fixed by three screws, two in the same places as the outside clasps, with an additional one found at the inside corner near to the book's back spine.

---

[20] At this point in the handwritten text, we find a rare error that was corrected by Malan himself. He had first of all written the word "taking," but wrote over the last three letters the two letters "en," leaving the "g" dangling in a slightly subdued grey ink.

Though the back side of the book is still completely connected to the leather covering the book's spine, the front part has broken away from at least two thirds of the front cover. On the right side of the manuscript 31 leather taps protrude about one half inch from the manuscript itself. They appear in two rows, placed progressively lower on the open side of the manuscript; the first row contains 21 tabs, and the last row only ten. They clearly were meant to identify a place where the first verses of each of the 31 chapters of the biblical book of Proverbs begin. So, for example, on checking where the 22nd tab was located, I discovered that it revealed passages related to Prov. 22:2-4 (folio page 681), but the passages related to verse one in this same chapter were found quite a distance away, starting on page 672 verso.

With regard to the manuscript's internal nature, most of the paper pages are tan colored and of a strong character; some are light blue in hue, and a number of pages are half sized, obviously included later because the items written upon them refer to the themes of the one or more verses of the biblical book of Proverbs being dealt with in that context, and not in any special numerical, linguistic or thematic order. These passages were actually written down in the manuscript in their original languages, and many times with an English rendering added to the text, if it was originally from an unusual language source.

Since all of these texts were written down over a period of more than fifty years, and so necessarily included three different times when the bindings had to be redone to enlarge the text, this suggests how SCM continued to locate texts and make new discoveries in his readings from those different studies.

Generally speaking, SCM first wrote down with his own hand the relevant passages he had found in the original language, and then added his own English translation of the text, followed most of the time by a reference to the work where it was found.[21] At the front or top of these passages would be a number, especially on those pages that had been added later (and not necessarily so if they were written down on the page where the King James English version appeared), referring to the number of the verse that it was related to in the immediate context of these collected passages. Because of the nature of the different languages employed, most texts read from left to right and so were written that way; in some cases – in languages such as Chinese, Hebrew, and Sanskrit, for example – the classical texts are read from right to left, and are also written that way. Still others were written generally from top to bottom, including Manchurian, Mongolian, Japanese, and Korean. Chinese language passages were generally written in red ink with a pen or a brush, and were normally read from left to right, though not always. Some texts also do not include English translations; these generally involve passages in Latin and Greek, but also include some Hebrew and Aramaic texts. Some unusual cases in this regard

---

[21] At some points, though fortunately not too many, he did not refer to the exact bibliographic reference, but only the name of the work. This made his efforts to relocate those sources in the *ONBP* all the more difficult, because the vast majority of his books had been sent away to the Indian Institute in January 1885.

relate to some of the Manchurian passages, since they were actually translations of classical Chinese passages that had already been given an English rendering.[22]

When this large volume is viewed as a total work, we can begin to sense just how massive the whole manuscript is. The whole work includes 952 folio pages, each numbered in sequence in pencil on the top righthand corner of each folio page. This was probably done by a careful librarian after the book had been in the Indian Institute Library for some undetermined amount of time. This means, in essence, that the work was actually 1,904 pages in length.[23]

From the initial pages of the work we also find some unusual features that only appear in the ONBP Ms, and are not replicated in the *ONBP*. After two blank pages, one finds on three pages introductory quotations from different languages including Latin, Hebrew and English (1 verso); numerous others that probably include Georgian, Arabic, Sanskrit, Mongolian, Uighur (possibly), Greek, and Hebrew, among others; and on the final page (2 verso) Arabic, Hebrew, and Tibetan. Following this there are eight pages constituting a bibliographic list of some of the works cited, according to the main language in which they were written.[24] These appear on 3 recto to 6 verso. From this point on we start to find passages related to the work itself, but these are apparently only introductory statements about the nature of wisdom and proverbs. They follow one blank folio page,[25] and fill most of the next six pages.[26] A larger typed title announcing "The Proverbs." (with the period) appears in the middle of page 11 recto, but the quotations continue beyond it. The first time that passages parallel to verses in Chapter 1 of the Book of Proverbs appear in the ONBP Ms are found on 14 recto.

The ONBP Ms is not a perfect text, but it was obviously meant to be a sourcebook primarily for shared themes within wisdom literature written in the more than fifty languages. Some pages show signs of amendments and editing after the initial writing down of the text was done. Sometimes those corrected passages are covered over by another piece of paper suited to that particular part of the page. In a few places where errors occur they are simply crossed out, but these kinds of bold deletions appear relatively seldom within the manuscript. Most significantly, there are obviously additional pages accrued to the work during the second and third binding, obvious because the sequence of references to the verses of the biblical Proverbs are not systematically included on these pages. Generally speaking, these additions are initiated by the number of the verse to which they refer.

---

[22] In rare cases SCM added a critical comment to indicate where these Chinese and Manchurian texts differed in character or tone, adding an emphasis or a word in the Manchurian, for example, or noting an absence of a term that appears in the Chinese.

[23] Here I can add that the last page on which proverbs or sayings in foreign languages was written along with their English rendering is on 945v, followed by seven blank pages.

[24] These are very helpful, but they are not a comprehensive list, and because the titles are written in their original language, they cannot always be identified by every reader.

[25] That is, 7 recto/verso.

[26] That is, from 8 recto to 13 recto.

Throughout the work, SCM pasted passages from the biblical Proverbs as rendered in the King James version of that text. This version of the King James Bible was also one prepared as a study bible, so that these pasted sections of this text include cross-references to other passages in the Old and New Testaments of the Christian scriptures, as well as a few other critical-textual comments.

In most cases, it is the Chinese and Japanese passages that appear in calligraphy produced by a writing instrument using red ink; nevertheless, SCM sometimes also wrote the Chinese passages in normal black ink. A number of those Chinese and Japanese texts stem from renderings by Christian missionaries who collected various sayings, and so are sometimes expressed in rather quaint ways. For example, an early Jesuit collection of Japanese proverbs writes them all in *katakana*, and includes no Chinese characters (*kanji*) or *hiragana*, which is currently used to articulate the Japanese pronunciation of words that are considered indigenous, or express the Japanese grammatical and phonetic ways of handling the *Kanji*. This is really awkward for those who are used to more complicated and fluid contemporary Japanese texts.

From all these various comments, then, a sense of the nature of the manuscript can be discerned. I have added colored images from three selected pages within the ONBP Ms in Appendix II to illustrate their linguistic complexity, their various levels of calligraphic achievement and concomitant aesthetic qualities, as well as samples of the English renderings that SCM added to those apothems/sayings, all written together within each page of the ONBP Ms.[27]

3. Complexities in Studying the *ONBP* and the ONBP Ms

When I took time to begin to compare various pages of the published version of SCM's English renderings of proverbial literature from sources in over fifty languages within the *ONBP* with those found in the ONBP Ms, I began to realize the immense amount of creative work that was involved in that effort. First of all, there was no simple pattern of his copying the English renderings from the manuscript version into the published version. I believe that this was because each of those original proverbial statements were discovered at different times in SCM's studies and did not necessarily follow a single thread of thematic connections. What this does assume – and was apparently the case – is that SCM had memorized the whole of the biblical book of Proverbs (31 chapters, and over 900 verses), so that he knew it well enough to relate any saying in another text to some passage within that biblical text. Consequently, then, the thematic connections SCM made in the published version were done only after he had read all the passages he had written down from the various sources over a period of as much as fifty years, and each one cited in relationship to the particular biblical verse or verses that he was considering. When specific passages are identified within the published version and the manuscript version, it was not uncommon to notice that SCM had also retranslated the passage

---

[27] A fourth image of another page from the ONBP Ms has been included in Chapter 4 of this volume, and on p. 53.

in its English version, probably due to his personal growth in linguistic and cultural understanding that he had gained before he began to create the English published version sometime in 1885. These basic observations can be checked by anyone who is interested by using the comparative location chart found in Appendix I.

In addition to these basic observations, there were obviously no introductory notes related to philological studies of the Hebrew standard text in the ONBP Ms, but these did occur in most of the sections for each verse or set of verses in the *ONBP*. These involved further scholarly considerations and studies of specific versions of the Proverbs, often including critical insights that will be explained in more detail below.[28]

These observations regarding the relationship of the ONBP Ms and the *ONBP* prompted me to ask even more questions about the nature of the published version of this massive and complex work. For example, what exactly is the character of the *ONBP* and what constitutes its scholarly contribution(s)? Should it be considered as a dictionary of sapiential sayings? Or is it more like a *collectanea* or *leishu* 類書? Or is it essentially a biblical commentary with parallel quotations from other linguistic sources? Ultimately, it appears that the *ONBP* belongs to none of these categories, but does include a mixture of several of their elements. If this is so, where does its scholarly contribution lie? A tentative answer to this question requires us to consider several aspects of the *ONBP* which even ANM could not adequately elaborate in his overview.

The published version of the *ONBP* includes what are generally found to be brief etymological comments on Hebrew, Latin and Semitic versions of the biblical Book of the Proverbs. Though these are often extremely concise, their scholarly impact was manifest as SCM presented a number of critical judgments regarding the English renderings found not only in the KJV of the English Bible, but also of the much earlier Septuagint and Latin versions. Over 140 such critical comments are recorded in the published version of the *ONBP*, and though ANM mentioned this fact and illustrated some of them, he did not indicate how very unusual this was for his father, who was a well-known advocate supporting the cultural importance and authoritative standard set by the King James Version of the English Bible.

In answering questions related to the nature and content of the *ONBP*, I came up with some slight revisions of what even SCM himself had claimed about the character of the published text. Undoubtedly, it is constituted essentially by being a collection of sapiential sayings originating primarily, but not exclusively, from "Eastern sources." I have already hinted above at where some slight qualifications about this description of the content of the work have to be made, including the fact that there were a number of sayings drawn from classical Greek and Latin sources, as well as some proverbial sayings drawn from earlier or contemporary European languages. In addition, a sizeable amount of sayings from Hebrew and Aramaic texts were also quoted, so that the descriptive term "Eastern" cannot easily cover all of those additional linguistic corridors. Whatever the character of the original

---

[28] A full account of those critical philological notes in the *ONBP* has been offered in the fourth section of Chapter 5 within this volume, in particular pp. 89-94.

languages in which these sources of proverbial and wisdom literature were found, all of them were organized around themes that arose in parallel or in contrast with particular sayings of the biblical book of Proverbs. As James Hegarty has insightfully stated about this aspect of the *ONBP* and SCM's own missiological approach to these matters, it was clear that SCM assumed there was a shared realm of practical wisdom that went beyond any singular cultural or linguistic expression.[29]

Nevertheless, unlike Chinese *collectanea*, the text of the *ONBP* is not divided into thematic categories, but like commentaries it links up quotations from many traditions of wisdom literature to specific passages or particular ideas and phrases encountered in the process of reading through the thirty-one chapters of the biblical book of Proverbs.

The fact that SCM provided nearly 16,000 abbreviated footnotes in the *ONBP* has been noted already more than once before. Nevertheless, in the manuscript version (or ONBP Ms) references to the original texts occurred within the body of the calligraphed page, but in the *ONBP* they appear only in the bottom margin of each page. Due to the immense work of preparing a systematic database of all of those citations, I now can confirm that within the *ONBP* there are references to just over one thousand specific works representing resources published and written in 54 different languages, and involving more than seventy distinct religious, philosophical and cultural traditions. Most of these texts were originally composed in ancient and medieval languages; the vast majority of these are from cultures located outside of Europe.

These statistics prompted me to ask a number of questions for which we have only inchoate answers even at this point in time. How in the world did SCM obtain materials from so many cultural traditions and linguistic sources? From my account of the nature of the Malan Library, I have already indicated that some of these were available from publishers and book sellers within European academic settings, but there are still many that could not be obtained from those regional institutions.[30] A few extant letters also found in the Bodleian Libraries' collections indicate that SCM kept up a wide-ranging correspondence with various kinds of people, including missionaries living and working in overseas settings, consular officials, and intellectuals who were contacted because they could inform him about specific texts that might be interesting to him. The cost for the correspondence and purchase of these unusual volumes in an age before anything like e-mail correspondence existed could not have been anything but expensive and time-consuming. In the end, this too is another unusual feature involved in the creation of the ONBP Ms that deserves far more detailed study than I have been able to give it up to this point in time.[31]

---

[29] See his claims made in Chapter 10 of this volume.

[30] See the discussion of this point in Chapter 12 within this volume.

[31] For example, there are many questions regarding the quality of the works that he received that could only be answered by specialists in these cultural and linguistic traditions. Many times the volumes he obtained were excellent sources for wisdom literature and well-recognized works; sometimes they involved little known texts that have been set aside by professional scholars or have no longer had any impact in the study of that particular cultural tradition. Though I have done some of this work in relationship to the Chinese texts that he

Once again, due to the insights now gained from the extensive database that has been created, I can now confirm that the most often quoted sources in the *ONBP* come from twenty-four languages.[32] Intriguingly, only ten of those language sources involve ancient languages. Listed in alphabetical order, they include sources written in Aramaic, Chinese, Egyptian hieroglyphics, Greek, Hebrew, Hindi, Latin, Sanskrit, Tamil, and Telugu. There are ten other languages in which SCM also found resources for wisdom literature; most of these are essentially medieval and not modern languages. They include Arabic, Burmese, Cinhalese, Georgian, Japanese, Mazdagasnian, Mongolian, Persian, Tibetan, and Uyghur-Karluk or Middle Turkish. The four remaining proverbial traditions come from sources written in relatively modern languages; they are Italian, Javanese, Spanish and Welsh. Notably, from the list of these 24 languages that form the major part of the collection of proverbial sayings SCM had identified, eighteen of those "major resource languages" involve written scripts and cultures that stem from geographical locations east of the Mediterranean Sea. In this regard, then, something like 75% of all the proverbial and apothemic literature SCM cited were from "eastern" sources, as seen from his self-conscious starting point in western Europe. But that also means that a noticeable minority are not from these sources, and so this qualification regarding the major language sources in his study should be underscored.

Something more needs to be stated about the content of the main body of the *ONBP*. Besides the expected concatenation of proverbial sayings following particular themes related to the biblical passages SCM was considering, there are also found within the body of the work occasionally hints, and sometime very explicit statements, of SCM's own evaluations about the claims made within particular sayings within the *ONBP*. Notably, however, SCM never was able to offer any lengthy, independent, and systematically-thorough reflections about any particular linguistic corridor of proverbs or their representative cultures. Particularly in this light, we should raise a number of further interpretive questions related to his own worldview, Christian values, and missiological interests as they appear in the *ONBP*.

Sometimes SCM's collected quotations involve contrasting proverbs, appearing at times to be like what Wolfgang Mieder calls "anti-proverbs."[33] Sometimes they obviously reflect alternative worldviews to the Yahweh-ist monotheism of the biblical Proverbs. These passages indicate SCM's awareness of some dynamic cultural tensions which arise as sapiential proverbial sayings circulate and develop within their own and other linguistic traditions. In addition, and from an even more

---

collected, and others specializing in various disciplines related to specific languages and cultures have also offered their assessments here in this volume, many more of these kinds of critical assessments could be done for most of the main languages that will be mentioned in the following accounts.

[32] Whether this is also the case regarding the ONBP Ms can be assumed, but this would need much more careful comparative work between the two works before such a claim can be confirmed with any level of certainty.

[33] Consult Mieder – Dundes 1994.

expansive set of perspectives, SCM was clearly drawn to compare not only proverbs culled from classical literature and its elite authors (a form of elitism he admired), and so is vulnerable to criticism from liberation-critical perspectives, but also at times highlighted plebian proverbs and fables which reflected also the diversity and character of sayings within the biblical book of Proverbs itself.

Summarily speaking, the published English version of the *ONBP* is a compilation of a vast array of proverbs gathered mostly from classical works representing numerous ancient and pre-modern cultures, all either reflecting or standing in contrast to themes found in the biblical Proverbs. SCM's collection provokes cross-cultural comparisons in wisdom traditions, most of which came from Asian cultures, and which more or less explicitly involved comparative religious and comparative philosophical elements.

Consequently, when the *ONBP* is viewed in the light of studies of the biblical book of Proverbs during the past two centuries, we learn that one main scholarly emphasis in comparative studies in the 20th century involved the book of Proverbs and ancient sapiential literature from Egyptian, Mesopotamian and Arabic cultures. Therefore, what SCM actually accomplished by the early 1890s was largely unprecedented: while engaging proverbial literature from Egyptian and numerous Semitic cultures, he emphasized even more comparisons with sapiential literature from many Asian cultures which had rarely, if ever, been studied in this manner during the late Victorian era.

4. Noting Some Difficulties in Evaluating the *ONBP*

There is no doubt that an uninitiated reader would find a number of technical matters related to the content of the *ONBP* annoying, if not concretely obtrusive. For example, in many cases the abbreviations related to different sources as found in the footnotes might be almost completely indecipherable for those seeking to understand all of them by means of their own learning.

In this case, however, SCM did provide some relatively helpful clues. At the end of the first and third volumes he prepared some bibliographic notes, including not only a good number of book titles mentioned in those footnotes, but also some separate explanations about various personal names for authors, deities, and historical figures which appeared in the main text. Though these indices are nowhere near being comprehensive,[34] they are nevertheless helpful to some degree in aiding the

---

[34] Here I can provide more precise details about these two indices to indicate why these general evaluative statements are justified. In the index related to book titles, there are 223 titles included in the list, which is found only at the end of Volume 1 of the *ONBP*. Yet in that particular volume, SCM actually refers to just under 670 individual works, and in the whole of the three volumes, that number swells to just over one thousand titles. As a consequence, it is obvious that the vast majority of the titles are not included in the index. The personal name index is only slightly longer, appearing at both the end of Volumes 1 and 3, and including 243 names of various figures. Still, as one can easily imagine, there are hundreds of other names in various works that are mentioned which are not given any coverage. As a consequence, if one is not a specialist in a particular area, many of the author's names and figures mentioned in the quotations are not easy to identify. More complications come when, for

persistent reader to gain some basic background information. What makes these abbreviations particularly difficult to handle at times are several additional minor problems. For example, SCM used non-standardized transliterations or his own personalized renderings of various titles of the source texts he employed in the *ONBP*, so that they are forms of references that 21st century scholars might not immediately recognize. For example, as was also the case with a number of his Sinologically-minded contemporaries in the late 19th century, SCM was not always consistent in his use of transliterations in referring to the same person.[35] Furthermore, he at times did not even clarify which language a particular work was written in after he rendered its title or passages from it into English. One either recognized the source in the footnote and knew from which linguistic setting it came from, or one would be lost without expert help.

One can reflect on this problem from a more existential point of view: SCM was an elderly (and at times very ill) man[36] during the years when he was producing the *ONBP* and reviewing its galley proofs. Having completed all the scholarly effort related to creating this major work by 1893, SCM found it difficult to recollect and compile even a basic list of all the works he had referred to. Understandably, it was a massive project of its own, and involved probably as many as one thousand sources which he had mentioned in the course of writing those volumes. Suffering from physical problems that hindered both his sight as well as his physical strength in 1893, he no longer had the means or motivation to offer a comprehensive list of these interpretive tools, even though they would have made the evaluation of his work quite a bit more feasible.

Consequently, even after one might be able to identify a particular title for a source text employed in the work, one may not be able to find out from any of the indices or any other notes within the work which original language the source is in, or even who the author or editor of that particular source text was, not to mention anything more precise about bibliographic data that would normally be expected in

---

example, SCM was unaware that the person "Choo-He" or "Chu-Hi" is the same as "Choo-tsze" or "Chu-tsze" (all referring to Zhu Xi 朱熹, 1130–1200); he simply did not have the background knowledge to identify different forms of reference to the same person. Fortunately, this is the only quandary of this sort that I have found in the work, but it indicates how one must be careful in reading through various matters in the text. For this particular confusion of these Chinese names and titles, see the index in vol. 1, p. 486, at the bottom of the left-hand column.

[35] So, as indicated in the previous footnote, SCM offered four different transcriptions for the name and title of Zhu Xi in his Name Index, and I have seen at least two other alternative renderings in the body of the work. For any person who might not be so informed as to decipher these different forms of reference, these can become obvious sources of confusion.

[36] This would be from 1886 to 1893, when he was 74 to 81 years old. Quite unexpectedly, he was involved in a very serious accident in 1887, having been essentially run over by a horse-drawn coach one late evening in the coastal city of Bournemouth, where he and his wife had taken up residence after his retirement. He was so severely hurt that he remained basically a hobbling cripple for the rest of his days, not one that was completely unable to walk, but one who found it no longer comfortable to take the long walks (which he had previously so thoroughly enjoyed).

21st century contexts. This means that an interested scholar or motivated reader may not be able to learn in any easy way the date of publication of the source text, or to grasp which version of a famous text was being used by SCM. At times it is even unclear whether that source text is itself a monolingual or polylingual work. All of these factors will be important to some scholars, especially after they learn that SCM had at times collected more than one version of major works within his own personal library. All this being understood, I still can affirm that what SCM did provide in the indices offers general hints for a persistent and thoughtful reader in identifying other means for discovering the necessary background information about these unusual texts in a good number of cases.

Undoubtedly, what is most significant in this regard is the need for organizing groups of scholars who can bring their expertise to bear on particular portions of the *ONBP*, so that a more precise and thorough account of the nature of the overall work might ultimately be attained.[37] My own strategy initiated in 2008 in this regard was to put the majority of my own energies into studying those aspects of the work that deal with Chinese sources, while relying on one other colleague[38] to look into the Tibetan and Mongolian texts. This selective approach, fortunately, has provided enough motivation to make the harder work of seeking to comprehend the more general features of SCM's published text somewhat more manageable. Since that time the group has grown to include all of those who have contributed to this volume, as well as a few more who have shown interest.

In speaking about the fact that SCM employed non-standard transliterations or transcriptions of the titles of works he cited in his footnotes, I should note that this was not because he was a willful rebel against transliteration systems in general, but because in most cases a standardized transliteration system for many languages he referred to had not yet been created or accepted.[39] This makes it difficult for

---

[37] It is particularly this strategy which I have been using since 2012. After introducing the work to various colleagues with expertise in languages and literatures I do not have, I have solicited their help in doing this kind of collaborative work. As a consequence, a larger team of competent scholars from a number of different areas of studies has been formed, so that I have hope that a far wider and more precise account of SCM's scholarly contributions in this work can be suitably achieved. After this volume is published, more work by means of such scholarly collaboration could be and should be done.

[38] This colleague is Karénina Kollmar-Paulenz, then Dean of the Humanities Faculty and also the Head of the Institute of the Science of Religion at the University of Bern.

[39] ANM highlighted the fact that his father disliked using transliterations because they could not always adequately portray subtleties in languages where differences in consonants and vowels were not always able to be highlighted by use of a Roman-based script. Unfortunately, later biographers have taken this to be another sign of his anachronous attitudes, or of his lack of scholarly attentiveness, but in fact this is an unfair judgment. His complaints were justified, and in many cases there were no standard renderings for a particular language that prevailed in England at the time. For example, the Wade-Giles transcription system for Chinese language only became a dominant feature in English speaking worlds in the early 20th century and was later largely replaced by the Pinyin system developed in the 1960s and generally dominating by the 1990s in this same English environment. This should also be seen in the larger historical context that there have been as many as over fifty different transcriptions

readers, and even for scholars in specific fields, to identify all the works that in the 21st century might otherwise be known by other names or transliterated titles.

5. Breaking the Code of the ONBP Ms and the *ONBP*

It has been my privilege to have a part in breaking through the fairly large number of obstructions that have been part and parcel of pursuing research on the life and works of SCM. Without a doubt, the most demanding and challenging of those hindrances has been figuring out ways to deal with the complexities of relating the content of the ONBP Ms to that found in the *ONBP*. What has been accomplished now within this volume, after more than a decade of toil, is a new level of understanding of this "monstrous" work that offers us many new insights and quite a few new motivations for pursuing further focused research within varying aspects of this seminal and difficult work. I am convinced that this can be done by interdisciplinary research that involves willing scholars who can employ the database we have created in order to explore both the ONBP Ms and the *ONBP* within specific linguistic and cultural contexts. The present volume has been the result of that form of research work and has moved us all to take up critical perspectives we have learned from our own 21st century disciplines to seek to understand this unusual man and his *magnum opus*. If this volume and its contents can stimulate further work on the man, his life, and some of his most important works, including the ONBP Ms and the *ONBP*, then our intellectual efforts expressed in conferencing, researching, and writing these chapters within this monograph will have received their most satisfying reward.

Select Bibliography

Legge, James. 1872. "Sketch of the Life of Ho Tsun-sheen." Manuscript located in the Christian World Mission Archives, SOAS Library, London. CWM/South China/Personal/Legge/Box 7.

Mieder, Wolfgang – Alan Dundes (eds.). 1994. *The Wisdom of Many: Essays on the Proverb*. Madison: University of Wisconsin Press.

Pfister, Lauren F. 1999. "A Transmitter but not a Creator: The Creative Transmission of Protestant Biblical Traditions by Ho Tsun-Sheen (1817–1871)." In: Irene Eber,

---

systems created by various Roman Catholic, Protestant, and other Sinological scholars for Chinese language since the 16th century. So that in the case of Chinese language transcriptions, one can understand why SCM would be frustrated by both the inherent inadequacy of various systems that he encountered as well as the effort it took to attempt to be systematic in his own right (especially since he had never really learned the language as a resident of China, and so was necessarily dependant on those who made attempts to transcribe various terms). One need only look at Herbert Giles' dictionary of Chinese language, where he added the pronunciation of single characters from a number of Chinese dialects and some other East Asian languages (particularly Korean and Japanese) to see how difficult these complications were in the last two decades of the 19th century.

Sze-Kar Wan, Knut Walf, and Roman Malek (eds.), *Bible in Modern China: The Literary and Intellectual Impact*. Nettetal: Steyler Verlag, pp. 165-197.

———. 2004. *Striving for 'The Whole Duty of Man': James Legge (1815–1897) and the Scottish Protestant Encounter with China*. 2 vols. Frankfurt am Main: Peter Lang.

———. [Fei Leren 費樂仁]. 2011. "Yiwei tongxiao duoguo yuyan de Ruishiren dui 'Zhongguo zhihui' de faxian" 一位通晓多国语言的瑞士人对"中国智慧"的发现 [A Swiss Polyglot's Discovery of "Chinese Wisdom"]. In: Pan Derong 潘德荣 (ed.), *Guoxue Xijian: Guoxue dui Xifang de yingxiang guiji* 国学西渐——国学对西方的影响轨迹 (Chinese [National] Studies Flowing Westward: The Tracks of Influences of Chinese [National] Studies in the West]. Hefei: Anhui renmin chubanshe, pp. 81-112.

———. 2012. "A Swiss Polyglot's Discovery about the Chinese Search for Wisdom: Solomon Cæsar Malan's (1812–1894) Comparative Philosophical Contributions in His Original Notes on the Book of Proverbs," *minima sinica* 2012/1, pp. 1-52.

Appendix I

Comparative Locations in the ONBP Manuscript and the *ONBP*

Prov = Chapter/Verses in Proverbs
PV = Printed Version
MS = Manuscript
v = verso/backside
1st Q = Location of first relevant quotation
* = these verses stand in a particular grouping in the ONBP Ms
(?) = Uncertainty based on the research notes

Prov	PV	MS	1st Q
1:1	I, 1	21*	14
1:2	I, 3	21*	"
1:3	I, 7	21*	"
1:4	I, 9	21*	"
1:5	I, 13	21*	"
1:6	I, 15	21*	"
1:7	I, 20	21v*	21v
1:8	I, 25	21v*	"
1:9	I, 27	21v*	"

Prov	PV	MS	1st Q
1:10	I, 29	30*	27
1:11	I, 30	30*	"
1:12	I, 32	30*	"
1:13	I, 32	30*	"
1:14	I, 33	30*	"
1:15	I, 34	30*	"
1:16	I, 36	30*	"
1:17	I, 36	30v*	30v
1:18	I, 37	30v*	"
1:19	I, 39	30v*	"
1:20	I, 40	30v*	"
1:21	I, 41	30v*	"
1:22	I, 41	30v*	"
1:23	I, 43	30v*	"
1:24	I, 45	37*	34v
1:25	I, 45	37*	"
1:26	I, 46	37*	"
1:27	I, 47	37*	"
1:28	I, 49	37v*	"
1:29	I, 50	37v*	"
1:30-31	I, 50	37v*	"
1:32	I, 51	37v*	34v
1:33	I, 53	37v*	"

2:1	I, 55	44*	40
2:2	I, 57	44*	"
2:3	I, 58	44*	"
2:4	I, 59	44*	"
2:5	I, 63	44*	"

Prov	PV	MS	1st Q
2:6	I, 65	44v*	44v
2:7	I, 68	44v*	"
2:8	I, 69	44v*	"
2:9	I, 70	44v*	"
2:10	I, 73	54*	48v
2:11	I, 76	54*	"
2:12	I, 84	54*	"
2:13	I, 85	54*	"
2:14-15	I, 85	54*	"
2:16	I, 85	54v*	51v
2:17	I, 88	54v*	"
2:18	I, 90	54v*	"
2:19	I, 91	54v*	"
2:20	I, 91	61*	56v
2:21	I, 98	61*	"
2:22	I, 99	61*	"

Prov	PV	MS	1st Q
3:1	I, 101	61v*	61v
3:2	I, 102	61v*	"
3:3	I, 105	61v*	"
3:4	I, 110	61v*	"
3:5	I, 115	70*	62v
3:6	I, 118	70*	(62v)
3:7	I, 120	70v*	70v
3:8	I, 122	70v*	"
3:9-10	I, 122	70v*	"
3:11-12	I, 125	74	71v
3:13	I, 131	74*	71v
3:14	I, 134	74*	"

Prov	PV	MS	1st Q
3:15	I, 135	74v*	71v
3:16	I, 137	74v*	"
3:17	I, 138	74v*	"
3:18	I, 139	74v*	"
3:19	I, 141	93*	77v
3:20	I, 171	93*	"
3:21	I, 174	93v*	93v
3:22	I, 175	93v*	"
3:23	I, 176	93v*	"
3:24	I, 178	93v*	"
3:25-26	I, 180	93v*	"
3:27	I, 183	101*	96v
3:28	I, 185	101*	"
3:29	I, 187	101*	"
3:30	I, 187	101v	100v
3:31-32	I, 188	101v	101v
3:33	I, 189	104*	102
3:34	I, 191	104*	"
3:35	I, 192	104*	"

Prov	PV	MS	1st Q
4:1-2	I, 194	104v*	104v
4:3	I, 196	104v*	"
4:4	I, 200	104v*	"
4:5	I, 201	104v*	(104v)
4:6	I, 202	104v*	"
4:7	I, 203	113*	108?/108v
4:8	I, 205	113*	"
4:9	I, 208	113*	"
4:10	I, 211	113v*	113v

Prov	PV	MS	1st Q
4:11	I, 213	113v*	"
4:12	I, 215	113v*	"
4:13	I, 216	113v*	"
4:14-15	I, 220	124*	116v
4:16-17	I, 223-224	124*	"
4:18	I, 224	124*	115v
4:19	I, 231	124*	"
4:20-22	I, 233	124v	124v
4:23	I, 235	137*	125v
4:24	I, 245	137*	"
4:25	I, 246	137*	"
4:26-27	I, 248	137*	"

Prov	PV	MS	1st Q
5:1-2	I, 254	137	131v
5:3-4	I, 255	137v*	137
5:5-6	I, 257	137v*	"
5:7	I, 259	137v*	"
5:8-9	I, 259-260	137v*	"
5:10-11	I, 260-261	137v*	"
5:12-14	I, 264	137v*	140v
5:15	I, 270	149*	"
5:16-17	I, 272	149*	"
5:18-19	I, 273	149*	"
5:10-21	I, 277	149v	149v
5:22	I, 280	149v*	149v
5:23	I, 282	149v*	"

Prov	PV	MS	1st Q
6:1-2	I, 285	154*	152v
6:3	I, 287	154*	"

Prov	PV	MS	1st Q
6:4-5	I, 288	154*	"
6:6-8	I, 289	154v	154v
6:9-11	I, 300	160	157
6:12-15	I, 303	160v	159v
6:16-19	I, 307	165	161v
6:20-23	I, 314	165v	165v
6:24	I, 323	172*	167v
6:25-26	I, 324-325	172*	"
6:27-28	I, 329	172v*	172v
6:29	I, 330	172v*	"
6:30-31	I, 331	172v*	"
6:32-33	I, 333	177*	173
6:34-35	I, 336	177*	"

Prov	PV	MS	1st Q
7:1-3	I, 339	177v*	177v
7:4-5	I, 340	177v*	"
7:6-10	I, 341	180	179
7:11-12	I, 345	180v	180v
7:13-15	I, 346	180v	"
7:16-21	I, 348	180v	"
7:22-23	I, 352	180v	"
7:24-27	I, 357-358	188	185v

Prov	PV	MS	1st Q
8:1-3	I, 361	188v*	188v
8:4-6	I, 362	188v*	"
8:7-9	I, 363	188v*	"
8:10-11	I, 365	193	189v
8:12	I, 367	193*	189v
8:13-14	I, 369	193*	"

Prov	PV	MS	1st Q
8:15-16	I, 371	193v	193v
8:17-18	I, 373	193v	193v
8:19-21	I, 375	197	196
8:22	I, 376	197v*	196v
8:23	I, 380	197v*	"
8:24-26	I, 384	197v*	"
8:27-28	I, 387	197v*	"
8:29	I, 390	197v*	"
8:30-31	I, 392	197v*	"
8:32-33	I, 395	206v*	203v
8:34-36	I, 396	206v*	"

Prov	PV	MS	1st Q
9:1-2	I, 398	210*	207v
9:3-5	I, 403	210*	"
9:6	I, 404	210v	210v
9:7-9	I, 405	210v	210v
9:10-11	I, 408	215*	211v
9:12	I, 413	215*	"
9:13	I, 415	215v*	215v
9:14-18	I, 416	215v*	"
10:1	I, 420	220	218v
10:2	I, 422	220v	218v
10:3	I, 424	220v	220v
10:4	I, 425	225	221v
10:5	I, 430	225v	225v
10:6	I, 432	228	228
10:7	I, 432	228v	227
10:8	I, 436	228v	228v
10:9	I, 437	231*	229v

Prov	PV	MS	1st Q
10:10	I, 438	231*	"
10:11	I, 439	231v	231v
10:12	I, 439	231v	231v
10:13-14	I, 440	234	232v
10:15	I, 442	234v	234v
10:16	I, 450	240	238
10:17	I, 453	240v	240v
10:18	I, 454	243	242
10:19	I, 456	243v	243v
10:20	I, 460	248*	247
10:21	I, 461	248*	"
10:22	I, 462	248v	248v
10:23	I, 465	251	251
10:24	I, 466	251	251
10:25	I, 467	251v	251v
10:26	I, 469	255	255
10:27	I, 469	255	254
10:28	I, 471	255v*	254
10:29	I, 474	255v*	"
10:30	I, 476	255v*	"
10:31	I, 476	258*	256v
10:32	I, 478	258*	"

11:1	II, 1	258	257v
11:2	II, 3	258v	258v
11:3	II, 6	262	259v
11:4	II, 9	262	261
11:5	II, 11	262v*	262v
11:6	II, 14	262v*	"

Prov	PV	MS	1st Q
11:7	II, 15	262v	262v
11:8	II, 16	267	267
11:9	II, 16	267	264v
11:10	II, 21	267v	267v
11:11	II, 22	267v	267v
11:12	II, 23	270	268v
11:13	II, 26	270v	269
11:14	II, 30	272	272
11:15	II, 32	272	272
11:16	II, 33	272v	272v
11:17	II, 37	276	274
11:18	II, 42	276v*	276v
11:19	II, 44	276v*	"
11:20	II, 45	278v*	277v
11:21	II, 46	278v*	"
11:22	II, 50	282	279
11:23	II, 53	282v	280v
11:24	II, 57	282v*	282v
11:25	II, 65	282v*	"
11:26	II, 70	282v*	"
11:27	II, 72	293v	293
11:28	II, 76	293v	291v
11:29	II, 79	297	296v
11:30	II, 82	297v	297v
11:31	II, 86	297v*	(297v)

12:1	II, 91	303	301
12:2	II, 96	303v*	302
12:3	II, 97	303v*	"

Prov	PV	MS	1st Q
12:4	II, 97	309	305v
12:5	II, 107	309v*	309v
12:6	II, 108	309v*	"
12:7	II, 108	309v*	"
12:8	II, 109	311	310v
12:9	II, 111	311v	311
12:10	II, 113	311v	311v
12:11	II, 115	315	313v
12:12	II, 120	315v*	315v
12:13	II, 121	315v*	"
12:14	II, 121	318	317
12:15	II, 123	318v	318v
12:16	II, 128	322	321v
12:17	II, 130	322v*	321
12:18	II, 133	322v*	"
12:19	II, 137	324v	324v
12:20	II, 139	327v	326v
12:21	II, 141	327v	327
12:22	II, 142	329	329
12:23	II, 144	329v	329v
12:24	II, 145	329v	329v
12:25	II, 150	333v	331
12:26	II, 151	333v	332v
12:27	II, 153	336	334v
12:28	II, 155	336v	336v

13:1	II, 156	336v	336v
13:2	II, 161	342*	339v
13:3	II, 162	342*	"

Prov	PV	MS	1st Q
13:4	II, 164	342v	342v
13:5	II, 165	342v	342v
13:6	II, 166	346	343
13:7	II, 169	346v*	344v
13:8	II, 173	346v*	"
13:9	II, 174	351	347v
13:10	II, 176	351	349
13:11	II, 178	351v	350v
13:12	II, 184	351v	350v
13:13	II, 186	358*	356v
13:14	II, 188	358*	"
13:15	II, 189	385	356v
13:16	II, 190	358v	358v
13:17	II, 191	358v	358v
13:18	II, 193	361	361
13:19	II, 194	361	361
13:20	II, 195	361v	361v
13:21	II, 206	361v	361v
13:22	II, 209	372*	269v
13:23	II, 211	372*	"
13:24	II, 212	372	372
13:25	II, 214	372v	372v

14:1	II, 215	372v	372v
14:2	II, 218	375*	374
14:3	II, 218	375*	"
14:4	II, 219	375	374v
14:5	II, 220	375v	375v
14:6	II, 221	375v*	375v

Prov	PV	MS	1st Q
14:7	II, 224	375v*	"
14:8	II, 226	384*	377v
14:9	II, 232	384*	"
14:10	II, 233	384	381v
14:11	II, 235	284v	284v
14:12	II, 236	384v	284v
14:13	II, 237	390	386
14:14	II, 239	390	386v
14:15	II, 245	390v*	386v
14:16	II, 251	390v*	"
14:17	II, 254	390v	390v
14:18	II, 256	397	397
14:19	II, 256	397	397
14:20	II, 257	397v	396v
14:21	II, 260	397v	397v
14:22	II, 263	405	401
14:23	II, 264	405	401
14:24	II, 268	405v	405v
14:25	II, 269	405v	405v
14:26	II, 270	411	406v
14:27	II, 274	411	408v
14:28	II, 274	411	407v
14:29	II, 279	411v	411v
14:30	II, 284	411v	411v
14:31	II, 287	419	418v
14:32	II, 288	419	416
14:33	II, 294	419v	419v
14:34	II, 296	419v	419v
14:35	II, 299	425	422

Prov	PV	MS	1st Q
15:1	II, 304	425	422v
15:2	II, 307	425v	424
15:3	II, 308	425v	425v
15:4	II, 312	431	429
15:5	II, 313	431	429v
15:6	II, 314	431v	431v
15:7	II, 315	431v	431v
15:8-9	II, 316	433	432v
15:10	II, 318	433	433
15:11	II, 319	433v	433v
15:12	II, 320	433v	433v
15:13	II, 322	439	434v
15:14	II, 325	439	434
15:15	II, 328	439v	438v
15:16	II, 333	439v*	439v
15:17	II, 337	439v*	"
15:18	II, 340	448	448
15:19	II, 341	448	446v
15:20	II, 343	448v	448v
15:21	II, 343	448v	448v
15:22	II, 344	453	452
15:23	II, 347	453	450v
15:24	II, 349	453v	453v
15:25	II, 353	453v	453v
15:26	II, 353	456	455v
15:27	II, 355	456	455
15:28	II, 357	456v	456v
15:29	II, 358	456v	456v
15:30	II, 361	456v	456v

Prov	PV	MS	1st Q
15:31	II, 362	462*	459
15:32	II, 364	462*	"
15:33	II, 365	462	460

Prov	PV	MS	1st Q
16:1	II, 367	462v*	462v
16:2	II, 368	462v*	"
16:3	II, 370	462v*	"
16:4	II, 376	468	464v (?)
16:5	II, 377	468	466v
16:6	II, 378	468v	468v
16:7	II, 379	468v	468v
16:8	II, 380	472	469v
16:9	II, 383	472	470v
16:10	II, 385	472v	472v
16:11	II, 386	472v	472v
16:12	II, 386	472v*	472v
16:13	II, 392	472v*	"
16:14	II, 393	472v*	"
16:15	II, 394	472v*	"
16:16	II, 396	478v	478v
16:17	II, 397	478v	478v
16:18	II, 398	486*	480
16:19	II, 403	486*	"
16:20	II, 405	486*	479v
16:21	II, 407	486*	"
16:22	II, 408	486v*	486v
16:23	II, 409	486v*	"
16:24	II, 412	486v	486v
16:25	II, 416	495	490v

Prov	PV	MS	1st Q
16:26	II, 416	495	488v
16:27	II, 424	495v	495v
16:28	II, 424	495v	494v
16:29	II, 426	449*	496v
16:30	II, 427	449*	"
16:31	II, 428	449*	496v
16:32	II, 432	499v	497v
16:33	II, 444	499v	499v

Prov	PV	MS	1st Q
17:1	II, 446	507	505
17:2	II, 451	507	503v
17:3	II, 452	507v	507v
17:4	II, 452	507v	507v
17:5	II, 453	510	509v
17:6	II, 454	510	508
17:7	II, 456	510	510
17:8	II, 457	510v	510v
17:9	II, 459	510v	510v
17:10	II, 461	514	513v
17:11	II, 462	514	513v
17:12	II, 463	514	513v
17:13	II, 463	514v	514v
17:14	II, 464	514v	514v
17:15	II, 467	514v	514v
17:16	II, 468	523	517v
17:17	II, 472	523	518v
17:18	II, 481	523v	523v
17:19	II, 481	523v	523v
17:20	II, 483	523v	523v

Prov	PV	MS	1st Q
17:21	II, 485	527	526
17:22	II, 485	527	526v
17:23	II, 487	527v	527v
17:24	II, 489	527v	527v
17:25	II, 493	532	530v
17:26	II, 493	532	532
17:27	II, 494	532v*	532v
17:28	II, 501	532v*	"
18:1	II, 504	539	536
18:2	II, 509	539	536v
18:3	II, 511	539	536v
18:4	II, 511	539v	539v
18:5	II, 512	539v	539v
18:6	II, 513	539v*	539v
18:7	II, 514	539v*	"
18:8	II, 515	543	541v
18:9	II, 516	543	542v
18:10	II, 517	543	541v
18:11	II, 518	543v	543v
18:12	II, 520	543v	543v
18:13	II, 521	550	546
18:14	II, 523	550	546v
18:15	II, 531	550	549
18:16	II, 532	550v	550v
18:17	II, 533	550v	549v
18:18	II, 536	550v	550v
18:19	II, 536	553	549v
18:20	II, 538	553	552v

Prov	PV	MS	1st Q
18:21	II, 539	553v	553v
18:22	II, 542	561	553v
18:23	II, 548	561	554v
18:24	II, 556	561v	559v

Prov	PV	MS	1st Q
19:1	II, 564	569	565v
19:2	II, 567	569	565v
19:3	II, 571	569v	569v
19:4	II, 573	569v	564v
19:5	II, 578	573	573
19:6	II, 580	573v	572v
19:7	II, 583	573v	570
19:8	II, 589	580	580
19:9	II, 590	580	578v
19:10	II, 591	580	579
19:11	II, 592	580v	580v
19:12	II, 598	580v	580v
19:13	II, 601	590	587
19:14	II, 603	590	586v
19:15	II, 608	590v	588v
19:16	II, 610	590v	590v
19:17	II, 612	596	592v
19:18	II, 619	596	593v
19:19	II, 621	596v	595
19:20	II, 623	596v	595
19:21	II, 628	603	598v
19:22	II, 632	603	598v
19:23	II, 636	603	601v
19:24	II, 638	603v	603v

Prov	PV	MS	1st Q
19:25	II, 639	603v	603v
19:26	II, 641	603v*	603v
19:27	II, 643	603v*	"
19:28-29	II, 645	607	605v

Prov	PV	MS	1st Q
20:1	II, 646	607	605v
20:2	II, 649	607v	607v
20:3	II, 650	607v	607v
20:4	II, 651	607v	607v
20:5	II, 655	616	610
20:6	II, 657	616	610v
20:7	II, 667	616	615v
20:8	II, 669	616v	615v
20:9	II, 671	616v	615v
20:10	II, 675	616v	616v
20:11	II, 675	616v	616v
20:12	II, 680	624	623v
20:13	II, 681	624	620v
20:14	II, 684	624	621v
20:15	II, 686	624v	624v
20:16	II, 687	624v	624v
20:17	II, 688	624v	624v
20:18	II, 688	629	625v
20:19	II, 692	629	625v
20:20	II, 696	629v	629v
20:21	II, 697	629v	629v
20:22	II, 698	629v	629v
20:23	II, 701	635	631
20:24	II, 701	635	631

Prov	PV	MS	1st Q
20:25	II, 704	635	631
20:26	II, 706	635	632
20:27	II, 708	635v	633v
20:28	II, 714	635v	633v (?)
20:29	II, 723	635v	635v
20:30	II, 726	635v	635v
21:1	III, 1	645	643 (?)
21:2	III, 1	645	643v
21:3	III, 2	645	642
21:4	III, 5	645v	645v
21:5	III, 6	645v	645v
21:6	III, 10	645v	645v
21:7	III, 11	651	650v
21:8	III, 12	651	648v
21:9	III, 15	651	649v
21:10	III, 16	651v	649
21:11	III, 18	651v	651v
21:12	III, 19	651v	651v
21:13	III, 19	655	653
21:14	III, 20	655	655
21:15	III, 21	655	654v
21:16	III, 21	655v	655v
21:17	III, 22	655v	655v
21:18	III, 23	655v	none found*
21:19	III, 23	659	656v
21:20	III, 26	659	657
21:21	III, 28	659	656v
21:22	III, 29	659v	659v

Prov	PV	MS	1st Q
21:23	III, 30	659v	659v
21:24	III, 32	659v	659v
21:25	III, 32	668*	661v
21:26	III, 35	668*	"
21:27	III, 44	668	663v
21:28	III, 46	668	668
21:29	III, 46	668v	668v
21:30	III, 47	668v*	668v
21:31	III, 49	668v*	"
22:1	III, 52	668v	668v
22:2	III, 61	681	675v
22:3	III, 64	681	675v
22:4	III, 68	681	675v
22:5	III, 73	681v	681v
22:6	III, 74	681v	681v
22:7	III, 84	689	683v
22:8	III, 88	689	689
22:9	III, 88	689v	689
22:10	III, 99	689v	689v
22:11	III, 99	696	695v
22:12	III, 100	696	696
22:13	III, 101	696	695v
22:14	III, 101	696v	696v
22:15	III, 102	696v	696v
22:16	III, 103	701	697v
22:17	III, 105	701*	697v
22:18	III, 105	701*	700
22:19-20	III, 107	701*	698v

Prov	PV	MS	1st Q
22:21	III, 108	701*	698
22:22-23	III, 112	701v	700
22:24-25	III, 114	701v	701v
22:26-27	III, 120	708	702v
22:28	III, 123	708	706
22:29	III, 124	708	705v

Prov	PV	MS	1st Q
23:1-3	III, 129	708v	708v
23:4-5	III, 135	708v	708v
23:6-8	III, 145	719	715
23:9	III, 149	719	716v
23:10-11	III, 151	719	715v
23:12	III, 153	719v	719v
23:13-14	III, 155	719v	719v
23:15-16	III, 157	723*	722
23:17-18	III, 158	723*	720v
23:19-21	III, 165	723v	723v
23:22-23	III, 175	723v	723v
23:24-25	III, 186	736	733v
23:26-28	III, 189	736	733v
23:29-32	III, 192	736v*	736
23:33-35	III, 199	736v*	736v

Prov	PV	MS	1st Q
24:1-2	III, 206	743	742v
24:3-4	III, 206	743	741v
24:5-6	III, 208	743v	743v
24:7	III, 213	743v	743v
24:8	III, 215	743v	743v
24:9	III, 216	752	748

Prov	PV	MS	1st Q
24:10	III, 218	752	748
24:11-12	III, 225	752v	752v
24:13-14	III, 232	752v	752v
24:15-16	III, 237	762	758
24:17-18	III, 243	762	760
24:19-20	III, 245	762v	761
24:21-22	III, 246	762v	762v
24:23-25	III, 253	768	766v
24:26	III, 255	768	766v
24:27	III, 256	768	765v
24:28-29	III, 259	768v	767v
24:30-34	III, 263	768v	769 (?)
25:1	III, 266	774	774
25:2-3	III, 266	774	773/772v
25:4-5	III, 268-269	774	772
25:6-7	III, 271	774v	774v
25:8-10	III, 273	774v/779	774v/775v
25:11	III, 281	779	778v
25:12	III, 283	779v	779v
25:13	III, 285	779v	779v
25:14	III, 287	779v	779v
25:15	III, 293	789	784v
25:16-17	III, 295	789	789/785v
25:18	III, 299	789v	788v
25:19	III, 300	789v	789v
25:20	III, 303	794	790v
25:21-22	III, 304	794	790v
25:23	III, 309	794	790v
25:24	III, 310	794v	794v

Prov	PV	MS	1st Q
25:25	III, 311	794v	794v
25:26	III, 313	794v	794v
25:27	III, 314	799	797
25:28	III, 318	799	797v

Prov	PV	MS	1st Q
26:1	III, 319	799v	799v
26:2	III, 320	799v	799v
26:3	III, 321	799v	799v
26:4-5	III, 322	805	800v
26:6	III, 323	805	803
26:7-9	III, 324	805*	801v
26:10	III, 326	805*	801v
26:11	III, 329	805*	801v
26:12	III, 332	805v	805v
26:13-16	III, 337	805v	805v
26:17	III, 340	810	807v
26:18-19	III, 341	810	808v
26:20-21	III, 345	810v*	810v
26:22	III, 346	810v*	"
26:23-25	III, 347	819*	812v
26:26	III, 357	819*	814
26:27	III, 358	819v	818v
26:28	III, 361	819v	819v

Prov	PV	MS	1st Q
27:1	III, 363	824	821
27:2	III, 372	824v	821v
27:3	III, 375	824v	824v
27:4	III, 376	831	825v
27:5-6	III, 380	831	825v

Prov	PV	MS	1st Q
27:7	III, 387	831v	830v
27:8	III, 389	831v	831v
27:9-10	III, 396	842	831v (?)
27:11	III, 409	842v	842v
27:12	III, 410	842v	842v
27:13-14	III, 411	842v/845	842v (?)
27:15-16	III, 414	845	843v
27:17	III, 416	845v	845v
27:18	III, 418	845v	845v
27:19	III, 420	845v	845v
27:20	III, 422	851	851
27:21	III, 423	851	848v
27:22	III, 425	851	848
27:23-27	III, 430	851v	850
28:1	III, 439	857	856v
28:2	III, 440	857	856
28:3	III, 441	857v	857v
28:4	III, 443	857v	857v
28:5	III, 444	857v	857v
28:6	III, 444	860	858v
28:7	III, 448	860	860
28:8	III, 449	860v	860v
28:9	III, 454	860v	860v
28:10	III, 455	867	864v
28:11	III, 455	867	861v
28:12	III, 459	867	866v
28:13	III, 460	867v	867v
28:14	III, 465	867v	867v
28:15	III, 467	876	872

Prov	PV	MS	1st Q
28:16	III, 469	876	870v
28:17	III, 474	876v	876v
28:18	III, 476	876v	876v
28:19	III, 476	881	877v
28:20	III, 480	881	878v
28:21	III, 482	881	881
28:22	III, 483	881v	881v
28:23	III, 485	881v	881v
28:24	III, 487	884	*none in MS
28:25	III, 488	884	884
28:26	III, 488	884	883v
28:27	III, 489	884v	884v
28:28	III, 493	884v	*none in MS

Prov	PV	MS	1st Q
29:1	III, 494	884v	884v
29:2	III, 495	889	886v (?)
29:3	III, 496	889	889
29:4	III, 497	889v	888v
29:5	III, 502	889v	889v
29:6	III, 503	889v	889v
29:7	III, 503	894	891v
29:8	III, 504	894	892
29:9	III, 506	894	891
29:10	III, 509	894v	894v
29:11	III, 509	894v	894v
29:12	III, 510	894v	895v
29:13	III, 513	899	895v
29:14	III, 514	899	898v
29:15	III, 517	899v	899v

Prov	PV	MS	1st Q
29:16	III, 522	899v	899v
29:17	III, 522	899v	*none in MS
29:18	III, 523	906	903v
29:19	III, 524	906	904
29:20	III, 526	906	906v
29:21	III, 528	906v	906v
29:22	III, 529	906v	906v
29:23	III, 530	906v	908
29:24	III, 532	911	910v
29:25	III, 533	911	910v
29:26	III, 534	911	907v
29:27	III, 535	911v	*none in MS
30:1	III, 537	911v*	911v
30:2	III, 538	911v*	"
30:3	III, 539	911v*	"
30:4	III, 539	914	913v(?)
30:5-6	III, 542	914	912
30:7-9	III, 543	914v	914v
30:10	III, 547	918	917
30:11-14	III, 548	918	*none in MS
30:15-16	III, 548	918v	918v
30:17	III, 550	918v	918v
30:18-20	III, 552	921	920
30:21-23	III, 554	921	920v
30:24-28	III, 555	921v	921v
30:29-31	III, 558	924	922v
30: 32-33	III, 559	924	922v

Prov	PV	MS	1st Q
31:1-2	III, 561	926v*	926v
31:3-7	III, 562-563	926v*	"
31:8-9	III, 569	935	927v
31:10-12	III, 570	935	927v
31:13-17	III, 580	935v*	935v
31:18-19	III, 583	935v*	"
31:20-22	III, 584	938	937v
31:23-25	III, 586	938v	938v
31:26-28	III, 586-587	942*	939v
31:29-31	III, 594	942*	939v

Appendix II

These three images of pages from the ONBP Ms were provided by the Bodleian Libraries in Oxford, and copyright privileges have been obtained to publish them here in this volume. Identification of the text as found in the ONBP Ms is documented in bottom margin of each image, and provided here in another format. A fourth image from another page within the ONBP Ms appears in Chapter 4 within this volume (see Fig. 6, p. 53).

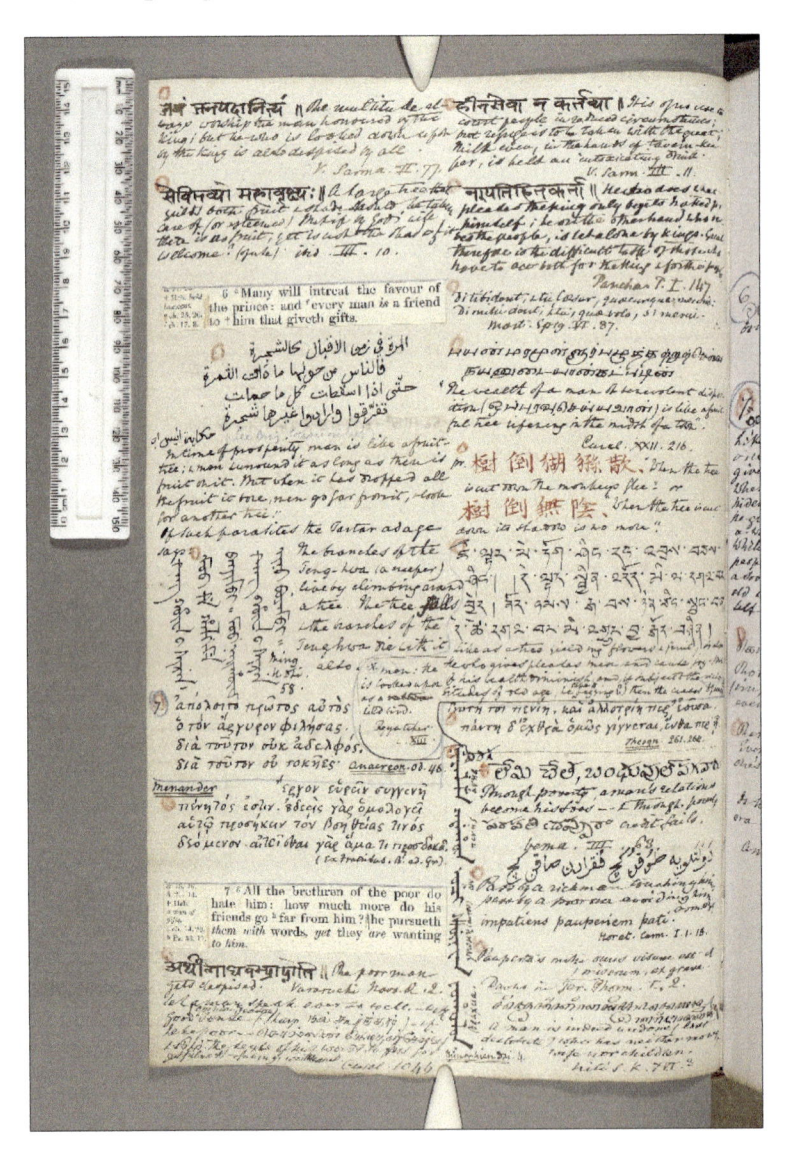

Fig. 20: Bodleian Color Image (ONBP Ms), MS.Ind.Inst.Misc. 10, f. 573 verso. Reprinted with permission of the Bodleian Library, University of Oxford

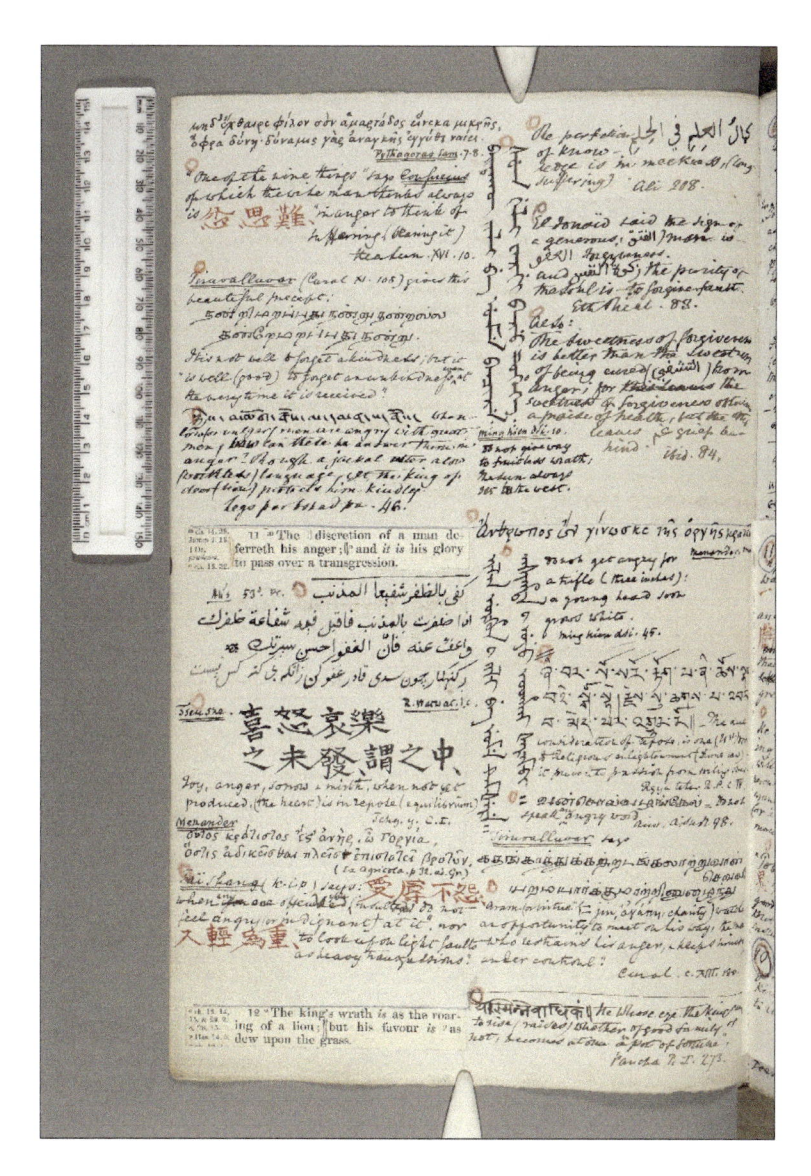

Fig. 21: Bodleian Color Image (ONBP Ms), MS.Ind.Inst.Misc. 10, f. 580 verso. Reprinted with permission of the Bodleian Library, University of Oxford

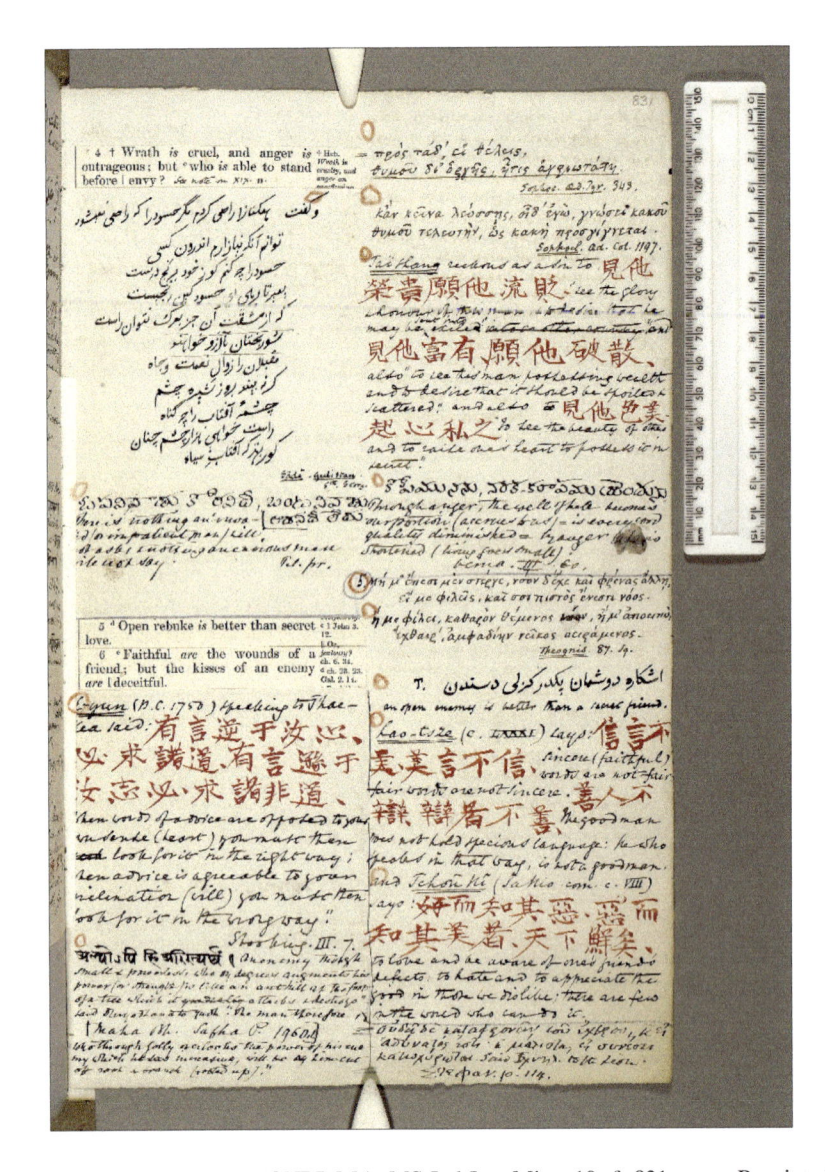

Fig. 22: Bodleian Color Image (ONBP Ms), MS.Ind.Inst.Misc. 10, f. 831 recto. Reprinted with permission of the Bodleian Library, University of Oxford.

NOTES ON CONTRIBUTORS

Frédéric Amsler is a senior professor at the Faculty of Theology and Sciences of Religions (FTSR) of the University of Lausanne, and the former director of its French-speaking Swiss Institute of Biblical Sciences. He holds a Doctorate of Theology (1994) from the University of Geneva. His fields of research are Christian apocryphal literature and history of Christianity in Antiquity, on one side, and the history of theology in the nineteenth century on the other side. Recent publications include: "La construction de l'homme ennemi ou l'anti-paulinisme dans le corpus pseudo-clémentin" in: *Receptions of Paul in Early Christianity: The Person of Paul and His Writings Through the Eyes of His Early Interpreters*, ed. J. Schröter, S. Butticaz and A. Dettwiler, Berlin – Boston, W. de Gruyter, 2018, pp. 729-747; *Alfred Loisy et la Grande Guerre*, F. Amsler éd. in *Modernism* 7 (2021), pp. 8-143.

T. H. (Tim) Barrett is professor emeritus of East Asian History in the University of London, where he taught at the School of Oriental and African Studies, for the latter part of his time there in the Department of Religions and Philosophies; he has also taught at Cambridge and Stanford. He graduated from Cambridge in 1971 in Chinese Studies and was awarded a Ph.D. from Yale in Buddhist Studies in 1978. His main publications concern historical aspects of the Buddhist, Daoist and Confucian traditions of China and Japan, such as the religious aspects of early printing in East Asia, published as *The Woman Who Discovered Printing* (New Haven: Yale University Press, 2008). He has also written extensively on the understanding of China in Britain.

John Edwards is a senior research professor at St Francis Xavier University (Antigonish), and is a fellow of the British Psychological Society, the Canadian Psychological Association, and the Royal Society of Canada. His main research interest is in group identity, with particular reference to language in both its communicative and symbolic aspects. Edwards's books include *Language, Society and Identity* (Oxford: Blackwell, 1985), *Multilingualism* (London: Penguin, 1995), *Language and Identity* (Cambridge, 2009), *Minority Languages and Group Identity* (Amsterdam – Philadelphia: Benjamins, 2010), *Multilingualism: Understanding Linguistic Diversity* (London – New York: Continuum, 2012) and *Sociolinguistics: A Very Short Introduction* (Oxford: Oxford University Press, 2013). His works have been translated into a dozen foreign languages.

James Marcel Hegarty is the professor of Sanskrit and Indian Religions at Cardiff University. His work takes up the role of religious narrative in South Asian history and culture. In particular, he focuses on the role of the Sanskrit *Mahābhārata* in the transmission and adaption of understandings of the significant past, of place and of understandings of religious and political authority. He is the author of *Religion, Narrative and Public Imagination: Past and Place in the Sanskrit* Mahābhārata

(London: Routledge, 2012). More recently, he has published on the arrival of Christianity in India, the internal structure of the foundational text of Swami Narayana Hinduism, the *Vachanamrut*, and early South Asian religious movements and their relationship to each other.

Loretta Kim (Kim Eumie 金由美) is an associate professor and coordinator of the China Studies program at the School of Modern Languages and Cultures, University of Hong Kong. She is a historian of late imperial and modern China. Her primary research areas include the comparative history of borderlands and frontiers, Sino-Russian cultural relations, and Chinese ethnic minority languages and literatures. She is the author of *Ethnic Chrysalis: China's Orochen People and the Legacy of Qing Borderland Administration* (Cambridge, Mass. – London: Harvard University Press, 2019) and the forthcoming *The Russian Orthodox Community in Hong Kong: Religion, Ethnicity, and Intercultural Relations* (to be published in 2021).

Rita Kuzder is a docent at the Dharma Gate Buddhist College in Budapest, Hungary, teaching Classical Tibetan Language, Tibetan Philosophy, and Buddhist Symbology. In 2012 she earned a Ph.D. in Hungarian and Contemporary Folkloristics from the University of ELTE, Budapest. Currently she works on an exercise book in classical Tibetan, and teaches an online course for students studying classical Tibetan. Her research interests are in the study of the genre of written and oral Tibetan folklore and topics in Tibetan Buddhism. She has published articles in Hungarian dealing with "A Selection of Gems from Tibetan proverbs" and "On Necshung, the Tibetan state oracle."

William Y. Ng 吳有能 (Ph.D., Toronto) teaches Chinese Philosophy and Religion, Matters of Life and Death, Environmental and Animal Ethics, and Buddhism at the Hong Kong Baptist University. His major publications including the following monographs and edited volumes: *Dangdai Gang Tai zhexue lunheng* 當代港台哲學論衡 [Comparative Horizon: Discourses on Contemporary Philosophy in Hong Kong and Taiwan] (Taipei: Liberal Arts Press, 2009); (ed.), *Duoduo liansheng* 朵朵蓮生——真佛宗研究論集 [The Lotus Blossoms: A Study of the True Buddha School] (Taipei: Literature, History, and Philosophy Press, 2016); (ed. with Ka-fu Keith Chan), *Paul Tillich and Asian Religions* (Berlin – Boston: De Gruyter, 2017); (ed. with Kwan Kai-man and K. T. Ip), *Quanren jiaoyu: Zhong Xi duihua* 全人教育——中西對話 [Whole Person Education: East and West] (Taipei: National Taiwan Normal University Press, 2017).

Gyula Paczolay, Ph.D., is a chemical engineer and a professor emeritus in that field, later becoming a researcher in proverbial sayings (paremiology). Awarded in 2000 UNESCO's European Folklore Medal and Diploma, in that same year he became an honorary member of the Hungarian Ethnographic Society. His major publications in paremiology are *European, Far-Eastern, and some Asian Proverbs: A Comparison of European, Chinese, Korean, Japanese, Vietnamese, and other*

Addenda to the European, Far-Eastern, and some Asian Proverbs (Veszprém: Central Library of the University of Veszprém, 1996) and *European Proverbs in 55 Languages with Equivalents in Arabic, Persian, Sanskrit, Chinese and Japanese / Európai közmondások* (Veszprém: Veszprémi Ny., 1997).

Lauren F. Pfister (Fei Leren 費樂仁) is a professor emeritus from Hong Kong Baptist University. His scholarly works explore issues in Chinese philosophy and its history, Sino-European comparative philosophical studies, and Sino-Anglo-European comparative religious studies. His major publications on James Legge (1815–1897) and other 19th and 20th century missionary-scholars in English and Chinese have been considered important contributions to studies in the history of Sinology. Most recently he has published a major volume entitled *Vital Post-Secular Perspectives on Chinese Philosophical Issues* (Lanham *et al.*: Lexington Books, 2020).

Rolf Gerhard Tiedemann (Di Deman 狄德満, 1941–2019) was a professor of Modern Chinese History at Shandong University in the PRC, before he passed away in 2019. Previously he taught for many years in the School of Oriental and African Studies in the University of London. His major research interest was the history of Chinese Christianity in the 19th and early 20th centuries. He was the editor of the immensely important and encyclopedic volume, *The Handbook of the Study of Christianity in China: 1800 to the Present* (Leiden – Boston: Brill, 2010). Since then he had produced a number of major articles in Chinese and English as well as a monograph on articles and books dealing with one of his major areas of expertise, the Boxer Rebellion.

Thomas Zimmer is a Sinologist and currently working as a distinguished professor at the Sino-German Center for Cultural Exchange at Tongji University in Shanghai. His major research focuses on studies of traditional and contemporary Chinese narrative art, with a current interest in the reconstruction of traditional Chinese worldviews based on historical sources. Most recently he has published (as co-editor) a book on competence on China in Germany and competence on Germany in China: *China-Kompetenz in Deutschland und Deutschland-Kompetenz in China: Multi- und transdisziplinäre Perspektiven und Praxis* (Wiesbaden: Springer, 2021).

GENERAL INDEX

A

Ackland, Valentine (1906–1969) 47
Alden, Robert (1937–1996) 95-96, 98
Aleni, Giulio (Ai Rulüe 艾儒略, 1582–1649) 156, 158, 159
Amenemope/Amen-em-Ope 95-97
Analects or *The Confucian Analects*, see *Lunyu*
Anglican Church / Church of England 19, 24, 26n55, 42, 80, 242, 257n14, 276, missionaries of the ~ 20, priest(s) of the ~ 18, 28; see also Church Missionary Society
Anglo-Saxon (language) 82
Anii/Ani 97
anti-proverbs 302
Arabic (language) 57, 86, 88, 93, 129, 212, 263n35, 267-268, 285-286, 298, 302-303
Aramaic (language) 86, 88, 97, 268, 297, 300, 302
Armenia 59n68, 87n33, 278
[Royal] Asiatic Society of Bengal 25, 51, 212, 231, 234, 238, 241
Assyrian (language) 265, 278n98, 285
Atisha (982–1054) 176, 189
autism 63-65, 67, 70, 73
Avestan (language) 87

B

Bactrian (language) 265, 267n54
Bai er laoren yulu 百二老人語錄 / *Emu tanggū juwan sakda gisun sarkiyan* (Manchu: Words of One Hundred and Twenty Old Men) 160
baoying 報應, see retribution
Barnes, William (1801–1886) 35-37
Bengali/Bengalese (language) 31, 33, 263n35 and 37, 264, 285
Bible: Authorized Version 79, 82, 99; Gospel of John 82, 83, 89, 91; Greek New Testament 83-84; King James Version (KJV) 89-90, 91n43, 216n30, 239, 291-292, 294, 299-300; Latin Vulgate 82, 91, 99, 225, 291; Proverbs, the biblical book of 52, 90, 95-98, 125-126, 129-130, 137-138, 185-186, 194, *et passim*; Revised English Version (of the New Testament) 79, 273n77; Septuagint (Greek Version of the *Tanakh* / Old Testament) 91, 93, 99, 300
Bishop's College 175, 212, 214, 229, 231, 241, 273, 276, 289
Boden, Joseph (ca. 1760–1811) 20, 212, 248n80, 276n88
Bodleian Library/Libraries 85-86, 128, 177, 185, 253-254, 261, 274, 283, *et passim*
Bonaparte, Napoléon (1769–1821) 4
Book of Ahiqar 97
Brāhūi (language) 265
Bridport News 39
British citizen(ship) 19n11, 129, 233
Broadwindsor 37-40, 42, 44, *et passim*
Budapest/Buda and Pest 39-40, 175-177
Buddhism/Buddhist: Chinese ~ 126, 188; Burmese ~ 30, 268; Pali texts 30, 186, 210, 219; Sanskrit texts 30, 176, 178, 185, 186, 188, 193, 199; Tibetan ~ 131, 188-189, 200, 230, 232n18, 237n39; Tibetan texts 194, 201-205
Burmese (language) 262-263, 265, 267, 285, 302
byang chub lam gyi sgron ma བྱང་ཆུབ་ལམ་གྱི་སྒྲོན་མ་, see *Lamp for the Path to Enlightenment*

C

Calcutta 39, 48, 51, 79, 83, 175-177, 211-214, 231, 234-238, 241-242
Calvin, Jean (1509–1564) 3, 11, see also catechism(s), Geneva
Calvinists/Calvinism 3, 11, 235-236, 257, see also Geneva
Cape of Good Hope/The Cape 23, 26, 60n75
catechism(s) 12, 158n42, 263, Calvin's ~ 3
cause and effect (*yinguo* 因果) 107
Chadwick, Owen (1916–2015) 50-51, 60-62
Chaldean (language) 86, 93, 285

Chapel of Witnessing / *Chapelle du Témoignage* 12
Chiang Yee 蔣彝 (1903–1977) 41
Chinese (language) 17, 25-27, 30, 35-37, 41, 83-84, 86, 88, 256, 259-261, 267, 285
Ching, Julia (Qin Jiayi 秦家懿, 1934–2001) 142
Christian scholarship / scholarly reflection 80, 83-84, 87, 98-100
Church of England, see Anglican Church
Church of Geneva, Protestant Reformed 2, 3, 8, 12, 19
Church Missionary Society 18, 20
Cobo, Juan (Gao Muxian 高母羨, ca. 1546–1592) 108
commentary/ies: biblical ~ 96, 284, 300; Chinese ~ 105, 128, 143n89, 144, 301; classical Sanskrit ~ 214; Jewish ~ 86, 285; Manchurian ~ 168n75, 169n83
Communes réunies 5, 7
comparative wisdom literature 95, 259
Confucianism/Confucian 27, 112, 157
congshu 叢書 (literary collections) 110
conversion/converts 3, 10, 11-12, 20n21, 27, 212, 267-268, 272n74, 280n119
Coptic (language) 48-49, 83, 93, 130n21, 286
creativity 67, 73-74, 192
Csoma Bequest 176-177, 188, 240, 247-248, 274n82; see also Malan Bequest
Csoma de Kőrös, Alexander (Kőrösi Csoma Sándor, 1784–1842) 25, 39, 51, 95, 175, 183, 229-252
cultivation, see self-cultivation, self-transformation
cultural accommodation 29

D

Dalai Lama, see Ngawang Lobsang Gyatsho (1617–1682)
Dandin (ca. 6–7th c.) 177
Daxue 大學 (The Great Learning) 124, 135, 136nn46,47, 144, 146n102, 148, 156, 168n75
dao 道 112, 137, cultivating the ~ (*xiudao* 修道) 107

Daoism/Daoist 103, 105-108, 112, 123n3, 126, 136n45, 160, 168, 259, 262
database (related to the *ONBP*) 88, 178n17, 294, 301-302, 306
deva (a god) 208, 223
Doctrine of the Mean, see *Zhongyong*
doedra (*zlos sgra* ཟློས་སྒྲ་) 181
Dorset/Dorsetshire 33, 87, 207, 226, 241, 250, 253, 258
Dsang-Lun (*mdzang blun zhes bya ba'i mdo* མཛངས་བླུན་ཞེས་བྱ་བའི་མདོ་, The Sutra of the Wise and the Foolish) 180, 193n75, 198-199, 239-240
Duin felehe oyonggo šošohon (Manchu: Four Volumes of Pithy Sayings), see *Si ben jianyao*
Duka, Theodore (1825–1908) 230n7, 233-234, 237, 241, 243-249, 274

E

East India Company 18, 211n12, 212
Egyptian hieroglyphics 95, 98n69, 259, 272n72, 302
Emu tanggū juwan sakda gisun sarkiyan (Manchu: Words of One Hundred and Twenty Old Men), see *Bai er laoren yulu*
Endlicher, Stephan Ladislaus (1804–1849) 36
Enduringge di giyūn kuwan mafa-i jalan de ulhibure boobai tacihiyan-i nomun bithe (Manchu: Precious Teachings for the Edification of the World), see *Guansheng di jun jueshi baoxun jing*
English (language) 18, 25-26, 48, 55, 95, 192n73, 285
Ethiopian/Ethiopic (language) 48, 80, 82, 83, 267n47, 268, 273n74, 280n120, 285
etymology/etymological 81n9, 82, 86, 100, 223
Evangelicalism/evangelical 12n37, 19-20, 24, 26n55, 80, 87, 99-100, 236
Extensive Play Sutra (*rgya cher rol pa* རྒྱ་ཆེར་རོལ་པ་) 178, 190

F

Fanyi liushi zhenyan 繙譯六事箴言 / *Ubaliyambuha ninggun baita targabun gisun* (Manchu: Admonitions Regarding Six Subjects) 160

French (language) 47-48, 55, 71, 94, 234n31, 265, 285

Four Books, see *Sishu*

footnotes (in *ONBP*) 88, 103, 145, 177, 183, 201, 254, 294, 301

Freemasons Lodge of Geneva 3

G

Gampopa Sonam Rinchen (1079-1153) 187

Ganyingpian 感應篇, see *Taishang ganyingpian*

Geneva 19-20, 80, 99, Constitution of the Republic of ~ 3; Napoleonic Annexation of ~ 4; see also Church of Geneva

Georgia 48n5, 87n33, 278

Georgian (language) 48n5, 82, 83, 88, 130n21, 264, 286, 298, 302

German (language) 47-48, 71, 113, 234n31, 285

ghost(s), see *gui/guishen*

Gospel of John, see Bible

Gothic (language) 82

Great Learning, see *Daxue*

Greek (language) 55n42, 83, 88, 131, 199, 211-212, 264, 285, 298, 302; see also Bible: ~ New Testament, Septuagint

Guansheng di jun jueshi baoxun jing 關聖帝君覺世寶訓經 / *Enduringge di giyūn kuwan mafa-i jalan de ulhibure boobai tacihiyan-i nomun bithe* (Manchu: Precious Teachings for the Edification of the World) 160

gui 鬼 / *guishen* 鬼神 (ghosts / ghosts and deities) 139-142

Gujarati/Gujarate (language) 263, 285

H

Han-i araha ubaliyambuha duin bithe (*Sy su bithe*) (Manchu: Imperially Commissioned Translation of the Four Books), see *Yuzhi fanyi sishu*

Han-i araha duin hacin-i hergen kamciha Manju gisun-i buleku bithe (Manchu: Imperially Commissioned Four-language Manchu Mirror), see *Yuzhi siti Qingwen jian*

Han-i araha inenggidari giyangnaha sy su-i jurgan be suhe bithe (Manchu: Explanations of the Four Books of Confucianism for Daily Tutoring), see [*Yuzhi*] *Rijiang sishu jieyi*

harmony (*he* 和) 128, 137, 144

Heath, Rev. William Mortimer (1822-1917) 38

Heaven (*tian* 天) 119, 139, 150

Hebrew (language) 55n42, 57, 86, 90, 93-97, 125, 129-131, 179, 186, 285, 297-298, 300

Hindi (language) 31, 285

Hitopadesa 86, 199

Huguenot, French 5, 11

humanism, religious 123-124

Hungarian/Magyar (language) 246, 285

Hungarian Academy of Sciences 39, 51, 157, 175-176, 188, 233, 244, 246-248, 274; see also Duka, Theodore

Huzuāresh (language) 265

hyperpolyglossia/hyperpolyglot(s) 17, 68, 70, 72, 80, 182, 260; see also polyglossia

hyperthymesia 66n103

I

India, British colonial government in 230-231

Indian Institute (Oxford) 48-52, 85-86, 241, 247, 253-254, 262n31, 264n40, 266, 281-284, 296

Italian (language) 47-48, 55, 88, 264-265, 284, 302

J

Japanese (language) 88, 264, 267, 271, 272n73, 280, 285, 297, 299, 302

Javanese (language) 285, 302

junzi 君子 (princely man/wise man/gentleman/superior man) 112, 136-137, 139, 141, 146

K

Kaqimna (or Kakimna) 97
Karen (Northern Burmese language) 263n37, 265, 285
khape (*kha dpe* ཁ་དཔེ་) 180
King James Version (of the Bible), see Bible
Korean (also Corean, language) 253n1, 267n46, 297, 306n39, 285
Kurdish (language) 265, 285

L

Ladakh 40
Lamp for the Path to Enlightenment (*byang chub lam gyi sgron ma* བྱང་ཆུབ་ལམ་གྱི་སྒྲོན་མ་) 176, 188
languages, see individual languages; see also hyperpolyglossia, polyglossia
Laozi 老子 ("Old Master") 105n6, 106
Latin (language) 47-48, 82-83, 159, 199, 211, 258, 265, 284, 297-298, 302
Legge, James (1815–1897) 26, 84, 139, 256, 280
legs par bshad pa ལེགས་པར་བཤད་པ་, see *Treasury of Good Words*
leishu 類書 (collectanea) 300
Letters to a Young Missionary (*LYM*) 28-31, 84-85
Li Changling 李昌齡 (*fl.* 1233) 106n8, 107
London Missionary Society 25-26, 27n56, 155, 280
Lord on High / Supreme Lord (*shangdi* 上帝) 138, 162
Lord's Prayer 49, 273n77
Lunyu 論語 (*Analects*) 104n1, 124, 134, 135, 140, 143, 146, 147n105

M

Malan, Arthur Noel (also ANM, 1846–1933) 1, 3, 17, 39, 129, 151, *et passim*
Malan Bequest 247
Malan, César Jacques (1821–1889) 1-2
Malan family archives 1n5, 256, 293
Malan, Henri Abraham César (1787–1864) 1-3, 5, 8-13, 19, 129, 257

Malan Library 85-86, *et passim*, ~ Book List 261-264, 268, 276n89, 277, 282
Malan, Solomon [Jean] Caesar (also SCM, 1812–1894), *passim*, bookbinding 32, 52, 56, 257, 270, 295-296; calligraphy 48, 52, 163, 167n70, 170, 242, 270-272, 280, 295, 299; correspondence (by letter) 37, 223n43, 233n27, 243-244, 246-247, 249, 267n49, 277, 279-280, 301; drawing(s) 31, 38, 42, 55, 59-60; illness 22, 32; painting(s) 59; sketching/sketches 59, 258, 278n98; worldview 87, 118, 120, 179, 204, 250, 302
Maltese (language) 263n35 and 37, 265
Man Han chengyu duidai 滿漢成語對待 / *Manju Nikan fe gisun be joforo acabuha bithe* (Manchu: Manchu–Chinese Concordance of Idioms) 156
Man Hanzi Qingwen qimeng 滿漢字清文啟蒙 / *Manju Nikan hergen-i Cing wen ki meng bithe* (Manchu: Manchu Script / Chinese Character Primer of the Qing Language) 155n24, 156
Manchurian (language) 86, 116, 193n74, 250, 273n74, 297-298
Manju gisun-i oyonggo jorin-i bithe (Manchu: Main Points of the Manchu Language), see *Qingwen zhiyao*
Manjuristics 151, 154, 170n84, 171
Manual of Daily Prayers Translated from Eastern Originals 40
Mazdagasnian (language) 302
mdzang blun zhes bya ba'i mdo མཛངས་བླུན་ཞེས་བྱ་བའི་མདོ་, see *Dsang-lun*
Medhurst, Walter H. (1796–1857) 162, 280
Memphitic (language) 82
Mengzi 孟子 124, 132, 134-135, 136n46 and 47
Mezzofanti, Cardinal Giuseppe (1774–1849) 17, 68-72
Middlemarch 37n14, 43-44
Middleton, Thomas Fanshawe (1769–1822) 18
Milarepa (ca. 1030–1120) 187, 189

GENERAL INDEX

ming 命 (fate/fortune) 118
Mingxianji 名賢集 (A Collection with Sayings from the Wise Men of the Past for Enlightenment) 103, 109-110, 116-119
Mingxin baojian 明心寶鑒 (The Precious Mirror to Enlighten the Mind) 103, 108, 110, 113n32, 120
The Mirror of Sweet Words (*snyan ngag me long* སྙན་ངག་མེ་ལོང་) 176
Mission(ary work), Christian humanist approach to 84-85, 100
Mongolian (language) 84, 86, 88, 152, 157, 161-163, 170, 184, 199, 267n49
Monier-Williams, Monier (1819–1899) 49, 50, 213, 248n80
Moorcroft, William (1765–1825) 177n13, 229n5, 231
Mortlock, Mary Marsh (1813–1840, SCM's first wife) 19-20
Moule, Henry (1801–1880) 36
Moule, Arthur Evans (1836–1918) 36
Moule, George Evans (1828–1912) 36-37
Mount, Caroline Selina (1821–1911, SCM's second wife) 33, 242

N

Ngawang Lobsang Gyatsho (1617–1682), Fifth Dalai Lama 177
Nīlakaṇṭha 209, 213

O

Orientalism 41, 212, 226, 230, 232, 235n33,
Original Notes on the Book of Proverbs: Eastern (original) sources in ~ 300; manuscript of ~ 242, 294-299, *et passim*; published volumes of ~ 51-52, 289-294, *et passim*
Orissa/Oriya (language) 262, 263n35, 285, 286
Orthodox Christianity: Armenian 81; Coptic 81; Georgian 48n5, 81; Greek 81; Russian 159; Syrian (Syriac) 81
Osmanli (language) 88, 94, 264
Oxford Movement / Tractarianism 24, 57

Oxford University 156, 231, 253n3, 275, 283

P

Pahlavi 19, 86
Pali (language) 30, 186, 210, 219, 263n37, 267, 285, 286,
Pandit 214
Pattison, Mark (1813–1884) 43-44
pechoe (*dpe chos* དཔེ་ཆོས་) 181
Persian (language) 17, 35, 48, 199, 262, 263, 267, 268, 285, 286, 302
Phonecian (language) 265
Pinney family (Broadwindsor) 44
polyglossia 68-72; see also hyperpolyglossia
polyglot: human polyglots 17, 50n18, 68-72, 230n7; ~ manuscripts and books 103, 225, 226, 267, 268
Protestants, see Calvinists/Calvinism, Chapel of Witnessing / *Chapelle de Témoinage*, Church of Geneva, Huguenot, Revival/Revivalism/ *Réveil*
proverb (form of speech) 54, 110, 124-127, 179-182
Proverbs, the biblical book of 91, 93, 95-100, 113, 116-119, 185, 224, 299-303, *et passim*
Ptah-hotep 97
Punjabi (language) 263

Q

Qianlong 乾隆, emperor (1711–1799) 152
Qingwen zhiyao 清文指要 / *Manju gisun-i oyonggo jorin-i bithe* (Manchu: Main Points of the Manchu Language) 168

R

retribution (*baoying* 報應) 106, 107, 111
Revival/Revivalism/*Réveil* 1n5, 8-12, 19
Roman Catholic Christianity 4, 6-7
Royal Asiatic Society 20, 231, 234, 238, 241, 247
Ruism/Ruist, see Confucianism

S

Sacra Privata 152, 170, 269, 295
sage (*shengren* 聖人) 136, 141-142
Sahidic (language) 82
Sakya Paṇḍita (or Kunga Gyeltsen Pal Sangpo ཀུན་དགའ་རྒྱལ་མཚན་དཔལ་བཟང་པོ།, 1182–1251) 177, 178, 182, 184
Samaritan Aramaic (language) 268
san le 三樂, see three joys
Sanzijing 三字經 (Three-Character Classic / Triliteral Classic) 27, 84, 104. 119
Sanskrit/Sanscrit (language) 17, 20, 31, 88, 170n86, 177, 178, 184, 185, 207-226, *et passim*
Śāntiparvan 215, 221-223
Sardinia 5n23, 6n26, 7
savantism 62, 68
Schönenberger, Salomé Georgette Jeanne (d.u., SCM's mother) 10
Sclavonic/Slavonic (language) 51n22, 82, 83, 234n31, 284
self-cultivation (*xiushen* 修身) 107, 126, 134, 142, 148; see also *dao*
self-transformation 132-133, 140, 144, 148
Šengdzu gūsin hūwangdi-i boo-i tacihiyan-i ten-i gisun (Manchu: The Kangxi Emperor's Noble Family Precepts), see *Shengzu jiaxun gaolun*
Septuagint, see Bible
shengren 聖人, see sage
Shengyu guangxun 聖諭廣訓 / *Enduringge tacihiyan neileme badarambuha bithe* (Manchu: The Sacred Edicts) 160
Shengzu jiaxun gaolun 聖祖家訓高論 / *Šengdzu gūsin hūwangdi-i boo-i tacihiyan-i ten-i gisun* (Manchu: The Kangxi Emperor's Noble Family Precepts) 160
Si ben jianyao 四本簡要 / *Duin felehe oyonggo šošohon* (Manchu: Four Volumes of Pithy Sayings) 160
Sishu 四書 (Four Books) 124, 127-128, 136-138, 144-147
Sindhi (language) 265, 268n54
Sinhalese/Singalese/Cingalese (language) 262, 263, 267, 269n58, 285, 286,

Slavonic (language), see Sclavonic
Smart, Ninian (1927–2001) 128
snyan ngag me long སྙན་ངག་མེ་ལོང་།, see *The Mirror of Sweet Words*
Society for Promoting Christian Knowledge (SPCK) 18, 21
Society for the Propagation of the Gospel in Foreign Parts (SPG) 18, 21-22
Socinianism / Socinian Church of Geneva 2, 8
Spanish (language) 47, 48, 108, 130, 284, 302
superior man, see *junzi*
Sutra of the Wise and the Foolish (*mdzang blun zhes bya ba'i mdo* མཛངས་བླུན་ཞེས་བྱ་བའི་མདོ།), see *Dsang-Lun*
synaesthesia 67-68, 72-73
Syrian (ancient and modern, language) 93

T

Taiping tianguo 太平天國 (Taiping Heavenly Kingdom, Taiping Insurgency, Heavenly Kingdom of Supreme Peace, 1850–1864) 27, 84
Taishang ganyingpian 太上感應篇 86n28, 103, 105-108, 114-116, 168
Taishang ganyingpian tu shuo 太上感應篇圖說 / *Tai sang-ni acabume karulara bithe* (Manchu: Illustrated Books of Rewards and Punishments) 168
Tamil (language) 31, 88, 263, 264, 269n57, 273n74, 285, 302,
Tammet, Daniel 64, 66n101, 71-72
tampe (*gtam dpe* གཏམ་དཔེ།) 180-181
Telegu (language) 88
three joys (*san le* 三樂) 146
Tian 天, see Heaven
Tibetan (language) 88, 95, 100, 176-205, 229-230, 286, 298, 302, *et passim*
Tibetology/Tibetan studies 25, 230-235, 243, 255
Toumen tschaki ounengi segiyen (Manchu: The Origins of a Myriad Things), see *Wanwu zhen yuan*
translation: ~ of the Bible / Christian Scriptures 84, 130, 158-162, 253,

263; ~ of religious literature 48-49, SCM's ~ technique 54-55, 82-83, 91, 110-120, 169, 191-201, 223-224
Treasury of Good Words (*legs par bshad pa* ལེགས་པར་བཤད་པ, also known as *Elegant Sayings*) 178
Triliteral Classic, see *Sanzijing*
Tuckwell, Rev. William (1829–1919) 42-43, 48, 55
Tulu (language) 265
Tungusic, language family 151, 155, 162; ~ script(s) 152
Turkish, including Middle Turkish (language) 55n42, 180n27, 199, 246, 267, 285, 302

U

Ubaliyambuha ninggun baita targabun gisun (Manchu: Admonitions Regarding Six Subjects), see *Fanyi liushi zhenyan*
Udyogaparvan 215, 220-221
Uighur, including Uighur-Karluk (language) 285, 298
University of Edinburgh 239, 243, 249

V

Vanaparvan 215-219
Vulgate, see Bible

W

Wanwu zhen yuan 萬物真原 (The Origins of a Myriad Things) / *Toumen tschaki ounengi segiyen* (Manchu) 156
Wang Lixi 王禮錫 (1901–1939), a.k.a. Shelley Wang 41
Warner, Sylvia Townsend (1893–1978) 41-42
Welsh (language) 71, 94, 170n86, 180n27, 284, 302
Wilson, Daniel (1778–1858) 19, 21-24, 32
Wilson, Horace Hayman (1786–1860) 212-214, 223
wisdom: apothemic/proverbial literature 240, 302; Chinese ~ 160, 169, 256, 292; divine ~ 207; Manchu ~ 160-161; Tibetan ~ 175-206; Sumerian ~ 182; practical ~ 192, 301; sapiential literature 82, 95, 100, 104, 108, 300, 303; ~ literature 192, 215-226, 292, 298, 301-303
Wong, Anna May (1905–1961) 41

X

xiushen 修身, see self-cultivation

Y

yinguo 因果, see cause and effect
Yuzhi fanyi sishu 御製翻譯四書 / *Han-i araha ubaliyambuha duin bithe* (*Sy su bithe*) (Manchu: Imperially Commissioned Translation of the Four Books) 160
[*Yuzhi*] *Rijiang sishu jieyi* [御製]日講四書解義 / *Han-i araha inenggidari giyangnaha sy su-i jurgan be suhe bithe* (Manchu: Explanations of the Four Books of Confucianism for Daily Tutoring) 157
Yuzhi siti Qingwen jian 御製四體清文鑑 / *Han-i araha duin hacin-i hergen kamciha Manju gisun-i buleku bithe* (Manchu: Imperially Commissioned Four-language Manchu Mirror) 156

Z

Zend (language) 265, 268n53 and 54, 285
Zhongyong 中庸 (The Doctrine of the Mean) 124, 135, 136n46 and 47, 138, 140, 142, 145n95, 146, 148, 168n75
Zigong shizhuan 子貢詩傳 (Zigong's Book of Songs) 167

COLLECTANEA SERICA – NEW SERIES
No. 2

GAIL KING

"A Model for All Christian Women"
Candida Xu, a Chinese Christian Woman of the Seventeenth Century

Institut Monumenta Serica, Sankt Augustin • Routledge, Abingdon, Oxon 2020
xvi, 162 pp., Bibliography, Index, 11 b/w ill., £ 120.00 (hbk), £ 36.99 (eBook).
ISBN 978-0-367-68290-3 (hbk) • 978-1-003-13677-4 (eBook)

"A Model for All Christian Women" recounts the life of Candida Xu (1607–1680), foremost Chinese Christian woman of the seventeenth century. A granddaughter of the prominent Chinese Christian convert and statesman Xu Guangqi (1562–1633), Candida Xu was raised from birth as a Christian in a Christian household, due to the earlier conversion of grandparents and parents. This circumstance of her family background was formative, since her childhood was shaped by both her native Chinese culture and by Christian influences that helped root in her receptive spiritual nature a strong, living faith. Her story, seen in the context of Christian families, marriage alliances, and conversions in the Shanghai area in the seventeenth century, points up the importance of the family in the transmission and continuance of Christianity in China. Sources for the book include the biography of Candida Xu titled *Histoire d'une dame chrétienne de la Chine* (Paris, 1688) written by her confessor Philippe Couplet, S.J. (1623–1693), an obituary of his mother and other writings by her eldest son, the Xu family history, and other European missionary and Chinese language sources.

Contents

Preface by D.E. Mungello; Introduction; Chapter One: Roots of the Xu Family: The Generations before Candida Xu; Chapter Two: Childhood and Married Life; Chapter Three: The Widowed Years; Chapter Four: The Legacy of Candida Xu; Appendices:1: "Baolun tang gao" 寶倫堂稿. Autobiographical Preface by Hesha 鶴沙 (Xu Zuanzeng 許纘曾). Translation of Portions Related to Candida Xu, 2: Xu Zuanzeng's Biography of His Mother Candida Xu. Translation of "Compendio de la vida y la muerte de Doña Candida, sacado de un librito,que imprimió su hijo D. Basilio Hiù," 3: Xu Yunxi, Foreword to the 1938 edition of *Yiwei Zhongguo fengjiao taitai* 一位中國奉教太太; Bibliography; Index with Glossary

Place order with your local bookseller or:
https://www.routledge.com/A-Model-for-All-Christian-Women-Candida-Xu-a-Chinese-Christian-Woman/King/p/book/9780367682903

COLLECTANEA SERICA – NEW SERIES
—————— No. 1 ——————

MIECZYSŁAW JERZY KÜNSTLER

The Sinitic Languages
A Contribution to Sinological Linguistics

Monumenta Serica Institute, Sankt Augustin
Abingdon, Oxon – New York: Routledge, 2019
xiii, 322 pp., £ 120 (hbk), £ 36.99 (eBook)
ISBN 978-0-367-18620-3 (hbk) • 978-0-429-19723-9 (eBook)

The Sinitic Languages is the quintessence of Mieczysław Jerzy Künstler's (1933–2007) thirty years of research into the Chinese languages. Originally published in Polish in 2000 as *Języki chińskie*, this work collected Künstler's various lectures on the fascinating world of this branch of the Sino-Tibetan language family. It marked the apogee of linguistic research of Chinese languages in Poland. With a keen, intuitive understanding of the workings of these languages, Künstler introduces his readership to the historical development of spoken Sinitic languages. Besides analyzing the various stages of Standard Chinese, he also makes a convincing case for classifying Cantonese, Pekinese, Nankinese, Minnanese, Wu, and other so-called "dialects" as distinct languages. Künstler's work offers an insightful and detailed overview about synchronic and diachronic research on the major language groups of Chinese, a fast-growing academic field until today.

The present English version was begun by Künstler himself before his untimely demise in 2007. However, it is not merely a translation of the Polish work, but a revised edition that introduces a shift in Sinological linguistics from a genetic to an areal description of Modern Chinese languages. Both amateurs and experts interested in this topic are invited to follow Künstler on his intellectual journey into Sinological linguistics.

Contents: Editor's Foreword; About the Author; Introduction to the English Version; Introduction; Chapter 1: Typology, Kinship, and Areal Features; Chapter 2: Writing and Language; Chapter 3: The Oldest Phase of the Chinese Language; Chapter 4: The Archaic Chinese Language; Chapter 5: The Post-Archaic Period; Chapter 6: From the Han Dynasty to the Tang Dynasty; Chapter 7: The Middle or Ancient Chinese; Chapter 8: Transitory Times; Chapter 9: The Modern Period; Chapter 10: The Contemporary Pan-national Language; Chapter 11: The Chinese Tower of Babel; Chapter 12: Mandarin Languages; Chapter 13: Southern Chinese Languages; Addendum – Bibliography – Index with Glossary

Place order with your local bookseller or:
https://www.routledge.com/The-Sinit-ic-Languages-A-Contribution-to-Sinological-Linguistics/Kunstler/p/book/9780367732004

MONUMENTA SERICA MONOGRAPH SERIES
─────────── Vol. LXXI ───────────

Hu Baozhu

Believing in Ghosts and Spirits
The Concept of *Gui* in Ancient China

Institut Monumenta Serica, Sankt Augustin • Routledge, Abingdon, Oxon 2021
xxvi, 280 pp., Bibliography, Index, £ 120.00 (hbk), £ 36.99 (eBook)
ISBN 978-0-367-62634-1 (hbk) • 978-1-003-11004-0 (eBook)
ISSN 0179-261X

The present book by Hu Baozhu explores the subject of ghosts and spirits, thus mapping the religious landscape of ancient China. The main focus is on the character *gui* 鬼, an essential key to the understanding of spiritual beings there. The author analyses the character *gui* in various materials – lexicons and dictionaries, excavated manuscripts and inscriptions, and received classical texts. *Gui* is examined from the perspective of its linguistic root, literary interpretation, ritual practices, sociopolitical implication, and cosmological thinking.

The *Shuowen jiezi*'s interpretation of *gui* as a sort of negative force tending to harm people's properties or even their lives greatly influenced later understandings of the concept. In addition to early lexicons, the present study also traces the understanding of *gui* in oracle bone script (*jiaguwen*) and bronze script (*jinwen*) where *gui* chiefly referred to concrete persons, groups or places, seen as remote, foreign, vigorous or malevolent, and then to ghosts/spirits of the dead. Linguistically the compound phrase guishen came later to denote all spiritual beings. The book further investigates essential layers of meaning of *gui* and its literary functions as a part of speech in some Chinese classics, the *Zuozhuan*, *Liji*, *Lunyu*, *Zhuangzi* and *Mozi* as well as in popular traditions, namely the *Rishu* (Day Book) unearthed in 1975.

Contents

Chapter 1: The Preliminary Understanding of *Gui*; Chapter 2: The Original Meaning of the Character *Gui*: An Examination of *Jiaguwen* and *Jinwen*; Chapter 3: What's in a Character? Definition and Variegated Characteristics of *Gui* in the *Zuozhuan* and *Liji*; Chapter 4: Confucian, Daoist, and Mohist Perspectives on the Concept of *Gui*; Chapter 5: Folk-oriented Usages of *Gui* in the *Rishu* Manuscript; Conclusion; Appendix I: Table of the Radical *Gui* and Its Related Characters; Appendix II: *Gui*-related Oracle Bone Inscriptions; Appendix III: Investigations: Annotated Translation of the "Jie" 詰 Section; Bibliography; Index with Glossary

Place order with your local bookseller or:
https://www.routledge.com/Believing-in-Ghosts-and-Spirits-The-Concept-of-Gui-in-Ancient-China/Baozhu/p/book/9780367626341

MONUMENTA SERICA MONOGRAPH SERIES
Vol. XLIII

Bible in Modern China
The Literary and Intellectual Impact

Edited by
IRENE EBER, SZE-KAR WAN and KNUT WALF
in collaboration with ROMAN MALEK

Institut Monumenta Serica, Sankt Augustin
Steyler Verlag, Nettetal 1999, 470 pp., £ 120 (hbk)
ISBN 978-3-8050-0424-4 (hbk) • ISSN 0179-261X

The volume presents the contributions of an international workshop held in Jerusalem in 1996. It includes a general index with glossary.

Contents:
NICOLAS STANDAERT, The Bible in Early Seventeenth-Century China • ARNULF CAMPS, O.F.M., Father Gabriele M. Allegra, O.F.M. (1907–1976) and the Studium Biblicum Franciscanum: The First Complete Chinese Catholic Translation of the Bible • JOST ZETZSCHE, The Work of Lifetimes: Why the *Union Version* Took Nearly Three Decades to Complete • LIHI YARIV-LAOR, Linguistic Aspects of Translating the Bible into Chinese • KNUT WALF, Christian *Theologoumena* in Western Translations of the Daoists • IRENE EBER, The Interminable Term Question • LAUREN PFISTER, A Transmitter but not a Creator: Ho Tsun-Sheen (1817–1871), the First Modern Chinese Protestant Theologian • JOAKIM ENWALL, The Bible Translations into Miao: Chinese Influence *versus* Linguistic Autonomy • LEWIS S. ROBINSON, The Bible in Twentieth-Century Chinese Fiction • RAOUL DAVID FINDEISEN, Wang Jingzhi's *Yesu de fenfu* (The Instructions by Jesus): A Christian Novel? • MARIÁN GÁLIK, Mythopoeic Warrior and *femme fatale:* Mao Dun's Version of Samson and Delilah • FRANCIS K. H. SO, Wu Ching-Hsiung's Chinese Translation of Images of the Most High in the Psalms • SZE-KAR WAN, The Emerging Hermeneutics of the Chinese Church: Debate between Wu Leichuan and T. C. Chao and the Chinese Christian Problematik • GONG LIANG, Twenty Years of Studies of Biblical Literature in the People's Republic of China (1976–1996) • WOLFGANG KUBIN, "The Sickness God" – The Sickness Man: The Problem of Imperfection in China and in the West • General Index with Glossary

Place order with your local bookseller or:
https://www.routledge.com/Bible-in-Modern-Ch-in-a-The-Literary-and-In-tellectual-Impact/Eber/p/book/9783805004244

Monumenta Serica Monograph Series
(ISSN 0179-261X)
Edited by Zbigniew Wesołowski, s.v.d. • Institut Monumenta Serica

I.–VIII. Out of print.

IX. Karl Bünger, *Quellen zur Rechtsgeschichte der T'ang-Zeit*, Peiping 1946, Fu Jen Catholic University Press. Neue, erweiterte Ausgabe, mit einem Vorwort von Denis Twitchett. Sankt Augustin – Nettetal 1996, 535 S. ISBN 3-8050-0375-7

X.–XIV. Out of print.

XV. Ch'en Yüan, *Western and Central Asians in China under the Mongols – Their Transformation into Chinese*. Translated and annotated by Ch'ien Hsing-hai and L. Carrington Goodrich, Los Angeles 1966, 328 pp. Reprint: Sankt Augustin – Nettetal 1989 (paperback). ISBN 3-8050-0243-2

XVI. Yen Yüan, *Preservation of Learning. With an Introduction on His Life and Thought*. Translated by Mansfield Freeman, Los Angeles 1972, 215 pp.

XVII. Claudia von Collani, *P. Joachim Bouvet S.J. – Sein Leben und sein Werk*, Sankt Augustin – Nettetal 1985, 269 S., Abb. ISBN 3-87787-197-6

XVIII. W. South Coblin, *A Sinologist's Handlist of Sino-Tibetan Lexical Comparisons*, Sankt Augustin – Nettetal 1986, 186 pp. ISBN 3-87787-208-5

XIX. Gilbert L. Mattos, *The Stone Drums of Ch'in*, Sankt Augustin – Nettetal 1988, 497 pp., Illustr. ISBN 3-8050-0194-0

XX. Out of print.

XXI. Karl-Heinz Pohl, *Cheng Pan-ch'iao. Poet, Painter and Calligrapher*, Sankt Augustin – Nettetal 1990, 269 pp., Illustr. ISBN 3-8050-0261-0

XXII. Jerome Heyndrickx (ed.), *Philippe Couplet, S.J. (1623–1693). The Man Who Brought China to Europe*. Jointly published by Institut Monumenta Serica and Ferdinand Verbiest Foundation, Leuven, Sankt Augustin – Nettetal 1990, 260 pp., Illustr. ISBN 3-8050-0266-1

XXIII. Anne S. Goodrich, *Peking Paper Gods. A Look at Home Worship*, Sankt Augustin – Nettetal 1991, 501 pp., Illustr. ISBN 3-8050-0284-X

XXIV. Michael Nylan, *The Shifting Center: The Original "Great Plan" and Later Readings*, Sankt Augustin – Nettetal 1992, 211 pp. ISBN 3-8050-0293-9

XXV. Out of print.

XXVI. Julia Ching – Willard G. Oxtoby, *Moral Enlightenment. Leibniz and Wolff on China*, Sankt Augustin – Nettetal 1992, 288 pp. ISBN 3-8050-0294-7

XXVII. Maria Dorothea Reis-Habito, *Die Dhāraṇī des Großen Erbarmens des Bodhisattva Avalokiteśvara mit tausend Händen und Augen. Übersetzung und Untersuchung ihrer textlichen Grundlage sowie Erforschung ihres Kultes in China*. Sankt Augustin – Nettetal 1993, 487 S., Abb. ISBN 3-8050-0296-3

XXVIII. Noel Golvers, *The "Astronomia Europaea" of Ferdinand Verbiest, S.J. (Dillingen, 1687). Text, Translation, Notes and Commentaries*. Jointly published by Institut Monumenta Serica, Sankt Augustin and Ferdinand Verbiest Foundation, Leuven, Sankt Augustin – Nettetal 1993, 547 pp. ISBN 3-8050-0327-7

XXIX. Gerd Wädow, *T'ien-fei hsien-sheng lu. „Die Aufzeichnungen von der manifestierten Heiligkeit der Himmelsprinzessin". Einleitung, Übersetzung, Kommentar*, Sankt Augustin – Nettetal 1992, 374 S., Abb. ISBN 3-8050-0310-2

XXX. John W. Witek, S.J. (ed.), *Ferdinand Verbiest (1623–1688): Jesuit Missionary, Scientist, Engineer and Diplomat*. Jointly published by Institut Monumenta Serica, Sankt Augustin and Ferdinand Verbiest Foundation, Leuven, Sankt Augustin – Nettetal 1994, 602 pp., Illustr. ISBN 3-8050-0328-5

XXXI. Donald MacInnis, *Religion im heutigen China. Politik und Praxis*. Deutsche Übersetzung herausgegeben im China-Zentrum von Roman Malek. Eine gemeinsame Veröffentlichung des China-Zentrums und des Instituts Monumenta Serica, Sankt Augustin – Nettetal 1993, 619 S. ISBN 3-8050-0330-7

Monumenta Serica Monograph Series

XXXII. PETER WIEDEHAGE, Das „Meihua xishen pu" des Song Boren aus dem 13. Jahrhundert. Ein Handbuch zur Aprikosenblüte in Bildern und Gedichten, Sankt Augustin – Nettetal 1995, 435 S., Abb. ISBN 3-8050-0361-7

XXXIII. D.E. MUNGELLO (ed.), The Chinese Rites Controversy: Its History and Meaning. Jointly published by Institut Monumenta Serica, Sankt Augustin and The Ricci Institute for Chinese-Western Cultural History, San Francisco, Sankt Augustin – Nettetal 1994, 356 pp. ISBN 3-8050-0348-X

XXXIV. Der Abbruch des Turmbaus. Studien zum Geist in China und im Abendland. Festschrift für Rolf Trauzettel. Hrsg. von INGRID KRÜßMANN, WOLFGANG KUBIN und HANS-GEORG MÖLLER, Sankt Augustin – Nettetal 1995, 314 S. ISBN 3-8050- 0360-9

XXXV/1-2. ROMAN MALEK (ed.), Western Learning and Christianity in China. The Contribution and Impact of Johann Adam Schall von Bell (1592–1666), 2 vols. Jointly published by the China-Zentrum and Monumenta Serica Institute, Sankt Augustin – Nettetal 1998, 1259 pp. ISBN 3-8050- 0409-5.

XXXVI. EWALD HECK, Wang Kangnian (1860–1911) und die „Shiwubao". Sankt Augustin – Nettetal 2000, 353 S. ISBN 3-8050-0432-X

XXXVII. SECONDINO GATTA, Il natural lume de Cinesi. Teoria e prassi dell' evangelizzazione in Cina nella Breve relatione di Philippe Couplet S.I. (1623–1693), Sankt Augustin – Nettetal 1998, 241 pp. ISBN 3-8050-0404-4

XXXVIII. ZBIGNIEW WESOŁOWSKI, Lebens- und Kulturbegriff von Liang Shuming (1893–1988). Dargestellt anhand seines Werkes Dong-Xi wenhua ji qi zhexue, Sankt Augustin – Nettetal 1997, 487 S. ISBN 3-8050-0399-4

XXXIX. TIZIANA LIPPIELLO, Auspicious Omens and Miracles in Ancient China. Han, Three Kingdoms and Six Dynasties, Sankt Augustin – Nettetal 2001, 383 pp. ISBN 3-8050-0456-7

XL. THOMAS ZIMMER, Baihua. Zum Problem der Verschriftung gesprochener Sprache im Chinesischen. Dargestellt anhand morphologischer Merkmale in den bianwen aus Dunhuang, Sankt Augustin – Nettetal 1999, 287 S. ISBN 3-8050-0428-1

XLI. ULRICH LAU, Quellenstudien zur Landvergabe und Bodenübertragung in der westlichen Zhou-Dynastie (1045? – 771 v. Chr.), Sankt Augustin – Nettetal 1999, 419 S., Abb. ISBN 3-8050- 0429- X

XLII. TIZIANA LIPPIELLO – ROMAN MALEK (eds.). "Scholar from the West." Giulio Aleni S.J. (1582–1649) and the Dialogue between China and Christianity, Sankt Augustin – Nettetal 1997, 671 pp. ISBN 3-8050-0386-2

XLIII. IRENE EBER et al. (eds.), Bible in Modern China. The Literary and Intellectual Impact, Sankt Augustin – Nettetal 1999, 470 pp. ISBN 3-8050- 0424-9

XLIV. DONALD DANIEL LESLIE, Jews and Judaism in Traditional China. A Comprehensive Bibliography, Sankt Augustin – Nettetal 1998, 291 pp. ISBN 3-8050-0418-4

XLV. JOST OLIVER ZETZSCHE, The Bible in China: The History of the Union Version or the Culmination of Protestant Missionary Bible Translation in China, Sankt Augustin – Nettetal 1999, 456 pp. ISBN 3-8050-0433-8

XLVI. From Kaifeng ... to Shanghai. Jews in China. Ed. by ROMAN MALEK. Joint Publication of the Monumenta Serica Institute and the China-Zentrum, Sankt Augustin – Nettetal 2000, 706 pp., Illustr. ISBN 3-8050-0454-0

XLVII. DOMINIC SACHSENMAIER, Die Aufnahme europäischer Inhalte in die chinesische Kultur durch Zhu Zongyuan (ca. 1616–1660), Sankt Augustin – Nettetal 2001, 472 S. ISBN 3-8050-0455-9

XLVIII. JEONGHEE LEE-KALISCH, Das Licht der Edlen (junzi zhi guang). Der Mond in der chinesischen Landschaftsmalerei, Sankt Augustin – Nettetal 2001, 188 S. und 80 S. Abb. ISBN 3-8050- 0457-5

XLIX. SHEN WEIRONG, Leben und historische Bedeutung des ersten Dalai Lama dGe 'dun grub pa dpal bzang po (1391–1474). Ein Beitrag zur Geschichte der dGe lugs pa- Schule und der Institution der Dalai Lamas, Sankt Augustin – Nettetal 2002, 476 S., Faksimiles. ISBN 3-8050-0469-9

L/1. ROMAN MALEK, S.V.D. (ed.), The Chinese Face of Jesus Christ, vol. 1, Sankt Augustin – Nettetal 2002, 391 pp. ISBN 3-8050- 0477-X

L/2. ROMAN MALEK, S.V.D. (ed.), The Chinese Face of Jesus Christ, vol. 2, Sankt Augustin – Nettetal 2003, 480 pp. ISBN 3-8050- 0478-8

L/3a. ROMAN MALEK, S.V.D. (ed.), The Chinese

Face of Jesus Christ, vol. 3a, Sankt Augustin – Nettetal 2005, 480 pp. ISBN 3-8050-0524-5

L/3b. ROMAN MALEK, S.V.D. (ed.), *The Chinese Face of Jesus Christ*, vol. 3b, Sankt Augustin – Nettetal 2007, xii, 429 pp. ISBN 978-3-8050-0542-5

L/4a. ROMAN MALEK, S.V.D. (ed.), *The Chinese Face of Jesus Christ. Annotated Bibliography*, vol. 4a, Sankt Augustin – Leeds 2015, 658 pp., Illustr. ISBN 978-1-9096-6268-1

L/4b. ROMAN MALEK, S.V.D. (ed.), *The Chinese Face of Jesus Christ. Supplementary Anthology, General Index, Addenda*, vol. 4b, Sankt Augustin – Abingdon, Oxon – New York 2020 [published 2019], xix, 354 pp., Illustr. ISBN 978-0-367-35697-2

LI. WU XIAOXIN (ed.), *Encounters and Dialogues. Changing Perspectives on Chinese-Western Exchanges from the Sixteenth to Eighteenth Centuries*, Sankt Augustin – Nettetal 2005, 406 pp., Illustr. ISBN 3-8050-0525-3

LII. CHEN ZHI, *The Shaping of the Book of Songs. From Ritualization to Secularization*, Sankt Augustin – Nettetal 2007, 380 pp., Illustr. ISBN 978-3-8050-0541-8

LIII/1-2. W. SOUTH COBLIN, *Francisco Varo's Glossary of the Mandarin Language*. Vol. 1: *An English and Chinese Annotation of the Vocabulario de la Lengua Mandarina*; Vol. 2: *Pinyin and English Index of the Vocabulario de la Lengua Mandarina*, Sankt Augustin – Nettetal 2006, 1036 pp. ISBN 3-8050-0526-1

LIV. DONALD DANIEL LESLIE – YANG DAYE – AHMED YOUSSEF, *Islam in Traditional China. A Bibliographical Guide*. Sankt Augustin – Nettetal 2006, 398 pp., Illustr. ISBN 3-8050-0533-4

LV. NICOLAS STANDAERT – AD DUDINK (eds.), *Forgive Us Our Sins. Confession in Late Ming and Early Qing China*, Sankt Augustin – Nettetal 2006, 268 pp., Illustr. ISBN 978-3-8050-0540-1

LVI/1-2. Kouduo richao. *Li Jiubiao's Diary of Oral Admonitions. A Late Ming Christian Journal*. Translated, with Introduction and Notes by ERIK ZÜRCHER, Sankt Augustin – Nettetal 2007, 862 pp. ISBN 978-8050-0543-2

LVII. *Zurück zur Freude. Studien zur chinesischen Literatur und Lebenswelt und ihrer Rezeption in Ost und West. Festschrift für Wolfgang Kubin*. Hrsg. von MARC HERMANN und CHRISTIAN SCHWERMANN unter Mitwirkung von JARI GROSSE-RUYKEN, Sankt Augustin – Nettetal 2007, 917 pp. ISBN 978-3-8050-0550-0

LVIII. CHRISTIAN MEYER, *Ritendiskussionen am Hof der nördlichen Song-Dynastie 1034–1093: Zwischen Ritengelehrsamkeit, Machtkampf und intellektuellen Bewegungen*, Sankt Augustin – Nettetal 2008, 646 pp. ISBN 978-3-8050-0551-7

LIX. NICOLAS STANDAERT, *An Illustrated Life of Christ Presented to the Chinese Emperor. The History of* Jincheng shuxiang *(1640)*, Sankt Augustin – Nettetal 2007, 333 pp. ISBN 978-3-8050-0548-7

LX. *The People and the Dao. New Studies in Chinese Religions in Honour of Daniel L. Overmyer*. Ed. by PHILIP CLART and PAUL CROWE, Sankt Augustin – Nettetal 2009, 542 pp. ISBN 978-3-8050-0557-9

LXI. *Miscellanea Asiatica. Mélanges en l'honneur de Françoise Aubin. Festschrift in Honour of Françoise Aubin*. Edited by DENISE AIGLE, ISABELLE CHARLEUX, VINCENT GOOSSAERT and ROBERTE HAMAYON, Sankt Augustin – Nettetal 2010, 812 pp. ISBN 978-3-8050-0568-5

LXII. JACQUES GERNET, *Die Begegnung Chinas mit dem Christentum*. Neue durchgesehene Ausgabe mit Nachträgen und Index, Sankt Augustin 2012, xxi, 413 S. ISBN 978-3-8050-0603-3

LXIII. URSULA TOYKA, *The Splendours of Paradise. Murals and Epigraphic Documents at the Early Ming Buddhist Monastery Fahai Si*, Monumenta Serica Institute, Sankt Augustin 2014, 2 vols., 990 pp., 279 colour illustr., 13 black and white illustr., ISBN 978-3-8050-0617-0

LXIV. BERNARD S. SOLOMON, *On the School of Names in Ancient China*, Sankt Augustin 2013, 161 pp. ISBN 978-3-8050-0610-1

LXV. DIRK KUHLMANN, „Das Fremde im eigenen Lande". *Zur Historiographie des Christentums in China von Liang Qichao (1873–1929) bis Zhang Kaiyuan (geb. 1926)*. Sankt Augustin 2014, 452 S. ISBN 978-3-8050-0624-8

LXVI. PIOTR ADAMEK, *A Good Son Is Sad if He Hears the Name of His Father. The Tabooing of Names in China as a Way of Implementing Social Values*. Sankt Augustin – Leeds 2015, xvii, 392 pp. ISBN 978-1-9096-6269-8

LXVII. HU QIUHUA, *Konfuzianisches Ethos*

Monumenta Serica Monograph Series

und westliche Wissenschaft. Wang Guowei (1877–1927) und das Ringen um das moderne China. Sankt Augustin – Abingdon, Oxon 2016, xviii, 445 S. ISBN 978-1-9096-6270-4

LXVIII. *Rooted in Hope: China – Religion – Christianity / In der Hoffnung verwurzelt: China – Religion – Christentum. Festschrift in Honor of Roman Malek S.V.D. on the Occasion of His 65th Birthday / Festschrift für Roman Malek S.V.D. zu seinem 65. Geburtstag.* Edited by BARBARA HOSTER, DIRK KUHLMANN and ZBIGNIEW WESOŁOWSKI S.V.D. Sankt Augustin – Abingdon, Oxon 2017, 2 vols., cviii, 907 pp., Illustr., Tables. ISBN 978-1-1387-1808-1

LXIX. SONG GANG, *Giulio Aleni,* Kouduo richao, *and Christian–Confucian Dialogism in Late Ming Fujian.* Sankt Augustin – Abingdon, Oxon – New York 2019, xvi, 420 pp., Illustr. ISBN 978-1-138-58912-4 (hbk); 978-0-429-49187-0 (eBook)

LXX. THOMAS JÜLCH, *The* Zhenzheng lun *by Xuanyi: A Buddhist Apologetic Scripture of Tang China.* Sankt Augustin – Abingdon, Oxon – New York 2019, xi, 194 pp. ISBN 978-0-367-18285-4 (hbk); 978-0-429-06051-9 (eBook)

LXXI. HU BAOZHU, *Believing in Ghosts and Spirits: The Concept of* Gui *in Ancient China.* Sankt Augustin – Abingdon, Oxon – New York 2021, xxvi, 280 pp. ISBN 978-0-367-62634-1 (hbk); 978-1-003-11004-0 (eBook)

Place order with your local bookseller or:
www.routledge.com/Monumenta-Serica-Monograph-Series/book-series/MSM

Collectanea Serica
Edited by ZBIGNIEW WESOŁOWSKI, S.V.D. • Institut Monumenta Serica

- ANNE SWANN GOODRICH, *The Peking Temple of the Eastern Peak. The Tung-yüeh Miao in Peking and Its Lore*, with 20 Plates. Appendix: *Description of the Tung-yüeh Miao of Peking in 1927* by JANET R. TEN BROECK. Nagoya 1964, 331 pp., Illustr.
- STEPHAN PUHL, *Georg M. Stenz SVD (1869–1928). Chinamissionar im Kaiserreich und in der Republik*. Mit einem Nachwort von R.G. TIEDEMANN (London): „Der Missionspolitische Kontext in Süd-Shantung am Vorabend des Boxeraufstands in China". Hrsg. von ROMAN MALEK. Sankt Augustin – Nettetal 1994, 317 S., Abb. ISBN 3-8050-0350-1
- DAVID LUDWIG BLOCH, *Holzschnitte*. 木刻集. *Woodcuts. Shanghai 1940–1949*. Hrsg. von BARBARA HOSTER, ROMAN MALEK und KATHARINA WENZEL-TEUBER. Sankt Augustin – Nettetal 1997, 249 S., 301 Abb. ISBN 3-8050-0395-1
- ROMAN MALEK (Hrsg.), *„Fallbeispiel" China. Ökumenische Beiträge zu Religion, Theologie und Kirche im chinesischen Kontext*. Sankt Augustin – Nettetal 1996, 693 S. ISBN 3-8050-0385-4
- ROMAN MALEK (Hrsg.), *Hongkong. Kirche und Gesellschaft im Übergang. Materialien und Dokumente*. Sankt Augustin – Nettetal 1997, 564 S., 97 Abb. ISBN 3-8050-0397-8
- ROMAN MALEK (Hrsg.), *Macau: Herkunft ist Zukunft*. Sankt Augustin – Nettetal 2000, 666 S. ISBN 3-8050-0441-9
- *Gottfried von Laimbeckhoven S.J. (1707–1787). Der Bischof von Nanjing und seine Briefe aus China mit Faksimile seiner Reisebeschreibung*. Transkribiert und bearbeitet von STEPHAN PUHL (1941–1997) und SIGISMUND FREIHERR VON ELVERFELDT-ULM unter Mitwirkung von GERHARD ZEILINGER. Herausgegeben von ROMAN MALEK SVD. Sankt Augustin – Nettetal 2000, 492 S., Abb. ISBN 3-8050-0442-7
- *Martino Martini S.J. (1614–1661) und die Chinamission im 17. Jahrhundert*. Hrsg. von ROMAN MALEK und ARNOLD ZINGERLE. Sankt Augustin – Nettetal 2000, 260 S. ISBN 3-8050-0444-3
- CHRISTAN STÜCKEN, *Der Mandarin des Himmels. Zeit und Leben des Chinamissionars Ignaz Kögler S.J. (1680–1746)*. Sankt Augustin – Nettetal 2003, 440 S. ISBN 3-8050-0488-5
- KARL JOSEF RIVINIUS, *Das Collegium Sinicum zu Neapel und seine Umwandlung in ein Orientalisches Institut. Ein Beitrag zu seiner Geschichte*. Sankt Augustin – Nettetal 2004, 176 S. ISBN 3-8050-0498-2
- ELEANOR MORRIS WU, *From China to Taiwan. Historical, Anthropological, and Religious Perspectives*. Sankt Augustin – Nettetal 2004, 274 pp. ISBN 3-8050-0514-8
- MARIÁN GÁLIK, *Influence, Translation, and Parallels. Selected Studies on the Bible in China*. Sankt Augustin – Nettetal 2004, 351 pp. ISBN 3-8050-0489-3
- THORALF KLEIN und REINHARD ZÖLLNER (Hrsg.), *Karl Gützlaff (1803–1851) und das Christentum in Ostasien. Ein Missionar zwischen den Kulturen*. Mit einem Vorwort von Winfried Scharlau†. Sankt Augustin – Nettetal 2005, 375 S. ISBN 3-8050-0520-2
- ROMAN MALEK (ed.) in connection with PETER HOFRICHTER, *Jingjiao. The Church of the East in China and Central Asia*. Sankt Augustin – Nettetal 2006, 701 pp. ISBN 3-8050-0534-2
- *Contextualization of Christianity in China. An Evaluation in Modern Perspective*. Ed. by PETER CHEN-MAIN WANG. Sankt Augustin – Nettetal 2007. ISBN 978-3-8050-0547-0
- *Richard Wilhelm (1873–1930). Missionar in China und Vermittler chinesischen Geistesguts. Schriftenverzeichnis – Katalog seiner chinesischen Bibliothek – Briefe von Heinrich Hackmann – Briefe von Ku Hung-ming*. Zusammengestellt von HARTMUT WALRAVENS. Mit einem Beitrag von THOMAS ZIMMER. Sankt Augustin – Nettetal 2008. ISBN 978-3-8050-0553-1
- OTTO FRANKE, *„Sagt an, ihr fremden Lande". Ostasienreisen. Tagebücher und Fotografien (1888 –1901)*. Herausgegeben von RENATA FU-SHENG FRANKE und WOLFGANG FRANKE. Sankt Augustin – Nettetal 2009, ISBN 978-3-8050-0562-3
- *Light a Candle. Encounters and Friendship with China. Festschrift in Honour of Angelo S. Lazzarotto P.I.M.E.* Ed. by ROMAN MALEK S.V.D. and GIANNI CRIVELLER P.I.M.E. Sankt Augustin – Nettetal 2010, 564 pp. ISBN 978-3-8050-05 63-0
- MIROSLAV KOLLÁR, *Ein Leben im Konflikt. P. Franz Xaver Biallas SVD (1878–1936). Chinamissionar und Sinologe im Licht seiner Korrespondenz*. Sankt Augustin – Nettetal 2011, 910 S., Abb. ISBN 978-3-8050-0579-1
- JOHN DEFRANCIS, *Die chinesische Sprache. Fakten und Mythen*. Sankt Augustin – Net-

tetal 2011, 379 S., Abb. ISBN 987-3-8050-0582-1
- JOHN T.P. LAI, *Negotiating Religious Gaps. The Enterprise of Translating Christian Tracts by Protestant Missionaries in Nineteenth-Century China*. Sankt Augustin – Nettetal 2012, 382 S., Abb. ISBN 987-3-8050-0597-5
- S.-J. DEIWIKS, B. FÜHRER, T. GEULEN (eds.), *Europe meets China – China meets Europe. The Beginnings of European-Chinese Scientific Exchange in the 17th Century*. Sankt Augustin, 2014, viii, 224 pp., Illustr. ISBN 978-3-8050-0621-7
- MIECZYSŁAW JERZY KÜNSTLER, *The Sinitic Languages: A Contribution to Sinological Linguistics*. Translated by Mieczysław Jerzy Künstler and Alfred Franciszek Majewicz. New Series, 1. Sankt Augustin – Abingdon, Oxon – New York, 2019, xiii, 322 pp., Illustr. ISBN 978-0-367-18620-3 (hbk); 978-0-429-19723-9 (eBook)
- GAIL KING, *"A Model for All Christian Women": Candida Xu, a Chinese Christian Woman of the Seventeenth Century*. New Series, 2. Sankt Augustin – Abingdon, Oxon – New York, 2021, xv, 162 pp., Illustr. ISBN 978-0-367-68290-3 (hbk); 978-1-003-13677-4 (eBook)

Place order with your local bookseller or:
www.routledge.com/Collectanea-Serica/book-series/CS